SELECTED WORKS OF MODERN CHINESE LEARNING

THE ECONOMIC PRINCIPLES OF CONFUCIUS AND HIS SCHOOL

Chen Huan-Chang

2015 · BEIJING

First Edition 2015

All rights reserved. No part of this publication may be reproduced or transmitted in any form or by any means, electronic or mechanical, now known or to be invented, without permission in writing from the publishers, except for brief quotations by reviewers.

ISBN 978 - 7 - 100 - 11220 - 8
© 2015 The Commercial Press

Published by
The Commercial Press
   36 Wangfujing Road, Beijing 100710, China
   www.cp.com.cn

CHEN HUAN-CHANG

(1880–1933)

Editorial Note

One hundred years ago, Zhang Zhidong tried to advocate Chinese learning by saying: "The course of a nation, be it bright or gloomy, the pool of talents, be it large or small, are about governance on the surface, and about learning at the root." At that time, the imperialist powers cast menacing eyes on our country, and the domestic situation was deteriorating. The quick infiltration of Western learning made the long-standing Chinese tradition come under heavy challenge. In those days, Chinese learning and Western learning stood side by side. Literature, history and philosophy split up, while many new branches of learning such as economics, politics and sociology were flourishing, which made many Chinese dazed. However, there appeared a vital and vigorous learning climate out of the confusing situation. It was at this critical moment that modern Chinese scholarship made the transition—by exchanging views, basing on profound contemplation and even with confrontation of idea and clash of views, the scholarship made continuous progress, bringing up a large number of persons of academic distinction and creating numerous innovative works. Changes in scholarship and in general modes of thinking made transition in all aspects of the society possible, thus laying a solid foundation for revitalizing China.

It's over a century since the journey of modern Chinese learning started, during which various schools of thought stood in great numbers, causing heated discussions. The journey sees schools of thought as well as relevant arguments rising and falling, waxing and waning instantly, leaving complicated puzzles to followers. By studying and reviewing the selected works, one may gain new insights into that journey; and it is the editor's sincere hope that readers would ponder over the future by recalling the past. That's why we have compiled "Selected Works of Modern Chinese Learning". The effort includes masterpieces of celebrated scholars from diverse fields of study and different schools of thought. By tracing back to the source and searching for the basis of modern Chinese learning, we wish to present the dynamics between thought and time.

The series of "Selected Works of Modern Chinese Learning" includes works (both in Chinese and in foreign languages) of scholars from China—mainland, Hong Kong, Macau, and Taiwan—and from overseas. These works are mostly on humanities and cover all fields of subjects, such as literary theory, linguistics, history, philosophy, politics, economics, jurisprudence, sociology, to name a few.

It has been a long-cherished wish of the Commercial Press to compile a series of "Selected Works of Modern Chinese Learning". Since its foundation in 1897, the Commercial Press has been privileged to have published numerous pioneering works and masterpieces of modern Chinese learning under the motto of "promoting education and enlightening people". The press has participated in and witnessed the establishment and development of modern Chinese learning. The series of "Selected Works of Modern Chinese Learning" is fruit of an effort to relay the editorial legacy and the cultural propositions of our senior generations. This series, sponsored by National Publication Foundation, would not be possible if there were no careful planning of the press itself. Neither would it be possible without extensive collaboration among talents of the academic circle. It is our deeply cherished hope that titles of this series will keep their place on the bookshelves even after a long time.

Moreover, we wish that this series and "Chinese Translations of World Classics" will become double jade in Chinese publishing history as well as in the history of the Commercial Press itself. With such great aspirations in mind, fearing that it is beyond our ability to realize them, we cordially invite both scholars and readers to extend your assistance.

Editorial Department of the Commercial Press

December 2010

FOREWORD

DR. CHEN HUAN-CHANG, the author of *The Economic Principles of Confucius and His School,* has seen some service as a mandarin in one of the metropolitan offices in Peking; he is deeply versed in his native literature, of which the so-called Confucian classics have occupied him for many years; he is a personal friend and has been a pupil of Kang Yu-wei, one of the originators of the modern Chinese reform movement and himself a profound connoisseur of Chinese literature. Thus armed, he came to New York about five years ago to study English and take courses in political economy at Columbia University. Kang Yu-wei's moral success among the masses of China was largely due to the fact that, while being thoroughly convinced of the necessity of reform in social and political life, he continued to be an eager adherent of Confucian principles. Dr. Chen proves a disciple worthy of his great teacher. His enthusiasm for the great sage and his doctrine could not be surpassed; western readers will find in his book the representation of Confucianism from the purely Confucianist point of view by an author who is a Confucianist himself and has had the advantage of sifting his ideas through the methods of western science.

FRIEDRICH HIRTH,
Professor of Chinese, Columbia University.

NEW YORK, OCTOBER 15, 1911.

PREFACE

In presenting the economic teachings of Confucianism, Dr. Chen has adopted the same order of arrangement that has become usual in English treatises on political economy. The danger which this plan involved of creating the impression of a more systematic exposition of economic principles than is to be found in the sacred writings, is much more than outweighed by the large number of clear anticipations of the accepted economic teachings of today which it reveals. Incidentally it enables the author, with his wide acquaintance with the best English economic literature, to bring out many interesting contrasts between Chinese civilization and the civilization of the Occident. His discussions of such institutions as the family, marriage, private property and the position of woman have an interest and value quite apart from their relation to the main purpose of his study.

No one can read these pages without becoming convinced that Confucianism is a great economic, as well as a great moral and religious, system and that it contains most, if not all, of the elements necessary to the solution of the serious problems that confront China to-day. That these problems may be speedily and happily solved and that Dr. Chen may take the prominent and distinguished part in the reformation of his country for which his high character and unusual attainments so well fit him is the earnest hope of his American friends.

HENRY R. SEAGER,
Professor of Political Economy.

COLUMBIA UNIVERSITY, OCTOBER 15, 1911.

AUTHOR'S PREFACE

THE following treatise includes a discussion of the economic principles of the chief disciples of Confucius in successive dynasties, as well as of the teachings of the Master himself, and, briefly for purposes of comparison, of the leaders of other schools, *e. g.*, those of Kuan Tzŭ, Lao Tzŭ, Mo Tzŭ, Shang Yang, and Hsü Hsing. It was deemed best to combine with the discussion of economic theory some consideration of economic history. Consequently the conditions out of which the theories arose and to which they were to be applied have usually been described. The canonical writings were taken as primary sources, and the historical writings as secondary. In connection with every theory and institution considered, the attempt has been made to throw light upon its origin and earliest development. Because of the wealth of material, only the most important or most interesting historical facts since the Han dynasty have received attention. Although some information in regard to conditions in China to-day is given, it was not thought desirable to go very much into detail, because these conditions are in process of revolutionary change and many questions are still unsettled.

The treatise is, therefore, essentially a study of the old régime in China. It is a survey of the Chinese thought and Chinese institutions which developed independently of the Occident. Although my arrangement of the material follows that which has become conventional among western writers and my understanding of the old texts was greatly helped by western thinkers, I have been very careful not to read into the writings of the ancient Chinese ideas drawn from modern western economists. All my statements are based upon the words or the spirit of the words of the original texts, and are in harmony with the whole system of Confucius as revealed by a comparative study of the various sources. In support of my interpretation numerous quotations and references are given. The Confucian writings may be compared to a great mountain containing rich mineral resources. I am in the position of a miner, extracting a particular ore and contributing it to the world's production. As the miner does not create the ore itself, but through his labor in exploring, digging and refining makes it available for human use, so I have tried to add something to human knowledge. My task has been so great that I have doubtless made some mistakes, but I have earnestly tried to be accurate in all my statements. This is the first attempt to present the economic principles of Confucius and his school in a systematic form in any language. At some future time I intend to translate this book into Chinese.

I am under heavy obligations to many persons. My greatest indebtedness is to Kang Yu-wei, my former teacher, from whom I obtained a general view of Confucianism. From my American friends, especially among the professors and students of Columbia University—e. g. Professors John Bates Clark, Edwin R. A. Seligman, Friedrich Hirth and Warren B. Catlin—I received many ideas and secured assistance in various ways. My greatest obligations, however, are to Dr. and Mrs. B. M. Anderson, Jr., who corrected the greater part of my manuscript; to Professor Henry Rogers Seager, who made numerous suggestions and corrections throughout the whole book; and to Professor Henry Raymond Mussey, who read all the proof sheets.

CHEN HUAN-CHANG.

COLUMBIA UNIVERSITY, NEW YORK, *the seventh day of the seventh month, two thousand four hundred and sixty-two years after Confucius, (August 30, 1911 A. D.).*

CONTENTS

VOLUME I

FOREWORD. By Professor Friedrich Hirth vi
PREFACE. By Professor Henry R. Seager..................... vii
AUTHOR'S PREFACE ix

PART I

INTRODUCTION

BOOK I. CONFUCIUS AND HIS SCHOOL

CHAPTER	PAGE
I. Life of Confucius.................................	5
II. The Fundamental Concepts of Confucius............	17
III. Writings of Confucius and His Disciples............	25
IV. Historical Movements of Confucianism	41

BOOK II. RELATION OF ECONOMICS TO OTHER SCIENCES

V. Economics and Other Sciences in General	50
VI. Economics and Sociology	54
VII. Economics and Politics..............................	75
VIII. Economics and Ethics	96

BOOK III. GENERAL ECONOMIC PRINCIPLES

IX. Economic Development as the Chief Cause of Progress	121
X. Economic Organization	141
XI. Economic Policies and the Divisions of Economics....	170

CONTENTS

PART II
CONSUMPTION

BOOK IV. CONSUMPTION

CHAPTER   PAGE
- XII. General Principles of Consumption 187
- XIII. Happiness for Both Rich and Poor 209
- XIV. Different Ways of Getting Pleasure 218
- XV. General Standard of Expenditure 244
- XVI. Particular Expenditures 271

PART III
PRODUCTION

BOOK V. FACTORS OF PRODUCTION

- XVII. Three Factors of Production 295
- XVIII. Labor–Population 299
- XIX. Nature and Capital 341

VOLUME II

PART III

PRODUCTION

BOOK VI. BRANCHES OF PRODUCTION

- XX. Branches of Production in General 367
- XXI. Agriculture 380
- XXII. Industry 398
- XXIII. Commerce 411

BOOK VII. DISTRIBUTION

- XXIV. General Principles of Distribution: Rent, Interest and Profits 460
- XXV. Wages 480

BOOK VIII. SOCIALISTIC POLICIES

CHAPTER		PAGE
XXVI.	The Tsing Tien System	497
XXVII.	Monopoly	534
XXVIII.	Exclusion of the Ruling Class from the Economic Field	543
XXIX.	Government Control of Demand and Supply	552
XXX.	Government Control of Grain	568
XXXI.	Government Loans and Public Relief	586

PART IV

PUBLIC FINANCE

BOOK IX. PUBLIC FINANCE

XXXII.	Public Expenditures	605
XXXIII.	Taxation in General	621
XXXIV.	Direct Taxes	638
XXXV.	Indirect Taxes	683

PART V

CONCLUSION

XXXVI.	Conclusion	717
APPENDIX I	Table of Chinese Chronology	731
APPENDIX II	List of Authorities in English and Chinese	733
INDEX		737
VITA		757

VOLUME I

PART I
INTRODUCTION

BOOK I. CONFUCIUS AND HIS SCHOOL

CHAPTER I

LIFE OF CONFUCIUS

An objective attitude toward the ideals and sages of one's own country is not easily to be attained. There is a corresponding difficulty in gaining a sufficiently sympathetic attitude toward the ideals and sages of a strange people. For these reasons it has seemed best to the writer to undertake a general estimate of the worth of Confucius and of Confucianism at the end, rather than at the beginning, of this study. The reader who has gone with him to the conclusion can better judge how far the estimate is objective, after seeing the evidence on which it is based; and he will also be better enabled to view the problem sympathetically. The words of a western writer shall, therefore, serve as our introduction.

Von der Gabelentz says:

Quite unique is the position occupied by him who, as no other man, was a teacher of his people, who, I venture to say, has become and continued to be a ruler of his people, the Sage of the family K'ung in the State of Lu, whom we know by the name of Confucius. Unique is his position, not only in the history of philosophy, but also in the history of mankind. For there is hardly any other man who, like Confucius, incorporated in his own person all the constituent elements of the Chinese type and all that is eternal in his people's being. If we are to measure the greatness of an historic personage, I can see only one standard applicable for the purpose: the effectiveness of that person's influence according to its dimensions, duration, and intensity. If this standard be applied, Confucius was one of the greatest of men. For even at the present day, after the lapse of more than two thousand years, the moral, social, and political life of about one-third of mankind continues to be under the full influence of his mind.[1]

Confucius has indeed been the maker of the Chinese people, but he himself did not spring from an uncivilized world. The date of the beginning of Chinese history is unknown, but it is certain that China has existed as a nation for at least six thousand years. The first legendary emperor, Pao Hsi, or Fu Hsi, is placed 2402 years before the Confucian era (2953-2839 B. C.). After the period of the Five Emperors, came the period of the Three Kings of as many dynasties, and it was during the Chou dynasty, the last of these three, that Chinese civilization reached maturity. It was after long periods of so-called sage rulers who were regarded as the heads of both religion and government, at the highest development of Chinese civilization under the Chou dynasty, and in the most cultured state of the Duke of Chou, that Confucius appeared. Confucianism, the new religion founded by Confucius, is therefore not the religion of a primitive tribe, but the religion of a civilized people.

While this was the general stage of development preceding the advent of Confucius, it must not be imagined that actual conditions during his time were so perfect as to make the work of a reformer unnecessary. The age of Confucius was quite remote from that of the sage rulers. With

[1] *Confucius und seine Lehre*, p. 4 *et seq.*, quoted in Friedrich Hirth's *The Ancient History of China, pp.* 242-3.

the beginning of Ping Wang's reign (219 B. K.[1] or 770 B. C.), the Chou dynasty had practically fallen, and all the emperors of the Eastern Chou line were without real power. It was the age of feudalism. Each feudal estate was an independent nation, each prince of each nation fought for its supremacy, and the power of the princes was greater than that of the emperor. During Confucius' time, the power of the prince in each state had generally fallen into the hands of a few noble families, and the government had become a form of oligarchy. Sometimes the private officials of these families took public affairs into their own hands. The confusion and disorder brought about by the ruling class extended over the whole empire, while the common people, who were not sufficiently educated to help themselves, were entirely neglected.

Although the great mass of the people in Confucius' time was uneducated, there was a middle class which had educated itself. Since China had been civilized for so long a time, the people were naturally developed to some extent. During the period of the Eastern Chou dynasty, although the power of the imperial government declined, the intellectual growth of the people increased. The greater importance acquired by the different independent states with the diminishing power of the emperor gave rise to much peaceful diplomatic intercourse as well as to many hostile military expeditions, and these forms of contact had an educative influence upon a considerable class of the people. Further, as the political power was shifting from class to class and from person to person within each state, some noble families had been ruined, and some common people had risen. Thus the profession of learning was also shifted

[1] We use the forms B. K. and A. K. to avoid confusion with the C. in the western chronology, as in B. C. The Chinese form of the name, Confucius, is K'ung Fu Tzŭ.

and more widely diffused. Moreover, in such a struggle, every one had absolute freedom of movement and of speech. It was a condition very favorable to the development of the minds of the people.

Such was the time in which Confucius was born. But the birthplace of Confucius was no less important than his time. His family had settled in the state of Lu, which was the state of the Duke of Chou. As the Duke himself remained with the imperial government, he gave the administration of his estate over to his son, who conducted it according to his father's principles and under his direction. Lu had become the center of Chinese civilization. About Confucius' time, Lu, although subordinate to the great states in military force, was supreme in art, literature, philosophy and morality.

Among Confucius' ancestors was Ch'êng T'ang, the founder of the Yin dynasty (1215-1203 B. K. or 1766-1754 B. C.). After the fall of this dynasty, Wei Tzŭ, brother of the fallen emperor, was enfeoffed by Chou Ch'êng Wang in the dukedom of Sung. The tenth ancestor of Confucius resigned his dukedom to his younger brother, and thus it passed out of the direct line of Confucius. Five generations later, K'ung-fu Chia, the sixth ancestor of Confucius, invented the surname of K'ung from his adult designation indicating separation from the house of the duke in conformity with the ancient custom. On account of some political trouble, the great-grandfather of Confucius fled from Sung to the state of Lu, and became mayor in the city of Fang. Confucius' father, Shu-liang Ho, was mayor in the city of Tsou, and distinguished himself as a brave soldier. Since on reaching the age of sixty-four he had no heir who could be his successor, he was obliged to marry a young girl, Yen Chêng-tsai, who became the mother of Confucius.

The year of Confucius' birth, according to the Commentaries of Kung-yang and Ku-liang, was the twentieth year of Chou Ling Wang's reign (552 B. C.); but the beginning of the Confucian era is dated one year later (551 B. C.) on account of a mistake made by Ssŭ-ma Chien, the greatest historian.[1] His birthday, according to the present Chinese calendar, is the twenty-first day of the eighth month. His birthplace is in the present district of K'ŭhfeu, Shantung province. K'ung was his family name; Ch'iu, his personal name; and Chung-ni, his adult designation. The word Confucius has come from three Chinese words, K'ung Fu Tzŭ, *Fu Tzŭ* meaning master.

Confucius was powerful in body and keen in mind. He studied under many masters and in many places, becoming a many-sided and versatile man.

The greatest service of Confucius to his contemporaries was as a teacher. Opening his school at the age of twenty-two,[2] he taught continuously to the time of his death. When he was thirty-five, a noble of one of the leading families of Lu, on his death-bed, ordered his two sons, Mêng Yi-tzŭ and Nan-kung Ching-shu, to become pupils of Confucius, and these two noble pupils undoubtedly increased his influence. When at this time he wished to visit the imperial capital, Nan-kung Ching-shu advised the Marquis of Lu to furnish a carriage, two horses and a servant for him, and himself accompanied his teacher. During this visit a very significant interview occurred between Confucius and Lao Tzŭ, the earliest philosopher of the Chou dynasty, then keeper of the imperial archives, and later regarded as the founder of Taoism. Confucius consulted this learned man concerning the rites, questioned Chang Hung, a high im-

---

[1] He began to write the *Historical Record* in 448, and finished it in 455 (104-97 B. C.).

[2] *Canonical Interpretation of the Ts'ing Dynasty*, vol. xxxiii, ch. i.

perial officer, about music, and studied many other things. After his return home, his pupils increased in number.

One year later, on account of a civil war, Confucius went to the neighboring state of Ch'i. The Marquis of Ch'i wished to confer upon him a territory, but this was objected to by a courtier named An Tzŭ. As he could not hold a good office there, Confucius returned, at the age of forty-two, to Lu.

After his return, he devoted himself exclusively to teaching and writing for a period of ten years. At forty-eight, he prepared the Canons of *Poetry*, of *History*, of *Rites* and of *Music*. Many pupils now came to him from remote regions. But he was so anxious to secure political power in order to reform the Chinese world that he even considered accepting the invitations of the rebels. At fifty-one, when Kung-shan Fu-jao, who held the city of Fei in rebellion against the minister of Lu, invited him to come, Confucius was disposed to comply. He said that if any one would employ him, he might create a new dynasty of Chou in the East.[1] Ten years later, at sixty-one, he also considered accepting the invitation of Pi Hsi, who rebelled with the city of Chung-mou against the minister of Tsin.[2] Although he did not go to see these two rebels at all and refused their invitations, it is clear that his love and faith were directed much more toward the general public than toward any personal ruler.

The political career of Confucius, although not an important part of his life, is proof of his practical talents. At fifty-two, he was appointed magistrate of the city of Chung-tu by the Marquis of Lu. His administration was very successful, and the princes of neighboring states took it as a

[1] *The Chinese Classics*, vol. i, pp. 319-20.
[2] *Ibid.*, p. 321.

model.¹ At fifty-three, the Marquis appointed him Minister of the Interior, and then Minister of Justice. A courtier of the state of Ch'i, which was jealous of its neighbor Lu, warned his prince that the increasing influence of the latter state under the administration of Confucius would endanger the balance of power. His prince, therefore, invited the Marquis of Lu to come to a friendly meeting in order to catch him and make him prisoner. Confucius accompanied his prince as substitute for the prime minister. He defeated the treacherous plot through his speeches and through a show of military force, so that Ch'i was obliged to apologize and as a mark of friendship to restore the former conquests which it had made from Lu. At fifty-five, Confucius strengthened the ruling house by having the walls of the cities of the noble families pulled down. Reaching the height of civil greatness, he became, at fifty-six, the acting prime minister. Within seven days, he ordered the execution of a great demagogue, Shao-chêng Mao, as being dangerous to the public welfare. Within three months, his moral influence prevailed over the whole state. But the neighboring countries began to fear that under Confucius' reformation, Lu would overtop and subdue them all. To prevent this, the Marquis of Ch'i, above referred to, sent eighty beautiful dancing girls and one hundred and twenty fine horses as a gift to the prince of Lu for the purpose of bringing about a separation between him and Confucius. The result was the demoralization of the government, as both the prince and the real prime minister neglected their duties. Confucius lost his influence, and soon left his native country for travel.

Confucius' travels were in the nature of missionary work. He aimed to establish his kingdom in the actual present

---

¹ *Cf.* the *Historical Record*, ch. xlvii, on which this chapter is based.

world through the influence of a government. He was not a narrow patriot. He presented himself for official employment before seventy-two princes, and even in the barbaric state of Ch'u. But he was not able in any case to realize his purpose. He was satirized by many of his contemporaries who felt the world to be evil and kept aloof from it. Confucius' declaration is at once sane and pathetic: " The bird and beast," said he sorrowfully, " cannot be in the same society with us. If I do not associate with my fellow-men, with whom shall I associate? Had the world been perfect, I would not care to change it!"[1] This was the spirit of Confucius: to love the world, to serve the world, and to busy himself restlessly in his mission.

Upon four different occasions during his travels, his life was placed in jeopardy. First, at fifty-seven, he was imprisoned by the people of the city of K'uang for five days. His pupils were fearful, but he said: " After the death of Wên Wang, was not the cause of truth lodged here in me? If God had wished to let this cause of truth perish, then I, his successor who later must die, should not have been placed in such a relation to that cause. But so long as God does not let the cause of truth perish, what can the people of K'uang do to me?"[2] Again, at fifty-eight, when with his pupils he was performing religious ceremonies under the shade of a large tree, Huan Tui, the minister of war of the state of Sung, who wished to kill him, had the tree cut down. Then his pupils warned him to go away at once. " God has produced," said he, " the virtue that is in me.

---

[1] *Classics*, vol. i, p. 334.

[2] Confucius here indentifies himself with the line of the great sage rulers to whom God had intrusted the instruction of men. In all the six centuries between himself and Wên Wang (673-584 B. K.), he does not admit of such another. *Ibid.*, pp. 217-8.

What can Huan Tui do to me?"[1] It is clear that he felt that God had committed to him the right way, and that he bore a charmed life until his work was done. Again, at fifty-nine, he was stopped by the rebels in the city of Po. But one of his pupils, Kung-liang Yü, who was following his master with five private chariots, fought bravely for him, and he was allowed to proceed. Once more, at sixty-four, he was surrounded by the officials of the states of Chên and Tsai. He was without food for seven days, and his pupils were so sick as to be unable to rise. But he never stopped preaching, reading, playing on the harp and singing. Finally he was rescued by the military force of the state of Ch'u.

When he arrived at Ch'u, the king wished to confer upon him a territory of seven hundred square miles. But the prime minister objected, because he feared Confucius' power and virtues, saying that the latter's pupils were much better than any of their own officials, and that if Confucius could occupy any territory, he himself would eventually be a real king and this would not be good for their state.

Having spent fourteen years in traveling abroad, Confucius was now, at sixty-nine, called back by the government of his native state. But the government did not finally employ him, and he himself at this period had no desire to be employed. About this time, his son died; his wife had died two years previously.

Confucius was destined, however, not chiefly to serve his own immediate period, but to influence endless ages of the future. He now spent all his time in writing, and this was, in the final analysis, his greatest work. As he had at the age of forty-eight already prepared the greater part of the Canons of *Poetry*, of *History*, of *Rites*, and of *Music*,

[1] *Classics*, vol. i, p. 202.

he now finished them, and also the *Canon of Changes*. The *Spring and Autumn* was written at the age of seventy-two.

What he wrote was very much the same as what he was teaching to his three thousand pupils, particularly the Canons of *Poetry, History, Rites* and *Music*. Those who graduated in the six arts—rites, music, archery, charioteering, writing and mathematics—which were all prescribed courses for each person, were seventy-two in number. His best students were those who specialized in morality, oratory, politics and literature. There were many special students. Therefore, the number of his followers amounted to sixty thousand.

Confucius was already an old man when he finished his writings; they were the product of his most mature wisdom. He now felt that his work was done. One morning, he got up early, and as he walked back and forth before his door with his hands behind his back dragging his staff, he sang the following words:

> The Tai Mountain must crumble!
> The strongest beam must break!
> The wisest man must fade!

Seven days later, the death of " The Perfect Holy Man " took place.[1] He was seventy-four years old (479 B. C.).

The highest honors were bestowed upon him after his death. The Marquis of Lu came to pass eulogy upon him. He was buried in what is now called the Forest of K'ung, to which the trees were originally brought from different states by his pupils. His pupils stayed there until the end of three years' mourning, but Tzŭ-kung (his pupil) alone built a house near his tomb and lived there for three years more. Some of his pupils and some of the people of Lu,

---

[1] According to the present Chinese calendar, the corresponding date is the eleventh day of the second month.

more than one hundred families in all, moved to the vicinity of his tomb and formed what was called the Village of K'ung. The people sacrificed to his tomb for many generations, and the Confucian scholars also practised different ceremonies about it. His house was then converted into a temple in which his clothes, hats, harp, carriage and books were stored. The first emperor who came to worship him was Han Kao Ti (357 A. K. or 195 B. C.). When new princes and governors first came to the state, they always worshiped him before they took up their official duties. Since 504 A. K. the descendants of Confucius have been a permanent nobility. The present duke of his descendants is in the seventy-sixth generation from him. In 610 A. K. (59 A. D.), Han Ming Ti first ordered the Imperial University and all the government schools in each district to worship Confucius. Since that time the school houses have been at the same time Confucian churches, and they have been established throughout the whole empire.

In conclusion, then, we may say that Confucius was a great philosopher, a great educator, a great statesman, and a great musician; but, above all, that he was the founder of a great religion. This is well stated by Tzŭ-kung when he says: "Certainly God has endowed him unlimitedly as a great sage, and, moreover, his ability is various."[1] Yu Jo, pupil of Confucius, said, "From the birth of mankind till now, there never has been one so complete as Confucius," and the same statement is also given by Tzŭ-kung and Mencius (180-263 A. K. or 372-289 B. C.).[2] In the *Analects*,[3] Confucius, by tacit implication, compares himself with God, and in the "Doctrine of the Mean,"[4] Confucius is

[1] *Classics*, vol. i, p. 218.
[2] *Classics*, vol. ii, pp. 194-6.
[3] *Classics*, vol. i, p. 326.
[4] *Ibid.*, p. 429.

called "the equal of God". The Chinese worship him not from any superstitious idea, but on the philosophical ground that "the individual possessed of the most complete sincerity is regarded as divine",[1] and that "when the sage is beyond our knowledge, he is what is called divine."[2] Although Confucius died about twenty-five centuries ago, the Chinese believe that his fundamental teachings will remain true forever. This is because, on the one hand, the teachings, based on the doctrine of the mean, never go to extremes; and on the other, being subject to the doctrine of changes, they easily adapt themselves to the environment. Confucius is called by Mencius "The Sage of Times". In fact, the teachings of Confucius are based on the nature of man,[3] and as long as we are human beings, no matter in what age or in what region we may live, we can learn from him. Hence, the Chinese believe that there has been no other man so great as Confucius.

[1] *Classics*, vol. i, p. 418.
[2] *Classics*, vol. ii, p. 490.
[3] *Classics*, vol. i, p. 393.

CHAPTER II

THE FUNDAMENTAL CONCEPTS OF CONFUCIUS

HAVING reviewed the more important facts of Confucius' life, we pass now to the fundamental concepts of the whole Confucian philosophy. There are two general classes of these concepts, one class based on the law of variety, and the other on the law of unity; the one, changeable with the needs of the times, the other unchangeable, rooted in the nature of man. Of the first type are the principle of the Three Systems and the principle of the Three Stages; of the second is the principle of love, which is to be practised on the basis of reciprocity.

I. THE THREE SYSTEMS

Confucius is like a great physician, and his teachings are like prescriptions. Just as the great physician never gives a single kind of medicine as a remedy for all diseases, so Confucius never gives a single form of teaching as the law of all ages. In the *Spring and Autumn,* he sets forth the principle of the Three Systems, and we meet this principle in all his writings. The Three Systems are represented by the Three Dynasties, Hsia, Yin and Chou, and he makes everything in three different forms. For example, the new year begins with either the first month, or the second, or the third; the new day begins either in the morning, or in the middle between morning and midnight, or at midnight; the principal color is either black, or white, or red. There is not a certain form, but the one is as good as the others. Hence the principles of the Three Dynasties are as in a cycle,

—the one succeeds the other, whenever the former principle does not work well. The fundamental concept is that all human civilization and social life are necessarily changed in order to reform the evil of the past and meet the need of the present. Any good thing must come to a period of decay and become an evil. Civilization may run through a long course to the original principle and then start again, although such a principle may not take exactly the original form. Or, in different places, different civilizations and institutions may exist at the same time.

II. THE THREE STAGES

A principle more important than the Three Systems is the Three Stages. In the first of these, the Disorderly Stage, primitive civilization is just arising from chaos, and the social mind is still very rude. There is a sharp distinction between one's own country and all other civilized countries. Hence attention is paid more to conditions at home than abroad, and, except the great powers, the small countries are neglected. In the second, the Advancing Peace Stage, there is a distinction only between all the civilized countries and the barbarians. The limit of civilization is broader, and the friendship of nations is closer; by the equal right, even the small countries can have their representatives. In the third, the Extreme Peace Stage, there is no distinction at all. The barbarians become civilized countries, and obtain the same title in the diplomatic circle. Whether the nations are remote or near, small or great, the whole world is as one unit, and the character of mankind is on the highest plane.

The principle of the Three Stages, illustrated by the international relation, is established in the *Spring and Autumn*.[1]

---

[1] It is very strange that Professor James Legge apparently does not know the international view of Confucius at all. He says: "Confucius

But we can find this principle in all Confucius' writings, whatever the subject. For example, in politics, despotism, constitutionalism and anarchism are three stages; in religion, polytheism, monism and atheism are three stages. The three stages can be subdivided into nine, eighty-one, and so on. It is simply the theory of progress, or evolution. But we must remember this principle in order to understand that the teachings of Confucius, although sometimes apparently inconsistent, are all fitted to different stages, and that we must not make the mistake of applying the theories of the low stage to the advanced stage.

The Advancing Peace Stage is also called the Small Tranquillity, and the Extreme Peace Stage, the Great Similarity. The marked difference between these two stages is described by Confucius himself. It is a most important passage, and

makes no provision for the intercourse of his country with other and independent nations. He knew indeed of none such. China was to him 'The Middle Kingdom,' 'The multitude of Great States,' 'All under Heaven.' Beyond it were only rude and barbarous tribes." (*Chinese Classics*, vol. i, pp. 107-8.) This statement is quite misleading. Confucius has made many provisions for the intercourse of his country with other and independent nations; and we can compile the International Law of Confucius even from the *Spring and Autumn* only. In Confucius' time, China was divided up into many nations. The number of leading nations was twelve, and the total number of nations was over one hundred. Therefore, his country was not China, but Lu. Since Lu had intercourse continuously with other and independent nations, why should Confucius know nothing about them? These nations were called "The multitude of Great States" and "The Middle Kingdom." This was the international society, and the term Middle Kingdom was like the term Christendom. Beyond this, there were at this time only rude and barbarous tribes, so far as the Chinese knew. This was the condition under which Confucius lived. By the term "All under Heaven," however, Confucius really meant the whole world, and it included not only the multitude of great states, but also all the barbarous tribes. Although it was sometimes used to cover only the Chinese world, such a term, everyone can see, could never mean a national state. In fact, Confucius always keeps the whole world in his mind.

we must quote it fully. In the "Evolution of Civilization," Confucius says:

When the Great Principle [of the Great Similarity] prevails, the whole world becomes a republic; they elect men of talents, virtue, and ability; they talk about sincere agreement, and cultivate universal peace. Thus men do not regard as their parents only their own parents, nor treat as their children only their own children. A competent provision is secured for the aged till their death, employment for the middle-aged, and the means of growing up to the young. The widowers, widows, orphans, childless men, and those who are disabled by disease, are all sufficiently maintained. Each man has his rights, and each woman her individuality safe-guarded. They produce wealth, disliking that it should be thrown away upon the ground, but not wishing to keep it for their own gratification. Disliking idleness, they labor, but not alone with a view to their own advantage. In this way selfish schemings are repressed and find no way to arise. Robbers, filchers and rebellious traitors do not exist. Hence the outer doors remain open, and are not shut. This is the stage of what I call the Great Similarity.

Now that the Great Principle has not yet been developed, the world is inherited through family. Each one regards as his parents only his own parents, and treats as his children only his own children. The wealth of each and his labor are only for his self-interest. Great men imagine it is the rule that their estates should descend in their own families. Their object is to make the walls of their cities and suburbs strong and their ditches and moats secure. Rites and justice are regarded as the threads by which they seek to maintain in its correctness the relation between ruler and minister; in its generous regard that between father and son; in its harmony that between elder brother and younger; and in a community of sentiment that between husband and wife; and in accordance with them they regulate consumption, distribute land and dwellings, distinguish the men of military ability and cunning, and achieve their work with a view to their own advantage. Thus it is that selfish schemes and enterprises are constantly taking their rise, and war is inevitably forthcoming. In this course of rites and justice, Yü, T'ang, Wên, Wu, Ch'êng Wang and the Duke of Chou are the best examples of good government. Of these six superior men, every one was attentive to the rites, thus to secure the display of justice, the realization of sincerity, the exhibition of errors, the exemplification of benevolence, and the discussion of courtesy, showing the people all the constant virtues. If any ruler, having power and position, would not follow this course, he should be driven away by the multitude who regard him as a public enemy. This is the stage of what I call the Small Tranquillity.[1]

This is the most important statement of all Confucius' teachings. The stage of Great Similarity or Extreme Peace is the final aim of Confucius; it is the golden age of Confucianism. If we make a comparison between the Great Similarity and the Small Tranquillity, we may get a clear view. Every one knows that Confucianism has five social relations and five moral constants: ruler and subject, father and son, elder and younger brothers, husband and wife, friend and friend, make up the five social relations; love, justice, rite, wisdom and sincerity, make up the five moral constants. But, according to the statement of Confucius himself, they belong only to the Small Tranquillity. Every one knows that Confucianism is in favor of monarchical government and of filial piety. But they are good only in the Small Tranquillity. In the Great Similarity, the whole world is the only social organization, and the individual is the independent unit; both socialistic and individualistic characters reach the highest point. There is no national state, so that there is no war, no need of defence, nor of men of military ability and cunning. Men of talents, virtue,

---

[1] *Li Ki*, bk. vii, pp. 365-7. "The exhibition of errors" refers to wisdom, and "the discussion of courtesy" to rites.

and ability are chosen by the people, so that the people themselves are the sovereign, and the relation between ruler and subject does not exist. Man and woman are not bound by the tie of marriage, so that the relations between husband and wife, between father and son and between brothers, do not exist. The only relation that remains is friendship. There is no family, so that there is no inheritance, no private property, no selfish scheme. There is no class, so that the only classification is made either by age or by sex; but whether old, middle-aged, or young, whether man or woman, each satisfies his needs. The Great Principle of the Great Similarity prevails, so that everyone is naturally as good as every one else and the distinction of the five moral constants is gone. Each has only natural love toward others, regardless of artificial rites and justice. Speaking of the Small Tranquillity, Confucius gives six superior men as examples, but for the Great Similarity, he does not mention any one, because it has never existed. In the *Canon of History*, Confucius takes up Yao and Shun to represent the stage of Great Similarity as they did not hand down their thrones to their sons, yet he does not mention them here. The principle of the Three Stages is the principle of progress; we must look for the golden age in the future; the Extreme Peace or the Great Similarity is the goal.

III. LOVE

Both the Three Systems and the Three Stages come under the law of variety in accordance with external conditions; the law of unity is based on the inner nature of man. It is the principle of love. From the religious point of view, the unity is called God; from the philosophical point of view, it is called *Yüan;* from the ethical point of view, it is called love.¹ These three names are based on the same principle, because it is a unity. The unity of the universe is nothing but love. The cement of the universe is called God or *Yüan*, and that of society is called love. Confucius says " Love is man ", and Mencius repeats the same words.² If we put it into negative form, any one who does not conform to the principle of love is not a man.

IV. RECIPROCITY

There is a question as to how we should practice the principle of love. After Confucius said to Ts'êng-Tzŭ, his pupil, " My doctrine is that of an all-pervading unity ", Ts'êng-Tzŭ explained to other pupils that the unity is simply faithfulness and reciprocity.³ Confucius himself says: " Faithfulness and reciprocity are not far from the way. What you do not wish when done to yourself, do not do to others." ⁴ We can see, therefore, that faithfulness and reciprocity both make up the unity, but faithfulness is included in the principle of reciprocity. When Tzŭ-kung asked, " Is there one word which may serve as a rule of practice for all one's life?" Confucius said, " Is not reciprocity such a word? What you do not want done to yourself, do not do to others." ⁵ Stating this golden rule positively, Confucius says: " The man who practices the principle of love, wishing to establish himself, seeks also to establish others; wishing to develop himself, he seeks also to develop others. To be able to take one's inmost self for

---

[1] See *Yi King*, pp. 408, 415. Legge's translation is obscure. The word *Ch'ien* means God, and also the word *Yüan*, " the great and originating." The word benevolence is love.

[2] *Classics*, vol. i, p. 405; and vol. ii, p. 485.

[3] *Classics*, vol. i, pp. 169-170.

[4] *Ibid.*, p. 394.

[5] *Ibid.*, p. 301.

the judging of others may be called the art of applying the principle of love." [1] This principle makes egotism and altruism into one and the same thing, and makes one regard others as oneself. In short, the principle of love is the end, and the law of reciprocity is the means. This is the unity of Confucianism.

[1] *Classics*, vol. i, p. 194.

CHAPTER III

WRITINGS OF CONFUCIUS AND HIS DISCIPLES

1. WRITINGS OF CONFUCIUS

WE have said that the work of Confucius is no greater than his writings. Let us now consider what his writings are. Since they are called the Holy Bible,[1] and are the oldest and best literature of the Chinese, they occupy the first department of the Chinese library. The study of them is very difficult; many good scholars, spending their whole lives, study thoroughly merely a part of them; yet their principles can never be exhausted. The writings on the subject of the Confucian Bible, therefore, are most numerous. But we shall give the essentials in the most condensed way.

[1] Since the Chinese word for "Bible" was mistranslated by Professor James Legge into the word "Classic," there has been much misunderstanding of the nature of Confucius' writings. It must be contended that these writings are regarded as divinely inspired, because Confucius himself is considered to have been divinely sent and appointed. (Cf. passage from the *Adjunct to the Spring and Autumn*, quoted in the *Annotation of Kung-yang*, 14th year of Duke Ai). An account given in the *Adjunct to the Canon of Filial Piety*, in which Confucius is represented as reporting to God the completion of his writings and as receiving divine approval in the form of a red rainbow coming down from above and transmitting itself into yellow jade with words sculptured upon it, would seem to give to the religion and writings of Confucius in the minds of the Chinese people the same claim to a sacred character as other religions and Bibles possess for the people who accept them. But the real value of the writings of Confucius is not based on such a story.

All the different writings of Confucius himself are called Bibles. But as the word is not ordinarily used in the plural in English, we are obliged to adopt the word "Canon." Originally, the Chinese called them *Ching*, which means Bible. We shall review them according to their original order, as follows:

1. The *Canon of Poetry* contains three hundred and five poems. Except the first two poems of " The Odes of Pin," they were all written by different authors in the Chou dynasty (about 631-47 B. K. or 1182-598 B. C.), but they are edited by Confucius according to his own principles. How many corrections have been made by him we do not know, but we are sure that he must have changed the original words in some way. The poems are divided into three kinds: the *Fêng*, spirits of different nations; the *Ya*, politics of the imperial government; the *Sung*, praises in the temples. Because politics is concerned with great and small questions, the *Ya* is divided up again into Small *Ya* and Great *Ya*. Hence, this Canon has four parts. All the poems are the expression of human nature; the description, narration, or criticism of social and political conditions. Their character is somewhat like that of a newspaper, and they serve as a comparative study of political science. This Canon is also a song book, as all the poems can be sung in harmony with music.

2. The *Canon of History* has twenty-eight books. It covers the history of China from Yao (1806-1707 B. K. or 2357-2258 B. C.) to Duke Mu of Ch'in (108-70 B. K. or 659-621 B. C.), and gives all the most important documents of this period. These documents were written by different authors, and edited by Confucius. But the labor Confucius put on this Canon is evidently greater than that put on the *Canon of Poetry*. The " System of Yao," the " Tribute of Yü," the " Great Model," and the " Code of

WRITINGS OF CONFUCIUS AND HIS DISCIPLES

Po," are apparently the works of Confucius himself, because their style is different from that of the other documents and similar to the style of Confucius. This Canon is a study of history and political science.

3. The *Canon of Rites* has seventeen books, and describes the details of the eight rites. These eight rites are: (1) capping for the indication of maturity, (2) marriage, (3) funeral, (4) sacrifice, (5) district-drinking, (6) game of archery, (7) diplomatic intercourse, and (8) visiting of the emperor by the princes. These eight rites are the rules governing the five social relations: The rites of capping and marriage govern the relation of husband and wife; the rites of funeral and sacrifice, that of father and son; the rites of district-drinking and archery, that of seniors and juniors; the rites of diplomatic intercourse and visiting of the emperor, that of ruler and minister. For the relation of friends, there are the third book on social intercourse, the twelfth book on feasting, and the fifteenth book on the rites of entertaining great officials by a prince. Moreover, through all the different rites there must be two parties, host and guest; hence the relation of friend to friend is within all the rites. Such rites are the old customs and manners, but they are collected and prescribed by Confucius. This Canon is now miscalled *Yi Li*.

4. The *Canon of Music*. Since the songs are all in the *Canon of Poetry*, and the different uses of music are prescribed in the *Canon of Rites*, there was no need to have a canon for music like the other *Five Canons*. But there must originally have been a *Canon of Music*, though different in form from the others, having notes instead of words. Unfortunately it was lost during the Han dynasty, (after 636 A. K. or 85 A. D.). Therefore, we generally speak only of the *Five Canons*.

5. The *Canon of Changes*. Although Pao Hsi first drew

the eight trigrams, and Wên Wang multiplied them into sixty-four hexagrams, the text of this Canon is virtually the exclusive work of Confucius. It is divided into two parts, and has sixty-four books. The first two books of the first part refer to heaven and earth respectively; those of the second part, to the relation between husband and wife; the last two books of this Canon are called "Success" and "Failure". Heaven and earth are the basis of the universal system, and husband and wife that of the social system. As the world never comes to the stage of perfection, and everything must have an end, this Canon ends at the book of Failure. The thought is mystical; the words are figurative; the illustrations are mathematical. The word "changes" has three distinct meanings: easy, changeable, unchangeable; and the principles of this Canon have these three qualities. In fact, the *Canon of Changes* is the doctrine of evolution, and we may adopt the word evolution instead of changes.

6. The *Spring and Autumn*. This Canon was originally the annals of Lu, but Confucius changed them into the present form. It covers the period of two hundred and forty-two years (171 B. K.-71 A. K. or 722-481 B. C.), and records the events during the reigns of twelve dukes. For the preparation of this Canon, Confucius sent fourteen pupils to get the sacred books from one hundred and twenty nations. It is an inductive work, written entirely by Confucius himself. This Canon is the most important of all his works. It is not historical in character; the words drawn from history are but the figures by which Confucius has illustrated his principles. "I should like to convey my ideas as pure theories," said he, "but it is deeper, truer, clearer, brighter, to represent them through the actions of men." He claims the rights of a king, represents his kingdom under the name of Lu, and gives numerous laws along

WRITINGS OF CONFUCIUS AND HIS DISCIPLES

with historical events. Censuring the emperors, abasing the princes, and attacking the great officials, he establishes his kingdom on earth through the *Spring and Autumn*. On this account, Confucius said: "It is only the *Spring and Autumn* which will make men know me, and it is only the *Spring and Autumn* which will make men condemn me."[1]

Of the *Five Canons*, the *Canon of Changes* and the *Spring and Autumn* are the most important. The Canons of *Poetry*, of *History*, and of *Rites* contain materials drawn from the ancients and remodeled by him, but the *Canon of Changes* and the *Spring and Autumn* are written entirely in his own words. The other three are his ordinary teachings; these two, his most important teachings. The *Canon of Changes* is a deductive work, beginning with abstract principles and proceeding to their practical application, while the *Spring and Autumn* is inductive, coming to the general theories through the analysis of facts.[2]

Both the inductive and the deductive method are employed by Confucius. He recognizes the equal importance of them, and points out the dangers of using either exclusively. He says: "Learning without thought is labor lost; thought without learning is perilous."[3] The word learning means induction, and the word thought, deduction. They must be combined and neither one can get along without the other. He tells us from his own experience that the single method of deduction is useless. He says: "I have been the whole day without eating, and the whole night without sleeping—occupied with thinking. It was of no use. The better plan is to learn."[4] Again, he speaks of his

[1] *Classics*, vol. ii, pp. 281-2.
[2] *Historical Record*, ch. cxvii.
[3] *Classics*, vol. i, p. 150.
[4] *Ibid.*, pp. 302-3.

inductive method as follows: "There may be those who write something without the knowledge of it. I have no such fault. Hearing much, and selecting what is good and using it; seeing much, and selecting what is good and writing it down: this way of getting knowledge is second only to having knowledge by birth." [1] From these two passages, it seems that he is more in favor of induction than of deduction.

We must understand, however, that since Confucius was not a historian, but the founder of a religion, his writings are not of a historical but of a religious character. All the data given in his writings, although often true, are primarily figurative illustrations of his own ideas, and he did not necessarily regard them as facts. In the *Analects* he says:

I can describe the civilization of the Hsia dynasty, but the state of Chi cannot sufficiently prove my words. I can describe the civilization of the Yin dynasty, but the state of Sung cannot sufficiently prove my words. It is because of the insufficiency of their literature and scholars. If those were sufficient, I could adduce them in support of my words.[2]

This passage indicates that Confucius himself fails to find historical data on which to base his doctrines, and that the descriptions of the ancient civilization given by him are simply from his own mind. In the "Doctrine of the Mean,"[3] and in the "Evolution of Civilization,"[4] Confucius gives passages similar to the above, so that we are assured that he creates the ancients out of his own mind. Moreover,

---

[1] *Classics*, vol. i, p. 201.
[2] *Ibid.*, p. 158.
[3] *Ibid.*, p. 424.
[4] *Li Ki*, bk. vii, p. 368.

when Mencius was asked by Pei-kung Yi about the arrangement of dignities and emoluments determined by the Chou dynasty, he replied, "The particulars of that arrangement cannot be learned, for the princes, disliking them as injurious to themselves, have all made away with the records of them."[1] We can see, therefore, that in Confucius' time, not only the civilization of the Hsia and the Yin dynasties had no authentic history, but also that of the Chou dynasty was without complete records. How much more doubtful were the things beyond these three dynasties to which he refers? Yet Confucius describes many matters which refer not only to the Three Dynasties, but also to the legendary periods.

When we compare his writings with those of other schools, we find no agreement among the different writers as to the facts, because they all utilize the ancient kings as figures to portray their own theories. Chuang Tzŭ (a pupil of the disciple of Confucius, who, however, turned to Taoism), is such a writer of the extreme type, and Confucius is one of the moderate type. Mo Tzŭ, a young pupil of Confucius, and later the founder of the rival school of Moism, said, "Between two philosophers, their words condemn each other, and their actions oppose each other. Yet they both say, 'I transmit from the ancients the principles of Yao, Shun, Yü, T'ang, Wên, and Wu.'"[2] Han Fei Tzŭ (died 319 A. K. or 233 B. C.), the greatest philosopher of the Law School, formerly a Confucian, said, "Confucius and Mo Tzŭ both speak of Yao and Shun, but what they select or reject is different. Yet they both claim to be the true representatives of Yao and Shun. As Yao and Shun cannot be alive again, who can be sent to determine the truthfulness of Confucius and Mo Tzŭ?"[3] Han Fei Tzŭ, living

[1] *Classics*, vol. ii, p. 373.
[2] Bk. xxv.
[3] Bk. l.

near to the age of Confucius, yet failed to assert whether the things ascribed by Confucius to the ancient kings were true or not; how can we assert such things to-day? It is evident that Confucius creates them himself.

The reason Confucius uses the names of the ancient kings to father his theories is told by himself, when he says to Ts'êng Tzŭ, "I humble myself in order to avoid danger, and refer to the ancient kings in order to borrow authority."[1] On the one hand, he escapes danger from the princes, and on the other, he wins the confidence of the people. Moreover, as China had a glorious history long before his time, and he was a great scholar, it was natural for him to utilize historical materials for his own purpose. But at bottom, all his writings are the fruit of his own mind and for his own religious teachings.

Some people think, however, that Confucius was "a transmitter and not an originator, believing in and loving the ancients," and quote this phrase from his own words in the *Analects*.[2] But these words simply express the characteristic modesty of the Chinese, a quality which Confucius shows in extreme form. Yet he was not always so modest, sometimes confessing that he was an originator. In the *Adjunct to the Spring and Autumn*, he said, "A sage is never born to do nothing; he must produce something in order to show the mind of God. I am 'the wooden-tongued bell', and make laws for the world." In the *Adjunct to the Canon of Filial Piety*, he said, "I am the law-making lord." Confucius was the real creator of his new religion, although incidentally transmitting some elements from the ancients.[3]

---

[1] *Adjunct to the Canon of Filial Piety.*

[2] *Classics*, vol. i, p. 195.

[3] *Cf. Research on the Reformation of Confucius*, published in 2449 (1898 A. D.) by Kang Yu-wei.

WRITINGS OF CONFUCIUS AND HIS DISCIPLES

II. WRITINGS OF THE DISCIPLES OF CONFUCIUS

The *Five Canons* do not give all the teachings of Confucius. So if we wish to learn his teachings, besides studying his own works, we must study also the writings of his disciples. For they are very closely related to each other, and both together make up the religion of Confucianism. If we neglect the writings of his disciples and take up only his own writings, it means that we omit a great part of his teachings, and that therefore we cannot understand him so well, or do him justice.

We shall now point out the names of the writings of his disciples, calling them Records and Commentaries, in order to distinguish them from the Canons of Confucius.

1. *Records and Commentaries*

1. The *Analects*. This is a record of the monologues and conversations of Confucius and his disciples. It was written by his disciples, Chung-kung, Tzŭ-yu, Tzŭ-hsia, and others.

2. The *Canon of Filial Piety*. This may have been written by the pupils of Ts'êng Tzŭ, and it serves as the gateway to the *Five Canons*.

3. The twelve "Records" and the "Commentary of Mourning." These Records are the complements to the twelve books of the *Canon of Rites,* which were written by the pupils of Confucius. The Commentary explains the mourning system prescribed in the Canon itself, and in the Record, and was written by Tzŭ-hsia alone. Both these Records and the Commentary are now contained in the *Canon of Rites*.

4. *Elder Tai's Record of Rites*. It was compiled by Tai Tê. The number of its original books is disputed. It has thirty-nine books now.

5. *Younger Tai's Record of Rites*. It was compiled by Tai Shêng, second cousin of Tai Tê. This has forty-nine

books now, but its original number is also disputed. It is now called the *Record of Rites* (*Li Ki*).

There was originally a compilation entitled *The Records of the Seventy Disciples and Their Followers,* which included all the books written by the disciples of Confucius, even the *Analects* and the *Canon of Filial Piety*. The number of books was two hundred and four. But the scholars of the *Canon of Rites* took many books out of it, and formed a particular encyclopaedia on the subject of rites. The Elder Tai and the Younger Tai, both great scholars of the *Rites* during the reign of Han Hsüan Ti (479-503 A. K. or 73-49 B. C.), compiled these two Records, and they are later called the *Records of Rites*.

6. The "Appendix" of the *Canon of Changes* was written by the disciples of Confucius, and is now contained in the *Canon of Changes* just after the sixty-four books of this Canon.

7. *Kung-yang's Commentary*. In order to understand the principles of the *Spring and Autumn*, nay, in order to understand the principles of Confucius at all, it is necessary to study *Kung-yang's Commentary*. Fearing the injury which the princes would do to his writings, Confucius omitted all detailed explanation in the *Spring and Autumn*, and such explanation is given by this Commentary, which records the oral teachings of Confucius. In fact, it is the keystone of Confucianism. It and the Canon are now contained in a single book.[1]

8. *Ku-liang's Commentary* is also a commentary on the *Spring and Autumn*, and a record of the oral teachings of Confucius. This Commentary is inferior to that of Kung-yang. It also is compiled with the Canon in a single book. These two Commentaries were written by the disciples of Tzŭ-hsia.

[1] The *Annotation of Kung-Yang* given by Ho Hsiu (680-733, or 129-182 A. D.) is very valuable and reliable.

9. The *Seven Adjuncts*. They were seven separate books, each of them supplementing respectively the *Six Canons* and the *Canon of Filial Piety*. The Canons are the warp, the Adjuncts the woof. Some scholars say that they were written by Confucius himself.[1] Since they appeared in the Former Han dynasty, and their interpretations agree with the Canons and the Modern Literature School, they are very valuable, because they give many oral teachings of Confucius. We are sure that they were written by his disciples, although many statements were added to them by the Confucians of the Former Han dynasty. In character, they were religious, mystical and prophetical. Unfortunately, they were prohibited by several emperors, and burned entirely by Sui Yang Ti (about 1156, or 605 A. D.). To-day, there is only a collection of their fragments.

2. Independent Works

There is another kind of writing, which is not the record of the words of Confucius, nor the commentary on his works. Such a kind is called *tzŭ* philosophy. It is a name given to the works either of the founders of different schools, or of the most prominent followers of any school. There are some original and independent thoughts in such writings. Among the Confucians, the most important works of this kind are those of Mencius and Hsun Tzŭ.

1. *Mêng Tzŭ* is the work of Mencius himself, and has seven books.

2. *Hsun Tzŭ* is the work of Hsun Tzŭ (218-339, or 334-213 B. C.), and has thirty-two books.

Although these two books are the independent works of the authors, they are exponents of the principles of Confucius. Therefore, they are not the exclusive products of

---

[1] *History of Sui*, ch. xxxii.

Mencius and Hsun Tzŭ, and form a part of the religion of Confucius.

III. CONCLUSION

Passing through the Ch'in dynasty and the Former Han dynasty, to the time of Liu Hsin (died 574, or 23 A. D.), all the Confucian literature remained the same as the original works of Confucius and his disciples. Unfortunately, when the political usurper, Wang Mang, came to power (551-574, or 1 B. C.-23 A. D.), there was also a religious usurper named Liu Hsin. At that time, books were scarce. Liu Hsin in 545 (7 B. C.) succeeded his father, Liu Hsiang,[1] as the reviewer in the imperial library. Both he and his father were great scholars; but he, under such favorable conditions, made many corruptions in the whole Confucian Bible in order to satisfy his literary purpose and the political purpose of Wang Mang. In 560 (9 A. D.) he was made by Wang Mang the National Teacher. He changed the order of the *Six Canons*—the *Canon of Changes* first, the *History* second, the *Poetry* third, *etc*. Since he had no way to destroy the Bible, he changed the original text somewhat and put some spurious words, statements, chapters, and books into it. Then he wrote or compiled many books for the interpretation of his spurious Bible. He found an ingenious pretext to help him. There had been a burning of literature by the Ch'in Dynasty (339 A. K. or 213 B. C.), but the existence of the Confucian literature was not affected. Yet Liu Hsin pretended that the existing Confucian literature was not complete on account of that fire, and that his spurious books were the only

---

[1] Liu Hsiang (473-544, or 79 B. C. to 8 A. D.) became the reviewer in the imperial library in 526 (26 B. C.), and his son, Liu Hsin, was his assistant. He was the author of the *Park of Narratives*, the *New Narration*, the *Biography of Noteworthy Women*, *etc*. He was one of the greatest authorities in the Modern Literature.

WRITINGS OF CONFUCIUS AND HIS DISCIPLES

old texts rediscovered, in the period between 397 and 423 (155-129 B. C.), which had escaped this burning. Hence, he called his spurious books the Ancient Literature.

Liu Hsin's chief works are these: 1. He compiled the *Official System of Chou* under the feigned name of the Duke of Chou, making the Duke a rival to Confucius. 2. He wrote the spurious *Tso's Commentary*, formed from the greater part of Tso-ch'iu Ming's *Narratives of Nations*, in order to interpret the *Spring and Autumn*. This was a great calamity.[1]

Opposing this spurious Ancient Literature are the true Canons interpreted by the great authorities of the Former Han dynasty. These interpretations are called the Modern Literature. Of course, it is very difficult to distinguish the true Canons from the spurious Canons, especially as many of the books of the Modern Literature have been lost.[2] But,

---

[1] Although the *Official System of Chou* and *Tso's Commentary* are the compilations of Liu Hsin, they give much information about the old customs, institutions and facts, because the materials of the *Official System of Chou* are drawn from the old books, and the *Narratives of Nations* is a history. Therefore, for the sake of mere facts, we cannot help making use of these two books.

[2] Chêng Hsüan (678-751, or 127-200 A. D.) was the chief figure among all the Confucians of the Han dynasty. He studied both the Modern and the Ancient Literature, but his works were based on the latter more than on the former. He was a very good man, and a very good scholar, though he mixed up the Modern and the Ancient Literature. He commented on nearly all the canonical books, taking up the interpretations from both the Modern and the Ancient Literature, but he used the text of the Ancient Literature for his annotation. Therefore, when his annotations were generally accepted, nearly all the Modern Literature was lost, but the Ancient Literature remains. From the time that Liu Hsin made the Ancient Literature, there had always been a bitter rivalry between the two schools, who had never come to any compromise. If such a condition had lasted forever, the Modern Literature would never have been lost. But, since Chêng Hsüan mixed up the two, a great confusion had been interwoven through them, and it is very difficult to distinguish them. Through his influence, the

since some still remain, and since there are many collections of the fragments of the Modern Literature, a most careful study has determined what the true Canons are. While every word cannot be made out, still the *Five Canons* are at least ninety per cent authentic.

Both these two classes of books—the Canons of Confucius, and the Records, Commentaries and the independent works of his disciples—are sources from which we have learned the principles of Confucius. In addition to these authorities, we use many interpretations suggested by the Confucians of different ages, from the Han dynasty to the present day, and information supplied by different philosophers from the Chou dynasty to the Former Han dynasty. But these need not be mentioned here. The details of distinguishing the Modern Literature from the Ancient Literature are very complex, and we have not space to discuss them here.[1] We have been very careful to base this study on the works of the School of Modern Literature, to leave out entirely spurious passages and books, and to present the principles of Confucius with all possible accuracy.

It should be noted that the influence of the writings cited above is exceedingly great. Nearly all Chinese institutions are based upon them. This appears from a consideration of the great events in Chinese history in their chronological order. The abolition of the feudal system, the abolition of

---

forged books of Liu Hsin were diffused and accepted. The people read him, and through him believed Liu Hsin. Therefore he was unconsciously a strong supporter of Liu Hsin, and a betrayer of Confucius. Despite this, he was a great authority, and from him we learn some of the oral teachings of Confucius. His chief works which remain are the *Annotation of the Canon of Peotry*, the *Annotation of the Canon of Rites*, the *Annotation of the Record of Rites*, and the *Annotation of the Official System of Chou*.

[1] The best book for it is the *Research on the False Bible of the School of Hsin*, published in 2442 (1891 A. D.) by Kang Yu-wei.

hereditary officials, the election system, the educational system, the adoption of the calendar of the Hsia dynasty, the three years' mourning, the distribution of the public land—all these were the products of Confucius himself. The theories of these writings are called by the Chinese "canonical principles," and they are of value not only for study, but even more in their application to practical affairs. Therefore, even a single word or a single phrase may be of great importance in the solution of problems of the day. For example, the Chinese want constitutional government, but they refer to Confucius for the support of their demand. Confucius is the chief authority, and it is the habit of the Chinese to seek from these writings sanction or guidance in the determination of important questions. It is necessary to bear these facts in mind in order to understand the significance of the quotations from these writings, no matter how short or how figurative they may be.

It should be noted also that Confucius was not primarily an economist. He was a general philosopher, interested in many things. Throughout all his writings, there is scarcely a single book treating exclusively of economic subjects. But there are many passages and chapters referring to economic life and giving economic principles. When we combine these two classes of writings, we find that economic principles are quite abundant. But the difficulty is that they are scattered through all the writings, and in such a chaotic way that they are not easily collected and arranged. Moreover, when there is an economic principle, it is generally mixed up with something else. Therefore, in bringing together the economic teachings of Confucius from these writings, we shall arrange them in the order of modern economists. That is to say, that while materials are old, the arrangement is quite new.

For the interpretation of these writings, we shall, so far

as possible, pick out the best from among the many old scholars. But, if we are not satisfied with the old interpretation, we are obliged to make a new one according to the original texts. Therefore, while the author does not pretend to any originality, he does claim to have discovered some new truths contained in the old texts.

CHAPTER IV

HISTORICAL MOVEMENTS OF CONFUCIANISM

CONFUCIANISM is the name of the new religion founded by Confucius. The word Confucianism in Chinese is called *Ju*, which may be applied both to the religion of Confucius and to his followers. Since Confucianism has been made the state religion, and practically every Chinese has been a Confucian, the word *Ju* is used narrowly as equivalent to scholar or litterateur,[1] but in its original sense it signifies simply those who believe the teachings of Confucius. Among the whole body of *Ju*, there are still many different classes. Confucius said to Tzŭ-hsia: "You shall be a great man of *Ju*, and shall not be a small man of *Ju*."[2] Hsun Tzŭ[3] classifies the people as these:—the common people, the common *Ju*, the regular *Ju*, and the great *Ju*. In the time of Hsun Tzŭ, Confucianism did not yet rule the whole Chinese people, so that the heathen of Confucianism were called common people. But even within the limit of *Ju*, there were still varying degrees. For the governing of his people, Confucius sets forth the "Conducts of Ju"[4] as the Confucian creed.

Confucianism is the new religion of China, but what was

---

[1] James Legge says: "We must bear in mind that the literati in China do in reality occupy the place of priests and ministers in Christian kingdoms. Sovereign and people have to seek the law at their lips." *Chinese Classics*, vol. ii, p. 53.

[2] *Classics*, vol. i, p. 189. [3] Bk. viii.

[4] *Li Ki*, bk. xxxviii, pp. 402-410.

her old religion? Her old religion was polytheism, and had no special name. According to the *Official System of Chou*[1] there were four classes of spirits—the spirits of heaven, of earth, of the dead, and of all material things—but above all there was a Supreme God. For the communication between the spirits and men, rose the priesthood, which was a body of scholars. They divided their profession into six departments:—(1) astrology, (2) the almanac, (3) the five elements (water, fire, wood, metal and earth), (4) milfoil and tortoise, (5) miscellaneous foretelling (dream-interpreting, devil-driving, prayer, *etc.*), (6) physical laws (the features of geography, of cities, of building, of human beings, of animals, of things, *etc.*). The *History of Han*[2] puts these six professions into the class of " magic ", but they were really a mixture of magic and science which is unintelligible and forgotten to-day.

Under this old religion, the whole empire was ruled by superstition. Confucius was a great religious reformer who swept away the old and established the new. He did not like to talk about extraordinary things and spiritual beings.[3] " To give one's self earnestly," said he, " to the duties due to men, and, while respecting spiritual beings, to keep aloof from them, may be called wisdom."[4] In Confucianism, there is no prayer. Confucius being very sick, Tzŭ-lu, his pupil, asked leave to pray for him. The master said: " My praying has been for a long time."[5] In other words, he had no need of prayer. The *Canon of Poetry* speaks of " seeking for much happiness by yourself,"[6] which Mencius explains as meaning, " Calamity and happiness are in all

---

[1] Chs. xviii, xxvii.   [2] Ch. xxx.
[3] *Classics*, vol. i, p. 201.
[4] *Ibid.*, p. 191.   [5] *Ibid.*, p. 206.
[6] *Ibid.*, vol. iv, pt. ii, p. 431.

cases of man's own seeking."¹ Confucius frees all mankind from supernatural power, and lays stress on the independent cultivation of one's own personality. Any individual, who has reached the highest standard of the means and harmony, can fix the Heaven and Earth and can nourish all things.² In fact, such a religion not only was new to China in ancient times, but is also new in the Western World to-day, where it is only now appearing in such forms as the Ethical Culture Society, though we find its essentials also in the teachings of Aristotle and of the stoics.

Confucianism is a religion of the highest development, so we must not think Confucius unreligious. In the *Canon of Changes,* Confucius said, " The sages took the spiritual way to establish religion, and hence the world submitted to them." ³ " To combine ghost and spirit," said Confucius, " is the good form of religion. . . . The sages framed distinctly the names of ghost and spirit, to constitute a pattern for the black-haired race; and all the multitudes were filled with awe and the myriads of the people constrained to submission." ⁴ All this shows that Confucius recognized the usefulness of the old religion, and so did not destroy it entirely. In his writings, we still find some of the old elements. Because he knew that the world could not attain the final stage at once, he did not carry his ideal too far, and this was one reason why Confucianism was accepted as the state religion of China. From the beginning of Chinese history, the old religion had been combined with politics, and the sage rulers had been the heads of both government and church; but ever since the new religion arose, Confucius,

¹ *Classics*, vol. ii, p. 198.   ² *Ibid.*, vol. i, p. 385.

³ *Yi King*, p. 230. The two words " spiritual way " in Chinese are pronounced *shên tao*. Hence, the Japanese call their religion Shên-taoism.

⁴ *Li Ki*, bk. xxi, pp. 220-221.

coming from an ordinary family, has been "The Throneless King," and religion has been separated from politics—the great sage was not necessarily to have a crown.

We must not think, however, that Confucianism was to become a state religion without a struggle for supremacy. In the periods of Spring and Autumn (171 B. K.-71 A. K. or 722-481 B. C.) and of Warring States (149-331 A. K. or 403-221 B. C.), great philosophers with creative genius were numerous, and each fought for his own doctrines. According to the *History of Han*,[1] there were nine sects: (1) Confucianism, (2) Taoism, (3) Spiritualism (the old religion), (4) The School of Law, (5) The School of Logic, (6) Moism, (7) The School of Diplomacy, (8) The School of Generalization, (9) The School of Agriculture. The most powerful of these were Confucianism, Taoism and Moism. Yang Chu was a great disciple of Lao Tzŭ, and he made Taoism a religion of extreme egoism, while Mo Tzŭ established his own school, which was one of extreme altruism. Yang was like Epicurus, and Mo was like Jesus. During the time of Mencius, the doctrines of Yang and Mo ruled the whole empire, and endangered the existence of Confucianism.[2] A little later, however, as society would not accept the doctrine of Taoism, now made extremely egoistic by Yang Chu, the only rivals were Confucianism and Moism. At the end of the Chou dynasty and the beginning of the Han dynasty, the names of Confucius and Mo Ti had equal prominence, and a life and death struggle between the two coming religions was now going on.

Let us consider the fate of Confucianism. After the death of Confucius, his pupils scattered over the whole empire. Some became teachers and ministers in the govern-

---

[1] Ch. xxx.   [2] *Classics*, vol. ii, pp. 282-3.

ments of different states, some private teachers. In 145 A. K. (407 B. C.), the Marquis Wên of Wei accepted the Confucian Bible from Tzŭ-hsia. This was the first time that Confucianism was recognized as a state religion. About 231 A. K. (321 B. C.), the Marquis Wên of Têng put Confucianism into practice on the advice of Mencius.[1] During this same period, we find that five states—Lu, Ch'i, Wei, Sung, and Ch'in—had established the Board of Great Scholars, (*Po Shih*), the government professorship of Confucianism. Confucianism attained this dominance largely because of the achievements of its disciples. According to *Han Fei Tzŭ*,[2] Confucianism was at that time divided up into eight branches. But the greatest Confucians fighting against all other schools were Mencius and Hsun Tzŭ. When the First Emperor of the Ch'in dynasty consolidated the whole empire, and Li Ssŭ, pupil of Hsun Tzŭ, became the prime minister, Confucianism was made in 339 (213 B. C.) a universal religion throughout the Chinese world, although this tyrannical emperor did not give religious freedom to the people, but confined authority of interpretation to the government.[3] The life of the Ch'in dynasty, however, was short, and the influence of the different schools was still felt during the beginning of the Han dynasty. It was not until 412 (140 B. C.) that Han Wu Ti accepted the proposal of Tung Chung-shu, the greatest Confucian of the Han dynasty, to abolish all other religions and to establish Confucianism as the only one. Then all the other schools, including Moism, died out, and the supremacy of Confucianism was complete.

During the Han dynasty (346-771, or 206 B. C.-220 A. D.), the influence of Confucianism was so great that its

[1] *Classics*, vol. ii, pp. 235-247. [2] Bk. 1.
[3] *Cf. Classics*, vol. i, pp. 7-9.

Bible served not only as a religious book, but also as a legal code. The whole Confucian school in this dynasty may be styled the canonistic school. During the Latter Han dynasty (576-771, or 25-220 A. D.) especially, the moral influence produced by Confucianism was the best in Chinese history. Personal honor and personal liberty were the first considerations; and, during the decay of this dynasty, the students fighting against the bad government sacrificed even their lives. The moral standard of society as a whole was very high. In fact, the Han dynasty, although not following the best principles of Confucius, proved the applicability of Confucianism to practical as well as theoretical problems.

After the Han dynasty, Confucianism fell into a period of decline. Tsao Tsao, the founder of the Wei dynasty, in 761 (210 A. D.) openly decreed official employment of bad men, and destroyed the moral influence that Confucianism had exerted. During the Wei and the Tsin dynasties (771-867, or 220-316 A. D.), Taoism was powerful; and during the Southern and the Northern dynasties, and the Sui and the Tang dynasties (868-1458, or 317-907 A. D.), Buddhism prevailed. Confucianism, although remaining nominally the state religion, had lost its supremacy. Nevertheless, the governments, especially those of the Northern Wei, the Northern Chou and the Tang dynasties, did apply some Confucian principles to political and economic problems, so that the people still enjoyed some of its benefits. There was only one scholar, Han Yü (1319-1375, or 768-824 A. D.), who fought for Confucianism, and against Taoism and Buddhism. Han Yü, not a deep philosopher, but the greatest writer since the Han dynasty, gave a death-blow to Taoism and Buddhism by attacking them from the economic standpoint. But the popular study of this period was literature in the narrow sense, and the Confucian philosophy

HISTORICAL MOVEMENTS OF CONFUCIANISM 47

was the study of but few. Then came the age of the Five Dynasties (1458-1511, or 907-960 A. D.) which, for Confucianism, was worst of all.

But such a decline had to come to an end, and during the Sung dynasty there were many great Confucians. The greatest of these was Chu Hsi (1681-1751, or 1130-1200 A. D.), who was the Martin Luther of Confucianism and whose influence is still strong at the present time. He, however, was a one-sided reformer who emphasized the ethical teachings of Confucius, and omitted his religious views; laid stress on individual character and neglected social welfare. In this dynasty, there was a great statesman named Wang An-shih (1572-1637, or 1021-1086 A. D.), who tried to change the whole of society by economic reforms. There was also a school called Yungchia (about 1714-1775, or 1163-1224 A. D.), that advocated material welfare as well as moral cultivation. But both failed to overcome the general influence of public opinion, and the scholars usually paid much attention to philosophical controversies and forgot practical problems. Passing through the Yüan and the Ming dynasties, the learning was not different from that of the Sung dynasty, although in the Ming dynasty there was Wang Shou-jen (2023-2079, or 1472-1528 A. D.) who was rival to Chu Hsi. For this period (1511-2194, or 960-1643 A. D.) the whole Confucian school may be styled the philosophical school.

In the present dynasty, beginning in 2195 (1644 A. D.), Confucianism has been in the period of renaissance. There were three great Confucians at the beginning of this dynasty: Ku Yen-wu (2163-2232, or 1612-1681 A. D.), Huang Tsung-hsi (2160-2246, or 1609-1695 A. D.), and Wang Fu-chih (2178-2230, or 1627-1679 A. D.). They did not belong to any particular school, but were great in many lines. Then came the school of the canonists. First (about 2287-2371, or 1736-1820 A. D.), they turned from the learning of all the mediæval and modern dynasties to the school of Ancient Literature of the Latter Han dynasty. Second (about 2372-2425, or 1821-1874 A. D.), they went back to the school of Modern Literature of the Former Han dynasty, and new thoughts sprang up. Kung Tsi-chin (born in 2343, or 1792 A. D.) and Wei Yüan (died in 2407, or 1856 A. D.) were the representatives of this movement. In the present day, the greatest exponent of Confucius is Kang Yu-wei, the personal advisor of Tê Tsung in the political reforms of 2449 (1898 A. D.).

We may roughly sum up the historical movements of Confucianism under six heads: (1) the school of the doctrine of Great Similarity, emphasizing liberty, handed down from Tzŭ-yu, Tzŭ-ssŭ to Mencius; (2) the school of the doctrine of Small Tranquillity, emphasizing government, handed down from Chung-kung to Hsun Tzŭ. Li Ssŭ applied it to the government of the Ch'in dynasty (331, or 221 B. C.), and it has lasted to the present day; (3) the theological school, drawn from the whole Bible, and especially from the "Great Model" of the *Canon of History*, the *Canon of Changes*, and the *Spring and Autumn*. Tung Chung-shu and Liu Hsiang were conspicuous representatives, but this school was practically ended after the Han dynasty; (4) the ethical school, the chief element of Confucianism, and highly developed in the Sung and the Ming dynasties; (5) the historical school, based on the *Canon of History* and the *Spring and Autumn*. Ssŭ-ma Chien and other great historians were the representatives; (6) the school of literary research and scientific study, set forth by Confucius, and popularly, but narrowly, applied in the present dynasty.

So far as we can see, we have not yet come to the best principles of Confucius. There have been many causes for this, but the influence of the government on religion has been the most important one. With a few exceptions, the mind of the great mass of students has been controlled by the direction of the government and this has greatly hampered the natural development of Confucianism. As soon as the Chinese shall have established a constitutional government, and secured perfect freedom of thought, Confucianism must enter on a new life. Then we may hope to have the stage of Great Similarity for the whole world.

BOOK II RELATION OF ECONOMICS TO OTHER SCIENCES

CHAPTER V

Economics and Other Sciences in General

1. DEFINITION OF ECONOMICS

THE equivalent of the English term " economics " in Chinese is " administering wealth." Such a term explains itself, and calls for no definition. Let us, however, trace the origin of the term. It occurs first in the " Appendix " of the *Canon of Changes* as follows: "That which enables men to live collectively, is wealth. Administering wealth, formulating rules, and prohibiting the people from doing wrong—this is called justice."[1] Since the " Appendix " was written, the Chinese have usually used the term " administering wealth " for the art of political economy, and also for the science of economics. But the modern Japanese has adopted another Chinese term, *ching chi,* for the word economics; and Herbert A. Giles has put this term, *ching chi,* in his *Chinese-English Dictionary* for " political economy ". The term *ching chi,* however, has a very broad meaning, and is not a good equivalent for the word economics. It generally means statesmanship, and covers the whole field of governmental action. It thus belongs to politics rather than to economics. It will be well, there-

[1] *Yi King*, p. 381.

fore, to keep the old term "administering wealth" as the equivalent of economics, since it is much more accurate and comprehensive than the term *ching chi.*

As we have taken the scientific term from the Confucian text, let us also adopt its definition. The term "administering wealth" covers the whole field of economics. "Formulating rules" and "prohibiting the people from doing wrong" refer respectively to the ethical and political life. All three of these aspects of life should be directed by the principle of justice, and their relations will be stated later. But we must remember that the object of "administering wealth" is man. Our reason for administering wealth is simply that men are living collectively and need wealth to support them. Man is our end, and wealth our means. From this we get as a definition: Economics is the science administering wealth according to the principle of justice, for the sake of men who live collectively.

II. GENERAL RELATION TO OTHER SCIENCES

From the above-quoted passage from the "Appendix" of the *Canon of Changes,* we can understand not only the meaning of economics, but also its relation to other sciences. Since the chief object of "administering wealth" is man, and man living collectively, when we administer wealth, we must deal with the whole body of men. Thus economics is very close to sociology. All the social sciences relate to man, so they all are also connected with economics. But there are two groups, most closely related to economics, that is, the moral and the political sciences. We cannot administer wealth in society without "formulating rules" as to what is right and what is wrong. The way to "formulate rules" is through moral teachings, and under this heading come the sciences of language, education, ethics and religion. We cannot administer wealth in a society without " prohibiting the people from doing wrong ". This we must do by political organizations, and in this group come the sciences of politics and law. All of these sciences —economics, ethics, and politics—are part of the science of justice, and they form a single group. But of them all, economics comes first, and is the most important. If we cannot maintain our economic life, we do not care to formulate our rules, and moral science is useless; we do not fear the prohibition of wrongdoing, and political science is without force. If there is to be any ethics or politics, there must be economic life before them. The "Appendix," therefore, tells us not only the close connection of economics with other sciences, but also the relatively higher importance of economics.

In the "Great Model" contained in the *Canon of History*, there are eight objects of government: " The first is called food; the second, commodities; the third, sacrifices; the fourth, the minister of works; the fifth, the minister of education; the sixth, the minister of justice; the seventh, the entertainment of guests; and the eighth, the army." [1]

These eight objects of government are simply the eight objects of human activities. We can understand their relation to each other from their order. First of all, food is most important, to satisfy hunger; and this word indicates agricultural life. The word commodities includes all other economic goods, among which money holds a prominent place, and indicates commercial and industrial life. These two words, " food and commodities ", represent the whole economic life, and they stand first before any other human activities. After the material wants are satisfied, religious worship begins. Then comes in the minister of works, to improve the physical environment; the minister of education,

[1] *Classics*, vol. iii, pt. ii, p. 327.

to develop the intellectual and moral power; and the minister of justice, to enforce the law. Now, the life of polite society is developed, and this is called the entertainment of guests. Finally, the army is maintained to keep the whole society in peace.

If we compare the eight objects of the "Great Model" with the seven sciences that Roscher groups together—language, religion, art, science, law, the state and economy—we may say that art and science are included in the functions of the minister of works and the minister of education, that language is implied in education, and that the state is represented by all eight objects. If we compare them with the eight groups of Prof. R. T. Ely—language, art, education, religion, family life, society life, political life, economic life—we may say that the family life is a concern of the minister of education. It is remarkable that the statement of the Confucian Bible is so similar to that of the modern economists.

It should be noted that all the great historians, except Ssŭ-ma Chien, have entitled all the economic histories of different dynasties "Record of Food and Commodities". This shows what great influence Confucianism exercises upon the economic thought of the Chinese.

From the "Great Model," we have seen the relation of economics to other sciences in general; and from the "Appendix", we have seen the relation of economics to sociology, politics and ethics in particular. Now, we shall study the relation of economics to these three sciences separately.

CHAPTER VI

Economics and Sociology

1. ECONOMICS AS THE BASIS OF SOCIOLOGY

SINCE economics is the science which administers wealth within human society, we shall consider first the relation between economics and sociology. In order to understand this relation, we must first raise the question, How does society come to exist? For the answer to this question, the "Appendix" has given the statement quoted above, "That which enables men to live collectively, is wealth." Therefore, sociology is dependent upon economics. If there were no wealth, men could not live collectively, and there would be no society. Before many men can live collectively, man must live individually. The individual man cannot live without wealth, but can live without society, because he can get wealth from nature instead of men. Therefore, economics precedes sociology.

For the explanation of the fundamental cause of the formation of co-operative groups, Hsun Tzŭ gives a good sociological theory, and it answers the question as to why society comes to exist. He says:

The water and fire have breath, but without life. The herb and wood have life, but without knowledge. The bird and beast have knowledge, but without justice. Man has breath, life, knowledge, and also justice; hence he is the noblest being in the world. His strength is not equal to that of the bull, and his running is not equal to that of the horse; yet the bull and horse are subjected to him. Why? It is because man is able to be social and they are not. How is man able to be social? It is by the principle of individual right. How can the individual right be realized? By justice. Therefore, justice and individual right make men harmonious. Since men are harmonious, they form one unity. Since they form one unity, they increase their strength. Increasing their strength, they become strong. Since they are strong, they conquer the natural things. Hence, the house can be secured for their safety. Hence, they arrange the four seasons, master all things, and benefit the world universally. It is for no other cause than that man possesses right and justice. Therefore, when man is born, he cannot get along without society. But if society did not distribute the individual right justly, men would quarrel. If they were to quarrel, society would be disorderly. If society were disorderly, men would be disunited. If men were disunited, they would be weak. If they were weak, they could not conquer natural things. Hence, the house could not be secured for their safety. All of which means that rites and justice cannot be left out for a moment.[1]

According to the theory of Hsun Tzŭ, society is based on legal rights, and legal rights are based on ethical justice. But the reason men form a society is simply because they want to unite in order to conquer the natural things through their collective activities. Therefore, the struggle between men and animals is the chief cause for the formation of society. Having society, they are strong enough to conquer these things, otherwise they cannot; and so men survive through being social—a foreshadowing of the principle of "natural selection" in explaining the development of sociality. Indeed, in men's economic needs is found the primary cause of the formation of society.

Pan Ku (583-643 A. K. or 32-92 A. D.) says:

Imitating the manner of heaven and earth, embracing the

[1] Bk. ix.

nature of the five moral constants, man, who is wise, subtile and pure, is the most intelligent being of all the species. His finger nails and his teeth cannot supply his wants. His running cannot escape dangers. He himself has no fur nor feather against heat and cold. He must enslave natural things in order to provide for his nourishment. Trusting to intellectual power and not to physical strength, he is the noble being. Therefore, if men did not love each other, they could not be social. If they were not social, they could not conquer natural things. If they could not conquer natural things, their nourishment would be insufficient. When they gather together, but their nourishment is insufficient, the warring spirit arises. The great sage first superexcellently practises the virtues of respect, deference, and universal love, so that the mass of people love and follow him. If the people follow him and form a society, he is the ruler. If the people come and go to him, he is the king.[1]

According to the theory of Pan Ku, society is based on love. But why should men love each other and form a society? This is simply because men have to conquer nature for their nourishment. Here, Pan Ku gives the same reason for the formation of society as that which is given by Hsun Tzŭ, namely, economic utility. But Hsun Tzŭ mentions the house because he emphasizes the struggle for safety, while Pan Ku mentions nourishment, because he emphasizes the struggle for subsistence. Yet their fundamental point is the same.

The social constitution is established not always according to the idea of the sages, but mostly through the historical development of actual conditions. And this actual condition is based on economic causes, namely, the struggle

[1] *History of Han*, ch. xxiii. The word "society" and the word "ruler" in the Chinese language are both pronounced *chün*, and the words "go" and "king," *wang*. In the Chinese characters, the words in each pair have also marked similarity in form.

for existence. In his "Essay on Feudalism", Liu Chung-yüan (1324-1370 A. K. or 773-819 A. D.) says:

In the beginning man is born at the same time with other things. The vegetable kingdom is wild, and the animal kingdom is cruel. Man cannot fight with his hand and eat with his mouth, as can the beast. He also has no feathers, as has the bird. He is unable to be self-supporting and self-protecting. Hsun Tzŭ has said that he must borrow some material things from outside for his use. Generally, if he borrows some material things from outside, struggle or war must arise. If the war is ceaseless, he must come to one who can decide the dispute, and must obey his dictate. Those who are the wise men must have a great number of subjects. When the wise men tell them what is right and they do not correct themselves, punishment must be used to increase their fear. In this way, the ruler, the leader, laws and politics arise. Therefore, the men of the neighborhood organize themselves into a society. But, when the society is formed, the division is sharper, and the war must be greater. When the war is greater, military force and personal virtue are more important. If there are those who possess the greater virtue, the leaders of various societies will come to them and obey their dictate, in order to keep their members peaceful. Hence, the class of feudal lords exists; but the war is still greater. If there are those who possess still greater virtue, the feudal lords will come to them and obey their dictate, in order to keep their territory peaceful. Hence, some sort of leading princes exist; but the war is still greater. If there is a man whose virtue is greatest of all, the leading princes will come to him and obey his dictate, in order to keep all the people peaceful. Then the whole world is united into one. Therefore, there must be first the masters of towns, then the magistrates of districts. Having the magistrates, then come the feudal lords. Having the feudal lords, then come the leading princes. Having leading princes, then arises the emperor. From the emperor to the town-master, if their virtue has impressed the mind of the people, the people certainly support their posterity, after their death, in holding their office through hereditary right. Therefore, feudalism is not the idea of the sages, but only the necessity of the condition.

According to Hsun Tzŭ, society is based on justice; according to Pan Ku, on love; and according to Liu Chung-yüan, on necessity. These three theories—legal, ethical and historical—are correct, although they are from different points of view. But why does society come to exist? On this point, they give the same answer. Man is physically weaker than other animals. If he wants to conquer other things, or enslave them, or borrow them from outside, he must make himself stronger. If he wants to make himself stronger, he must co-operate with his fellows. If he co-operates with his fellows, such a society must be based on justice, love and necessity to avoid war and keep peace. Therefore, society is the result, but economic life is the cause. Had the human being had no economic needs, society would not exist. Why do men regard social justice and observe individual right? Why do men love each other and restrain the warring spirit? Why do men make war against each other before society is formed, and why is the war still greater when that society is larger? Why do the warlike animals subdue their passions and come to the arbitrator, obey the law of the ruler and keep peace among themselves? It is simply for their own interest. But their own interest is nothing greater than the economic interest In a word, society is an organization carrying on the struggle for existence in collective form. Ethics and law, religion and politics, love and hatred, peace and war, justice and injustice, all of them are the results of economic causes. Indeed, economic interest is the basis of everything. According to Liu Chung-yüan, war continues among the diferent sizes of societies, and it ceases only in the unification of the whole world. It is the doctrine of "great uniformity" of Confucius. But, in the past, the world from the Chinese point of view was fictitious; in the present, the world is the real one. By the application of "great uniformity" to the real world, the whole world will be equalized into a single economic unit, and industrialism instead of militarism will dominate the globe. In short, world economy is the solution of the problems of world sociology, and it is the step to the stage of Great Similarity.

II. ECONOMICS AS THE BASIS OF RELIGION

As religion is a great force in social life, we may ask how it comes to exist. The answer to this question is given by Confucius, who says:

The first development of religion began with food and drink. Primitive people roasted millet and pieces of pork on heated stones; they excavated the ground in the form of a jar, and scooped the wine from it with their two hands; they fashioned a handle of clay, and struck with it an earthen drum. Simple as this economic life was, they yet seemed to be able to express by these things their reverence for spiritual beings.[1]

That is, food and drink follow heaven and earth, and worship follows food and drink. This means that immediately after the creation of heaven and earth, as soon as there is a man, there must be economic life; and that the religious life comes next. The "Great Model," therefore, puts "sacrifices" next only to "food and commodities". Indeed, economic satisfaction is the condition necessary for the development of religion.

[1] *Li Ki*, bk. vii, p. 368.

III. ORIGIN OF MAN

Since economics and sociology are interdependent, we should study the sociological teachings of Confucius in order the better to understand his economic teachings. Among all his sociological teachings, there is nothing more important than the doctrines of the fatherhood of God and the brotherhood of man. With these doctrines as a basis, there arise the principle of universal love, the principle of universal equality, and the principle of individual independence. We may designate these doctrines by a phrase—the origin of man. One cannot understand the foundations of society until he knows the origin of man, but he cannot think of the origin of man until he satisfies his economic wants.

We have already said that the word *Yüan* is similar to the word God and that they are different only from different points of view. However, we shall discuss them more fully, and take up the doctrine of *Yüan* first. The word *Yüan* is the first word of the *Spring and Autumn*, and it is the chief principle of Confucius' philosophy. Ordinarily, one says the first year of the reign of so and so, but Confucius says, " *yüan* year " instead of the first year. Ho Hsiu comments: " *Yüan* is the infinite breath, from which the immaterial things arise and the material things are separated. It creates heaven and earth, and it is the beginning of heaven and earth." This is the theory of creation in Confucianism. The *Many Dewdrops of the Spring and Autumn*[1] says: " Only the holy man can relate the myriad of things to one and subject them to the *Yüan*. ... *Yüan* means the origin. ... *Yüan* is the root of everything, upon which the origin of man depends. Where is the origin of man? It precedes heaven and earth." The

---
[1] Written by Tung Chung-shu, bk. xiii.

Canon of Changes says: "How great the masculine *Yüan* is! All things owe to it their beginning. It governs the heavens." [1]

Yüan is the ruling power governing the whole universe. It is interpreted most clearly by Ho Hsiu, who says, "*Yüan* is the infinite breath." In fact, it is the natural and originating force of everything. In the "Evolution of Civilization," it is called Grand Unity.[2] In the "Appendix," it is called Grand Summit.[3] But the name of Grand Unity can be changed into the word Heaven in the "Evolution of Civilization," and the word Heaven is identified with the word God in many places. Therefore, the word *Yüan* is identified with the word God. The reason Confucius prefers the word *Yüan* to the word God is because *Yüan* is infinite, while God is personal. Indeed, Confucius writes from the philosophical rather than from the religious point of view.

Since *Yüan* is the origin of everything, the origin of man must be derived from it. But it is not only the origin of man, but also the origin of the heavens. Therefore, man may originally have come from *Yüan* either at the same time with the heavens, or afterward, or even before them. This doctrine is the highest theological stage. It makes every man free from supernatural power, and dependent upon his own conscience. According to this doctrine, we may call *Yüan* our father, instead of God; and we may call not only all men our brothers, but even all the heavens. Wearing the heavens, and standing upon the earth, how noble is man! All that man can do and all that he ought to do are merely the duties of man, and nothing else. The object of man is simply to be a man. Man is not only the son of God, but also his assistant and his co-ordinate.

[1] *Yi King*, p. 213.
[2] *Yi King*, p. 313.
[3] *Li Ki*, bk. vii, p. 386.

We now come to the doctrine of the fatherhood of God proper, stated very clearly in *Ku-liang's Commentary*, which says:

The female alone cannot give birth; the male alone cannot give birth; and God alone cannot give birth. The three must unite together, then there is a birth. Therefore, we may call anyone either the son of his mother, or the son of God. But, according to his social position, the honorable person takes the honorable designation, while the common people take the common one. That some one is called king is simply because the people come to him.[1]

This is the doctrine of the trinity in the Confucian religion; it means that the union of father, mother, and God, gives birth to everyone. The *Many Dewdrops of the Spring and Autumn* says: "There never has been a birth without the influence of God. God is the father of everything."[2]

The doctrine of the brotherhood of man has already been included in the doctrine of the fatherhood of God. But we may quote two passages showing this doctrine separately. Confucius says: "All within the four seas are brothers."[3] Again he says: "A holy man is able to make the whole world as one family, and the Middle Kingdom as one person."[4] Therefore, from Confucius' point of view, the whole world is but a single family, and all the men are brothers of this same family.

The best explanation for the principle of universal love is given by Chang Tsai, a great Confucian in the Sung dynasty (1571-1628, or 1020-1077 A. D.). He says:

The virtue of Heaven is called our Father, and the virtue of Earth is called our Mother. Although we are small beings, we

[1] 3rd year of Duke Chuang.   [2] Bk. lxx.
[3] Quoted by Tzŭ-hsia, *Classics*, vol. i, p. 253.
[4] *Li Ki*, bk. vii, p. 379.

are their mixture and stand firmly in the middle. Therefore, the full breath of Heaven and Earth is our body, and the strong spirit of Heaven and Earth is our mind. All people are our brothers, and all things are our companions. The great ruler is the heir of our Parents, and the great minister is his steward. To respect the seniors of the world is to honor our older brothers, and to pity the weak is to help our younger brothers. The holy men are those who possess virtue equal to that of our Parents, and the wise men are the leaders of ourselves. All the unfortunate persons of the world, through physical weariness, old age, severe sickness, the brotherless, childless, widowers and widows, are calamitous and helpless brothers of our own.[1]

As to the principle of universal equality, we may look at it from two aspects. First, from the religious aspect, not only the founder of a religion is the son of God, but everyone is the son of God. On this point, Confucianism is more democratic than Christianity, because the Confucians never say that Confucius is the " only begotten son " of God. Mencius says: " The holy man and we are the same in kind."[2] The Confucian religion gives full freedom of thought to everybody,[3] and promotes everybody to the highest position, equal to God. The Confucian church has never had such a head as the pope, and the Chinese emperor is not the head of the church. Throughout the whole of Chinese history, no blood has ever been shed on account of religious controversy. In a word, China enjoys complete religious freedom.

Second, from the political aspect, not only is the emperor the son of God, but every one is the son of God. In Confucianism, there is no such thing as the " divine right " theory. Five hundred and seventy-one years be-

[1] *Correction of the Youth*, ch. xvii.
[2] *Classics*, vol. ii, p. 405.　　　[3] *Yi King*, p. 389.

fore Confucius, Chou Wu Wang cut off the head of the Emperor Chou, and put it on the top of a flag. Confucius said that the revolution of Wu Wang was in accordance with the will of God.[1] Mencius also said that the act of Wu Wang was not that of a regicide, but simply the execution of an outcast.[2] From 343 to 350 A. K. (209-202 B. C.) China had as great a revolution as had France in 2341 A. K. (1790 A. D.). By this great revolution, the common people began to rule the empire. Hence, China has been at the stage of democracy since this revolution, although in many respects she did not change the monarchical form. The *General Discussion in the White Tiger Palace*[3] says: " The nomination, ' The Son of God,' [emperor], is merely an honorable title." Indeed, China has been the most democratic country of the world, with the exception of the really constitutional states at the present time.

The best illustration of the principle of individual independence is given in the *General Discussion in the White Tiger Palace*. It says:

Why should a father be executed for killing his son? "Among all the lives given by Heaven and Earth, that of man is the noblest." All men are the children of God, and are merely born through the breath of father and mother. The emperor should nourish and teach them. Hence the father has no absolute power over his son.[4]

This is a very important principle of Confucius. Unless we understand it, we might make the mistake of thinking that in accordance with the teachings of Confucius a father has the power of life and death over his son, and the son has no independence. But this is not the case. In a family,

---

[1] *Yi King*, p. 254.   [2] *Classics*, vol. ii, p. 167.
[3] Written by Pan Ku in 630 (79 A. D.), bk. i.   [4] Bk. v.

one is the son of his father; in a state, he is the citizen of the emperor; in the universe, he is the son of God. Therefore, according to the *Canon of History*, the punishment for the unkind father is equal to that for the undutiful son, and no member of the family is responsible for the crime of any other member.[1]

This is personal liberty. But we should consider also personal responsibility. Confucius puts great emphasis on the cultivation of personality. The " Great Learning " says: " From the emperor down to the mass of the people, all must consider the cultivation of personality the root of everything besides."[2] Ts'êng Tzŭ says: " One cannot be a student without breadth of mind and vigorous endurance. His responsibility is heavy and his way is long. He assumes universal love as his own responsibility;—is it not heavy? Only with death does his way come to an end;—is it not long?"[3] This is the type of student from the Confucian standpoint. After Mencius, Lu Chiu-yüan (1691-1743 A. K. or 1140-1192 A. D.) and Wang Shou-jen distinguished their school on the basis of personal liberty and personal responsibility. The teachings of Lu Chiu-yüan are as follows: " Even if I do not know a single word, I must try my best to become a man gloriously." " While above is heaven and below is earth, man lives in the middle. Unless he is able to become a man, his life is of no use." Indeed, the Confucians put a great deal of emphasis on personal responsibility, since man is the son of God and is independent.

IV. POSITION OF WOMAN

Next to the origin of man, the most important question is the position of woman. Since man and woman are the

[1] *Cf. Classics*, vol. iii, pt. ii, pp. 392-3.
[2] *Classics*, vol. i, p. 395. [3] *Ibid.*, pp. 210-211.

two component parts of society, her position is very important, not only for the social life, but also for the economic life. Therefore, we shall study her position from the point of view of Confucius.

First, according to the teachings of Confucius, the position of woman is equal to that of man. From the emperor to the common people, the wife of each is his equal. Therefore, the word wife means equal. And the *Canon of Changes* even says that with the repression of the one for the satisfaction of the other, man is placed below woman in relative position.[1] Hence, the relation of husband and wife is called " brothers " by Confucius.[2] And the *Canon of Poetry* also says: " Love your bride as your brothers."[3]

For the equality of man and woman, Confucius prescribes the rite of " personal receiving " as a necessary ceremony for marriage, that is, the bridegroom must go to the bride's home to receive her personally. This rite is necessary for all classes, not excepting even the emperor. In the *Canon of Poetry* and the *Spring and Autumn*, there are many condemnations of those who do not observe this rite. Confucius was asked by Duke Ai of Lu if to wear a crown for the exercise of " personal receiving " would be too ceremonious. Confucius answered him by saying that an emperor must pay respect to his wife.[4] Indeed, the rite of " personal receiving " is to indicate the principle of respect for woman. Mo Tzŭ attacked Confucius on this point by saying that one is as respectful and humble as a servant to his wife; that the ceremony of taking her to the carriage is like the service due to one's parents; and that all the

[1] *Yi King*, p. 238.
[2] *Cf. Li Ki*, bk. v, p. 320. But it is incorrectly translated.
[3] *Classics*, vol. iv, pt. i, p. 54.
[4] *Li Ki*, bk. xxiv, pp. 264-6.

ceremonies of marriage are as solemn as those of sacrifices.[1] From the argument of Mo Tzŭ, we know clearly that Confucius raised the position of woman very high.

Another example illustrating the equality of man and woman is that the married woman preserves her own name after marriage. We shall see that Confucius regards the name of anyone as very important as it identifies the personailty and is dearer even than life.[2] If anyone cannot have his own name, it means that he loses his personality and cannot leave any mark upon the world. This is the worst of calamities. Europeans and Americans are proud of the high position of their women, but the married woman must give up her own name, and adopt the name of her husband, being known as Mrs. So-and-so. This means that she cannot keep her individuality and is merely a dependant of her husband; whereas, among the Chinese, the married woman has her individual name. In the *Spring and Autumn,* Confucius always gives the name of the women themselves, such as Po-chi, Shu-chi, Chi-chi, Chung-tzŭ, Ch'êng-fêng, *etc.* It shows that woman does not lose her individuality after marriage, and that she is equal to man.

Second, we shall consider the separation of the two sexes. This was an old custom, and was recognized by Confucius. The " Details of Rites " says:

Man and woman should not sit together in the same apartment, . . . nor let their hands touch in giving and receiving. A sister-in-law and brother-in-law do not interchange compliments about each other. . . . When a young lady has been engaged, . . . no man should enter the door of her apartment, unless there be some grave occasion [such as great sickness, or death, or other great calamity]. When a married aunt, or sister, or daughter, returns home on a visit, no brother of the

[1] Bk. xix.   [2] See *infra.*

family should sit with her on the same mat or eat with her from the same dish. Even father and daughter should not occupy the same mat. Man and woman, without the intervention of the matchmaker, do not know each other's name. Unless the engagement has been accepted, there should be no communication or affection between them.[1]

Since human nature is universally the same, the social life of the Far East cannot differ very much from that of the West. Therefore, the separation of the two sexes was not the original plan in China. In the *Canon of Poetry*, there are many poems describing a social life quite like that of the West to-day. We may select two stanzas from two poems for examples. The one reads this way:

> The Tsin and the Wei,
> Now present their broad sheets of water.
> Ladies and gentlemen
> Are carrying flowers of valerian.
> A lady says, "Shall we go to see?"
> A gentleman replies, "I have already been."
> "But let us go again to see.
> Beyond the Wei
> The ground is large and fit for pleasure."
> So the gentlemen and ladies
> Make sport together,
> Presenting one another with small peonies.[2]

The other reads as follows:

> [The girl] goes out on a fine morning;
> Then [the boy and girl] proceed together.
> "I look on you as the flower of the thorny mallows;
> You give me a stalk of the pepper plant!"[3]

[1] *Li Ki*, bk. i, pp. 77-8.
[2] *Classics*, vol. iv, pt. i, p. 148.   [3] *Ibid.*, p. 207.

From what has been described by the two stanzas, the reader may not find any difference in the social life of the West and China; and he may not see any wrong in such a gathering of the two sexes. But Confucius puts them in the *Canon of Poetry* as bad examples of a lewd custom. The separation of the sexes was indeed generally approved by the ancient Chinese, but such a theory was strengthened very much by Confucius.

The separation of the sexes was developed on historical facts. Formerly, when the princes called on each other, the princess came out with her husband for the " great entertainment " of the guests. But, the Marquis of Yang, on such an occasion, killed the Marquis of Mu, and stole away his wife. This is something like the story of the Trojan War, when Paris visited the Spartan king, Menelaus, and took away secretly his wife, Helen. According to Confucius, the abolition of the practice of making a princess part of the " great entertainment " was due to the Marquis of Yang.[1] From this instance, we can see that the sexes were not formerly separated so severely as in later times. But such a custom was gradually developed in many cases, even long before the age of Confucius.

The simple reason for the separation of the sexes is for the preventing of illicit intercourse. Confucius says:

The ceremonial usages prevent the people from excesses; they display the separation which should be maintained between the sexes; and they make the people free from suspicion, in order to define the relations of the people. Therefore, man and woman do not make friendship when there is no go-between, and they do not meet together when there is no ceremonial present;—these are for the distinction between the two sexes.[2]

[1] *Li Ki*, bk. xxvii, p. 298.

[2] *Ibid.*, p. 297. But its translation has left out a few sentences.

Although the separation of the two sexes has raised the standard of morality, it has retarded economic development. Montesquieu says:

The society of the fair sex spoils the manners and forms the taste; the desire of giving greater pleasure than others establishes the embellishments of dress; and the desire of pleasing others more than ourselves gives rise to fashions. This fashion is a subject of importance; by encouraging a trifling turn of mind, it continually increases the branches of its commerce.[1]

From this statement of Montesquieu, we may understand why the economic condition of China has been stationary for so long a time. The chief reason for it is that the Chinese woman has been separated from the man, so that social life is dry and commercial development slow. Setting aside the question of right and wrong, woman is, indeed, the spice of society, and the promoter of economic progress. But the ancient Chinese, although they might have realized the economic advantage of letting woman share society with man, were afraid of the moral disadvantage, her possible loss of chastity.

We must understand, however, that the separation of the sexes does not mean that woman is not the equal of man. Of course, in a paternal society, woman inevitably suffers many disadvantages. But, as far as the separation is concerned, woman is equal to man. Though women cannot join the social gatherings of men, and so lose a great amount of social pleasure, on the other hand, men cannot share the social gatherings of women, and they, too, suffer the loss of such social pleasure. On this point, man never can have more privileges than woman,

[1] *Spirit of Laws*, vol. i, p. 318. Bohn's Library, George Bell & Sons, 1906.

although he belongs to the more fortunate sex and may enjoy some things which woman cannot have. Thus, the fundamental principle of equality is not altered by the separation.

Third, we shall see that Confucius has sanctioned the social intercourse of man and woman. According to his *tsing tien* system, during the winter, from the tenth month to the first, men and women should work together at weaving in the same street from evening to midnight. This is an extremely unusual example of the commingling of the sexes and the promotion of social intercourse. Moreover, during these four months, whenever men and women have any dissatisfaction, the two sexes may sing together to express their discontent.[1] This affords great freedom of social contact of the two sexes.

Again, according to the principles of *Spring and Autumn*, the queen and princess must have teachers and nurses. The teachers, who are selected from the old great officials, look after their conduct. The nurses, who are selected from the wives of the great officials, look after their physical welfare.[2] This principle is quite significant. As soon as the old great officials can be selected as the teachers of the queen and princess, the separation of men and women is destroyed. Therefore, separation is not the ideal of Confucius, but only a necessary custom for the time being.

Fourth, the political rights of woman are given to her by Confucius, and these rights are indicated in the instance of holding office. This principle is one of the most valuable things mentioned in the *Spring and Autumn*. Under the *tsing tien* system of Confucius, if the women have no children at the age of fifty, they are to be given clothes and food by the government; and they are to be appointed

[1] The *Annotation of Kung-yang*, 15th year of Duke Hsüan.
[2] 30th year of Duke Hsiang.

commissioners for the collection of poetry from the people.[1] This shows that Confucius thinks that women are qualified to hold government office. Since the commission of collecting poetry is equal to the imperial commission of to-day, it is quite different from inferior service. Moreover, it implies that the education of women should be very high, otherwise they could not take the office and could not understand poetry. This principle will have great importance in the future.

Fifth, we may learn that the absolute independence of woman is the final stage of the doctrine of Confucius. We have already seen that in the Great Similarity there is no marriage, but we shall discuss this more fully here. The stage of Small Tranquillity accepts all the present institutions, but that of Great Similarity does not. The fundamental difference between these two stages is the independence of woman, and it forms the basis for the changes from Small Tranquillity to Great Similarity. Therefore, in the Small Tranquillity, Confucius mentions all the family relations, such as father and son, brothers, husband and wife. But, in the Great Similarity, he does not mention them at all, and says that "men do not regard as their parents only their own parents, nor treat as their children only their own children." Here Confucius does not use the words husband and wife, but uses the words man and woman. "Each man has his rights, and each woman her individuality safeguarded," are the two fundamental bases of Great Similarity. But how can this be? It is simply that they have to abolish the institution of marriage.

What Confucius means by "each woman has her individuality safeguarded" is that she is not the wife of any man. She has her individual personality, and in all things

---

[1] 15th year of Duke Hsüan.

depends upon herself. She does not lose any individuality on account of sexual relations to man. When she loves a man, it is simply like the act of shaking hands or dancing with a man, and she does not become the property of man. Kang Yu-wei, in the fifth book of his *Book on the Great Similarity*,[1] has given a very good explanation of this principle. His theory is something like this. The institution of marriage is changed to a legal agreement of love, and the names of husband and wife are abolished. Such an agreement must be limited to a certain length of time. When it expires, the contracting parties may either dissolve immediately, or renew it successively until the end of their life, or dissolve first and renew it again in later times. In fact, there is perfect freedom for them to do what they want in accordance with their true love. The time limit of an agreement is not longer than one year, nor shorter than one month.

If the tie of marriage is destroyed, however, the functions of the family must be handed over to the state. Therefore, the sixth book treats of the substitution of the state for the family. In the Great Similarity, the state is a world republic. All the people are cared for by the state. As soon as a woman is pregnant, she must go to the " school of gestatory education " in order to teach the child before he is born. At the age of twenty, the child's education is completed, and he is independent and may go his own way. After the age of sixty, he can live in the " house of old age " until he dies. Indeed, the state is the large family for everybody. Only in this way can woman get absolute independence.

Apart from the doctrine of Great Similarity given by Confucius, the ancient Chinese never talked of the abolition

[1] This book has not been published yet, but Kang Yu-wei kindly sent the author a duplicate of the manuscript.

of marriage. The only exception to this was Lieh Tzŭ, a philosopher in the period of Warring States. He describes a Utopian state called Extreme North, where everything is very happy and pleasant. As to the social relations, he gives the following four sentences: " The old and young live equally; there is no ruler, nor minister. The men and women ramble together; there is no matchmaker, nor engagement."[1] This is a picture somewhat like that of the Great Similarity.

In conclusion, the position of woman is this: fundamentally woman is the equal of man. But, in the Disorderly Stage, the separation of the two sexes is advisable; in the Advancing Peace Stage, social intercourse between the sexes is suitable; in the Extreme Peace Stage, the absolute independence of woman is most lovely and just. All these are harmonious with the doctrine of the Three Stages of Confucius.

[1] Bk. v.

CHAPTER VII

Economics and Politics

1. ECONOMICS AS THE BASIS OF POLITICS

In order to understand the relation between economics and politics, let us take the " System of Yao," the first book of the *Canon of History,* written by Confucius to represent his political program. According to this, the whole government is divided into nine departments. The first one is the department of water and earth, the interior department assigned to the prime minister; the second, that of agriculture; the third, that of education; the fourth, that of justice; the fifth, that of labor; the sixth, that of natural resources, charged with the forests, the animals and the mines; the seventh, that of religion; the eighth, that of music; the ninth, that of communication, the mediator between the emperor and the people. Of the nine departments, none is for personal service to the emperor, showing the principle of democracy, and none for the preparation of war, indicating the principle of peace. But four departments out of the nine—the first, the second, the fifth and the sixth—are charged with economic functions. From the second book of the *Canon of History,* it appears that the functions of commerce are included in the first department.[1] Therefore, the whole government is, in large part, a tool for economic development. Indeed, if there were no economics, there would be no politics; the government exists chiefly for

---

[1] See *infra.*

economic reasons. It is not a military, but an industrial society.

In the *Analects,* also, there is a chapter showing very clearly the relation between economics and politics. When Yen Yüan, Confucius' best pupil, modestly puts his question with reference to the government of a state, he really asks how the government of a universal empire should be administered. The answer of Confucius is:

Adopt the calendar of the Hsia dynasty. Ride in the state carriage of the Yin dynasty. Wear the crown of the Chou dynasty. Imitate the music of Shao and Wu. Banish the tunes of Chêng, and keep far from specious talkers. The tunes of Chêng are licentious; specious talkers are dangerous.[1]

This chapter has been highly praised by all scholars through all ages, but none has understood the meaning of it. Its exact meaning is similar to that of the last chapter of the "Great Learning." The subject of that chapter is the governing of the state and the equalizing of the whole world, and there are only two ways to realize such a purpose, namely, administering wealth and employing the best men. This chapter has exactly these two principles. Keeping far from specious talkers is the negative form of stating the principle of employing the best men. All the four positive rules are economic principles. The calendar of Hsia is most seasonable; to adopt it means to keep the agricultural works in the best time. The carriage of Yin is most economical and lasting; to ride in it means to promote commerce by means of economical and lasting transportation. The crown of Chou is most beautiful; to wear it means to raise the standard of workmanship. These three things, calendar, carriage and crown, refer to agri-

[1] *Classics,* vol. i, pp. 297-8.

culture, commerce, and industry respectively. These three sentences are more concerned with the production of wealth than with its consumption, while the fourth sentence, which mentions music, refers to consumption. The music of Shao belonging to Shun and that of Wu belonging to Wu Wang, both are the best music of the ancients; to imitate them means to better the standard of life in the most refined stage, while to banish the tunes of Chêng is simply to prevent excess of pleasure. Therefore, Confucius gives Yen Yüan six rules, four positive and two negative; but five rules out of the six are economic principles. In fact, the first way of governing either a state or a universal empire is to reform economic life, and the second way is to employ good men. These are the essential meanings of this chapter, although Confucius uses figures of speech. Unless we understand that Confucius refers to economic principles, how can we explain how a calendar, a carriage, and a crown have anything to do with the governing of a state or a universal empire? According to the old interpretation, the answer of Confucius has no significance. But according to our interpretation, it means that the chief concern of a government is economic life.

Mencius also recognizes that economics is the chief object of politics. When the Marquis Wên of Têng asks him about the proper way of governing a state, he replies: "The business of the people should not be remissly neglected." What he means by the business of the people is their economic life. Then he explains the importance to the people of permanent property as that which he has told the King Hsüan of Ch'i,[1] and his conclusion for the betterment of their economic condition is the *tsing tien* system.[2] The answer of Mencius is quite significant. What

---

[1] See *infra*.   [2] *Classics*, vol. ii, pp. 239-245.

the Marquis asks about is the business of the state—politics. But what Mencius discusses in his answer is the business of the people—economics. It seems that Mencius does not answer directly the question of the Marquis. But he really answers him from the fundamental point of view. For the business of the people is the chief business of the state; and if a ruler can attend to such business earnestly, he will govern the state well. In short, besides economics, there is no politics, and true politics is economics.

II. POLITICS AS THE PROMOTER OF ECONOMIC LIFE

While economic forces form the basis of political organization, political organization in turn promotes economic development. Mencius says: "Without the great principles of government and its various activities, wealth will not be sufficient."[1] Therefore, the economic needs are the causes for the existence of government, and a good government is also the cause of successful economic life.

The simplest reason for the economic development of a good government is given in the "Great Commentary":

When a ruler attaches importance to the state, he loves the people. When he loves the people, punishments and penalties are just. When punishments and penalties are just, the people are peaceful. When people are peaceful, wealth is sufficient. When wealth is sufficient, all purposes can be realized.[2]

Judging from this reasoning, economic development is based on legal development. When legal development comes to the stage of just punishments and penalties, the people can engage peacefully in different occupations, and the production of wealth may be sufficient. This is the type of

[1] *Classics*, vol. ii, p. 483.
[2] *Li Ki*, bk. xiv, p. 67.

patriarchal government. But, even in the democratic government of modern time, economic development is still based on legal justice. If there were no good law, there could not be great industries. Therefore, good government is necessary for economic development, and politics paves the way for economics.

III. GENERAL PRINCIPLES OF GOVERNMENT

Since politics paves the way for economics, we should study the political teachings of Confucius in order to understand the background for his economic principles. Therefore, we shall study first his principles of government in general, and then his system of instruction in particular. If we take these as illustrating Confucius' political views, we shall understand the economic principles in his mind.

1. *Imperial Democracy*

According to Confucius, the external form of government is monarchical, but the fundamental principle of it is democratic. The four parts of the *Canon of Poetry* all begin with Wên Wang, who represents the type of constitutional monarchy. The *Canon of History* begins with Yao and Shun, who represent the type of republic. The *Spring and Autumn* begins with Wên Wang and ends with Yao and Shun. These are enough to show that in the ideal government of Confucius the sovereign power is in the hands of the people. Of course, Confucius teaches the people to be loyal to their ruler; but what he means by a ruler is the man who has the best character and talents. The " Great Learning " gives a very good definition of the patriarchal government of Confucius. It says: " Loving what the people love, and hating what the people hate: this is he who is called the parent of the people." As soon as the people turn away from their ruler, he is no longer to be a ruler, but a single fellow. If he is a bad man, according to the

" Great Learning," he will be executed by the people of the whole world.¹ Tyrannicide is recognixed as a great deed by all great Confucians, because they do not recognize the tyrant as a ruler.

Confucius himself has the revolutionary idea; in the *Canon of Changes,* he gives a book entitled " Revolution." He says: " Heaven and earth are revolutionary, so that the four seasons complete their functions. The revolutions of T'ang and of Wu were in accordance with the will of God and in response to the wishes of men. Great indeed is what takes place in a time of revolution." ² When Confucius reads the *Poetry* about the revolution changing the Yin dynasty to the Chou dynasty, he exclaims: " If there were no revolution, what could make the emperor and princes take precaution, and what could make the common people keep up their ambition?" ³ From this exclamation, we know that Confucius does not regard the king as sacred, and that he gives the common people the right of being king. The reason Confucius is sometimes in favor of imperialism or absolute monarchy is because, for the time being, he wants to do away with feudalism; but his fundamental idea is democracy.

The principle of democracy is most clearly set forth by Mencius as follows: " The people are the most important element; the state is the next; and the ruler is the least. Therefore, to gain the mass of people is the way to become emperor; to gain the emperor is the way to become a prince of a feudal state; and to gain the prince is the way to become a great official." ⁴ By this statement, Mencius means that

¹ *Classics,* vol. i, p. 374.
² *Yi King,* p. 254.
³ *History of Han,* ch. xxxvi.
⁴ *Classics,* vol. ii, pp. 483-4.

the emperor should hold his place by popular consent, and the prince should be appointed by the emperor, and the great official by the prince. Since the appointive governor of the province took the place of the hereditary prince of the feudal state, the last two things have been realized in China; but the first never has been realized, except in the negative form of revolution. But that the sovereign power is in the hands of the people is the fundamental concept of the Confucians.[1]

2. *State Government*

For the government of the feudal state, Confucius gives the following general principles: " To rule a state of a thousand chariots, there must be reverent attention to business, and sincerity to the people; economy in expenditure, and love for the people; and the employment of the people at the proper seasons." [2] These principles are the theories of Confucius' political economy. Under such a government, the people are encouraged to work and enjoy their occupations, to care first for public, and then for private welfare.

3. *Local Government*

By the *tsing tien* system of Confucius, a village is a unit of political division, which consists of eighty families. In a village, the people elect aged and virtuous men called patriarchs, and eloquent and strong men called justices. The official rank of the patriarchs is equal to that of the subordinates of the educational department, and that of the justices is equal to that of the common people who are employed about the government offices. Both of them receive double shares of land, and ride on horseback. They are the people themselves; but at the same time, they are offi-

[1] *Classics*, vol. ii, pp. 354-9.   [2] *Ibid.*, vol. i, p. 140.

cials among the people. Therefore, their administration is so efficient in detail as to extend from the morning to the midnight, from the field to the town, from the man to the woman, and from the physical to the intellectual and moral life. These numerous things can be done only by the system of self-government.

4. *Freedom of Speech*

In an imperial democracy, the government is really ruled by public opinion, and the way to get public opinion is by freedom of speech in the form of poetry. According to the *tsing tien* system of Confucius, from the tenth month to the first month, the people live in town. If they have any cause for dissatisfaction, men and women sing together to express their discontent in the form of poetry. Those who are hungry sing about their food; and those who are tired, about their business. Indeed, their economic conditions are their principal subjects. They have, however, the absolute freedom of choosing any subject, referring either to themselves or to the court and government. The principal thing is the style in which the reproof is cunningly insinuated. The authors of the poetry give no offence, but the hearers of it are warned.

Men at the age of sixty and women at that of fifty, if they have no children, are supported by the government, and are appointed commissioners for the collection of poetry. In the first month, when the people are about to leave the town for the field, the commissioners ring out the wooden-tongued bell along the roads in order to collect poetry from the people. From the village, the poetry is transferred to the town; then to the capital of the feudal states; and at last it comes to the imperial government. After the Grand Music-master arranges the poetry according to its style and tune, it is presented to the emperor.

Therefore, even if the emperor does not go out of the door, he understands all the grievances of the empire; and even if he does not come down from the palace, he knows about the four quarters. Hence poetry forms the basis of government.

In the *Canon of Poetry*, the three hundred and five poems are the remainder of ancient poetry edited by Confucius. Their functions are equal to those of newspapers; both are the description of daily life of the people and the expression of public opinion. That the poetry had fulfilled such functions shows that there had been freedom of speech.

5. *Morals v. Law*

Under the *tsing tien* system, people can live sufficiently well, so that they can understand what is honor and what is dishonor. As their virtue has been refined, they become moderate in their concern for wealth, and are complaisant toward others. Hence, there is no dispute nor litigation. Men are governed not by the legal code, but by the moral law. Such a society is higher than the so-called law-governed society, because there is self-respect without the need of law. The legal code must be limited to a certain number of acts, and the people may escape the law when it does not literally specify the act; but the moral law is unlimited and is a matter of spirit rather than letter. Legislation is enforced by external power after the deed is done, and prevents only the bad act, while moral law is enforced by internal conscience. Not only does it prevent the bad thought, but it also makes them good. Therefore Confucius says: "In hearing litigations, I am like any one else. What is necessary, however, is to cause the people to have no litigations."[1] Again, Confucius says:

If the people be led by laws, and uniformity be sought to be

---
[1] *Classics*, vol. i, p. 257.

given them by punishments, they will try to avoid the punishment, but have no sense of shame. If they be led by virtue, and uniformity be sought to be given them by the rules of propriety, they will have the sense of shame, and moreover will become good.[1]

In fact, in the government system of Confucius, there is much legislation, but more emphasis is laid on the moral than on the legal side.

IV. SYSTEM OF INSTRUCTION

The system of instruction is the fountain of democracy in the political system of Confucius. The reason we use the word instruction instead of education is because the former is broader in sense than the latter. We may divide the word instruction into three great branches, namely, education, religion, and election. They are all together the same stream. Education is one source, and religion is the other, while election is the flow. In Confucianism, religion is really included in education, because the word education itself means intellectual education, while the word religion means ethical education. For the convenience of our readers, however, we may put religion in a separate section in order to make a comparison between China and the West. The only thing we should remember is that the system of instruction is a whole. According to the political system of Confucius, the *tsing tien* system and the instruction system are the two greatest things, and they must go together, although the former precedes the latter. Therefore, if we are going to study the economic system of Confucius represented by *tsing tien*, we should know something about his system of instruction.

1. *Universally Free Education*

After the people can make their living and thus satisfy

[1] *Classics*, vol. i, p. 146.

ECONOMICS AND POLITICS

their physical needs, development of mind and character is necessary. Then the educational system arises. According to Confucius, in the center of a village which contains eighty families, there is a schoolhouse. The aged and virtuous men are elected " patriarchs ", and are teachers of the school; usually, they come from the retired officials of the government. Such a school of a village is called a local school. It opens in the tenth month when the agricultural work has been finished, and closes in the first month, when this work begins again. At eight years of age, the children begin to go to school, and study reading and writing, mathematics and geography, and the ethical rules of family and society. This is the most popular education, and is the basis of all the higher schools.

There are different grades of schools. The local school of the village is the lowest grade. Then come successively the district school, the provincial college, and the national university. The highest one is the imperial university. The local school is in every village; the district school, in every district; the provincial college, in every province; the national university, in every capital city of every feudal state; and the imperial university, in the imperial capital.[1] Thus, educational institutions exist over the whole empire. They are all public schools and are maintained by the different governments; hence they are all free. The school system was an actual system of the ancients, although it may not have been so complete as the Confucians prescribe. In ancient times, the different institutions were used not only as schools, but also as churches, and for political meetings, social gatherings, and even military councils.[2]

Regarding the training of the different schools, all those below the imperial university are called small learning; the

---

[1] *Li Kï*, bk. xvi, p. 83. [2] *Ibid.*, bk. iii, p. 220.

latter is called great learning. The lowest age for the great learning is fifteen, and the highest is twenty. The subjects of study are the different civilizations of the ancients and the social and political institutions of the present. The " Record of Education " says:

Every year new students may enter the imperial university, and every alternate year there is a comparative examination. At the end of the first year, the examination is to see whether they can read the texts intelligently, and what the individual taste of each is; in the third year, whether they are reverently attentive to their work, and what companionship is most pleasant to them; in the fifth year, how they extend their studies and seek the company of their teachers; in the seventh year, how they can discuss the subjects of their studies and select their friends. They are now said to have made some small accomplishments. In the ninth year, when they know the different relative subjects and have gained general intelligence, establishing themselves firmly so that they cannot be moved, they are said to have made some great accomplishments.[1]

In every one of these five examinations, the students are examined from two points of view: one is knowledge, and the other is character. To balance mental and moral training is the Chinese system of education, handed down from Confucius. In fact, the educational system of Confucius has been partially carried out in different periods.

2. *Social Religion and Freedom of Belief*

In the Chinese language, the word religion is not exactly the same as in English. The Chinese word *chiao* means instruction; hence it stands for education as well as for religion. But the word *chiao* in the religious sense of the Chinese means moral teachings; sometimes it in-

[1] *Li Ki*, bk. xvi, pp. 83-4.

cludes even the whole of civilization. Therefore, what the Chinese call religion is moral, social and philosophical rather than spiritual. As the word *chiao* means both education and religion, an educational institution is a church as well as a school. According to Mencius, the object of all the schools of the Three Dynasties is to illustrate the human relations.[1] Even in the present day, in the Confucian Churches over the whole empire, there is a hall called " Illustrating-Human-Relations Hall "; and the Chinese call the Confucian Church by the name of Holy Temple, or Civil Temple, or School House. This is the reason why under the *tsing tien* system there is no church, because the religious function is absorbed by education. The patriarchs, although the teachers of the school, are like the pastors or fathers of the church. But what are the subjects of their sermons? According to Mencius, the most important teachings of the schools are the filial and fraternal duties; and their results are that the gray-haired men do not need to carry any burdens on their backs or on their heads along the roads.[2] Therefore, we can see that the Chinese religion has been directed toward man more than toward God. Indeed, the religion of Confucius is based on sociology rather than on theology. Hence, China has given full freedom of belief to the people, since spiritual worship has not been the essential of the Chinese religion.

In modern times, there is a conflict between religion and science, but this can never be the case in Confucianism. Confucianism is based on scientific principles. When Confucius teaches Tzŭ-lu what knowledge is, he says: " When you know a thing, to hold that you know it; and when you do not know a thing, to allow that you do not know it—this is knowledge." [3] In the *Spring and Autumn*, " to leave out

[1] *Classics*, vol. ii, p. 242. [2] *Ibid.*, vol. ii, pp. 131-2.
[3] *Ibid.*, vol. i, p. 151.

the doubtful points" is a great principle. With such a scientific nature, Confucianism differs from all other religions, and is a religon of the highest type. On this account, the Chinese can identify religion with education, and church with school; and there will never be any conflict between science and Confucianism, because Confucianism itself is also a science.

In modern times, there is also a conflict between religion and politics, but this is not the case in Confucianism. The Roman Catholics have a pope who assumes political power as an emperor, and the ecclesiastical body forms a specially-favored class exercising political privileges over and against the common people. This is an unnatural and unjust thing. Therefore, conflict between church and state arises, and European and American statesmen separate church from state. How is this in the religion of Confucius? He did not choose a special successor, and no one dared to call himself the only successor of Confucius. In fact, Confucianism is a democratic religion, and has no such monarchical idea. Confucius did not distinguish his followers from the common people, and they never formed such a special class as the priesthood. Therefore, the Confucians never got political privileges. Although the student class always has more access to the government than the common people, it is through educational qualifications, and not through religious privilege. Therefore, since the Confucians have never taken any political power from the state, the state has no trouble with the Confucian religion at all, and there is no need to separate it from the state.

Moreover, Christianity is a simple religion, and has nothing to do with government; hence it can be separated from the state. But Confucianism is a complex religion, and has very much to do with government; hence it can never be separated from the state. The missionary work of Confucius himself was mostly in court; he taught the people not on the subject of theology, but on that of social relations; he taught his pupils not in order to make priests of them, but to make them statesmen and teachers. His teachings are at least half on political subjects; and the whole Chinese society is built up under his teachings, although not under the best of them, and even opposing some of them. In a word, China never can separate Confucianism from the state, unless she would destroy her whole civilization. It is not only unwise and unnecessary, but also impossible. This is the main characteristic of the religion of Confucius.

4. *Educational Election as a System of Popular Representation*

As regards politics, Confucius lays much stress on the power of man. He says:

The principles of the government of Wên and Wu are always displayed in the records—the tablets of wood and bamboo. But, when there are the right men, such a government flourishes; while without such men, such a government decays and ceases. With a good quality of men, the growth of government is rapid, just as vegetation is rapid in land of good quality. Thus a government is like an easily-growing rush. Therefore, the administration of government depends upon man.[1]

Having such a theory of government, Confucius thinks that to get good men is the fundamental thing for a good government. But how shall we get them? By the system of educational election.

According to Confucius, the school is not only a system of education, but also a system of election; hence, it combines politics with education. His political doctrine is

[1] *Classics*, vol. i, p. 405.

democratic, and no aristocracy is allowed. The *Record of Rites* says: " Even the eldest son of the emperor by his legitimate queen is only as an ordinary student. In the world, there is nowhere such a thing as being born noble."[1] In the *Spring and Autumn,* Confucius denies the hereditary right of aristocracy, and gives educational election as a substitute.[2] This was at that time a revolutionary idea in social life; it was realized by the recommendation of Tung Chung-shu (412 A. K. or 140 B. C.). According to the " Royal Regulations," the sons of the emperor, the princes, and the officials, are to study at the same university with the students chosen from among the common people; and their classes are to be divided up, not by ranks, but by ages.[3] Hsun Tzŭ says: " Even among the sons of the emperor, the princes, and the great officials, if they were not qualified to rites and justice, they should be put down to the class of common people; even among the sons of common people, if they have good education and character and are qualified to rites and justice, they should be elevated to the class of ministers and nobles."[4] In short, under the system of Confucius, there is no distinction of classes; and education is the only determining force in social standing. We may say that there is an educational aristocracy, but such an aristocracy is unavoidable, unless human characteristics be equal by birth. The only thing that human power can do is to make education universal and free, in order to give everyone equal opportunity; and this is the way of Confucius.

The way Confucius combines politics with education is something like this: the best students of the local school are elected and transferred to the district school; the best of the

---

[1] *Li Ki*, bk. ix, p. 438.
[2] Third year of Duke Yin.
[3] *Li Ki*, bk. iii, p. 233.
[4] Bk. ix.

ECONOMICS AND POLITICS

district school, to the provincial college; and the best of the provincial college, to the national university. Every three years, the feudal princes send the best students from their national universities to the emperor, and let them study at the imperial university. The best students of the imperial university are called "complete scholars". If their conduct and capability are equal, they are distinguished by archery. Then titles are conferred upon them. In this way, the students promote themselves by their capability; and the emperor appoints the officials by the examination of their merit.[1] This sytem may be called educational election.

The system of educational election may also be called a system of representation. Since the students elected from the common people become high officials, the different institutions are really the places where the representatives of the people are elected. As the elections are held in schools and the representatives are confined to the body of students, education is the exclusive qualification. The educational test takes the place of universal suffrage. But choosing education as a qualification is much better than choosing anything else, especially when education is universally free. Although there is no popular vote, this should not be far from popular sentiment, because those chosen are the best students. Since they come from different political divisions, although there is no legal responsibility between them and their native localities, they should be regarded as the representatives of the people as a whole. The *Great Commentary of the Canon of History*[2] speaks thus of the election of students. "It lets the wise men have their way to come up, and co-operate with their ruler in the government. It

---

[1] *Annotation of Kung-yang*, 15th year of Duke Hsüan, *etc.*

[2] Written by Professor Fu of the Ch'in dynasty, the oldest and greatest authority on the *Canon of History*.

shows that a ruler alone should not control the government. This is the way to give the greatest importance to the people."

What we have mentioned is the ideal system of Confucius, and it has been essentially carried into effect. But the system of representation was also a fact of the ancients, although it may not have been so perfect as the Confucians describe. The *Official System of Chou* says: " Let the people elect the virtuous to be their leaders outside, and let them also elect the able to be their governors inside." [1] " Outside " means the central government out of their province, and " inside " means the local government, the word leaders meaning representatives. In ancient times, the students were at the same time the farmers, so that the farmers could easily elect the students among themselves. The *Canon of Poetry* tells how the prince goes to the field to preside over the election: " Now, I go to the south-lying acres, where some are weeding and some gather the earth about the roots. The millets look luxuriant. And in a spacious resting place, we elect our eminent students." [2] From this poem, we can understand that the farmers, outside of the school, still had the right to choose their representatives, although the election was controlled by the government.

Historically, the system of representation was changed from election by the people into selection by the government, that is, civil-service competitive examinations. Even by this change, the graduates who passed examinations still had the qualifications of representatives, because the number of graduates was proportionate to the population and the amount of taxation of their native province. So China had the representative system. But the great trouble was that China did not develop a legal organi-

---

[1] Ch. xii. [2] *Classics*, vol. iv, pt. ii, p. 377.

zation of the representative body to assume the sovereign power. In ancient times, although there was a popular council of the people in the central government,[1] it had not been legally well organized. And so those representatives were only the advisors of the ruler.

According to the ideal of Confucius, before the officials take office, there is an educational election; and after they come to office, there is also an examination of merit every three years. Hence, there can be no corruption. The examination is based entirely on the economic conditions of the people. After three examinations, officials are either degraded or promoted according to the value of their service to the people. They are required to have such conditions that not only is capital increased, but also labor is improved. In short, economic prosperity is the only test of a good government, and it is the chief task of the officials who are subjected to the examination of merit. Ho Hsiu says: " The wise ruler gives reward to the officials according to their obvious service, so that the undeserving cannot be promoted by popular praise; and gives punishment to them according to their obvious guilt, so that the innocent cannot be dismissed by popular slander."[2] This principle has been put into actual law.

In conclusion, the word representatives includes all the officials of the government. Although there are three powers—legislative, administrative and judicial—they are not sharply divided into distinct branches. Therefore, the representatives of the people, the students, may take office in any branch of the government, not being confined to legislative power only.

[1] *Cf. Classics*, vol. iii, pt. i, pp. 41, 224, 233-4. F. Hirth's *The Ancient History of China*, p. 124. *Kuan Tsu*, bk. lvi.
[2] Third year of Duke Yin.

Under the influence of Confucius, the Chinese government has been that of imperial democracy, and everyone has the chance to be prime minister, although it is not necessary that everyone should have the ambition to be emperor. In China, " linen prime minister " and " white house duke and minister " have become popular terms. " Linen " and " white house " indicate the poor conditions from which they arise to the highest office. Indeed, China has been the most democratic country of the world in this point. Even in the United States, a republican government, it is difficult for one to hold an elective public office, no matter how high or how low, unless he is an active member of one of the two great parties. This means that many good men are excluded from the government, and it tends to make men lose their personality, and to deny them the opportunity for showing their political ability in rendering public service. Although the form of the American government is republican, it is very tyrannical in this respect; or at least it is something of an aristocracy. How much worse are the monarchical governments of the world! All the modern European countries and Japan are only now doing away with aristocracy; and in most of them the nobility is still a great element in their government. But China had largely destroyed the nobility with the election system of the Han dynasty (418 A. K. or 134 B. C.), and has extinguished it entirely since the *Chin Shih* examination of the Sui dynasty (1157 A. K. or 606 A. D.). In the present day, all the titles of nobility are merely nominal honors, and have no political power whatever attached to them. The only material gain they bring is the hereditary salary received in the form of pension. Even the members of the imperial family have no political power, unless they are officials. Any student, poor in the economic sense, studying quietly and even laboring hard, may expect to become prime minister and carry out his principles. He does not need to spend his time, energy and money in self-advertisement.

If the ruler should always be as good as Confucius requires, the system of educational election would be perfect. But, since the ruler is not always good, and the world has been progressive, China is going to change her absolute to a constitutional government. As soon as she shall have a constitutional government, she will have a party government. And as soon as she has a party government, she will have party elections, and modern aristocracy will grow in China. But, as the educational election is a system peculiar to the Chinese, they should keep the best of their own, and adopt only the best of their neighbors' systems, without their defects. By extending the principle of popular suffrage to just the right point, China will have a governmental system which surpasses the most sanguine hopes of American civil service reformers.

The election system of Confucius is the chief weapon for the destruction of class interests. This was appreciated by the physiocrats. They hold up as the ideal of political government, not Switzerland or England, but China,[1] because in other countries one did not find individual interest coming to the front. In England the political system gives too much power to the merchants; on the other hand, democracy gives too much power to the lower classes, and aristocracy, too much power to the higher classes. In China alone no one class tends to become dominant. This view of the physiocrats is very true. It is doubtless true that Quesnay was theorizing, and used China as a model because it was far away and he knew little about it, but in this instance his theory was justified by the facts.

[1] *Cf.* Quesnay's *Despotisme de la Chine*, first published in the *Éphémérides du Citoyen* in 1767 and reprinted in *Oeuvres Économiques et Philosophiques de Quesnay*, ed. Oncken, 1888, pp. 563-660.

CHAPTER VIII

ECONOMICS AND ETHICS

I. ECONOMICS AS THE BASIS OF ETHICS

In the Confucian system, there are two great principles. One is called love, or humanity; the other, justice, or righteousness. It may be interesting to notice that, according to the Chinese etymology, the word love is formed from the word denoting man, or others, and the word justice from the word denoting self. Thus the primary meaning of the word love is a relation between persons; and that of the word justice is an aspect of the self. We love others, but we justify ourselves. Hence we should strictly control ourselves, according to the highest standard of morality, and treat others liberally, according to the ordinary level of human nature. Confucius says: "The superior man reasons about theoretical principles from the standpoint of himself, but lays down practical laws from the capabilities of the people."[1] Therefore, regarding ourselves, Confucius puts ethical teaching above economic life,—in some cases, life itself should be sacrificed for the sake of virtue; but regarding society as a whole, he puts economic life before ethical teaching.

The best illustration of this principle is given in the *Analects*. When Confucius went to Wei, Jan Yu acted as driver of his carriage. Confucius observed, "How numerous are the people!" Jan said, "Since they are thus nu-

---

[1] *Li Ki*, bk. xxix. p. 333.

merous, what more shall be done for them?" "Enrich them," was the reply. "And when they have been enriched, what more shall be done?" Confucius said, "Instruct them"[1]

Before we can instruct the people, we must enrich them, no matter how few or many they are. This is a universal principle. The *Canon of Poetry* repeats three times the following two sentences: "Give them drink and give them food. Instruct them and teach them."[2]

If we understand in the beginning that Confucius gives two principles for the two classes of men, one for the officials and students, the other for the mass of common people at large, we shall avoid confusion. For the higher class, ethical life is first, but for the lower class, economic life is first. Confucius says: "The mind of great men is conversant with justice; the mind of small men is conversant with profit."[3] In speaking of great men and small men, he refers to their social standing. This theory is very clearly stated by Tung Chung-shu when he says: "Busily seeking for wealth and profit, and fearing only the condition of want, this is the mind of common people; busily seeking for love and justice, and fearing always that they could not influence the people, this is the mind of ministers and great officials."[4] Such a statement, of course, is only a theory, not fact. Yet we must understand that Confucius has these two classes in his mind, and sets forth two different principles for them. On the one hand, he forbids the higher class, from emperor to student, to seek private gain. They should confine themselves to the ethical life. On the

---

[1] *Classics*, vol. i, pp. 266-7.
[2] *Classics*, vol. iv, pt. ii, pp. 418-420.
[3] *Classics*, vol. i, p. 170.
[4] *History of Han*, ch. lvi.

other hand, he allows the lower class to make profit, and thinks that they ought to do so. Hence, for the governing of society, Confucius takes up the economic life of the people for the first consideration. The " Great Learning " describes the effects of a good government as follows: " The common people find pleasure in what they call their pleasure, and find profit in what they call their profit." [1] We are sure that Confucius, in the program of his reformation, feels that economic betterment is the first item.[2]

Unfortunately, since the Confucians of the Sung dynasty did not wholly understand the principles of Confucius and thought that he did not approve even talking about profits, the teachings of Confucius failed to be considered of great importance in the practical world, and the Chinese suffered a great deal through need of economic reforms. They made such a great mistake because they misunderstood the statements of Mencius and Tung Chung-shu. Mencius tells the King Hui of Liang: " Why must your Majesty use that word profit? What I am provided with are counsels concerning the principles of love and justice, and these are my only topics." [3] Tung Chung-shu tells the Prince of Kiang-tu: " The man of perfect virtue is thus: following strictly justice, not for the sake of profit; discussing thoroughly principle, not with the expectation of success." [4] This simply means virtue for virtue's sake. These two statements given by Mencius and Tung Chung-shu are quite good in themselves, but they do not mean that the economic problems should be entirely left out. They have their own writings, and we can find their economic principles even from the

---

[1] *Classics*, vol. i, p. 364.
[2] *Classics*, vol. ii, p. 131.
[3] *Classics*, vol. ii, p. 126.
[4] *History of Han*, ch. lvi.

quotations of this treatise. They are talking to the king and the prince, and such men, of course, are forbidden by Confucius to talk about profits. We never expect to use the same prescription for everybody; why should we apply those statements to every one? Neither Confucius, nor Mencius, nor Tung Chung-shu, nor any great Confucian before the Sung dynasty, has ever said that the common people should not talk about profits. Moreover, the Confucians of the Sung dynasty did not distinguish the public profits from private profits, and left them both out of consideration. This has been a great obstacle to the economic development of China.

II. HARMONY OF ECONOMICS AND ETHICS

The reason the Confucians of the Sung dynasty fear to talk about profit is because they make the distinction between profit and justice too sharp, and think they are necessarily opposed to each other. But true Confucianism harmonizes economics and ethics, and identifies profit with justice. A true profit, it holds, is justice, and the immediate profit which opposes justice is, in the long run, not a profit at all. The essential of these two words, profit and justice, is the same thing, but expressed in different terms.

As Confucius lived in the stage of feudalism, and generally talked with princes, he did not like to mention the word profit, but used the word justice for its substitute. Since princes, as we know, generally care for profit, but not for justice; for wealth, but not for virtue; why should Confucius talk to them about profit instead of about justice? But, if Confucius only says to them that justice is good, and does not say that justice is a profit, they will not believe him, and will not practice justice. Therefore, Confucius points out very clearly that justice is a real profit, and that to prefer the immediate profit is only a suicidal policy.

This principle is thus set forth in the " Great Learning ":

The superior man will first take pains about his own virtue. .... Virtue is the root, and wealth only the result. If he make the root his secondary object, and the result his primary, he will only wrangle with his people, and teach them rapine. Hence, the concentration of wealth is the cause of driving the people away, and the diffusion of it among them is the way to collect the people. And hence, ... the wealth, got by improper ways, will take its departure by the same. ... The virtuous man, by means of his wealth, makes his personality more distinguished. The vicious man accumulates wealth at the expense of his life. Never has there been a case of the sovereign liking love, and the people not liking justice. Never has there been a case where the people have liked justice, and the affairs of the sovereign have not been carried to completion. And never has there been a case where the wealth in such a state, collected in the treasuries and arsenals, did not continue in the sovereign's possession.

For the explanation that the real profit of a state is not pecuniary profit, but justice, it quotes from Mêng Hsien-tsŭ: "It is better to have an officer who steals, than to have one who collects unjust imposts from the people." Indeed, losing wealth is better than losing justice.

The conclusion of the "Great Learning" is this:

When he who presides over a state or a family makes wealth his chief business, he must be under the influence of some mean fellow. He may consider this fellow good; but when such a person is employed in the administration of a state or family, calamities from nature and injuries from men will befall it together. And, although a good man may take his place, he will not be able to remedy the evil. This illustrates the saying, that a state does not take the pecuniary profit as a real profit, but takes justice as a real profit.[1]

The same principle is also given by Mencius. When he

[1] *Classics*, vol. i, pp. 375-381.

meets King Hui of Liang, he first rejects the word profit, which is mentioned by the king, and supplies the two words love and justice. Then he points out that profit in the common sense is not a profit. If the king, the great officials, the students and the common people, all try to snatch this profit the one from the other, the state will be endangered. He says: "If justice be put last, and profit be put first, they will not be satisfied without snatching all."

Now, he turns to the real profit of love and justice, and says: "There never has been a man who practiced the principle of love and neglected his parents. There never has been a man who practiced the principle of justice and made his sovereign an after-consideration.[1]

What has been said in the "Great Learning" and by Mencius is for princes or for the government. But the principle that justice is a profit holds true among all mankind. The Chinese take this principle as the fundamental law of economics, and carry it into practice in daily life. This is why the Chinese merchants have the highest moral standard. Indeed, "honesty is the best policy." If justice is not a profit, the morality of man would be as low as that of the beast. But to-day, as human progress has risen to the present stage, it proves that justice is a profit. The more just we are, the more we shall prosper.

Since justice is a profit, why do not the Confucians use the word profit as often as the word justice? Human nature is already selfish, and society is already a profit-seeking society. The people know profit in the narrow sense by birth, and do not need any more teaching about it. If a great teacher like Confucius were to talk constantly about profit, it would make the people think about profit still more and about justice still less. They would care much more for money than for character. They would excuse them-

[1] *Classics*, vol. ii, pp. 125-7.

selves on the ground of the teachings of Confucius, and would use Confucius' word for their pretext. Therefore, Confucius does not use the word profit very often, but uses the word justice for its substitute. This idea is very well explained by Adam Smith. He says:

Those principles of the human mind which are most beneficial to society are by no means marked by nature as the most honorable. Hunger, thirst, and the passion for sex are the great supports of the human species, yet almost every expression of these excites contempt. In the same manner, that principle in the mind which prompts to truck, barter, and exchange, though it is the foundation of arts, commerce, and the division of labor, yet it is not marked with anything amiable. . . . The plain reason for this is that these principles are so strongly implanted by nature that they have no occasion for that additional force which the weaker principles [*e. g.*, generosity] need.[1]

Moreover, social profit is harmonious with social justice, while individual profit is not always harmonious with individual justice. Confucius says: " Riches and honors acquired by injustice are to me as a floating cloud."[2] He recognizes that there are some individual profits without the principle of justice. Yang Hu was a bad officer at the time of Confucius, but Mencius quotes his words as follows: " He who seeks to be rich will not be benevolent. He who wishes to be benevolent will not be rich."[3] Mencius thinks that there is sometimes a contradiction between economic gains and ethical principles. Hence, Confucius speaks of the superior man as one who, when he sees gain, thinks of justice.[4] And hence, the *Record of Rites*

[1] *Lectures of Adam Smith*, p. 232.
[2] *Classics*, vol. i, p. 200.
[3] *Classics*, vol. ii, p. 240.
[4] *Classics*, vol. i, p. 314.

ECONOMICS AND ETHICS

says: " When you find wealth within your reach, do not try to get it by improper means." [1]

III. CHOICE BETWEEN ECONOMIC LIFE AND ETHICAL LIFE

Even though the economic principles are finally harmonious with those of ethices, under some circumstances economic life cannot exist along with ethical life. Hence, we shall see how Confucius makes a choice between these two things.

When Tzŭ-kung asks Confucius about government, Confucius says: " The requisites of government are that there be sufficiency of food, sufficiency of soldiers, and the faith of the people." Tzŭ-kung says: " If it cannot be helped, and one of these must be dispensed with, which of the three should be foregone first?" " The soldiers ", says Confucius. Tzŭ-kung again asks: " If it cannot be helped, and one of the remaining two must be dispensed with, which of them should be foregone?" Confucius answers: " Part with the food. From of old, death has been the lot of all men; but if the people have no faith in their hearts, there is no standing for any one."[2]

This dialogue is very important and very interesting; the questions and the answers are both very good. The word food includes all economic life; the word soldiers, all military forces and equipments; and the word faith, all religious and ethical life. So far as we have seen, Confucius emphasizes economic life as the first thing in society. And even in this dialogue, he puts food before the other two. But, when the economic life and ethical life cannot both be preserved, economic life must be sacrificed. This seems a foolish policy, and an impracticable theory. Moreover, it seems contradictory to his own principle that economic

[1] *Li Ki*, bk. i, p. 62.
[2] *Classics*, vol. i, p. 254.

life should come before ethical life. In reality, however, there is great harmony here. In the primary stage, when the people do not know much about faith, and their immediate need is food, if you talk to them on any subject, such as religion or ethics, before they can satisfy their hunger, they will not listen to you. Food, therefore, must come before all other things. In the advanced stage, when they have built a society as high as a state, they must know something about faith, and faith is the strongest social tie. If the getting of food were their sole aim, or escaping from death their highest ideal, they would do anything in any way for the sake of their lowest self. Without faith, the world would be a wilderness; no one would trust others, and every one would be an enemy to others. Society could not exist; and at last, not even the individual could exist. Only the strongest would survive. In the beginning, the people would sacrifice their faith to escape death; but ultimately, they would fall together into death because they had no faith. A great teacher like Confucius must prefer faith to food. Or, in other words, he must choose to die with faith rather than to live without it. Food is the primary means of building up society, but faith is the final end in maintaining it. These two theories of Confucius are not contradictory. Hence, this policy is not only honest, but also wise. Nor is it impracticable.

To show that the ethical life should be preferred to the economic life, Mencius cites this concrete case, and shows that every one has such conscience. He says:

We desire fish, and we also desire bear's paws. If we cannot have the two together, we will let the fish go and take the bear's paws. So, we desire life, and we also desire righteousness. If we cannot keep the two together, we will let life go and choose righteousness. We desire life indeed, but there is that which we desire more than life, and therefore we will not seek to possess it by any improper ways. We dislike death indeed, but there is that which we dislike more than death, and therefore there are occasions when we will not avoid danger. . . .

Therefore, men have that which they desire more than life, and that which they dislike more than death. They who have this conscience are not men of distinguished talents and virtue only. All men have it; what distinguishes such men is simply that they do not lose it.

Here are a small basket of rice and a platter of soup, and the case is one in which the getting them will preserve life, and the want of them will be death; if they are offered with an insulting voice, even a tramp will not receive them, or if you first tread upon them, even a beggar will not stoop to take them.[1]

This statement of Mencius, that even the tramp or the beggar still cares for his personal honor, and that he preserves it even at the expense of his life, is very true. Hence, there is really no such man as may be called the purely economic man, and the ethical motive is rooted in human nature as well as the economic motive. For this reason, we can harmonize the economic life with the ethical life.

IV. ACCEPTANCE OF WEALTH

When we discuss economics and ethics, the important question is the acceptance of wealth. As men are living in society, they have to give and receive wealth in daily life. But what are the principles which govern those matters? On this question, it is best to look at the teachings of Mencius. For the principles of both giving and receiving wealth, he says: " When it appears proper to take a thing, and afterwards not proper, to take it is contrary to moderation. When it appears proper to give a thing, and after-

---

[1] *Classics*, vol. ii, pp. 411-3.

wards not proper, to give it is contrary to kindness."¹ Again, when he speaks of Yi Yin, he says that Yin would neither have given nor have taken a single straw, if it were contrary to justice and principle.² Therefore, he wants the people to act in the proper way not only in their taking, but also in their giving; foolish generosity and unwise alms are not approved by Mencius.

But the principles governing the taking of wealth are more important than those governing the giving of it, because human nature is more often too covetous, rather than too liberal. For the taking of wealth, Mencius gives this general principle: if there be not proper ground for taking it, a single bamboo-cup of rice may not be received from a man; but if there be such proper ground, then Shun's receiving the empire from Yao is not to be considered excessive.³ Therefore, the taking of wealth, no matter how great or how little, must be governed by moral considerations.

The greatest difficulty, however, is to determine what is proper and what is not. On this point, there is no certain rule. But we may refer to concrete cases and take them as examples. When Mencius was in Ch'i, the king sent him a present of 2000 taels of fine gold, and he refused it. But he accepted a present of 1400 taels when he was in Sung, and accepted one of 1000 taels when he was in Hsieh. Chen Tsin, his pupil, asked him if there were not something wrong in one of the two cases. But Mencius said that they are all right. When he was in Sung, he was about to take a long journey. It is a custom of the Chinese to present a traveler with a traveling present. Therefore, the message of the prince was the sending of such a present. Why

---

[1] *Classics*, vol. ii, p. 328.
[2] *Ibid.*, p. 362.
[3] *Ibid.*, p 269.

should he have declined the gift? When he was in Hsieh, he was apprehensive for his safety, and taking measures for his protection. The message was, " I have heard that you are taking measures to protect yourself, and send this to help you in procuring arms." Why should he have declined the gift? But when he was in Ch'i, he had no occasion for money. To send a man a gift when he has no occasion for it, is to bribe him. How is it possible that a superior man should accept a bribe?[1] These are concrete cases showing the principles of accepting and declining wealth.

There is a most interesting discussion between Mencius and Wan Chang, his pupil, about the acceptance of wealth. The point of Mencius is that, when the donor offers his gift on a reasonable ground and in a manner in accordance with propriety, even Confucius would have received it. " Here now," says Wan Chang, " is one who stops and robs people outside the city gates. He offers his gift on a ground of reason and in a proper manner;—would it be right to receive it when so acquired?" The answer of Mencius is, of course, negative. " The princes of the present day," pursues Wan Chang, " take from their people just as a robber despoils his victim. Yet if they put a good face of propriety on their gifts, the superior man receices them. I venture to ask you to explain this." Here Wan Chang alludes to Mencius himself. Mencius answers:

Do you think that, if there should arise a truly imperial sovereign, he would collect the princes of the present day and put them all to death? Or would he admonish them, and then, if they did not change their ways, put them to death? Indeed, to call every one who takes what does not properly belong to him a robber is pushing a point of resemblance to the utmost

[1] *Classics,* vol. ii, pp. 215-6.

and insisting on the most refined idea of righteousness. When Confucius was in office in Lu, the officials struggled together for the game taken in hunting, and he did the same. If that struggling for the captured game was proper, how much more may the gifts of the princes be received![1]

According to the reasoning of Mencius, we may receive a gift offered on a reasonable ground and in a proper manner, and need not push the idea of absolute justice to the extreme. For instance, we may receive donations from a trust in a proper way, and need not regard the trust as a robber. Although the trust may take what does not properly belong to it, we cannot call it a robber because the whole structure of present society is not an ideal society. Under present conditions, we cannot judge every one according to the ideal standard. We should need to change the condition itself first. This is the explanation of Mencius, and it may be also the principle of Confucius.

V. THREE DOCTRINES DIRECTLY OPPOSED TO ECONOMIC MOTIVE

Confucius has very many teachings on the subject of ethics, but we shall leave them out entirely, and take up only three doctrines which are directly against the economic motive. The first is the doctrine of fate; the second is the doctrine of name; and the third is the doctrine of soul. All are very important teachings of Confucius.

1. *Doctrine of Fate*

In order to understand the doctrine of fate, we must ask first what is meant by the word fate. Here is a definition given by Mencius: "That which is done without man's doing is from Heaven. That which happens without man's causing is from fate."[2] These two words, Heaven and

---

[1] *Classics*, vol. ii, pp. 379-383.   [2] *Ibid.*, p. 359

fate, are interchangeable. According to the *Adjunct to the Canon of Filial Piety*, there are three kinds of fate. Doing good and getting good is called receiving fate; doing good but getting evil is called encountering fate; doing evil and getting evil is called following fate. Therefore, Mencius says: "There is a fate for everything. A man should receive submissively what may be correctly ascribed thereto."[1] Indeed, the word fate has three points of view. From the religious viewpoint, it is a supernatural power predetermining everything. From the philosophical viewpoint, it is the law of necessity. From the ethical viewpoint, it is the right principle, doing the right thing at the right moment and in the right way. The doctrine of fate of Confucius embraces these three points of view; hence he says that without recognizing fate, it is impossible to be a superior man.[2]

Believing in fate and having no anxiety to acquire wealth, Confucius gives himself as an example. He says: "If the search for riches were sure to be successful, though I should become a groom with whip in hand to get them, I should do so. As the search may not be successful, I will follow after that which I love."[3] What he loves is the study of truth, and not the search for wealth. Hence he says: "Death and life have their fate; riches and honors depend upon Heaven."[4] The word Heaven and the word fate are the same thing expressed differently.

Since man's fate is determined in Heaven, and his nature is also given by Heaven, how can he harmonize these two things when his nature has wants and his fate cannot satisfy them? According to Confucius, man should subject

[1] *Classics*, vol. ii, p. 449.
[2] *Classics*, vol. i, p. 354.
[3] *Ibid.*, p. 198.
[4] Quoted by Tzŭ-hsia, *ibid.*, pp. 252-3.

his nature to fate. He says: "The superior man proclaims the doctrine of fate as a barrier against material wants."[1] As the human wants rooted in nature are very numerous, and never can be completely controlled by anything, he proclaims the fate which is in Heaven and beyond the power of man, in order to prevent unlawful ambition and to lessen unlimited desires. Mencius gives the same principle. He says:

For the mouth to desire sweet tastes, the eye to desire beautiful colors, the ear to desire pleasant sounds, the nose to desire fragrant odors, and the four limbs to desire ease and comfort: these wants are of human nature. But there is fate in connection with them, and the superior man does not say of his pursuit of them, "It is my nature."[2]

Mencius recognizes what human nature is, but he teaches men to respect fate and not to excuse their pursuit of gratification on the pretext of nature. Therefore, the doctrine of fate is an ethical teaching directly modifying the economic wants.

From the doctrine of fate spring two policies. The first policy is negative, passive, taking everything when it comes, but not running risks to get it. This is primarily for the weakening of economic wants, and especially so in the individual case. For the individual himself, if he takes the natural course and does not try to get anything by improper means, frees his mind from physical desires, and enjoys a great amount of happiness. It is said in the "Appendix" of the *Canon of Changes* that a sage rejoices in Heaven and knows fate, hence he has no anxieties.[3] This is the view

[1] *Li Ki*, bk. xxvii, p. 284.
[2] *Classics*, vol. ii, p. 489.
[3] *Yi King*, p. 354.

of optimism. If one does not believe in fate, he will be the slave of passion and the hunter of fortune. Therefore, Confucius says: "The superior man lives in safe ways in order to wait for fate, while the mean man walks in dangerous paths in order to catch luck."[1]

But we must not misunderstand and think that the passive policy excludes the principle of self-help. When one dies in the discharge of his duties, it is a regular fate; but when one dies of his own fault, it is not a regular fate. Therefore, Mencius says that the one who knows fate will not stand beneath a precipitous wall.[2] Therefore, according to the principle of rites, those who die either from an unreasonable attack which they do not wisely escape, or through the fall of some dangerous thing, or by drowning through heedlessness, should have no condolence offered for them.[3] Indeed, if anyone does not help himself, fate never can help him, and he would be punished by his own fault. Fate is the final cause which operates after man has tried his best, but not a mere chance for the careless man. "Trust in God and keep your powder dry" is the real meaning of waiting for fate. The only difference between those who recognize fate and those who do not is that the former do everything morally, legally, reasonably, and that the latter do the opposite thing. But fate does not make men do nothing. Mencius says: "The superior man performs the law of right, and thereby waits simply for fate."[4]

The second policy is positive, active, trusting one's own principles, and disregarding all circumstances. This is primarily for the fulfillment of ethical duties, and especially

[1] *Classics*, vol. i, p. 396.
[2] *Classics*, vol. ii, p. 450.
[3] *Li Ki*, bk. ii, p. 131.
[4] *Classics*, vol. ii, p. 496.

so in the social case. In the social relations and conditions, it is usually very difficult for men to carry out their ethical principles; and there is fate. But we should be true to our nature, and should not discourage ourselves by saying that there is a fate.[1] The spirit of Confucius is that although he knows the impracticable nature of the times, yet will he be striving to do something.[2] He makes himself responsible for the betterment of the world, and exhausts all his mental powers. This is the principle of "establishing fate."

The active policy is not to disregard fate, but to believe it, and such a belief makes the character of man very strong. When Confucius was in the state of Wei, he lived with Yen Ch'ou-yu, a worthy of Wei. But Mi Tzŭ, an unworthy favorite of the court, informed Confucius through his pupil, that if he would lodge with him, he might obtain a position as a minister. The answer of Confucius was that there is fate. Mencius comments as follows: "Confucius went into office according to propriety, and retired from it according to righteousness. In regard to his obtaining office or not obtaining it, he said: 'There is fate.'"[3] When Confucius was informed that Kung-po Liao, an officer of Lu, slandered Tzŭ-lu to Chi-sun, the prime minister, Confucius said: "If my principles are to be carried out, it is fate. If they are to fall to the ground, it is fate. What can Kung-po Liao do to fate?"[4] Therefore, the doctrine of fate makes man believe firmly his own principles, and not move on account of anything outside of himself. Even the question of life and death cannot affect him,—how

---

[1] *Classics*, vol. ii, pp. 489-490.
[2] *Classics*, vol. i, p. 290.
[3] *Classics*, vol. ii, p. 365.
[4] *Classics*, vol. i, p. 289.

can the question of obtaining office or wealth affect him? Mencius says: " When neither a premature death nor long life causes a man any double-mindedness, but he cultivates his personal character, and waits for whatever issue;—this is the way in which he establishes fate." [1] Every one has his own fate; if he does not believe it, he will be disturbed and changed by even very little things, and he destroys by himself what he has done before. This is a lack of self-confidence. Therefore, the doctrine of fate is good not only for those who discharge their ethical duties, but also for those who carry on their economic business. Indeed, it applies to the problems of daily life.

The doctrine of fate is accepted by Taoism, but rejected by Moism. Mo Tzŭ gives three books against this doctrine, but he cannot attack it on any exact point. He says that by the doctrine of fate, the ruler and officer must be lazy regarding the works of government, and the men and women must also be lazy regarding production of wealth.[2] But this is not the doctrine of fate at all.

2. *Doctrine of Name*

The second principle directly against the economic motive is the doctrine of name. The name of a man is the identification of his personality, and what a man cares for is not merely the name but the merits which make the name famous. Confucius says: " The superior man hates that his name will not be praised after his death." [3] Since the name is the invariable concomitant of merit, and no one can have been a superior man without his name being remembered, the name is necessary to the superior man. This does not mean that he should seek for his name from others,

---

[1] *Classics*, vol. ii, p. 449.
[2] Bk. xxxvii.
[3] *Classics*, vol. i, p. 300.

but that he should make his name for himself. Again, he says: " When we have established our personality and diffused our principles, so as to make our name famous in future ages, and thereby glorify our parents: this is the end of filial piety." [1] From this statement, we know that Confucius regards the name as the final aim of ethical life. It is said by Ssŭ-ma Chien that establishing a name is the highest of conduct.[2]

The doctrine of name is to make the ethical motive stronger than the economic motive, and to make people disregard their economic conditions through attachment to virtue. Confucius says:

Riches and honors are what men want. But, if they are obtained in an improper way, they should not be held. Poverty and low estate are what men hate. But, even though they befall one who does not deserve them, they should not be evaded.

If a superior man abandon the virtue of love, how can he completely make his name? The superior man does not, even for the space of a single meal, act contrary to the virtue of love. In moments of haste, he cleaves to it. In times of danger, he cleaves to it.[3]

This is the ethical teaching which directly opposes economic wants. What we must cling to is the virtue of love, and it is the means by which to make our name complete. Therefore, we must cleave to the virtue of love and must not prefer riches to poverty. This is the way of making a name.

Since desire for riches and hatred of poverty are very strong human motives, how can Confucius make men indifferent to these two conditions and careful for their name? In order to preach the doctrine of name, not only are ethical theories needed, but also historical facts. Hence, Confucius

---

[1] *Sacred Books of the East*, vol. iii, p. 466.
[2] *History of Han*, ch. lxii.
[3] *Classics*, vol. i, p. 166.

gives these facts to show that a name is independent of riches, and that it is much more lasting and important. He says:

The Duke Ching of Ch'i had a thousand teams, each of four horses, but on the day of his death, the people did not praise him for a single virtue. Po-yi and Shu-ch'i died of hunger at the foot of the Shou-yang mountain, but the people, down to the present time, praise them. "It is certainly not on account of material wealth, but merely on account of personal distinction"—is not that saying illustrated by this?[1]

The rich prince cannot live longer than the day of his death, and all his riches cannot be of any use to him; but the two starved men can live forever by their names. This is proof that the name has much more value than riches, and man should not deceive himself when he makes a choice between them. Therefore, Chia Yi (352-384 A. K. or 200-168 B. C.) says: "The coveteous man dies for the sake of wealth, but the heroic man dies for the sake of his name."[2]

Some people would say that the doctrine of name is based on selfishness, and that it is not the highest principle of ethics. This might be somewhat true, but we must discuss it further. To care for the name may be a form of selfishness, but we never can get away from selfishness in that sense, no matter how perfect the ethical principle. The highest principle is that virtue is for virtue's sake. Confucius says: "The determined scholar and the man of virtue will not seek to live at the expense of injuring their virtue, but will sacrifice even their lives to preserve their virue complete."[3] This is the highest type of man. But

[1] *Classics*, vol. i, p. 315.
[2] *Historical Record*, ch. lxxxiv.
[3] *Classics*, vol. i, p. 297.

when we ask why they sacrifice their lives to preserve their virtue complete, it must be explained that in this way they satisfy their ethical wants. It is a feeling that they cannot withstand, and for the satisfaction of this feeling they sacrifice even their lives. This may be selfishness, but how can we get any better than this? In fact, man is a living creature with feelings and wants, and he never can be an absolutely unselfish man from this point of view, unless he is not a man.

Since men are generally very anxious to make profit, Confucius cannot weaken such an economic interest without arousing the ethical interest; hence he preaches the doctrine of name as a substitute for profit. Human nature is so weak that it does not want to do good unless there is some gain either in the form of profit or in that of name. Confucius says: " In the whole world, there is only one man who loves what is proper to humanity without some personal object in the matter, or who hates what is contrary to humanity without being apprehensive of some evil." Again, he says: " The philanthropist practices the virtue of humanity easily and naturally; the wise man practices it for the sake of advantage which it brings; and those who fear the guilt of transgression practice it by constraint." [1] We should not expect all men to be philanthropists practicing virtue without aiming at any advantage, and we should give some reward to anyone who practices this virtue. If we taught the people not to make profit, and denied them also the interest of making a name, it would be too cruel, and unjust, and human society would not progress at all. Therefore Confucius establishes the doctrine of name in order to draw the people away from the economic world to the ethical world, and to give them ethical gain instead of economic gain.

[1] *Li Ki*, bk. xxix, pp. 332-3.

According to Confucius, the name has two kinds of use, one for reward and the other for punishment. In the *Spring and Autumn*, he exercises his authority to praise and to condemn men, from the emperor to the common people, by the use of name. When he praises a name, even a single word is more honorable than the position of emperor; and when he condemns a name, even a single word is more severe than the death penalty. Therefore, when he speaks of Wu Wang, he says that he does not lose his famous name in the world.[1] Mencius says: "If a ruler is called after his death by the name of the Dark or the Cruel, even though he may have filial sons and affectionate grandsons, they will not be able to change his bad name even after a hundred generations."[2] Hence, the people are impelled to do good in the hope of getting a good name, and are afraid to do wrong for fear of getting a bad name. This illustrates the usefulness of the doctrine of name.

Taoism destroys the doctrine of name. Lao Tzŭ raises the following question: "Which is dearer to you, your name or your life?"[3] He means that the life is dearer than the name, and that we should not care for our name at the expense of our life. Taoism is egoistic, and Yang Chu carries it to the extreme. His doctrine is that everyone must come to the same end, death, no matter how good or how bad he may be. The good men have a good name after their death, but they lose enjoyment during their life; the bad men have a bad name after their death, but they have the enjoyment of gratifying their wants during their life. Both the good name and the bad name are no more to the dead than to the trunk of a tree or a clod of earth: they do not know either the praise or the condemna-

---

[1] *Classics*, vol. i, p. 400.
[2] *Classics*, vol. ii, p. 293.
[3] *Tao Tê King*, ch. xliv.

tion. How can a name do any good to the rotten bones?[1] Such a doctrine is extreme Epicureanism, and it is directly against Confucianism. But it was swept away by Mencius.

3. *Doctrine of Soul*

The third principle directly against the economic motive is the doctrine of soul. With the word soul, we must include its synonyms. In the "Great Learning," soul is also called "brilliant virtue"; in the "Doctrine of the Mean," it is called "the nature of Heavenly endowment", "the virtuous nature", and "sincerity"; in the "Evolution of Civilization", "intelligent spirit"; in the "Appendix" of the *Canon of Changes*, "essential spirit"; in *Mêng Tzŭ* (Mencius), it is called "the spirit of the greatest and strongest", "the good conscience", "the good mind," "the original mind", and "mind". According to Confucianism, we can look at soul from two points of view. From the ethical viewpoint, there is the soul of the living which is the best part of the mind. From the religious viewpoint, there is the soul of the dead which is apart from the body. It is the same soul, only in different times of the life. If we can keep our soul here in the ethical way, we shall preserve it hereafter as the essential spirit shining in Heaven; if we cannot keep it right, it will be dissolved and changed.[2]

To contrast it with the economic motive, we shall discuss the doctrine of soul only from the ethical point of view. On this account, the teachings of Mencius are best fitted to our purpose. He usually employs the word mind instead of the word soul, but its meaning is the same. He first points out that the spiritual wants are just as strong as the physical wants. To illustrate this principle, he indicates that the senses of the mouth, the ears and the eyes all have standards of taste, of sound and of beauty. Why should

[1] *Cf. Classics*, vol. ii, pp. 93-7. [2] *Yi King*, p. 354.

the mind alone have no standard at all? The standard of the mind is one of reason and justice. Therefore, reason and justice satisfy the needs of our mind just as the best foods satisfy the needs of our appetite.[1]

Now, Mencius is going to show that the soul is more important than the body. He says:

There is no part of the person which a man does not love, and as he loves all, so he must nourish all. . . . But some part of the person is noble, and some ignoble; some great, and some small. The great must not be injured for the small, nor the noble for the ignoble. He who nourishes the little belonging to him is a little man, and he who nourishes the great is a great man. . . . The man of only eating and drinking is counted mean by others, because he nourishes what is little to the neglect of what is great.[2]

What he means by the noble and great part of the person is the soul; and by the ignoble and small part, the body. A man should love both his soul and his body, and he should nourish them both. But he should nourish the soul more than the body. He who cares more for the body is a little man. What Mencius calls "the man of only eating and drinking" is what we may call the economic man who cares only for the body. According to the principle of Mencius, the chief object of man is the soul and not the body, and he should subject the economic life to the ethical or spiritual life.

The question arises as to how he can make the soul more important than the body, or in other words, how he can use the soul as the master of the whole body. Why does not every one take more care for his soul than for his body? To answer this question, Mencius gives a very good principle which is the key to the ethical religion of Confucius. He says:

[1] *Classics*, vol. ii, pp. 405-7. [2] *Ibid.*, pp. 416-7.

The senses of hearing and seeing do not think, and are obscured by external things. When the external things come into contact with the senses which are also only things, as a matter of course they lead them away. To the mind belongs the office of thinking. By thinking it gets the right view of things; by neglecting to think it fails to do this. Both the senses and the mind are what Heaven has given to us. If a man can first establish the supremacy of the nobler part of his constitution, the inferior part will not be able to take it from him. It is simply this which makes the great man.[1]

From this statement, we know that the superiority of the mind over the senses is that the mind can think about anything and the senses cannot. Although both are the endowments of Heaven, the one is nobler than the other. The mind is like the sovereign, having the full powers of will and reasoning, while the senses are like the ordinary officials, performing their functions only in a passive way. The senses are material things themselves, and of course they are subjected to the material things outside. But the mind is the soul, which has the power of thinking and is independent of anything. If a man can make his soul supreme, how can the senses snatch it away? But how can he establish the supremacy of the soul? Simply by thinking, and thinking is sufficient to make a great man. It is said in the *Canon of History* that the effect of thinking is perspicacity, and that perspicacity becomes the quality of the holy man.[2] Therefore, thinking is the way of establishing the soul, and establishing the soul is the way of controlling economic wants. In fact, the doctrine of soul is an ethical teaching, but it is practiced in the economic life. Hence, according to Confucianism, we can live in the economic world, and yet we can be holy men.

[1] *Classics*, vol. ii, p. 418.
[2] *Classics*, vol. iii, pt. ii, pp. 326-7.

BOOK III GENERAL ECONOMIC PRINCIPLES

CHAPTER IX

Economic Development as the Chief Cause of Progress

I. ECONOMIC DEVELOPMENT

WE have already seen that Confucius is in favor of the inductive method; his statements are generally based on historical facts. When he discusses with Tzŭ-yu the evolution of civilization, he takes up the economic development of the remotest time as the starting point. The discussion of the first stage is concerned only with primitive technique, such as the building of houses, the cooking of food, and the making of clothes. Indeed, technical invention is the basis of civilization.

Confucius begins his discussion with the so-called root-grubbing period which was supplemented by the hunting stage. Such an economic condition was before the age of Pao Hsi. His exact words are as follows:

Formerly the ancient kings had no houses. In winter they lived in caves which they had excavated, and in summer in nests which they had framed. They did not yet know the transforming power of fire, but ate the fruits of plants and trees, and the flesh of birds and beasts, drinking their blood, and swallowing also the hair and feathers. They did not yet know the use of flax and silk, but clothed themselves with feathers and furs.

The later sages then arose, and men learned to make use of fire. They molded the metals into articles and fashioned clay into pottery. By using fire, metals and earth, they built towers with structures on them, and houses with windows and doors; they toasted, grilled, boiled and roasted their foods; they produced must and sauces; they dealt with the flax and silk so as to form linen and silken fabrics. They were thus able to nourish the living and to give burial to the dead, to serve the ghosts, the spirits, and God. In all these things the people still follow the example of that early time.[1]

Food, clothes and housing are the three most important things in economic life. But they never can be made by the human hand until the development of technique. The utilization of fire is the most important of all, and the molding of metals and baking of earth come next. Then these crafts can be used for the purpose of getting food, clothes and houses. After the economic life has been satisfied, the religious life begins. This is the origin of civilization, based on economic development.

In the "Appendix" of the *Canon of Changes,* just after the first paragraph speaking about "administering wealth" which has been partly quoted above,[2] there are thirteen paragraphs pointing out the historical facts of "administering wealth" by the ancient emperors. The whole chapter is really an outline of the economic development of China. The order of paragraphs is chronological, and everything is traced back to the age of invention and discovery.

The first emperor the "Appendix" mentions is Pao Hsi. It says:

---

[1] *Li Ki*, bk. vii, pp. 369-370.
[2] See *supra*, p. 50.

ECONOMIC DEVELOPMENT

Anciently, when Pao Hsi had come to rule the world, looking up, he contemplated the brilliant forms exhibited in the sky; and looking down, he surveyed the patterns shown on the earth. He contemplated the ornamental appearances of birds and beasts, and the different possibilities of the soil. Near at hand, in his own person, he found things for consideration, and the same at a distance, in things in general. From this he devised the eight trigrams, in order to show fully the attributes of spiritual and intellectual life, and to classify the natures of the myriads of things. He invented the making of nets of various kinds by knitting strings, both for hunting and fishing.

By his name and inventions we may know that the age of Pao Hsi was in the hunting and fishing stage, and also in the pastoral stage.[1]

The Chinese really have no accurate knowledge about the earliest history of China, but it is said that the reign of Pao Hsi lasted one hundred and ten years, and that the fifteen reigns which followed all adopted the name of Pao Hsi. It is certain that the period between Pao Hsi and Shên Nung must have been very long. Since Shên Nung was a great inventor, the "Appendix" mentions him next. It says: "He fashioned wood to form the share, and bent

---

[1] The name of Pao Hsi has some significance. Pao means kitchen, and Hsi domestic animal. Such a name would mean that he was the inventor of kitchen and cookery. He is also called by the name of Fu Hsi. Fu means subjugating or domesticating, and such a name would mean that he was the inventor of the domestication of animals. At that time, both hunting and fishing were by means of different nets. The eight trigrams were the first invention of writing. For example: ☰ represents heaven; ☷ , earth; ☳ , thunder; ☴ , wind; ☵ , water; ☲ , fire; ☶ , mountain; and ☱ , marsh. They are really eight characters. In the Chinese language, they are called *pa kua*; *pa* means eight, and *kua* means hanging. The latter means that the phenomena of things are hung in order to show them to the people. This was the first step toward civilization.

wood to make the plough-handle. The advantages of ploughing and weeding were then taught to the whole empire." The age of Shên Nung was thus the beginning of the agricultural stage.[1]

This age was also, however, the beginning of the primitive commercial stage. The "Appendix" says: "He caused markets to be held at midday, thus bringing together all the people, and assembling in one place all their commodities. They made their exchanges and retired, everyone having got what he wanted." This was a very important advance of civilization. Since the "Appendix" does not mention money, it would seem that the exchanges of this period were mostly in the form of barter.

According to the historians, the reign of Shên Nung lasted one hundred and twenty years. After seven subsequent reigns, Huang Ti arose. His reign lasted one hundred years (2147-2048 B. K. or 2698-2599 B. C.). After two hundred and forty-one years, came the Emperor Yao whose reign lasted ninety years, and the Emperor Shun whose reign lasted fifty years. Huang Ti, Yao and Shun were the three greatest emperors, and they were in the historical periods; hence, the "Appendix" mentions them as a whole. It says:

After the death of Shên Nung, there arose Huang Ti, Yao and Shun. They carried through the necessary changes of material things, so that the people would not get tired of them. They transformed the economic conditions miraculously in order to make them fit the people. They were harmonized with the principle of the *Canon of Changes:* when the course of any

---

[1] The name of Shên Nung also has some significance. Shên means divine, and Nung means farmer. As he was called Divine Farmer, it is very clear that he was the discoverer of agriculture. Especially from the word "fashioned", we know that there was the utilization of metal, although the share was made of wood.

thing comes to an end, it should be changed; when it is changed, it passes through freely; when it passes through freely, it can continue for a long time.

The principle of the *Canon of Changes* is the theory of evolution, but the "Appendix" illustrates it by the economic development of these three emperors.

Indeed, economic changes form the most powerful elements in evolution in the course of civilization. K'ung Ying-ta (1125-1199 A. K. or 574-648 A. D.), for the explanation of this point, gives this illustration:

Preceding the time of Huang Ti, the people wore the furs of animals. Later, the population grew larger, and the animals became fewer; hence the material for such a dress would be somewhat exhausted. Therefore, the adoption of silk and flax for the making of clothes was a miraculous transformation, in order to adapt them to the people.

This is quite an economic interpretation of history. In short, the age of Huang Ti, and that of Yao and Shun, marked an epoch-making advance in the history of civilization, and such an advance was chiefly based on economic development. Therefore, the "Appendix" does not mention anything but the material civilization.

Concerning the material civilization of these three emperors, the "Appendix" mentions only nine things. The nine things were all invented in the time of Huang Ti, and were completed or improved in the time of Yao and Shun. Therefore, the "Appendix" does not make any distinction among them. The nine things are in the following order.

(1) They made the new system of dress and established the social order by the means of it. Hence, the "Appendix" says: "Huang Ti, Yao and Shun simply wore their upper and lower garments, as patterns to the people, and good order was secured throughout the whole empire." It shows

the peaceful, graceful, orderly, and industrial society of that time, and it takes dress first as a sign to mark the distinction between this age and the ages previous.

(2) They discovered the means of navigation. The "Appendix" says: "They cut open trees to form boats, and cut others long and thin to make oars . . . . They could now reach the most distant parts, and the whole empire was benefited." In the making of the boats and oars, they made use of metal.

(3) They discovered the means of transportation. The "Appendix" says: "They used oxen in carts, and yoked horses to chariots, thus providing for the carriage of what was heavy, and for distant journeys, thereby benefiting the whole empire."

(4) After navigation and transportation had been developed, there was need of protection for the cities. Hence, the "Appendix" says: "They made the system of double gates, and the warning of the clapper, as a preparation against the approach of marauding visitors."

(5) For the refinement of the food, they made the pestle and mortar. The "Appendix" says: "They cut wood and fashioned it into pestles; they dug in the ground and formed mortars. Thus the myriads of the people received the benefit arising from the use of the pestle and mortar." As the "Appendix" takes them as a great invention among all other great things, we can see how much importance the Chinese ascribe to rice.

(6) Since society was now highly developed, and the double gates and clapper were not sufficient for protection, there was need of good weapons. The "Appendix" says: "They bent wood by means of string so as to form bows, and sharpened wood so as to make arrows. The utility of bows and arrows was to produce a feeling of awe over the empire." These things seem more military than economic,

but they really are for economic purposes, because they are for the protection of wealth.

(7) They changed the form of shelter. The "Appendix" says: " In the highest antiquity, they made their homes in winter in caves, and in summer dwelt in the open country. In subsequent ages, for these the sages substituted houses, with the ridgebeam above and the projecting roof below, as a provision against wind and rain."

(8) As we shall see, the Chinese always consider the funeral as a part of economic life;[1] the "Appendix" mentions the invention of coffins as follows:

When the ancients buried their dead, they covered the body thickly with pieces of wood, having laid it in the open country. They raised no mound over it, nor planted trees around it; nor had they any fixed period for mourning. In subsequent ages, the sages substituted for these practices the inner and outer coffins.

(9) So far as the physical needs had been satisfied, there should be mental and legal development, and the most important thing was the complete invention of writing. The "Appendix" says:

In the highest antiquity, government was carried on successfully by the use of knotted cords to preserve the memory of things. In subsequent ages, the sages substituted for these written characters and bonds. By means of these, the doings of all the officials could be regulated, and the affairs of all the people accurately examined.[2]

This was the last thing in the economic development of ancient China.

[1] See *infra*.
[2] *Yi King*, pp. 382-5.

The age of Huang Ti, Yao and Shun was in the agricultural stage. Through the improvements of navigation and transportation, it belonged also to the stage of primitive commerce. But what made this age a great advance was that it had reached the beginning of the primitive industrial stage. The ships and oars, the carts and chariots, the gates and clappers, the pestles and mortars, the bows and arrows, the ridgebeams and projecting roofs, the different coffins, and the tablets which were to be written, all these things required some kind of skilled labor. And above all, there was the silk industry. It changed the face of the whole society, and distinguished the social order by the system of dress. It marked a great advance not only in the economic development, but also in the social and political organization.

Looking at the whole chapter of the "Appendix," we can see it is really a historical treatise on Chinese economic development. Or, since the writer of the "Appendix" would be interested in the general development of Chinese civilization as a whole, and not in the economic development particularly, we may better say that it is certainly an economic interpretation of history. From its beginning to its end, it mentions thirteen things; and, except four things only—namely, the eight trigrams, the double gates and clappers, the bows and arrows, and the written characters and bonds—all of them are absolutely essential to economic civilization. Moreover, even among those four things, the double gates and clappers and the bows and arrows are mainly for the protection of economic life; and the different forms of writing, from the eight trigrams to the written characters and bonds, are partially for the development of economic life. In short, economic development is the principal factor of civilization, while writing is the most important tool to promote civilization.

The "Appendix" was written by the immediate pupils of Confucius, and its importance is equal to that of the "Great Learning" and the "Doctrine of the Mean." It was the basis of the philosophical schools of the Sung dynasty, and it gave a great impetus to thought. But the Schools of the Sung did not understand this chapter well, so that the economic development of China has been retarded since that time. The reason was simply that they did not know that technical invention and material welfare are the chief cause of civilization. If we read this chapter carefully, we see how important to the progress of civilization economic development is from the point of view of the Confucians.

Besides this chapter, we should like to quote four passages more from the "Appendix," in order to show that Confucianism is somewhat materialistic and praises technical invention very highly. It says: "The sages, fully understanding the way of Heaven, and having clearly ascertained the experience of the people, invented these divine things as a provision for the use of the people."[1] As the "Appendix" calls such material things "divine things" and the results of "the way of Heaven", we can see how materialistic is Confucianism; nay, we may even say that Confucianism is a religion of the economic world. It gives its explanation as follows:

The first appearance of anything as a bud is what we call a semblance; when it has received its complete form we call it an article. How to make and how to use it is what we call a law. The utilities arising from it in external and internal matters, so that the people all use it, stamp it with a character which we call divine.[2]

Again, it says: "In preparing material things for the reali-

[1] *Yi King*, p. 372. [2] *Ibid.*, p. 373.

zation of practical use, and inventing the complete articles for the benefit of the whole world, there are none greater than the sages." [1] Hence, the Confucians call all the great inventors by the name of sages. It says again:

That which is antecedent to the material form exists, we say, as a principle, and that which is subsequent to the material form exists, we say, as an article. Transforming and shaping it is what we call change. Carrying it out and putting it in operation is what we call success. Taking the result and setting it forth for all the people of the whole world is what we call the business of life.[2]

This passage is simply an explanation of the process of invention. It traces back to the beginning when there is merely a principle without anything existing, and comes down to the end when the article is utilized in the business of life. By these four passages, we can understand perfectly that the Confucians take technical invention as the basis of economic development, and the economic development as the basis of all civilization.

What Confucius discusses in the " Evolution of Civilization " and what the "Appendix" narrates is the economic development of the earliest China. But we should like to say something about the economic progress made about the time of Confucius. The Chou dynasty, as we know, was the period of maturity of the Chinese civilization. In the beginning of this dynasty (about 571 B. K. or 1122 B. C.), there were two great statesmen; the Duke of Chou and T'ai Kung. They both were very efficient in developing Chinese economic civilization. But T'ai Kung, especially, after he withdrew from the imperial government and came to his feudal state, Ch'i, devoted all his attention to economic development, and made Ch'i the chief state for industry

---

[1] *Yi King*, p. 373. [2] *Ibid.*, p. 377.

ECONOMIC DEVELOPMENT 131

and commerce in the Chinese world. This was the first time that China rose to the stage of national economy; and even began to reach that of international economy.

Later, Ch'i declined; but Kuan Chung, or Kuan Tzŭ (died 93 B. K. or 644 B. C.), minister of Ch'i, raised Ch'i again to the chief state of industry and commerce, and its prosperity lasted until the end of its political life (331 A. K. or 221 B. C.). In the period of Spring and Autumn (171 B. K.—71 A. K. or 722—481 B. C.), there were many industrial and commercial states besides Ch'i; hence, economic civilization in the time of Confucius was highly developed. This period was really in the stage of international economy or world economy. Of course, what the ancient Chinese called world was simply the Chinese world. But we must understand that the territory of the leading states of this period was really equal to that of the leading European states in modern times. Therefore, there is no reason why we should not call it world economy. In the period of Warring States (149-331 A. K. or 403—221 B. C.), the whole Chinese world was divided up into only seven states, and economic development was still higher. This period was the most dynamic in the whole history of China, and it marked the sharp distinction between ancient and modern China. Such a dynamic condition was ended at the beginning of the Han dynasty (about 412 A. K. or 140 B. C.).

Taking Chinese history as a whole, we may divide the economic stages as follows: From the standpoint of the relation of production to consumption, the period from the beginning of Chinese history to the beginning of the Chou dynasty was the stage of self-sufficing or isolated economy; that from that period to the period of Spring and Autumn was the stage of local or village economy; and that from that period to the present day was and is, the stage of national economy. Of course, such a division is very rough.

If we want to get a finer division, we may say that the period preceding the age of Spring and Autumn was ancient economy; that the period covering the age of Spring and Autumn and that of Warring States was a transitional period; and that the period from the Ch'in dynasty (331, or 221 B. C.) to the present was modern economy. From the political point of view, the period preceding the Ch'in dynasty was feudalism, and that after that dynasty was absolute monarchy; and from the economic point of view, the former period was marked by the government ownership of land, and the latter period, by its private ownership. These are the only general statements we can make.

If we wish to make a general comparison between China and Europe, we may say that China passed through the pastoral stage in a short period, but has stayed in the agricultural stage for a very long time; and that Europe had stayed in the pastoral stage for a very long time, but passed through the agricultural stage in a short period. We do not wish to go into the details of history, but we may pick out some features of the present day in order to show some of the more striking contrasts between the Chinese and the European economic civilizations.

First, we may take up foods. In the western world, steaks and chops are the principal meats, but their cooking is quite simple, because they are merely burned by fire. Milk is a common drink, and butter is used as oil. These foods are quite similar to those consumed by the Huns described in the Han dynasty. In China, the people have much more varied food, and their cutting, seasoning and cooking are much finer and more complex. Milk is not a common drink in China, and the Chinese do not use butter, but peanut oil.

Second, we may take up the subject of dress. In the western world, wool is the principal material for clothes and hats, and leather for shoes. The men's dress is simple in color; and the children in most countries wear only short trousers and short dresses, having their legs below the knees covered only by stockings. Furs and feathers are still used by women, not only for warmth, but also for fashion. In China, silk, linen and cotton are the principal materials for clothes, hats, or shoes. The men's dress has different colors, and the children do not purposely expose any part of their body. The people wear furs only as fur coats, but never use feathers. All these things show that Europe has passed the pastoral stage only a short time ago, and still has indications of the survival of that stage; and that China has long since come to the agricultural stage, and has the indications of the agricultural life.

It is fortunate for Europe and unfortunate for China, however, that Europe has come to the true industrial stage much earlier than China. The great difference is marked by machinery. Besides food and dress, moreover, the building of Europe is better than that of China. It is probably because in the ancient times, Greece and Rome had slaves for erecting their buildings, and in the medieval times, the church and the feudal princes had great power to build up the churches and castles. But in China, there was no slavery; the church had no such power; and the feudal princes were not so oppressive as those in Europe. Whatever the cause may have been, there can be no doubt that Chinese buildings are inferior to those of Europe. The chief defects of Chinese buildings are that the material of the walls is brick instead of stone, and that the inside structure is finished in wood, for the most part, that is, there are wooden beams and wooden pillars to support the roof, and wooden floors. Hence they do not endure very long. Moreover, the Chinese have not shown any great interest in preserving their old buildings. Therefore, even though

II. THEORY OF PROGRESS

there have been many good buildings, they have been destroyed during the revolutions of different dynasties.

From different writings, we may infer the theory of progress of Confucius. There is no better example than the principle of The Three Stages, as pointed out above,[1] for proof that Confucius believed in progress. But the principle of The Three Stages is very general, and it can be applied to every case. If we wish to get a specific theory about economic progress, we may come to the *tsing tien* system, and see how Confucius expects that general progress of every kind will result from this system. On this specific point, his theory of progress is periodical, and can be measured by the length of one year, three years, nine years, eighteen years, twenty-seven years, and thirty years. According to his theory, progress can be realized within three years, and it can be completed within thirty years. It comes from the *tsing tien* system, and we shall take the interpretation of Pan Ku from his " Economic History."[2]

Under the *tsing tien* system, in the cultivation of three years, the people have a surplus of food sufficient for one year. Hence, the sense of pride and shame is developed, and quarrels and litigations do not exist. Therefore, every three years, an examination of merit is given to the officials. Confucius says: " If there were any of the princes who would employ me, in the course of twelve months, I should have done something considerable. In three years, the work would be accomplished."[3] In saying that the work would be accomplished in three years, he refers to the *tsing tien* system. From his point of view, *tsing tien* is not only a

[1] See *supra*, pp. 18-22.
[2] *History of Han*, ch. xxiv.
[3] *Classics*, vol. i, p. 267.

theoretical system, but a practical one; and the period of three years is the first step of progress. In nine years, after three examinations have been held, the undeserving officials are degraded, and the deserving promoted. There is a surplus of food sufficient for three years; and the improvement of the occupations of the people is called " advancement." In eighteen years, there are two periods of " advancement ", and such a condition is called " peace "; the surplus of food is sufficient for six years. In twenty-seven years, there are three periods of " advancement ", and this is called " extreme peace "; the surplus of food is sufficient for nine years. Then virtue prevails, and the government is perfected. Confucius says: " If a true king were to arise, it would still require a generation, and then the benevolent government would be complete." [1] He means that the completion of the *tsing tien* system requires thirty years. *Kung-yang's Commentary* says: " If the system of tithes, [the whole system of *tsing tien*], shall prevail, the praise of peace will arise."

Although the tendency of the *tsing tien* system is to level the whole society into a static condition, there is, at the same time, a dynamic principle. In every period of nine years, it requires a total improvement in all the different occupations;—that is, among all the agricultural and industrial occupations no stationary condition is allowed. Such an improvement is called by the name of advancement; two steps of advancement are called by the name of peace; three steps of advancement, extreme peace. It is peculiar enough that the name of peace or extreme peace is assigned for the advancement of the occupations of the people; it means that we can obtain the stage of peace only by the improvement of productive power. Therefore, for the in-

[1] *Classics*, vol. i, p. 267.

dividuals, the *tsing tien* system does not give anyone an advantage; it is a static model. But for society as a whole, advancements are necessary; and it is the dynamic principle. This is the theory of progress of Confucius.

His theory of progress, however, is based on many phases. Some of them have been discussed above, and the others will be discussed later. If we want to sum up his whole theory of progress in a few words, it will be:

> I. The Abolition of War. A peaceful society is necessary for industrial development.[1]
> II. Technical Invention. It is the basis of economic progress, and is also the basis of all other progress.[2]
> III. The Control of Nature. It makes man the rival and the assistant of Heaven and Earth.[3]
> IV. The *Tsing Tien* System. Everyone has an equal share of the most important part of the means of production.[4]
> V. The Universally Free Education. It gives everyone equal opportunity for intellectual and moral development.[5]
> VI. The Election System. It makes a representative government based on the educational system.[6]
> VII. The Great Similarity. It abolishes such social institutions as state, family and private property.[7]

[1] See *infra*.
[2] See *supra*, pp. 121-130.
[3] See *infra*.
[4] See *infra*.
[5] See *supra*, pp. 84-86.
[6] See *supra*, pp. 89-95.
[7] See *supra*, pp. 20-22.

ECONOMIC DEVELOPMENT 137

VIII. The Change of Human Nature. The end of the Confucian system is to make human nature perfect.

All other phases are discussed in other places, and we shall discuss here only the last one, the change of human nature. Since there are many different views regarding human nature, we must go back to Confucius first. He says: " By nature, men are nearly alike; by practice, they get to be wide apart." Again, he says: " There are only the wise of the highest class, and the stupid of the lowest class, who cannot be changed." [1] From this point of view, therefore, human nature is about the same everywhere and in everyone, but it generally can be greatly changed. What Confucius means by nature is the qualities received by birth, the same meaning that has been given by the *Adjunct to the Canon of Filial Piety* and by Kao Tzŭ. Mencius and Hsun Tzŭ both differ from Confucius in their views, and each opposes the other. Hsun Tzŭ holds that human nature is evil; hence education is the most important thing for the correction of human nature. Mencius holds that human nature is good; hence the only thing which is needed is to extend what man already has. They both are not quite correct, but each has established his doctrine. If we make a compromise, we may say that Hsun Tzŭ speaks of human nature in the stage of Small Tranquility, and that Mencius speaks of it in that of Great Similarity. If they have different stages in mind, their doctrines are both correct.

According to the theory of Confucius, in the stage of Great Similarity or Extreme Peace, human nature is good. As we have quoted before, in the Great Similarity selfish schemings are repressed and find no way to arise. This means that the selfishness of human nature is changed. In

[1] *Classics.* vol. i, p. 318.

the *Spring and Autumn*, the Extreme Peace Stage is that in which everyone in the world conducts himself like the superior man, and all the barbarians become civilized. Therefore, changing human nature so that it will be perfectly good is the final aim of Confucianism.

But how can we go about changing human nature? Simply by means of those seven things just mentioned above, but the chief thing is economic prosperity. Mencius is the chief representative of those who advocate that human nature is good, yet he still says that in good years the children of people are most of them good, while in bad years the most of them abandon themselves to evil.[1] Therefore, the human nature changes to either good or evil in accordance with the economic condition. If there is economic prosperity equally distributed to everyone, the nature of the people must be good. Mencius says: " When a sage governs the world, he will cause pulse and grain to be as abundant as water and fire. If pulse and grain are as abundant as water and fire, how shall the people be other than virtuous?"[2] Therefore, if we shall come to the highest development of the economic world, we shall come also to the highest development of the ethical world. The former is the cause, and the latter is the effect. Hence, Confucius regards economic progress as the means, and moral perfection as the end. If we understand this, we have the general view of his theory of progress.

Besides economic prosperity as a general condition, Confucius has a special device for changing human nature. As we have seen, Confucius makes universally free education a necessary institution; it is really a most important force for modifying human nature. But the educational system of Confucius begins not only in the school age of a child,

---

[1] *Classics*, vol. ii, p. 404.   [2] *Ibid.*, p. 463.

but even before his birth. This is a peculiar doctrine of Confucius, and it is known as gestatory education.

According to *Elder Tai's Record of Rites*, the first thing in gestatory education is the choice of the mother. Therefore, when the parents choose the wife of their son, they must select her from among those families which have had a high standard of morality for all generations. There are five women who are not to be taken in marriage: (1) the daughter of a rebellious house; (2) the daughter of a disorderly house; (3) the daughter of a house which has produced criminals for more than one generation; (4) the daughter of a leprous house; (5) the daughter who has lost her mother and has grown old.[1]

When a woman is pregnant, the rules are as follows: While sleeping, she should lie on her back; while sitting or standing, the body should be in an upright position, and the weight evenly distributed. She should not laugh too loudly; nor eat food of bad flavors, nor anything which is not cut properly; nor sit down on anything which is not placed properly. The eyes should not see bad colors, the ears should not hear bad sounds, and the mouth should not utter bad words. She should read good poetry, and tell good stories. By this means, the child will be physically, morally, and mentally excellent. Whenever a woman is pregnant, she must be very watchful in regard to the things by which the mind is affected. If she is affected by good things, the child will be good; if by bad things, he will be bad. These are the rules of gestatory education. The mothers of Wên Wang and of Ch'êng Wang are good examples of such educators.

When a child is born, moreover, he receives the family education for a long time before he goes to school. There-

[1] Bk lxxx.

fore, Confucius says: " When a child is trained completely, his education is just as strong as his nature; and when he practices anything perpetually, he will do it naturally as a permanent habit." [1]

This is Confucius' plan for changing human nature. If every generation of the world would put it in practice, human nature would soon be perfect. It is the same principle as that man should control nature in the economic world. Man must control nature not only without him, but also within him, so that progress will be complete and continuous.

[1] Bk. xlviii.

CHAPTER X

Economic Organization

I. THE WHOLE WORLD AS THE LARGEST ORGANIZATION

When we come to the topic of economic organization, we must say that according to the view of Confucius, there are two organizations. The one is the largest—the world; the other, the smallest—the family. As Chinese philosophy is mostly synthetical, going from the whole to the part, and as world economy is a special theme of Confucius, we shall take up the largest organization first, in order to show the economic thought of Confucius prominently and clearly.

How do we know that Confucius regards the world as an economic organization? It is found in the "Great Learning." The "Great Learning" may be called the catalogue of the teachings of Confucius. The objects of the principles of the "Great Learning" are three: to brighten the brilliant virtue, to renovate the people, and to rest in the highest excellence. The first object is to care for the individual himself; the second for the other people as a whole; the third is the perfect state which forms the goal for the other two objects. Having understood these three objects, we now come to its eight subjects: (1) the investigation of things; (2) the extension of knowledge; (3) sincerity of thought; (4) composing the mind; (5) the cultivation of the personality; (6) the regulation of the family; (7) the governing of the state; (8) the equalization of the whole world. These eight subjects are taken step by step, one following another; yet the student must have the whole world in view from the beginning. Among all the eight subjects, the cultivation of the personality is the root of everything. From this point, Confucius regards the individual as the unit. But sincerity of thought is, in turn, the root of cultivating the personality.

Having understood the whole outline of the "Great Learning," we come now to see how Confucius regards the whole world as an economic unit. We have already seen that Confucius ascribes very much importance to economic life. But, in the "Great Learning," he does not say a single word about economic life until the last chapter—namely, the equalization of the whole world. It is not for the cultivation of the personality, not for the regulation of the family, not for the governing of the state, but for the equalization of the whole world, that Confucius gives his economic principles. He feels that the whole world is the economic unit, and that the economic life can never be confined to any particular person, family or state. The student can never study economics completely unless he takes the world as a whole. And the world can never be equalized unless the economic life of the whole world is equal. This is a special concept of Confucius.

The economic principles given in the "Great Learning" are conspicuous above all the other economic principles given in other Confucian books. The reason is simply that the "Great Learning" simplifies the principles for equalizing the world into only two things—namely, employing the best men, and administering wealth. Hence, everyone knows that a part of the "Great Learning" is devoted to the principles of economics. What we wish to emphasize is, however, that Confucius has the world economy in his mind, and that he thinks about the world as an economic unit.

But we must understand that the economic principles of the "Great Learning" are very general. Although they are given in the chapter on the equalization of the world it does not mean that they are fitted only for world economy. Indeed, they can be applied to either a person, a family, or a state.

All other economic principles given in the " Great Learning " are quoted in other places, and we shall quote here only one, the fundamental principle of world economy;—namely, the principle of reciprocity. It is stated in a metaphorical sense as follows:

What you do not like above, do not place below; what you do not like below, do not place above; what you do not like in front, do not shift to the back; what you do not like in back, do not turn to the front; what you do not like on the right, do not bestow on the left; what you do not like on the left, do not bestow on the right;—this is what is called the principle with which we are, as with a measuring-square, to establish the law of justice.[1]

The principle of reciprocity, as stated in the second chapter, is one of the fundamental concepts of Confucius. But there it is discussed from the purely moral point of view. Here we must consider it from the economic and political point of view. The principle is the same, but its application is a little different. Taking this principle as the basis of world economy, it develops commercial policy and international law. It is the golden rule of the business world, and we cannot say that there is no moral standard for politics and diplomacy.

The economic system of Confucius is not nationalism, but cosmopolitanism. Before Confucius, economic theories were mostly like the doctrines of the mercantile school and took the nation as the unit. The chief representative was Kuan Tzŭ, who was the most successful minister for the

[1] *Classics*, vol. i, pp. 373-4.

realization of mercantilism and of state socialism. He was the first one to have a complete economic system which we can see to-day. But we have no room to deal with his economy, and the only reason we mention him is to contrast him with Confucius.

1. *Doctrine of Peace*

The most important principle for international relations is the doctrine of peace. This doctrine is based not only on the principle of humanity, but also on that of utility. Confucius says: " Talking about sincere agreement and cultivating universal peace are what are called the advantages of men. Fighting, plundering, and killing each other are what are called the calamities of men." [1] In the *Spring and Autumn*, Confucius records about four hundred wars within the period of two hundred and forty-two years, and condemns them all, for war is contrary to the principle of humanity. Therefore, Mencius says that in the *Spring and Autumn* there are no righteous wars. He holds that military force is used only as a punishment by the supreme authority to its subjects, but that the independent states have no right to engage in such punitive war against one another.[2]

For the condemnation of war, Mencius gives many passages in very strong language. He says:

When contentions about territory are the ground on which they fight, they slaughter men till the fields are filled with them. When some struggle for a city is the ground on which they fight, they slaughter men till the city is filled with them. This is what is called " leading on the land to devour human flesh ". Death is not enough for such a crime. Therefore, those who are skilful in fighting, should suffer the highest punishment.[3]

---

[1] *Li Ki*, bk. vii, p. 380.
[2] *Classics*, vol. ii, p. 478.   [3] *Ibid.*, p. 305.

ECONOMIC ORGANIZATION 145

He says again: "Those who say that we can, for our sovereign, form alliances with other states, so that our battles must be successful, are nowadays called good ministers, but anciently they were called pests of the people."[1] Mencius also calls such persons the destroyers of the people.[2] Moreover, he condemns not only the ministers, but also the rulers. When he speaks of King Hui of Liang, who to gain territory, tore and destroyed his people in battle, he condemns him as brutal.[3] Therefore, according to the principle of Confucius, there is no absolute justification for any war; it is only that some wars are relatively better than others. Hence, war should be abolished.

The doctrine of peace is harmonious with economic principles. First, it makes the life of man more valuable than the land. In the *Analects*, Confucius attaches the chief importance to the life of the people; even food ranks only second. In the *Spring and Autumn*, he condemns those who employ the people in a bad year for the reparation of an old house, because they exploit the people in hard labor. But how much more strongly would he condemn those who injure the people? And how much more strongly still would he condemn those who kill the people in war? Generally, the object of war is getting land. But, getting land by sacrificing numerous lives of the people is a most costly enterprise, and will not pay. This is what Mencius calls sacrificing what is really dear on account of what is not so dear.[4] This is also what he calls "leading on the land to devour human flesh."

Second, it makes the people's production continuous, and their consumption satisfactory. As a matter of fact, war is most injurious to the people, although it may give a use-

[1] *Classics*, vol. ii, p. 441.
[2] *Ibid.*, p. 439.
[3] *Ibid.*, pp. 477-8.
[4] *Ibid.*, p. 478.

less glory to the ruler. Mencius describes the suffering of the people on account of war as follows: "The rulers of those states rob their people of their time, so that they cannot plough and weed their fields in order to support their parents. Their parents suffer from cold and hunger. Brothers, wives, and children are separated and scattered abroad." [1] In fact, the evils of war are the interruption of production, the lessening of consumption and the destruction of the family. It is only peace that can cure these evils.

Third, it saves the economic waste in the preparation for war. Confucius condemns not only actual war, but also the preparation for it. Preparation for war is a great waste of wealth, and a heavy burden upon the people. Therefore, the doctrine of peace is based partially on economic principles.

Abolishing war and changing the military society into an industrial one is the common wish of Confucious and his best pupil, Yen Yüan. The *Park of Narratives* [2] tells us that when Confucius went up to the Nung Mountain, Tzŭ-lu, Tzŭ-kung and Yen Yüan accompanied him, and Confucius asked them each to tell his individual wishes. Tzŭ-lu said that he wished to raise an army and to attack the enemy, so that he was sure to take the territory for a thousand miles. Tzŭ-kung said that he wished to wear a white garment and a white cap to persuade the two armies under the white swords, in order to take away the calamity of the two nations. Yen Yüan said:

I wish to have a wise king or a sage ruler and to become his minister. I shall cause the city walls to have no need to be repaired, the ditches and moats to have no foe to cross over them, and the swords and spears to be melted for the making of agricultural implements. I shall cause the whole world to

[1] *Classics*, vol. ii, pp. 135-6.   [2] Bk. xv.

have no calamity of war for thousands of years. Under such a condition, how can Yu go to fight angrily? And how can Tz'ŭ go to make arbitration cheerfully?

Then Tzŭ-lu asked what the wish of Confucius was. He said: "What I wish to do, is the plan of the son of Yen. I wish to carry my clothes and hats and to follow him." This conversation shows clearly the common wish of Confucius and Yen Yüan. The aim of Tzŭ-lu is but that of a soldier; that of Tzŭ-kung is but that of a diplomatist; but that of Yen Yüan and Confucius is that of the highest statesmanship, and the plan of a sage. The most important sentence is "the swords and spears are melted for the making of agricultural implements." Thus one would turn the instruments for killing men into instruments for nourishing men, and change the soldiers to farmers; in short, the military society would be entirely destroyed, and an industrial society would be universally and permanently established. This is the ideal of Confucius.

The evils of feudalism, with its constant wars, impressed Confucius profoundly, and led him to the vision of a world-state and world-peace. Plato's ideal state, on the other hand, is a small city-state, ever ready for war. The spirit of the Chinese people, under the influence of Confucius' teachings, is such that they are more nearly ready than any western people for the realization of this lofty vision.[1]

II. THE FAMILY AS THE SMALLEST ORGANIZATION

While the whole world is the largest economic organization, the family is the smallest one, and the one having closest economic relation to the individual. As long as there is a family, the individual never can make his economic

[1] In the second book of Kang Yu-wei's *Book on the Great Similarity*, the details of how the world is to be united are given.

life absolutely independent. Therefore, the family life is very important in affecting the economic life. Whenever we use the term family we mean that there are at least two generations, although the principal factor of production is only of one generation. For example, a family means husband and wife. But it may have either old parents, or young children, or both. Hence, it may include three generations at the same time. But in any case it must have two generations, if it has children. Therefore, we may consider the family as an economic organization from two points of view,—namely, the relation of husband and wife, and that of father and son.

The happy life of the family in Confucius' mind is given in the "Doctrine of the Mean." It first quotes from the *Canon of Poetry*, as follows:

> Loving union with wife and children,
> Is like the music of lutes and harps;
> When there is concord among brothers,
> The harmony is delightful and enduring.
> Thus you make your family happy,
> And enjoy pleasure with your wife and children.

Then it quotes from Confucius, who gives to this poem the following appreciation: "In such a state of things, parents have entire complacence!"[1] The poem itself mentions only wife and children, and brothers. But Confucius adds to them the parents, in order to make the happy life of the family complete. This is what Confucius thinks a happy family.

1. *Relation of Husband and Wife*

According to the social system of Confucius, the relation of husband and wife is the starting-point. He always puts the matrimonial significance at the beginning of all his writ-

---

[1] *Classics*, vol. i, pp. 396-7.

ings. The "Doctrine of the Mean" says: "The way of the superior man, [Confucius], is beginning with its course from the relation of husband and wife. But in its utmost reaches it shines brightly through heaven and earth."[1]

(a) *Marriage*

It is well known to the Western world that marriage in China is a matter arranged primarily by the parents of the parties, and through the services of a go-between. This was an old custom, and it is in accordance with the teachings of Confucius. It has, of course, the disadvantage that the contracting parties cannot be sure in advance that they are perfectly suited to each other. It is not the practice, however, for parents to disregard the wishes of their children in these matters. These marriage customs are a necessary consequence of the Chinese custom which forbids social intercourse between the sexes prior to marriage—the obvious reason for which is, of course, to prevent not alone any improper relations, but even the suspicion of them. In China there is no marriage license and no church to take charge of the ceremony. The parents' order takes the place of the license, and the go-between takes the place of the minister or justice of the peace.

The ninth book of the *Record of Rites* says: "Once mated with her husband, all her life she will not change her feeling of duty to him; hence, when the husband dies she will not marry again."[2] This is the ideal of marriage. But, at the death of her husband, if her age is below fifty, and that of her son below fifteen, and he has no close relatives on his father's side to take the economic responsibility, the widow may marry again. Therefore, according to the *Canon of Rites*, a step-son should mourn for his step-father,

[1] *Classics*, vol. i, p. 393.
[2] *Li Ki*, bk. ix, p. 439.

who is the second husband of his mother.¹ The fact that Confucius allows the woman to marry a second husband under some circumstances shows the practicality of Confucianism. It is Ch'êng Yi (1584-1658 A. K. or 1033-1107 A. D.) who first says that a woman should not marry a second husband, even if she should die in hunger. But this is not the teaching of Confucius.

(b) *Divorce*

Having understood the proceeding of marriage, we now come to the subject of divorce. According to *Elder Tai's Record of Rites*, there are seven grounds for divorcing a wife: (1) disobedience to parents-in-law; (2) not giving birth to a son; (3) adultery; (4) jealousy of her husband's attentions, that is, to the other inmates of his harem; (5) leprosy; (6) talkativeness; (7) thieving. But there are three considerations which may overrule these grounds: (1) having no family for her return; (2) having passed through the three years' mourning for his parents; (3) his condition formerly poor and mean, and now rich and honorable.² But these rules are entirely applied only to the classes of the great officials, the students, and the common people. The prince can divorce his wife on six other grounds, but not because she has no son. And the emperor cannot divorce the empress on any ground, but simply separates from her. These rules are adopted even in the *Law Code of the Ts'ing Dynasty*, the present dynasty.

Because the emperor, the prince, and also the great officials, have not so much freedom of divorce as those below them, they do not consummate the marriage upon the date of marriage. When the wife comes in, she lives apart from the husband. After the period of three months, she is presented to the ancestral temple, and begins to be called wife.

---

¹ Ch. xxxi. ² Bk. lxxx.

This period is just long enough for the examination into her character and for her special training. If the parents-in-law and husband cannot get along with her, she can return to her family a virgin, and can marry another without any trouble. This is for the benefit of both sides, although the men get more advantage. But the student and the common people have more freedom of divorce, so that they consummate the marriage the same night. This was an old custom.

As to the third reason for the prohibition of divorce, that one should not divorce his wife if his condition formerly was poor and mean, and is now rich and honorable, this provision is very just. But, as a matter of fact, divorce is generally caused by economic conditions. In the *Canon of Poetry*, there is a poem against the corrupt custom of divorce. The people of Wei loved new wives and abandoned the old ones. Therefore, the poet, speaking for the divorced wives, made this a subject for satire. We should like to quote a few lines of this poem, which refer to the economic aspect of the affair.

Whether you had plenty or not,
I exerted myself to be getting
    *   *   *   *   *   *   *
Formerly, I was afraid our means might be exhausted during our old age,
And I worked hard with you in the struggle for existence.
Now when your means are abundant and you are old,
You compare me to poison.
    *   *   *   *   *   *   *
Feasting with your new wife,
You think of me as a provision only against your poverty.[1]

Disapproving such a divorce, Confucius puts this poem in this Canon to serve as a warning.

[1] *Classics*, vol. iv, pt. i, pp. 55-8.

It is true that, in the Confucian writings, there is no statement about divorce issued to the woman. Though this is not wholly just, in a paternal society it must be so. In ancient time, the Disorderly Stage, if woman should be allowed to have the right to divorce her husband, the paternal family could not be established, and social life would be disorderly. This is the reason a woman cannot divorce her husband. Han Fei Tzŭ, however, speaks of T‘ai Kung as a divorced husband of an old woman. This shows that in ancient times, even long before Confucius, a woman did have the right to divorce her husband. It might have been that a woman could divorce her husband if her husband agreed to it, but that there was no legal ground for her doing so. The *Law Code of the Ts‘ing Dynasty* says that if the husband and wife are not harmonious and both wish to be separated, they may be allowed to do so.[1] Therefore, in the present day, the woman is legally allowed to divorce her husband, with his consent.

However, when we say that the Confucian writings have no statement about divorce issued to the woman, we are simply referring to the ordinary case. If in the unusual case, a woman shall have the absolute right to divorce her husband. The *General Discussion in the White Tiger Palace* says: " If the husband should either violate the social relations, or kill his parents-in-law, or break down the most important laws, it would be the greatest of disorder. In such cases, the ethical relation between husband and wife is cut off, and the wife may divorce her husband."[2] According to the *Law Code of the Ts‘ing Dynasty*, whenever the ethical relation between husband and wife is cut off, they must be separated, and are not permitted to remain in union. From this point, we can see that the Chinese re-

---

[1] Ch. x.   [2] Bk. x.

gard the ethical relation as very important, and that the husband and wife cannot remain in union, even though they love each other.

The Chinese consider the marriage tie as very strong, and continue it through the whole life. Although their marriages are not directly arranged by themselves, husbands and wives love each other and do not get divorces. The fundamental reason is that they have a habit of bearing moral obligations for which they sacrifice their sentimental feelings. Second, they accept the philosophical doctrine of fate, and content themselves on the ground that their marriage had been predestined. Third, their social condition does not allow either husband or wife to have any sweetheart beside the other. These are the most important reasons why the Chinese have very few, practically no, divorces. And we must understand that the Chinese are not concerned with formal law at all, when they either marry or divorce, but merely with the rites prescribed by religion and custom. Yet they keep their marriages sacred, and make them even stronger than if they were fixed by law. At the present day, there is practically no divorce, unless in the case of adultery; and such cases are rare.

(c) *Economic Position of Woman*

Since we have discussed above the social position of woman, we should now discuss her economic position, in which we are especially interested. Inside the family, the housewife is the chief worker. First of all, she must care for the children. The " Great Learning " says: " There never has been a girl who learned to nourish a child, that she might afterwards marry."[1] This implies that every married woman must know how to nourish a child without special training, and that it is a duty of woman. The

---
[1] *Classics*, vol. i, p. 370.

"Pattern of the Family" says: "The son of the great official has a nurse. The wife of the student nourishes her child herself."[1] Therefore, the wives of students and common people must nourish their own children, although the empress, the princess, and the noble ladies may hire nurses. This is the chief work of woman.

Second, she must take charge of the food. The *Canon of Poetry* says: "It will be hers neither to do wrong nor to do good. Only about the spirits and the food will she have to discuss."[2] The *Canon of Changes* says: "She does nothing of her own initiative, but stays at home for the preparation of food."[3] These two passages are sufficient to indicate the principal work of the housewife.

Third, she must take charge of the clothes. According to the "Pattern of the Family," when a girl reaches the age of ten, she ceases to go out from the home. Her governess teaches her to handle the hempen fibres, to deal with the cocoons, to weave silks and form fillets, and to learn all woman's work in order to furnish garments.[4]

In ancient times, all, from the empress to the wives of the common people, had to make clothes for their husbands. The *Record of Rites* tells us that the emperor must be personally a farmer, and the empress a weaver. This has three significances: First, it indicates religious piety, because the emperor and empress personally furnish the materials for the food and clothes used for sacrifices. Second, it indicates political democracy, because it makes the emperor and empress not entirely different from the farmer and weaver. Third, it indicates economic productivity, because it makes even the emperor and empress produce material things.

[1] *Li Ki*, bk. x, p. 476.
[2] *Classics*, vol. iv, pt. ii, p. 307.
[3] *Yi King*, p. 137.
[4] *Li Ki*, bk. x, p. 479.

There is a silk-worm's house. From the washing of the seeds in the stream, gathering of the leaves from the mulberry trees, feeding the worms, to the presenting of the cocoons to the empress, all the processes of work are done by the honorable ladies. Then the empress rinses some of them thrice in a vessel, begins to unwind them, and distributes them to the honorable ladies to complete the unwinding. After the dyeing and embroidering have been finished, garments are made for use in sacrifices.[1] This custom still exists to-day. In the *Canon of Poetry*, there is a poem directed against the Emperor Yu and his wife. In criticism of his wife, it says that she leaves her silkworms and weaving.[2] Since even an empress must take up the work of silkworm culture and weaving, it goes without saying that the women in general must take charge of the clothes.

In order to show that woman is in an honorable position which is equal to that of her husband, here is a good example. Though we have seen that the preparation of food is the principal work of woman, still this does not mean that she is a slave in the kitchen. One chief function of food is for religious sacrifices, and in such sacrifices the wife participates in the ceremonies with her husband. Because they are both equal in the family, they both sacrifice to the ancestor. When a girl of ten, she watches the sacrifices, supplies the liquors and sauces, fills the various stands and dishes with pickles and brine, and assists in setting forth the appurtenances for the ceremonies.[3] Such an education is simply for the duty of a housewife. But, if a housewife is required to take part with her husband in sacrifice to his ancestor, how honorable is her position!

[1] *Li Ki*, bk. xxi, pp. 223-4.
[2] *Classics*, vol. iv, pt. ii, p. 562.
[3] *Li Ki*, bk. x, p. 479.

There is a Confucian principle giving respect to woman. This principle is clearly indicated, as we have seen, in the ceremony of the personal receiving of the bride. But there is another example which illustrates the respect for woman in regard to her economic position. According to Confucianism, although a woman should work for the family, she should be treated nicely, and should not be employed only for financial gain. Therefore, when a woman is married, she need not take up any household work until the end of three months. If her husband causes her to work within this period, it seems cruel to Confucius. In the *Canon of Poetry*, there is a poem directed against a man of the official family, who makes his wife sew within the period of three months. It reads as follows:

Shoes thinly woven of the dolichos fibre
May be used to walk on the hoarfrost.
The delicate fingers of a bride
May be used in making clothes.
Putting the waistband to his lower garment and the collar to his upper,
The beautiful woman fixes them.

The beautiful woman moved gracefully,
And politely stood aside to the left [when she just came into the family];
From her girdle hung her ivory comb-pin.
But it is the narrow-mindedness [of her husband],
Which makes the subject for satire.[1]

This poem describes the woman beautiful in every way, as a contrast to the work of making clothes, and it censures expressly the mean character of her husband. It serves as an example to indicate that Confucius regards the housewife as in a respected position.

Since the wife is equal to her husband, and husband and wife are considered to be one body, she shares all the various

[1] *Cf. Classics*, vol. iv, pt. i, pp. 163-4.

conditions with her husband. Even though she may have no title of her own, she holds the title of her husband. And, in all social positions, she takes her seat according to the rank of her husband.[1]

Regarding the ownership of property, the ownership of woman is included in the name of her husband. If her husband is dead and she has no son, she may succeed to the property of her husband, or may sell it for her support, if she is poor. If she marries a second husband, the property of her former husband and her dower should belong to the family of her former husband, and she cannot take them away. These are stated in the *Law Code of the Ts'ing Dynasty*.[2] But, according to the recent commercial law (2454 A. K. or 1903 A. D.), a wife, or a daughter above the age of sixteen, may be a merchant and may use her own name to own the business. A wife or a daughter, however, must register as a merchant either directly or indirectly in the Department of Commerce in Peking (now the Department of Agriculture, Industry and Commerce); and a wife must also get the written consent of her husband, while he still cannot relieve himself from liability.

2. *Relation of Father and Son*

(a) *The Love for the Same Kind*

The relation between father and son is the strongest tie of Chinese society, and it is the basis of Confucius' philosophy and religion. This relation is fixed by birth, so that the love between father and son is quite natural, without any other consideration. But there is one thing which causes such a love and which is independent of the blood relationship:—namely, " the love for the same kind." The *Record of Rites* says: "All living creatures between heaven

---

[1] *Li Ki*, bk. ix, p. 441.   [2] Ch. viii.

and earth, being endowed with blood and breath, have a certain amount of knowledge. Possessing that amount of knowledge, there is not one of them but knows to love its own kind." [1] The love for kind is a feeling common to all creatures,[2] and man especially develops such a feeling to a great extent. This is the foundation upon which human society is built. Of course, when parents give birth to a son, they love him. But why do they do so? It is not merely because he is their product, but also because he is of the same kind with them. Among different sons, the father will love the one most who is most similar to himself, and that one who is least similar he will love least. Indeed, the degree of his love given to his sons is according to the degree of similarity which they show to him. In the case of a step-son, although he is not the child of the father, the father will love him, if he is similar to him. In fact, the love for the same kind is the basis of the relation between father and son. And the one who can extend such a feeling and love all of mankind, is called a man of great filial piety. The *Canon of Poetry* says: " The love of a filial son can never be exhausted; it is given to your same kind for ever." [3]

(b) *Doctrine of Filial Piety*

Taking such a natural love as the basis, Confucius establishes the doctrine of filial piety, a doctrine that has much to do with economic life. In the *Canon of Filial Piety*, he thus sums up the duties of a son:

The service which a filial son renders his parents is as follows:

[1] *Li Ki*, bk. xxxv, p. 392.
[2] Confucius' conception is very closely kin to Professor Giddings' conception of " the consciousness of kind."
[3] *Cf. Classics*, vol. iv, pt. ii, p. 477.

In his general conduct to them, he manifests the utmost reverence; in his nourishing of them, his endeavor is to give them the utmost pleasure; when they are ill, he feels the greatest anxiety; in mourning for them dead, he exhibits every demonstration of grief; in sacrificing to them, he displays the utmost solemnity. When a son is complete in these five things, he may be pronounced able to serve his parents.[1]

In the *Canon of Filial Piety*, there are five chapters describing respectively the different duties among the five classes,—namely, the emperor, the princes, the great officials, the students, and the common people. It is the last chapter of the five that interests us especially. Although it is an ethical teaching of Confucius, it is really of great economic significance. He says: "They follow the course of heaven in the revolving seasons, they distinguish the advantages afforded by different soils, they are careful of their conduct, and they are economical in their expenditure, in order to support their parents: this is the filial piety of the common people."[2] It is very interesting to see that Confucius identifies the filial piety of the common people with economic efficiency. The first two phrases refer to production, and the last two to consumption. Although the third phrase is mixed with an ethical element, it is a provision for the control of personal expenditure, because to be careful for the conduct means a moral control of material wants. Therefore, if a man among the common people is diligent in production and frugal in consumption for the support of his parents, it suffices to make him a filial son. This is the type for the farmer.

Among all the pupils of Confucius, Ts'êng Tsŭ is the chief representative of filial piety. He says: "There are

[1] *Sacred Books of the East*, vol. iii, p. 480.
[2] *Ibid.*, pp. 471-2.

three degrees of filial piety. The highest is to honor our parents; the second is not to disgrace them; and the lowest is to be able to support them." Again he says: " To prepare the fragrant flesh and grain which he has cooked, tasting and then presenting them before his parents, is not filial piety, it is only nourishing them." Yet he says that the fundamental lesson for all is filial piety, and the practice of it is seen in the support of parents.[1] Therefore, although the support of parents is the lowest type of filial piety, it is a necessary step. There may be some who cannot be called filial sons, because they can only support their parents, but there never has been anyone who could be called a filial son without fulfilling the duty of supporting his parents. Based on such ethical and social teachings, the chief economic burden of the Chinese is the support of parents.

Since all these teachings are in the positive form, let us now consider the support of parents on the negative side. When Mencius enumerates the five things which are pronounced in common usage to be unfilial, the first four out of the five are economic. The first is laziness in the use of one's four limbs, without attending to the support of one's parents. The second is gambling and chess-playing, and being fond of wine, without attending to the support of one's parents. The third is being fond of commodities and money, and selfishly attached to wife and children, without attending to the support of one's parents. The fourth is following the desires of one's ears and eyes, so as to bring one's parents to disgrace. The fifth is being fond of bravery, fighting and quarreling, so as to endanger one's parents. Among the first four things which are economic, the first refers to production, the second and the fourth, to consumption; and the third, to distribution. To sum them

---

[1] *Li Ki*, bk. xxi, pp. 226-7.

up in a word, what the Chinese call unfilial is failure to attend to the support of parents on account of any one of these five causes.

The third of the five unfilial things has a great significance. In China, the son must support his parents first; and his wife and children are regarded as secondary, because the parents are much more to be respected. It is true that the parents never want to sacrifice their daughter-in-law or grandson for their own sake, and that they usually do sacrifice themselves for them. But the Chinese think they ought to care for parents first. In the first place, they cannot work very well; and even though they can work, they ought to be given a rest, because they have worked for a long time. In the second place, they cannot live very long, so that a son ought to discharge his filial duty as soon as possible, otherwise in no way can he pay off his moral debt.

The most conspicuous fact which marks the difference between China and the West is that the Chinese regard their parents above their wives and children, and the people of the West regard their wives above anything else. In a word, China emphasizes the relation between father and son, while the West emphasizes that between husband nad wife. This is the fundamental difference which causes many other differences in the social and economic life. Such a difference not only is found in modern times, but also existed in ancient times. It is the chief antagonistic point between Confucianism and Christianity. Although the fifth of the Ten Commandments say, " Honor thy father and thy mother," [1] Genesis says, "A man shall leave his father and his mother, and shall cleave unto his wife." [2] Jesus [3] and Paul [4] repeat the same words, commending them. Hence, it has become

[1] *Exodus* 20:12.
[2] *Genesis* 2:24.
[3] *Matthew* 19:5.
[4] *Ephesians* 5:31.

the fundamental basis of western society. Whenever the son marries a wife, he leaves his parents and cleaves to her only. As soon as the relation between husband and wife begins, the relation between father and son becomes less important.

As human nature is everywhere about the same, the Chinese do not love their parents more than the western people, and the western people do not love their wives more than the Chinese. Mencius says:

The desire of a child is towards his father and mother. When he becomes conscious of the attractions of beauty, his desire is towards young and beautiful women. When he comes to have a wife and children, his desire is towards them. . . . But the man of great filial piety, to the end of his life, has his desire towards his parents.[1]

Therefore, a man turns his heart away from his parents not only when he marries, but also when he becomes conscious of the attractions of beauty. There is no need to teach a man to leave his father and his mother, and to cleave unto his wife, because this is his strongest passion. Even in China, there is always a tendency this way. But, by the teachings of Confucius, this natural passion is controlled by the ethical doctrine. Hence, it has become the general spirit of the Chinese that they should support their parents first and above the support of their wives and children. This is the fundamental point, marking the differences between China and the West.

Accepting the teachings of Confucius, the Chinese embody them in their laws. In the *Law Code of the Tsing Dynasty*, there is a provision that those who purposely do not give sufficient support to their grandparents or parents shall be punished with one hundred blows with the long

---

[1] *Classics*, vol. ii, p. 345.

stick. For the infliction of this punishment, however, the complaint must be lodged by the grandparents or parents. If a son, who is poor, but who does not work for the making of a living and for the support of his parents, causes his parents to resort to suicide, he shall be punished with one hundred blows with the long stick, and shall be exiled for the distance of three thousand miles from home.[1] If the age of his grandparents or parents is above eighty, or they have severe sickness, and there is no other son attending to them, the son or grandson shall not leave them at home and go to take official employment in another place. If he does so, he shall be punished with eighty blows with the long stick, and compelled to go home for the support of his parents.[2] Even among criminals, under certain conditions, one may be saved from capital punishment or from exile, for the support of his grandparents or parents.[3] Therefore, the support of parents is a positive institution, which is established not only by the moral law, but also by the legal law.

According to the regulations of the present day, when a filial daughter whose parents have neither son nor grandson, serves them till their death, remaining unmarried for that purpose, she shall be honored as the filial sons; *e. g.*, an arch shall be built for her in her locality, and her name shall be dedicated in the " Temple of Faithfulness, Righteousness, Filiality and Fraternity," *etc.* Therefore, although a daughter is not compelled to support her parents by the punitive law, she is encouraged to do so by the honorary reward.

In the *Principle of Population*, the first edition, Malthus does not approve the Chinese law which requires that a son support his aged and helpless parents. He says: " It seems at any rate highly improper, by positive institutions, which render dependent poverty so general, to weaken that dis-

---

[1] Ch. xxx. [2] Ch. xvii. [3] Ch. iv.

grace, which for the best and most humane reasons ought to attach to it."[1] His argument is true. But he looks only at the side of parents, and not at the side of children. According to the view of the Chinese, they may say that, while the parents should maintain their economic independence, the sons should nevertheless support their parents in order to return something for their kindness. If the sons are not obliged to support their parents, although it may strengthen the economic motive of the parents and promote their desire of saving, it weakens the economic motive of the sons and their desire of working. For the economic society as a whole, it may have no gain. It simply makes the old and weak people live in a harder way, and the young and strong people in an easier way. Even though it should be of some advantage to society, it is unjust and unkind.

Moreover, according to human nature, at least Chinese nature, the old people are generally diligent and frugal to acquire and to accumulate wealth not only for their own sake, but mainly for the sake of their sons, grandsons, great-grandsons, great-great-grandsons, *etc.* Therefore, Confucius says that, when the superior man is old, and the animal powers are decayed, he guards against covetousness.[2] In fact, there are very few parents who like to be dependent upon their sons. If they are compelled to depend upon them, they have a sense of disgrace, because none will feel good if he falls into dependent poverty. The really fortunate parents are those who themselves are very prosperous and independent, while their sons are also very rich and dignified, and contribute their service and honor to their parents in order to please them. Therefore, the public has no fear that the parents will lower themselves to be a

[1] Ashley's *Economic Classics*, p. 33.
[2] *Classics*, vol. i, p. 313.

dependent class, and it ought not to deprive them of their claim upon their sons. We are afraid only that the sons will not support their parents when there is need of it, and not that the parents will not take care of themselves.

(c) *Holding of Property*

Since Confucius attaches much importance to the doctrine of filial piety, he gives the parents great power over the property of the whole family. He says: "When his parents are alive, a son should not dare to consider his body as his own, nor to hold his wealth as his private property. .... His gifts or presents should not extend to the carriage and horse."[1] The controllers of the property of a family are not the sons, but the parents.

The "Pattern of the Family" says:

A son and his wife should have no private commodities, nor animals, nor vessels; they should not presume to borrow from, or give anything to, another person privately. If her relatives give the wife an article of food or dress, a piece of cloth or silk, a handkerchief for her girdle, an iris or an orchid, she should receive and offer it to her parents-in-law. If they accept it, she will be as glad as if she were receiving it afresh. If they return it to her, she should decline it; and if they do not allow her to do so, she will take it as if it were a second gift, and lay it by to wait till they may want it. If she wants to give it to some of her relatives, she must ask leave to do so, and that being granted, she will give it.[2]

When her father-in-law is dead, her mother-in-law retires from the open headship of the family, and hands her duties to the wife of her eldest son; but the latter, on all occasions of sacrificing and receiving guests, must ask her

[1] *Li Ki*, bk. xxvii, p. 295.
[2] *Li Ki*, bk. x, p. 458.

directions in everything, while the wives of the other sons must ask directions from her.[1]

In this type of family, wealth is acquired by the father, and it is owned in common by all the members of the family. Therefore, the father is the head of the family, and the mother is the head of the household. Or, the wealth is acquired by any one of the brothers, usually the eldest, but he is willing to give it up to the family as a whole, and regards his parents as the heads. In Chinese history, some families can hold their property under the common ownership for nine generations. But the management of this is very difficult. In the present day, the tendency is towards the limitation of family, basing it on the husband and wife only. But as long as the institution of family exists, the Chinese can never separate their parents from the family, just as they cannot separate their children from it.

Moreover, the marriage of a son is usually arranged by his parents, before he has become a producer. Under such circumstances, he has nothing to call his own, and he and his wife are economically dependent upon his parents. How can he be the real head of a family? During this period, his mother takes charge of the household, and his wife works merely as a student or an assistant to her. In reality, it is much better for his wife to work under his mother, because Chinese social life is very complex, and a young woman can never understand all the affairs of her new home. Of course she may own some private property, such as the dower; but, when she receives, or borrows, or gives anything beyond the limit of the family, it is polite for her to ask leave from her mother-in-law. Since her mother-in-law must treat her reasonably, the asking for leave is simply a formal ceremony, otherwise the Chinese could not

[1] *Li Ki*, bk. x, pp. 457-8.

have held such a family type for thousands of years. A few years later, when she has more experience, or more children, or when her husband becomes economically independent, she may be separated from her mother-in-law and manage a family of her own. But, even after such a separation, it is natural for her to seek direction from her mother-in-law, and to regard her at least as an honorary head of the family. If the new family is less prosperous than the old one, the son and his wife may still draw benefit from the latter; if the old family is less prosperous than the new one, the son must support his parents. In short, since the son and his wife owe a great debt to the parents and parents-in-law, they can never sever the economic relation between them. Even in a very poor family, when the son establishes himself, arranges his marriage himself, and maintains his family himself, he still must support his parents, and serve them as the honorary heads of the family. This is the type of Chinese family which still exists to-day. The difference between this and the type of family organization prevalent in the West is obvious, and will help to explain the Chinese emphasis on the duties of sons to parents, already discussed.

Basing them on the Confucian doctrine, the Chinese draw the following laws. According to the *Law Code of the Ts'ing Dynasty*,[1] if grandsons or sons whose paternal grandparent or parent is still alive, separate themselves from their homes to settle elsewhere, or detach parts of the family possessions, they shall be punished with one hundred blows with the long stick. For the infliction of this punishment, however, it is required that the complaint be lodged by a paternal grandparent or parent. During the life of their paternal grandparents or parents, no sons or grandsons shall

[1] Ch. viii.

be allowed to divide the family possessions or to dwell apart. But they may split up their possessions if their parents approve thereof, or order them to do so. If brothers, while in mourning for one of their parents, separate themselves from the home to fix their domicile in another locality, or detach parts of the patrimony, eighty blows with the long stick will be inflicted upon them. It is, however, required that a complaint be first lodged by a superior or senior from among the relations who are to be mourned for during one year or longer. Should such separation from the family or division of the patrimony have taken place in obedience to the testamentary dispositions of a paternal grandparent or parent, it does not fall under this law.

Within the family which holds a common possession, if a member of the lower generation or younger age, without asking the authority of the higher generation or older age, presumes to use the money or goods of the family privately, he shall be beaten with a small stick twenty times, when the money or goods used amount to ten taels. The number of blows shall be proportionately increased for every ten taels which he shall use privately. But the punishment is limited to one hundred blows. If a member of the higher generation or older age, who has the power to divide up the wealth of the family, does not divide it up proportionately and equally, the punishment is the same. Although the junior must ask the permission from the senior, he has a right to the common possessions. Although the senior controls the affairs of the family, he has no right to divide up its wealth unequally among the members. In short, the head of a family is but a trustee.

When there is any title or office which is given to the descendant of a man, it shall be first received by the eldest son or grandson of his wife. But, when his property, personal and real, is divided, it shall be distributed equally according to the number of sons, without difference between the son of his wife and that of his concubine. If he has an illegitimate son, this son may have only half the portion of those sons who are the children of his wife or concubine. If he has no son but an illegitimate one, he shall adopt a step-son who has the proper relation with him, and the stepson shall divide his property equally with the illegitimate son. If he cannot adopt a proper step-son, the illegitimate son is allowed to inherit the whole portion of his property.

When a family is extinguished without any proper stepson, the daughter of the family may receive its property. If it has no daughter, the magistrate shall report it to the superior, and it may be taken by the public.

These are the laws of the present dynasty concerning the holding of property. In conclusion, the institution of family has been most highly developed in China, because of the doctrine of filial piety of Confucius. The rest of the world has no clan system so complete and highly developed as that of China. A clan which is composed of many families under a common remote ancestor, may occupy a whole town for over a thousand years, may number over one hundred thousand souls, and may hold its property as long as the clan exists. It has its own history, and it has its own law, not contrary to the national law, however. It is a very strong local government, taking charge of birth and death, marriage, religion, education, charity, election, arbitration, punishment, taxation, police, public work, *etc.* It is a Confucian system of the Disorderly Stage, but it has developed into a refined form. But we must understand that a family is an economic organization, while a clan is only a social organization, although holding common property for unlimited generations.

CHAPTER XI

Economic Policies and the Divisions of Economics

I. GOVERNMENT REGULATION

Since economic life is very important to man, everyone naturally considers first what he is to get, rather than what he ought to do. Each man is concerned primarily about his own interests. It is because of this fact that competition arises. According to the theory of the *laissez-faire* economists, if competition is absolutely free, everyone will get just what he ought to get, because everyone is careful for his own interest. Hence these economists advocate competition as necessary to economic life, and believe government interference should be reduced to a minimum. The Confucian doctrine is just the opposite; government interference is necessary for economic life, and competition should be reduced to the minimum. In order to explain this doctrine, we shall indicate first why competition should not be absolutely free, even if it could be so.

First, let us consider the principle of natural selection. In the Chinese language, the word *tien* has three meanings: the first is God; the second, Heaven; and the third, nature. We now use this word only in the second and third senses. Confucius is an evolutionist. He says, " In its production of things, Heaven is sure to give addition to them, according to their own qualities. Hence, when the things or men are flourishing, Heaven nourishes them; when they are ready to fall, it overthrows them." [1] This statement suggests the principle of natural selection.

[1] *Cf. Classics*, vol. i, p. 399.

Mencius, also, says:

When the good principle prevails over the world, men of little virtue are submissive to those of great, and those of little worth to those of great. When the good principle does not prevail over the world, men of small power are submissive to those of great, and the weak to the strong. Both these cases are the rule of Heaven. They who accord with Heaven are preserved, and they who rebel against Heaven perish.[1]

Therefore, Heaven does not help anyone in competition; it simply stands on the side of the few who can help themselves, and eliminates the many who cannot help themselves.

What Heaven is, is a problem transcending the question of good or evil, because Heaven is neither good nor evil. The "Appendix" says, "The cosmic processes give their stimulus to all things, but have not the same anxiety as the sage."[2] On the natural side, Heaven represents cosmic processes; while on the social side, the sage represents ethical processes. These two can never be harmonized, because the one has purpose, and the other has not. In a religious sense, we may say that God helps the virtuous; but in reality, we are bound to admit that God does not help anyone but the strongest. If we should follow closely the *laissez-faire* policy, and should let competition be absolutely free, the world would be left to the few strongest only. Although we cannot do very much against nature, how can we bear to see the sufferings of the weak, who constitute the greatest part of mankind? Therefore, no great religious teachers, nor great moralists, nor great statesmen, let nature alone without some sort of regulation. Since natural selection is good, not for the weak, but for the strong only, artificial adjustment for society as a whole is necessary. The *Canan of Changes* says: " The sage sov-

---

[1] *Cf. Classics*, vol. ii, p. 296.   [2] *Yi King*, p. 356.

ereign regulates the natural course of heaven and earth, and assists the application of the adaptations furnished by them. —in order to help the people." [1]

Second, let us consider the nature of man. The strong are never satisfied unless they take all from the weak. Ho Hsiu says: "When the rich compete with the poor, even though the law were made by Kao Yao, [the judge of Emperor Shun], no way can prevent the strong from pressing upon the weak." When anyone has a little power over others, he usually employs that power without any hesitation to sacrifice the interest of others for his own sake, if it be allowed. Everyone is looking after his own interest indeed; but some can protect themselves, and prosper, and some cannot, although they may know the need of it perfectly. Therefore, human nature being as it is, competition should not be unlimited. For, although the minority may profit by absolute freedom of competition, the majority have no free hand to take part in competition with the minority, and must be overcome by them. Hence, self-interest cannot be the regulator of economic life, and government regulation is necessary.

Confucius does not abolish competition, but proposes instead many governmental regulations to control consumption, production and distribution. We shall mention them below under these different headings. What we shall discuss here is the general policy of Confucius. On this point, it is best to refer to the "Great Model." According to the "Great Model," the final end of a government is to enable the people to enjoy the five blessings and to escape the six calamities. The five blessings are: (1) abundance of wealth, (2) long life, (3) good health, (4) love of virtue, (5) good looks. Contrasted with these are the six calamities: (1) premature death, (2) sickness, (3) sorrow, (4)

[1] *Yi King*, p. 281.

poverty, (5) ugliness, (6) weakness. It is to be noticed that, among these eleven things which sum up Confucius' conception of human happiness, only three, love of virtue, sorrow, and weakness, pertain to man's moral and mental condition, while all the others refer to physical and material enjoyment.

Having stated what is the final end of government, let us now see what are the duties of a sovereign. The central point of the " Great Model " is the standard of royal perfection: " The sovereign must establish a perfect standard first. Then he concentrates in his own hand the sources of the five blessings, in order to diffuse and to confer them on all the people." In fact, his most important duties are only two, namely, distribution of wealth and selection of men. It admonishes him specially by saying, " Do not insult the widowers and widows; do not fear the high and honorable." In short, the sovereign should establish universal and equal laws in order to help the weak and to curb the strong. Then it points out: " Even among all the right men, they have begun to be good only after they had been enriched." Therefore, the distribution of wealth should be very just; and the condition of the whole society should be as follows :

> Without deflection, without unevenness,
> Pursue the royal righteousness;
> Without any selfish likings,
> Pursue the royal way;
> Without any selfish dislikings,
> Pursue the royal path.
> Without deflection, without partiality,
> The royal way is broad and long;
> Without partiality, without deflection,
> The royal way is level and easy;
> Without perversity, without onesidedness,
> The royal way is right and straight.
> All concentrates to the perfect standard;
> All comes to the perfect standard.

This form of government is the ideal of Confucius. The emperor is the parent of the people.[1]

Such a government regulates not only the economic life of the people, but also many other things. Yet their economic life is the most important and the chief source of all the five blessings. The reason why the "Great Model" puts wealth first among the five blessings is told by the *Park of Narratives*. It says that wealth is the cause that makes the state prosperous, men and women beautiful, morality prevailing, and the mind satisfied.[2] Therefore, when the sovereign concentrates in his own hand the sources of the five blessings in order to diffuse and to confer them on all the people, he controls all the means of production, and distributes equally the benefits of them to the people. This resembles the principle of state socialism. The only difference is that, in state socialism, there is no personal sovereign, while in Confucius' mind, there is an unselfish, wise, just, and benevolent sovereign of perfect character. Since wealth is the first thing among the five blessings, and the fountain of the other four blessings, the government must control the economic life of the people above anything else.

The *Great Commentary of the Canon of History* says:

The mothers can give life to the people and can feed them; the fathers can instruct and can teach them; but the sage king includes the two functions of father and mother together with all the details. . . . He makes the city walls for their settlement; builds the houses for their dwelling; establishes the different schools for their education; and divides the lands and fixes the number of acres for their nourishment. . . . The emperor is the parent of the people, to whom the people of the world will go.

From this statement, we can see that the emperor takes

[1] *Classics*, vol. iii, pt. ii, pp. 328-333, 343.   [2] Bk. iii.

charge of the economic life of the people even more than do their parents.

Concerning government interference with the economic life of the people, the *Canon of History* gives the words of the Emperor Yao as follows: " I wish to help the people on the left and the right."[1] K'ung Yin-ta thus explains this: " To establish a sovereign is for the shepherding of the people. Therefore, when the people are working for the production of wealth, the sovereign should assist and help them." Such a conception is general among the Confucians.

To describe the evils which spring from the absence of regulations, Pan Ku gives an example. His statement refers to the age of Spring and Autumn and to that of Warring States, but it is also a picture of the capitalistic stage of the present day. He says:

Under the influence of luxury and extravagance, the students and the common people all disregarded the regulations and neglected the primary occupation. The number of farmers decreased, and that of merchants increased. Grain was insufficient, but luxurious goods were plenty. After the age of Duke Huan of Ch'i and Duke Wên of Tsin, moral character was greatly corrupted, and social order was confused. Each state had a different political system, and each family had different customs. The physical desires were uncontrolled, and extravagant consumption and social usurpation had no end. Therefore, the merchant transported goods which were difficult to obtain; the artisans produced articles which had no practical use; and the student practised ways which were contrary to orthodoxy; all of them pursued the temporary fashion for the getting of money. The hypocritical people turned away from truth in order to make fame, and the guilty men ran risks in order to secure profit. While those who took the

[1] *Classics*, vol. iii, pt. i, p. 79.

states by the deed of usurpation or regicide became kings or dukes, the men who founded their rich families by robbery, became heroes. Morality could not control the gentlemen, and punishment could not make the common people afraid. Among the rich, the wood and earth wore embroidery, and the dog and horse had a superabundance of meat and grain. But, among the poor, even the coarsest clothes could not be completed; beans made their food, and water was their drink. Although they were all in the same rank, of common people, the rich, by the power of wealth, raised themselves to kings, while the others, although their actual condition was slavery and imprisonment, had no angry appearance. Therefore, those who were deceitful and criminal were comfortable and proud in the world, but those who held principles and followed reason could not escape hunger and cold. Such an influence came from the government, because there was no regulation to control the economic life.[1]

This statement represents the general theory of the Confucians. They always have the socialistic idea in mind. The best thing is the equal distribution of wealth, while the worst thing is the division of people into the rich and the poor. Such a theory is not communism, but rather state socialism.

In practice, however, the Chinese government very seldom takes up a positive policy of interference with the economic life of the people. According to history, whenever the government adopted any minute measure, it failed, with few exceptions. The territory of the empire is large, the term of the magistrate is short, and the people by nature do not like to have anything to do with the government. Therefore, since the Ch'in dynasty, the government of modern China has not controlled the economic life of the people as did the government of ancient China.

[1] *History of Han*, ch. xci.

On account of the teachings of Confucius, however, the people respect social order and public interest. Hence, their competition is not very sharp, and moral influences still control their economic motives. Therefore, although their production is not very great, their distribution is comparatively equal. It is not the result of government regulation, but the outcome of Confucius' teachings.

II. LAISSEZ-FAIRE POLICY

By the word *laissez-faire*, we do not mean to imply that Confucianism leaves every thing wholly unregulated. It simply indicates that the Confucian socialism depends not upon any revolutionary force, but upon the development of the natural course of things; that human nature can be developed to perfection, and that there is no need of too many artificial laws to restrain it and to retard its progress, except in special cases. Universal equality, universal opportunity, and economic freedom are the most important doctrines of Confucius. The class system, monopoly, and the tariff, are the objects of his condemnation. According to the true Confucian theory, a full chance is given to the people for their natural development. This is the way to realize Confucian socialism. On the one hand, we find that Confucianism is in favor of social legislation; on the other, we find also that it is in favor of the *laissez-faire* policy. They are both advantageous. Confucianism is the golden mean, and it never goes to extremes. What is fitted to the time or condition is the best. In a word, the Confucian social legislation is by means of moral, rather than governmental laws.

For the exact statement of the *laissez-faire* policy, we find a general economic principle given by Confucius himself. When Tzŭ-chang, his pupil, asks Confucius about the art of government, he enumerates for him the five excellent things. The first of them is "bounteousness without any cost." Tzŭ-chang asks again: "What is meant by bounteousness without any cost?" "Follow what is the profit of the people, and profit them," answers Confucius; "is this not bounteousness without any cost?"[1] This statement is most general and comprehensive, and needs no particular explanation.

In the *Many Dewdrops of the Spring and Autumn*, Tung Chung-shu also expresses the principle of the *laissez-faire* policy as follows: "If a sage governs a state, he must follow the nature of heaven and earth, and the personal interest of the senses of man."[2] This is the general policy of leading the economic life of the people in the natural way.

Among all the Confucians, Ssŭ-ma Chien is the one who advocates the *laissez-faire* policy most strongly. His theory is based on human wants. He says:

Before the time of Shên Nung (2287 B. K. or 2838 B. C.), I do not know; but since the dynasties of Yü and Hsia, told of by the Canons of *Poetry* and *History*, the ear and eye want to exhaust the fineness of sound and beauty; the mouth wants to exhaust the taste of meat; the body wants to be easy and pleasant; and the mind wants to be proud of the glory of power and ability. These economic wants have produced a general habit and have fixed the nature of the people for a very long time. Even though we should persuade them from door after door with a fine speech, we cannot change their habits. Therefore, the best policy is to follow the economic activities of man; the second is to lead them on profitably; the third is to teach them; the fourth is to regulate them; and the worst is to fight with them.

This is the basis of his theory. In a word, economic wants;

[1] *Classics*, vol. i, pp. 352-3.
[2] Bk. xx.

ECONOMIC POLICIES

or self-interest, is the foundation upon which economic policy is based.

Then he comes to the process of production and says:

Society depends upon the farmer for the supply of food; upon the miner for the development of the mine; upon the artisan for the manufacturing of goods; and upon the merchant for the exchange of them. Has this natural process anything to do with either political action, or religious teaching, or special order and meeting? It is simply that everyone respectively employs his own ability, and exhausts his own energy, in order to get what he wants. Therefore, when the commodity is cheap, it calls forth demand, and raises its price; and when it is dear, it calls forth supply, and lowers its price. Everyone respectively encourages his own occupation, and enjoys his own work. Such a natural thing is like the water drifting to the low place through day and night without any cessation. There is no one to call for it especially, but it comes itself; there is no one to demand it especially, but the people offer it themselves. Is it not the result of the natural law and the proof of the natural course?

The reason he is in favor of the *laissez-faire* policy is because he is afraid that the natural process of production would be interrupted if it were interfered with by the government. He quotes the four following sentences from the *Book of Chou*: " If there were no farmer, society would be in want of food; no artisan, it would be in want of business; no merchant, the three kinds of money [copper, silver and gold] would disappear; no miner, wealth would be exhausted and insufficient."

He emphasizes the last sentence by saying that, if wealth were exhausted and insufficient, the natural resources of the mountains and marshes could not be developed. By this he points out the importance of capital. Then he concludes this quotation with the following remarks:

These four branches of production are the sources of the economic life of the people. When the sources are great, the people are rich; and when the sources are small, they are poor. Such sources are the causes for the enrichment, both of the state and of private families.

Here he means that there should be large production. If production be large, the sources of wealth are great, and it is good not only for the private families, but for the public as a whole. Therefore, the natural process of production should be left free, because it will bring great sources of wealth to society.

In regard to distribution, he says: " The reason why there are the rich and the poor is not by reason of taking something from the one and giving it to the other. It is simply that the clever get more than sufficient, and the stupid get less than they need." Thus, the division of the people into rich and poor is merely the result of free competition.

After describing the different lives of rich men, and the various economic conditions of great cities, he continues as follows:

Among the common people generally, if a man's wealth is tenfold, the people respect him; if one hundredfold, they fear him; if one thousandfold, they serve him; and if ten thousandfold, they enslave themselves to him. It is the nature of things. Generally, if one wishes to acquire wealth from a poor condition, to be a farmer is not so good as to be an artisan; to be an artisan is not so good as to be a merchant; and to make embroidery is not so good as to speculate in the market. This means that the commercial and industrial occupations are the resorts of the poor.

According to this statement, Ssŭ-ma Chien admits that there is an inequality of wealth on account of free competition, yet he points out that the employment of the poor depends upon the rich.

ECONOMIC POLICIES

Through the ages of Spring and Autumn and of Warring States to the beginning of the Han dynasty, the economic condition of China was very dynamic, and great capitalists were numerous. Great capitalists would control whole provinces; smaller ones, whole districts; and still smaller ones, whole towns. Their wealth was accumulated by different occupations, such as agriculture, animal-breeding, mining, manufacture, trade and commerce. Since there had been a great amount of production and of accumulation, Ssŭ-ma Chien believed in the *laissez-faire* policy.

However, he does not go to the extreme. In conclusion, he says:

When wealth is not confined to any certain occupation, goods have no permanent owners. They go to the efficient as all the trains come to the central station, and dissolve from the grasp of the inefficient as the tiles fall from the roof to the ground. A millionaire is equal to the prince of a feudal state, and a billionaire even enjoys the same pleasure as a king. Are they not the so-called titleless lords? No.[1]

At the very end of the whole chapter, he puts this negative answer for the withdrawal of his former statements. In fact, on the one hand, he likes large production, so that he thinks free competition is worth while; on the other hand, he hates unequal distribution, so that he employs sarcasm against the rich. To enlarge production and to equalize distribution is his final aim. Therefore, in his conclusion, he comes to the common point of the Confucians.

Taking Chinese history as a whole, we may say that the Chinese have enjoyed a great deal of economic freedom.

[1] *Historical Record*, ch. cxxix. It is interesting to compare this theory of Ssŭ-ma Chien with that of Pan Ku in the last section, since they wrote on the same subject.

Except for a few laws regulating consumption for social reasons, the people really do what they please. The fundamental cause is that, since the Chinese Empire is very large and its government is monarchical in form, it is impossible for the government to interfere closely with the economic life of the people. Therefore, although there are some laws respecting economic life, the people need not come in touch with them at all. In fact, the commercial community of the Chinese is governed by custom rather than by law.

III. DIVISIONS OF ECONOMICS

For the divisions of economics in the Confucian school, there is no passage more comprehensive than that in the "Great Learning." It reads: "There is a great principle for the increase of wealth: those who produce it should be many; and those who consume it, few. Those who create it should be rapid; and those who use it, slow. Then wealth will always be sufficient."[1] According to this great principle, there are only two things, namely, production and consumption. While the terms many and few refer to the number of men, the terms rapid and slow refer to the process of production and consumption. This is a most comprehensive principle covering the whole field of economics.

This great principle makes production and consumption equal in rank, but recommends that production should be over and above consumption. This is quite correct. If production were just equal to consumption, there could be not only no increase of production, but also no increase of consumption. The only means of extending consumption, is to produce wealth over and above the limit of consumption. This is the way to accumulate capital, and to make wealth always sufficient. Such terms as many and few, rapid and slow, are only comparative expressions. They

[1] *Classics*, vol. i, p. 379.

ECONOMIC POLICIES 183

mean that the consumers should be fewer than the producers, and the using of wealth slower than the creation of it. This does not mean that the consumers should be so few as to check the producers, and the using of wealth so slow as to block its creation. Should it mean this, it would be not only inadvisable, but also impossible.

This great principle holds true not only in ancient times, but also to-day. As the words many and few refer to the number of men, their meaning is self-evident, and needs no explanation. The word rapid, however, has great significance. It includes all the improvements in economic life. In short, all those things which can quicken the process of creating wealth are embraced. Therefore, time-saving machines, transportation and communication, the money and banking system, business organizations, *etc.*, all are included in the principle that those who create wealth should be rapid. Hence, this sentence covers not only production, but also exchange and distribution.

According to Professor J. B. Clark, exchange is only a part of production, because it produces either form utility, or place utility, or time utility. Distribution is intimately linked with production, because distribution to each member is according to the amount he has contributed to the product. Indeed, production continues up to the time when consumption begins. Therefore, the " Great Learning " in dividing economics into two parts, instead of four, covers the whole ground.

Following the statement of the " Great Learning," we shall divide our treatise on the same basis,—that is, we shall divide the economic principles of Confucius and his school into only two parts, namely, production and consumption. Within the part of production, we shall include the principles of exchange and distribution. In the natural order, production precedes consumption. For the convenience of our arrangement, however, we shall take up consumption first. In the first place, human wants are the basis of economic life and the object of production. In the second place, the part dealing with production needs to be much fuller than that dealing with consumption, so that it seems best to discuss the more simple subject first and then the more complex one.

PART II
CONSUMPTION

BOOK IV. CONSUMPTION

CHAPTER XII

GENERAL PRINCIPLES OF CONSUMPTION

I. HUMAN WANTS

ALL founders of religions turn their attention to God, but Confucius turns his to man. In the "Evolution of Civilization," he says: "Man is the product of the attributes of Heaven and Earth, by the interaction of the dual forces of nature, the union of the animal and intelligent souls, and the finest subtle matter of the five elements."[1] By this statement he means that man is a spiritual being. Again, he says: "Man is the heart and mind of Heaven and Earth, and the visible embodiment of the five elements. He lives in the enjoyment of all flavors, the discriminating of all notes of harmony, and the enrobing of all colors."[2] By this passage, Confucius means that man is also a material being. He takes the feelings of man as the basis of his philosophy. Or, as Confucius himself puts it: "The sage cultivates the feelings of man as the fields, so that man regards the sage as the landlord."[3]

Now, what are the feelings of man? According to Confucius, man has seven feelings which are given to him by nature and not by learning, namely, joy, anger, sadness, fear, love, hatred and desire.[4] The last one, desire or want,

---

[1] *Li Ki*, bk. vii, p. 380.
[2] *Ibid.*, p. 382.
[3] *Ibid.*, p. 384.
[4] *Ibid.*, p. 379.

is the strongest of all. Confucius says: "For food and drink and sexual pleasure, there is the greatest desire of man; against death and poverty, there is the greatest hatred of man. Thus desire and hatred are the two great elements in the mind of man." [1]

In fact, Confucianism is more human than any other religion. Mankind is the object of its teaching. Human feeling is the field of its work. Since desire is the strongest feeling of man, no matter how spiritual he may be, the economic wants for food, drink and sexual pleasure, are the corner stones of human society. Therefore, human desire is the starting point both of ethics and of economics.

Kao Tzŭ, a Confucian living in the time of Mencius, says: "The appetite of food and of sex is the nature of man." [2] Mencius says: "A beautiful woman is what man desires . . . Wealth is what man desires . . . Political dignity is what man desires." [3] Of course, Confucius and his followers do not mean that man should be enslaved by his desires. Yet they recognize that the human wants are necessary to man. Therefore, the Confucians, since Confucius, never advocated the doctrine of extinguishing desires until the time of Chou Tun-yi (1568-1614, or 1017-1073 A. D.). The true doctrine of Confucius is not that man should have no desires, but that the fewer he has, the better. The "Details of Rites" says: "Desires should not be indulged; . . . pleasure should not be carried to excess." [4] This is the true teaching of Confucius in regard to human wants.

It should be noticed that the theory of Malthus is formulated upon the same basis as that of Confucius. The two postulata made by Malthus are: "First, that food is necessary to the existence of man. Secondly, that the pas-

[1] *Li Ki*, bk. vii, p. 380. [2] *Classics*, vol. ii, p. 397.
[3] *Ibid.*, p. 344. [4] *Li Ki*, bk. i, p. 62.

sion between the sexes is necessary, and will remain nearly in its present state."[1] These two postulata are similar to those of Confucius. However, Malthus develops from these wants his famous doctrine of population, while Confucius works out a general system of philosophy. This is because Malthus is a specialized economist, while Confucius is a great teacher, in the broadest sense. Taking parts of his general system, however, Confucius, too, shows himself an economist.

Human wants, however, are progressive and unlimited. Such characteristics are described by Hsun Tzŭ, as follows:

In the nature of man, in his eating, he wants flesh of grass- and grain-fed animals; in his dressing, he wants silk of beautiful dye, and embroidery; in his traveling, he wants carriages and horses. Besides these, he wants the riches of accumulated surplus. But, year after year, and generation after generation, man still does not know what "enough" is; this is the characteristic of human nature.[2]

II. THE DOCTRINE OF RITES

Although Confucius recognizes human wants, and sanctions their gratification, he does not allow the human wants to be uncontrolled. Therefore, he sets forth rules for their regulation, known as rites. This means what is proper, in every way. The scope of this word is too broad; it has no real equivalent in English, except that the word civilization might cover its whole sense.[3] As we are considering the principles of consumption, however, we shall confine ourselves to those rites which are connected with consumption. We shall divide the functions of rites into two heads:

[1] *Principle of Population.* Ashley's edition, p. 6.
[2] Bk. iii.
[3] *Cf.* Montesquieu's *Spirit of Laws,* vol. i, pp. 324-5.

the one for the satisfaction of wants, and the other for their regulation. These are the chief aspects of rites. There are many other details, but we shall study them under other sections.

1. *Satisfaction of Wants*

The first function of rites is the satisfying of human wants. This is pointed out most clearly by Tsun Tzŭ:

Where do the rites come from? Man is born with wants. When he wants something and cannot get it, he must try to acquire it with all his effort. When people acquire things without measure or limitation, they must fight with one another. When they fight with one another, society becomes disordered. If society became disordered, it would come to an end. The ancient kings hated social disorder, so they established rites and justice to mark the social distinctions, in order to satisfy the wants of man and to supply his demands. Preventing the wants from exhausting the commodities, and not allowing the commodities ever to fail the wants, two elements that help each other and keep society going—this is the point from which the rites arose.

Therefore, the rites are made for the satisfying of wants. The flesh of grass- and grain-fed animals, the rice and millet, made savory with the five flavors, are used to satisfy the sense of taste. The scents of the spice-plants and orchids satisfy the sense of smell. Sculptures, embroideries and the different colors satisfy the eyes. The bell, drum, flute, sounding-stone, lute, harp, reed-pipes and reed-organ satisfy the ears. And the pleasant room, magnificent buildings, rush mat, bed, chair and table satisfy the body. Therefore, the rites are necessary for satisfaction.[1]

From what Hsun Tzŭ has indicated we know that the fundamental purpose of rites is to satisfy wants. Rites have not grown out of the religious or ethical sense, but out of

[1] Bk. xix.

economic wants.¹ Therefore, economic wants are at the basis of civilization.

A particular characteristic of Confucius' system is that he takes human wants as the foundation of his philosophy, and combines the economic and ethical elements into one single principle. He says:

> The rites have their origin in Heaven; their movement reaches to the earth; their distribution extends to all the business of the world; they change with the times; they agree with the variations of condition and skill of man. When they come down to man, they serve to satisfy the human wants. They are practiced by means of wealth, efforts of labor, words and postures of courtesy, eating and drinking, in the observances of capping, marriage, funeral, sacrificing, games of archery, district-drinkings, princely visiting to the emperor, and diplomatic intercourse.
>
> Therefore, rites and justice are great elements of man. They are the instruments to express truth and to promote harmony in dealing with others; and to strengthen the union of the cuticle and cutis, the binding together of the muscles and bones, in dealing with one's self. They are the great systems to nourish the living, to give funeral to the dead, and to serve the spirits and gods. They are the great channels through which we carry out the principles of Heaven and satisfy the feelings of man.²

This is the most wonderful system of Confucius. He brings his principles from Heaven, and establishes his real kingdom upon the earth. His system is not unhuman, but human; not theoretical, but practical; somewhat spiritual,

---

[1] What the Confucians call rites are simply rules of consumption for the satisfaction of wants. The reason Confucius uses the word rites, instead of an economic term, is merely because he is not a pure economist.

[2] *Li Ki*, bk. vii, p. 388-9.

but very material; ethical, but at the same time economic. He especially emphasizes that, when the rites come down to man, they serve to satisfy the human wants. He takes care of not only the heart and mind, but also the body; he regards not only the individual, but also society and the diplomatic world. Indeed, he takes the economic needs as the basis of his ethical teachings, and prescribes social systems for the satisfaction of economic wants. The principles of Heaven are included in the desires of man, and the social and spiritual duties are discharged by the physical and material means: without economics there would be no ethics. Hence, he makes economics and ethics one system, and the satisfaction of human wants the first function of rites.

It is at this point that Confucius establishes his religion differently from that of Lao Tzŭ and that of Mo Tzŭ. They were the two great rivals of Confucius; but they were surpassed by him. It is because their religions, Taoism and Moism, do not satisfy the human wants. Lao Tzŭ says:

The five colors make the eyes of man blind. The five notes of music make the ears of man deaf. The five tastes make the mouth of man lose its sense. Riding and hunting make the mind of man insane. The articles which are hard to be obtained make the conduct of man harmful.[1]

This is exactly opposite to the doctrine of Confucius. On this point, Lao Tzŭ is similar to Mo Tzŭ. The economic doctrine of Mo Tzŭ depends entirely upon parsimony. He reduces the consumption of man to a bare living. He opposes the practice of rites and the use of music, and makes life as uncomfortable as possible. Taoism and Moism are

[1] *Tao Tĕ King*, ch. xii. The five colors are green, red, yellow, white, black. The five notes correspond to c, d, e, g, a. The five tastes are sour, bitter, acrid, salt, sweet.

very unnatural and impracticable, because they do not satisfy human wants. But Yang Chu changed Taoism to resemble Epicureanism.

Basing it on economic principles, Confucius makes his religion not only different from Taoism and Moism, two religions native to China, but also from the foreign religion that had been introduced into China, that is, Buddhism.

In the *Canon of History*, there is the "Announcement About Drunkenness," in which Chang Shih (1684-1731 A. K. or 1133-1180 A. D.) gives a famous interpretation to show the differences between Confucianism and Buddhism. We shall quote it as follows:

Strong drink is a thing intended to be used in offering sacrifices and in entertaining guests; such employment of it is what Heaven has prescribed. But men by their abuse of such drink come to lose their virtue and destroy their persons; to such employment of it Heaven has annexed its terrors. The Buddhists, hating the use of things where Heaven sends down its terrors, put away as well the use of them which Heaven has prescribed. It is not so with our Confucians;—we only put away the use of things to which Heaven has annexed its terrors; and the use of them of which it approves remains as a matter of course.

For instance, in the use of meats and drinks, there is such a thing as wildly abusing and destroying the creatures of Heaven. The Buddhists, disliking this, confine themselves to a vegetable diet, while our Confucians only keep away from the wild abuse and destruction. In the use of clothes, again, there is such a thing as wasteful extravagance. The Buddhists, disliking this, will have no clothes but those of a dark and sad color, while our Confucians only condemn the extravagance. They, further, through dislike of criminal connection between the sexes, would abolish the relation between husband and wife, while our Confucians only denounce the criminal connection.

194   THE ECONOMIC PRINCIPLES OF CONSUMPTION

The Buddhists, disliking the excesses to which the evil desires of men lead, would put away, along with them, the actions which are in accordance with the justice of heavenly principles, while our Confucians put away the evil desires of men, and what are called heavenly principles are the more brightly seen. Suppose the case of a stream of water. The Buddhists, through dislike of its being foul with mud, proceed to dam it up with earth. They do not consider that when the earth has dammed up the stream, the supply of water will be entirely cut off. It is not so with our Confucians. We seek only to cleanse away the mud and sand, so that the pure, clear water may be available for use. This is the difference between Buddhism and Confucianism.[1]

Along this line, we may make a comparison between Confucianism and Christianity. The position of St. Paul in Christianity is more important even than that of Mencius in Confucianism, because Paul is the real founder of Christianity. When we study his first epistle to Timothy, he speaks of "forbidding to marry and commanding to abstain from meats which God created to be received with thanksgiving" as the doctrine of demons.[2] This seems quite similar to Confucianism, but there is a difference. In regard to marriage, Confucius not only does not forbid it, but recommends it as a necessary thing. Among all great Confucians, none has spoken of celibacy, although anyone might practice it from personal choice. But Jesus regards the unmarried men as those who "have made themselves eunuchs for the kingdom of heaven's sake."[3] And Paul says also: "It is good for a man not to touch a woman."[4] This is really the orthodoxy of Christianity; hence, apostles and fathers of the church alike have ever looked upon

[1] *Classics*, vol. iii, pt. ii, p. 402.
[2] *I Timothy* 4:3.
[3] *Matthew* 19:12.   [4] *I Corinthians* 7:1.

marriage as a necessary evil, and even to-day the Catholic Church still clings to the orthodox view. This is similar to Buddhism, but entirely different from Confucianism.

Concerning marriage, Christianity goes further than Confucianism, but concerning the eating of meat, it is a little behind it. Paul says that God has created meats "to be received with thanksgiving by them that believe and know the truth. For every creature of God is good, and nothing is to be rejected." Comparing such a theory with that of Confucius, it seems narrow-minded, and not very humane. Man is also a creature of God; but how can we say that we may eat his flesh with thanksgiving? To say that every creature of God is not to be rejected is not very good reasoning. Of course, we may, and ought to, eat meat now; but we should not base the eating of it on such a theory.

Confucius, although not abstaining from meat entirely, has a tendency to such abstinence. In the " Royal Regulations," there is a rule that no one should kill animals without sufficient cause.[1] Confucius says: " To fell a single tree, or kill a single animal, not at the proper season, is contrary to filial piety."[2] And there is a suggestion that the tendency of Confucianism is toward abstaining from meat, because there is the principle of " keeping away from the kitchen " where the victims are both killed and cooked. Mencius says: " For the relation of the superior man to animals, having seen them alive, he cannot bear to see them die; having heard their dying cries, he cannot bear to eat their flesh. Therefore, the superior man keeps away from the kitchen."[3] This is the way to develop the spirit of humanity. The *Record of Rites* says: "A superior man

---

[1] *Li Ki*, bk. iii, p. 227.   [2] *Ibid.*, bk. xxi, p. 228.
[3] *Classics*, vol. ii, p. 141.

keeps away from the kitchen, and does not tread wherever there is such a thing as blood or tainted air."[1] The *Many Dewdrops of the Spring and Autumn* says: " Sincerely love the people; and love also even the animals and insects. If we do not love them all, how can it be called humanity?"[2] The reason the Confucians extend their love to animals is exactly because they are the creatures of God. But, since Confucianism is very practical, it does not insist on abstinence from meat under existing conditions. Mencius says: " The superior man is affectionate to his relatives, and lovingly disposed to people generally. He is lovingly disposed to people generally, and kind to creatures."[3] This is the standard of giving love, and it is harmonious with the principle of the Three Stages. According to Kang Yu-wei, when we shall have a suitable substitute for meat, we shall abstain from meat entirely. This will be the Extreme Peace Stage of Confucius.

In short, concerning abstinence from meat, from the point of view of love, Buddhism is the highest, but it is impracticable. The theory of Paul is somewhat cruel, although it is an unavoidable fact. Confucianism here takes the middle ground between Buddhism and Christianity. It embraces the whole principle of love, but practices it step by step. It is the golden mean.

All these discussions are introduced not as a comparative study of religions, but merely to indicate the fact that Confucius combines the economic and ethical elements into one system, and that this is a characteristic peculiar to his religion.

[1] *Li Ki*, bk. xi, p. 4.
[2] Bk. xxix.
[3] *Classics*, vol. ii, p. 476.

2. The Regulation of Wants

(a) Moral Control

Although the primary function of rites is for the satisfaction of wants, a secondary function is for their regulation. There are many bases according to which the regulation of consumption is made. But the ethical basis is the first one, that is, self-control. The "Record of Music" says:

The ancient kings, in their institution of rites and music, did not seek to extend the wants of the appetite and of the ears and eyes to an extreme; but they intended to teach the people to regulate their passions of liking and disliking, and to bring them back to the normal course of humanity.

When man is born, he is still; it is the nature given by God. When he is affected by external things, he is active; it is the wants coming out from his nature. When things come to him more and more, his knowledge is increased. Then arise the passions of liking and disliking. If these are not regulated by anything within, growing knowledge leads him more astray without, and he is unable to come back to himself: his principle given by God will be extinguished.

Now, the moving power of things upon man is ceaseless; and if his passions of liking and disliking are not subjected to regulation from within, he is changed into the nature of things as they come before him; that is, he destroys the principles of God and gives utmost indulgence to the wants of man. From this we have the rebellious and deceitful heart, together with licentious and violent disorder. Therefore, the strong oppress the weak; the many are cruel to the few; the intelligent impose upon the ignorant; the bold make it bitter for the timid; the diseased are not nursed; the old and young, orphans and those who are solitary are neglected: such is the great disorder that ensues.[1]

---

[1] *Cf. Li Ki*, bk. xvii, p. 96.

From this passage, we can understand why the ethical element comes into the economic field. First, man by nature has wants. Second, his wants become more active when he is affected by external things. Third, his wants increase as his knowledge increases, and the latter is the result of the coming of things. Fourth, things that affect man are ceaseless, and the wants of man are limitless. With all these four reasons, if man were driven only by economic wants without any ethical consideration, society would surely become disordered, and the majority of the human race would be unable to satify their wants.

In order to make everyone able to satisfy his wants to some degree, it is necessary to make everyone able to regulate his wants. And such regulation is best made by each for himself. Everyone has a good nature given by God; if he can come back to himself, he will make his own mind the master of his body, and his passions will be controlled within. This is an ethical regulation upon the human wants, but it has two objects. On the one hand, it prevents the existence of the rebellious and deceitful heart, and of licentious and violent disorder. This is the ethical result. On the other hand, it helps to supply the material needs for the weak, the few, the ignorant, the timid, the diseased, the old and young, the orphans and the solitary. This is the economic result. Therefore, we may ethically control our consumption, but its effect will help the consumption of others, and the distribution of wealth throughout the whole society.

(b) *Social Control*

The second basis for the regulation of economic wants is the social order. In Confucian literature, society is divided into five orders; namely, emperor, princes, great officials, students, and common people. Each class has its own standard, and regulates its own consumption. For all food, clothes, dwellings, furniture, decorations, *etc.*, there are certain rules prescribed by law. For example, the emperor has seven ancestral temples; each prince five; each of the great officials three; each student one; the common people have none, but worship their ancestors in their houses.[1] Again, when a son is three days old, there is a ceremony of receiving him. If he is the eldest son of the emperor, or of a prince, three animals are killed for the occasion; of a great official, two small animals; of a student, a single pig; of the common people, a sucking pig. If he is not the eldest son, the provision is diminished in every case one degree.[2]

The *Many Dewdrops of the Spring and Autumn* says:

The ordinary people do not dare to wear different colors; the artisans and merchants do not dare to wear the thick furs of fox and badger; those criminal people who have been punished by bodily penalty do not dare to wear silk, or deep azure and purple colors, nor do they dare to ride on horses. This is called the system of dress.[3]

All these regulations are ancient customs, and they are recognized by Confucius. Of course, they prevent the economic development a good deal, but they have three essential purposes.

First, they have the ethical reason. *Han's External Commentary of the Canon of Poetry*[4] says:

The ancients have the "appointed people." When those people, who are able to respect the old, to help the orphan,

---

[1] *Li Ki*, bk. iii, p. 223.
[2] *Ibid.*, bk. x, p. 472.   [3] Bk. xxvi.
[4] Written by Han Ying, one of the three oldest and greatest authorities on the *Canon of Poetry*. He was professor during the reign of Han Wên Ti (373-395 A. K., or 179-157 B. C.). Bk. vi.

to be moderate in their getting and diligent in their working, are commended to their ruler, the ruler appoints them to have the right to ride with decorated carriage and two horses. Those who have no such appointment cannot have the right; if they do ride with decorated carriage and two horses, they shall pay a penalty. Therefore, if the people had no rites, justice, merit, and virtue, even though they have superfluous wealth and luxurious things, they could not use them. Therefore, the people rise for love and justice, and look down on wealth. Looking down on wealth, they do not struggle for money. Not struggling for money, the strong do not oppress the weak and the many do not hurt the few.

Similar statements are given by the *Great Commentary of the Canon of History*, and the *Park of Narratives, etc.* This is an important principle of Confucius, to raise the standard of morality above the standard of living. You cannot raise the standard of living, unless you raise the standard of morality. The moralist can get all the material enjoyments, but the financier can get nothing. Therefore, the people will struggle for virtue rather than for wealth, and the two standards will be identified.

Second, they have the social reason. That all are born equal is a theory, but that all are not equal is a fact. Therefore, the superior man should occupy the high position, and the common man the low position. Again, those who occupy the high position should enjoy high living, and those who stay in the low position should content themselves with low living. If the common people can use everything which is used by the ruling class, they will have no respect for their authority, and fight for usurpation. Then society will become disordered, and depend only upon force. This is especially true under a monarchical government. Therefore, the social scale should have order, and the dress should have system. The *Canon of History* says: " The carriage and the clothes are according to service. Who will dare not to cultivate a humble virtue? Who will dare not to respond to this rule with reverence?"[1]

The significance of social distinction is also indicated by N. W. Senior as follows:

We do not, of course, mean it to be inferred that all personal expenditure beyond mere necessaries is necessarily unproductive. The duties of those who fill the higher ranks in society can seldom be well performed unless they conciliate the respect of the vulgar by a certain display of opulence.[2]

This is a theory similar to that of Confucius.

Third and last, they have an economic reason, and this is the most important. If wealth were always unlimited for the satisfaction of human wants, even though there were no regulation of consumption, there would be neither moral corruption nor social disorder. But the great trouble is that wealth is limited, and that it cannot satisfy the wants of everybody. Hence the principles of distribution come in. Before the wealth is distributed, the Confucians believe that standards of consumption according to the social standing should first be set forth. If consumption had no legal standard, and were regulated only by the law of final utility, no one would feel quite satisfied, even though the distribution were very just. This is because human wants are unlimited. The *Many Dewdrops of the Spring and Autumn* says: "The objects of wants are limitless; their quantity never can be enough. Hence, there is the suffering of poverty."[3]

The modern economic theory is to increase consumption in order to increase production. But the theory of Con-

[1] *Classics*, vol. iii, pt. i, pp. 83-4.
[2] *Political Economy*, pp. 56-7.   [3] Bk. xxvii.

fucius is to limit consumption. Why so? In ancient China, there was no machinery; there was no slavery; agriculture was the principal occupation; and every kind of work depended upon the two hands. Under such conditions, how could the existing production be increased? Of course, Confucius appreciates invention and improvement. But, before the modern machine came to exist, there was no epoch-making advance in the increase of production. At that age, when everyone was afraid that production would fall short of consumption, who should dare to advise the people to extend consumption in order to stimulate the increase of production? Therefore, the regulation of consumption, although not a happy thing, was, nevertheless, at that time, a necessary measure for economic society.

Furthermore, the limitation of consumption had the effect of encouraging production. By production, we mean both the material and immaterial production of value. If the higher class can consume more than the lower, and the lower are jealous of the higher, the lower class will endeavor to raise themselves to the higher scale, and will enjoy the same. According to the principles of Confucius, there is no fixed social order, but every one can find his own place by his contribution to society. The higher classes are open to everybody; or anyhow a man can become one of the " appointed people " very easily. If he wants to consume more, he has to raise himself higher. If he raises himself higher, he produces more value to society; and if he consumes more, the aggregate of material production must be larger. Therefore, the regulation of consumption does not prevent the progress of society, but helps it along.

(c) *Financial Condition*

The third basis for the regulation of human wants is the financial condition of individuals. One day Tzŭ-lu says:

GENERAL PRINCIPLES OF CONSUMPTION

"Alas, for the poor! While their parents are alive they have not the means to nourish them; and when they are dead, they have not the means to perform the mourning rites for them." Confucius gives him the lesson as follows:

Bean soup, and water to drink,[1] while the parents are made happy, may be pronounced filial piety. If a son can only wrap the body round from head to foot, and inter it immediately, without a shell, that being all which his means allow, he may be said to discharge all the rites of mourning.[2]

Again, when Tzŭ-yu asks about the articles to be provided for the mourning rites, Confucius says: "They should be according to the means of the family." Tzŭ-yu urges: "How can one family that has means and another that has not have things done in the same way?" "Where there are means," replies Confucius, "let there be no exceeding of the prescribed rites. If there be a want of means, let the body be lightly covered from head to foot, and forthwith buried, the coffin being simply let down by means of ropes. Who in such a case will blame the procedure?"[3] Moreover, the "Details of Rites" gives a general princple that the poor need not use goods and wealth to discharge the rites.[4]

Everyone knows that Confucius has given very many details of rites. When he comes to economic questions, however, he describes them most simply and convincingly. Confucius, indeed, is a very practical man. The principles of life are summed up by him thus:

The superior man does what is proper to the position in which he is; he does not desire anything outside of it. In a position

---

[1] Even at the time of Confucius, drinking water was considered a mark of poverty. But, at present, America uses water as a national drink.

[2] *Li Ki*, bk. ii, p. 182.

[3] *Ibid.*, pp. 153-4. [4] *Ibid.*, bk. i, p. 78.

of wealth and honor, he does what is proper to a position of wealth and honor. In a poor and low position, he does what is proper to a poor and low position. Situated among barbarous tribes, he does what is proper to a situation among barbarous tribes. In a position of sorrow and difficulty, he does what is proper to a position of sorrow and difficulty. The superior man can find himself in no situation in which he is not himself.[1]

One may say that consumption according to means is a very common thing, and needs no special teaching from Confucius. This might be true. When we study the human wants, however, we find that those who have means will spend more than is proper for them, and that those who have no means will spend more than they can bear. In the former case, it disturbs the social order, or at least it must be an economic waste. In the latter case, it makes the poor poorer. Although the poor cannot spend beyond a certain limit, they may still use up all they have, or borrow money in the expectation of future income, or come to the worst, corruption and robbery. That is an economic and social evil. Furthermore, even if a man spends what his means allow, but is not satisfied with his poor condition, his mind still suffers great pain. By the teaching of Confucius, he will not only maintain his financial condition, but also enjoy a good deal of happiness in life. The "Details of Rites" says: "When the rich and noble know to love rites, they do not become proud nor dissolute. When the poor and mean know to love rites, their minds do not become cowardly."[2]

(d) *Time Element*

The fourth basis for the regulation of wants is the time element. Tzŭ-ssŭ says: "I have heard that when there are

---

[1] *Classics*, vol. i, p. 395.   [2] *Li Ki*, bk. i, p. 65.

certain rites to be observed, and he has not the necessary wealth, a superior man does not observe them, and that neither does he do so, when there are the rites, and he has the wealth, but the time is not suitable."[1] When he speaks of the rites, he refers to the ethical considerations, the social orders, and all the other proper rules. These principles have been discussed above. We shall discuss the time element now.

The principle of the time element is very broad; it takes into consideration all the things that are related to the period when the wealth is spent. Above all, however, the national spirit is a most important consideration. Ts'êng Tzŭ says: " When a nation is not well governed, the superior man is ashamed to observe all rites to the full. When a nation is extravagant, he shows an example of frugality. When a nation is frugal, he shows an example of the strict observance of all rites."[2] Therefore, the national spirit is the chief barometer of the time, and determines the scale of spending. But we must understand that the superior man does not bend himself to follow the national spirit, but raises himself as a guide for the correction of his nation. This is the principle of the golden mean, that is to say, not adding anything to the prevailing habit, or tending toward either extreme, but drawing the nation of that age back and keeping it in the middle way.

Confucius says: " When good order does not prevail in the state, one should not use the full dress as prescribed."[3] And " Small Rules of Demeanor " also says: " When a state is at the time of luxury and decay, the carriages are not carved and painted; the buff-coats are not adorned with ribbons and cords; and the dishes are not carved; the super-

---

[1] *Li Ki*, bk. ii, p. 152. [2] *Cf. ibid.*, p. 175.
[3] *Ibid.*, bk. xi, p. 11.

ior man does not wear shoes of silk; and horses are not regularly supplied with grain." [1] These five things are given as examples of showing frugality during times of national extravagance.

As China is an agricultural country, the condition of the crops is very important in judging of the time element. If the crop fails, consumption ought to be cut down. The eleventh book of the *Record of Rites* says: "If the year is not good and fruitful, the emperor wears white and plain robes, rides in the plain and unadorned carriage, and has no music at his meals." It says again: "If the year is not good and fruitful, the ruler wears linen, and sticks in his girdle a tablet made of bamboo instead of ivory ... No earthworks are undertaken. The great officials do not make any new carriage for themselves." [2] Its first book says:

In bad years, when the grain of the season does not come to maturity, the ruler at his meals will not make the usual offering of the lungs [that is, he will not take more than one kind of meat]; nor will his horses be fed on grain. His special road will not be kept clean and swept, nor even at sacrifices will his musical instruments be suspended on their stands. Great officials will not eat the large-grained millet; and the students will not have music, even at their drinkings.[3]

In the *Spring and Autumn*, there is a principle that the construction of any public work should not be performed during a bad year. The fundamental idea is that, in a bad year, all expenditures should be cut down to the minimum. Since the work of construction is most expensive, the *Spring and Autumn* takes it as an example. But we must understand that, in ancient times, the public work was done by

---

[1] *Li Ki*, bk. xv, p. 81. [2] *Ibid.*, bk. xi, pp. 2, 4.
[3] *Ibid.*, bk. i, p. 106.

GENERAL PRINCIPLES OF CONSUMPTION 207

forced labor; hence, if the people were employed in a bad year, they would suffer more severely than usual. Since hired labor was established in the Sung dynasty,[1] public work is now advisable for the help of the poor in a bad year. This scheme is carried out in order to give the people public employment instead of alms, because thus they can receive wages.

When a crop is bad, not only should human beings cut down their consumption, but the gods also should suffer for it. The ninth book of *Record of Rites* says:

The *Cha* with its eight sacrifices serves to record the condition of the people throughout all the quarters of the empire. If in any quarter the year has not been good, the gods of that quarter are excluded from such sacrifices held in the imperial state, in order to notify these people that they should be very careful in the use of their wealth. If those quarters have had a good year, such sacrifices are opened to their gods, in order to please those people, that they should have enjoyment.[2]

By this rule, the gods share sorrow and joy with the people. In fact, in a bad year, religious expense must be cut down. Confucius says that "victims lower than a man's standard requires should be used."[3]

Supplementing the time element, is a consideration for the place. The *Canon of History* says: "Loving the products of your land only, the heart will be good."[4] This means that you will not fall into temptation, if you have no desire for the luxurious things from other lands. This seems more ethical than economic.

[1] See *infra*.
[2] *Cf. Li Ki*, bk. ix, p. 434.
[3] *Ibid.*, bk. xviii, p. 166.
[4] *Cf. Classics*, vol. iii, pt. ii, p. 403.

But there is also a real economic teaching on this point. The *Record of Rites* says:

What the land does not produce will not be used by a superior man in performing the rites. . . . If mountaineers were to seek to use fish and turtles in their rites, or the dwellers near lakes, deer and pigs, the superior man would say of them that they did not know the nature of those usages.[1]

This is both economic and economical. On the one hand, the rites are easily performed, because they do not require certain things from another land. But on the other hand, money is saved, because it spares the unnecessary expense of getting something away from their own land.

[1] *Li Ki*, bk. viii, pp. 395-6.

CHAPTER XIII

HAPPINESS FOR BOTH RICH AND POOR

WHEN we study the proposition that consumption should accord with one's financial condition, we see that Confucius would make everyone contented with his own lot. But we shall inquire further to see how Confucius creates happiness for both the rich and the poor. For, if we say that one's consumption should be according to his means, the consumer might still feel economic pressure because he cannot do otherwise. But, if we say that one always finds pleasure in whatever he consumes, independent of the amount, then the consumer is really a happy man; and this is especially true when he is poor. In the former case, the consumer adapts himself to his condition, and needs some effort to regulate his wants. In the latter case, the consumer raises himself above his condition, and pays no attention to his wants. It is the highest ideal in economic life, and it is nevertheless very practicable for everyone. This is the value of the teachings of Confucius.

I. HAPPINESS OF THE RICH

1. *Contentment with Means Possessed*

For the consumption of the rich, the principle is contentment with means possessed. Wealth does not make the rich happy, but contentment does. Confucius sometimes said of Prince Ching of Wei that he knew the economy of a family well. When he began to have means, he said, "Ha! here is a collection!" When they were a little increased, he said, "Ha! this is complete." When he had become rich, he said, "Ha! this is admirable!"[1] These utterances are not the exact expressions of Prince Ching, but they represent his feelings as described by Confucius. He sets forth Prince Ching as a good example of managing the household. The essential thing is that Ching did not care much for getting wealth, because his wants were few and were easily satisfied. He was contented with what he had, so that he was very cheerful through all the three periods of his economic life.

Everyone ought to be contented with what he possesses; then he may find himself rich. If he is not contented, even if he be an emperor, he will still find himself poor, and his hunting for wealth will never cease. But how can he be contented? He should accept his economic condition as it is, and not extend his wants beyond his means.[2] In modern times, if the millionaire followed the teaching of Confucius, there would be no suicide on account of economic troubles.

II. HAPPINESS OF THE POOR

1. *Personal Pride*

For the consumption of the poor, the primitive principle is that personal pride should not be affected by one's economic condition,—that is, personality is worthier than any material thing outside of oneself. Confucius says: "A student, whose mind is set on truth, and who is ashamed of bad clothes and bad food, is not fit to be discoursed with."[3] To respect oneself as the most valuable object in the world, and to pay no attention to whatever one consumes, this is

---

[1] *Classics*, vol. i, p. 266.
[2] *Han's External Commentary of the Canon of Poetry*, bk. v.
[3] *Classics*, vol. i, p. 168.

HAPPINESS FOR BOTH RICH AND POOR

the first step to obtain the truth of Confucius. And it is a very simple, but very effective, way to make the poor happy.

Confucius speaks of Tzŭ-lu, whose personal name is Yu. He says:

Dressed himself in a tattered robe quilted with hemp, yet standing by the side of men dressed in furs of fox or badger, and not ashamed;—ah! it is Yu who is like this!

> " He has no jealousy and no entreaty;—
> What is not good when he does anything?"[1]

The last two sentences are quoted from the *Canon of Poetry* in admiration of Tzŭ-lu. When anyone is ashamed because he is poor, he may either be jealous of the rich, or entreat them for something. But neither is good. The best thing is to maintain personal dignity and disregard material welfare.

When Confucius describes the different types of the conducts of the Ju, the Confucian, he gives one type as this:

The Ju may have a house in only one acre of ground; its apartment is ten feet in width and height; the outer door is made of thorns and bamboos, and its side door is simply an opening of the wall, long and pointed; the inner door is stopped up by brushwood, and the little round window is like a jar's mouth. The members of the family may have to exchange alternately the same clothes when they go out. They may have to make one day's food serve for two days. Despite such a condition, if the ruler responds to him, he does not lose his confidence; and if the ruler does not respond, he does not offer any flattery. This is the type when the Ju take the small office for the relief of poverty.[2]

---

[1] *Classics*, vol. i, p. 225.
[2] *Li Ki*, bk. xxxviii, pp. 405-6.

From this passage, we can see how strong is the character of a Confucian. No matter how poor may be his shelter, clothing and food, he is confident of his principles, and is honorable because of his personality. This law is given by Confucius to dignify his followers.

The poor feel unhappy about their consumption not only because it is difficult for them to satisfy their physical needs, but mainly because they cannot reach a higher social standard, and so they fear to have no standing in society. To cure such a feeling, and to raise oneself above petty social ambitions, it is well to read the passage of Mencius. He says:

To desire to be honored is the common feeling of men. But all men have in themselves that which is truly honorable. Only they do not think of it. The honor which some men confer on others is not good honor. Those whom Chao the Great [1] ennobles he can make mean again. It is said in the *Canon of Poetry:* " He has filled us with wine; he has satiated us with virtue." " Satiated us with virtue " means satiated us with love and justice, and he who is so satiated, consequently does not wish for fat meat and fine millet of men. When a good reputation and far-reaching praise fall to him, he does not desire the elegant embroidered garments of men.[2]

When one reads this chapter, he will certainly find himself very worthy, and he will get from himself real satisfaction, even truer and better than that from material things. Such a theory is not based upon an ideal imagination, but upon real facts. As Mencius points out, " those whom Chao the Great ennobles he can make mean again ". How can such a temporary and uncertain honor be worth while

[1] This title was borne by four ministers of the family of Chao, who at different times held the chief sway in the state of Tsin.
[2] *Classics*, vol. ii, pp. 419-20.

to a man who is really noble in himself? One can make no comparison between the virtue and reputation which a worthy man enjoys and the food and clothes which a rich man consumes, because the satisfaction in the former case is too great to be compared with that in the latter. As soon as one understands this truth, he will occupy the most honorable position in society, no matter how poor he may be.

Mencius has a great deal of pride and expresses this most frankly. He says:

Those who give counsel to the great should despise them, and not look at their pomp and display. Halls several times eight cubits high, with beams projecting several cubits,—these, if my wishes were to be realized, I would not have. Food spread before me over ten cubits square, and attendants and concubines to the number of hundreds,—these, though my wishes were realized, I would not have. Excessive pleasure in drinking, and the dash of hunting, with a thousand chariots following after me,—these, though my wishes were realized, I would not have. What they esteem are what I would have nothing to do with; what I esteem are the rules of the ancients. Why should I be afraid of them?[1]

In fact, if we maintain our high moral standard, although our standard of living be low, we are never afraid of the rich.

The superiority of virtue over wealth is a principle of Confucius, and it has become the national spirit of the Chinese. Adam Smith points out four causes of subordination, namely, (1) the superiority of personal qualifications —strength, beauty, and agility of body, wisdom and virtue, prudence, justice, fortitude, and moderation of mind; (2) the superiority of age; (3) the superiority of fortune; and (4) the superiority of birth. Mencius enumerates only three things worthy of honor; he sums up the personal quali-

[1] *Classics*, vol. ii, p. 496.

fications in the word virtue, combines the two elements, fortune and birth, in the word nobility, and counts age as a separate one.[1]

The classification of Mencius is essentially the same as that of Adam Smith. But their theories are entirely different. The theory of Smith is based on general facts, so that he thinks fortune is the most important of all the four causes in getting authority. The theory of Mencius is an ideal, though also based on facts, so that he puts virtue as the most honorable thing. Smith's theory may be true when he refers to the western world, but Mencius' theory also is true when he speaks of China. China has honored virtue above anything else, and this is a peculiar product of Confucius. Smith says: "There never was, I believe, a great family in the world whose illustration was entirely derived from the inheritance of wisdom and virtue."[2] But, in China, besides the family of Confucius, there still are many families of his disciples, and of the greatest Confucians of the Sung dynasty, whose illustriousness is derived entirely from the inheritance of wisdom and virtue. Although their descendants do not possess virtue equal to that of their ancestors, the Chinese confer upon them special nobility in honor of the virtue of their ancestors. Creating the real nobility in honor of virtue, leaving the descendants of the great princes, great kings and great emperors in the background, and giving no honor at all to the millionaires, —this is the influence of Confucius. Under his influence, the poor really do not lose social standing on account of their low standard of life, if they in themselves are worth anything.

Confucius first teaches the poor how to maintain personal

[1] *Classics*, vol. ii, pp. 213-4.
[2] *Wealth of Nations*, vol. ii, pp. 204-6. Cannan's edition.

dignity over and against material wealth, and second, he teaches society how to appreciate the honor of virtue over and above the power of fortune. Following his teaching, virtue really holds the place of honor in the Chinese social life. Such a national spirit, during the Latter Han dynasty, and the Sung and the Ming dynasties, flourished at its best times; even at the present day, it still prevails over the whole empire. It is the flower of China, and the fruit of Confucius. Although it may retard material development to some extent, it has brought a large sum of happiness to society. Indeed, Confucius makes man far nobler than wealth.

2. *Pleasure in Truth*

The highest principle for the consumption of the poor is that the pleasure in truth should not be affected by the economic condition; that is, pleasure in truth is the most enjoyable thing, and there is nothing else able to attract the mind. This is the highest type of living for the poor. It is an advance over the primitive principle. For, if we maintain personal pride against material wealth, we still feel that we are poor in something, and that the wealth is there, in our minds. We must make a comparison between our immaterial riches and the material riches of others. Hence, we hold our honor with some purpose, and struggle for social standing with some effort. But, if we enjoy the pleasure of truth, and have no concern whatever when we consume anything, we really forget our own condition, and ignore the wealth of others. Hence, we live naturally with great pleasure, and raise our minds far above the economic world. This is the happiest type of the living of Confucians.

To illustrate this principle, Confucius gives his own case. He says: " With coarse rice to eat, with water to drink, and my bended arm for a pillow, I still have pleasure in the midst of these things. Riches and political position acquired by unrighteousness are to me as a floating cloud."[1] He takes great pleasure in truth; even in great poverty, he does not suffer any pain, nor is his pleasure affected. We must understand that he does not regard those things as his pleasure, but simply that those things have no influence upon his pleasure.

Confucius gives also the case of Yen Yüan, whose personal name is Hui. He says:

Admirable indeed is the virtue of Hui! With a single bamboo dish of rice, a single gourd dish of drink, and living in his mean, narrow lane, while others could not have endured the distress, he does not allow his pleasure to be affected by it. Admirable indeed is the virtue of Hui![2]

This is an extreme case showing that happiness can be independent of poverty. Yen Yüan did not take his poverty as a pleasure, but enjoyed his own pleasure, which was not affected by poverty.

Confucius does not forbid the people to make a living; he simply teaches them that they should not let their happiness depend upon material wealth. The creating of true happiness beyond the material world, and the elevating of the mind to be independent of physical needs, are the essentials of his teaching. Moreover, the type of Confucius and Yen Yüan is the highest standard, especially for those who devote themselves to the study of truth. Hence, they should find great pleasure in truth, and should not disturb their minds with material things. But, for the common people in general, to make a living is their duty. Even though their happiness is affected by their economic condition, Confucius excuses them. Therefore, while Confucius is anxious

---

[1] *Classics*, vol. i, p. 200. [2] *Ibid.*, p. 188.

to provide a good condition for the common people, he gives the highest standard to inspire the superior man. But, although the common people are not expected to realize this highest principle, they may still know that happiness is independent of the mode of living, when they study the teachings of Confucius. Hence, they may enjoy their life better, even though they are poor.

CHAPTER XIV

DIFFERENT WAYS OF GETTING PLEASURE

When we consume anything, we get pleasure; hence, whenever we get pleasure out of material things, it is consumption. According to Confucius, there are many ways to get pleasure. But we may study a few things which particularly belong to Confucius, and serve as means of obtaining pleasure.

There is a general principle of enjoying pleasure, which is given by Mencius. To enjoy pleasure by one's self alone, is not so pleasurable as to enjoy it with others. To enjoy pleasure with a few is not so pleasurable as to enjoy it with many.[1] Bearing this general principle in mind, we shall know that the ways of getting pleasure are really good ways.

1. MUSIC

First, Confucius was very fond of music. When he was in Ch'i, he heard the Shao, the music of Emperor Shun, and he did not know the taste of flesh for three months. "I did not think", he said, "that music could have been made so excellent as this!"[2] Again, he said: "From the beginning of singing of Music-master Chih, to the end of the six pieces[3] of which Kuan Chü is the first one,—how magnificently it fills the ears!"[4] These two expressions

---

[1] Cf. *Classics,* vol. ii, p. 151.   [2] *Ibid.,* vol. i, p. 199.

[3] They are the first three poems in the first and second books of the *Canon of Poetry.*

[4] *Classics,* vol. i, p. 213.

show how Confucius delights in the enjoyment of music. In fact, his liking for music was much greater than that for flesh, and its pleasure, appealing to his ears, was much greater than that which appealed to his appetite.

Confucius regards music as necessary to daily life. The "Details of Rites" says: "Without some sad cause, a great official should not remove his music-stand away, nor a student his lutes."[1] We learn from the *Analects*, that Confucius sang every day, except after he had wept for a mourning on the same day. When Confucius was singing together with some one, if the one sang well, he usually made him repeat it, and then he followed it with his own voice.[2] The word sing in the old sense of the Chinese always means that there is an accompaniment of musical instruments. Therefore, Confucius got pleasure from music, not only as a listener, but mostly as a player and a singer.

Confucius taught music not only to his pupils, but also to the officials. He gave instruction to the Grand Musicmaster of Lu as follows:

The spirit of music may be known. At the commencement of music [ringing out the bells for the playing of the piece of Ssŭ Hsia], there is a movement in the hearts of men. A little later [when the men sing together], there is a harmony. [When the organ is played only with tunes to which there are no words], there is a distinction among the different tunes. [When the singing of men and the playing of organ take place alternately], there is a continuation. [After the music is closed with the six pieces of which Kuan Chii is the first], it is complete.[3]

[1] *Li Ki*, bk. i, p. 106.
[2] *Classics*, vol. i, pp. 197, 205.
[3] *Cf. ibid.*, p. 163.

This was the arrangement of music by Confucius himself, and he described his appreciation of it.

A great achievement of Confucius was the reformation of music. He said: "Since I have returned from Wei to Lu, the music is reformed and the tunes of *ya* and *sung* find their proper places."[1] Confucius loved music, but he hated vulgar music. He said: "I hate the tunes of Chêng which confound the music of the *ya*."[2] Cheng was a commercial state during the Eastern Chou dynasty; its influence was immoral, and its music was licentious; hence all kinds of vulgar music were called the tunes of Cheng. Therefore, the reformation of music of Confucius was the reformation of tunes. The tunes of *ya* and *sung* found their proper places, and they were not confounded by those of Cheng. Confucius made music an object of pleasure, but did not allow it to be licentious. He said: "Kuan Chü [and the two following pieces][3] are expressions of pleasure without being licentious, and of grief without hurtful excess." This is the principle of the music of Confucius.

The theory of music is given in the "Record of Music," and we may select a few passages from it, and rearrange them.

For the origin of music, the "Record of Music" says:

All the modulations of the voice arise from the mind, and the various affections of the mind are produced by things external to it. The affections thus produced are manifested in the sounds that are uttered. Changes are produced by the way in which those sounds respond to one another; and those

[1] *Cf. Classics*, vol. i, p. 221.

[2] *Ibid.*, p. 326.

[3] They are the first three poems in the first book of the *Canon of Poetry*.

[4] *Classics*, vol. i, p. 161.

DIFFERENT WAYS OF GETTING PLEASURE 221

changes constitute what we call the modulations of the voice. The combination of those modulated sounds, so as to give pleasure, and the direction in harmony with them of the shields and axes, the plumes and ox-tails, constitute what we call music.[1]

This is the definition of music which includes the movement of dance or pantomime. In short, music is the product of the human mind.

Anything arising from the mind of man, however, is not artificial, but natural. The "Record of Music" says: "The influences of heaven and earth and all the various things flow forth and never cease; and they join together to form one great harmony, and then produce the changes: —in accordance with this, there is music."[2] Indeed, music is a natural product of the universe, and man is but an imitator of nature.

Concerning the reasons why music was made an institution, the "Record of Music" says:

Music is an object of pleasure, that which the nature of man cannot be without. Pleasure must be expressed in the modulations of the voice and manifested in the movements of the body; such is the rule of humanity. These modulations and movements are the changes required by human nature, and they are found complete in music. Thus men will not live without pleasure, and pleasure will not exist without its embodiment; but if that embodiment be not conducted according to principle, it is impossible to prevent disorder. The ancient kings, feeling that they would be ashamed in the event of such disorder, appointed the tunes and words of the *ya* and the *sung* to guide the pleasure. They made the notes give sufficient pleasure without any intermixture of what was bad, the words afford sufficient for discussion without ex-

[1] *Li Ki*, bk. xvii, p. 92.   [2] *Ibid.*, p. 102.

hausting their senses. And they directed the voice in singing, whether tortuous or straight, the sounds of musical instruments, whether increasing or diminishing, whether small or great, and the process of playing, whether pausing or starting; all sufficient to stir up in the minds of the hearers what was good in them, without inducing any looseness of thought, or depraved air. Such was the way of framing music of the ancient kings.[1]

Music has two functions: the one is for the administration of pleasure, and the other is for the guidance of it, in order to keep it in the right way.

The relation between music and society is very close. First, society has its influence upon music as the " Record of Music " says:

The airs of an age of good order are peaceful and pleasant; they indicate the harmony of the government. The airs of an age of disorder are dissatisfied and angry; they indicate the confusion of the government. The airs of a state going to ruin are grievous and gloomy; they indicate the suffering of the people. The spirit of the airs is connected with the government.[2]

In turn, music has its influence upon society. The " Record of Music " says:

When the airs are quick, small, dry and short, the people are gloomy and sad. When the airs are gentle, harmonious, slow, and easy, having various styles, but in a simple way, the people are comfortable and pleasant. When the airs are coarse and violent, so as to excite the body and cause anger, the people are resolute and daring. When the airs are pure, straightforward, strong, correct, grave, and true, the people are sober and respectful. When the airs are liberal and graceful, as a re-

---

[1] *Li Ki*, bk. xvii, p. 127.   [2] *Ibid.*, pp. 93-4.

sult of orderly performance and harmonious action, the people are kind and loving. When the airs are uncontrolled, perverse, immoral, dissipated, barbarous, and irregular, the people are licentious and disordered.[1]

Therefore, at first, music is a product of the mind of man; whenever his mind is affected by either a good or a bad thing, his music will be either good or bad. But, at the last, man is a subject under the influence of music; whenever the music is either good or bad, he will be moved either way. Man and music interact upon each other. Hence, man should be very careful about the affections, which come to his mind from external things and then express themselves through music; but man should be also careful about music, which in turn influences him.

As to the usefulness of music, we may divide it up into four categories. First, music has ethical value. The "Record of Music" says:

Rites and music should not for a moment be neglected by anyone. When one has mastered completely the principles of music, and regulated his heart and mind accordingly, the natural, honest, loving, and sincere heart is easily developed, and with this development of the heart comes a great pleasure. . . . If the heart be for a moment without the feeling of harmony and pleasure, meanness and deceitfulness enter it.[2]

Second, music has physical value. The "Record of Music" says:

From the manner in which the shields and axes are held and brandished, and from the movements of the body in the practice with them, now turned up, now bent down, now retiring, now stretching forward, the carriage of the person receives

---

[1] *Li Ki*, bk. xvii. p. 108.   [2] *Ibid.*, p. 125.

gravity. From the way in which the pantomimes move to their several places, and adapt themselves to the several parts of the performance, the arrangement of their ranks is made correct, and their order in advancing and retiring is secured.[1]

In fact, in this way, music is something like a gymnasium, a theater, or a dancing school. It gives physical training to the body.

Third, music has social and political value. The "Record of Music" says:

When rulers and ministers, high and low, listen together to the music in the ancestral temple, all is harmonious and reverent. When old and young together listen to it at the clan, village and district, all is harmonious and deferential. When the fathers and sons, brothers and cousins, together listen to it within the gate of the family, all is harmonious and affectionate. . . . In this way, fathers and sons, rulers and subjects, are united in harmony, and the people of the myriad states are associated in love.[2]

Fourth, music has economic value. The "Record of Music" says:

Music is an object of pleasure. The superior man finds his pleasure in it because it satisfies his principles, and the common man finds his pleasure in it because it satisfies his wants. . . . When one enjoys alone the pleasure of music in his mind, he will not tire of his principles. When he keeps his principles fully, he will not satisfy his wants in a selfish way. . . . Hence it is said, "Of the principles of political economy, music is the greatest one."[3]

It is very interesting, this fact that the Record regards music as the greatest principle of political economy. It

---

[1] *Li Ki*, bk. xvii, p. 128. [2] *Ibid.*, p. 128. [3] *Ibid.*, pp. 112-3.

DIFFERENT WAYS OF GETTING PLEASURE 225

gives this quotation which may come from an old saying, from Confucius himself, or from his disciples. However it may come, it is certainly a principle of Confucius. It is because music can satisfy the economic wants without danger to the ethical principles. This is the characteristic of Confucius' economy.

The component parts of music are four, namely, musical instruments, poetry, singing and the dance. The "Record of Music" says: "Poetry gives expression to the thought; singing prolongs the notes of the voice; dance puts the body into action in harmony with the sentiments. These three things originate in the mind, and the musical instruments accompany them."[1]

Let us consider only singing and the dance. As to the beauty of singing, the "Record of Music" gives the following description:

In singing, the high notes rise as if they were borne aloft; the low descend as if they were falling to the ground; the turns resemble a thing bending itself and then turning around; the stops resemble a dead tree without motion; emphatic notes seem to be made by the square, quavers are like the hook of a spear; and those prolonged on the same key are like pearls strung together.[2]

From this description, we may get some idea about the singing of Confucius' time.

The dance of the ancient Chinese was something like a play. There were two kinds of dance; civil and military. In a civil dance, the plumes and ox-tails were waved, and in a military one, the shields and axes were brandished. Their general style is indicated by the "Record of Music" as follows:

[1] *Li Ki*, bk. xvii, p. 112.   [2] *Ibid.*, pp. 130-1.

At first, there are three strokes on the drum to warn the performers to be in readiness, and then there are three steps to show the gradual start of the dance. On the second beginning, the dance really takes its place, and it is going on. At the end, they return to their position in good order.[1]

It is said that the wheelings and revolutions of the dance are like the wind and rain.

The ancient dance was the origin of the Chinese drama. Let us take the military dance for our example, as we cannot get the civil one. Confucius said:

Regarding the music of Wu, in the first scene, the pantomimes proceed towards the north to imitate the marching of Wu Wang against Shang, [or the Yin dynasty]. In the second scene, they show the extinction of Shang. In the third scene, they exhibit the victorious return to the south. In the fourth scene, they play the annexation of the southern states. In the fifth scene, they manifest the division of labor of the dukes of Chou and Shao, one on the left and the other on the right, in charge of the empire. In the sixth scene, they return to the point of starting to show that the work of the emperor is complete and that the whole empire recognizes him as the supreme ruler.[2]

These are the outlines of the music of Wu. Because it was a military dance, Confucius said, " It is perfectly beautiful, but not perfectly good." [3]

In ancient times, singing and the dance were taken by different persons and at different places. The singers were on the higher stage, and the dancers below it. But they worked together in harmony, and all the characteristics of the play were made intelligible. In modern times, the actors are both singing and acting at the same time, in harmony with music.

[1] *Li Ki*, bk. xvii, p. 113. [2] *Ibid.*, pp. 122-3.
[3] *Classics*, vol. i, p. 165.

We must understand that, according to Confucius, women should not take part in the dance at all. It was only in the vulgar music that women came on the stage. Ssŭ-ma Chien tells us that the tunes of Chêng arose from the feudal princes who competed with each other for fame and honor in such things.[1] This kind of music was composed either only of girls or of a mixture of both boys and girls.[2] But Confucius condemned it. Under his influence, China had no actresses in the theater. Very recently, however, Shanghai has plays performed entirely by girls, and Tientsin has plays performed by both sexes together. This is merely the beginning of the foreign influence.

Confucius generally does not approve of the social mixture of the two sexes; hence he does not approve of the dance between them. The ancient Chinese, however, had such a custom as the European or American dance, participated in by both boys and girls. In the *Canon of Poetry*, there is a poem indicating that in the morning the son of Tzŭ-chung and the daughter of Yüan danced at the marketplace.[3] This is the only example we can find; it means that such a dance was a local custom only. Confucius puts this poem in this Canon only to condemn such a dance. Under his influence, China never has the social dance between men and women.

Confucius says: " For changing the influence of the people and altering their customs, there is nothing better than music."[4] Hence, his principle is to develop the taste for music among the people. To attack the principle of Confucius and establish his own, Mo Tzŭ has written three

---

[1] *Historical Record*, ch. xxiv.
[2] *Li Ki*, bk. xvii, p. 117.
[3] *Classics*, vol. iv, pt. i, p. 206.
[4] *Sacred Books*, vol. iii, p. 482.

books entitled "Condemnation of Music". His theory is based entirely upon the economic argument; for the player of music and the listener are wasting their time and checking their production of wealth. This is a very good example to illustrate the difference between Confucius and Mo Tzŭ, the one an advocate of music, and the other against it. Both defend their views with economic reasons. As Confucius looks at it from the point of view of consumption, he thinks music necessary. Mo Tzŭ looks at it only from the point of view of production, ignoring the principles of consumption entirely, so he thinks music a waste. This is the weakest point of Mo Tzŭ.

Since Confucius lays so much importance on music, why is the Chinese music so poor? To explain briefly, it is the fault of the Chinese scholars. In the Han dynasty, the *Canon of Music* of Confucius had been lost. Hence the tunes of the *ya* and the *sung* were unknown. Moreover, the pitch-tubes were also lost, so that the musical instruments of the classical music were also unknown. Whatever had remained was called vulgar music. The scholars found it impossible to trace back to the notes of Confucius; but they did not pay attention to the so-called vulgar music, and left it to the poor musician whose only object was money-making. They were much too conservative, and did not know the evolution and progress of music. Or it is better to say that they were influenced by Confucius too much on the ethical side, and forgot his most important principle, that music is an object of pleasure. Therefore, on the one hand, they tried to reproduce the old instruments, but did not get any result. On the other hand, they regarded the prevailing music as the tunes of Chêng, and would have nothing to do with it. Hence, the so-called classical music did not produce any pleasure, and the so-called vulgar music has necessarily become popular.

Since the vulgar music did not secure any help from the scholars, and lost their moral support, too, it was retarded in its development. As a matter of fact, although the vulgar music cannot be classical, it is by no means entirely licentious. If the scholars would accept it as a base and then reform it, China would have a natural development of music. Unfortunately, they made the great mistake of not dealing with the popular music, and it became a great loss to China. Indeed, they were not good followers of Confucius. Confucius says: " ' It is music ', they say; ' it is music ', they say. Are bells and drums all that is meant by music?" [1] According to the principle of Confucius, the essentials of music are harmony and pleasure. If any music can produce these essentials without excess, it is good music. But most of the old scholars did not understand this principle. Even the few who did understand it had no influence.

II. DISTRICT-DRINKING

The second way of getting pleasure is the rite of district-drinking. It is one of the eight rites of Confucius. There are four occasions on which this rite is performed. First, when the best students are elected and sent to the ruler; second, when the ministers and great officials give entertainment to the best men of that state; third, when the head of the county collects the people to practice archery; fourth, when the president of the town observes the *Cha* sacrifice; —all these occasions have the rite of district-drinking. But we shall discuss the fourth only, as it is the most democratic one.

Before we go into the rites of drinking, we must explain what the *Cha* means. The word *Cha* expresses the idea of searching out. In the twelfth month of the year, they

[1] *Classics*, vol. i, p. 324.

brought together some of all the products of the harvest, and sought out the authors of them to present these products to them as offerings. There were eight objects to which the sacrifices were offered;—namely, the Father of Husbandry, the Oldest Minister of Agriculture, the discoverers of the various grains, the ancient overseers of husbandmen, the spirit of the buildings marking out the boundaries of the fields, the spirits of cats and tigers, the spirit of dykes, and the spirit of water-channels. These sacrifices were expressions of thanks. The principle was that when anything renders you service, you must give it a return. As the cats devoured the rats and mice of the field, the tiger devoured the wild boars, and the dykes and water-channels performed their business, they should receive return. Such a custom was originated in legendary times. In fact, it is a festival day of thanksgiving.

After these eight sacrifices, they proceeded to sacrifice to their ancestors and the five spirits of the house. They wore yellow robes and yellow caps for the performance of sacrifice, in order to indicate that the farmers should take a rest. The yellow-caps were the dress of the country, and they were the signs of the farmers. The harvest time being past, the people had nothing to do but to rest. Therefore, after the *Cha,* the ruler did not commence any public work for the employment of the people.[1]

On such an occasion, the rite of district-drinking takes place. There must be a great gathering of the people in the school house, and the president of the town is the host. Many details are given in the *Canon of Rites,* but we shall omit them, picking out three following passages from the " Principles of District-Drinking."

First, this rite has an ethical significance. The " Principles of District-Drinking " says:

[1] *Li Ki,* bk. ix, pp. 431-434.

DIFFERENT WAYS OF GETTING PLEASURE 231

The host bows to the coming guest as he receives him outside the door of the school. They enter and three salute one another, till they come to the steps. There each three yields the precedence to the other, and then they ascend. In this way they carry to the utmost their mutual demonstrations of honor and humility. The host washes his hands, rinses the cup, and raises it,—to give the highest idea of purity. The host bows when the guest arrives in the hall; the guest bows when the host washes the cup, and bows again when the cup is received; the host bows after the cup has been sent away; and the guest bows when the drinking is over,—in this way carrying to the utmost their mutual respect.[1]

Honor, humility, purity and respect are the manners of social intercourse. They will keep men away from quarrels and disputations, and prevent the evils of violence and disorder.

Second, it has a social significance. The "Principles of District-Drinking" says:

Those who are sixty years old sit down, and those who are only fifty stand up and wait for any order of service;—thus illustrating the honor which is paid to elders. Before those who are sixty, three additional dishes are placed; before those of seventy, four; before those of eighty, five; and before those of ninety, six:—thus illustrating how the aged are cherished and nourished. When the people know how to honor their elders and nourish their aged, they will be able to practice filial piety and fraternal duty in their own homes. Filial and fraternal at home, and honoring the elders and nourishing the aged outside of their family, the religion is complete, and this leads to the peace and tranquillity of the state.[2]

Third, it contains an economic lesson. The "Principles of District-Drinking" says:

[1] *Li Ki*, bk. xlii, p. 435.   [2] *Ibid.*, pp. 439-440.

When the guest sips some of the liquor . . . at the end of the table, it means that the middle of the table is not only for the purpose of eating and drinking, but also for the performance of rites. It shows that the rites are made valuable, while wealth is made of little account. When the guest drains the liquor of the cup at the top of the western steps, it means that the table is not merely for the purpose of eating and drinking, and shows the principle that rites stand at the first place and wealth at the last. When rites have the first place and wealth the last, the people become respectful and yielding, and are not contentious with one another.[1]

From this point of view, the district-drinking combines economic and ethical elements into one principle.

The "Miscellaneous Records," however, tells that this drinking harmonizes with a purely economic principle, that is, the balance between working and enjoying. Tzŭ-kung, having gone to see the festival of *Cha*, found all the people drunk. Confucius asked him, "T'zŭ, does it give you pleasure?" The answer was, "The people of the whole state appear to be mad; I do not know in what I could find pleasure." Confucius said:

For their hundred days' labor in the field, the husbandmen receive this one day's enjoyment from the state;—this is what you do not understand. Even Wên and Wu could not keep a bow in good condition, if it were always drawn and never relaxed; nor did they leave it always relaxed and never drawn. To keep it now strung and now unstrung is the principle of Wên and Wu.[2]

This dialogue shows the difference between Confucius and his pupil. Tzŭ-kung was too strict and thought that the people should not have the pleasure of drinking. Confucius was sympathetic with the laborers, and thought that

[1] *Li Ki*, bk. xlii, p. 439.   [2] *Ibid.*, bk. xviii, p. 167.

the festival day was necessary for them. " Now strung and now unstrung" is a good rule for keeping the physical strength of the people in good condition, and it suggests the principle of labor legislation.

Confucius says: " When I observe the district-drinking, I know that the principles of a royal government are very easy to carry out." There is a distinction between the honorable guest and the common guests: this exhibits the principle of social order between the noble and the mean. There is a difference in the number of ceremonies paid to the different guests: this illustrates the proper degree of using ceremonies. After the formal music is finished, a superintendent is appointed to look over the ceremonies: this means that they get harmony and pleasure without disorder. They pledge one another according to age, and even the keepers of the vases and the cup-washers enjoy the same: this is a practice of fraternity, without omitting anyone. Finally, taking off their shoes below the hall, and sitting in the hall for the feast, they drink as much as they can stand, and play music as much as they please; but the ceremonies are nevertheless observed: this shows that they are able to enjoy the feast without any confusion. These five qualities form the reason why Confucius says that the principles of a royal government are very easy to carry out.[1]

This rite still exists to-day, but only in a very aristocratic form. Its essentials are found in the country life when there is a social drinking; but it does not use its name, and has no so much ceremonies.

III. GAME OF ARCHERY

The third way of getting pleasure is by the game of archery. It is also one of the eight rites of Confucius. Its beginning and its end are the same as the rite of district-

[1] *Li Ki*, bk. xlii, pp. 440-442.

drinking, and the game takes place at the middle part. After the formal music is finished, and before the general pledging begins, there is the game of archery. We shall describe the game as simply as possible according to the *Canon of Rites.* There are one host, one guest, and the common guests, sometimes with great officials. The game is presided over by the master of archery and the superintendent, and has many curators. Two men make up one pair;—the one is called upper archer, standing on the right; and the other, lower archer, standing on the left. The distance between the two is about the length of a bow. Each one shoots four arrows; the lower archer follows the upper archer in each shooting, and the arrow of the winner must pierce the target which is made of cloth.

The game is divided into three parts. In the first part, there is the game of the three pairs who are made up of young students for the practice of archery. At first, the master of archery himself gives an example. Then he directs the three pairs in the game. But the score is counted later.

In the second part, there is the game of all the members. At first, they arrange the pairs; the host is with the guest; the great officials, even though their number may be many, are coupled with the students; and the common guests are coupled with one another; the host and the great officials act as the lower archers. After taking their arrows and coming to their positions, the score of the first game is counted. Then the three pairs take the first part of this second game; the guest and host follow them; the great officials come in third, and the common guests at the end. The score is counted in two ways. First, all the pairs are generally divided into right and left, the upper and the lower archers, and the accountant finds which set wins more than the other. Then he reports which is the better set;

if two sides are equal, he says that the left and right are equal. Secondly, the game is counted according to each individual in each pair. The master of archery gives an order that all the winners should show their left arms, their bowstring thimbles and armlets, and should hold the bows strung; that all those who are defeated should cover their left arms, take off their thimbles and armlets, leave their bows unstrung and hold the strip of bamboo by both hands. The victorious partner ascends to the hall a little earlier than the defeated partner; the latter drinks a cup of liquor as a fine, and then comes down a little earlier than the former.

In the third part, there is the principal game. Every part of it is the same as that of the second part; the only difference is the using of music for the regulation of the discharging of arrows. The same notes of music are repeated five times without any variation, the first note for the preparation of the archer, and the others for the discharging of the four arrows. If any arrow is not in harmony with the music, although it pierce the target, it is not counted as a point.

After the game is all over, the ceremonies are like those of district-drinking. The guest first pledges the host, and then comes the general pledging. Then the feast takes place; there is no limit as to the number of cups to be drunk, nor to the amount of music to be played. When the guests are about to go out, music is being played, and the host escorts them out of the door and bows.

The game of archery was the national game of ancient China. It was practiced by every man, from the emperor to the common people. When a boy was born, a bow was placed on the left of the door; and when he was only three days old, he began to be carried for the shooting of six arrows.[1] This showed that archery was a necessary pro-

---

[1] *Li Ki*, bk. x, pp. 471-2.

fession for any boy. Hence it is one of the six arts of Confucius. If a man was unable to take part in this game, it was a very shameful thing. In the *Canon of Rites*, there is a book entitled the " Ceremonies of Great Archery," which describes the game participated in by the feudal princes and their officials. What we have mentioned above is district-archery. It was practiced twice a year, in the spring and autumn; and it was held at the school-house of a county. But it might be practiced at any time. If it was at a social gathering, it was called social archery. District-archery and great archery were quite similar to each other, with only a little modification. For our purpose, district-archery should be given because it was much more popular than the other.

There is a description of an archery meeting that Confucius directed. When he takes part in the game in a vegetable garden at Kuo-hsiang, the lookers-on surround it like a wall. He appoints Tzŭ-lu as the master of archery, and orders him to go out with his bow and arrows to introduce those who wish to shoot and to see. Tzŭ-lu says to the crowd: " The general of a defeated army, the great official of a fallen state, and anyone who has schemed to be the successor and heir of another, will not be allowed to enter, but the rest may all enter." Owing to this, one half goes away, and the other half enters.[1] From this description, we know that the game of archery can be held at any place, and that it may be participated in by any stranger. This is true of both district-archery and social archery. Indeed, it was the most favored and popular game.

The game of archery is very useful. First, it has educational value, and this value may be divided into two parts. In the first place, it is a moral education. The " Principles of Archery " says:

[1] *Li Ki*, bk. xliii, pp. 449-450.

DIFFERENT WAYS OF GETTING PLEASURE

The archers, in advancing, retiring, and in all their movements, are required to observe the rules. Internally, the mind is correct; and externally the carriage of the body is straight; then they hold their bows and arrows skilfully and firmly. When they do so, they may be expected to hit the mark. In this way, their moral characters can be seen from their archery.[1]

Confucius says: " In archery we have something like the way of the superior man. When the archer misses the center of the target, he turns around and seeks for the cause of his failure in himself."[2] He says again: " To shoot exactly in harmony with the note given by the music, and to shoot without missing the center of the target:—it is only the archer of superior virtue who can do this! How shall a man of inferior character be able to hit the mark?"[3] In the second place, it is a military education. In ancient times, archery was the chief art of war; hence it was necessary for the national defence. Archery was a great ceremony, and required men of great vigor and strength to go through with it. The *Record of Rites* says:

[When men of great vigor and strength are about to engage in archery], though the liquor is clear and they are thirsty, they do not venture to drink it; though the stalks of flesh are dry and ready to their hand, and they are hungry, they do not venture to eat them; at the close of the day, when they are tired, they continue to maintain a grave and correct deportment. . . . Therefore, such men, bold and daring, full of vigor and strength, when the empire is at peace, employ their gifts in the exercise of propriety and righteousness; and, when there is trouble in the empire, employ them in the battlefield and in the gaining of victory.[4]

---

[1] *Li Ki*, bk. xliii, p. 446.
[2] *Classics*, vol. i, p. 396.
[3] *Li Ki*, bk. xliii, p. 453.
[4] *Ibid.*, bk. xlv, pp. 462-3.

From this point of view, this part of the educational system of Confucius is very wonderful. It trains the body as well as the mind and the character, and it can stand in time of war as well as in time of peace.

Second, it has a political value. In ancient times, the emperor used archery as an additional test for selecting the feudal princes, the ministers, the great officials, and the students.[1] And the princes, ministers, and great officials all selected the students for their employment in the same way. In fact, archery was one kind of civil examination throughout the whole political life, and one qualification for election.

Third, it has social value. District-archery includes the rite of district-drinking, hence gets all its benefits. It fixes the relation between seniors and juniors in good order, and makes society harmonious.

Fourth, it has economic value. In the first place, it gives immaterial pleasure. (a) There is the social pleasure in the gathering of different classes and different ages of men. (b) There is the physical pleasure in the exercise of the whole body for the whole day. (c) There is the pleasure in winning the game, by showing personal qualities. In the second place, it gives material pleasure. (a) There is the pleasure of drinking, both before and after the archery. (b) There is the pleasure of listening to music, before, during, and after the game. (c) There is the great pleasure of the feast.

Similar to the game of archery, there is the rite of pitchpot. It takes place in the middle of a feast for the pleasure of the guests. In the *Record of Rites*, there is a book describing the game,[2] but we shall give only a little of it. The neck of the pot is seven inches long; its belly, five inches long; and its mouth is two and a half inches in

---

[1] *Li Ki*, bk. xliii, p. 448.   [2] *Ibid.*, bk. xxxvii, pp. 397-401.

DIFFERENT WAYS OF GETTING PLEASURE

diameter. It is filled with small beans to prevent the arrows from leaping out. Regarding the length of the arrows, if the game is held in the chamber, it is two cubits; in the hall, two cubits and eight inches; in the courtyard, three cubits and six inches. The size of the arrows is one-seventh of an inch. This game can be practiced anywhere according to the sunlight; if at noon, it is held in the chamber; if in the afternoon, in the hall; if in the evening, in the courtyard. In all three places, the distance of the pot from the players is equivalent to the length of two and a half arrows; that is, in the chamber, five cubits; in the hall, seven; and in the courtyard, nine.

The partners of the game are two; and there are as many sets of partners as there are players. The party of the guests is in the right, and that of the host in the left. Each partner throws four arrows in each part of the game. Its rules are: when the arrow goes straight in, it is reckoned an entry; when it is not thrown according to the alternation, it is not reckoned. During the game, the pitching is in harmony with music. After the result of the game is announced, the cup-bearers of the successful side give drink to the unsuccessful side as a fine. When the three parts of the game are all over, the superintendent begs to set up figures of horses in honor of the victorious party. There are three horses, one for each part of the game. If the side wins only one part of it, it should give up its one horse to the stronger side to unite the three horses for the celebration of victory. Then the defeated partner personally offers drink to the winning partner for congratulation. After it is over, the horses are removed, and the feast is in order, with unlimited drinking.

IV. PUBLIC PARK AND HUNTING

The fourth way of getting pleasure is by the public park

system. According to the principle of the *Spring and Autumn*, the proportion of the ground of the public park to the total territory is one to ten. Based on the theory of Confucius, the territory of the imperial state is a thousand miles square; that of the states of a duke or a marquis, one hundred miles square; that of the state of an earl, seventy miles square; that of the states of viscount or baron, fifty miles square. Therefore, the area of the park of the emperor is one hundred miles square; that of a duke or a marquis, ten; that of an earl, seven; that of a viscount or a baron, five.[1] This proportion of public parks is quite sufficient for the pleasure both of the rulers and of the people.

When Mencius visits King Hui of Liang, the king leads him into the park, and stands with him by a pond. Looking round at the geese and deer, he asks Mencius, "Do wise and good rulers also find pleasure in these things?" Mencius replies: "Being wise and good, they may have pleasure in these things. If they are not wise and good, although they have these things, they may have no pleasure." To illustrate the two cases, Mencius first quotes the words from the *Canon of Poetry* which tell about the park of Wên Wang. Part of the quotation is as follows:

> When the king is in the Good Park,
> The does are lying down,
> The does are so sleek and fat,
> And the white birds shine glistening.
> When the king is by the Good Pond,
> How full is it of fishes leaping about!

Mencius remarks: "The ancients took the people with them for participation in their pleasure, and therefore they were enabled to have pleasure." Contrary to this, Mencius points out, that, if the people wish their ruler to die, although the ruler may have towers, ponds, birds, and animals,

[1] Eighteenth year of Duke Ch'êng.

DIFFERENT WAYS OF GETTING PLEASURE 241

how will he be able to have pleasure alone?[1] Taking people for the participation of pleasure is the fundamental principle of Confucianism, and it determines whether or no the ruler can have his pleasure. This is the principle of the public park system.

Wên Wang had a park of seventy miles square, and yet his people looked on it as small; King Hsüan of Ch'i had a park only of forty miles square, and yet his people looked on it as large. This difference is explained by Mencius, who says that the park of Wên Wang was open to the people, and that of King Hsüan was kept for his own interest. Mencius describes the system of the park of Wên Wang as follows: The grass-cutters and fuel-gatherers have the privilege of entrance into it, and so also have the catchers of pheasants and hares. Then Mencius says: "He shared it with the people, and was it not with reason that they looked on it as small?" The park of Wên Wang is an example of the public park system.[2] In a word, a park should be shared with the people.

Included with the park system, is the system of hunting, and this is also a source of pleasure. The public park is very large, outside of the city, and it has forests and wild animals; hence it can be used as a hunting ground. According to the *Spring and Autumn*[3] and the "Royal Regulations,"[4] the emperor and the princes have three huntings in every year, when they have no special business in hand. The three huntings are in spring, in autumn, and in winter. The game of the first grade furnishes dried flesh for the sacrificial dishes; that of the second grade is for the entertainment of guests and visitors; and that of the third grade is to supply the kitchen of the rulers. These

[1] *Classics*, vol. ii, pp. 127-9. [2] *Ibid.*, pp. 153-4.
[3] Fourth year of Duke Huan. [4] *Li Ki*, bk. iii, p. 220.

are not for the purpose of acquiring wealth, but serve only as regulations of the hunt. Besides the three grades of games, a hunting can also kill wild animals for the benefit of the farms, and it can practice the art of war. These are the grounds on which Confucius approves hunting.

In primitive life, hunting is production; but in civilized life, hunting is often consumption, because it gives a psychic pleasure, greater than that given by the game killed. When Mencius talks about pleasure with King Hsüan of Ch'i, he mentions only two things,—music and hunting. So he considers hunting a great source of pleasure. But, when a ruler does not share his pleasure with the people, they feel his hunting bad; and when he shares his pleasure with them, they feel his hunting good. The conclusion again is that a ruler must share his pleasure with the people.[1]

According to the system of Confucius, the common people have hunting as well as the emperor, the prince and the great officials. There were catchers of pheasants and hares in the park of Wên Wang. By the "Royal Regulations," the hunting of the common people is held during the winter. In the *Canon of Poetry*, two of the poems of Ch'i tell about the hunting of the common people.[2] In fact, the people just as their rulers, ought to have pleasure.

Though Confucius allows the rulers and people to have their pleasure in hunting, he does not allow them to have excessive pleasure. The second and the eighth of the poems of Ch'i just referred to are directed against the inordinate love of hunting. The *Canon of History* says: "Wên Wang did not dare to go to any excess in his excursions or his hunting." [3] Mencius quotes the words from An Tzŭ that

---

[1] *Classics*, vol. ii, pp. 150-153.
[2] *Ibid.*, vol. iv, pt. i, pp. 131-2, 158.
[3] *Ibid.*, vol. iii, pt. ii, p. 469.

pursuing the chase without satiety is called being wild.[1] Therefore, Confucius forbids hunting in summer time, and gives many rules in the "Royal Regulations." In short, Confucius prescribes always the happy medium; he approves social institutions as safety-valves for human passions, but he establishes regulations to control them. This is the doctrine of the golden mean.

[1] *Classics*, vol. ii, p. 160.

CHAPTER XV

GENERAL STANDARD OF EXPENDITURE

I. HAPPY MEDIUM BETWEEN PARSIMONY AND EXTRAVAGANCE

The principles of Confucius always seek the golden mean, and this is especially true as regards consumption. There is only one proper way, neither parsimony nor extravagance. Confucius says:

Kuan Chung had carving on the square vessels for holding the grain of his offerings, and red ornaments for his cap; he set up a screen where he lodged on the way, and had a stand of earth on which the cups he had used in giving a feast were replaced; he had hills carved on the capitals of his pillars, and pondweed on the lower pillars supporting the rafters. He was a worthy great official, but made it difficult for his superiors to distinguish themselves from him. An Ping-chung, in sacrificing to his father and other progenitors, used a sucking-pig, even with its shoulders not large enough to cover the dish. He was a worthy great official, but made it difficult for his inferiors to distinguish themselves from him. A superior man will not encroach on the observances of those above him, nor put difficulties in the way of those below him.[1]

Kuan Chung is the representative of extravagance, and An Ping-chung of parsimony. They both depart from the rule of moderation, and both are condemned by Confucius.

Confucius says: " The rites should be most carefully con-

---

[1] *Li Ki*, bk. xviii, p. 165.

GENERAL STANDARD OF EXPENDITURE 245

sidered. Rites are different; they are the standards above which it is too much and below which it is too little." [1] Hence, consumption should not be too great; if so, it is extravagant. Nor should it be too little; if so, it is parsimonious. Both are against the principle of rites.

Confucius gives an example to represent the proper way of spending. He says:

I can find no flaw in the character of Yü. He himself used coarse food and drink, but displayed the utmost filial piety toward the spirits. His ordinary garments were poor, but he displayed the utmost elegance in his sacrificial cap and apron. He lived in low, mean houses, but expended all his strength on ditches and water-channels. I can find nothing like a flaw in Yü.[2]

Food, clothes, shelter, are the three necessities of life. Confucius takes them to test the character of Yü, and their standard is low. Yet Confucius applauds it. However, when he judges Yü from the viewpoint of social expenditure, such as religious sacrifices and public works, he praises his liberal spending. From this example, we see that when one spends money for his individual interest, he should be frugal, and that when it is for the social interest, he should be liberal.

II. EVILS OF LUXURY AND EXTRAVAGANCE

Speaking generally of the evils of luxury and extravagance, Confucius sums them up in a single word—injurious. He says: " There are three things that men find enjoyment in which are injurious . . . To find enjoyment in extravagant pleasure; to find enjoyment in luxurious excursions; to find enjoyment in the pleasure of disorderly feasting:—these are injurious." [3]

[1] *Cf. Li Ki*, bk. viii, p. 401.
[2] *Classics*, vol. i, p. 215.   [3] *Ibid.*, pp. 311-2.

In the *Canon of History*, there is a book entitled "Against Luxury." It thus pictures luxurious people: " When the parents have diligently labored in sowing and reaping, their sons often do not understand this painful toil, and abandon themselves to luxury and pleasure, and become quite disorderly, without any rule. They cast contempt on their parents, saying, ' Those old people have heard nothing and know nothing.'" Then it criticizes the emperors of the later generations of the Yin dynasty, and says: " From their birth enjoying luxury, they did not understand the painful toil of sowing and reaping, nor hear of the hard labors of the inferior people. They only sought after excessive pleasures, and so not one of them enjoyed the throne for a long period." It gives many good emperors as examples, who were all diligent and did not dare to indulge in luxurious ease. The most conspicuous example is Wên Wang. It says:

Wên Wang dressed meanly and gave himself to the work of settlement and to that of husbandry. . . . From morning to mid-day and from mid-day to sundown, he did not allow himself time to eat; thus seeking to secure the universal harmony of the myriads of the people. Wên Wang did not dare to go to any excess in his excursions or his hunting, but carefully devoted his attention to the work of government only.

The conclusion is that all the succeeding emperors shall not indulge themselves to excess in drinking and in the luxury of excursions and hunting.

This book is directed against luxury; but it does not go to the extreme, and allows a reasonable luxury. In the very beginning of the book, it says: " The officials shall not live the life of luxury. But, after they have first understood the painful toil of sowing and reaping, they may then be allowed luxury; and thus they can understand the suffering of the inferior people."[1] Wang Chung (578-648, or 27-97. A. D.) explains this principle by saying that the muscle and bones of a man are not like wood and stone, and that they cannot get along without some reasonable indulgence. This is the principle of Confucius, when he talks about the drinking in the festival of *Cha.*[2]

The evils of luxury and extravagance are frequently condemned in the *Spring and Autumn*. The chief object of condemnation is the work of building, because it is expensive and lays the heaviest burden upon the people. For instance, in the twenty-third year of Duke Chuang, it records that the pillars of Duke Huan's temple were painted red. This was a usurpation of the right of the emperor, because the legitimate color of the pillars of a prince is black. In the following year, it records the carving of the rafters of Duke Huan's temple. This is worse than before, because it requires more labor than painting.

The reason Confucius always takes the work of building to illustrate his condemnations of extravagance is because it hurt the people to a great extent, besides taking much money. In ancient times, there was no slavery, and all constructive works were done by forced labor. When the princes were extravagant, the people were compelled to give painful labor in order to satisfy the wants of the princes. Or, at least, the people must have paid more taxes. Of course, Confucius does not want to sacrifice the labor and money of the people for the personal gratification of the princes. This is the reason he condemns extravagance in buildings. However, after forced labor was abolished, the condition of the people was quite different. But the Chinese did not understand the idea of Confucius very well, and clung to the old custom concerning buildings, because they

[1] *Classics*, vol. iii, pt. ii, pp. 464-470.   [2] *Cf. supra*, p. 232.

were afraid of being condemned as extravagant. This explains why the Chinese buildings are, in general, inferior.

Besides the extravagance of building, the *Spring and Autumn* condemns all other extravagance. For the condemnation of extravagance in general, the *Spring and Autumn* records the fire of the altar of Poh in the fourth year of Duke Ai. The altar of Poh represented the ruined dynasty of Yin, and it was placed outside the gate leading to the ancestral temple in all the feudal states to serve as a warning to the princes to guard against the calamity of losing their states. According to the *Many Dewdrops of the Spring and Autumn*,[1] Chou, the last emperor of the Yin dynasty, is the strongest example of extravagance. His foods, drinks, clothes, buildings, parks, animals, different kinds of art, colors, forms, music and women, were all of the most luxurious and extravagant. But his empire was lost, and his head was cut off. This was the punishment of extravagance. Recording the fire of the altar of Poh, Confucius gives a warning against the danger of luxury and extravagance. Since it can ruin even an emperor and an empire, how much more easily will it ruin an ordinary man or an ordinary family?

However, Confucius condemns the evils of luxury and extravagance on social, as well as economic, grounds. In the third book of the *Analects*, there are many chapters about this point. Picking out the most conspicuous chapters, we may classify them into two parts. First, we may take up the usurpation of the class of great officials. In the first chapter, Confucius condemned the head of the Chi family, because he usurped the right of emperor and had eight rows of pantomimes in his area. Confucius said: " If this be allowed, whatever else may not be allowed?" In

[1] Bk. vi.

GENERAL STANDARD OF EXPENDITURE 249

the sixth chapter, Confucius condemned him again, because he usurped the right of princes and sacrificed to the Tai Mountain. In the second chapter, Confucius censured the three families—the Chi family, the Chungsun, and the Shusun—because they used the song of the emperor at the conclusion of sacrifice. In the twenty-second chapter, Confucius censured Kuan Chung on the ground that he married three girls and had many officers performing separate duties, and that he had a screen at his gate and had a stand for the returning of cups. Those things belong to the class of princes, but Kuan Chung usurped them. Second, we may take up the usurpation of the class of princes. In the tenth chapter, Confucius condemned the prince of Lu who performed the great sacrifice which belongs to the emperor only.

In all cases, Confucius regards this from the social point of view. But, at the same time, it is an economic principle. Since Confucius regulates consumption according to the social order, if any class usurps the right of a higher one, it is a social usurpation on the one hand, but it is also an economic extravagance on the other. Usurpation and extravagance are the same thing, and the difference comes only from the differing view-points.

1. *Principles of Simplicity and Moderation*

Preventing the tendency to luxury and extravagance there is the principle of simplicity, which is illustrated in the ceremonies of sacrifices. The *Record of Rites* says:

Admirable as are the spirits and sweet spirits, a higher value is attached to the dark spirit and the bright water,[1]—in order to honor that which is the source of the five flavors. Beautiful as is the elegant embroidery of robes, a higher value is

---

[1] Dark spirit and bright water both are simply the pure spring water.

set on plain, coarse cloth,—going back to the commencement of woman's work. Inviting as is the rest afforded by the mats of fine rushes and bamboos, the preference is given to the coarse ones of reeds and straw,—distinguishing the sacrifice to God. The "grand soup" is unseasoned,—in honor of its simplicity. The "grand symbols of jade" have no engraving on them,—in admiration of their simple plainness. There is the beauty of the red varnish and carved border of a carriage, but a plain one is used for riding,—doing honor to its plainness.[1]

All these things, of course, are for some religious reason. But, fundamentally, there is an economic reason. As pointed out by Ssŭ-ma Chien, they are used for the prevention of luxury, and for the remedy of decay.[2]

In the *Canon of Changes,* there is a book entitled "Diminution", which illustrates the principle of moderation. It says: "If there be sincerity in the method of diminution, . . . even in sacrifice, only two baskets of grain may be presented. But these two baskets ought to be offered at the fitting time. . . . Diminution and increase, overflowing and emptiness:—these take place in harmony with the conditions of the time." This means the cutting down of expenditure at the proper time, and the two baskets stand only as an illustration. Sincerity is worthier than material things; and yet material things should not be diminished at all times. This is the principle of moderation, and it is not parsimony. But, how can we be moderate? Bearing on this question, this Canon suggests the term, "repressing wants".[3] If we have ethical control over economic wants, we shall be moderate in a proper way.

[1] *Li Ki,* bk. ix, pp. 435-6.
[2] *Historical Record,* ch. xxiii.
[3] *Yi King,* pp. 246, 317.

III. EVILS OF PARSIMONY

Confucius' system is an advanced civilization, and not a primitive doctrine. Therefore, in his theory of economics, he does not put too much emphasis on frugality. On the contrary, he sets a check against the excess of frugality. In the *Canon of Poetry,* he gives the first poem of the nation of Wei for the condemnation of extreme parsimony in the higher class.[1]

Once again, Confucius sets forth the first two poems of the nation of Tang for the condemnation of extreme parsimony. The first one has three stanzas, all of which express practically the same thing, though in a rising scale. The first is as follows:

> The cricket is in the hall,
> And the year is drawing to a close.
> If we do not enjoy ourselves now,
> The days and months will be leaving us.
> But let us not go to great excess;
> Let us first think of the duties of our position.
> Let us not be wild in our love of enjoyment.
> The good man is anxiously thoughtful.[2]

The second one also has three stanzas, one of which we here quote:

> On the mountains are the thorny elms,
> In the low wet grounds are the white elms.
> You have suits of robes,
> But you will not wear them;
> You have carriages and horses,
> But you will not drive them.
> You will drop off in death,
> And another person will enjoy them.[3]

---

[1] This poem is given *supra,* p. 154.
[2] *Classics,* vol. iv, pt. i, p. 174.
[3] *Ibid.,* p. 176.

All these poems emphasize the same principle, and are arranged by Confucius in a most conspicuous place, as representing the spirit of the two nations. The poem of Wei is expressly against narrow-mindedness. The two poems of Tang are in encouragement of the enjoyment of things. When the first of these two considers the passing away of time, it looks only at the present day; but when the last one assumes the taking away of ownership by another person, it shares in the sadness of the future. The first one thinks of duty, but the last one only of pleasure. Yet Confucius takes them all for the indication of his economic principle against niggardliness. In fact, consumption is the end of economics, and production is only its means; if man does not consume in a moderate way what he produces, he will destroy the object of production, and there can be no economic progress.

Moreover, if extreme parsimoniousness is the general spirit of a nation, besides these economic defects there will be many defects of an ethical and social nature. When the people are stingy, their minds are narrow, their natures cruel, their characters mean; their ambition amounts to nothing; their lives are unhappy; they have no generosity in social relations, and social conditions are unpleasant.

1. *Principles of Aesthetics*

Confucius lays much emphasis on moral duties, and yet he does not entirely leave out material enjoyments. He has a sense of beauty, and suggests aesthetic principles for consumption. Unfortunately, since the Sung dynasty, the Confucians pay too much attention to internal character, and neglect almost entirely external well-being. They care only for the mind or heart, and not for the body; only for what is good, and not for what is beautiful. They narrow Confucianism into a sect like Puritanism. Hence, Chinese ma-

GENERAL STANDARD OF EXPENDITURE 253

terial development has been retarded. But we must go back to Confucius himself, and see how he cared for the aesthetic. For this purpose we may distinguish three forms of consumption: (1) food; (2) clothes, and (3) dwellings.

First, let us consider the foods which were consumed by Confucius. The *Analects* tells us:

He does not dislike to have his rice finely cleaned, nor to have his minced meat cut quite small. He does not eat rice which has been injured by heat or damp and turned sour, nor fish or flesh which has been spoiled. He does not eat what is discolored, or what is of a bad flavor, nor anything which is ill-cooked, or is not in season. He does not eat meat which is not cut properly, nor that which is served without its proper sauce. Though there might be a large quantity of meat, he does not allow what he takes to exceed the due proportion for the rice. It is only in wine that he lays down no limit for himself, but he does not allow himself to be confused by it. He does not partake of wine and dried meat brought in the market. He is never without ginger when he eats. He does not eat too much.[1]

From this description, we can imagine how careful Confucius was about the consumption of his food.

In the *Record of Rites,* there is a book entitled the "Pattern of the Family"; and we may say that it is a sort of domestic science, or economy of the household. It gives many details about the foods and the art of cooking. We may take a few passages from it as examples:

Of grain food, there are millet, the glutinous rice, rice, maize, the white millet, and the yellow maize, which are cut when ripe, or when green.

Of prepared meats, there are beef soup, mutton soup, pork

[1] *Classics,* vol. i, pp. 232-3.

soup, and roast beef; pickle, slices of beef, pickle and minced beef; roast mutton, slices of mutton, pickle, and roast pork; pickle, slices of pork, mustard sauce, and minced fish; pheasant, hare, quail, and partridge.

Of drinks, there is must in two vessels, one strained, the other unstrained, made of rice, of millet, or of maize. In some cases, either the gruel is fermented for one night, as the must, or simply as millet gruel. There are four more kinds of drink—soup of rice, pure water, syrup of prunes, and cold broth mixed with different grains and fruits.

Of wines, there are clear wine and white wines.

Of confections, there are dried cakes, and rice-flour scones.

For relishes, snail-juice and a condiment of the broad-leaved water-squash are used with pheasant soup; a condiment of wheat with soups of dried slices and of fowl; broken glutinous rice with dog soup and hare soup; the rice-balls mixed with these soups have no smart-weed in them. A sucking-pig is stewed, wrapped up in sonchus leaves and stuffed with smart-weed; a fowl, with the same stuffing, and along with pickle sauce; a fish, with the same stuffing and egg sauce; a tortoise, with the same stuffing and pickle sauce. For meat spiced and dried, the brine of ants is placed; for soup made of sliced meat, that of hare; for a ragout of elk, that of fish; for minced fish, mustard sauce; for raw elk flesh, pickle sauce; for preserved peaches and plums, egg-like suet.[1]

It is not necessary for the common people to possess all these articles of food. It is simply that, if they have such things, they ought to use them according to these rules. For religious worship, social entertainment, and the nourishment of parents, these are domestic arts for the women to learn. There are many rules, but we shall quote only one more:

For the art of baking, take a sucking-pig or a young ram.

---

[1] *Li Ki*, bk. x, pp. 459-60.

Having cut it open and removed the entrails, fill the belly with dates. Wrap it round with straw and reeds, which are plastered with clay; and then bake it. When the clay becomes all dry, break it off. Having washed the hands for the manipulation, the crackling is removed, and it is macerated with rice-flour, so as to form a kind of gruel which is added to the pig. Then the whole is fried in such a quantity of melted fat as to cover it. In the middle of a large pan of hot water, place a small tripod, which is filled with fragrant herbs and the slices of the creature which is being prepared. Care must be taken that the hot water does not cover this tripod, and that the fire has no intermission for three days and nights. After this, the whole is served with the addition of pickled meat and vinegar.[1]

From these passages, we can see how beautiful and intricate Chinese cooking was, even at the time of Confucius. It is no wonder that Chinese food is the best in the world.

Second, let us consider the clothes of Confucius. The *Analects* tells us:

The superior man [Confucius] does not use a deep purple, or a puce color, in the ornaments of his dress. Even in his négligée, he does not wear anything of a red or reddish color. In warm weather, he has a single garment of either coarse or fine texture, but he wears it displayed over an inner garment. Over lamb's fur he wears a garment of black; over fawn's fur, one of white; and over fox's fur, one of yellow. The fur robe of his négligée is long, with the right sleeve short. He requires his sleeping dress to be half again as long as his trunk. Staying at home, he uses thick furs of the fox or the badger. When he puts off mourning, he wears all the appendages of the girdle. His lower garment, except when it is required to be of the curtain shape, is made of silk cut narrow above and wide below. He does not wear lamb's fur or a

---

[1] *Li Ki*, bk. x, pp. 468-9.

black cap, on a visit of condolence. On the first day of a month, he puts on his court robes and presents himself at court. When fasting, he requires his underwear to be brightly clean and made of linen cloth.[1]

Here we get some idea about the dress of Confucius. It is timely, and most suitable in color, style and combination.

The theory of dress of Confucius is to make the clothes the symbols of personality. Hence they must have colors for distinction, and the colors must be classified according to the social orders. The *Canon of History* says: " God graciously appoints the virtuous;—are there not the five habiliments, and the five decorations belonging to them? "[2] According to Confucius' theory, all the officers should be virtuous, and should be awarded decorations according to their virtue. Thus, the decorations of the emperor are of yellow fowl, white tigers, red flames, and green dragons, all upon a black background. Those of a marquis are the same as those of the emperor, leaving out the yellow fowl. The viscount or baron has only the white tigers, the red flames, and the green dragons. The decorations of the great officials consist of only the red flames and the green dragons, while the decoration of the student is only the green dragons.

According to the *Canon of History*, the dress of the emperor is something like this: All his upper and lower garments are made of fine embroidered cloth. They all have the embroidery of (1) the drawing lines, (2) the grains of rice, (3) the combination of white and black, and (4) the combination of black and green. But, while the lower garment has only these four kinds of embroidery, the upper one has five kinds more, namely, as mentioned above, the

---

[1] *Classics*, vol. i, pp. 230-232. [2] *Ibid.*, vol. iii, pt. i, p. 74.

GENERAL STANDARD OF EXPENDITURE 257

green dragons, the yellow fowl, the white tigers, the red flames, and the black color of the garment itself. The *Canon of History* says: "Take the five colored silk threads, and apply them brilliantly to the five colors which are drawn for the base of embroidery, in order to make clothes."[1]

One sees that the costume of Confucius' system is by no means simple. On the contrary, it is intricate and very beautiful, and has social value. It is the mark of personal distinction, hence it inspires the people to do good and guards them against falling into disgrace. It is used as a means of reward and punishment of society. There is no plain dress, except at the time of mourning, during a bad year, and for receiving punishment. For example, a cap of white silk with edging of silk rough and plain, and with strings hanging down five inches, serves to mark the idle and listless student; a dark-colored cap with a roll of white silk marks exclusion from society.[2]

In civilized society, human wants go beyond the bare necessities; hence clothes are required not only for warmth, but also for display and beauty. Confucius is not like Buddha, whose system of dress is like that of a mourner. Nor does Confucius resemble Jesus, under whose church the dress of monk and nun is also very simple. The religion of Confucius is in the world, and does not seclude itself; this is the explanation of the whole thing.

Under the system of Confucius, even for the dress of a boy under twenty years old, there are regulations. The *Record of Rites* tells us: "His upper garment is of black linen, with an embroidered edging. His sash is embroidered, and also the strings for the button-loops of his girdle. With such a string he binds up his hair. All the embroid-

[1] *Cf. Classics*, vol. iii, pt. i, p. 80.
[2] *Li Ki*, bk. xi, pp. 9-10.

ered border and strings are red."[1] This is for his decoration. But he should not wear furs, nor should he wear jacket or trousers of silk, because both are too warm for children.[2] For the convenience of doing service, he should not wear the lower garment.[3] And because he has not come to maturity, he should not wear the ornamental points on his shoes.[4]

There are many details about dress in the *Record of Rites*, but we shall not go into them. The only other thing we care to mention is the "long dress." It is the most simple and most common dress of the Confucian system. It can be worn on all occasions, by both sexes, and by all classes, from the emperor to the common people. It is next only to the court and sacrificial robes. It is lasting and not expensive, and yet it has an ornamental border. Its details are given in a small book entitled the "Long Dress."[5] In fact, Confucius has given a complete system about the dress of the head, the feet, and the whole body. So far as their dress is concerned, the Chinese all say that their costume is most genteel and comfortable.

Third, let us consider dwellings. Unfortunately, we cannot find any description of the house of Confucius. The only thing we know is that the present temple of Confucius is his old house, which was also occupied by his pupils. As his house was at the same time a school-building, and his pupils were very numerous, such a house must have been very large. His school-house has been called by the name of Apricot Arena, so it must have presented a very beautiful scene with the apricot flowers. Its situation was good, as we can see at the present day.

[1] *Li Ki*, bk. xi, pp. 19-20.   [2] *Ibid.*, p. 20.
[3] *Ibid.*, bk. x, p. 478.   [4] *Ibid.*, bk. xi, p. 20.
[5] *Ibid.*, bk. xxxvi, pp. 395-6.

While we have no description of his own house, we still can get his ideas about buildings from his writings. In the *Canon of Poetry*, there is a poem praising Hsüan Wang (276-231 B. K. or 827-782 B. C.), who built a new palace according to the principle of frugality. Frugality is the essential of this poem, and yet it gives the sense of beauty. We shall quote a few lines about this palace.

> Like a man on tip-toe, in reverent expectation,
> Like an arrow, flying rapidly,
> Like a bird which has changed its feathers,
> Like a pheasant on flying wings,
> Is the hall which our noble lord will ascend.
>
> Level and smooth is the court-yard,
> And lofty are the pillars around it.
> Pleasant is the exposure of the chamber to the light,
> And deep and wide are its recesses.
> Here will our noble lord repose.[1]

This poem about the palace shows in the first stanza how magnificent and conspicuous is the hall, and in the second, how grand and lovely the private apartment.

Scattered throughout the *Canon of Rites* is the description of a house which is about the same as the ancestral temple. It was an old custom, adopted by Confucius. The Chinese house to-day still seems somewhat similar to this. Such a system was common to all classes, from the emperor to the student, the difference being only in size and details. Let us now consider the house of the student.

Imagine an oblong space enclosed by four brick walls. In the front, or southern wall, (a house must always face the south), is the "external entrance." Some distance behind it is a second wall, in the center of which is the "main entrance." Both entrances are roofed over, with oblong

[1] *Classics*, vol. iv, pt. ii, p. 305.

buildings, running east and west, on each side, each building divided into two lobbies, one within, one without, the entrance. The house proper, about square in outline, is situated well toward the back of this enclosed space. It consists of a great hall and behind it three apartments.

The great hall stretches clear across the front of the house, its front open, having two pillars instead of a dividing wall, one at the east, one at the west. This great hall is approached by two flights of steps, one toward the east, one toward the west. At the center of the northern wall of the hall, between a door on the east leading into the apartment behind and a window on the west, is the honorable place for guests. The east and west ends of the hall are partitioned off into long, narrow " assistant apartments."

Behind the great hall is the " principal apartment," used as a business office. At each side of this is a chamber. The northern half of the " eastern chamber " is called the " northern hall." It has an open front in the north, and it is for the exercising of ceremony by the ladies. The " western chamber " stores the valuable things. The whole house proper is covered by a peaked roof made of tile, sloping to back and front.

Behind the house proper are the " private apartment " for eating and sleeping, and several small buildings for the children, or perhaps for a son and his family. In the homes of those of higher rank, this third and back part may be expanded indefinitely.

The open space in front of the house proper is the court, which is usually three times the length of the hall.

The house of the common people is similar to that of the student. The only great differences are that it has only one entrance, without lobbies in its two sides, and that the court is only as long as the hall. It has not the " private apartment ", and the principal apartment is used for eating, sleeping, *etc.* Besides these, there is no great difference in the house proper. In fact, according to the economic principles of Confucius, there is no pauper; and even the lowest people must have for their houses plenty of sunlight and good air.

The most beautiful building in the Confucian system is the " Brilliant Hall." The *Many Dewdrops of the Spring and Autumn* says: " The Brilliant Hall is round; its building is high, imposing, magnificent and round."[1] According to *Elder Tai's Record of Rites*, the Brilliant Hall has nine apartments in all. Each apartment has four doors and eight windows; in the whole hall, there are thirty-six doors and seventy-two windows. The roof is covered with grass, to symbolize cleanliness. The upper part is round, the lower part square. It is surrounded by a round body of water.[2] This is the most important building for all great exercises of the emperor: to worship God together with the founder of the dynasty, and to observe many other important ceremonies.

IV. CHOICE BETWEEN PARSIMONY AND EXTRAVAGANCE

If we are obliged to choose either extravagance or parsimony, however, which one is preferable? When Lin Fang asks Confucius what the essential of rites is, Confucius replies: " In festive rites, it is better to be sparing than extravagant."[3] This statement is clear enough to show his opinion in favor of parsimony. Again, Confucius says: " Extravagance leads to insubordination, and parsimony to meanness. It is better to be mean than to be insubordinate."[4] Therefore, we are sure that, if one cannot act in the proper way, Confucius would prefer parsimony rather than extravagance.

[1] Bk. xxiii.
[2] Bk. lxvi.
[3] *Classics*, vol. i, p. 155.
[4] *Ibid.*, p. 207.

V. SOCIAL STANDARD OF LIVING

1. *General Survey*

We have discussed above the doctrine of rites, and have seen how the standard of living enters into the Confucian system. We must now study it especially and definitely. In every age and every place, there must be different standards among different classes, and this holds in the teachings of Confucius. Since there are five classes, as we know, there are five standards,—that is, those of the emperor, the princes, the great officials, the students and the common people. But, on some occasions, the standard of the prince may be the same as that of the emperor, that of the great official as that of the prince, and so on down.

We must keep in mind that social standards have a great influence upon the economic life, in addition to marking social distinctions. They make everyone satisfy his wants according to the standard of his class. They help to make the wealth that is produced suffice for the needs of consumers. They stimulate everyone to do his best in production for the sake of raising himself to a higher class. Therefore, Confucius prescribes the different standards for the different classes.

Take religious expense, for example. The " Royal Regulations " says:

In sacrificing at the altars to the spirits of the land and grain, the emperor uses in each case a bull, a ram and a boar; the princes, only a ram and a boar. The great officials and students, at the sacrifices in their ancestral temples, if they have land, observe the full ceremonies of regular sacrifice; and, if they have no land, they simply present their offering, [that is, the great official offers a lamb, and the student a sucking-pig]. The common people, in the spring, offer scallions; in summer, wheat; in autumn, millet; and in winter, rice. The scallions are set forth with eggs; the wheat with fish; the millet with a sucking-pig; and the rice with a goose.¹

This represents the standards of their worship; and it is somewhat according to their means.

Let us take their foods for another example. When there is any occasion, the emperor and prince may kill an ox; the great official, a sheep; the student, a dog or a pig; and the common people may eat delicate food. But, among all of them, nobody should do so simply to satisfy his appetite and without any other reason.²

The " Pattern of the Family " says:

The cupboards of the emperor are five in the assistant apartment to the left, and another five in that to the right; those of dukes, marquises, and earls are also five, but all in one chamber; those of great officials are three in the assistant apartment; and the students have only one on their buffet.³

It does not speak about the number of cupboards of the common people, but it may be understood that it is equal to that of the students.

The ancient Chinese liked to have a large area for a house, rather than many stories. Hence the standard of a house is generally measured by its size instead of its height. And yet there is a rule to regulate the height of a house. Such a rule is illustrated in the steps of a hall. According to the *Record of Rites*, the hall of the emperor has nine steps, each of one cubit, that is, it is nine cubits higher than the ground; that of the prince, seven; that of the great official, five; and that of the student, three.⁴ The text does not say

---

¹ *Cf. Li Ki*, bk. iii, p. 226.
² *Ibid.*, p. 227, and bk. xi, p. 4.
³ *Ibid.*, bk. x, p. 464.
⁴ *Ibid.*, bk. viii, p. 400.

how high the hall of common people should be; but, judging from what has been described above, and drawing authority from Chia Yi and modern scholars, the hall of the common people must have one step, that is, be one cubit higher than the ground. Here we get some idea about the standard for their dwelling.

The Chinese have a peculiar index of social status; that is, the use of jade. The reason the Chinese set a high value on jade is explained by Confucius. His full explanation is given in the *Record of Rites*,[1] but it can be summed up in one line—jade has all the qualities which are similar to the virtues of a gentleman. The same book tells us:

All the girdles must have the pendant of jade, except during the mourning only. At the end of the middle string is the tooth-like piece, colliding with the others. Without some sad cause, a gentleman will never let the jade leave his person; he regards the pieces of jade as emblematic of the virtues which he should cultivate.

The pendant of the emperor is composed of beads of white jade, hung on dark-colored strings; that of a duke or marquis, of jade-beads of hill-azure, on vermilion strings; that of a great official, of beads of aqua-marine, on black strings; that of an heir-son, of beads of *yü* jade, on variegated strings; that of a student, of beads of jade-like quartz, on orange-colored strings. As for Confucius, he sometimes wears at his pendant an ivory ring, five inches round, on variegated strings.[2]

These are the different standards in connection with the use of jade for pendants, and this is a good example of the significance ascribed to ornaments.

[1] *Li Ki*, bk. xlv, pp. 463-4.
[2] *Ibid.*, bk. xi, p. 19.

2. Standard of the Class of the Great Officials

We are not much interested in the standard of living of the emperor and princes, but we are interested in that of the great officials, because they are of the middle class. In the *Record of Rites*, there is a passage telling about the daily life of great officials, which may be taken as a description of the higher standard of living. It says:

A gentleman washes his hands five times a day. He uses millet-water in washing his head, and maize-water in washing his face. For his hair, when wet he uses a comb of white-grained wood, and an ivory comb for it when dry. After his toilet, there are brought to him the usual sup of wine and some delicacy; and the musicians come up the raised hall and sing. In bathing he uses two towels; a fine one for the upper part of his body, and a coarser one for the lower part. When he gets out of the tub, he steps on a straw mat; and having washed his feet again with hot water, he steps on the rush one. Then in his bathing robe of cloth, he dries his body again, and puts on his shoes; and a drink is then brought to him.[1]

Confucius once belonged to the class of great officials, and, when he lost his position, he belonged to the class of students. But, after he was called back to his state, he received his old title as a retired official, although he did not take the actual position. Therefore, he kept the standard of living of a great official. When Yen Yüan died, Yüan's father asked Confucius to sell his carriage in order to get an outer shell for the coffin of Yüan; but Confucius refused to do so. He referred to the fact that, when his own son died, he did not give up the carriage to get an outer shell for him. He said: "It is because that, having belonged to the class of great officials, it is not proper for me to

[1] *Li Ki*, bk. xi, p. 5.

walk on foot." From this instance, we can see how careful Confucius was to maintain his standard of living. Of course, this is a little more social than economic; but it is a very good example of the attention Confucius paid to the standard of living.

3. *Standard of the Class of Students*

In the "Pattern of the Family," there are many details of daily life, and they are essentially common to all classes. We may select some details in order to represent the standard of the class of students. This class is very important, because their living is similar to that of common people. Although the common people may not observe those rules as fully as the students, the rules are nevertheless the pattern of the people to whom the following lessons are taught.

When the sons serve their parents, on the first crowing of the cock, they all wash their faces and rinse their mouths, comb their hair, draw over it the covering of silk, fix this with the hair-pin, bind the hair at the roots with the fillet, brush the dust from the hair-tufts hanging over the forehead, and then put on their caps, leaving the ends of the strings hanging down. They then put on their square black robes, knee-covers, and girdles, fixing in the last their tablets. From the left and right of the girdle they hang their articles for use:— on the left side, the duster made of a handkerchief, the knife and whetstone, the small ivory spike for the opening of knots, and the metal speculum for getting fire from the sun; on the right, the archer's thimble for the thumb, and the armlet, the tube for writing instruments, the knife-case, the larger spike, and the borer for getting fire from wood. Finally, they put on their leggings, and adjust their shoe-strings.

This description seems to have too many details, but it gives a very good picture of the young men in ancient times. When the young women serve their parents or parents-in-law, they dress like these young men, with this difference: they wear the square black silk robes, also with girdles; leaving out such articles as the thimble and armlet, the tube and knife-case, they hang the needle-case, thread and floss, all bestowed in the satchel; then they fasten their necklaces which serve as bags for perfume.

When the young men and young women have thus dressed, they go to their parents and parents-in-law, and care for them in every way. They ask whether they want anything, and then respectfully bring it. They bring to their parents gruel, thick or thin, spirit or must, soup of vegetables, beans, wheat, spinach, rice, millet, maize, and glutinous millet,—whatever they wish, in fact; and their parents are also furnished with dates, chestnuts, sugar and honey, to sweeten their dishes; with the ordinary or the large-leaved violets, leaves of elm-trees, fresh or dry, and the most soothing rice-water to lubricate them; and with fat and oil to enrich them. Waiting till the parents have tasted them, the young people may withdraw.

As to the younger boys and girls, they do not take the full dress of young men and young women, but they all use necklaces as ornamental bags of perfume. At daybreak, they begin to pay their respects to their parents—later, however, than their older brothers and sisters. Their duty is to do the small services for their parents.

All the members living in the inner and outer parts of the house, at the first crowing of the cock, should wash their faces and mouths, put on their dresses, gather up their pillows and fine mats, sprinkle and sweep out the apartments, hall, and courtyard, and spread the mats—each doing his proper work. After sunrise, each attends to his special business.

Besides the old parents who are treated especially well, the children also receive favorable treatment. They go earlier to bed, and get up later. Everything is ready according to what they want; there is no fixed time for their meals. Whenever the parents leave something after their eating, although the sons and their wives may finish the remainder, the sweet, soft, and oily things are specially for the children.[1] This example is given to illustrate the principle of "loving the young".

4. *Standard of the Common People*

The most important of all is the standard of living of the common people. Of course, the living of the common people must be simple, and we cannot expect to have many details about it in the Confucian system. Under the system of *tsing tien*, however, they enjoy a very good living, and their standard is thus summed up by Mencius:

Around the house of five acres, the space beneath the walls is planted with mulberry trees, with which the woman nourishes silkworms, and thus the old are able to have silk to wear. Each family has five brood hens and two brood sows, which are kept to their breeding seasons, and thus the old are able to have flesh to eat. The husbandman cultivates his farm of one hundred acres, and thus his family of eight mouths are secured against hunger.

According to Mencius, the people of fifty years old cannot be kept warm without silk, and those of seventy cannot be satisfied without flesh. If they are not kept warm by silk, or not satisfied by flesh, it is said that they are starved and famished.[2] Therefore, the silk for dress and flesh for food are not the luxuries of the old, but their necessities. From this point of view, we may say that the standard of the common people is by no means low.

[1] *Li Ki*, bk. x, pp. 449-453.
[2] *Classics*, vol. ii, pp. 461-2.

"Nourishing the old" is a special principle of Confucius, and it raises the standard of living. According to the "Royal Regulations," for those of fifty, the grain is fine and different from that used by the younger people. For those of sixty, flesh is kept in store waiting for their order at any time. For those of seventy, there is a second service of savory meat. For those of eighty, there is a constant supply of delicacies. For those of ninety, food and drink are never out of their chamber; wherever they wander to another place, it is required that savory meat and drink should accompany them.[1] There is a strict rule that the old of the common people should not eat their meal without flesh.[2] Therefore, the standard of the common people is kept up by the old, and it can never be lowered.

According to the *tsing tien* system, however, although the persons fifty years old may be clothed with silk, and those of seventy may eat flesh, nothing is said about those who are younger than fifty or seventy years. We may suppose that the young people cannot consume such things in daily life, and that they are especially given to the old, because the productive power of ancient times was very limited.

What we have described of the standard of common people, however, is mixed up with the theoretical points of Confucius. But we want to know the actual condition of the people at that time. There is a valuable statement given by Li K'o,[3] the pupil of Tzŭ-hsia, and the minister of Marquis Wên of Wei (128-165 A. K. or 424-387 B. C.), indicating exactly the economic condition of the

[1] *Li Ki*, bk. iii, p. 240.

[2] *Ibid.*, p. 244, and bk. x, p. 462.

[3] His name is correctly recorded in the *Historical Record* (chs. xxx and cxxix) and in the *History of Han* (ch. xci). But the latter makes a mistake in ch. xxiv, where his name is given as Li Kuei.

farmers. Since Li K'o lived shortly after Confucius, but much earlier than Mencius, his statement probably shows the facts of Confucius' age. He says:

Now, one man, having five mouths in all, cultivates the land of one hundred acres. He reaps annually from each acre one bushel and a half of grain; the total amount is one hundred and fifty bushels. Subtracting fifteen bushels for the taxation of one-tenth, there remain one hundred and thirty-five bushels. For food, each person consumes one bushel and a half monthly; five persons consume ninety bushels for the whole year. There remain forty-five bushels. One bushel is worth thirty coins; the total value is one thousand three hundred fifty coins. Subtracting three hundred coins for the expense of social gathering and religious worship, there remain one thousand fifty coins. For clothing, each person spends three hundred coins on the average; five persons spend one thousand five hundred for the whole year. There is a deficit of four hundred fifty. If they are so unlucky as to have expense for sickness and funeral, or for the extra impositions of government, such expenditure still has not been included in this account.[1]

This statement gives a statistical view of the unhappy condition of farmers, and is the most reliable information which we now have. Since agriculture was the principal occupation of the ancient Chinese, the economic condition of the whole people must have been very bad. Hence Li K'o introduced his famous system of equalizing the price of grain for their relief.[2] Such a bad condition was probably not confined to the state of Li K'o, but prevailed over the whole empire. It is no wonder that Confucius devotes his attention first to the economic life of the people.

[1] *History of Han*, ch. xxiv.
[2] See *infra*.

CHAPTER XVI

PARTICULAR EXPENDITURES

ALTHOUGH the standard of living may include all kinds of expenditures, we prefer to discuss some particular expenditures separately, in order to show the characteristics of Confucius' system. These expenditures are: the expenditure for a marriage, the expenditure for a funeral and mourning, the expenditure for ancestor-worship, and the expenditure for social intercourse. The theories of these expenditures are extremely complex; they are not only economic, but also sociological, political, philosophical, ethical and religious. Of course, we are most interested in the economic aspect. But, as we are studying the system of Confucius, we have to consider many other aspects which are peculiar to Confucius and are correlative to economics.

1. MARRIAGE

First, we shall discuss the expenditure for a marriage. Since Confucius makes marriage a necessity of human life, he reduces its expense to the minimum. According to the *Canon of Rites,* there are six rites for marriage. After the family of the girl has accepted the proposal, the first rite is " giving a choice " to her father; the second is " inquiring into the name " of the girl. These two rites are consummated at one time. The third is " giving the lucky result " of divination; the fourth is " giving engagement;" the fifth is first " asking about the date " of the wedding, and then announcing it. All these five rites are performed by a proxy sent by the father of the bridegroom. The sixth rite is "personal receiving," an act of the bridegroom himself.

The rite of "giving engagement" is performed by the use of a bundle of silk and two pieces of the fur of a deer. The bundle of silk contains five rolls; each roll is folded double, and is forty cubits in length.[1] Three rolls are black, and the other two crimson. The two pieces of deer's fur can be used for dress. Besides "giving engagement," the other five rites are all performed by the use of a domestic goose for a present. This token is intended to represent the regularity and faithfulness of the relation of husband and wife. Requiring only five geese, five rolls of silk and two pieces of deer's fur, this ceremony of marriage is inexpensive. Of course, the expense of an American marriage can cut down to even less than this, but, according to Confucius' system, this is the lowest limit.

In the *Canon of Poetry*, there is a poem written by a heroic girl. She has promised to marry a man of Fêng, but his family wants to receive her before the rites of marriage are completed. She refuses to allow them to do so, on the ground that marriage is a most sacred thing and cannot be consummated without the full observance of rites. His family prosecutes her and causes her to be brought to court. But she insists that, if one single thing has not been presented, and one single rite has not been completed, she will not leave her home even if she sacrifices her life. Her poem runs as follows: "Although you have brought me to court, your offerings for the rites of marriage are not sufficient." It says again: "Although you have brought me by prosecution, I will not follow you."[2]

By selecting this poem in his Canon for an example of a

---

[1] *Li Ki*, bk. xviii, p. 172.
[2] *Classics*, vol. iv, pt. i, pp. 27-8.

marriage that is good, not only morally, but also legally, Confucius shows that he does not approve of allowing people to marry without going through the six rites, on the pretense that they have not the means. Indeed, he regulates the relation of husband and wife very carefully in the beginning, and does not make marriage too easy for the young couple.

Although Confucius does not make marriage too easy, he makes it as simple as possible. He is most fond of music, and employs it for all fortunate occasions; yet he omits music from the ceremonies of marriage. Confucius says:

The family whose daughter is married, does not extinguish its candles for three nights, thinking of the separation that has taken place. The family that has received the bride, for three days has no music; the bridegroom is thinking that he is about to take the place of his parents.[1]

According to this expression, marriage is not a gay ceremony, but a solemn business through which the son assumes responsibilities of his own and feels that his parents are getting older. It should be quiet and sober. Therefore, the *Record of Rites* says that at the marriage ceremony, music is not employed, and that there is no congratulation on marriage.[2]

Confucius limits the expense of marriage to a minimum, but he cannot help making the feast necessary. Since he separates the two sexes very severely, he must not allow the new couple to keep so quiet as not to give a conspicuous notice to society. In order to mark the new relation between bride and bridegroom, a feast is necessary to notify the public. The *Record of Rites* says: " The bridegroom should make a feast and invite the people of the town and

[1] *Li Ki*, bk. v, p. 322.   [2] *Ibid.*, bk. ix, p. 442.

his friends to attend it, in order to give its due importance to the separate position of man and woman."¹ Of course, this feast must cost something, but its expense cannot be saved because it has social and ethical value.

As the feast must necessarily be given by the bridegroom to his townsmen and his friends, although there is to be no congratulation, the guests cannot simply attend the feast without any social obligation. Hence the congratulation takes place under another name. It is not said to be a congratulation upon the marriage, but only a present for the entertainment of the guests. The language used by the messenger for such a congratulation is given by the "Details of Rites:" "So-and-so has sent me. Having heard that you are having guests, he has sent me with this present."² Such a present may consist of four pots of spirits, ten pieces of dried meat, and a dog.³ Although it may not be too expensive, it will yet cost a family a good deal. As marriage is necessary in the social life, this expenditure is also necessary. In the present day, however, such a congratulation is directly expressed for the happiness of the wedding, and not for the gathering of the guests.

To-day, the Chinese still observe these rites of marriage in their essentials. But they increase the expense greatly. It would be much better to return to the rules of Confucius, and make marriage again simple and economical.

II. FUNERALS

Second, we shall study the expenditure for the rites of a funeral and mourning. This is the most important point in the religion of Confucius, and we cannot help discussing it at some length. We shall take up certain details first, and discuss the theory later.

---

[1] *Li Ki*, bk. i, p. 78. [2] *Ibid.* [3] *Ibid.*, bk. xv. p. 76.

At the ceremony of "slighter dressing" of the dead, the sheet for a ruler's body is embroidered; for that of a great official, white silk; for that of a student, black silk;—each has one sheet. But there are nineteen suits of clothes for each of them; a suit is made up of a long robe and a shorter one placed over it, and there must be the upper garment together with the lower garment. At the "fuller dressing," each of them has two sheets; but a ruler has one hundred suits of clothes; a great official, fifty; and a student, thirty. For the coffins, the largest or outermost coffin of a ruler is eight inches thick, the next, six inches, and the innermost, four inches. The larger coffin of a great official of the highest grade is eight inches thick; and the inner, six inches; for one of the lowest grade, the dimensions are six inches and four. The coffin of a student is six inches thick. For the outer shell of the coffin, a ruler uses pine; a great official, cypress; a student, various kinds of wood.[1] When Confucius became the magistrate of Chung-tu, he made an ordinance that the coffin of the common people should be four inches thick, and its shell five.[2] This is only an instance to show the expenditure for the funeral.

Now, we come to the contributions for the funeral. As the funeral system is so expensive, there is really a need of contributions, besides the fact that they have ethical and social reasons. According to the *Canon of Rites* and the *Spring and Autumn*, we may divide these contributions into three kinds. First, there are the contributions for the dead. Some are called "shroud," such as the sheets and clothes. Some are called "gift," such as the "spiritual vessels." This gift is not regular, but just according to what the contributor has. If a prince of state gives it to a student, it will be one hundred eighty cubits of silk. When

---

[1] *Li Ki*, bk. xix, pp. 185-199. [2] *Ibid.*, bk. ii, p. 150.

the contributor knows the dead, his contribution should be of the first kind. Second, there are the contributions for the mourner. This is called " help," and is performed by the use of money and other articles of wealth. When the contributor knows the mourner, his contribution should be of the second kind, in order to form a mutual help and to supply the deficiency. Third, there are the contributions for the dead and the mourner both. These are called " covering." Such things are the bundle of silk, carriage, horse, sheep, *etc.* They are used both for the obsequies of the dead, and for the financial assistance of the mourner. When the contributor knows them both, his contribution should be of the third kind. By these contributions, society is interwoven like a net, and wealth is distributed to and fro like the tide. But they form an expenditure to the contributor. If a poor man cannot contribute anything, it is a custom of the Chinese for him to help his relatives and friends by his labor instead of wealth. Generally a man, for the funeral of his relatives and close friends, contributes both labor and wealth.

The reasons Confucius makes the rites of funeral so expensive are four: (1) ethical, (2) aesthetic, (3) social and (4) economic. Let us first consider the ethical reason. We already know that, under Confucius' teaching, filial piety is one of the chief virtues of his moral code. We have already seen that, when the parents are living, the rites of serving them are very numerous; but how is it when they are dead? When one treats his parents well at the beginning, he must treat them well at the end. If he is careful for their living and careless for their death, it means that he is respectful to those who have knowledge and disrespectful to those who have no knowledge; it denotes a rebellious heart and is the practice of the unfaithful man. Even if we have a rebellious heart toward a servant, we are still ashamed; how can we have such a heart toward our parents? Death is the end of human life; it affords our last chance to render service to our parents.[1] Confucius says: "Man may not have shown his self-devotion to something else, but he must show it at the funeral of his parents."[2] Mencius says: "The nourishment of parents when living is not sufficient to be accounted the great thing. It is only in the performing of their obsequies when dead that we have what can be considered the great thing."[3] According to Confucius, if a man, at the death of his parents, has no devotion, he must be a hard-hearted creature, without any feeling of humanity. Therefore, Confucius establishes his funeral rites to make it necessary for the people to observe them. This is really an advancing step to lead the people to do their duty; since they must serve their parents faithfully even after they are dead, how faithful must they then be when their parents are alive!

Ethical reasons are of fundamental importance in connection with the funeral rites, and yet we cannot explain on ethical grounds why such rites should be as expensive as Confucius prescribes. This is because of aesthetic considerations. Tzŭ-yu says: "Among the rites, some are intended to lessen the display of feeling, while others purposely introduce things to excite it. To give direct vent to the feelings and display them without restraint is the way of barbarism." Therefore, the funeral rites are not simply to express the feeling of sorrow, but also carefully to regulate it in a proper way, for the direction of average people. He continues: "Whenever a man dies, there arises a feeling of disgust at the corpse. . . . On this account, there is the wrapping of it in the shroud, and there are the cur-

[1] *Hsun Tsŭ*, bk. xix.
[2] *Classics*, vol. i, p. 344.
[3] *Ibid.*, vol. ii, p. 322.

tains, plumes and other ornaments of the coffin, to preserve men from that feeling of disgust." [1]

Hsun Tzŭ has given the same reason as that of Tzŭ-yu. If the dead has no decoration, it becomes a bad thing; and if it becomes a bad thing, man will have no sorrow for it. Just losing a parent within a single day, and burying him, nevertheless, without any sorrow, it is similar to the death of a beast. How can it be done in such a way without great shame? Therefore, in the ordering of funeral rites, there are added more decorations at each step of the ceremony, in order to counteract such a tendency.[2]

Beside the ethical and aesthetic reasons, there is the social reason. As Confucius marks the social distinctions for the living, he also marks them for the dead. An emperor is placed in his coffin on the seventh day after his death, and interred in the seventh month. A prince of a state is placed in his coffin on the fifth day, and interred in the fifth month. A great official, a student, and the common people are placed in the coffin on the third day, and interred in the third month.[3] The reasons why the funeral is thus delayed are, (1) that the articles required for the dead may be completed, and (2) that the guests coming to attend the funeral may arrive. But we must understand that during such a period there is great expense.

There is, however, the significance of social distinction. The funeral of an emperor is attended by all the princes under the imperial jurisdiction; that of a prince, by those of the states which have diplomatic relations; and that of a student and the common people, by all their relatives and friends. But the funerals of those who have been punished by criminal law are not allowed to be attended by any

[1] *Li Ki*, bk. ii, p. 177. [2] Bk. xix.
[3] *Li Ki*, bk. iii, pp. 222-3.

PARTICULAR EXPENDITURES 279

people, except the wives and sons. There are only three suits, and the coffins are only three inches thick. The coffins are not allowed to have any decorations, or to be conveyed away in the day time. They are buried at night, and excluded from the regular ceremony. There is no mourning at all for them; after the burial everything is over. This is a most disgraceful thing. Therefore, the scale of the expenditure for a funeral is a reflection of the life of the dead; and, if the financial condition allows it, a man should not let his parents fall into the class of criminals. When a man is living, he should be glorious, and when he dies, he should be bitterly lamented.[1] This is the social reason for the expensive funeral.

Finally, and most important for our treatment, there is an economic reason,—the satisfaction of human wants. This is explained very clearly by Mencius. He says:

In the most ancient times, there were some who did not inter their parents. When their parents died, they took them up and threw them into some water-channel. Afterwards, when passing by them, they saw foxes and wild-cats devouring them, and flies and gnats biting at them. The perspiration started out upon their foreheads, and they looked away, unable to bear the sight. It was not due to other people that this perspiration flowed. The emotions of their own hearts affected their faces and eyes, and instantly they went home, and came back with baskets and spades and covered the bodies.[2]

This is a description of the development of the funeral in the rudest stage, and it indicates that funeral is necessary to satisfy the psychological wants of man.

Since society is higher in civilization, the human wants for a funeral are more complex; hence Confucius' system

[1] *Classics*, vol. i, p. 349.   [2] *Ibid.*, vol. ii, pp. 259-260.

arises. Man does not satisfy his wants by a simple covering of the body of his parent, but in a very handsome way. This is characteristic of human wants. After Mencius had buried his mother, Chung Yü, his pupil, questioned him about the wood of the coffin, which seemed too good. Mencius replied:

Anciently, there was no rule for the size of either the inner or the outer coffin. In middle antiquity [the Hsia and the Yin dynasties], the inner coffin was made seven inches thick, and the outer one the same. This was done by all, from the emperor to the common people, and not simply for the beauty of the appearance, but because they thus satisfied the natural feelings of their hearts. If prevented by statutory regulations from making their coffins in this way, men cannot have the feeling of pleasure. If they have not the money to make them in this way, they cannot have the feeling of pleasure. When they were not prevented, and had the money, all the ancients used this style. Why should I alone not do so? Moreover, is there no satisfaction to the natural feelings of a man, in preventing the earth from getting near to the bodies of his dead? I have heard that the superior man will not, for all the world, be niggardly to his parents.[1]

Again, Mencius says: "To make the people have no dissatisfaction about the nourishment of the living and the funeral of the dead, is the first principle of a good government."[2] In other words, the economic condition of the people is the first object of a good government, and such a condition must be satisfactory. But what we should understand is that the Confucians put the nourishment of the living and the funeral of the dead in the same rank, as the two necessities of economic life.

These four reasons explain why Confucius made the

[1] *Classics*, vol. ii, pp. 221-2. [2] *Ibid.*, p. 131.

funeral rites. But we may raise a question as to whether he was so superstitious as to believe that the dead really have knowledge or power. The answer must be no. On such an important point, we must quote him directly. Confucius says:

In dealing with the dead, if we treat them as if they were entirely dead, that would show a want of affection, and should not be done; or, if we treat them as if they were entirely alive, that would show a want of wisdom, and should not be done. On this account, the vessels of bamboo used in connection with the burial of the dead are not fit for actual use; those of earthenware cannot be used to wash in; those of wood are incapable of being carved; the lutes are strung, but not evenly; the pan pipes are complete, but not in tune; the bells and musical stones are there, but they have no stands. These things are called " spiritual vessels ", because the dead are treated as the unknowable spirits.[1]

From this statement, we know that Confucius treats the dead as midway between dead and alive, in order to avoid being either unkind or unwise. There is another statement of his which is very striking. When Tzŭ-kung asks him whether or not the dead have knowledge, he replies:

If I were to say that the dead have knowledge, I am afraid that filial sons and dutiful grandsons would injure their substance in paying the last offices to the departed; and if I were to say that the dead have no knowledge, I am afraid that unfilial sons and undutiful grandsons would leave their parents unburied. If you wish to know whether the dead have knowledge or not, you will know it yourself when you die. There is no need to discuss this point at the present.[2]

[1] *Li Ki*, bk. ii, p. 148.
[2] *Park of Narratives*, bk. xviii. *Cf. Classics*, vol. i, p. 99.

Confucius regulates not only the rites of funeral, but also the periods of mourning, which have great importance for economic life. We shall not go into any details of mourning, except the mourning for parents. The period of mourning for parents in ancient times was one year only. Confucius doubles this period; the actual length of time is twenty-five months, and the nominal title is "three years' mourning." Within this period, the son should not drink wine, not eat meat, not live with his wife. Confucius says: "A superior man, during the whole period of mourning, does not enjoy pleasant food which he may eat, nor derive pleasure from music which he may hear. He also does not feel at ease, if he is comfortably lodged. Therefore, he does not do such things at all."[1] Mencius says: "For the three years' mourning, the garment of coarse cloth with its lower edge even, and the eating of congee, are common to all, from the emperor to the mass of the people."[2] This is a return by the son for the benefits he has received from his parents. Confucius explains: "It is not till a child is three years old that it is allowed to leave the arms of its parents. Hence the three years' mourning is a universal system of the empire."[3]

The rites of funeral and mourning are the creeds of Confucius. When Confucius and his disciples preach the doctrine of filial piety, these rites are used as the means for conversion. But the anti-Confucians attack them as the weakest points. Among all the anti-Confucians, Mo Ti is the chief. He is a pupil of Confucius, but he is not satisfied with the rites of funeral and mourning, so he establishes his new school against his old master. These rites are the fundamental differences between Confucianism and Moism.

---

[1] *Classics*, vol. i, p. 328. [2] *Ibid.*, vol. ii, p. 236.
[3] *Ibid.*, vol. i, p. 328.

PARTICULAR EXPENDITURES

But why does Mo Ti differ from Confucius at this point? His argument is based entirely upon economic grounds. As we are treating the economic principles of Confucius, we may take up some points from the argument of Mo Ti, in order to enable us to understand Confucianism better.

The economic argument of Mo Ti has two points: first, these rites cannot increase wealth; and second, they cannot increase population. By the expensive funeral, too much wealth is buried, and by the long period of mourning, production is stopped too long. The existing wealth which has been accumulated from the past is thrown away, and the coming wealth which will be produced in the future is prevented for a long time. This is against the law of increasing wealth. During the different periods of mourning for the different relatives, the physical condition is undermined, and the living is also too coarse; hence many persons die on this account. Moreover, the rites of mourning destroy the sexual relations to a great extent. This is against the law of increasing population. Therefore, Mo Ti establishes his funeral laws as follows: In winter time, the winter clothes are used for the dead; in summer, the summer clothes; but there are no more than three suits. The coffin is only three inches thick. The period of mourning is only three months. As soon as the dead is buried, the living must immediately return to the production of wealth.[1]

Mo Ti uses the economic argument as the strongest point to attack Confucius, and yet he is defeated on the economic ground. He cares too much for production, and too little for consumption; hence he sacrifices the end to the means. This is the point for decisive battle between Confucianism and Moism. Chuang Tzŭ has given the best criticism on Moism, in the following:

[1] *Mo Tsŭ*, bk. xxv.

For life, it is hard; for death, it is cruel; its principle is too dry. It makes men grieve and lament. Its practice is difficult to carry out. I am afraid that it cannot be the principle of a sage. It opposes the natural feeling of the world, and the world cannot accept it. Although Mo Tzŭ can bear it alone, how can he do anything against the world? As he is different from the world, he is too far away to be a king.[1]

From this judgment of Chuang Tzŭ, we need not wonder why Mo Ti has lost his influence, and why Confucius has become " The Throneless King." It is simply an economic reason; Confucius satisfied human wants, and Mo Ti did not.

We must not misunderstand and think, however, that the funeral rites of Confucius are too expensive. He uses still the principle that consumption should be according to the means. His social system is based on the scale of virtue; those of greater virtue occupy the higher position and get more wealth; hence they should have better funerals. Moreover, he is the real reformer of the funeral system of his time. During the Chou dynasty, life was luxurious, and the expenditure for funerals was most excessive, even to burying men alive for the service of the dead. It became much better when Confucius regulated the funeral of different classes by a certain standard, beyond which they could not go. According to Confucius, all the things used for the dead should be entirely different from those used by living men. For examples, the carriages of clay and the figures of straw simply represent spiritual ideas but do not have much economic value. Even using a wooden image to bury with the dead Confucius condemns severely,—how can he approve a funeral which is really too expensive?[2]

[1] *Cf. Sacred Books*, vol. xl, p. 219.
[2] *Li Ki*, bk. ii, p. 173.

Therefore, in the *Spring and Autumn*, he records the sepulture of Huan Wang in order to condemn the extravagant burial even of an emperor.[1]

Confucius uses exactly the same principle for three years' mourning; it cannot be made longer for the superior men, but it cannot be made shorter for the inferior men. All the rites of funeral and mourning are based on the golden mean, and they satisfy the human wants.

III. ANCESTOR-WORSHIP

Third, we shall study the expenditure for ancestor-worship. This is also a most important point in the religion of Confucius, and we must study it at its root. According to Confucius, ancestors should be worshiped by all classes, from the emperor to the common people.

This means an increase in expenditure. First, they must build the ancestral temples; and such temples must be better than, or at least equal to, the residential houses. When a superior man is about to engage in building, he should build the temple first, and the residence last. Although the common people cannot have the right to build a temple, they must give up some part of their house for the worship of their ancestor, and it must cost them something. Second, they must have sacrificial dress. Those officials who receive land for salary should make such dress without delay. Even though they were cold, they should not wear the sacrificial dress for protection. Third, they must make the sacrificial vessels. Although the common people who do not receive land as salary cannot have them, the family of officials must make them first, and the vessels for the use of the living afterwards. Even though they were poor, they should not sell the sacrificial vessels.[2] Fourth, they must have the offerings. When the offerings are presented by

[1] Third year of Duke Chuang.   [2] *Li Ki*, bk. i, pp. 103-4.

the emperor, there are the small things, such as the sauerkraut of water plants, and pickles from the produce of dry grounds; the fine things, such as the stands for the bodies of the three victims and the supplies for the eight dishes; and those things produced under the best influences of light and shade, such as strange insects, and the fruits of plants and trees. Whatever the heaven and the earth have produced, if they can be used for offerings, are all exhibited there to show the great abundance of things.[1] Even among the offerings of the common people, we have already seen that they should present the different things according to the four seasons.[2] Therefore, in ancestor-worship, there must be an expenditure added to the cost of living.

Let us now consider why Confucius approves ancestor-worship. This is the fundamental basis of Confucius' religion. He advocates one supreme God, but he has also a companion of God, that is, one's father. Hence his religious system is dualism. God is our common father, without whom we cannot have life; but we have also a specific father, without whom we still cannot have life. If God is our only father, we may be born into any other life and it is not necessary that we be human beings. If the specific father is our only father, we may lose the best elements of nature and have no spiritual life. Hence Confucius recognizes these two fathers; adding a mother to them there is the Confucian doctrine of trinity. If we leave out the common father, we shall be too narrow-minded, too egotistic, unkind to the human race, and against the law of love. If we leave out the specific father, we shall be too loose in the family relation, too altruistic, undutiful to our own father, and against the law of wisdom. As love and

[1] *Li Ki*, bk. xxii, p. 238.
[2] See *supra*, pp. 260-261.

wisdom are the balance of Confucius, he combines the two principles, and establishes his dual religion.

Confucius says:

By the ceremonies of the sacrifices to Heaven and Earth, we are to serve the Supreme God, and by the ceremonies of the ancestral temple, we are to worship the ancestors. One who understands the ceremonies of the sacrifices to Heaven and Earth, and the meaning of the several sacrifices to ancestors, will find the governing of a kingdom as easy as to look into his palm.[1]

By this statement, he points out that the worship of God and that of ancestor are equally important on different occasions. But he has still another statement to point out that the worship of God and that of ancestor can be held on the same occasion. He says:

In filial piety there is nothing greater than the reverential awe of one's father. In the reverential awe shown to one's father there is nothing greater than making him the correlate of Heaven. The Duke of Chou was the man who first did this. Formerly the Duke of Chou at the border altar sacrificed to Hou Chi as the correlate of Heaven, and in the Brilliant Hall he honored Wên Wang, and sacrificed to him as the correlate of God.[2]

Indeed, as long as we have not reached the stage of Great Similarity, and have the tie of family, ancestor-worship is quite justifiable.

There arises a question as to whether Confucius believes that the ancestor is really equal to God. The answer must be no. It is simply that the descendant contributes the greatest honor to his ancestor. Because it is only a social

[1] *Classics,* vol. i, p. 404.
[2] *Sacred Books,* vol. iii, pp. 476-7.

honor, Confucius makes the emperor the only one to have the right of sacrificing to God; otherwise, as Confucius recognizes that everyone is the son of God, why should everyone not sacrifice to him, and why should everyone not make his own father equal to God? In the social system of Confucius, the emperor is the chief personality, and in his moral system, filial piety is the chief virtue; hence the father or ancestor of the emperor can enjoy the greatest honor, and the emperor sacrifices to him for the showing of the practice of filial piety to the empire. Moreover, the ancestor who is made the correlate of God must be the most famous one of the dynasty; the number of those ancestors never can be more than two, and the one must be separated from the other when the one is placed as a companion of God. Therefore, we are sure that Confucius does not regard the ancestor as God.

Does Confucius believe in a soul? Yes. It is the soul to which the worship is directed. As soon as the dead is buried, its soul is received home immediately, and it is represented by a tablet. Confucius says: "The physical body goes downwards, but the intelligent spirit is on high."[1] He says again: "The bones and flesh molder below, and, hidden away, become the earth of the fields; but the spirit issues forth, and is displayed on high in a condition of glorious brightness."[2] The *Record of Rites* also says: "The spiritual soul returns to heaven, while the physical body returns to earth."[3]

However, Confucius does not prove the existence of the soul. The *Record of Rites* says: "The flesh of the victim may be presented raw and as a whole, or cut up in pieces, or sodden, or thoroughly cooked; but how can we know

---

[1] *Li Ki*, bk. vii, p. 369.   [2] *Ibid.*, bk. xxi, p. 220.
[3] *Ibid.*, bk. ix, p. 444.

whether the spirit does enjoy it? It is simply that the sacrificer shows his reverence to the utmost of his power."[1] A similar statement is found in many places of the *Record of Rites*.[2] In fact, the mind of Confucius is not only religious, but also scientific; hence, according to him, the soul is an unknowable spirit.

If the soul is unknowable, why does Confucius make ancestor-worship necessary? It is only on the ethical ground. As we have already said that filial piety is the chief virtue of his moral system, should a son stop observing such an important principle after the death of his parents? Certainly not. It is by ancestor-worship that the nourishment of parents is followed up and filial duty to them perpetuated.[3] Confucius says: "Serving the dead as they were served when alive, and serving the departed as if they were still abiding among us; this is the summit of filial conduct."[4] Therefore, ancestor-worship is exclusively for the sake of virtue, and the worshiper does not seek anything for his own benefit.[5] This is the noblest character of the religion of Confucius.

Since China has adopted Confucianism as the state religion, everyone must conform to the filial duties. According to the *Law Code of the Ts'ing Dynasty*, all the monks and nuns of the churches of Buddhism and Taoism are required to kneel before their parents, to worship their ancestors, and to follow the mourning system. If they do not obey this law, they shall be punished with one hundred blows with the long stick, and shall be driven out of their monastery to stay at home.[6] This shows the peculiar character of the Chinese. Although they allow everyone to have

[1] *Li Ki*, bk. ix, p. 446.
[2] *Ibid.*, bk. ii, pp. 169, 177.
[3] *Ibid.*, bk. xxii, p. 237.
[4] *Classics*, vol. i, p. 403.
[5] *Li Ki*, bk. xxii, p. 237.
[6] Ch. xvii.

perfect freedom of belief, they compel him to perform the social and ethical duties. Therefore, according to the view of the Chinese, ancestor-worship is not a religious rite, in the English sense, but a social and ethical obligation.

In conclusion, for the funeral rites, the mourning system, and ancestor-worship, the Chinese not only observe the teachings of Confucius, but also go a little farther, although changes in many details are necessary.

IV. SOCIAL INTERCOURSE

Fourth, we shall study the expenditure for social intercourse, namely, "the presents of introduction." According to the ceremonies of Confucius, when anyone calls on another for the first time, he must bring a present to express his respect and sympathy. When the feudal princes pay their visit to the emperor, or visit among themselves; when a man first becomes an officer, or first advances to a higher official rank, and then pays his first visit to his ruler, or his superior, or his compeer; when officials call on the foreign princes who have just come to visit their own county; when the boy first meets his teacher; when a woman first sees her parents-in-law, and the princess or queen; and, indeed, when all persons first meet other persons of higher rank or the same rank; it is necessary to take presents. But such presents are not made by superiors to their inferiors.

The things used for presents of introduction are regularly prescribed. They are different according to the social standing of the callers, and have representative significance referring to their personal characters. The present of the emperor is spirits of black millet. He is too high to be a guest of the feudal princes, and yet, when he comes to inspect their state, he uses the spirits in their ancestral temple in order to show the ceremony of his arrival. The present of the feudal princes is their symbols of jade. The present of a high minister is a lamb; and that of a great official, a goose; both are alive. The present of a student is a dead pheasant; but in summer time, the pheasant is dried in order to avoid its smelling. The present of the common people is a duck; that of a boy, ten pieces of dried meat. The present of a woman is entirely different from that of a man; throughout all classes, women use the fruits of the *hovenia dulcis,* and of the hazel tree, dried meat cut fine, and hash with spices, jujube dates, and chestnuts. If in an army out of the towns, having no regular present, a tassel from a horse's breast, an archer's armlet, or an arrow, one may use for the present. Judging from this instance, if one cannot find the regular present in some locality, he may use any seasonable thing.[1]

These presents are only to represent the respect of the guest, and the host cannot make use of them for his own advantage. When the princes visit the emperor or visit each other, the presents of different jades are immediately returned to them. When the inferior calls on the superior, the presents of different animals are not accepted, or they are returned after the calling is over. If men of the same rank call on each other, the presents will be returned to the guest when the host repays his visit, on the same day, or another day. It is only the prince who can accept presents from his officials without return, and yet he may give them a banquet. At all the callings of the same rank, as soon as the formal meeting is over, the guest is invited to dine with the host.[2]

So far as the present of introduction is necessary for the first calling, no matter whether it will be returned or not, it is a necessary expenditure. It makes the life of society

[1] *Li Ki,* bk. i, p. 119.   [2] *Canon of Rites,* ch. vii.

harmonious and respectful, but it cannot occur without the use of wealth. As regards the expenditure of social intercourse, there are many kinds of gifts to show friendship according to different occasions. But we need not go into them, because they are not necessary expenses.

In the present day, the custom of bringing presents of introduction for the first visit has been changed to other forms or other names, and has been practically abolished. The only remaining trace of this custom is in the group of pupils. When a student goes to school, he must give something, mostly in the form of money, as the present of introduction to his teacher or teachers at least the first year, or at the beginning of every year. Very recently, since schools of the modern type have been established, this custom is abolished in some schools, while it remains in others. The difference is that when one is considered as a personal pupil to his personal teacher, he brings the present of introduction; but when the institution takes the place of his teacher, he is under no obligation to do so. China as regards this custom is thus in a transitional period.

PART III
PRODUCTION

BOOK V. FACTORS OF PRODUCTION

CHAPTER XVII

Three Factors of Production

For the three factors of the production of wealth, we may select the following passage from the "Great Learning":

The superior man must be careful about his virtue first. Having virtue, there will be the man. Having the man, there will be the land. Having the land, there will be the wealth. Having the wealth, there will be its use. Virtue is the root, and wealth is only its outcome.[1]

This principle is originally applied to the ruler. If a ruler has virtue, he can rule the man, hold the land, accumulate the wealth, which means here, capital, and have many things for use. But this principle can be applied to everybody, generally. Take the business man, for instance. He must possess some virtue first, either physical, mental or moral—the word virtue is used in its broad sense. If competition were perfectly free, he would get wealth in proportion to the virtue he possessed. If he have no virtue at all, or if he, in some way, fail to show his virtue (such as being able to work, and not working at all), he would be an outcast, and he could not get any wealth by himself. In society, there is no such person. If there is any, he cannot live very long. The loafer, the

[1] *Classics,* vol. i, p. 375.

parasite, and the thief, although they are bad men, still have some particular virtue for getting wealth. Therefore, virtue is the root, and wealth is only its outcome.

Thus, according to the " Great Learning," the factors of production are three. The first is the man who has any virtue; the second is the land, and the third is capital. All the three factors belong to the productive sphere. Then the word " use " appears. With the word " use," consumption begins.

The principle of dividing the productive factors into three is a general economic principle. It can be applied even to a single man in savage life. First, he himself must be a human being. Second, he must live on some kind of land, and use either fishing land or hunting land. Third, he must have some kind of capital to help his fishing or hunting. In primitive life, the capital must be subordinate to the land, because he can live without capital, but he can never live without land. In social life, land is only a part of capital, and man can have many other capital goods without owning land. Therefore, in social life, there are only two factors—man and capital goods. But, in Confucius' time, it was not so. Under the *tsing tien* system, every man accepted a portion of land, otherwise he could have no other capital goods, or very few. Therefore, land was a separate factor, and played the most important part among all capital goods. Moreover, in economic dynamics, the difference between land and artificially made goods becomes prominent, because land is not made and not perishable. The " Great Learning " is correct in treating these three factors separately.

Taking a nation as an economic unit, this principle is still more true. The first element of the wealth of a nation is man, the second is land, and the third is capital. Unoccupied land never can form a nation, unless it belongs to man. Those who have merely perishable capital goods never can form a nation, unless they own some land. There are the stateless people, who have men, land, and capital, but have no nation. But there is no nation that has neither men, nor land, nor capital.

According to the order of the "Great Learning," we shall discuss human beings first, and then nature. In other words, we shall make the man precede the land. It is true that the land is not made by man, even existed before man. But it is equally true, that the land is useful to man simply because man comes into it, otherwise the whole world is only a wilderness. Economics is not a natural science, but a human science. We should care for the man first. Moreover, since human power has been developed, nature is subject to man. All the natural forces are only machines, helping to produce wealth, but the real ruler of the natural world is man. For these reasons, we shall discuss man before discussing land.

This order has produced a special economic influence upon the Chinese. Why does China have a large population? Why do the Chinese like to have even more children than their fortune can support? Why do Chinese scholars never think of such a theory as limiting the population? It is because the "Great Learning" states that man is the first factor of production. According to this principle, land and capital both come after man. This principle is familiar to all the Chinese. They have a proverb: "Money is made by man." For their greetings, their first phrase is "increasing sons," and the second is "accumulating capital." When a new year comes, the people write or say, "The man and the capital both are successful." They are very glad to have more members in a family, in a community, or in the whole nation, not only for social pleasure, but also for economic production, because they think that man is the chief productive factor. This is undoubtedly due to the influence of the "Great Learning."

Henry George says: "It is not the increase of food that has caused this increase of men; but the increase of men that has brought about the increase of food. There is more food, simply because there are more men."[1] Such a theory is the common idea of the Chinese. And the "Great Learning," in putting man before land and capital, has exactly the same theory.

In the very beginning of the subject of political economy, the first part of his *General History of Institutes,* Tu Yu (died 1363 A. K. or 812 A. D.) also enumerates the three factors of production. He says:

The grain is the controller of the life of man; the land is the ground upon which the grain is grown; and the man is the object for which the ruler administers his government. Storing the grain, the national reserve will be abundant; distinguishing the land for agricultural purposes, the food will be sufficient; and making an investigation of the men, the service of the public labor will be equal. When a ruler understands these three things, it is called a good government.

His statement is from the standpoint of a ruler, but the three things are common to all economic life. The word grain is the chief representative of capital, which we shall discuss later; while the words land and man have no need of explanation. Therefore, according to Tu Yu also, the factors of production are three,—namely, capital, land and man. His order is just the reverse of that of the "Great Learning." But they are essentially th same, because he names them in the order of a climax, while the "Great Learning" does the opposite.

[1] *Progress and Poverty,* p. 97.

CHAPTER XVIII

Labor – Population

1. IMPORTANCE OF POPULATION

SINCE man is the first factor of production, we should first discuss man in the collective sense—that is, the population. The *Analects* tells us, "To anyone bearing the tables of population, Confucius bowed forward to the crossbar of his carriage."[1] This shows that Confucius attached much importance to the tables of population. Chu Hsi comments:

The action of Confucius was due to the importance of the number of people. Man is the most intelligent of all the creatures, and the people are regarded as the heaven of the emperor. Therefore, according to the *Official System of Chou*, when the number of people was presented to the emperor, he accepted it kneeling. How should one whose position was lower than that of the emperor not give respect to the number of population?

From the example of Confucius, the Chinese always think that population is the chief element of the national assets.

The *Official System of Chou* has many passages in regard to population. We shall select only a few of them. Among the duties of the vice-president of the department of people are these: he shall investigate the number of males and

[1] *Classics*, vol. i, p. 236.

females who live in the city, the suburb and the country, and pay the different kinds of taxes. He shall distinguish the noble and the common, the old and the young, and the sick people. He shall denote those who are exempted from taxation, and state their rules of worship, of drink and food, of funeral, *etc.* He shall send the statistical laws to each of the local governors, ordering him to record the size of the population of his province and also the number of their horses, cows, sheep, pigs, dogs, hens, carriages, wagons, and vehicles, and to distinguish their various kinds of wealth. The governors are required to report quarterly those numbers to this department in order to form the basis of administration. Every three years there is a " great comparison " of all the population and capital. During the " great comparison " this department shall accept the statistics from all the feudal states and the crown provinces.[1]

There is the bureau of people for registering the size of the population. All the people, from the babe who has teeth up to the man, are recorded in the census. This bureau distinguishes their residence, whether in the city, the suburb, or the country, classifies them according to sex, and adds births and deducts deaths annually. During the " great comparison " of every three years this bureau reports the census to the department of justice. In the tenth month the minister of justice presents the census to the emperor. The emperor accepts it kneeling, and keeps it in the sacred college. The imperial historian, the auditor and the prime minister, respectively, keep duplicates in order to help the administration of the emperor.[2]

According to the *Official System of Chou*, there is a statistical comparison of the distribution of population by sex. In order to facilitate a study of the statistics of population.

---

[1] Ch. xi. [2] Ch. xxxv.

we may present its statements in the form of a table, as follows:[1]

Province	Male	Female
Yang Chow	2	5
King Chow	1	2
Yü Chow	2	3
Ts'ing Chow	2	3
Yèn Chow	2	3
Yung Chow	3	2
Yu Chow	1	3
Ki Chow	5	3
Ping Chow	2	3

However far from the truth these figures may be, the table shows that in the majority of the provinces the number of females was greater than that of males. It is interesting to know that a predominance of females is not merely a modern phenomenon, but was a phenomenon of ancient times. This is probably because hard work and nervous strain have chiefly fallen upon men.

From the *Official System of Chou* we see how careful the emperor was to learn the size of the population. The statistics described not only the population, but also all kinds of capital goods. In a word, the governmental power touched the actual life of the people in every aspect. It was, however, not a despotism, but a democracy, because the local officers who exercised the governmental power were the people themselves. In the Chou dynasty, under feudalism, the political division was small and somewhat independent, and the ruler held by hereditary right, so that the ruling class and the subject knew each other very well, and administration was easy. Since the Ch'in dynasty (331 A. K. or 221

[1] Ch. xxxiii.

B. C.), however, under the absolute monarchy, the central government has directly controlled the whole empire, and the governors have been only temporary officers, so that the mandarin and the people are strangers, and the administration is necessarily inefficient. Therefore China could not get even an accurate census, because the government has kept aloof from the people.[1]

The importance of the study of population is summed up by Hsü Kan (died in 768 A. K. or 217 A. D.) as follows:

A peaceful government is dependent upon the prosperity of industry, the prosperity of industry upon the equality of public labor, and the equality of public labor upon the accuracy of the census. Therefore, the accuracy of the census is the foundation of the administration of a state. . . . Indeed, the number of population is the source of everything, and everything takes it as a standard. To distribute the land, to impose the taxes, to produce the products, to regulate salaries and wages, to do the public work, to raise the army, to establish the national institutions, to adjust the household economy, to observe the social and moral laws, and to set aside the punishment, all these are the results of a careful study of the number of population.[2]

In short, population is the basis of social, political, and economic adjustments.

II. LAW OF POPULATION

1. *Population and Land*

In connection with the policy of dealing with population, the first thing is the work of settlement. According to the

---

[1] *Cf. infra.*

[2] *General Research on Literature and Authorities*, written by Ma Tuan-lin, a great authority at the beginning of the Yüan dynasty, published in 1873 (1322 A. D.), ch. xii.

"Royal Regulations" this is in charge of the minister of works. With the various instruments he measures the land for the settlements of the people. He distinguishes the geographical situations, such as the mountains and rivers, the oozy ground and marsh; and he observes also the temperature of the four seasons.[1] In short, the first principle is that the population must be adjusted to the natural environment.

Second, the density of population must agree with the extent of the land. The "Royal Regulations" says:

In settling the people, the land is measured for the formation of cities, and then measured again in smaller portions for the allotments of the people. The land and the population must agree with each other. There is no land left out of use, and none of the people left to wander about idle.[2]

We should not miss, however, the most important point which governs these two principles, namely, governmental control of population. Since the minister of works has charge of the settlement of the people, it is he who distributes the people in accordance with the natural environment and the land, and not the people themselves. Although the government may simply follow what the people want, it takes very active measures. Therefore, the distribution of population is a function of the government.

The government, however, must be in harmony with the real interest of the people, and it should not change their adaptation to the environment. Confucius says:

The sage kings showed their sense of the state of harmony in the following way: they did not make the occupants of the hills remove and live by the streams, nor the occupants of the

---

[1] *Li Ki*, bk. iii, p. 228.   [2] *Ibid.*, p. 230.

islands remove and live in the plains; and thus the people complained of no hardship.[1]

The commentator says that the inhabitants of the hills are interested in the animals; those of the islands in the fishes and salt; and those of the plains in the different kinds of grain. The government should let them live respectively in those localities to which they have been accustomed, and should not change their occupations and make hardships for them. If the people lose their occupation, they will be poor; and if they are poor, they will give way to unbridled license. Therefore, the governmental distribution of population is necessarily harmonious with the people themselves.

The principle that the population must agree with the extent of the land is held by all the scholars. In 702 (151 A. D.), Tsui Shih says that the ancient sages distributed the cultivated land to every man, and the land was proportional to the population. Now, in some provinces the population is dense and the land is insufficient to support it, while in other provinces the population is sparse but the land is uncultivated, although it is fitted for the growing of grain. The old plan of removing the poor people who cannot have their own occupation to those places where the land is plenty should here be followed. This is a policy for the development of the land and the help of the people.[2] This theory of Tsui Shih's represents the common idea of the Chinese.

In the Southern Sung dynasty, the capital was in Hangchow, Chekiang province, and surrounding the capital there was an over-population. Therefore, Yeh Shih (1701-1774 A. K. or 1150-1223 A. D.) proposed to remove the surplus from the over-populated regions to those that were under-populated. He says:

[1] *Li Ki*, bk vii, p. 392.   [2] *General Research*, ch. ii.

The importance of the administration of a state lies in the possession of the people. If the people are many, the land is developed, the taxes are increased, the public laborers are numerous, and the army is strong. . . . Therefore, when there are people, they must be directed to the development of the land. If the land is developed, the taxes are increased. Therefore, when they live at home they can do the public labor, and when they go abroad they can become soldiers. But this is not the case now. They are caused to live in poverty and suffering, because they have no land to establish their own occupation. Those who are dull and unskilful become loungers or dependent servants, and those who are strong and selfish become small dealers or robbers. They can roughly get food for the morning and evening, but cannot make a home. Even during a good year, when food is cheap, the people are afraid that they cannot get even a pint or a peck of it. Generally, those who can pay the taxes and serve the public labor are less than one-third of the whole population. The landowners do not till the land themselves, and the tillers own no land. Therefore, although the population multiplies and prospers, it cannot be of any use to the state. . . . Under such circumstances no land can be developed and no tax be increased. The people simply gather together for the getting of food and clothes by means of robbery and stealth. It makes their habits covetous, licentious, deceitful, luxurious, and without faithful and honest conduct. Such a people, however, how can it be thrown away like spoiled fish or flesh?

His conclusion is that they should be removed to the underpopulated provinces. By this means more land will be developed, more taxes will be collected, and the people can be either soldiers when they are abroad, or public laborers when they are at home. Therefore, the wealth of a nation will naturally grow up without special effort. This he considers a very important part of public policy.[1]

[1] *General Research*, ch. xi.

It should be noticed that both Tsui Shih and Yeh Shih are more in favor of agriculture than of industry. Although the commercial and industrial cities can maintain more population, they think that the condition of the poor is very bad, because they are merely dependents. Hence, they both use the term " own occupation " for the object of their advocacy. In order to make the poor have their own occupation and become independent of the rich, the only thing the state can do is to give them free land. Since the land of the cities where the poor concentrate is not enough, they cannot have any free land unless they are removed to the under-populated places. Therefore, the theory of Tsui Shih and Yeh Shih is to enable the poor to have an occupation which can be called their own. In other words, they want to make the dependent laborers become independent farmers. If they should see the factory system of to-day, they would advocate their plan still more strongly.

The above-mentioned policy of moving the population is based on economic pirnciples, and we have entirely omitted those policies based on military defense. But we should give a few details about the removal of population in ancient times. In 383 A. K. (169 B. C.) Chao Tso (died 398 A. K.) says:

I have heard that, in ancient times, the moving of population from a distance to the empty land was like this: In the first place, the temperature of the climate is examined into, the taste of the water tested, the fitness of the soil judged, and the richness of the plants looked into. Then the city is established and the walls built, the streets fixed and the houses separated, the roads of the farms connected and the boundaries of the field divided. Their houses are first built. Each house has one hall, two chambers, and the different doors. Within the house the articles and instruments are laid down. The people may have residence when they come, and have something for use when they work. Therefore the people are encouraged in moving to the new city, and do not mind leaving their old homes. Furthermore, they are given doctors for the cure of their sickness and priests for the exercise of their worship. Between the two sexes, the people have marriage; for birth and death, they help each other; for the funeral, they have a common cemetery. Their plants are flourishing, their animals are growing, and their houses are complete and comfortable. All these make the people feel their place pleasant and dispose them to live there permanently.[1]

From such a description we can see how active the government was when it moved the people. This is a very valuable statement, because it gives some details of the ancient system.

Since the Han dynasty, the policy of moving population has been carried into effect many times. For an example we may select the decree of Ming T'ai Tsu, which was given in 1921 A. K. (1370 A. D.). It runs thus:

The five prefectures, Suchow, Sungkiang, Kiahsing, Huchow and Hangchow,[2] are over-populated. The people cannot have land for cultivation, and usually pursue the secondary occupations without getting sufficient food. In Linhao,[3] my native prefecture, the land is not developed, and there is unopened wealth in the ground. The people of those five prefectures who own no land should be directed to go there for the cultivation of land. The land which they may cultivate shall be given to them for their private property. They shall be supplied with money, food, oxen and seed, and they shall be exempted from taxation for three years. The distribution of land shall be according to the number of men and their

[1] *History of Han,* ch. xlix.
[2] In the provinces of Kiangsu and Chekiang.
[3] The present prefecture of Fungyang, Anhui province.

physical sufficiency, but none shall be allowed to own too much land.[1]

This decree is a general provision for the removal of population.

This question will arise: Why should the government control the distribution of population? Under the theory of free competition, the population would naturally distribute itself nicely. But there are many circumstances under which competition is not free, and especially among poor people. In the first place, they will not care to move, because it is human nature to become attached to the old place. In the second place, they do not know how to move, because they do not know what place is good for them. A number of obstacles, such as the differences of dialects, customs and climates, and especially the poor transportation, all prevent them from moving. In the third place, they cannot move themselves by their empty hands. Therefore, the moving of population by the government is a necessary thing. It is a good policy, first, for the poor themselves, and next, for the nation as a whole. It is good not only for their economic life, but also for their moral and social conditions, and many other things. Moreover, this policy is not compulsory, but voluntary. The government gives only the inducement to encourage their hope, but not force to increase their fear. Therefore, government control of population is a good thing.

In the present day, as the population of China is dense in the east and the south, but sparse in the west and the north, she should move the people from the former to the latter. She should move not only the poor, but also the rich, be-

---

[1] *Continuation of the General Research on Literature and Authorities*, edited under the imperial direction of Kao Tsung, and published in 2335 (1784 A. D.), ch. ii.

cause the rich have capital. She should move not only the manual laborers, but also the professional men, because those men have more intellectual power. Such a great movement must be carried on by the state, in order to make Manchuria, Mongolia, Chinese Turkestan and Tibet nearly equal to China proper. Building railroads, increasing political districts, establishing public schools, distributing free land, starting factories, and developing every kind of industry—all of these will encourage the immigrants and improve the natives. The state should give a number of immunities and privileges to the immigrants; otherwise they will not migrate. Moreover, she should select the best natives from among those regions to come to the most important cities to study everything, in order to assimilate the Chinese civilization and spread it among their own people. In a word, she should unify the whole empire for the realization of the " great uniformity " of Confucius. There is no reason why there should be a distinction between China proper and the rest of the state. This has become the public opinion in China to-day.

2. *Population and Food*

The relation of population and food is indicated by Confucius himself. He says: " The important things for a government are the people and food." [1] The commentator says that the people are important because they are the root of a state, and that the food is important because it is the life of the people. Therefore, it has become the common saying of the Chinese: " The state regards the people as its root, and the people regard the food as their heaven."

The relation between population and food is familiar to every one, and especially since the doctrine of Malthus was

[1] *Classics*, vol. i, p. 351.

set forth. According to him, if the population increases beyond the proportional increased or acquired produce of the country, the deaths will shortly exceed the births, unless an emigration takes place.[1] Therefore, the increase in population is dependent upon the supply of food. For the misery of the unfortunate population, Mencius gives a similar expression. When he talked to King Hui of Liang, he said that the rulers of Ch'in and Ch'u robbed the people of their time, so that they could not plough and weed their fields. The results were that their parents suffered from cold and hunger, and that their brothers, wives, and children were separated and scattered abroad.[2] Again, when he talked to Duke Mo of Tsau, he said that, in calamitous years and years of famine, the old and weak have been found dying in the ditches and water-channels, and the able-bodied have been scattered about to the four quarters.[3] Therefore, according to Mencius, when there is an insufficiency of food, there are two things for the people—emigration and death. These are the two positive checks to population.

For the adjustment between population and food, Mencius has the great principle of political economy, shown in the conservation of natural resources, the *tsing tien* system, the control of prices, *etc.*; that is, to increase wealth in general and not to increase food in particular. How can he approve a half measure which does not increase the food at all, but simply distributes it in accordance with the condition of the people? The King Hui of Liang said to Mencius that, when the year was bad on the inside of the river, he removed as many of the people as he could to the east of the river, and conveyed grain to the country on the inside; and that when the year was bad on the east of the river, he

---

[1] *The Principle of Population,* Ashley's edition, pp. 39-40.
[2] *Classics,* vol. ii, pp. 135-6. [3] *Ibid.,* p. 173.

acted correspondingly. He spoke of such measures with great pride, but Mencius did not give him his approval. The reason is that a ruler should adopt the fundamental principle for the permanent increase of the wealth of the people, and should not resort to the temporary removal of either people or food, as a great measure.[1]

3. *Population and Wealth*

The most important support of the population is not land, nor food, but wealth. If we have more wealth, we may utilize the land either more extensively, or more intensively, or both; and we may produce more food. Therefore, the relation between population and wealth is the fundamental thing. This principle was recognized by Confucius. When he went to Wei, as we have mentioned above,[2] he gave his impression from his carriage by saying, " How numerous are the people!" " Since they are thus numerous," asked Jan Yu, " what more shall be done for them? " " Enrich them," was the reply. By this answer Confucius indicated that wealth is most important for the population. As soon as the population is large, the first thing is the increase of wealth. Although he did not give the details as regards how the enrichment was to be made, such a general statement covers the whole economic field. Indeed, whatever can make the people rich is the thing which should be used for the support of population.

Confucius appreciated a large population, because it is an indication of national prosperity. But he did not think that a large population is good when its wealth is not equally distributed. He said that we should not be troubled lest the people should be few, but should be troubled lest they should

[1] *Classics*, vol. ii, pp. 129-132.
[2] *Cf. supra*, pp. 96-97.

not have equality of wealth. If they have equality of wealth, they will have no poverty, and they will be in a condition of harmony. If they are harmonious, their number will not be few.[1] Therefore, no matter whether the population is large or small, wealth is most important for avoiding poverty and bringing harmony. Since Confucius was not a pure economist, but a general reformer, he spoke of the wealth of the people from the distributive, rather than from the productive, point of view. But his view is quite correct. For if wealth were not equally distributed, the population as a whole would suffer from poverty and lack of harmony, even though its production were great.

The relation between population and wealth is also pointed out by the "Miscellaneous Records." First, a large territory must be sufficient to support a corresponding population. Second, the same number of population must have the same efficiency. "If there is a large territory, and the people be not correspondingly numerous, the superior man regards it as a shame. If another government has the same population as his own, but has a double efficiency, the superior man regards it as a shame."[2] The word superior man refers to either the ruler or the officer. The first defect comes from the fact that he cannot make the wealth sufficient to support a large population in correspondence with the extent of the land, and this causes the people to desert his territory. Therefore, even though the land is plentiful, the population is sparse, because population depends not merely upon the land, but upon the wealth. In the second case, although he possesses the same density of population as does his neighbor, the merit of his neighbor is double his. This means that he has the same number of men, but accomplishes only half the work of his neighbor.

[1] *Cf. infra.*
[2] *Cf. infra,* p. 167.

LABOR - POPULATION

This points out the difference between the size of the population and the efficiency of production. The mere possession of a large population is of no use, unless it gives a corresponding amount of production. Therefore, if the large territory cannot support a large population, and the large population cannot give a large production, these two cases are both regarded by the superior man as his shame. In short, wealth must be in accordance with the population.

III. MIGRATION OF POPULATION.

1. *Freedom of Movement.*

The fundamental principle underlying the problem of population is the freedom of movement. According to the principles of the *Spring and Autumn*, there is a division of territory, but there is no division of people. This means that the people may either emigrate or immigrate, without a permanent residence. Under such a principle the people have perfect freedom of movement. When the government is good the people immigrate, and when it is bad they emigrate. The number of people is the index of the political condition of the government and the economic condition of the people. Therefore, the merit of the officials is tested by the examination into the size of population.

The chief cause of emigration is economic. So long as the people are satisfied with their economic condition, they will stay even though there might be some other great evils. When Confucius passed by the side of Tai Mountain, and saw a woman who was wailing bitterly by a grave, he sent Tzŭ-lu to question her. She said: "Formerly, my father-in-law was killed here by a tiger. My husband was also killed by another; and now my son has died in the same way." Confucius said: "Why do you not leave the place?" The answer was, "There is no oppressive government here." He then said to his pupils: "Remember this, my little children. Oppressive government is more terrible than tigers."[1] In fact, the worst thing to drive the people away is an oppressive government, especially if it touches the economic life of the people by heavy taxation.

On the other hand, the chief cause for immigration is also economic. According to Chao Tso, people seeking their economic interest anywhere are like water running to a low place, and they do not choose any particular region in the four corners.[2] The mobility of population, then, is like water. If the economic interest of one locality is greater than that of another, the people will emigrate from the latter to the former, when there is no obstacle. Therefore, both emigration and immigration depend upon economic principles.

2. *Encouragement of Immigration in General*

Since Confucius regards immigration as a sign of good government, he advocates the encouragement of it. Confucius says:

If a ruler love propriety, the people will not dare not to be reverent. If he love righteousness, the people will not dare not to submit to his example. If he love good faith, the people will not dare not to be sincere. Now, when these things obtain, the people from all quarters will come to him, bearing their children on their backs.[3]

He thus shows that the immigration of the people is the result of a good ruler. When the Duke of Yeh asked Confucius about government, Confucius said, " Good government obtains when those who are near are made happy, and those who are far off are attracted to come."[4] By this

---

[1] *Li Ki*, bk. ii, pp. 190-191. [2] *History of Han*, ch. xxiv.
[3] *Classics*, vol. i, p. 265. [4] *Ibid.*, p. 269.

LABOR - POPULATION 315

statement he makes the immigratoin of the remote people one of the two objects of good government. Again, he says: " If remoter people are not submissive, all the influences of civil culture and virtue are to be cultivated in order to attract them to come; and when they have come, they must be made contented and tranquil." [1] Therefore, to attract the immigrants to come in is the doctrine of Confucius. This means to win the heart of the people, and to conquer them by culture and virtue.

Mencius has made a similar statement. When he talked to King Hsüan of Ch'i, he said:

Now, if your Majesty will institute a government whose action shall be benevolent, this will cause all the officers in the world to wish to stand in your Majesty's court, and all the farmers to wish to plough in your Majesty's fields, and all the merchants, both traveling and stationary, to wish to store their goods in your Majesty's market-places, and all traveling strangers to wish to make their tours on your Majesty's roads, and all throughout the world who feel aggrieved by their rulers to wish to come and complain to your Majesty.[2]

In fact, this is the condition of a royal government. It makes the state the center of the immigration of the whole world, and conquers the whole world by the institutions of benevolent government instead of military force. This is the real meaning of the word "king" or "royal" in the Confucian sense. It is universalism in contrast to imperialism.[3]

For the encouragement of immigration, exemptions are given to the immigrants. For example, we may quote this

[1] *Classics*, vol. i, pp. 308-9.

[2] *Classics*, vol. ii, pp. 146-7. The benevolent government means the *tsing tien* system; cf. *infra*, pp. 501-6.

[3] *Cf. infra.*

passage from the " Royal Regulations:" " When the people of the noble families move to the feudal states, they are discharged from service for three months. When the people move from the feudal states to the noble families, they are not required to take service for a round year."[1] For the explanation of the text, K'ung Ying-ta says:

In the feudal states, the land is larger, and the public labor requiring the people to do service is less; hence the people desire it. Therefore, they are exempted from service only for three months. . . . In the estates of the noble families, the land is smaller, and the public labor is more. In order to make the people like it, they are exempted from service for a round year.

From this passage we may get two points. First, it shows the freedom of movement. The people may move either from the noble estates to the feudal states, or *vice versa*, as they please. Second, it shows the real encouragement of immigration, because the immigrants get some material gain from such an exemption.

The Confucian theory is exactly the opposite of actual conditions in American and European countries. While the restriction and the exclusion of immigrants in the United States is based mainly on the economic struggle—that is, the laborers want to get more money—the theory of Confucius is based on politics, ethics and religion. Indeed, his theory tends to make a universal empire, a universal religion, a universal conception, a universal law, a universal custom, a universal route, a universal language, a universal calendar, *etc.* These ideas can be summed up in a single word—universalism. Confucius says: " When there is the teaching, there shall be no distinction between the races, nor be-

[1] *Li Ki*, bk. iii, p. 243.

tween the sexes, nor between the classes."[1] From such a point of view it is necessary to encourage immigration in order to realize universalism.

Under the influence of Confucius, China did realize universalism to a great extent, although it was imperfect. Unfortunately, or fortunately, the Opium War brought about by the English broke the Chinese peace and marked a most important epoch in Chinese history. In the past, China was a universal empire, and in the present, she is only one of the nations of the world. Since the Opium War, China has been forced to make unjust treaties, and such terms as "extraterritoriality," "sphere of influence," "shall China be partitioned," "open door," have been introduced. When foreigners come to China, they, although not every one of them, threaten the national sovereignty, deprive the individual of liberty, violate the law of the land, and do anything they please.[2] The Chinese, indeed, sincerely welcome well-behaved foreigners, but there can be none who like such men. The ideal of Confucian universalism is too advanced; it does not fit the world which is still full of injustice. Hence, China is forced back to the lower stage of a national military state. We hope, however, that after China shall be strong enough to maintain peace against any external interference, she will by herself open the door of every part to any foreigner under the Chinese jurisdiction, in order to realize Confucian universalism and to make a world state by means of the national state.

---

[1] *Cf. Classics,* vol. i, p. 305.

[2] A single instance must stand as a type of multitudinous insults and oppressions which the Chinese have to endure in consequence of the presence of foreigners, protected by extra-territorial rights. At the entrance of the Shanghai Public Garden on the Bund, there is a notice written in Chinese saying: "Dogs and Chinamen are not allowed to come in," posted by order of the Municipal Council, which is composed entirely of the representatives of foreign residents.

3. *Encouragement of Immigration of Artisans and Merchants*

Although immigration in general has a great effect upon the economic life of a nation, its influence is far beyond the economic field. Hence, we now come to immigration in particular—namely, the immigration of artisans and traveling merchants. When Duke Ai asked Confucius about government, he gave him the nine standard rules. Among these, the seventh is to induce all classes of artisans to come in, and the eighth is concerned with the indulgent treatment of foreigners. The former mentions the word artisans expressly, while the latter means foreign merchants especially, although it includes all foreigners in general.

The happy effects of these two rules and the details of practising them are given by Confucius as follows:

> By inducing all classes of artisans to come in, wealth is made sufficient. By indulgent treatment of foreigners, the people of all quarters will come. . . . By daily examinations and monthly trials, and by making their rations in accordance with their labors: this is the way to encourage all the classes of artisans. To escort them on their departure and meet them on their coming; to commend the good among them, and show compassion to the incompetent: this is the way to treat foreigners indulgently.

In short, the government should make the state a center of industry and commerce. In order to accomplish this aim it must encourage immigration.

It is very important to know that, although Confucius is in favor of agriculture, he leaves it out of the nine standard rules, and mentions only industry and commerce. In order to bring out this point we must give the nine standard rules fully. They are as follows: (1) the cultivation of the personality of the ruler, (2) the honoring of men of virtue and talents, (3) affection toward relatives, (4) respect toward the great ministers, (5) kind and considerate treatment of the whole body of officials, (6) dealing with the mass of the people as children, (7) inducing all classes of artisans to come in, (8) indulgent treatment of foreigners, and (9) the kindly cherishing of the princes of the feudal states. This is a complete program of government It begins with the personal character of the ruler himself; for such a purpose his familiar friends must be men of virtue and talents. Then he must be affectionate to the relatives of his family, and must be good to all the officials and the people. These six rules are all applied within the limit of his own state. Now, for international relations, they are governed by the last three rules. Excepting the last rule as a diplomatic principle, the other two are economic doctrines. It is interesting to see that Confucius always regards economic life not as a national phenomenon, but an international one. Therefore, he does not give any economic principle until he reaches the seventh and eighth rules. It is exactly for this same reason that the "Great Learning" does not touch any economic problem until under the last chapter, namely, the equalizing of the whole world.[1]

Now, we come back to our point. So far as the nine rules are concerned, none of them are economic principles except the seventh and the eighth. But these two rules refer to industry and commerce only, and agriculture is left out entirely. There may be several reasons for this. First, agriculture may be included in industry and commerce, because the one is the primary industry and the other two are secondary. Second, for international competition, industry and commerce may be preferred to agriculture.

[1] *Cf. supra*, pp. 141-144.

Third, since there is a great immigration of "all classes of artisans" and "the people of all quarters," industry and commerce, rather than agriculture, are needed to support such a large population. Confucius may have had all these three points in mind as reasons for referring to industry and commerce only and leaving agriculture out.

There is still another point. For the effect of the indulgent treatment of foreigners, Confucius mentions only that "the people of all quarters will come;" but for that of inducing all classes of artisans to come in, he points out very clearly that "the wealth is made sufficient." Therefore, if a state wants to make wealth sufficient, it must resort to industry. Industry alone can create new wealth, while commerce simply creates new value upon the existing wealth. From this point of view, we may say that Confucius knows the importance of industrial capital. All those points mentioned above are the economic principles of Confucius.[1]

Although the policy of "inducing all classes of artisans to come in" has not been realized in China, it has been carried out very successfully in England and the United States. During the reigns of Edward III and of Elizabeth, the immigration of Flemish workmen gave a great impetus to English industry. It has also contributed to the progress of the United States since 2371 A. K. or 1820 A. D. Had the immigrants not come, the United States would not have been so prosperous as at present. Unfortunately, since China stood as an isolated country for a long period, this policy did not have any marked effect upon her, because the workmanship of the surrounding countries was much lower than that of China. To-day, by the change of methods, China really demands a great number of skilled workmen. But the political interference of foreign countries is a

[1] *Classics*, vol. i, pp. 408-411.

temporary bar to block this demand. We are sure, however, that such a bar cannot last very long, and that the principle of " inducing all classes of artisans to come in " will have a great triumph in the future.

4. *Absence of Race Question*

According to the principles of the *Spring and Autumn*, a nation is called either civilized or uncivilized, not on account of blood, or of geography, but on account of true civilization—rites and justice. There is no race or state which can permanently assume the title of civilized nation unless its actions be just. This is the principle of Confucius; hence, the Chinese have no race question at all.

The absence of race questions in China is due, however, not only to the teachings of Confucius, but also to geographical causes. As China is located in the greatest continent, together with great mountains and rivers, she has produced one great people, and has had no opportunity for a race question. Every one can see from Chinese history that China has accepted any religion and any race from any part of the world. The so-called barbarians were made not only common citizens, but also prominent officials, either civil or military, and feudal princes. Although we have no full knowledge about the earliest history, from the Chou dynasty to the present day, China has had no race prejudice against any other nationality.

The best example of this was given by the Tang dynasty. In 1181 A. K. (630 A. D.), after the Turkish nation was destroyed, besides those who ran to the West, the number who surrendered to the Tang dynasty was about one hundred thousand. Tang T'ai Tsung ordered his courtiers to debate on the treatment of the Turks. Some one wanted to drive them back to their old place. But Wun Yen-po said:

An emperor to the myriad of things is like the covering of heaven and the containing of earth without any exclusion. Now, the Turks come to us because they are powerless. Why should we refuse them? Confucius said that when there is the teaching, there should be no distinction between the races. If we relieve them from death, give them economic occupations, and teach them rites and justice, after several years they will be entirely our citizens. Then we can select their chiefs to come to the capital and to become the imperial guards. Thus they will fear our power and love our virtue. What will be the danger in the future?

T'ai Tsung finally used this policy. He divided their territory into several provinces, and appointed their leaders as the governors. When the Turkish chiefs came to court, they were all appointed as military commanders, and occupied offices in the court. Above the fifth official rank, they amounted to more than one hundred persons, nearly half of the number of the Chinese courtiers. Hence, the Turks living in the capital were about ten thousand families.[1] This shows how broad-minded the Chinese people are. Even when the Turks were conquered, they gave them immediately equality of political rights. Indeed, they put the barbarian races upon the same footing with their own, and assimilated them.

We may ask a question: Why did, and does, the race problem arise in the western world? It seems that it is due to geographical smallness. Since Europe is not a real continent, but only a peninsula of Asia, there are many geographical subdivisions and many small islands and peninsulas. In such an environment, European sectional feeling has been fostered. In ancient times, the Greeks and the Romans, except Alexander and Caesar, knew only the city-

[1] *General Political History*, published in 1635 (1084 A. D.) by Ssŭ-ma Kuang, ch. cxciii.

state. Even in the *Republic* of Plato, his idea is only a city-state, and everything depends upon war. In modern times, the European race feeling is still worse. This seems to be the product of the geographical situation.

Now, we may turn to the United States of America. The United States was founded in the new world by virtuous men, and the Americans are more broad-minded than the Europeans. When the nation grew a little older, however, the old good-faith became less, and the Chinese Exclusion Act began (2433 A. K. or 1882 A. D.). It seems that race prejudice does not come from the American continent itself—such a great new world should not produce such a narrow idea—but from the European peninsula, and especially from the new immigrants. The Exclusion Act is an extremely bad example to the world, and is a serious blemish on the glorious American history. From this point of view, the Americans are inferior to the Chinese.

IV. CONDITIONS WITH REFERENCE TO POPULATION IN CHINA

The reasons for China's large population may be examined from two viewpoints—the relation of husband and wife and the relation of father and son. In other words, we may explain it by the customs of marriage and the doctrine of filial piety.

1. *Marriage*

(a) *Importance of Marriage*

The religion of Confucius is very different from Buddhism and Catholicism. It offers no objection to marriage. Confucius regards marriage not only as human happiness, but as human duty. Mencius says: " That male and female should dwell together is the greatest of human relations." [1] The aged widower and the aged widow are classified as

[1] *Classics*, vol. ii, p. 346.

324   THE ECONOMIC PRINCIPLES OF CONFUCIUS

the most unfortunate people. If marriage is too late, it is regarded as unhappiness. When Mencius describes the social life of the reign of Tai Wang (died in 680 B. K. or 1231 B. C.), the grandfather of Wên Wang, he says: "At that time, in the inside there were no dissatisfied women, and in the outside there were no lonesome men." This means that all married at the proper time. Such a theory has a great influence on the Chinese population. In China there are practically no unmarried people, except when under special circumstances they are forced to leave their families and become Buddhists. In fact, there are very few people who voluntarily remain in single life. Hence, the Chinese population is the largest in the world.

(b) *Day of Marriage*

Although Confucius thinks that marriage is necessary, he does not make the day of marriage early. A man takes the first ceremony of marriage—that is, the capping—at twenty years, and has a wife at thirty. A woman takes the first ceremony—that is, binding up the hair with the hair-pin—at fifteen, and marries at twenty. If she has not been engaged, she will assume the hair-pin at twenty, and under some circumstances she may marry at twenty-three.[1] This general rule is given in the *Record of Rites* and many other books. It makes the day of marriage so late not as a check to the growth of population, but as a provision for physical development and personal responsibility. The *Great Commentary of the Canon of History* says that the woman may marry at twenty years, because at that time she can understand all the family duties and domestic science, otherwise she could neither serve her parents-in-law, help her husband, nor breed her children.

During the Han dynasty (491 A. K. or 61 B. C.), Wang

[1] *Li Ki*, bk. x, pp. 478-9.

LABOR - POPULATION   325

Chi proposed his theory of marriage to the emperor. He thought that marriage is the primary form of social relationship and determines the length of life. If the day of marriage is too early, the pair may have children when they do not understand their parental duties. Therefore, the moral influence is weak, and the people frequently die prematurely. Moreover, if the expenditure on marriage has no limit, poor people, either men or women, cannot marry. Therefore, they do not want to raise children.[1] This theory, although it was not carried out by law, is a general thought of the Chinese.

There are two points in this discussion. One is to improve the physical condition of the people by the postponement of marriage, in order to increase the average length of life. The other is to encourage the marriage of the poor, in order to increase the population. They are not checks, but aids, to population. In China, as ceremony is very important and social relation is very close, marriage is very expensive on both the male and the female side, even among the poorest people. Therefore, the Chinese always try to reduce its expense by reforms of custom, in order to make marriage easy. In short, the people generally think that men or women are happier married than alone, and that wealth will be increased as the number of men increases. Generally speaking, the Chinese marry earlier than Confucius prescribes.[2]

---

[1] *History of Han*, ch. lxxii.

[2] In Confucius' time, Wu and Yüeh were the two rival states. When Wu conquered Yüeh (58 A. K. or 494 B. C.), she did not take it for her own possession. After peace was made, the king of Yüeh established this policy: The young men should not take the old women, nor the old men the young women. When a girl at seventeen, or a man at twenty, had not married, their parents were held guilty. When a woman was about to give birth to a child, the king should be informed beforehand; then she was cared for by the public physician. If the

(c) *Exogamy*

There are two important customs which have brought about the large population of China—the one is exogamy and the other polygyny. In *Tso's Commentary* the principle of the first institution is given as follows: "When husband and wife are of the same clan, their children do not prosper and multiply."[1] This is a biological principle discovered eighty-six years before Confucius. But this principle had been in practice, by law, since the time of the Duke of Chou (about 564 B. K. or 1115 B. C.). The *Record of Rites* says: "According to the rule of Chou, there is no intermarriage among the same clan, even after a hundred generations."[2] This means that there is no intermarriage of the male lines of the common remotest ancestor. This rule has been observed by all the Chinese. From this principle, on the one hand, the Chinese have enlarged their own race; on the other, they have assimilated all other races. About three thousand years ago different races commingled in China, as the Americans do now.

According to the principles of the *Spring and Autumn*, a man should not marry the relatives of his mother. The reason here is the same as that a man should not marry the daughter of the same clan. This principle is also applied to the lines of the sisters of his father. In the *Law Code of the Ts'ing Dynasty* this principle is applied to a very great

---

child was a boy, two pots of wine and a dog were given; if a girl, the same amount of wine and a pig. If the mother gave birth to three children, the king supplied a nurse; to two children, he supplied food. He took different kinds of food with him while traveling, in order to feed children. These were his policies for the increasing of population for military purposes. Twenty-one years later, he succeeded in conquering Wu and took it for his own.—*Narratives of Nations*, bk. xx.

[1] *Classics*, vol. v, pt. i, p. 187.

[2] *Li Ki*, bk. xiv, p. 63.

extent.[1] Such exogamy has two great reasons: On the ethical side, it promotes the moral sense and prevents the people from falling in love with their relatives. On the biological side, it gives physical betterment to the couple themselves and multiplies their offspring. This is the second point which has a great effect upon the question of population.

(d) *Polygyny*

For the explanation of the Chinese population, the practice of polygyny must also be referred to. It was an old custom, and it was not abolished, but reformed, by Confucius. According to his regulation, the emperor may have twelve females; the prince, nine; the great official, three; the student, two; the common people, only one. Some authorities say that the emperor and the prince both may have only nine females. Therefore we may take the marriage of the prince as the maximum example. When the prince marries a queen from a foreign nation, she takes her younger sister and niece along with her; then two other nations respectively send one companion to her, together with the companion's younger sister and niece, the whole party being nine females.

The reason the emperor and the prince may have nine females is that they represent the sovereignty of the state and their succession is very important. If they have no son from these nine females, however, they have no reason to take any more. Their marriage is finished at this one time; no second marriage is allowed. They must marry girls outside of their own state. All these regulations make them more respectful and prevent them from loving other women. The younger sisters and nieces, although they may be too young, must accompany the queen at the time of marriage,

[1] Ch. x.

but later return to their own states and remain there until the age of twenty. Why does the queen or the companion take her younger sister and niece along? It is that there may be no jealousy; when one of them has a son, the three will have the same pleasure. Why does she not take two younger sisters instead of the niece? It is because the physical condition of the niece may differ from that of her sister. Why does the prince take girls from three different states? It is for the diversification of the races, lest the girls of the same state have the same blood and give no son at all. In short, all these details make the emperor and the prince sure to have more sons—a political necessity.

The reason the great official may have three females is in honor of the wise and able man, and because of the importance of continuing his lineage. Below the class of great official, the student may have two females. For the common people there is monogamy; hence they are called " single man and single woman."

Although Confucius did not abolish polygyny, he did reform it. At that time the emperor regularly had one hundred and twenty-one females; the prince must have had more than nine; the great official more than three; the student more than two; and the common people more than one. But he reduced the number to a certain limit and did not allow the emperor and the prince to marry a second time. By these means he markedly checked the prevailing custom. During his age, all the great officials, not only the emperor and the princes, held their office by hereditary right; hence, the succession of their family was an important thing. Moreover, Confucius himself thought that the perpetuation of family is a great duty of man. Therefore, he did not, and could not, abolish polygyny entirely.

Confucius' reason for not abolishing polygyny—that is, that a family may perpetuate its lineage—applies especially to the feudal stage. But we must understand that Confucius is in favor of monogamy. Although the emperor, the prince, the great official, and the student may have more than one female, each of them has only one wife. The other females are concubines, simply for the producing of sons, and they cannot be called wives. Since a son is very important for the paternal family, and one wife may fail to give birth to a son, the concubine is recognized by Confucius. But Confucius himself did not have any concubine, although he had the right to have two. In the *Canon of Changes*, he says: " When two women live together, their minds do not move in the same direction." Again he says: " When two women live together, their minds do not agree with each other." [1] From his own practice and from these two passages, we may be sure that he is in favor of monogamy. Indeed, polygyny is for the Disorderly Stage, and monogamy for the Advancing Peace Stage.

As a matter of fact, the Chinese do not follow the regulations of Confucius. They may have as many concubines as their condition allows, although there must be a natural limit. This is an evil custom, indeed, but it still has some merit. From the moral and social point of view, since a man may have concubines openly, he will not resort to prostitution or illegitimate intercourse. From the economic point of view, it may relieve some poor girls from deep poverty. But most important of all is that the practice of polygyny has increased the population to a great extent. This is the reason why we discuss it here. The Chinese, however, are likely to change polygyny into monogamy before very long.

[1] *Yi King*, pp. 243, 253.

2. *Doctrine of Filial Piety*

(a) *Perpetuation of the Family*

In the world there is no nation that has perpetuated its people as a particular race so long as has China. It is the contribution of Confucius, because he preaches the doctrine of filial piety. According to this doctrine the perpetuation of the family is the chief duty of man. Confucius says: " Since the parents have given birth to a son, it is the perpetuation of the human race, and there is nothing greater than this." [1] Hence, a son must continue the line of his parents. Mencius says: " There are three things which are unfilial; but to have no posterity is the greatest of them." [2] The other two unfilial things are, according to Chao Ch'i (died 752 A. K. or 201 A. D.), the commentator, first, by a flattering assent to encourage parents in unrighteousness; and second, not to succor their poverty and old age by engaging in official service. To be without posterity is a fault greater than these, because it is an offense against the whole line of ancestors and terminates the sacrifices to them.

In short, by the statement of Confucius, to give birth to a son is the greatest contribution of the parents to society as a whole; and by that of Mencius, to have no posterity is the greatest offense of a son against all his ancestors. Therefore, the perpetuation of the family is the chief duty of both father and son.

Since we have already discussed the doctrine of filial piety (and the custom of ancestor-worship) from the religious and ethical point of view, we shall now look at it only from its influence on the Chinese population. Under the influence of Confucius, every one wants to marry in order to have sons. The parents can never be satisfied until they finish

---

[1] *Sacred Books*, vol. iii, p. 479.
[2] *Classics*, vol. ii, p. 313.

for their children the proceeding of marriage, which they regard as an obligation. Among very poor families, it is even the social duty of their friends to help them to marry.

If one has no son, he may take a concubine in the hope of having posterity, and his wife almost always agrees to it. If he has no prospect of having a son, he may adopt a son, either from his own clan or from another. Sometimes even, when he dies prematurely, not having married at all, his family adopts a son for him, in order to continue his lineage.

(b) *Return to the Parents*

While the perpetuation of the family is the strongest motive impelling the Chinese to have sons, another stimulus is the expected return to the parents. Since we have already discussed this principle, there is no need of any further explanation. We now simply point out that it has a great influence upon the Chinese population. As we have seen, China makes the support of parents a positive law. The parents usually derive their support from their sons. Although the sons are not necessarily dutiful enough to support their parents, the custom has behind it a very strong public opinion; hence, the return to the parents is a general expectation. Therefore, when one has no son, he regards it as the greatest of misfortunes. First, he is afraid that his lineage will be extinguished. Second, he has no hope of being supported in his old age. Third, even when he has no need of support, he needs a son as an object of pleasure, a performer of social and religious duties, *etc.* In fact, desire for sons among the Chinese is stronger than among any other people.

The return to the parents may be divided into two categories. One is the material return. Since the support of parents is an obligation of the sons, the parents claim the duties from their sons as creditors from debtors. Hence, the bringing-up of children may be regarded as a provision for the later part of life. Indeed, it is equivalent to an insurance policy, providing a sickness benefit, unemployment benefit, old-age benefit, funeral benefit, *etc*.

The other is the immaterial return, and it may be divided into three things. First, the son may return honor to his parents during their life. Ts'ĕng Tzŭ says: " He whom the superior man pronounces filial is he whom all the people of his state praise, saying with admiration, ' Happy are the parents who have such a son as this!'—that indeed is what can be called being filial." [1] Second, he may return honor to them after their death. Confucius says that to make our name famous in future ages, and thereby glorify our parents, is the end of filial piety.[2] The " Pattern of the Family " says:

Although his parents be dead, when a son is inclined to do what is good, he should think that he will thereby transmit the good name of his parents, and carry his wish into effect. When he is inclined to do what is not good, he should think that he will thereby bring disgrace on the name of his parents, and in no wise carry his wish into effect.[3]

Since Confucius regards the name as a very important thing, the parents have expectations from the glory of their sons. In China, whatever official title a son may get may be transmitted to his parents either during their life or after their death, and also to his grandparents and great-grandparents. Third, the son may return homage to his parents in the form of ancestor-worship. Thus we can see how the principle of the returns to parents helps to bring about China's great population.

---

[1] *Li Ki*, bk. xxi, pp. 226-7.   [2] See *supra*, p. 114.
[3] *Li Ki*, bk. x, p. 457.

V. HISTORICAL STUDY OF POPULATION

The word population is expressed in the Chinese language by two words, " door " and " mouth." " Door " means a family, and " mouth " a person. But we do not like to translate the word "door" into the word family, because China had the "door tax," which made the people conceal their families, and the word "door" cannot represent the word family. For the same reason, the people concealed their number in order to escape the " mouth tax," and so the word " mouth " cannot represent the word person. We shall use these original words, "door" and " mouth," to stand as a picture of the historical Chinese population, and give our population statistics in those terms. Although it is too far from the real figures, it is the only way by which we can get any idea about the history of Chinese population. Therefore, we shall give the most important figures, whether the largest or the smallest, of the most important periods, in the form of a table. From the table we can judge something not only about the real population, but also about the economic, social and political conditions.

Population of China at Different Periods

Era of Confucius	Era of Reigning Dynasties	Number of Doors	Number of Mouths	Era of Christ
1654 B. K. (about)	Hsia Yü		13,553,923	2205 B.C.
504 " (about)	Chou Ch'êng Wang		13,714,923	1115 "
132 " "	13th year of Chou Chuang Wang		11,941,923	683 "
219 A. K.	36th year of Chou Hsien Wang		30,000,000 (about)	333 "
352 "	7th year of Han Kao Ti		5,000,000 (about)	200 "
553 "	2d year of Han P'ing Ti	12,233,062	59,594,978	2 A.D.
608 "	The last year of Han Kuang-wu	4,279,634	21,007,820	57 "
707 "	Han Huan Ti	16,070,906	50,066,856	156 "
814 " (about)	Three Kingdoms	1,473,423	7,672,801	263 "
831 "	Tsin Wu Ti	2,459,804	16,163,863	280 "
1044 " (about)	Southern and Northern Dynasties	6,000,000 (about)	40,000,000 (about)	493 "
1131 " (about)	Southern and Northern Dynasties	4,090,000	11,009,604	580 "
1157 "	2d year of Sui Yang Ti	8,907,536	46,019,956	606 "
1178 " (about)	1st year of Tang T'ai Tsung	3,000,000 (less)		627 "
1305 "	Tang Hsüan Tsung	9,619,254	52,009,309	754 "
1311 "	Tang Su Tsung	1,933,134	16,990,386	760 "
1396 "	5th year of Tang Wu Tsung	4,955,151		845 "
1527 "	Last year of Sung T'ai Tsu	3,090,504		976 "
1653 "	2d year of Sung Hui Tsung	20,019,050	43,820,769	1102 "
1711 "	Sung Kao Tsung	11,375,733	19,229,008	1166 "
1744 "	Sung Kuang Tsung	12,302,873	27,845,085	1193 "
1774 "	Sung Ning Tsung	12,670,801	28,320,085	1223 "
1758 "	Kin Chang Tsung	7,684,438	45,816,079	1207 "
1758 " (about)	Sung and Kin	20,355,239	74,136,164	1207 "
1841 "	Yüan Shih Tsu	13,196,206	58,834,711	1290 "
1932 "	14th year of Ming T'ai Tsu	10,654,362	50,873,305	1381 "
1954 "	1st year of Ming Ch'êng Tsu	11,415,829	66,598,337	1403 "
2172 "	1st year of Ming Hsi Tsung	9,825,426	51,655,459	1621 "
2212 "	18th year of Ts'ing Shih Tsu		21,068,609	1661 "
2262 "	50th year of Ts'ing Shêng Tsu		24,621,334	1711 "
2300 "	14th year of Ts'ing Kao Tsung		177,495,039	1749 "
2334 "	48th year of Ts'ing Kao Tsung		284,033,755	1783 "
2393 "	22d year of Ts'ing Hsüan Tsung		413,020,000	1842 "

LABOR-POPULATION

The above table shows the size of the population of China proper throughout all the ages, and is based mostly upon the *Three General Researches*.[1] Their materials came from history, and those of history came from the official reports. All the figures of this table are quoted from the *Three General Researches* except those for the years 219 A. K. and 352 A. K., which are estimates. At the end of the Yüan dynasty, about 1918 A. K., although it is an important period, we cannot make an estimate, because there is no basis. All the dates of this table are also quoted from the *Three General Researches*; but in a few cases dates are uncertain, and we have inserted the word " about " to indicate that the dates may not be exact. All the figures and dates of this table are based on a very careful study.

1. *Inaccuracy of this Table*

The statements of this table are very far from accurate. (1) In the reigns of Hsia Yü, of Chou Ch'êng Wang and of Chou Chuang Wang, there are no real records in regard to the population, but only the estimates of Huang-fu Mi (766-833 A. K. or 215-282 A. D.), a great authority.

(2) The most trustworthy figures are those of the Han dynasty.

(3) Among the Three Kingdoms, about 814, the Wei kingdom and the Shu kingdom both had only 943,423 doors and 5,372,891 mouths. After Tsin Wu Ti succeeded to the Wei kingdom, which included the Shu kingdom, he conquered the Wu kingdom in 831 and took 530,000 doors and 2,300,000 mouths by his conquest. The total number of these two sets of figures in 831 was 1,473,423 doors and 7,672,891

---

[1] They are (1) the *General Research on Literature and Authorities*, chs. x-xi; (2) the *Continuation of the General Research on Literature and Authorities*, chs. xii-xiii; and (3) the *General Research on Literature and Authorities of the Present Dynasty*, ch. iii.

mouths. Why should Tsin Wu Ti in the same year (831) have 2,459,804 doors and 16,163,863 mouths? Although from 814 to 831 the number of the first would increase, it could hardly have doubled in the short space of seventeen years. It seems that the historian's mistake arose from taking the number of the population toward the close of Wu Ti's reign (about 840) and putting it in the year when he had just reunited the whole empire (831).

(4) The Tang dynasty began in 1169, and had lasted 137 years in 1305. At that time the people enjoyed a long golden age, and the population must have increased. Tu Yu says: " It should at least have thirteen or fourteen millions of doors." But, according to this table, in 1305 it had only 9,619,254 doors.

(5) In the Former Han dynasty, the average number of mouths for ten doors was more than 48; in the Latter Han dynasty it was 52 mouths, and in the Tang dynasty, 58 mouths. But in the Sung dynasty it was only 21 mouths. There is no reason why one family should have only two persons. For instance, in 1774, the 12,670,801 doors of the Sung dynasty had only 28,320,085 mouths. But in 1758, the 7,684,438 doors of the Kin dynasty had 45,816,079 mouths. There is no reason why the Sung dynasty, which had doors nearly double those of the Kin dynasty, should have about half as many mouths as the latter. According to this table, each door of Kin had more than six mouths. If we should take a rate as low as five mouths to each door, Sung should have 63,354,005 mouths. Adding the mouths of Kin on this reasonable estimate, China should have had at least 109,170,084 mouths in 1758.

(6) The census of the Ming dynasty is still worse. We select the figures only about its beginning and its end. In 1932 the revolutionary war had only recently ended, and in 1954 the civil war was just finished. If the population

LABOR - POPULATION

at those periods had grown as large as this table shows, why should it become smaller in the later peaceful time? In fact, China was never able to get a census that was even approximately accurate until 2300.

2. *Causes of the Inaccuracy*

Why did China not have an accurate census? There is a sound reason for it. Because China had a monarchical government it did not touch the people closely, and because the people did not directly enjoy political interest very much they tried to escape from the taxes. Since the "door tax" and the "mouth tax" depended entirely upon the number of the population, the people had to conceal their number in order to evade the taxes; hence, none understood the real population. In the Han dynasty the two taxes were very light, so that the numbers of the population were more trustworthy. After that time, the two taxes were higher, but the number of the population was lower. Why did the government, however, not exercise its force in order to get the full amount of taxes? It is because the government was under the Confucian influence. The Confucian doctrines, such as "Love the people," "light tax," and "benevolent government," were familiar to all the rulers. Hence, the Chinese government generally never dared to exercise a despotic force directly upon the people. If the people wanted to conceal anything, the government could not find it out, because it did not control the actual life of the people. Moreover, the mandarin would have some deep ideas. For example, when Ma Jên-wang [1] made his census he finished it in less than twenty days. Some one was surprised, and questioned him. He said: "If the numbers of population were taken inclusively without remainder, it will induce the

[1] He was made minister of the Liao dynasty in 1664 (1113 A. D.).

trouble of a heavy tax in the future. Generally, taking six or seven out of ten is quite enough." But we must not make such a mistake as to think that the Confucians do not care to have an accurate census. Indeed, the Confucians regard the population as the most important thing and value highly an accurate census. A light tax is one thing, but an accurate census is another. Yet, on account of the door tax and the mouth tax, China could not get a good census.

3. *Significance of this Table*

Although this table is inaccurate, it is still valuable. If one could completely understand these figures he would be able to master the whole Chinese history. The really hereditary monarchical empire was founded by Hsia Yü. At that time the population was more than thirteen millions. The beginning of the Chou dynasty was a golden age. As China in about 564 B. K. had more than thirteen millions of population, she should possess much more two hundred years later, because this peaceful period lasted for about three hundred years. We may think that this period fostered the most wonderful civilization of the period of Spring and Autumn (171 B. K.-71 A. K.) and that of Warring States (149-331 A. K.).

As a destroyer of population, war is the worst influence. According to this table, in the beginning of the Han dynasty the population lost five-sixths; in the beginning of the Latter Han dynasty, about two-thirds; in the Three Kingdoms, about six-sevenths; in the latter part of the Southern and Northern Dynasties, about three-fourths; in the beginning of the Tang dynasty, about two-thirds; in the reign of Tang Su Tsung, within the period of only five years, it lost over two-thirds: in the beginning of the Sung dynasty, about two-fifths; in the beginning of the Southern Sung dynasty, more than half; in the beginning of the Yüan dynasty, measured by the number of the "doors," it lost over one-third; in the beginning of the present dynasty it lost about three-fifths. From this point of view, the revolutionary war was a great calamity. It not only destroyed the population, but retarded civilization.

In Chinese history, when her civilization advanced to a high level, it was dragged down by warfare. When, after a long time, it rose again, it fell again. It is no wonder that the Chinese progressed so slowly. But, through modern inventions, such as the railroad, telegraph, telephone, *etc.*, which will enable her to change absolute monarchy into a really constitutional monarchy, China may avoid such internal wars as have troubled her in the past, and will permit her civilization continuously to progress. Moreover, as China can never be conquered by any external power, she will be able to change a constitutional monarchy into a real republic, and she might form a world-state with the leading nations, and might realize the Great Similarity of Confucius. Then the whole population of the world will enjoy the Stage of Extreme Peace without any war.

It should be noticed that the magnitude of the figures in this table does not necessarily reflect upon the reigning rulers. Generally, the ruler of the beginning of a dynasty was an able or good man, and that of its decay a weak or bad man. But at the beginning of a dynasty the population would be small, and about the time of its decay it would be large; for in the former case it would suffer from the hard times of the past, and in the latter case it would enjoy the good fortune of the past. This table indicates only the facts of history and does not show exactly what the governments were during the given years. As a rule, however, a large population would be produced under a good government, but such a result would of course follow only after a considerable period.

The most wonderful increase of population was during the Sui dynasty. In the first year of Sui Wên Ti's reign (1132 A. K.), he had only 9,009,604 mouths. In his ninth year (1140 A. K.), he took 2,000,000 mouths from the Southern Chen dynasty. The total number was 11,009,604 mouths. But in 1157 A. K., when only twenty-five years had passed, his son had 46,019,956 mouths. The population increased over fourfold within twenty-five years. It seems that the figures for population increased not on account of the birth-rate only, but mainly on account of the system of taxation. After the great statesman of Sui, named Kao Kung, established a system of taxation in favor of the free citizens by making the taxes light, the people did not like to be the dependents of the higher class for the purpose of evading taxes; hence the number of citizens who paid taxes increased rapidly. Indeed, the Sui dynasty was the richest one in Chinese financial history.

According to this table, before 2300 the population never numbered over one hundred millions. Why should the population figures of the present dynasty be much larger than those of all the past dynasties? It is because the present dynasty has neither "door tax" nor "mouth tax." In 2212 A. K. the number was 21,068,609, and in 2262, 24,-621,334. Throughout fifty peaceful years the population increased only 3,552,725. But in 2300 A. K. the number was 177,495,039. It increased more than seven times in the thirty-eight years. Why should the figures increase so rapidly as this? It was because Shêng Tsu had abolished these two taxes in 2263. His decree is as follows:

The empire has been peaceful for a long time, so that the population increases numerously. If I increase the amount of taxes according to the present number of population, it is not right; for, although the population becomes larger, the acreage of land does not become wider.[1] . . . To-day the public treasury is very rich. Although I have frequently given the exemption, which amounted to ten millions, for several years, the national expenditure has never any trouble of insufficiency. Therefore, I should take the number of people from the present tax-roll as a fixed number to be taxed, and the increased population of the future shall be exempted from any additional tax. What I want is merely the report of the true numbers.

Then the legislature established the law that the amount of poll tax is permanently fixed according to the number of the tax-roll in the year 2262, and that the new increased number, which is called " the increasing population of the prosperous age," shall never be taxed.

This marks a new epoch in Chinese economic history. The population began to show its approximate number in 2300 A. K. Through thirty-four years, to 2334 A. K., the population increased more than half. Through fifty-nine years, to 2393 A. K., it increased less than half. During the T'ai-p'ing rebellion (2401-2417 A. K.) it may have lost a hundred and fifty millions. Although the census of the present dynasty is still not very accurate, it is near the truth. In a few years, when China shall have a regular parliament, accurate statistics of population should be available.

[1] This suggests the Malthusian doctrine.

CHAPTER XIX

NATURE AND CAPITAL

I. NATURE

1. *The Five Elements*

SINCE land is only one part of nature, we should first consider all the elements of nature. For this reason we may take up the five elements as presenting an exhaustive classification of natural forces. Although the five elements are the basis of Chinese philosophy, we are concerned here with their economic aspects only.

The "Great Model" puts the five elements in the first of the nine categories. The first element is water; the second, fire; the third, wood; the fourth, metal; the fifth, earth. The five elements in the Chinese language are called "the five movements," because they move and revolve throughout heaven and earth without ceasing. In 6 A. K. (546 B. C.), Tzŭ-han, prime minister of Sung, says: "Heaven has produced the five elements which supply men's requirements, and the people use them all. Not one of them can be dispensed with."[1] The Chinese regard all the five elements as the natural forces upon which human life depends.

After having given the names of the five elements, the "Great Model" describes their nature. "The nature of water is to soak and descend; of fire, to blaze and ascend; of wood, to be crooked and to be straight; of metal, to obey and to change; while the virtue of earth is seen in seed-

---

[1] *Classics*, vol. v, pt. ii, p. 534.

sowing and ingathering." Then it gives the tastes of the five elements: "That which soaks and descends becomes salt; that which blazes and ascends becomes bitter; that which is crooked and straight becomes sour; that which obeys and changes becomes acrid; and from seed-sowing and ingathering comes sweetness."[1] The five elements have their several sounds, colors and airs, as well as tastes; but the text speaks only of their tastes, because they are of greater importance to the people than the others, and they can be the representatives of the others. Leaving out all philosophical points, we may say that the five elements are the basis of production and consumption.

The *Great Commentary of the Canon of History* says: "Water and fire are the things by which the people eat and drink; metal and wood are the things by which the people labor; earth is the thing upon which the life of everything depends. All these give their utilities to man." Therefore, the five elements are originally free goods, because they are produced by nature.

Adding the grain to the five elements, the Chinese call them "the six treasuries." Such a term first appears in the "Tribute of Yü." It says that the six treasuries are greatly regulated.[2] Because the grain is the food of the people, they regard it as equally important with the five elements. According to *Tso's Commentary*, water, fire, metal, wood, earth, and grain are called the six treasuries. They are called treasuries because they are the sources of wealth which depend upon nature. The rectification of the people's virtue, the conveniences of life, and the securing abundant means of sustenance, are called "the three businesses." The six treasuries and the three businesses are called "the nine services."[3] The distinction between the

[1] *Classics*, vol. iii, pt. ii, pp. 325-6. [2] *Ibid.*, pt. i, p. 141.
[3] *Classics*, vol. v, pt. i, p. 250.

six treasuries and the three businesses is that the former are produced by natural power. But the six treasuries, although they depend upon nature, are to be regulated by human power. Therefore, all these are called nine services.

The manner of regulating the six treasuries may be illustrated by a few examples. In ancient times there were many officers controlling these six things. During the reign of Shun, the chief duty of the prime minister was to regulate water and earth. Even after "the great floods" had been repressed (1725 B. K. or 2276 B. C.), the regulation of water remained important to man. Irrigation, navigation, and carrying off the floods are examples of regulating water. Anciently, the regulations of fire were numerous. According to the *Official System of Chou*, there is a bureau of fire. In procuring fire by boring wood, certain woods were assigned to be employed in the four seasons, in order to prevent the seasonal diseases. In spring the fire was taken from the elm and willow; in summer, from the date and almond trees; in the last month of summer, from the mulberry and the wild mulberry trees; in autumn, from the oak and the *yu*; in winter, from the *huai* and the *tan*. In the third month the people were ordered to use fire for pottery and foundery, and in the ninth month they were forbidden to use fire for this purpose. In the hunting of the second month fire was used for the burning of the old grass; after that time the people should be fined if they set fire to the field without permission.[1] Metals and woods were similarly regulated by rules in regard to the management of mines and forests. As to the regulating of the earth and of the grains, we shall speak later.

[1] *Official System of Chou*, ch. xxx.

2. *Control over Nature*

The acme of human power is to control nature. If man can control nature, he is equal to the Supreme Power. But how can man have such power? It is by the most complete sincerity. Indeed, it is the result of the most careful and thorough study of the truth. This is told by the " Doctrine of the Mean." It says:

It is only he who is possessed of the most complete sincerity that can exist in the world, who can give its full development to his nature. Able to give its full development to his own nature, he can do the same to the nature of other men. Able to give its full development to the nature of other men, he can give their full development to the natures of animals and things. Able to give their full development to the natures of creatures and things, he can assist the transforming and nourishing powers of Heaven and Earth. Able to assist the transforming and nourishing powers of Heaven and Earth, he may with Heaven and Earth form a triumvirate.[1]

The doctrine of controlling nature is very clearly given by Hsun Tzŭ. The seventeenth book of his work is entitled " Essay on Heaven ". He uses the word heaven most often in the sense of nature, but we may preserve the word heaven. He says:

Strongly clinging to the primary industry and saving expenditure, heaven cannot make you poor; when the subsistence is complete, and working at a due time, heaven cannot make you sick. . . . If the primary industry is neglected, and the expenditure is extravagant, heaven cannot make you rich; if the subsistence is insufficient, and the working time is contrary to the natural law, heaven cannot make you healthy.

[1] *Classics*, vol. i, p. 416.

This shows that the accumulation of capital and the preservation of labor are both dependent upon man, and not upon heaven.

According to the theory of Hsun Tzŭ, man is the one who can form a triumvirate with Heaven and Earth. What we call "divine" is simply "the natural deed." A sage does not care to know the Heaven, the supernatural power. When a man has "the natural feelings" and "the natural senses," the most important thing for the control of them is "the natural king," the mind. To use the mind for the control of those things outside of the human race is "the natural support," and "the law of natural selection." Therefore, when the natural king is supreme, man "can employ the heaven and earth as the officers and exploit all things as the slaves." This is a materialistic and scientific doctrine in regard to the relation of man and nature. The chief power is the human mind, the natural king.

Now, he makes a comparison between those who can control nature and those who cannot, as follows:

To honor nature and to expect something from it, is not as good as to accumulate things and to shape them. To follow nature and to praise it, is not as good as to control what nature has given and to employ them. To expect the time and wait for it, is not so good as to seize it and to use it. To increase the things according to themselves, is not so good as to transform them by the exercise of human power. To wish the thing and to get the thing as it is, is not so good as to deal with the thing and not to lose any utility of it. To expect the thing grown by nature, is not so good as to have the thing manufactured by man. Therefore, to set aside the power of man and to depend on the power of nature is to lose the nature of everything.

Hence, according to Hsun Tzŭ, man is not the dependent of nature, but its controller.

3. *Conservation of Natural Resources*

The conservation of natural resources takes three forms. The first is the conservation of the living creatures. In ancient times there were four huntings in each quarter of the year. But Confucius lays down a rule that no hunting should be held in summer, because at that season the creatures are growing. The " Royal Regulations " says: " To hunt without observing the rules for hunting is deemed cruelty to the creatures of Heaven." The rules of hunting and fishing are these: The emperor should not surround the hunting-ground, but should leave one opening for the game; and the princes should not take a whole herd by surprise. When the wolf sacrifices its prey, between the ninth and the tenth month, the hunting commences. Until the insects have all withdrawn into their burrows, the tenth month, fire should not be used for hunting. When the otter sacrifices its fish, the tenth month, the foresters begin to enter the meres and dams for fishing. When the dove changes into a hawk, the eighth month, the large and small nets begin to be set for the catching of birds. They should not take fawns, nor eggs. They should not kill pregnant animals, nor those which have not attained to their full growth. They should not throw down nests. These are the rules set forth in the " Royal Regulations."[1]

From the ethical point of view these rules are designed to foster kindness and sympathy, but from the economic point of view they are for the conservation of natural resources. Both points are the objects of these rules. For the practicing of them we may take Confucius as an example. The *Analects* tells that he angled, but did not use a net; and shot, but not at birds perching.[2] This is the

---
[1] *Li Ki*, bk. iii, pp. 220-221. The note of Prof. Legge makes a mistake, because it says that hunting is forbidden in autumn.
[2] *Classics*, vol. i, p. 203.

principle of humanity. On the other hand, Mencius points out the economic principle, as follows: " If close nets are not allowed to enter the pools and ponds, the fishes and turtles will be more than can be secured."¹ The meshes of a net were anciently required to be four inches in size, and the people might not eat fish under a foot long. Therefore, the conservation of the living creatures is preservation of food for the people.

The second is the conservation of the forests. Mencius says: " If the axes and hatchets enter the hills and forests only at the proper time, the wood will be more than can be used."² But what is the proper time? We may find this in the " Royal Regulations." It says, when the plants and trees drop their leaves, the tenth month, the people enter the hills and forests with the axes.³ According to the *Official System of Chou*, there is a forester to take charge of the rules of forests. For instance, in midwinter the trees on the south of the hill are cut down, and in midsummer those on the north. When the people are admitted to cut down the trees, they are regulated by the number of days. Although we do not know the length of the time period, we may be sure that this rule preserved the trees. In spring and autumn the people should not enter forbidden places to cut down trees, although they may cut the wild trees. If the people steal trees during the forbidden time, they should be fined.⁴ These rules are for the conservation of the forests.

The third is the conservation of the mines. The " Doctrine of the Mean " says that the precious treasuries are

¹ *Classics*, vol. ii, p. 130.
² *Ibid*.
³ *Li Ki*, bk. iii, p. 221.
⁴ *Official System of Chou*, ch. xvi.

found on the mountains,[1] but it does not touch the conservation of them. The " Royal Regulations " says that the famous mountains and great meres are not conferred on any feudal lords either within or without the imperial state.[2] This rule has two points. On the distributive side it is against monopoly, which will be discussed later. On the productive side it is for the conservation of natural resources. Since all the famous mountains and the great meres are under the control of the central government, no one can exhaust the natural wealth. According to the *Official System of Chou*, all the lands which produce gold, jade, tin, and precious stones are controlled by the miner, an official. He makes severe prohibitions, and orders the people of their neighborhood to guard them. If any mine is opened at a proper time, he draws a map of it, and gives it to those who dig the mine. Around those lands he looks after the prohibitions and orders.[3] These are the rules for the conservation of the mines.

The fundamental principle underlying the conservation of natural resources is the law of diminishing returns. Although this law is not expressed, it is clearly implied.

4. *Influence of Natural Environment*

While nature is a factor of production and is controlled by man, it has in turn a great influence, modifying man. The " Royal Regulations " says:

In all the settlements, the physical capacities of the people are sure to be according to the sky and earthly influences, as cold or hot, dry or moist. Where the wide valleys and the large rivers are different in shape, people born in them have differ-

---

[1] *Classics*, vol. i, p. 421.
[2] *Li Ki*, bk. iii, pp. 211-2.
[3] *Official System of Chou*, ch. xvi.

ent customs. The measure of their temperaments, as hard or soft, light or grave, slow or rapid; the taste of their preferences as to flavors; the fashion of their implements and weapons; and the suitability of their clothes—all are different.[1]

According to this statement the natural environment shapes the man. First, it fixes the physical capacities of the people; second, it fosters their temperaments; third, it produces different customs; fourth, it establishes different economic conditions, either in production or in consumption. The teaching is, further, that these differences should not be disturbed by government—a *laissez-faire* policy, in so far; and there is a recognition that in these differences is the basis of international trade.[2]

For the influence of the natural environment upon the people there is a general principle given by Ching Chiang, a widow of the noble family of Lu. She says:

Anciently, when the sage kings settled the people, they selected the poor land for the settlement of them, and made them work hard for the employment. Hence, they ruled the empire for a long time. For if the people are working hard, they will think. If they think, their good thoughts arise. If they are living in an easy way, they will be licentious. If they are licentious, they forget what is good. If they forget what is good, their bad thoughts arise. Therefore, the people of the rich land have no strong character, because they are licentious; and those of the poor land all direct their mind to righteousness, because they are working hard.[3]

Then she describes the different businesses of the two sexes of different classes, from the emperor to the common people.

[1] *Li Ki*, bk. iii, p. 228.   [2] *Cf. infra*, p. 450.
[3] *Narratives of Nations*, bk. v.

When Confucius has heard her words, he tells his pupils to record them.

The principle given by Ching Chiang is a mixture of economics and ethics. We now come to the pure economic principle. In the "Biography of Merchants," Ssŭ-ma Chien gives a commercial geography. He describes the geographical situations of the great cities, their natural resources, their population, their history, their prominent occupations, their customs, *etc.* We cannot enter into all the details, but we may condense his conclusion. According to him, in Southern China land was plenty, the population was sparse, the soil was rich, and food was abundant without the fear of famine. On this account the people were lazy, short-sighted, and had no saving. Therefore, there was none who suffered from hunger, but there was no family which possessed a thousand dollars. In Northern China the land was scarce, the population was dense, the soil was good for agriculture, but the people often suffered from flood and drought. Hence, they had a desire for saving. Therefore, they were diligent in different industries, such as agriculture, animal-breeding, silk-worm, commerce and speculation, in different localities. Such a difference between Southern and Northern China was true only in ancient times; it has gradually disappeared since the end of the Han dynasty (about 735 A. K. or 184 A. D.). But the theory of Ssŭ-ma Chien is held true by the general mind. His theory is like that of Ching Chiang; both are based on the idea that the people are spoiled if they make their living too easily. The only difference is that Ching Chiang looks at it from both economic and ethical points of view, while Ssŭ-ma Chien regards it from the economic viewpoint only. Indeed, natural environment has a great influence in determining the economic conditions and the characters of men. It is only when the human power grows greater that the natural power diminishes.

II. LAND

1. *Limited in Quantity*

Since the land is the chief representative of the natural things which help production, we may consider it separately. When we study the land question, the first thing that confronts us is that land is limited in quantity. The " Royal Regulations " says:

A space one mile square contains fields amounting to 900 acres. Ten miles square is equal to 100 spaces one mile square, and contains 90,000 acres. A hundred miles square is equal to 100 spaces ten miles square, and contains 9,000,000 acres. A thousand miles square is equal to 100 spaces one hundred miles square, and contains 900,000,000 acres. . . . All within the four seas, taking the length with the breadth, makes up a space 3,000 miles square, and contains 8,100,000,000 acres.

A space 100 miles square contains ground to the amount of 9,000,000 acres. Hills and mounds, forests and thickets, rivers and marshes, ditches and canals, city walls and suburbs, houses, roads, and lanes take up one-third of it, leaving 6,000,000 acres.[1]

2. *Various in Quality*

The second thing that confronts us is that land is various in quality. This is most clearly set forth in the " Tribute of Yü." After Yü repressed the great floods, he divided the Chinese Empire into nine provinces, and classified the land into nine gradations. For convenience of review we may reduce the statements [2] to the form of a table:

[1] *Li Ki*, bk. iii, pp. 244-6.
[2] *Classics*, vol. iii, pt. i, pp. 94-125.

Grades of Land	Names of Provinces	Present Provinces	Color and Nature of Soil
First	Yung Chow	Shensi and Kansu	Yellow and mellow
Second	Sü Chow	Shantung, Kiangsu and Anhui	Red, clayey and rich
Third	Ts'ing Chow	Shantung	Whitish and rich, salt
Fourth	Yü Chow	Honan	Mellow, rich, dark and thin
Fifth	Ki Chow	Chihli and Shansi	Whitish and mellow
Sixth	Yên Chow	Chihli and Shantung	Blackish and rich
Seventh	Liang Chow	Szechuan and Shensi	Greenish and light
Eighth	King Chow	Hunan and Hupei	Miry
Ninth	Yang Chow	Kiangsu, Anhui, Kiangsi, and Chekiang	Miry

This table shows the differences, in color and nature, of the soil with general reference to the whole province, and classifies the land into nine grades. Such a classification is very general and rough indeed, but it indicates that the comparative study of the quality of land had begun at a very early time.

The *Official System of Chou* also classifies the land into nine grades, but it differs from the "Tribute of Yü." While the latter judges the land collectively from the general view of the whole province, it judges the land specifically from the quality of the land itself. According to the *Official System of Chou*,[1] the quality of land is measured by its power of supporting population. It gives expressly only the middle class of land, by saying that a prescribed amount (one hundred acres) of the superior land can support a family of seven persons; of the ordinary land, one of six persons; and the same amount of the inferior land, one of five persons. These are the three kinds of land in the middle class. Such a statement, according to the com-

[1] Ch. xi.

mentary of Chêng Hsüan, implies that there are nine gradations of land, and that only the middle class is given as an example. In the highest class, the land can support either eight, or nine, or ten persons. In the lowest class, it can support either two, or three, or four persons. In the grand division, land is divided into three classes, and in its subdivision, it is divided into nine grades. Such a gradation is determined by the number of people which the land can support.

3. *Different in Location*

Difference in lands are due not only to their qualities, but also to their locations. According to the Confucian theory, the capital city of a state should be in its center. Taking the city as the central point, the land of the whole state is divided up into five zones. Outside of the city, it is called " suburb;" outside of the suburb, " country;" outside of the country, " forest;" outside of the forest, " frontier." [1] These five names are merely geographical divisions for the indication of the difference of location. The widths of all the zones are equal, and they vary only according to the extent of the whole state. In fact, the difference of location is measured from the central city. In a simple way, there are only three divisions, namely, the city, the suburb, and the country, which includes the forest and frontier.

4. *Form of Field*

For the division of the land we must study the system of *tsing tien*. This system is so important that we discuss it separately in another chapter. What we consider here is only the form of *tsing tien*.

In ancient China the land was divided up into the form of *tsing*. *Tsing* means well, which written in Chinese is

[1] *The Oldest Chinese Dictionary (Erh Ya)*, ch. ix.

NATURE AND CAPITAL

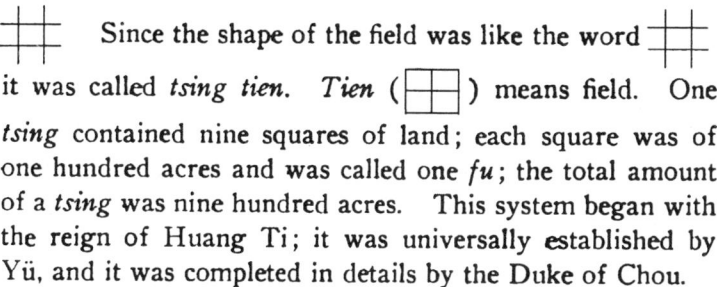

Since the shape of the field was like the word it was called *tsing tien*. *Tien* ( ) means field. One *tsing* contained nine squares of land; each square was of one hundred acres and was called one *fu*; the total amount of a *tsing* was nine hundred acres. This system began with the reign of Huang Ti; it was universally established by Yü, and it was completed in details by the Duke of Chou.

In one square of land the one hundred acres contained ten thousand paces. According to the ancient measures, six feet was one pace, and one hundred paces was one acre. Therefore, one acre was six feet wide and six hundred feet long. Hence, the *Canon of Poetry* says, "The grain is well cultivated all over the long acres."[1] Between two acres there was a small ditch. If there were one hundred acres, there were one hundred small ditches. The acre was higher, and the ditch was lower. Since one ploughshare was five inches wide, and two men using two ploughshares were called a pair, the cultivation of a pair was a foot wide and deep, and this was the form of a small ditch. In cultivation, the farmer first used the plough to turn over the grass, and then formed lines, such as the acres and ditches. This was the plan of one square of land, and the small ditch was the basis of the measure of all the water-channels.

For the system of *tsing tien* the water-channels were very important, because they determined the boundaries of the field and carried off the water of floods. Such a system of water-channels was originated by Yü. After he had fixed the natural waterway he devoted his attention to the artificial waterway along the fields.

In the Chou dynasty the *tsing tien* system was at its height, and the water-channels were complete. According to the

[1] *Classics*, vol. iv, pt. ii, p. 378.

"Record of Industry,"[1] the bureau of civil engineering is in charge of water-channels, and it gives the following standard measures for the making of different waterways: Within the *fu*, a field of one hundred acres, the small ditch running between two acres is one foot wide and deep. Hence, one *fu* has one hundred small ditches. Along the head-line of the field, the large ditch running outside of the *fu* is two feet wide and deep. Hence, three *fu* have only one large ditch in common. Outside of the *tsing* which contains nine *fu*, the ditch is four feet wide and deep. Hence, ten *tsing* have only one such ditch in common. Ten miles square make one *ch'êng*, which contains one hundred *tsing*, and outside of the *ch'êng* the larger ditch is eight feet wide and deep. Hence, ten *ch'êng* have only one larger ditch. One hundred miles square make one *tung*, which contains ten thousand *tsing*, and outside of the *tung* the largest ditch is sixteen feet wide and deep. The length of the largest ditch is uncertain, and its water flows to the natural stream directly. In a *tung*, the *tsing tien* system is complete, and it has five grades of water-channels: (1) the one-foot ditch, (2) the two-foot ditch, (3) the four-foot ditch, (4) the eight-foot ditch, and (5) the sixteen-foot ditch. This is the general rule, but it must be modified according to the geographical situation.

Along all the water-channels, except the one-foot ditch, there were different roads. Along the two-foot ditch the road was large enough for the ox and horse; along the four-foot ditch it was large enough for the wagon; along the eight-foot ditch, for one chariot; along the sixteen-foot ditch, for two chariots; and along the natural stream or artificial canal, for three chariots.[2] These waterways and roads were the general rules for the formation of *tsing tien*.

[1] It was a separate book written during the Chou dynasty. But it is now contained in the end of the *Official System of Chou*, ch. xlii.

[2] *Official System of Chou*, ch. xv.

According to the *Canon of Poetry*, there were two kinds of acres: one kind was called "southern acres," and the other "eastern acres." In the southern acres, the acres and the small ditches all ran east and west, and in the eastern acres they all ran north and south. Because looking from the north the southern acres were arranged in the south, they were called southern acres. Because looking from the west the eastern acres were arranged in the east, they were called eastern acres. The acres were southern or eastern in accordance with the river. Since the Chinese rivers mostly run from the west to the east, the greater part of the land became eastern acres. For, if the river was in the latitudinal line, the largest ditch should be in the longitudinal line; then the next smaller ditch was latitudinal and the four-foot ditch longitudinal; then the two-foot ditch was latitudinal and the smallest ditch longitudinal; hence, the acres were arranged in the east. The southern acres were arranged *vice versa*. The Chinese rivers sometimes run either toward the south or toward the north, so there were also the southern acres. Both the southern and the eastern acres were according to the natural situation of the land.

III. CAPITAL

1. *Capital and Wealth*

The word capital in Chinese is *pen*. Its original sense means the root of a tree; hence, it means the principal part or the basis of anything. The word *pen* used in the sense of capital first appears in *Kuan Tzŭ*, and it has been popularly used to the present day. But the word used in this sense is not to be found in the writings of Confucius. Instead, he uses the word *tzŭ*. The *Canon of Poetry* says: "Ruin and disorder are destroying the *tzŭ* [the capital], and do not show any kindness to our multitudes."[1] The

[1] *Cf. Classics*, vol. iv, pt. ii, p. 502. See also *ibid.*, p. 520.

Park of Narratives says that this sentence expresses grief that disorder is caused by luxury and extravagance, without saving.[1] Chen Huan says that the "accumulated wealth" is called *tzŭ*.[2] Therefore, the word *tzŭ* in Chinese is exactly the word capital in English. In the *Canon of Changes* there is a book on "Traveling," which refers especially to the traveling merchant, although it includes travelers generally. It describes the good condition of a traveling merchant as follows: " The traveler occupies the proper place, carries with him his *tzŭ*, and secures the trusty servants."[3] This statement includes the three factors of production; the word *tzŭ* means capital, while the proper place and the trusty servants refer to land and labor respectively. Indeed, the word *tzŭ* is used by Confucius as capital, because *tzŭ* means accumulation or storage. Hence, the Chinese combine the word *tzŭ* either with the word *tsai* (wealth), or with the word *pen*, for the term capital. The Japanese adopt the latter expression.

The word wealth in the Chinese language is sometimes the same as the word capital. Such a case has been already shown in the "Great Learning."[4] Sometimes the word wealth combining with the word commodity forms the term capital. For instance, Mencius says: " The fields and wilds not being developed, and the commodities and wealth not being accumulated, these are not the chief danger of a state."[5] The two words "commodities and wealth" stand as the English word capital, while " fields and wilds " stand for land. This is the style of Chinese expression.

Since the word wealth is sometimes identified with the

---

[1] Bk. vii.

[2] In his *Explanation of Mao's Commentary of the Canon of Poetry*, published in 2398 (1847 A. D.).

[3] *Yi King*, p. 188.   [4] See *supra*, p. 295.

[5] *Classics*, vol. ii, p. 291.

word capital, we may find out what is meant by wealth. Hsü Shên's *Dictionary*[1] says: "Wealth is what man regards as valuable." Chêng Hsüan says that wealth includes all money and grain. Money and grain, as we shall see, are the chief representatives of capital goods; hence, Chêng Hsüan takes them for the explanation of the word wealth. Even in the present day the Chinese still use the two words "money and grain" to cover the whole economic field. Although they are not so dignified as the term "food and commodities," they are synonyms. But the best definition of the word wealth is given by Hsiang An-shih (died in 1759 A. K. or 1208 A. D.). He says: "The word wealth is the collective name of all the things in which the people find their utilities." In short, wealth is the general term covering all production and consumption goods, while capital is the particular term covering only production goods and those consumption goods which are used for productive purposes. Hence, the Chinese use such terms as "funds," "principal money," "accumulated wealth" and "mother wealth" for the word capital.

To understand the meaning of wealth we may look at the problem from the standpoint of different classes. According to the "Details of Rites," each class has special representatives of its wealth.

When one asks about the wealth of the ruler of a state, the reply should be given by telling the extent of his territory, and the productions of its hills and lakes. To a question about the wealth of the great official, it should be said: "He has the lands allotted to him, and is supported by the taxes of his people. He needs not to borrow vessels or dresses for his sacrificial occasions." To a question about the wealth of the

[1] It was begun in 651, and presented to the emperor in 672 (100-121 A. D.).

student, the reply should be by giving the number of his carriages; and to one about the wealth of a common man, by telling the number of the animals that he keeps.[1]

According to this passage, the wealth of any class is a collective name for all material things. It does not confine the term wealth to any particular thing. If the people understand this, they never make the mistake of thinking that money is the only wealth, because it does not mention money at all. Indeed, wealth includes both production and consumption goods.

2. *Grain as Capital*

While grain is a consumption good, the Confucians regard it also as a very important capital good; hence, there is the principle of accumulating grain. The "Royal Regulations" says:

If in a state there is not an accumulation of saving sufficient for nine years, its condition is called one of insufficiency; if there is not enough for six years, one of urgency. If there is not a saving sufficient for three years, the state cannot continue. The husbandry of three years is held to give an overplus of food sufficient for one year; that of nine years, an overplus sufficient for three years. Going through thirty years in this way, though there might be bad years, drought and inundations, the people would have no lack, nor be reduced to eating merely vegetables.[2]

In short, every family must save grain at such a rate that every three years should yield a surplus sufficient for one year. This is the general rule of saving, and grain is only the example, as it was the most important thing in ancient times.

[1] *Li Ki*, bk. i, pp. 115-6.   [2] *Ibid.*, bk. iii, p. 222.

According to the "Royal Regulations," a state as a whole must have an accumulation sufficient for at least nine years. But the accumulation is of nothing but food. Therefore, food is not only a consumption good for the present, but also a capital good for the future. Since food is not a permanent article, it needs a successive renewal for the change of the old. But it serves as a capital good just the same. In fact, in ancient China grain was the chief among all the capital goods, since land was in a separate category; and the accumulation of grain was a national surplus.

In the Han dynasty the theory of accumulating grain was put into full effect. The chief representatives of this theory were Chia Yi and Chao Tso. Chia Yi pointed out to his emperor that if wealth is produced in limited amounts but is consumed without any limit, the capital must in time be exhausted. Now, the people run away from agriculture and turn to industry and commerce. Hence, the consumers are very many, and luxurious habits spread day after day. These two facts are the great injury and the great destroyer of the empire. Those who produce wealth are few, but those who waste it are many: how can the wealth and property of the empire fail to fall short? Indeed, on accumulating and storing up for the future the fate of the empire depends. If grain is plenty and wealth is superabundant, what can we not accomplish? In an attack, we can take what we want; in a defense, we can have a safeguard; in a battle, we can win the victory. In calling the enemy and absorbing the foreigners, who will not come at our invitation? Now, if we drive our people back to the farm for the attachment to primary industry, we shall make every one of the empire eat the produce of his own labor, and the people of little skill and the journeymen turn to the fields. Then the storage and accumulation will be sufficient and the people will enjoy their life. This policy is for the wealth and safety of the empire. Han Wên Ti was influenced by the words of Chia Yi, and he opened " the borrowing field " for his personal cultivation in order to set a good example to his people (374 A. K. or 178 B. C.).

In 384 (168 B. C.) Chao Tso also said to Han Wên Ti that, when the sage kings were in the government, their people did not suffer from cold and hunger. This came about, not because they could feed and clothe them by their own cultivation and weaving, but because they opened the sources of capital for them. Therefore, although Yao and Yü had the flood of nine years, and T'ang had the drought of seven years, the empire did not suffer from famine or pestilence. This was because saving and accumulation were abundant and preparation was completed beforehand. Therefore, the wise ruler encourages the people to take up agricultural occupation, lightens their taxes, and extends the accumulations for the filling of granaries and the preparation against flood and drought. The immediate policy of Chao Tso was to call upon the people for the sending of grain to the granaries in the northern boundary, where the Chinese guarded against the Huns. The people should receive titles from the government, and the gradation of the title should be according to the amount of grain which they sent. After Han Wên Ti had put his policy into effect, he proposed again to order the people to send their grain inland, and Wên Ti followed his advice again. Therefore, during the reigns of Wên Ti and Ching Ti (373-411, or 179-141 B. C.) China was very rich, both the government and the people.[1] It was the contribution of Chia Yi and Chao Tso, and their theory was drawn from Confucius.

[1] *History of Han*, ch. xxiv.

3. *Saving*

Since capital is the result of saving, we now come to the principle of saving. Confucius speaks of saving, not only for the private family, but also for the state. In ruling a state of a thousand chariots, one of the five things is saving in expenditure.[1] In the *Canon of Changes* there is a book called "*Chieh*," which means abstinence, control, restraint, economy, saving, *etc*. It includes three phases—law, ethics and economics. In the beginning of this book it is stated that abstinence is the basis of progress and attainment. But the reader is reminded that if the abstinence is very severe and difficult, it cannot be right.[2] This shows that the principle of saving in the teaching of Confucius is not cruel parsimony but reasonable abstinence.

The chief point of this book is this: "Basing on the principle of abstinence for the making of regulations, it will not injure the wealth, nor hurt the people."[3] This is an abstract economic principle. It refers to either public or private economy. As soon as wealth is injured people are hurt, even in the case of a private person. Therefore, if you wish not to injure the wealth, there must be some sort of regulations, such as financial legislation in a government, or as control of expenditure in a private person, according to the principle of abstinence. Hence, abstinence is the basis for the preservation of wealth and the benefit of the people.

When Confucius speaks of the filial piety of the feudal princes, he says: "Making the saving, and carefully observant of the regulations, they are full without overflowing. . . . To be full without overflowing is the way long to preserve riches."[4] Again, when he speaks of the filial piety

---

[1] See *supra*, p. 81.
[2] *Yi King*, p. 197.
[3] *Ibid.*, p. 262.
[4] *Sacred Books*, vol. iii, p. 468.

of the common people, he mentions saving in expenditure.[1] Therefore, every class, from the emperor to the common people, must observe the principle of saving.

The importance of saving is thus told by Hsun Tzŭ:

In the living of a man, he keeps fowls, dogs and pigs, and he keeps also oxen and sheep; but in his eating, he does not dare to have wine and meat. He has plenty of money and stores of grain, but in his dressing he does not dare to have silk. He has the deposit of the most valuable things, but in his going he does not dare to have carriage and horse. What is the reason? It is not because he does not want them, but because he has a long thought and cares for the future, lest nothing will succeed hereafter. Therefore, he saves expenditure, controls wants, and accumulates wealth for the succession. How good it is that he has a long thought and cares for the future in regard to himself! The short-sighted people who are careless for their living do not know even this. They consume food extravagantly, and do not care for the future. Then they exhaust quickly all the means. This is the reason they cannot escape from cold and hunger, and become beggars or victims dying in the ditches.[2]

Indeed, the opening of the sources of income and the saving of expenditure are the only ways for the increase of wealth. They are both familiar to all the Chinese, but the latter only is the way of increasing capital.

[1] See *supra*, p. 159.   [2] Bk. iv.

VOLUME II

BOOK VI. BRANCHES OF PRODUCTION

CHAPTER XX

Branches of Production in General

1. THE FOUR GROUPS OF PEOPLE

USING the principle of the division of labor as a basis, the Chinese have classified their people into four groups from a very early period. Such a classification is not a caste system, but a division of occupations, and it includes all the people. *Ku-liang's Commentary* says: " In the ancient time there were four groups of people: there was a group of people called students; there was a group of people called merchants; there was a group of people called farmers; and there was a group of people called artisans." [1] The definition of these four groups is given by Ho Hsiu. He says:

First, those whose virtue enabled them to occupy the public positions were called students. Second, those who cultivated land and produced grain were called farmers. Third, those who finished the goods by skilful mind and toilsome hand were called artisans. Fourth, those who exchanged wealth and sold goods were called merchants. The four groups worked separately and the labor of one group was not taken by the other three. Therefore, the wealth was sufficient.[2]

---

[1] First year of Duke Ch'êng.
[2] *Annotation of Kung-yang,* first year of Duke Ch'êng.

This was the system of the ancients and the same classification is still used now.

Under the influence of Confucius, China had no social class or caste. But by the division of labor, she had, and has, four groups of people. In the statements just quoted above we may note three points of special significance. The first is social equality. All the four groups are indiscriminately called people, and no group is higher than the others. The second is that the merchant is productive as well as the student, the farmer and the artisan. In the Chinese language the order of these four groups is usually this: the first is student, the second farmer, the third artisan, and the fourth merchant. But, according to *Ku-liang's Commentary*, the merchant is next to the student. It is obvious that the Confucians recognize the productivity of the merchant, and that they are not hostile to him, no matter whether he is put second or fourth in order. The third is the principle of division of labor. These four groups are divided in order to make the productive power more sufficient; and the people are not confined to any given group, but simply fall into one through the classification of occupations. These are the essentials of this grouping system.

In ancient times there was a static theory about the four groups. According to Kuan Tzŭ, the sage kings settled the students in the quiet place, the artisans in the factory, the merchants in the market-place, and the farmers in the country. Each group collectively lived in a special district by itself and attended to its own business day and night. They practised their occupation when they were young; their minds were satisfied; and they did not like to change their occupations, even when they saw strange things. Therefore, the teaching of their fathers and older brothers was effective without severity, and the learning of their sons and younger brothers was successful without difficulty.

Hence, the sons of each group usually took up the occupation of their fathers. Therefore, these four groups should live separately. Had they all lived together, their talking would be confused and their business would be changed.[1] Such a theory was carried out successfully by Kuan Tzŭ, and it was harmonious with the theory of the Confucians. In fact, the separation of the four groups was not for social distinction, but for occupational specialization.

Because the ancient Chinese had static economics in mind, they thought that it was a good thing for people not to change their occupations. When Tzŭ-nang, prime minister of Ch'u, described the good social conditions of Tsin (27 B. K. or 578 B. C.), he said: " The students of the prince of Tsin vigorously study their lessons; his common people attend diligently to agriculture; his merchants, artisans, and servants know nothing of changing their occupations."[2] According to this statement, Tzŭ-nang judged the economic condition of Tsin by the adherence to their occupations of the four groups. Such a judgment is correct. For, if the people are not satisfied with their occupations, they must change from group to group. So long as the people can remain in their own group without moving, it means that they can earn a living in their group, and there is no inducement offered by other groups. It is a static state, because the four groups stand on the same level and the people do not want to change their occupations.

II. FREEDOM OF OCCUPATION

Although by the system of four groups, the people are divided up on account of their different occupations, there is freedom of occupation. According to the theory of the

[1] *Narratives of Nations*, bk. vi.
[2] *Classics*, vol. v, pt. ii, p. 440.

Confucians, every one should have free choice of his own occupation, and this was the fact in ancient times. Mencius says:

Is the arrow-maker less benevolent than the maker of armor of defence? And yet, the arrow-maker's only fear is lest men should not be hurt, and the armor-maker's only fear is lest men should be hurt. So it is with the priest and the coffin-maker. The choice of a profession, therefore, is a thing in which great caution is required.[1]

According to this statement, Mencius refers to any kind of profession, and the arrow-maker, armor-maker, coffin-maker and priest are only examples. His essential point is that a man should be careful to choose his profession for the development of moral sense. An arrow-maker and a coffin-maker are not inhumane, but their professions make them wish men to die. Pan Ku says that the reason those who sell coffins wish to have an epidemic in the year is not because they hate men and wish to kill them, but because their profit depends upon the death of men.[2] His idea is the same as that of Mencius.

Indeed, a profession can generally affect the motives of man. For this reason the Chinese still have a general conception about the choice of an occupation from the standpoint of morality. Our discussion here, however, is not from the moral point of view, but from the economic. Since Mencius teaches men to be careful in choosing their professions, it indicates that there is freedom of occupation and every one may make his own choice freely. Otherwise, if there were no choice, how could a man be careful about his choice?

[1] *Classics*, vol. ii, p. 204.
[2] *History of Han*, ch. xxiii.

Since there is freedom of occupation, a son does not necessarily have to follow in the steps of his father. The reason a son usually takes up the profession of his father is not because he has no freedom of choice, but because it is easy for him to do so. According to the " Record of Education," a son may usually change from the occupation of his father, simply because he gets the education from his father's occupation, but applies it to another line. It says: " The son of a good founder is sure to learn how to make a fur robe. The son of a good maker of bows is sure to learn how to make a sieve." [1] Because the founder melts the different metals to make a complete article, or repairs the broken things by fixing the metals on it, such an art is similar to the making of fur robes by putting the different pieces of fur together. Because the bow-maker bends the wood in a good condition, it is similar to the making of sieves. Therefore, when the sons of the founder and the bow-maker have familiarly seen the practice of their fathers, they use similar principles for different applications. In a word, the sons utilize the occupations of their fathers as the basis of their education, but they specialize in their own occupations. Therefore, the son does not necessarily succeed to the profession of his father and has freedom of choice.

III. THE NECESSITY, JUSTICE AND HONOR OF WORK

Confucius never holds in contempt any kind of work, and he thinks that work is necessary, just and honorable. First, let us see why work is necessary. The *Canon of History* says: " When the farmer labors upon the fields and spends his strength in reaping, there is then a good harvest. . . . When the lazy farmer yields himself to ease, and is not strong to toil and to labor on his acres, he cannot have

[1] *Li Ki*, bk. xvi, p. 90.

either rice or millet." Therefore, P'an Kêng (850-823 B. K. or 1401-1374 B. C.) reproved his people by saying: " You, the myriads of the people, unexpectedly do not know how to produce wealth." And he encouraged them to move the capital city by saying: " Go! Produce wealth there." [1] Indeed, the production of wealth is the necessary business of the people, and they must not be lazy. Therefore, there is a proverb: " The life of the people depends on diligence; with diligence there is no want." [2]

According to Confucius, the lazy man is very bad. He says: " Hard is it to deal with him who will stuff himself with food the whole day without applying his mind to anything. Are there not gamesters and chessplayers? To be one of these would still be better than doing nothing at all." [3] Confucius does not teach man to be a gamester or chessplayer, but he still thinks that they are better than the idler. Therefore, either physical work or mental work is necessary for the life of man.

Second, let us see why work is just. Confucius says:

What the superior man calls justice, is that noble and mean all do their work in the world. The emperor himself ploughs the ground for the rice with which to fill the vessels, and the black millet from which to distil the spirit to be mixed with fragrant herbs, for the services of God; and the feudal princes are diligent in discharging their duties to the emperor.[4]

Indeed, in the world none should be idle. Even the emperor and the princes must have to do their work; it is what the superior man calls justice. In other words, not to work is unjust.

[1] *Classics*, vol. iii, pt. i, pp. 226-7, 239, 241.
[2] *Classics*, vol. v, pt. i, p. 318.
[3] *Classics*, vol. i, p. 329.   [4] *Li Ki*, bk. xxix, p. 338.

BRANCHES OF PRODUCTION IN GENERAL 373

Third, let us find out how work is honorable. Take Confucius for example. He was a good worker. He was once keeper of granaries, and his calculations were all correct. He was once in charge of the public fields, and the oxen and sheep were fat, strong, and superior.[1] Confucius worked in many ways, and was famous on account of his various abilities. But he himself spoke of it modestly: " When I was young my condition was low, and therefore I acquired my ability in many mean matters."[2] This was only a modest description of himself, but it indicates that he did not think work a dishonor to the worker.

For the illustration of this principle we may go to Mencius. He says:

Shun rose from among the channelled fields. Fu Yüeh was called to office from the midst of his building-frames; Chiao Ko from his fish and salt; Kuan Yi-wu from the hands of his gaoler; Sun-shu Ao from his hiding by the seashore; and Pai-li Hsi from the market-place. Thus, when Heaven is about to confer a great work on any man, it must first exercise his mind with suffering, and his sinews and bones with toil; expose his body to hunger; subject him to extreme poverty; and confound his undertakings. By all these methods it stimulates his mind, hardens his nature, and supplies his incompetencies.[3]

According to Mencius, all great men are developed by hardships. Therefore, the farmer, the artisan, or the merchant may become a great emperor or a great minister. His conclusion is this: " Life springs from sorrow and calamity, and death from ease and pleasure." Therefore,

[1] *Classics*, vol. ii, pp. 383-4. [2] *Classics*, vol. i, p. 218.
[3] Shun was the best emperor; Fu Yüeh and Chiao Ko were great ministers of the Yin dynasty; Kuan Yi-wu (Kuan Tzŭ), Sun-shu Ao, and Pai-li Hsi were great ministers of the states of Ch'i, Ch'u and Ch'in. *Classics*, vol. ii, pp. 446-7.

we should not dislike work, and should accept the hardship with thankfulness to Heaven. Indeed, poverty is a condition under which great men are produced, and a man's working does not bring him any dishonor at all. Under the influence of such teachings, the poor may keep their ambitions even higher than the rich, and workingmen may hold an honorable position in society.

IV. ABSENCE OF SLAVERY

In Chinese history there is a very glorious thing—that is, China has never had slavery existing as a general institution. Under the *tsing tien* system every one received one hundred acres of land from the government, so that every one was a landlord. Who would be a slave? And how could slavery come to exist? Since the land was rich and easily cultivated, and landholding was limited to one hundred acres, there was no need of slaves. Moreover, such intensive cultivation was not fitted to slave labor, and the free labor would not permit slavery to exist, under competition, because there was a large population. Furthermore, China has been an agricultural country, and the Chinese have been a diligent people, since the remotest times. Therefore, they made agriculture the fundamental and honorable occupation, and even the emperor took up such work. The theory that slavery becomes an institution most often in the agricultural stage seems refuted when we study Chinese history. Slavery may have existed in the prehistoric period, but if so there is no trace of it.

Although China had no slavery as a general institution, there were still a few slaves. According to the *Official System of Chou*, slavery resulted from crime. But no innocent man became a slave. It was only a kind of punishment, and it exempted those who had titles and those whose age was either above seventy or below eight.[1] But it was

---

[1] Ch. xxxvi.

not a social or an economic institution. Hence, Hsü Shên's *Dictionary* defines the word slave as the criminal of the ancients.

Such are the facts of history. Now, we come to the teachings of Confucius. According to him and his school, there should be no slavery. The social classes are five—emperor, princes, great officials, students, and common people. The groups of people are four—student, farmer, artisan, and merchant. But there is no such class or group as that of slave. According to his system, all the menial work in the family is done by the son, the daughter and the daughter-in-law; in society, by young men; in the government, by government employees. There is no need of slaves. Take Confucius himself for example. He lived in the style of the great official. Yet he had no slave, and not even a servant. The drivers of his carriage were his pupils, such as Fan Ch'ih and Jan Yu. When he employed a boy as the bearer of a visitor's card, he meant that it should teach the boy a lesson.[1] Even for himself, he said, "I will take up driving as a profession."[2] Therefore, Tzŭ-hsia taught his pupils to sprinkle and sweep the ground, to answer and reply, and to advance and recede.[3] These things are the necessary lessons of a servant, but Tzŭ-hsia took them to teach his pupils. This shows that everyone should learn the duties of a servant, because in the ordinary life there was no servant. Confucius says: "Among all the lives given by Heaven and Earth, that of man is the noblest."[4] According to the system of Confucius, there is absolutely no slavery.

Although China had no slavery before Confucius, and

[1] *Classics*, vol. i, p. 293.
[2] *Ibid.*, p. 216.   [3] *Ibid.*, p. 343.
[4] *Sacred Books*, vol. iii, p. 476.

although Confucius' system has no slavery, the economic condition changed in the Ch'in dynasty. After the *tsing tien* system was destroyed (202 A. K. or 350 B. C.), continuous wars went on, taxes were very heavy, and wealth was unequally distributed, so the poor people were unable to maintain their independent condition. Hence, the market of slaves was established, and there was traffic in slaves who came from the kidnapper and the robber.[1] Therefore, slavery arose during the Ch'in dynasty.

In 347 A. K. (205 B. C.), during the war between Han and Ch'u, a great famine occurred, so that the people ate human flesh. Then Han Kao Ti permitted the people to sell their sons. It was the first time that the people were allowed to sell themselves as slaves. But, in 350 A. K., when Han Kao Ti conquered Ch'u and became emperor, he issued a decree: "The people who have sold themselves to be slaves of others on account of famine are all emancipated as free citizens." This shows that slavery was not an institution. But it was bad enough that criminals became government slaves and that the poor sold themselves as private slaves. The slaves, however, were very few in number and did not form a special class. They should be called servants rather than slaves. For example, Wei Ts'ing (died in 446 A. K. or 106 B. C.) was a slave. But he was later the commander-in-chief of the army which conquered the Huns, the marquis of an honorary estate amounting to twenty thousand two hundred families, and the husband of the oldest sister of Han Wu Ti.

The first to make a public announcement against slavery was Tung Chung-shu. In 432 A. K. (120 B. C.) he petitioned Wu Ti in the following words: "We should abolish slavery, and prevent the master from killing the slave by

[1] *History of Han*, ch. xcix.

BRANCHES OF PRODUCTION IN GENERAL 377

arbitrary oppression."[1] But this proposal was not carried out by Wu Ti.

The first to abolish slavery was Wang Mang. In 560 A. K. (9 A. D.) he decreed that all slaves should be called "private dependents," and should not be bought and sold. But there was still slavery as a punishment. Since his government was not successful, in 563 A. K. he allowed the people to sell and buy the "private dependents."[2]

The Confucian emperor most influential in the abolition of slavery was Kuang-wu, whose reign was from 576 to 608 A. K. (25-57 A. D.). In 577 he decreed: "The people have formerly married their wives away and sold their sons; now they are all allowed to go back to their parents if they wish. Who dares to hold them shall be punished according to law." In 581 he decreed: "The officials and the commons who, during the time of Wang Mang, were subdued to slavery without the accordance of old law, are all emancipated to be free citizens." In 582 he decreed: "The officials and the commons who became slaves or inferior wives, either on account of famine and warfare or through the robbers of Sü Chow and Ts'ing Chow, are all allowed either to go or to stay, as they please. Who dares to hold them and not give them return shall be punished by the law of selling persons."

In the second month of 586 he decreed: "'Among all the lives given by Heaven and Earth, that of man is the noblest.' If anyone kills a slave, his crime cannot be less than ordinary murder." In the eighth month he decreed: "He who dares to torture a slave with fire shall be punished according to law, and those who are tortured are emancipated as free citizens." In the eleventh month he abolished the law that the slave who wounded any person was to be punished by death.

[1] *History of Han*, ch. xxiv.   [2] *Ibid.*, ch. xcix.

In 587 he decreed: "The people of Lung[1] and Shu[2] who were captured and made slaves, whether those who have appealed to the courts or those who have not been reported by the judges, are all emancipated to be free citizens." In 588 he decreed: "Since the eighth year [583], the people of Yi Chow[2] who were captured and made slaves are all emancipated to be free citizens. Those who depend on others as inferior wives are all allowed to go away if they wish. Who dares to keep them shall be punished by the law of capturing persons, as it has been applied to Sü Chow and Ts'ing Chow." In 589 he decreed: "Since the eighth year, the slaves of Yi Chow[2] and Liang Chow,[1] who have appealed to the local courts, are all emancipated to be free citizens. Those who were sold need not pay back the price to their owner.'"[3]

In Chinese history, although there were many emperors who freed slaves, Kuang-wu was the most important. He decreed freedom to the slaves nine times. Since his reign, China virtually has had no slaves at all. Some other emperors paid the price to the slave-owner, but he did not do so. He was the Abraham Lincoln of China, but he abolished slavery without civil war. In an absolute government, although the emperor can do wrong easily, he can also do good easily.

Unfortunately, during the disturbance of the Five Barbarians (855-990 A. K. or 304-439 A. D.) and the conquest of the Tartars and the Mongolians, slavery was introduced into China by those barbaric tribes. From the Northern Wei dynasty to the beginning of the present dynasty (937-2195 A. K. or 386-1644 A. D.), however, the slaves were generally not actual slaves. They were

---

[1] Kansu province.   [2] Szechuan province.
[3] *History of Latter Han*, ch. i.

mostly persons who pretended to be dependents of noble or rich families in order to escape taxes. At the end of 2460 (Jan. 1909 A. D.) slavery was absolutely abolished in China.

We cannot say that China had no slaves at all. But we deny that China had such slavery as that of ancient Greece and Rome or that of the United States before the Civil War.

CHAPTER XXI

Agriculture

I. IMPORTANCE OF AGRICULTURE

BASING our classification on the system of four groups, we shall divide the branches of production into three categories—namely, agriculture, industry and commerce. Although the group of students is productive like the other three groups, they do not produce material wealth. Therefore we shall take up the other three groups first, discussing the productivity of students later.[1] Among these three groups the farmers stand first; hence, we shall begin with agriculture. As man is supported by food, and food comes from the land, agriculture is always the primary occupation. And as the land of China is fitted to agriculture, and she has had a large population, the Chinese always attach the chief importance to agriculture. Therefore, the Chinese economy is mostly an agricultural economy.

The importance of agriculture is indicated in the " Great Model." We have already seen that the " Great Model " puts food and commodities as the first and second of the eight objects of government.[2] For this reason it says: " It is on the basis of agriculture that the eight objects of government can be attained." [3] It is very clear that the " Great Model " lays the emphasis on agriculture, because food is the first of the eight objects.

---

[1] See *infra*, pp. 487-8.
[2] See *supra*, p. 52.
[3] *Classics*, vol. iii, pt. ii, p. 324.

AGRICULTURE

Since ancient times there has been a system of "borrowing field". This field contains one thousand acres, and the emperor cultivates it personally. As the emperor has no time to finish the cultivation of the whole field, and so borrows the labor of the people, it is called borrowing field. In 276 B. K. (827 B. C.), when Hsüan Wang did not plough the borrowing field, Duke Wên of Kuo gave him a remonstrance. In its beginning, he pointed out the importance of agriculture as follows:

The greatest business of the people is agriculture. From agriculture, the millet which is used for the sacrifice to God is produced; the density of population grows; the expense of the businesses is supplied; social harmony and peace arise; the multiplication of wealth begins; and the characters of honesty, great-mindedness, integrity and solidity become a general habit of the people.[1]

According to the *Record of Rites*, in the first month, the emperor selects a good day, puts the plough in his own carriage, and conducts his three ducal ministers, nine high ministers, the feudal princes, and his great officials, for the personal cultivation of the " borrowing field." The emperor ploughs the land three times, each of the ducal ministers five, and the other ministers and feudal princes nine.[2] This system is significant from two points of view. In the first place, it touches religion. The " Principles of Sacrifices " says that this system is for the service of Heaven, Earth, the spirits of the land and grain, and the ancestors, because the new wine, cream, and vessels of grain are made from the products of the borrowing field. This procedure, then, is a great expression of reverence.[3] It is significant,

---
[1] *Narratives of Nations*, bk. i.
[2] *Li Ki*, bk. iv, pp. 254-5.
[3] *Ibid.*, bk. xxi, p. 322.

too, from the economic viewpoint. The emperor, honorable as he is, ploughs the field personally; it is an encouragement of agriculture. To-day this system still exists, and the emperor and his representatives all perform this service throughout the provinces. This shows well the importance ascribed to agriculture.

In the 28th year of the reign of Duke Chuang the *Spring and Autumn* records: " There is greatly no wheat and rice." This means that there was a great famine. In 432 A. K. (120 B. C.) Tung Chung-shu said to Han Wu Ti:

The *Spring and Autumn* does not record any other grain. But, when wheat and rice have no crop, it records them. By this statement it shows that the Holy Man gives the greatest importance to wheat and rice among the five grains.[1] Now, the people of the metropolitan province [2] have a custom of disliking to plant wheat. It loses annually what the *Spring and Autumn* regards as important, and diminishes the nourishment of the people. I wish your Majesty graciously to decree that the Minister of Agriculture order the people of this province to plant more wheat without delay.[3]

This proposal was carried into effect. Thus we see the theory of Confucius put into practice.

All the Confucians are in favor of agriculture, and it is needless to quote all their words on the subject. During the Han dynasty there was a popular theory that the great profit of the world, in last analysis, is ascribable to agriculture. In urging the importance of agriculture, Chao Tso speaks strongly. He says that poverty comes from insufficiency of food, and insufficiency of food from the neglect of agriculture. When the people neglect agricul-

---

[1] The five grains are rice, millet, panicled millet, wheat and pulse.
[2] Shensi province.
[3] *History of Han*, ch. xxiv.

ture, they do not become attached to the land. If they are not attached to the land, they leave their families and towns carelessly, like birds and animals. Hence, emigration takes place. Then he makes a comparison between the pearl, jade, gold and silver, and the grain, rice, cloth and silk, and says that a wise ruler should value grain more highly than gold and jade. His conclusion is this: the most important thing is to direct the people to work earnestly in agriculture. For this direction, the grain must be valued highly; and the policy of giving high value to grain is to make the grain an object of reward. Therefore, the government should order the people to turn over their grain to the government. If the people do so, they may either get honorable titles or be relieved from punishment. In this way the rich can receive titles and the farmer can make more money by the increasing demand for grain. Since those who can send grain to the government for the receiving of titles must be the rich, if the state takes the superabundance from them for its expenditure, the taxes of the poor can be reduced. This may be said to be diminishing superabundance to relieve insufficiency. The results of this policy will be three: to make public expenditure sufficient, to reduce taxation, and to encourage agricultural industry. This is the policy of Chao Tso, and it was carried out very successfully by Han Wên Ti. Although Chao Tso does not understand the law of diminishing returns since he says that the grain which is produced by the people will grow in the land without deficiency, his whole essay has had a great influence in emphasizing the importance of agriculture.[1]

II. AGRICULTURE NOT THE ONLY PRODUCTIVE OCCUPATION

Although Confucius thinks that agriculture is most im-

[1] *History of Han*, ch. xxiv.

portant so far as food is concerned, he does not think that every one should be a farmer, and that besides agriculture there is no productive labor. To prove this point there is a case in the *Analects*. One day Fan Ch'ih requested Confucius to teach him husbandry. He said: "I am not so good for that as an old husbandman." Then Fan requested Confucius to teach him gardening. He replied: "I am not so good for that as an old gardener."[1] Although Confucius had shown his disapproval of Fan Ch'ih's learning agriculture by these two answers, yet he was still afraid that Fan would fail to understand. Therefore, when Fan Ch'ih had gone out, he said: "A small man, indeed, is Fan Hsü!" Then he described the effect of a good government upon the people, and his conclusion was that there is no need of the knowledge of husbandry. Confucius said this, intending that it should be repeated to Fan Ch'ih.

The reason Confucius refused to teach Fan Ch'ih agriculture is that agriculture is an occupation of the common people only, and it should not be learned by the students. Since the students are the candidates for the public offices, they should learn how to manage the government and how to influence the people, but they should not learn how to practise agriculture. Moreover, as Confucius was a great reformer, and Fan Ch'ih was his pupil, why should he ask him about such a small thing as agriculture? It indicated that the ambition of Fan was not higher than to become a farmer. Therefore, Confucius pointed out the great influence of a good government affecting the people, and said that agriculture is not a necessary thing for a student. In short, Confucius taught Fan Ch'ih politics instead of agriculture. Therefore, according to Confucius, agriculture is the profession of only one of the four groups of people,

[1] From this conversation we know that there was the science of agriculture. *Classics*, vol. i, pp. 264-5.

AGRICULTURE

and the student may produce even more utility for society than the farmer.

For this reason most of the pupils of Confucius were not farmers. Take Tzŭ-lu, for example. When he followed Confucius and happened to fall behind, he asked an old farmer, "Have you seen my master?" The answer was: "Your four limbs are unaccustomed to toil; you cannot distinguish the five kinds of grain—who is your master?"[1] We may take the words of the old farmer as typical of the pupils of Confucius.

In Mencius' time there was a founder of the agricultural school named Hsü Hsing.[2] He pretended that he studied the doctrine of Shên Nung. He had a large number of disciples, "several tens" in all. All of them wore clothes of haircloth, and made sandals of hemp and wove mats for their living. His doctrine is this: A wise and able ruler should cultivate the land equally and along with his people, and eat the fruit of his labor. He should prepare his own meals morning and evening, while at the same time he carries on his government. A ruler should not have granaries, treasuries, and arsenals. If he has such things, it is oppressing the people for his own support.[3] His doctrine is extremely democratic, but it is impracticable, because it implies the abolition of government and advocates the universal application of a communistic scheme.

The argument of Mencius against the doctrine of Hsü Hsing is based on the principle of division of labor.[4] But here we wish to show simply that Mencius does not

[1] *Classics*, vol. i, p. 335.
[2] Hsü Hsing's doctrine might come from Shih Chiao, the teacher of Shang Yang, since Shih Tzŭ advocated the same theory.
[3] *Classics*, vol. ii, pp. 246-7.
[4] See *infra*, pp. 485-6.

think agriculture alone productive. He makes use of historical facts for the support of his argument. For instance, he says: "Yü was eight years away from his home, and though he thrice passed the door of it, he did not enter. Although he had wished to cultivate the land, could he have done so?" "When the sages were exercising their solicitude for the people in this way, had they leisure to cultivate the land?" "He whose anxiety is about his hundred acres not being properly cultivated is a mere husbandman." "In their governing of the empire, were there no subjects on which Yao and Shun employed their minds? There were subjects, only they did not employ their minds on the cultivation of the land." [1] Thus we see that Mencius believes that public officers also are producers and that they should not take up the work of a farmer.

III. METHODS OF AGRICULTURE

In describing the form of the field, we have already shown the methods of agriculture in a general way. But we must now study them in some detail. The chief feature is the system of "alternative fields." It was a very old system, Hou Chi, the minister of agriculture of Emperor Yao (about 1732 B. K. or 2283 B. C.), being the one who invented it. As the acre was six feet wide and six hundred feet long, the system of alternative fields was to make three low lines within one acre. The low line was made by two ploughshares, and was a foot wide and deep and as long as the acre. In the field of one hundred acres there were three hundred low lines, and parallel with them were three hundred high lines. The seed was sowed into the low line, and the blade sprang up. When the grass of the high line was weeded out, the soil of the high line was put down

[1] *Classics*, vol. ii, pp. 251-3.

to the low one, in order to protect the root of the blade. In every time of weeding the root was protected by the additional soil. Such a process was repeated and repeated; hence, the low line gradually became higher and the high line lower. By summer the high line had disappeared, and the root was very deep. Therefore, the grain was able to stand against the wind and drought.

The reason this system was called alternative fields was this: since there were three low lines and three high lines within one acre, the low one and the high one were alternated every year. Therefore, the power of the soil was annually recovered and the crop was very good. In 463 A. K. (89 B. C.) this old method was put in practice again, and the annual harvest of the alternative fields exceeded that of those fields which were not alternative by more than one bushel to every acre. If this method was properly employed by a good farmer, the surplus doubled this amount.[1]

The second feature is cultivation by pairs. As the ploughshare made of metal was eleven inches long and five inches wide, the cultivation of land was carried on by two men using two ploughshares. Since the strength of one man was sufficient for one ploughshare, why should the cultivation be carried on by two? It was because the co-operative labor of two men was better than the individual power. This method also was invented by Hou Chi. The *Canon of Poetry* says: "Attend to your cultivation, with your ten thousand men all in pairs." Again it says: " In thousands of pairs they remove the roots."[2] According to the *Official System of Chou*[3] and the *Record of Rites*[4]

[1] *History of Han*, ch. xxiv.
[2] *Classics*, vol. iv, pt. ii, pp. 584, 600.
[3] Ch. xv.
[4] *Li Ki*, bk. iv, p. 308.

there was a local officer to arrange the pairs in the twelfth month. Such an arrangement was to equalize their ages and physical conditions. In Confucius' time this method still existed. The *Analects* says that Chang-chü and Chieh-ni were cultivating in a pair.[1] This method lasted during the Han dynasty.

The third feature is the ploughing with oxen. According to the *Canon of Mountains and Seas*, this method was invented by the grandson of Hou Chi, whose name was Shu-chün. In Confucius' time this method prevailed. Among his pupils, one was named Jan Kêng, and his designation was Po-niu; another was named Ssŭ-ma Kêng, and his designation was Tzŭ-niu. Jan and Ssŭ-ma were family names, and Kêng meant cultivation. Since there was a connection between cultivation and the ox, they both used the word Niu for their designations, because Niu meant ox. Moreover, Confucius himself spoke of "the calf of a ploughing cow."[2] Therefore, the Chinese began to employ the ox or cow for ploughing a long time ago, but they still do the same to-day. They very seldom employ the horse for this purpose.

The fourth feature is the application of agricultural chemistry. According to the *Official System of Chou*, there are nine kinds of soils. The different seeds are chosen to fit the different soils. The bones of different animals are boiled and their juice is discriminately used to soak the different seeds for the different soils; or the bones are burned and their ashes are put on different soils.[3]

The fifth feature is the two-crop system. We do not know when this system began, but we find a statement given by Hsun Tzŭ. He says: " Now, the land is pro-

[1] *Classics*, vol. i, p. 333.   [2] *Classics*, vol. i, p. 186.
[3] Ch. xvi.

ducing the five grains. If man cultivates it well, each acre will yield several bushels, and he will reap the harvest twice in one year."[1] Although the two-crop system might not have prevailed over the whole empire on account of different climates and soils, it was a great advance.

All these five things are most important methods of the ancient Chinese.

IV. EXTENSIVE AND INTENSIVE CULTIVATION

For the cultivation of land there are two methods, extensive and intensive. If the land is poor, the farmer must cultivate a larger area than if it is good, in order to get the same return. This is extensive cultivation. If the land is good, he may cultivate it intensively by using more labor and capital on a smaller area, getting the same return. This is intensive cultivation. The margin of extensive cultivation is determined by the imaginary boundary beyond which the land is not fitted to be used at all. The margin of intensive cultivation is determined by the law of diminishing returns. In a static condition, the productivity of labor and capital at these two margins will be equal.

For the extensive cultivation, there is a theory given by Chia K'uei (581-652 A. K. or 30-101 A. D.), commentator of *Tso's Commentary*.[2] He divides the land into nine kinds, and takes the best kind as the standard. In the best kind of land, which is rich and plain, one *fu*, 100 acres, is the unit; and nine *fu* is one *tsing*. Now, if you measure all the other eight kinds of land by the extent of nine *fu*, 900 acres, the differences will be: in the second kind, which is low and wet, nine *fu* is a *mu*, and two *mu* equal one *tsing*; in the third kind, the land between the dikes, nine *fu* is a *ting*, and three *ting* equal one *tsing*; in the fourth kind,

---

[1] Bk. x.   [2] *Classics*, vol. v, pt. ii, p. 517.

the low land with water, nine *fu* is a *kuei*, and four *kuei* equal one *tsing*; in the fifth kind, the land having sand and small stones, nine *fu* is a *shu*, and five *shu* equal one *tsing*; in the sixth kind, poor and salt, nine *fu* is a *piao*, and six *piao* equal one *tsing*; in the seventh kind, the hills, nine *fu* is a *pien*, and seven *pien* equal one *tsing*; in the eighth kind, the marshes, nine *fu* is a *chiu*, and eight *chiu* equal one *tsing*; in the ninth kind, the wooded mountains, nine *fu* is a *tu*, and nine *tu* equal one *tsing*. These nine kinds of land are the classification for the land tax, but they represent at the same time the different degrees of extensive cultivation. One *tsing* of the best land is the standard; and if we want to get the same return from the lower grades of land as that from the best, we must extend our cultivation over an area from two to nine times as great. The poorer the land, the larger must be its area.

Such a mathematical calculation is only a general theory and cannot be the exact measure of the value of the land. Yet it was the classification of the land tax of Ch'u (4 A. K. or 548 B. C.). Since Ch'u was a new country in southern China where the land was plenty but poor, extensive cultivation would prevail. In the Middle Kingdom, the China proper of the ancient times, the land was good, and the population was dense; hence, there was intensive cultivation. Taking ancient China as a whole, cultivation was mostly intensive, because, under the *tsing tien* system, one family cultivated only one hundred acres.

According to Mencius and the "Royal Regulations," intensive cultivation is this: When a farmer cultivates one hundred acres of land, together with some capital, such as manure, he gets different amounts of return from the land according to the intensity of his cultivation. If he is the best farmer, the return can support nine persons; next to the best, eight persons; if he is an ordinary farmer, seven persons; next to the ordinary one, six persons; if he is a poor farmer, it can support only five persons.[1] In this case there is a certain area of land connected with a certain number of men. And yet the amount of return from the one hundred acres of land cultivated by one farmer varies. These differences come from the differences of cultivation. In fact, the amount of return is determined by the degree of intensity. However, why cannot the best farmer get more return than support for nine persons by putting more labor and capital in the one hundred acres of land? Because land is subject to the law of diminishing returns. Therefore, support for nine persons is the intensive margin of cultivation.

The theory of intensive cultivation was put into practice very successfully by Li K'o. His theory is called " the doctrine of exhausting land power." It is something like this: Within an area one hundred miles square, there are nine million acres. Taking away the mountains, marshes and city residences, one-third of this amount, there are six million acres of cultivable land. If the people cultivate it intensively, each acre can yield three additional pecks (*tou*) of grain. Therefore, even within an area one hundred miles square, the difference between an addition and a loss of grain will be one million eight hundred thousand bushels (*shih*). When this doctrine was applied to Wei, the state became rich and strong.[2] But why did Li K'o not say that the addition of grain per acre would be more than three pecks if the cultivation should be still more intensive? Because land is subject to the law of diminishing returns. Therefore, according to Li K'o, the additional amount of three pecks of grain is the intensive margin of cultivation.

[1] *Classics*, vol. ii, p. 376; *Li Ki*, bk. iii, p. 210.
[2] *History of Han*, ch. xxiv.

V. DIMINISHING RETURNS

For the law of diminishing returns, the Chinese do not give a complete principle. Yet they point out the facts. *Han's External Commentary of the Canon of Poetry* says: " The produce of the land cannot be increased, and the yielding of the mountains and marshes can be exhausted."[1] The first part of the sentence refers to agriculture, and the second to natural resources in general. This sentence shows a very good apprehension of essential elements of the law of diminishing returns.

When Yeh Shih describes the evils of congestion of the regions surrounding the capital,[2] he says:

In the over-populated land, the people dig the mountains and dam the sea, picking out any profit which is left. While the productivity of the land is limited, the cultivation of the people is endless. Hence, it hurts the natural phenomena and injures the five elements. Therefore, the power of land is exhausted without supplying the demand of men, and the air becomes dry without the natural harmony.

These are the ill effects of over-population upon natural resources. In fact, the reason a large population living on a small area of land is an economic evil is because land is subject to the law of diminishing returns, a point shown very clearly by Yeh Shih.

VI. AGRICULTURAL LIFE

Let us study the agricultural life of the ancients as a whole, beginning with the earliest we can find. In the *Canon of Poetry* there is a poem written by the people of Pin, describing the economic life of Pin, at the time of Kung Liu (about 1245 B. K. or 1796 B. C.). It was

---

[1] Bk. v.   [2] See *supra*, p. 305.

AGRICULTURE

presented by the Duke of Chou to the emperor as the foundation of the Chou dynasty. This poem is very valuable, giving us a picture of the actual life at that time. Therefore we shall give it fully.

In the seventh month, the Fire Star passes the meridian;
In the ninth month, clothes are given out;
In the days of the [eleventh] month, the wind blows cold;
In the days of the [twelfth] month, the air is cold.
Without the clothes and garments of hair,
How could we get to the end of the year?
In the days of the [first] month, we fix the ploughs;
In the days of the [second] month, we cultivate the fields.
Together with our wives and children,
We carry food to those southern acres.
The surveyor of the fields comes, and is glad to eat with us.

In the seventh month, the Fire Star passes the meridian;
In the ninth month, clothes are given out.
With the spring days the warmth begins,
And the oriole utters its song.
The young women take their deep baskets,
And go along the small paths,
Looking for the tender leaves of the mulberry trees.
As the spring days lengthen out,
They gather in crowds the white southernwood.
When the young ladies' hearts are wounded with hardship,
They begin to have the common idea with the princesses, wishing to marry.

In the seventh month, the Fire Star passes the meridian;
In the eighth month are the sedges and reeds;
In the silkworm month we strip the mulberry branches of their leaves,
And take the axes and hatchets,
To lop off those that are distant and high,
Only stripping the young trees of their leaves;
In the seventh month, the shrike is heard;
In the eighth month, we begin the spinning of flax.
We make dark fabrics and yellow;
Our red manufacture is very brilliant,
It is for the lower robes of our princesses.

In the fourth month, the small grass is in seed;
In the fifth, the cicada gives out its note;
In the eighth, we reap;
In the tenth, the leaves fall;
In the days of the [eleventh] month, we go after badgers,
And take those foxes and wild cats,
To make furs for our princesses;
In the days of the [twelfth] month, we have a general hunt,
And proceed to keep up the exercises of war.
The boars of one year are for ourselves;
Those of three years are offered to our lord.

In the fifth month, the locust moves its legs;
In the sixth, the spinner sounds its wings;
In the seventh, in the fields;
In the eighth, under the eaves;
In the ninth, about the doors;
In the tenth, the cricket enters under our beds.
Chinks are filled up, and rats are smoked out;
The northern windows are stopped up, and the doors are plastered.
Ah! our wives and children!
That the year is changing,
We enter these houses and dwell.

In the sixth month, we eat the sparrow-plums and grapes;
In the seventh, we cook the *kuei* and pulse;
In the eighth, we knock down the dates;
In the tenth, we reap the rice,
And make the spirits for the spring,
For the benefit of the bushy eyebrows;
In the seventh month, we eat the melons;
In the eighth, we cut down the bottle-gourds;
In the ninth, we collect the hemp-seed;
We gather the sowthistle and make firewood of the fetid tree,
To feed our husbandmen.

In the ninth month, we prepare the vegetable gardens for the stacks;
And in the tenth, we convey the sheaves to them,
The millets, both the early sown and the late,
With the rice, the hemp, the pulse, and the wheat.
O, our husbandmen,
Our harvest is all collected.
Let us go to the town, and be at work on our homes,

In the day time collect the grass,
And at night twist it into ropes,
Then repair quickly our houses in the fields,
For we shall have to recommence our sowing.

In the days of the [twelfth] month, we hew out the ice with harmonious blows;
And in those of the [first] month, we convey it to the ice-houses,
Which we open in those of the [second] month, early in the morning,
Having offered in sacrifice a lamb with scallions.
In the ninth month, it is cold, with frost;
In the tenth month, we sweep clean the stack-sites.
Every two bottles of spirits are arranged for the public banquet;
The lambs and sheep are killed.
We go to the public school,
Where we raise the cup of rhinoceros horn,
And wish our lord long life,—that he may live forever.[1]

This poem is a description of the economic life of the ancient Chinese. The first stanza covers all the ideas of the whole poem, and the other seven stanzas give the details. The most important things of economic life are food and clothes. The former is produced by the labor of men, and the latter by that of women. The different kinds of grain are the principal articles of food, and the vegetables and fruits are auxiliary. The silk and flax are the principal materials of clothes, and the furs are auxiliary. These two, food and clothes, are the chief subjects of this poem. Besides the economic life, all the family life, social life, and political life are indicated by this poem. In fact, it pictures the golden age of the ancients.

In the beginning of the Han dynasty there was a policy of suppressing the merchants for the encouragement of the farmers. Yet the condition of the farmers was very bad, and the merchants took advantage of them. Chao Tso says:

[1] *Classics*, vol. iv, pt. i, pp. 226-233.

Now, if a farmer has a family of five persons, the number for serving at public labor is not less than two persons. But the land which he can cultivate is no more than one hundred acres, and the harvest of one hundred acres can be no more than one hundred bushels of rice. In spring, he cultivates the land; in summer, weeds the field; in autumn, gathers the harvest; in winter, stores up the grain. He cuts the woods, repairs the public buildings, and serves the public labor. He cannot escape from the wind and dust in spring, nor the heat in summer, nor the soaking rain in autumn, nor the cold in winter. Within the four seasons he does not have a day of rest. Moreover, he must pay the expense for the coming and going of his guests, the funeral and sickness of his friends, and the nourishment and bringing-up of his children. Working hard as he does, he still suffers from the calamities of flood and drought, and from oppressive government and uncertain taxation, which is different from morning to evening. When he has goods, he is compelled to sell them at half price; when he has nothing, he must borrow money at the rate of one hundred per cent. Therefore, among the farmers there are those who liquidate their debts by selling their farms or houses, their sons or grandsons.

On the other hand, the great merchants accumulate money and get interest at the rate of one hundred per cent; and the small ones sell goods in the market. They control extraordinary profit, and speculate around the market day by day. Taking advantage of any immediate demand of the government, they raise their price to double. Therefore, although their men do not cultivate and weed the land, nor their women take up the silkworm and weaving, their clothes must be of beautiful silk, and their food must be the best rice, together with meat. Without the hardship of the farmer, they secure hundreds or thousands of large coins. On account of their wealth, they connect themselves with the princes and marquises. Their power is even greater than the influence of the officials, and they control society by money. Traveling over thousands of miles in a great style, their carriages, horses, hats and shoes all are of the first grade. Such a condition is the reason the merchants can crush the farmers, and the reason the farmers emigrate. To-day the law dishonors the merchants, but they are rich and honorable already; it honors the farmers, but they are poor and mean already.[1]

From the end of the Chou dynasty to the beginning of the Han dynasty, economic life was dynamic. Hence, the condition of the farmers was much worse than that of the merchants. What Chao Tso described referred to the beginning of Han, but it was true at the end of Chou. Such a condition began about the time of Confucius and it prevailed about the time of Mencius. But, since the policy of Chao Tso[2] was carried out by Han Wên Ti, the condition of the farmers was greatly improved, and during his reign and that of his son (373-411 A. K. or 179-141 E. C.) there was a golden age. In fact, this period was one of national prosperity based upon agriculture, and it was the result of encouraging agriculture.

[1] *History of Han*, ch. xxiv.
[2] See *supra*, p. 362.

CHAPTER XXII

INDUSTRY

THE occupation of the group of artisans is industry. By industry, we mean the making of things by the power of man. The word handicraft gives the exact meaning, but we are obliged to use the word industry. In the Chinese language, the word *kung* really means industry, although the industry of the ancients was done by hand. Therefore we cannot use the word handicraft in place of the word *kung*. If we do so, it means that we must put the word *shou* before the word *kung*, "hand industry;" and such a term will change the sense of the word *kung* from a general and abstract sense, which can be applied to all ages, to a narrow and definite meaning, which is fitted only to the ancient time.

I. IMPORTANCE OF INDUSTRY

The importance of industry is indicated by Confucius himself. As we have seen, among the nine standard rules of a government, he says: " By inducing all classes of artisans to come in, wealth is made sufficient." [1] Therefore, if a government wishes to make the national wealth sufficient, it must welcome all classes of artisans, because they are the industrial workmen. It is industry alone that can produce new wealth, at all independent of nature. Industry can produce wealth in greater degree and more easily than agriculture. Hence Confucius does not mention agriculture in the

---

[1] See *supra*, p. 320.

nine standard rules. Commerce can only add to the utility of the existing wealth; industry produces new items of wealth. Hence Confucius ascribes to industry only the power of making wealth sufficient. From this passage, it is clear that Confucius thinks that industry is more important than both agriculture and commerce.

The reasons the Chinese make agriculture precede industry are, in the first place, that agriculture supplies food, and in the second place, that it furnishes raw materials. Therefore, in the process of production, agriculture comes naturally before industry. But as regards the efficiency of production, industry is under the absolute control of human power. Hence industry is more important than agriculture. The reasons the Chinese make industry precede commerce are still clearer. First, there can be little if any commerce unless there is some sort of industry. A good must be finished in the workshop before it can go to the market for sale. Therefore, in the process of production, industry comes naturally before commerce. Second, commerce is only an exchange of goods which have been produced, but industry is a creation of goods which have never before existed. Therefore, as regards the efficiency of production, industry has creative power much greater than that of commerce. Hence industry is more important than commerce. Indeed, agriculture, industry and commerce are all necessary, but industry is the most important branch of production.

II. DIVISIONS OF INDUSTRY

In ancient times, the kinds of industry must have been very few. But there were still six grand divisions of industry. According to the "Details of Rites," the emperor had six treasuries for the storing of products, and there were six superintendents in charge of them. These were:

first, the superintendent of the land; second, the superintendent of the wood; third, the superintendent of the waters; fourth, the superintendent of the grass; fifth, the superintendent of the manufactured articles; sixth, the superintendent of the mineral commodities. At that time, the taxes were paid in kind much more than in money. Therefore, the imperial government established the six treasuries for the keeping of the different commodities. All the products paid by the farmers, the foresters, the inhabitants along the waters, the gardeners, the artisans, and the merchants, were stored up in these six treasuries. The stores of these six treasuries came from the taxes, but they were mostly raw materials; hence, they needed to be manufactured.

On this account there were six imperial factories. Hence industry was divided into six kinds, and thus there were workers in earth, workers in metal, workers in stone, workers in wood, workers in the skins of animals, and workers in twigs. These six factories were for working up the materials of those six treasuries.[1] The reason the six treasuries left out metal, stone, and the skins of animals, was because these were included in the manufactured articles and mineral commodities. For the same reason, the six factories left out the products of the water, the manufactured articles, and the mineral commodities, because they were included in the factories of metal-workers and stone-workers. The six factories, however, did not necessarily correspond with the six treasuries in details. For instance, the superintendent of the land had charge of the products of the farmer, which might be ready for consumption, but the factory of earth-workers was a factory of pottery. Therefore, the six treasuries were simply warehouses of the different products,

[1] *Li Ki*, bk. i, p. 110.

and their goods were not necessarily turned over to the six factories for production. On the other hand, the six factories were places for manufacturing different articles, and they did not necessarily take their materials from those six treasuries only. Of course, the six factories had a very close connection with the six treasuries, but there was no exact correspondence. The six treasuries and the six factories were the system of the Yin dynasty (1215-571 B. K. or 1766-1122 B. C.). Hence, we know that even at that time Chinese industry was divided up into six kinds.

During the Chou dynasty, industry was highly developed; yet there were still six kinds only. According to the "Record of Industry," there are the industry of wood, the industry of metal, the industry of skin, the industry of coloring, the industry of polishing, and the industry of earth. These are the grand divisions of industry.

For their sub-divisions, the branches of the industry of wood are seven—namely, the wheelwright, the carriagewright, the bow-maker, the maker of the handle of different weapons, the mason, the car-maker, and the carpenter. The branches of the industry of metal are six—namely, the maker of the knife (used as a pen), the maker of different weapons, the maker of bells, the maker of measures, the maker of agricultural implements, and the sword-maker. The branches of the industry of skin are five—namely, the maker of armors of defense, the tanner of hides, the maker of drums, the worker in leather, and the furrier. The branches of the industry of coloring are five—namely, the design-drawer, the maker of embroidery, the dyer of feathers, the drawer of baskets, and the steeper of silk. The branches of the industry of polishing are five—namely, the lapidary, the comb-maker, the sculptor, the arrow-maker, and the maker of musical stones. The branches of the industry of earth are two—namely, the maker of different pots, and the maker of different vessels. In the six grand divisions, four divisions are based upon materials, such as wood and metal; the other two, upon the nature of arts, such as coloring and polishing. The total number of the branches of industry is thirty, but this number is incomplete. These thirty branches are simply the representatives of the prominent skilled workmanship, and this Record does not give all the branches of industry of that time. Moreover, there is even a branch given in this Record which is not included in the thirty branches; the maker of the shaft where the yoke for the two inside horses is attached. Therefore, these thirty branches are merely examples.

All the thirty branches are government factories, and are controlled by officials. Hence they are subject to the promotion of the government. Since the progress of civilization is from simplicity to complexity, the division of labor follows the same law, and the domination of different industries changes along this direction. Therefore, in the Yü dynasty, the government promoted the industry of pottery; in the Hsia, that of masonry; in the Yin, that of carpentry; and in the Chou, that of carriage-making. Such a government promotion simply followed the natural course. In the Yü dynasty, society was simplest; hence, pottery was the prominent industry, because it was the simplest form of industry. In the Hsia dynasty, when "the great flood" had just been settled, there was a great demand for shelter, and the land needed the system of water-channels, so the industry of the mason was prominent. In the Yin dynasty, when civilization had advanced, and society had demands beyond the necessaries of life, the industry of the carpenter was dominant. According to the "Record of Industry," the works of the carpenter are: the making of the stands of the musical instruments, which are carved with the figures of animals; the making of drinking-cups; and the making of the poles of the targets which are for the game of archery. Those things are far beyond the class of necessaries. In the Chou dynasty, when the civilization was most complex, and the division of labor was marked, the industry of the carriage-wright was dominant. Among all these industries, the carriage is the chief thing which, although itself a single article, concentrates many kinds of labor. The wheelwright, the carriage-wright, the maker of the shaft, the car-maker, all are the workers of a carriage. Since the economic life of the Chou was comfortable, the industry of the carriage was made prominent. In fact, the government promotion of industry is harmonious with the need of society at large, and the need of society is harmonious with the stage of civilization. Therefore, the higher civilization is, the more complex is industry.

III. FOUR ELEMENTS OF INDUSTRY

According to the " Record of Industry," industry depends upon four things: the season of the heaven, the climate of the earth, the goodness of the material, and the skill of the workman. Combining these four things, the article will be excellent.

(1) In some seasons, the heaven gives birth to a thing, and in some seasons, it kills it. In some seasons, the grass and trees grow, and in some seasons, they die. The stone sometimes dissolves, as in the hottest summer; the water sometimes freezes, and sometimes flows. These are the differences of seasons. For the adaptation to the seasons, we may take the bow-maker as an example. The materials of a bow are six: the strip of wood, the horn of the cow, the sinew of the brash animals, the glue of the cow, silk and varnish. The wood should be taken in winter; the horn, in autumn; the silk and varnish, in summer. For the making of a bow, in winter, the strip is divided up; in

spring, the horn is steeped; in summer, the sinew is made ready; in autumn, these three materials are united by the glue, silk, and varnish; in winter, the bow is finished, and its condition is fixed by the cold. In short, the different processes of making a bow are in harmony with the seasons. This is an example of the adaptation to the seasons of heaven.

(2) The knife of Chêng, the adze of Sung (both in the province of Honan), the knife used as a pen of Lu (Shantung province), the sword of Wu (Kiangsu) and Yüeh (Chekiang), all are very famous. Yet they could not be excellent, if they were made of the same materials, but changed to other localities. Therefore, any industry should be in harmony with the climate of the earth.

(3) The horn of Yen (Chihli), the wood for bow of King, the wood for arrow of Hu (both in Hupei province), and the metals and tin of Wu and Yüeh, are the materials of superiority. Therefore, any industry should take its materials from those places where they are especially good for the industry.

(4) In Yüeh, anyone can make agricultural implements, because its soil needs such things and its mines supply the materials. In Yen, anyone can make armors of defense, because its boundary is near to the Huns. In Ch'in (Shensi), anyone can make handles of weapons, because its woods are fitted to this occupation. In Hu (where the Huns live), anyone can make the bow and the car, because it is a nomadic country. This shows the different workmanship of different nations. Indeed, the skill of workmen is determined by the natural resources and the natural environment. Where the place is fitted to a particular industry, the people are accustomed to it, and develop a special skill. Hence, any industry needs the skill of the workman.

All these four things are important for any industry. If

the materials are good, and the workmen are skilful, but the article is not excellent, it may be because the article is made either during the improper season, or in opposition to the climate. These four things are the grounds upon which any industry is built. But the skill of the workman is the most important of all, because it can modify the other three elements.

IV. IMPORTANCE OF TOOLS

In the "Record of Industry," there are many details about the methods of industry. But they are very technical, and we shall not enter into them. Since those four elements of industry mentioned above left out the element of tools, which might be included in the element of skill, we now point it out especially, and show the importance of the tools.

The *Canon of History* quotes these words from Ch'ih Jên, a good historian of the ancients: "While in the employment of men we seek the old friends, in the employment of tools we seek, not the old ones, but the new."[1] Therefore any industry needs new tools. Since the newer tools are the better, there should always be a change in the methods of production. This principle of seeking new tools is a dynamic force in economic life.

The importance of the tools is indicated by Confucius himself. He says: "The artisan who wishes to do his work well must first sharpen his tools."[2] Therefore, next to the artisan himself, tools are most important. This is why capital is as important as labor in production. And this is why tools are the determining forces of industry. The artisan should improve his tools all the time, if he wishes to do good work.

---

[1] *Classics,* vol. iii, pt. i, pp. 229-230.

[2] *Ibid.,* vol. i, p. 297.

V. POSITION OF THE ARTISANS

For the position of the artisans, it is best to refer to the beginning of the "Record of Industry." It says:

A state has six functions, and the "hundred artisans" take up one of them. Some are sitting down and discussing the principles. Some are rising and executing them. Some are judging the curve, the plane and all the conditions of the materials, for the utilization of the five elements and the preparation of the articles. Some are transporting the valuable and strange goods of the four corners and storing them up. Some are using their energy for the increase of wealth from the land. Some are making the silk and flax ready for the finishing of clothes. Those who are sitting down and discussing the principles are called emperor and princes. Those who are rising and executing them are called students and great officials. Those who are judging the curve, the plane and all the conditions of the materials, for the utilization of the five elements and the preparation of the articles, are called the hundred artisans. Those who are transporting the valuable and strange goods of the four corners and storing them up are called merchants. Those who are using their energy for the increase of wealth from the land are called farmers. Those who are making the silk and flax ready for the finishing of clothes are called working women.[1]

In this statement we find four important points. First, it shows industrial democracy. It classifies the emperor, the princes, the students and the great officials along with the hundred artisans, the merchants, the farmers and the working women. All of them are in the laboring class. No one is personally higher than any other, but everyone must fulfil one of the six functions of the state; hence there is a division into six groups. Such a grouping system is not a caste, but a division of labor. Second, it attaches the chief im-

[1] *Official System of Chou*, ch. xxxix.

portance to industry. In the beginning, it especially gives emphasis to industry by saying that the hundred artisans take up one of the six functions. This shows that the artisans play the most important part in the economic functions of a state. Therefore, it puts the artisans in the third order, preceding the merchants, farmers, and working women. Third, it indicates the economic position of woman. It classifies the working women with the emperor and the princes, *etc.* This shows that women have economic independence, in forming a separate group from men, and that they have political rights, in bearing the function of a state, like the emperor and princes. Chêng Hsüan says: " Cloth is the task of the female officials." As women can be officials in the state, the political rights of women are obvious. Fourth, it indicates that every kind of labor is productive. The emperor and the princes, who are sitting down and discussing the principles, and the students and great officials, who are rising and executing them, are just as productive as the other four groups. Indeed, no one should be unproductive. These are the four significant points. And the chief point to which we want to call attention is that the artisans occupy a prominent position in the state.

VI. CONDITION OF THE ARTISANS

Since we have described the position of artisans in the state at large, we now come to consider the artisans themselves. Under this head, we may note six points. First, the government controls all the industries. In ancient times, the government was not only a political organization, but also an economic one. In the whole society, there is no greater industrial enterprise than that of government. It receives all kinds of products as taxes, so it has all the raw materials and unfinished goods. Hence, it has the means of production. Since the government contains a large body of men, and is the richest organization of the whole society, it has the greatest power for consumption. Therefore the government factories rise. Every important industry has a factory, and all the factories belong to the department of labor. The artisans of high grade are government officers, while the common artisans are government employees. From this point of view, we may say that it is a factory system. The government is the employer, supplies all the materials and tools, takes the finished products, and pays the wages. But it does not sell the products which are produced in the factories, but consumes them itself. The employees are simply the wage-earners, dependent upon the government; but they may get good pay, because theirs is not forced labor, and the government does not lay the burden upon any particular group of people, as the artisans. Moreover, their work may be very regular, and unemployment is unknown to them. Therefore, we may venture to say that the conditions of artisans in the government factories are better than in the private factories.

Second, the different crafts are hereditary. The " Record of Industry " gives a definition of the word industry, as follows: " After the sage has invented a thing, the expert transmits it and holds it generation after generation—this is called an industry." Since the division of labor is not complete, the technical training is complex, and the secret of the industry is not written out, the artisans usually getting their special training from their fathers. Hence the craft becomes hereditary. This is not a caste system; but it necessarily comes about through specialization of industry, family education, and the careful transmission of secrets. Therefore, although the artisans have freedom of occupation, they usually take up the work of their fathers. But we must understand that any industry does not exclude the outsider who does not belong to the same family. The fundamental thing is this; since the government controls all industries, there is no room for any private family to monopolize any industry. Because the crafts are mostly hereditary, however, the artisans sometimes adopt the name of their industry for their surname—Ch'iu (furrier), T'ao (potter), *etc.*

Third, every industry has a master to preside over the whole of it. He is an officer of the government. According to the " Record of Industry," the industry of carpentry has a master; from this we may presume that there is a master for every industry. Mencius speaks of the master of the workmen.[1] The duties of the master are to choose and to inspect the materials, to oversee the work, to test the finished articles, to educate the workmen, *etc.* But teaching may be the chief duty of a master. Mencius says: " A master-workman, in teaching others, uses the compass and square, and his pupils do the same." [2] The relation between master and workmen is in part like that between teacher and pupils. Such technical training is open to anyone who wishes to specialize in the particular industry, but we do not know the length of the term of apprenticeship.

Fourth, the artisans are mostly confined to a single industry for a lifetime. According to the " Royal Regulations," all the public artisans, who serve the government with their particular arts, are not allowed to practise any other thing, or to change their offices outside of their industry.[3] There are two reasons for this: first, it makes them concentrate their attention on their own specialization; and second, they are not qualified for general activities.

Fifth, the artisans live together in a special district, and

---

[1] *Classics*, vol. ii, p. 167.   [2] *Ibid.*, p. 421.
[3] *Li Ki*, bk. iii, p. 235.

by themselves. Since we have stated above the theory of Kuan Tzŭ—that the four groups of people are separated [1] —we need not enter into details now. On the one hand, they can easily learn their profession within their group; and on the other, they do not pay any attention to the outside. This is a scheme for specialization of arts.

Sixth, we are sure that the group of artisans is in the true handicraft stage. All those five characteristics belong to the artisans of the government factories, but they are common to all the independent artisans, except that the first and the fourth characteristics should be somewhat modified. The independent artisans, too, are controlled by the government; their crafts are hereditary; there is a master in every industry; they confine themselves to a single industry for life; and they live in a special district. But they have their own factory or workshop; buy their own materials and tools; sell their own products; and are both employers and employees. They are different from the artisans of the government factories. The latter are really in a factory system, and they are simply wage-earners; but the former are in the handicraft system. Tzŭ-hsia says: "The artisans have their shops to dwell in, in order to accomplish their works." [2] Such shops are in the market place, for the display and sale of goods. In so far as the artisans dwell in the shops, they are not only artisans, but also merchants. This is a very important characteristic of the independent artisan.

All these six characteristics mark the life of the artisans of ancient China, and they show the industrial conditions of the time. To-day, China is coming from the domestic system to the modern factory system, and industrial conditions are quite different from those of the ancients.

[1] See *supra*, pp. 368-9.   [2] *Classics*, vol. i, p. 341.

CHAPTER XXIII

COMMERCE

THE occupation of the group of merchants is commerce. In it is included what economists call "exchange;" but we shall preserve the word commerce, because it is the usual designation of one of the four great groups of people. In the Chinese language, the group of merchants is divided into two classes. The one is called traveling merchant; he deliberates about the distance to be covered, makes calculations in regard to market conditions, and transports his goods to distant places. The other is called stationary merchant; he stores up goods, and waits for customers, in order to sell at a profit. Such a distinction might have been very important in ancient times, but it does not help us any to-day; hence, we shall use the word commerce to include these two classes of merchants, and make no distinction between them.

1. IMPORTANCE OF COMMERCE

Since the Chinese put merchants in the last of the four groups of people, a misconception has arisen. According to the common view, merchants belong to the worst class of people, because they do not make anything themselves, but simply pick up profit from things made by others. Moreover, they invite the hatred of the people by storing up commodities in order to raise their prices, and then selling them at a profit. This was the reason why Han Kao Ti (350-357 A. K. or 202-195 B. C.) forbade the merchants wearing silk and riding in carriages, and put a burden and disgrace upon them by heavy taxes. It was the first law applied to the whole empire for the suppression of merchants.[1] From that time on, there were several periods in Chinese economic history in which merchants suffered a great deal. But such a policy is not according to the principle of Confucius.

As we have seen, in *Ku-liang's Commentary,* merchants are ranked next only to students,[2] and are not the worst class of people at all. The reason why the Chinese usually put the merchants in the last of the four groups is simply this. Since the farmers produce the raw materials, and the artisans the manufactured goods, the merchants who exchange the raw materials and the manufactured goods should not come before them. It is the order of the processes of production, not the order of social position, nor of moral distinction. Therefore, the Chinese call agriculture the primary occupation, industry and commerce the secondary occupations. It is the natural order of production, but there is no contempt for industry and commerce.

Confucius never underestimates the merchants. And before the Han dynasty, no Confucian ever advocated the policy of suppressing the merchants for the encouraging of farmers. The principle that the four groups of people are equally useful to society is pointed out by Yeh Shih as follows: " It is because the four groups of people all together contribute their usefulness to society, that civilization can be advanced. To depress the secondary occupations and to promote the primary one, is not a correct theory.[3]

The relative importance of agriculture and commerce

---

[1] Shang Yang was the first one who established the policy of supressing merchants for the encouragement of farmers (192-214 A. K. or 360-338 B. C.). See *Book of the Lord of Shang,* bk. ii; *Historical Record,* ch. lxviii.

[2] See *supra,* p. 367.

[3] *General Research,* ch. xx.

varies with the times. This principle is stated by Ssŭ-ma Chien as follows:

The *Canon of History* tells of the interval of the Tang and the Yü dynasties, and the *Canon of Poetry* relates the ages of the Yin and the Chou dynasties: In time of calm and repose, they honored the school as the chief social institution; they preferred the primary occupation at first, and put the secondary ones in the background; they used the rites and justice to control personal interest. But things change, and in the complexity of many causes, it is necessary to take the opposite view. Therefore, when a thing is at its apogee, it decays, and when a time comes to the climax, it turns. Sometimes the simple reality predominates, and sometimes the complex civilization; such is the evolution of an end and of a beginning.[1]

According to his theory, in a dynamic state and a complex civilization, commerce is naturally more important than agriculture. Therefore, even though the moral influence is weakened by economic interest, and capitalistic production destroys the equality of distribution, it is a natural result which is bound to come. In fact, when there is a universal empire, without struggle outside, and the people live on the social income by themselves, the Chinese attach more importance to agriculture; it is looked at from the standpoint of distribution. But, when there is a national struggle, they attach more importance to industry and commerce; it is looked at from the standpoint of production.

II. COMMUNICATION AND TRANSPORTATION

The important things helping the growth of commerce are communication and transportation. These two things

---

[1] *Historical Record*, ch. xxx.

usually work along the same line. Regarding communication, in Confucius' time it depended on the strength of horses and the speed and endurance of man. Therefore, Confucius says: " The flowing progress of virtue is more rapid than the transmission of royal orders by stages and couriers." [1] Along the roads, there were stations at fixed distances. As the government dispatch reached any station, the station employed its own stage or courier to transmit it to the next station, and the next station did the same. In this way, the dispatch was rapidly sent forward.

According to the *Law Code of the Ts'ing Dynasty*,[2] every fifteen miles a post station is established; and at every station, there are one postmaster and four postmen. Within twenty-four hours, the dispatch must pass over three hundred miles. The postman must not delay midway. When any dispatch comes in, no matter how many or how few, the postmaster must give it immediately to the postman without waiting for the coming dispatch. Such a system is the survival of an old fashion, but it is gradually being abolished.

Formerly, private letters were delivered by a private post-office. Now, communication is usually through the new postal, telegraph and telephone system. These three things belong to the Department of Communication and Transportation which controls also steamships and railroads (established in 2457 A. K. or 1906 A. D.).

Since transportation is even more important than communication, we shall discuss it at greater length. Since transportation by land was naturally easier than transportation by water, it shall receive first attention. According to his-

[1] *Classics*, vol. ii, p. 184.
[2] Ch. xxii.

COMMERCE 415

tory,[1] Huang Ti was the inventor of the carriage; Shao Hao was the first one who used the ox to draw it; and Yao was the first one who used the horse. In ancient times, the use of oxen or cows for the drawing of carts was more common than that of horses.[2]

The "pointing-south car" was invented by Huang Ti. When he fought with Ch'ih Yu, the latter created a fog by magic power, and his soldiers missed their way. Huang Ti therefore invented the "pointing-south car" for the showing of direction. After the victory was won, this car was often used. During the Chou dynasty, when the envoy of Annam who came to pay the tribute to the court missed his way going home, the Duke of Chou made this car for him, and he arrived home in the length of one year. Therefore, this car always led the procession when the emperor went out, in order to impress the people. During the Latter Han dynasty, Chang Hêng (629-690, or 78-139 A. D.) began to make this car again. But the invention was lost during the revolutionary war of that dynasty. Under the reign of Wei Ming Ti (about 784-787, or 233-236 A. D.), Professor Ma Chün-shao was ordered to make it. On the top of the car, there was a wooden figure with hand raised, and always pointing south. But it was lost again during the revolution of the Tsin dynasty. In 968 (417 A. D.), this car was discovered, but its mechanism was not perfect. During the reign of Sung Shun Ti (1028-1029, or 477-478 A. D.), Tsu Chung-chih renewed and perfected it. In later times, there were many styles, but the essential, that is, pointing south, was always the same. The "pointing-south car" was of great importance to the development of transportation, because it was the origin of the compass.

[1] *General Research*, ch. cxvi.
[2] *Classics*, vol. iii, pt. ii, p. 404; vol. iv, pt. ii, pp. 356, 413.

According to the imperial procession, next to the "pointing-south car" was the "recording-miles-drum car." Within the car, there was a wooden person holding a hammer toward a drum, and striking the drum once when it passed each mile. It was discovered in 968, but the inventor is unknown. In later times, it had many modifications.[1] This original form of speedometer was also important to the development of transportation.

One of the most wonderful inventions along the line of transportation was the invention of "wooden oxen and flowing horses." In 782 (231 A. D.), Chu-ko Liang, the greatest statesman of the Three Kingdoms, invented the wooden oxen and the flowing horses for the transportation of food to his army.[2] They were labor-saving machines, and their operation was very successful. Unfortunately, after his death (785), no one was able to make use of his invention, although a description of it is still preserved.

Uniformity, which is a very important principle of Confucius, is especially applicable to the system of transportation. The "Doctrine of the Mean" says that all over the world carriages have wheels of the same size.[3] This is the theoretical view of the Confucians; it requires the roads of the whole world to be uniform. Such a theory will be easily realized when the railway system is perfected.

According to the "Royal Regulations," one road is divided up into three parts. Men take the right way; women take the left way; and carriages keep in the middle.[4] Therefore, the road is very broad; the two sexes are kept apart; and the carriages never can hurt the people. This is the general system of roads.

[1] *General Research*, ch. cxvii.
[2] *History of the Three Kingdoms*, ch. xxxv.
[3] *Classics*, vol. i, p. 424.
[4] *Li Ki*, bk. iii, p. 244.

COMMERCE 417

According to the *Official System of Chou,* the system of roads is very complete. There is the surveyor (*liang jên*)[1] to fix the different standards of different roads, which vary in width from eight feet to seventy-two feet. There is the superintendent of strategical positions (*ssŭ hsien*)[1] to connect the roads through the mountains and rivers, and to plant trees along the roads. There is the inspector of hotels (*yeh lu shih*)[2] to look after the roads of the whole imperial state, and the stations, hotels, wells and trees along the roads. There is a general rule.[3] Every ten miles, there is a station along the road, and food and drink are served there. Every thirty miles, there is a lodging place, where the hotel stands; and within the hotel, a small store of grain is kept. Every fifty miles, there is a market place, where a tower is built; and within the tower, a large store is kept. All these public buildings are for the convenience of travelers. There is the chief of guards (*hou jên*)[4] who sends the guards carrying lances and halberds on the roads, for the safety of travelers. Finally and most important for the economic life, there is the officer called the combiner of all directions (*ho fang shih*).[5] His function is to control all the roads of the empire, for the exchange of wealth. Through these regulations prescribing the duties of different officers, the operation of an efficient system of roads is assured.

For transportation by water, we must go back to the "Tribute of Yü." This book is a description of the different water-ways by which the tribute of the nine provinces was presented to the capital city. The capital city was in Ki Chow, the present provinces of Chihli and Shansi. Along

[1] Ch. xxx.
[2] Ch. xxxvi.
[3] Ch. xiii.
[4] Ch. xxx.
[5] Ch. xxxiii.

the three directions of Ki Chow, west, south and east, there is the Ho, the Yellow River. The reason why the capital was there was for the convenience of transportation. According to the theory of Confucius, a capital must be in a place where the water-way is good, in order to facilitate the paying of visits and tribute by the princes, and the exchanges of the merchants. Therefore, the "Tribute of Yü," after telling about the taxation and the tribute of different provinces, describes the water-ways connected with the capital. The fundamental point was the Ho, because, when anything came to the Ho, it was easily conveyed to the capital. The routes to be taken by boats from the different provinces are described in detail. This is the oldest system of water transportation in the history of the empire.[1]

Transportation by sea can be traced back to the "Tribute of Yü." When Yang Chow (Kiangsu, Anhui, Kiangsi, Chekiang, Fukien) sent its tribute, they followed the course of the Kiang (the Yangtze River) and the sea, and so reached the Hwai and the Sze; then they came to the Ho. From the mouth of the Kiang to the mouth of the Hwai, however, are only six or seven hundred miles. The long way of transportation by sea conducted by the government really began under the Tang dynasty. In 1290 (739 A. D.), the governor of Yu Chow (Chihli province) was appointed as a commissioner of sea transportation. At that time, the rice of Kiangsu was transported by sea to Chihli for the support of the soldiers. During the Yüan dynasty, sea transportation became very important. It began in 1833 (1282 A. D.), and ended in 1914, about the end of that dynasty (1918). It transported rice from Kiangsu and Chekiang to Peking twice a year, and the annual amount of rice at the highest point was more than three

[1] *Classics*, vol. iii, pt. i, pp. 92-127.

million bushels. All the officials and the people were dependent upon this transportation.[1]

The "Tribute of Yü" describes the natural waterways; we come next to the system of canals. In ancient times, there was no canal for the purpose of transportation, because there was no need of it. In 66 A. K. (486 B. C), the first canal, which was called the Han Canal, was built, and it was the most important one. *Tso's Commentary* says: "This autumn, Wu walled Han, and thence formed by a canal a communication between the Kiang and the Hwai."[2] Before that time, these two large rivers had never been connected. It was only when the king of Wu wished to get the supremacy over the northern states, that he first opened this canal for the transportation of food to his army. It was to lead the water of the Kiang to that of the Hwai, and it was the basis of the Imperial Canal. In 1138 (587 A. D.), Sui Wên Ti opened a new canal on the west of the Han Canal. This was the first time that the water of the Hwai was led to the Kiang, but it was not large enough for the navigation of battle ships. In 1156 (605 A. D.), Sui Yang Ti employed more than one hundred thousand laborers for the enlarging of the new canal. Its length was more than three hundred miles, and its width was forty paces. The "dragon boats" could be navigated. Along the two sides of the canal, the imperial roads were built, and willow trees were planted on the roads. In the same year, more than one million laborers, including men and women, were employed for the opening of the Tung-chi Canal, in order to connect the Loh with the Ho and the Ho with the Hwai. In 1159, a similar number of laborers were employed for the opening of the Yung-chi Canal, which

---

[1] *Continuation of the General Research*, ch. xxxi.
[2] *Classics*, vol. v, pt. ii, p. 819. Han is the present Yangchow.

led the Ts'in southward connecting with the Ho, and northward reaching Peking. In 1161 (610 A. D.), the Southern Canal was opened from Chênkiang to Hangchow. Its length was more than eight hundred miles, and its width more than one hundred feet. Thus the Imperial Canal was completed. Since the large rivers of China run mostly from the west to the east, there is only the Imperial Canal running from the north to the south for a great distance. In fact, it connected the north and the south, and had a great influence upon every aspect of Chinese life. Before the modern railway system began, there was no means of communication comparable with the Imperial Canal.

For transportation by water, the best invention was the "thousand-miles ship". It was the invention of Tsu Chung-chih, and was made between 1034 and 1051 (483-500 A. D.). It was moved by machine power. When it was tested, it sailed more than one hundred miles in one day.[1] It was like the modern steamship, but it produced no practical effect.

III. WEIGHTS AND MEASURES

Among the instruments of commerce, the different kinds of measures are very important. In ancient China, all the measures were based upon the standard tubes. The twelve tubes were originally made by Huang Ti of bamboo, then of jade, and in the Han dynasty of brass or copper. They were a little more than three-tenths of an inch in diameter, and the circumference of the bore was exactly nine-tenths. The longest, called the "yellow cup," was 9 inches long, and the shortest, the "responsive cup," only 4.66 inches. Six tubes of them gave the sharped notes in music, and the other six gave the flat notes; the twelve together formed a

[1] *History of Southern Ch'i*, ch. lii.

COMMERCE 421

chromatic scale. Besides their application to music, (1) the yellow cup was the standard measure of length. Since the breadth of a grain of millet made 1 *fên*, 90 grains determined the length of the yellow cup; 10 *fên* were 1 inch; 10 inches were 1 foot; 10 feet were 1 *chang;* and 10 *chang* were 1 *yin*. (2) The yellow cup was also the standard for measures of capacity. 13⅓ millet grains filled 1 *fên* of it, and 1200 grains filled the whole; so much made 1 *yo;* 2 *yo* made 1 *ko;* 10 *ko,* 1 *shêng* or pint; 10 *shêng,* 1 *tou* or peck; 10 *tou,* 1 *hu* or bushel. (3) This tube, again, supplied the standard for weights. 100 grains of millet weighed 1 *chu;* 24 *chu,* 1 *liang* or tael; 16 taels, 1 *chin* or catty; 30 catties, 1 *chün;* and 4 *chün,* 1 *shih* or stone. Therefore, it was said that the yellow cup was the basis of all human affairs.[1]

The comparison between the ancient measures and the modern measures we may state as simply as possible.[2] First, regarding the measure of length, the ancient foot was only 7.4 inches of the modern foot (the foot of the Department of Labor); and the modern foot is 1 foot 3.5 inches of the ancient foot. If we take this standard to measure the land, the ancient pace was 6 feet, and the modern pace is 5 feet; hence, the ancient pace was only 4 feet 4.4 inches of the modern pace, and the modern pace is 1 pace 7.5 inches of the ancient pace. In ancient times, 300 paces made 1 mile; and in modern times, 360 paces make 1 mile. Therefore, 100 miles of the ancient were little more than 55 miles and 22 paces of the modern. In ancient times, 100 paces made 1 acre; and in modern times, (from the Han dynasty to the present), 240 paces make 1 acre. According to the difference of measures, the 240 paces of the modern acre are little

---

[1] *History of Han,* ch. xxi.
[2] All the measures mentioned in this treatise refer to this paragraph.

more than 364 paces of the ancient. Therefore, 100 acres of the ancient were little more than 27 acres of the modern. Second, regarding the measures of capacity, the proportion is 10 to 2. For example, 10 pints of the ancient equaled only 2 pints of the modern.[1] Third, regarding weights, the proportion is 3 to 1. For example, the ancient weight of 3 catties equaled only 1 catty of the modern weight (since the Sui dynasty).[2] It thus appears that all the measures and weights of the modern are much greater than those of the ancient.[3]

Since the different measures are very important for human affairs, and especially for commerce, the government should pay much attention to them. According to the *Canon of History*, the Emperor Shun made a tour of inspection every five years; and during that time he made uniform the standard tubes, the measures of length, of capacity and of weight throughout the whole empire.[4] According to the *Record of Rites*, at the equinox of the second month, the government makes uniform the measures of length and capacity; the weight of 30 catties, the steelyard, and the weight of 120 catties. It corrects the peck and bushel, the steelyard weights and the bushel-scraper.

[1] *Canonical Interpretation of the Present Dynasty*, vol. xxxix, ch. ii.
[2] *General Research of the Present Dynasty*, ch. ii.
[3] A comparison of modern Chinese measures and weights with English, results as follows: (1) The Chinese foot (*chih*) is fixed by treaty at 14.1 inches English, or 0.3581 meters. The Chinese acre (*mou*) is fixed by treaty at 733½ square yards, or 6.6 Chinese acres equal 1 English acre. A Chinese mile (*li*) is 360 paces or 1800 feet, and it equals 1894.12 English feet. (2) A Chinese pint (*shêng*) is about one-fourth less than an English pint. (3) The Chinese catty (*chin*) is equal by treaty to 1⅓ lbs. avoirdupois, or 604.53 grams. Except that the measurement of the pint is quoted from a note of Legge (*Chinese Classics*, vol. i, p. 185), all these statements are quoted from the *Chinese-English Dictionary* of H. A. Giles.
[4] *Classics*, vol. iii, pt. i, p. 36

And, at the equinox of the eighth month, it does the same.[1] Thus the government regulated the different measures twice a year. From these statements, it appears that in ancient China, the government gave much attention to the different measures in order to prevent fraud in commercial life.

During Confucius' time, the government did not pay attention to the measures, and there either were no special officers in charge of them, or the officers did not do their duty. Therefore, Confucius sets forth the rules of a government as follows: " Carefully attending to the weights and the measures of capacity; examining the standard tubes and the measures of length; and restoring the discarded officers who take charge of them—the good government will be prevailing over the four corners."[2] According to the principle of Confucius, the weights and measures are the most important instruments of commerce, and they must be regulated carefully and uniformly by the government. If they are correct, it is good not only for commerce, but also for political affairs as a whole.

IV. VALUE AND PRICE

The value of a thing is dependent not only upon its utility, but also upon its scarcity. Such a principle is given by Mencius. He says:

The people cannot live without water and fire, yet if you knock at a man's door in the dusk of the evening, and ask for water and fire, there is no man who will not give them, such is the abundance of these things. A sage governs the world so as to cause pulse and grain to be as abundant as water and fire.[3]

According to this statement, water and fire have utility,

---

[1] *Li Ki*, bk. iv, pp. 260, 289.
[2] *Cf. Classics*, vol. i, p. 351.
[3] *Classics*, vol. ii, pp. 462-3.

because the people cannot live without them. But they have no value when they are abundant and can be obtained easily. On the other hand, pulse and grain have both utility and value, because they are limited in supply. Therefore, the sage wants to make them as abundant as water and fire. In other words, the sage wants to make economic goods as abundant as free goods. The multiplication of their quantity in supply is the fundamental cause of lowering their value, provided that there is a constant demand for them. If all the economic goods were converted into free goods, they would have no value, but utility, and the people would obtain them without payment; hence, the people would all be virtuous. This is the object of the sage who wants to solve the ethical problem by the solution of the economic problem; and this is also the principle of value.

The difference between economic goods and free goods is pointed out very clearly by Su Shih, a great writer of the Sung dynasty (1587-1652, or 1036-1101 A. D.). In one of his famous essays, he says:

Generally, in the world, everything has its owner. If it does not belong to us, we ought not to take even a little bit. But the gentle wind above the river which is obtained by the ear as a sound, and the radiant moonlight in the mountain which is met by the eye as a beauty, are to be taken without prohibition, and to be consumed without exhaustion. They are supplied by the unexhausted treasury of nature.

His essay is not a treatise on economic subjects at all, but this statement is a good principle of economics. According to it, economic goods are limited in supply, and belong to their owners; but free goods are not limited in supply, and belong to nature only. Hence, the former have value, and the latter have not. Therefore, economic goods differ from free goods as regards their supply; while as regards demand there is no difference between them.

Confucius very seldom speaks of price. But there is one statement in reference to price, and it is in harmony with economic principles. Tzŭ-kung asks Confucius: "There is a beautiful jade here. Should I lay it up in a case and keep it? or should I seek for a good price and sell it?" Confucius says: "Sell it! Sell it! But I would wait for some one to offer the price."[1] This conversation is not about an economic problem at all, but is allegorical. Tzŭ-kung takes the jade as the representative of Confucius, and then asks him why he should not offer himself for official employment. The answer of Confucius is that self-respect is more important and more proper than office-seeking. Therefore, he does not bend himself for the seeking of office. This is the whole meaning of this conversation. According to their words, however, it is a principle of price. Since price is determined by demand and supply, if the seller offers his commodity for sale before there is any demand for it, its price must be low; but, if he keeps it on his own hands and waits until the rise of demand, its price must be high. This is really a true principle of price, although it is stated in an illusive way.

Although Confucius very seldom spoke about price, he did influence the market price by his administration. According to Hsun Tzŭ, when he was about to become the minister of justice, the sellers of cows and horses in the state of Lu did not have fraudulent prices,[2] though fraudulent prices were common in ancient times. The sellers made devices to deceive the buyers for the purpose of raising prices, especially the sellers of animals. But, when Con-

---
[1] *Classics*, vol. i, p. 221.
[2] Bk. viii.

426   THE ECONOMIC PRINCIPLES OF CONFUCIUS

fucius was about to take that office, his moral influence prevailed even over the market place. Therefore, the whole market was free from fraudulent prices.

Mencius gave a very good principle about price, in his reply to Chen Hsiang, the follower of Hsü Hsing. After Chen Hsiang had been defeated by Mencius,[1] he advanced the following argument:

If the doctrines of Hsü Tzŭ were followed, then there would not be two prices in the market, nor any deceit in the state. If a boy of five cubits were sent to the market, no one would impose on him. Linen and silk of the same length would be of the same price. So it would be with bundles of hemp and silk, being of the same weight; with the different kinds of grain, being the same in quantity; and with shoes which were of the same size.

Mencius replied:

It is the nature of things to be of unequal quality. Some are worth twice, some five times, some ten times, some a hundred times, some a thousand times, some ten thousand times as much as others. If you reduce them all to the same standard, that must throw the world into confusion. If coarse shoes and fine shoes were of the same price, who would make the latter? For people to follow the doctrines of Hsü Tzŭ, would be for them to lead one another on to practise deceit. How can such doctrines avail for the government of a state?[2]

According to these arguments, Hsü's doctrine is that the price should be made uniform on the basis of the quantity of things; but Mencius' principle is that price should vary according to the quality of things. We cannot make a comparison between these two arguments, because the former

[1] See *supra*, p. 385, and *infra*, pp. 485-6.
[2] *Classics*, vol. ii, p. 256.

COMMERCE 427

is obviously wrong, and the latter is obviously correct. We now simply explain the principle of Mencius. According to him, the value of a thing is determined by its quality, not by its length, nor by its weight, nor by its quantity, nor by its size. Now, we may ask what is the determining factor of the quality of a thing? In fact, the quality of a thing depends on the cost of making it. Therefore, if coarse shoes and fine shoes were of the same price, no one will make the fine ones. If we put it into modern terms, price is determined by the cost of production. When the cost of a thing is twice, or five times, or ten times, or a hundred times, or a thousand times, or ten thousand times as much as that of others, its price will be in the same proportion. This is true in regard to manufactured goods, and even in regard to natural goods, such as pearl and jade, they cannot get away from the cost element, because they are difficult to obtain. This theory is from the standpoint of the producer, but the producer really has a greater power in the making of price than the consumer. Therefore, the cost of production is a great element in determining price. Moreover, if we return to the beginning of the argument of Mencius, we must say that the price of all things is determined by the nature of them. By the phrase " nature of things," on the one hand, he means the utility which can be derived from them, and it is looked at from the point of view of the consumer; on the other hand, he means the cost which has been put into them, and it is looked at from the point of view of the producer. Therefore, Mencius' statement that price is determined by the nature of things is quite correct and conclusive, because it combines the utility element and the cost element.

There is a very close relation between consumers' wants and prices, and it is shown by the " Royal Regulations." It says: " [When the emperor makes a tour of inspection throughout the empire], he orders the superintendents of markets to present lists of prices, that he may see what the people want. If their mind were luxurious, they would want the extraordinary things."[1] Chêng Hsüan explains: "If their wants are simple, the price of necessaries will be high; and if they are luxurious, that of luxuries will be high." Therefore, prices are the index of consumers' wants. If we do not know what is the characteristic of their wants, we may judge them by the lists of prices. In fact, the wants of consumers are usually the causes, and prices are their effects, although the latter may sometimes affect the former.

V. MONEY AND BANKING

1. *History of Money and Banking*

The history of Chinese money begins in the remotest time. It is said that money had been used since the reign of Pao Hsi (2402-2288 B. K. or 2953-2839 B. C.). During the dynasties of Yü and Hsia, three metals were used for money. Gold occupied first place as a standard, silver the next, and copper the lowest in the class of money.[2] According to the "Tribute of Yü," the provinces of Yang and King both sent these three kinds of metal to the imperial government as tribute.[3] We may say that the Chinese give us our oldest example of the gold standard.

During the beginning of the Chou dynasty, T'ai Kung established the nine treasuries to have charge of the money system. The gold money was an inch square, and its weight was one catty. The shape of copper money was round, and there was a square hole in its middle; its weight was counted

---
[1] *Li Ki*, bk. iii, p. 216.
[2] *Historical Record*, ch. xxx.
[3] *Classics*, vol. iii, pt. i, pp. 110, 115.

COMMERCE

by *chu*. The name of the gold coin was catty, and that of the copper was coin.[1] According to Chia K'uei, the monetary system of all the four dynasties, the Yü, the Hsai, the Yin, and the Chou, was the same. They used gold, silver, and copper as the three kinds of money.[2] Therefore, the state of Ch'u had the treasuries of three kinds of money.[3]

We do not know the ratio of the three kinds of money during ancient times, but we do know it during the Han dynasty. At the time of Wang Mang (561 A. K. or 10 A. D.), the smallest copper coin, weighing 1 *chu*, was the unit, and the largest one, weighing 11 *chu*, was worth 50 of the smallest coins; a silver coin, weighing 8 taels, was the unit, and was worth 1,000 of the smallest copper coins; the gold coin weighed 1 catty, and was worth 10,000 of the smallest copper coins. These were the ratios of the three kinds of money in the Han dynasty. According to these ratios, one tael of silver exchanged for a little more than one catty and ten taels of copper, and one tael of gold exchanged for a little more than eight catties and two taels of copper. In fact, one tael of gold was equal to only five taels of silver. According to Hu Wei (his book was published in 2252, or 1701 A. D.), in ancient times, the value of all commodities was measured by the copper coin, and the value of copper coin was measured by the gold and silver coins. When the payment was large, gold and silver took the place of copper; and when gold and silver were insufficient, copper took their place, even though they were to be paid. This system was used to make the three kinds of money supplement one another.[4]

[1] *History of Han*, ch. xxiv.
[2] *Narratives of Nations*, bk. iii (commentary).
[3] *Historical Record*, ch. xli.
[4] *Canonical Interpretation of the Ts'ing Dynasty*, vol. ix, ch. vii.

During the Ch'in dynasty, there were only two kinds of money. Gold was the higher money; its weight was one *yi*, twenty taels; and its name was therefore *yi*. Copper was the lower money; it was inscribed with the two words, "half tael," and its weight conformed to the inscription. Han Kao Ti changed the weight of the copper coin, making it lighter, and also that of the gold money, which was one catty. Therefore, in the Ch'in dynasty and in the beginning of the Han dynasty the money systems were similar.

As China had used gold as the standard of money since the Yü dynasty, why did she give it up after the Tsin dynasty? In the first place, it was because gold had decreased in quantity. During the Chou and the Han dynasties gold was used by both government and people. The Han and the Northern Wei dynasties allowed the punishment of crime to be commuted with gold. In the Northern Wei dynasty, however, on account of the scarcity of gold, ten rolls of silk were accepted as the equivalent of one tael of gold. In the Tang dynasty, the ransom was paid with copper instead of gold. Therefore, the decrease of gold began in the period of the Southern and the Northern Dynasties. The causes for such a decrease were four. First, there was a great consumption of gold; the Buddhist church was the chief consumer, and the court was the second. Second, the gold was exported to foreign countries. Third, it was hoarded by those who kept it secretly. Fourth, few gold mines were opened, hence there was no production on a large scale. These reasons made gold scarce, and prevented China from using gold continuously.

In the second place, it was subject to Gresham's law. Except during the reigns of Han Wu Ti and Wang Mang, the Han dynasty had only two kinds of money, and each was as much legal tender as the other; hence, copper drove out gold. Although these two metals were ranked, one higher and one lower, they were not equal in circulation, and the lower one became predominant. Moreover, as the commerce of the ancients was not highly developed, small payments were naturally carried on by the lower money. Therefore copper occupied the more influential place. The chief trouble was that, as there was no limitation put upon the quantity of the cheaper money, the people would use it not only for small payments, but also for large ones. They would either hoard gold or use it for other purposes, and gold gradually became only a commodity, but not money. Therefore, after the Tsin dynasty, gold ceased to be money.

Before the Ch'in dynasty, silver was used as one kind of money, ranking between gold and copper. But from the Ch'in dynasty to the Kin dynasty, silver was not money at all. It was used as money only during the reigns of Han Wu Ti and Wang Mang, but this system lasted but a short time. During the reign of Liang Wu Ti (1053-1100), southern China used gold and silver as money; during the Northern Chou dynasty (1110-1131), north-western China used them also; and through the Tang and the Sung dynasties, southern China still used silver. But such money was confined to certain localities. Under the Kin dynasty (1748, or 1197 A. D.), silver began to be coined as money, and it has been used by the whole society to the present day

Throughout Chinese history, the chief kind of money was copper. For the copper money, we can speak generally. From the Ch'in dynasty to the Sui dynasty, the best coin was the "five chu", which was first coined by Han Wu Ti (434, or 118 B. C.). "This coin," says H. B. Morse, "also easily obtainable to-day, is beautifully cast, 0.95 inch in diameter, weighing to-day from 46 to 51 grains." From the Tang dynasty to the present day, the Kai-yüan coin has been of the standard type, which was first coined by Tang

Kao Tsu (1172, or 621 A. D.). With a diameter of 0.95 inch, it was presumably one-tenth of the modern tael of 570 to 580 grains.[1]

Paper money was a Chinese invention. The *Official System of Chou* speaks of the *li pu*.[2] Chêng Chung, the commentator (died in 634, or 83 A. D.), says: "It was a piece of cloth, stamped with seals and written with words, two inches wide and two feet long. It was used as money for the exchange of things."[3] Ho Yi-sun, living at the beginning of the Yüan dynasty, says that it was like the paper money of modern times. According to the same book, there was the "written tally."[4] It was made of a piece of wood, which was divided into two parts with inscription in their edge. Such a tally was paid and accepted by the buyer and seller, and it was inspected by the auditor of price. It resembled the check of modern times. Therefore, the forms of paper money were developed in the Chou dynasty, although the materials were not paper because at that time there was no paper.

The paper money issued by the government was an invention of the Tang dynasty. During the middle part of that dynasty, there was a scarcity of money; hence, money was not allowed to be taken out of certain localities. Therefore, during the reign of Tang Hsien Tsung (1357-1371), when merchants came to the capital, they deposited their money in the offices which represented the different pro-

---

[1] Here the English inch. *Currency in China*, p. 4. Morse also says: "Under the Chou dynasty, on the evidence of the coins, the *liang* of 24 *chu* was probably 97.5 grains, giving 4.06 grains as the weight of the *chu*."—P. 8.

[2] Ch. xiv.

[3] Even though his commentary may not be correct, it is obvious that he had the conception of paper money.

[4] Ch. xv.

COMMERCE 433

vinces at the capital, and received bonds from them. In this way, wherever they went, they drew money with their bonds very easily. This was called "flying money." Such a practice, however, was prohibited by the central government, because it thought that the offices would keep the money out of circulation, and the prices of commodities would be lowered. But the result was still worse than before. Therefore, in 1363 (812 A. D.), the government opened its own offices at the capital for carrying on the business of flying money—that is, the government issued bonds to depositors, and they exchange bonds for money at the great cities of different provinces. This was the first time that the government issued paper money. This system prevailed during the earlier part of the Sung dynasty (1511-1573).

During the Sung dynasty, while the flying money was like the bill of exchange, true paper money was introduced by Chang Yung in the province of Szechuan. This also was a spontaneous growth. On account of the weight and troublesomeness of the iron money, about 1556 (1005 A. D.), the people of that province issued notes privately which were called "changelings," for the convenience of exchange, and the notes were managed by sixteen rich houses.. In later times, when the rich houses became bankrupt, and were unable to pay their debts, there arose many lawsuits. Therefore, about 1572, the government established a bank in that province for the management of the changelings. After 1574 this kind of paper money prevailed over the whole empire; and throughout the Sung dynasty, there were many kinds of paper money.

Passing through the Kin, the Yüan, and the Ming dynasties, the chief kind of Chinese money was paper, especially during the Yüan dynasty. The only difference was that before the Kin dynasty the paper money represented only copper, and that after the Kin dynasty it represented both copper and silver. But it would take too long to narrate the whole history of Chinese paper money, and the facts mentioned above are sufficient to show its origin.

We have no intention of discussing the private banking system,[1] but give only a general conception of the development of government banks. According to the *Official System of Chou*, there was a government bank called Money Treasury. It kept the money which came from different sources; bought and sold special goods; and lent money to the people either with or without interest.[2] This was the first government bank of China.

After the Chou dynasty, there was no government bank. Even during the Tang dynasty, when the flying-money system was in operation, there was no special bank, although there was a system of banking. The true government bank was established in the beginning of the Sung dynasty (1521, or 970 A. D.), for the operation of the flying-money system. It was called The Bank of Convenient Money. In later times, there were many banks for the management of the "changelings" and the "exchanges." During the Kin dynasty, the Exchange Bank was established in 1749 (1198 A. D.); and during the Yüan dynasty, the Level Standard Bank was established in 1814 (1263 A. D.), and its branches

---

[1] China has a very beneficial institution, known as the "money association." Each member contributes periodically a certain amount of money, and may get a large sum of it by offering the highest premium in a secret competitive bidding, or by lottery without interest when there is no demand for money. These associations are like co-operative banks, people's banks, and saving banks. We are told by tradition that this system was invented by Mang Kung, a hermit, living about the end of the Latter Han dynasty (771 A. K. or 220 A. D.).

The great existing banks were established by the people of the Shansi province centuries ago, and they have branches throughout the whole empire.

[2] See *infra*, pp. 587-8.

COMMERCE

were opened in different provinces. All these banks were for the issue and redemption of paper money.[1]

2. *Principles of Money*

(a) *General Principles*

Confucius does not give many principles about money, but we may set forth a few. First, money is necessary for the economic life of the people, and its importance is next only to that of food. Therefore, according to the "Great Model," first is food and second is commodities, among which money is the chief thing. Second, money is a commodity. It is a part of wealth, but it is not the only form of wealth. The "Great Model," therefore, includes it in the term commodities, and no one misunderstands and thinks that money is identified with all kinds of wealth.[2] Third, money is a medium of exchange. The *Canon of Poetry* says: "A simple-looking fellow brings money to buy silk."[3] Fourth, according to the "Tribute of Yü," there are three kinds of money—gold, silver and copper. Although this seems a trimetallic system, there is theoretically a gold standard, because gold is the highest kind of money, and silver and copper are the middle and the lowest. If we state it in modern terms, we may say that gold is the standard, and that the silver and copper are the subsidiary money.[4] These are the principles of Confucius himself.

Among the Confucians, there are many principles of money. Kuan Tzŭ was not a Confucian; but his theory was derived from the ancient kings, and it was common to the

[1] At the present time the money and banking system has not been well established. A central bank was opened, however, in 2456 (1905 A. D.), and the silver standard was adopted in 2461 (1910 A. D.).

[2] See *supra*, p. 52.

[3] *Classics*, vol. iv, pt. i, p. 97.

[4] See *supra*, p. 428.

Confucians. Therefore, we give his theory. According to him, money itself must have high value. Because it is an object which is difficult to obtain, it can measure the value of other things. Therefore, he puts pearl and jade as the highest kind of money, gold as the middle, and copper as the lowest. He says:

These three kinds of money cannot protect you against cold if you hold them, nor can they satisfy you against hunger if you eat them. By the use of them, however, the ancient kings guarded wealth, controlled human affairs, and equalized the world. Therefore, money was called standard, which means that it makes the rise and fall of price not affect the standard itself.

This theory has been accepted by the Confucians.[1] Indeed, the chief function of money is to serve as the standard of value.

(b) *Quantity Theory*

The most important theory is the quantity theory. It is the theory of the Confucians, but it had arisen before Confucius. According to the *Official System of Chou,* when there was a famine or epidemic, the government did not tax commodities, but coined money.[2] According to the *Narratives of Nations,* in 28 A. K. (524 B. C.), Duke Mu of Shan says:

In ancient times, when there was any natural calamity, the government coined money in accordance with its quantity and its value, for the relief of the people. If the people suffered from the cheapness of money, the government coined dear money and put it in circulation for them. Therefore, the dear money controlled the cheap money in the market, and all the

---

[1] *General Research,* ch. viii.
[2] Ch. xiv.

COMMERCE

people got the benefit. If they felt the money too dear, the government coined more cheap money and put it in circulation, but did not abolish the dear. Therefore, the cheap money controlled the dear money in the market, and all the people were also benefited.[1]

This theory needs much explanation. First, we must understand why there should be a coinage of money during a period of natural calamities. In ancient times, not only were the metals money, but grain, too, was used as money. Grain, however, was not a standard of value, but only a medium of exchange. Therefore, whenever there was any natural calamity, it was like a crisis of modern times, because grain was very dear, and was not sufficient to be used as money. Hence, the government supplied metallic money to take the place of grain, and save it from being circulated, in order to leave it for food of the people. This was why money was coined at such a time.

According to the quantity theory, if money is more plentiful, prices are higher. Now, when grain is dear during a bad time, why should money be coined at all? It would raise the price of grain. In order to answer this question, we must understand the situation of the ancients. At that time the people were mostly farmers. They possessed their own grain for food, but could not get other necessaries unless they exchanged for them their grain. If they did so, their grain would not be sufficient for their own use. Therefore, the government supplied money for them, in order to enable them to exchange it for other things. This was simply to enlarge their purchasing power, but not to increase the price of grain particularly. Even if the farmers had not sufficient food, they could buy it with money, otherwise they had no medium of exchange

[1] Bk. iii.

at all. Therefore, even though the increased money raised the price of food a little, it still would be better for them than if they had no money at all. But how could the farmers get the money? It would be lent or distributed to them by the government during such a bad time. In short, the ancient government coining money for such purposes was like the modern government issuing bank notes for the relief of a crisis. There was really great demand for money, but not an over-supply of it.

Moreover, during famine or epidemic, commodities in general were cheap, except grain. The purchasing power of society was diminished, and the demand for commodities was lowered. The merchants would be ruined or discouraged, and the whole society became stagnant. At such a time, copper was also very cheap. Therefore, the government took the cheap copper and transformed it into money. Then it issued the money to the market for the raising of the price of commodities, in order to aid the merchants; and, if the merchants could not sell their goods, it would buy them with the money, so that they could utilize the money to do their business anywhere, and the whole society was stimulated. This explains why the government coined money during a bad time. Indeed, it was not contrary to the quantity theory, but in harmony with it.

Second, let us take up the quantity theory proper. According to the Duke Mu of Shan, the coinage of money should be in accordance with its quantity and its value. When there is an over-supply of money, its value is low, and the price of commodities is high. Therefore, the government should reduce the quantity of cheap money, and issue dear money. The dear money which is higher in value is called mother, and the cheap money is called son. The mother should be used as the standard, and the son as subsidiary. For instance, if the price of a thing is the sum of eighty coins, fifty coins should be paid in the mother, and the other thirty in the son. This is a single standard. It is said then that the mother is controlling the son in circulation. This means a reduction of its quantity, and an increase of its value. Hence, price is lowered. On the other hand, when money is under-supplied, its value is high, and prices are low. Therefore, the government should issue more cheap money, but not abolish the dear money. Then the people can use the cheap money for general transactions, while the dear money is used only for large payments. The son, not the mother, becomes the standard. Then it is said that the son is controlling the mother in circulation. This means an increase in quantity, and a reduction in value. Hence the price is raised. This is a monometallic system, and the government controls the quantity of both kinds of money in order to adjust their value and the prices. Although there are two kinds of money, there is only one standard at a certain period of time. But the one standard is alternately changed with the other, according to the quantity of money. This is the quantity theory.

The quantity theory has been recognized by all the statesmen and scholars. Therefore, we shall not take up any other authorities, except to give the statement of Chia Yi. He says: "The government accumulates copper for the control of the value of money. When the value is low, it lessens the quantity by some policy; and when it is high, it distributes the money by some policy. Hence, the price of commodities must be equalized." According to this theory, the value of money is low because its quantity is too much; hence, it should be withdrawn. Its value is high because its quantity is insufficient; hence, it should be distributed. This is the control of the quantity of money by the government, and it adjusts the level of prices. This is the common theory of the Confucians.

(c) *Coinage*

From the beginning of history, money was always coined by the government. It was only during the reign of Han Wên Ti (377, or 175 B. C.), that the people were allowed to coin money. Against this law Chia Yi gave his protest. His theory is as follows: (1) It will induce the people to make great profit on a small part of illegal alloy, which cannot be stopped by punishment. (2) It will destroy the universal standard, and introduce confusion into the market. (3) It will encourage the people to leave the farms for the coining of unlawful money. These are the great calamities. On the other hand, if coinage is exclusively controlled by the government, there will be seven blessings. (1) The people are saved from crime. (2) The confidence of the people is established. (3) The miners and the coiners will return to their farms. (4) The government can control the quantity of money and equalize prices.[1] (5) The government can control the social order. (6) The government can control the demand for and the supply of commodities.[2] (7) It can compete with the Huns by financial control. Wên Ti did not accept Chia Yi's advice. In 408 (144 B. C.), this law was abolished by Ching Ti, and the law of punishing the coiner by death was enacted. Hence, the statement of Chia Yi has become a classical theory.

For the prevention of illicit coining, money should be according to the standard quality and weight. In 1033 (482 A. D.), K'ung Chi, a courtier, said that the reason illicit coining cannot be stopped by severe punishment is because the government coins bad money. Presuming that money is useless except as a medium of exchange, the government makes the money cheaper and more in quantity. Its object is simply to save the expense of metal and labor,

---

[1] See *supra*, p. 439.   [2] See *infra*, pp. 552-6.

COMMERCE 441

but the results are very bad. This theory was recognized as the fundamental principle of coinage by Lü Tsu-chien, a great Confucian of the Sung dynasty (1688-1732, or 1137-1181 A. D.). He said that the reason the state coins money is for the establishment of the standard of value, and not for the making of profit. Those who do not understand economic principles clearly, recognize as a profit only the amount of seigniorage; but it is merely a small profit, while the controlling power of the state is a great profit. If the government does not save the expense, coinage has no profit. If it has no profit, illicit coining will not arise. If there is no illicit coining, the state controls exclusively the power of issuing and withdrawing money. As the government does not lose the power of coining money, it is great profit. If it looks only for the small profit, the money will be debased in weight and quality. Then all the bad people can coin money, and the state loses the controlling power. It is a loss of great profit for the sake of small profit. Therefore, good money is the prevention of the illicit coining, because there is no profit in the coining of money.

According to history, the system of free coinage was developed in 1046 (495 A. D.). During the reign of Shao-wên Ti of the Northern Wei dynasty, the government opened the mints and prepared the coiners. If the people wished to coin money, they were allowed to coin it there. The copper was required to be of the standard quality without any mixture. This law was probably for the encouragement of using money and for the supply of copper to the mint, because Shao-wên Ti was the first one of the Northern Wei dynasty who decreed that people should use money and who established the mint. If we put this law into modern terms, it was free coinage.

(d) *Paper Money*

To regulate the value of paper money, some provision for redemption is necessary. This theory was advocated by Shên Kai, and approved by Sung Kao Tsung (1678-1713). They held that the government should always have cash amounting to one million strings. If the price of the "changelings" decreases, the government should immediately buy the paper with the cash. In this way paper money will have no evil consequences. Ma Tuan-lin also gives a very good theory about paper money. He says: "Formerly, making paper on account of the heaviness of cash, paper was really convenient; now, making paper on account of the scarcity of cash, paper is really evil." According to their opinions, paper can represent money, but cannot be money itself. In other words, paper can be used when there is specie payment; but it should not be used when there is no specie payment.[1]

There is a very conclusive theory given by Yeh Tzŭ-ch'i.[2] He says:

The paper money of the Yüan dynasty was like the "changelings" and the "exchanges" of the Sung dynasty, and the "changeable paper" of the Kin dynasty. During their good time, they all used paper to represent cash. But, during their decay, when their money was not sufficient, they simply manufactured a great quantity of paper to be money. Therefore, the paper money was unable to measure the value of exchange, and all commodities were blocked in the market. Now, if we want to establish paper money, it is necessary to reserve cash as a fund. It should be like the certificate of tea or salt;

---

[1] Since 1682 A. K. (1131 A. D.), the banking bureau has co-operated with the commodity-taxing bureau, and commodities such as tea, salt, incense, alum, *etc.*, have been used unconsciously for the redemption of paper money, besides cash redemption. *General Research*, ch. ix.

[2] His book was written in 1929 A. K. or 1378 A. D.

when the certificate is presented, the tea or salt can be obtained immediately. If paper money is like this, how can there be the evil of not accepting paper? During the year of their reformation, they should establish banks in every prefecture and district, for the keeping of a certain amount of cash; and should issue paper according to the system of money certificate. They should do as Chang Yung, who used the "changelings" in Szechuan, and should choose the rich houses to manage the banks. When the certificate comes, the cash goes out; and when the certificate goes out, the cash comes in. Take the cash as the mother, and take the certificate as the son. The mother and son supplement each other, and control the price of all commodities. When the price is low, paper should be issued; and when the price is high, it should be withdrawn. Judging and adjusting the price according to the times, there is no reason why paper money should not be used. It is like the water of a pond. When the way of coming-in and the way of going-out are equal, the water will naturally flow and always be fresh. If only the way of coming-in is open, but the way of going-out is closed, the water will be stagnant, and the only result will be an overflow.

According to his theory, the best policy for controlling paper money is redemption, which is the way of going-out. But how can it be redeemed? It is by the reserve fund of cash, which is the mother. This is the fundamental principle of paper money. Adding to this, it should be also in harmony with the quantity theory, namely, the paper should not be issued beyond a certain limit even though there is the reserve of cash. But how can we know the exact amount according to which so much paper should be issued? It is judged by the price of all commodities. Indeed, price is the barometer of the quantity of money, either paper or coin. This is the theory of Yeh Tzŭ-ch'i.

(e) *Gresham's Law*

Fourth, since paper money was used under the Sung dynasty, there was a theory like Gresham's Law. Yeh Shih says:

> The men who do not inquire into the fundamental cause simply think that paper should be used when money is scarce. But, as soon as paper is employed, money becomes still less. Therefore, it is not only that the sufficiency of goods cannot be seen, but also that the sufficiency of money cannot be seen.

His statement combines the quantity theory and Gresham's Law. For the former theory, he means that the wealth of a nation is dependent upon the increase of goods, and not upon the increase of money. When goods are abundant, they will be cheap, and the value of money will be high. If goods are not sufficient, they cause the value of money to be low. Therefore, he says that the sufficiency of goods cannot be seen, because he compares the quantity of money with that of goods. For the latter theory, he means that paper drives out money when they are both circulated in the same market. As paper is employed, money is kept out of circulation. Therefore, he says that the sufficiency of money cannot be seen. This is in principle like Gresham's Law. Hence, we may say that Gresham's Law was discovered by Yeh Shih, because he saw the fact that paper drives out money.

Yüan Hsieh states Gresham's Law still more clearly. In 1774 (1223 A. D.), he says:

> Now, the officials are anxious to increase wealth, and want to put both iron money and copper money in circulation. If money were suddenly made abundant during a period of scarcity, it should be very good. But the fact never can be so. Formerly, because the paper money was too much, the copper money became less. If we now add the iron money to it,

should not the copper money but become still less? Formerly, because the paper money was too much, the price of commodities was dear. If we now add the iron money to the market, would the price not become still dearer? . . . When we look over the different provinces, the general facts are these. Where paper and money are both employed, paper is superabundant, but money is always insufficient. Where the copper money is the only currency without any other money, money is usually abundant. Therefore, we know that the paper can only injure the copper money, but not help its insufficiency.[1]

According to Yüan Hsieh, the evil of bimetallism is very clear. If iron money is employed side by side with copper money, it simply makes the copper still less, because iron is cheaper than copper, and the cheaper money always drives out dearer money. It is exactly the case when paper is employed side by side with copper money. If they both are employed, the copper will be driven out. If copper is the only money, it will remain sufficient. Therefore, the monetary system should choose a single standard. This principle is true in every case. It is true between iron and copper, but also true between silver and gold. In fact, it is Gresham's Law.

VI. COMMERCIAL REGULATIONS

According to the theory of Confucians, the government should take positive measures to regulate the commerce of the people. The " Royal Regulations " says:

All who have charge of the prohibitions for the regulation of the multitudes do not forgive transgressions of them.

[1] Those who have rank-tokens, the long or the round, and gilt libation-cups are not allowed to sell them in the market places; [2] nor are any allowed to sell robes or chariots, the gift of the king; [3] or vessels of an ancestral temple; [4] or victims for sacrifice; [5] or instruments of war; [6] or ves-

---

[1] *Continuation of the General Research*, ch. vii.

sels which are not according to the prescribed measurements; [7] or chariots of war which are not according to the same; [8] or cloth or silk, fine or coarse, not according to the prescribed quality, or broader or narrower than the proper rule; [9] or of illegitimate colors, confusing those that are correct; [10] or cloth, embroidered or figured; or vessels made with pearls or jade; [11] or clothes, or food, or drink, in any way extravagant; [12] or grain which is not in season, or fruit which is unripe; [13] or wood which is not fit for the axe; [14] or birds, beasts, fishes, or reptiles, which are not fit to be killed. At the frontier gates, those in charge of the prohibitions examine travelers, forbidding such as wear strange clothes, and taking note of such as speak a strange language.[1]

There are fourteen prohibitions, and we may classify them into four classes. (a) From the first to the fifth prohibition, the things should not be possessed by the common people—rules for the maintaining of social order. (b) From the sixth to the ninth, the things are not good for consumption, and these four prohibitions maintain the legal standards. (c) From the tenth to the eleventh, the two prohibitions are for the prevention of extravagance and dissipation. (d) From the twelfth to the fourteenth, the rules refer to things which are not ready to be consumed; hence, these three prohibitions promote the mature growth of natural things on the one hand, and prevent the harm which may come from unseasonable consumption on the other. All these fourteen prohibitions are examples of commercial regulations.

According to the *Official System of Chou*, there is a controller of market (*ssŭ shih*) to take charge of commercial regulations. Under his administration, there are many subordinate officers. For the convenience of the reader, we may classify the commercial rules under the following six

---

[1] *Li Ki*, bk. iii, p. 238.

heads: First, the market-places are divided up in accordance with the offices of officers and the shops of merchants. The shops are also distinguished from each other by the different sorts of goods, that is, a certain group of shops is arranged together for the sale of certain goods. Second, the times of doing business are divided up into three periods —the noon, the morning and the evening. The most popular period is at noon, and all the different people are represented; hence, it is called the great market. In the morning market, the chief participants are the merchants; and in the evening market, the chief participants are the small sellers and buyers. Third, there is the inspector (*hsü shih*) in every twenty shops, and the subordinate places under him are filled up by business men, for the prohibition of false goods and the prevention of deceitful methods. If there is any misrepresentation or deceit, the seller shall be punished by him.

Fourth, prices are controlled by the government. For this object, there are six policies. (a) In every shop, there is the superintendent of the shop (*ssŭ chang*). Within a shop, the goods are arranged in a certain way. Those which have the same name but different value are separated in a great distance. For examples, the different pearls and jades are called by the names of pearl and jade, but their values show great differences. Since the merchants find it easy to impose upon farmers and ignorant people these goods must be arranged so as to be easily distinguished. On the other hand, if their quality is quite similar to each other, they may be arranged within a short distance. To distinguish the quality of goods is the basis of regulating price. (b) All goods have a fixed price, and its difference is simply according to the quantity. In this way, the buyers are encouraged to come in. (c) There is the master of merchants (*ku shih*) in every twenty shops, to fix the price according to the cost. When there is any natural calamity, the merchants are not allowed to raise their price. For example, during a famine grain should be sold at the natural price; and during a great epidemic, coffins should be sold in the same way.[1] Moreover, seasonal things are also regulated by the natural price. In short, the price should be constant. (d) There is the auditor of price (*chih jên*) to oversee the prices of the most valuable things, through whom the transactions are carried on. (e) By the raising and lowering of price, the government controls the supply. When a thing is not in existence, the government causes it to exist; when a thing is useful, it causes it to be abundant; when a thing is harmful, it causes it to be extinguished; when a thing is luxurious, it causes it to be lessened. The former two policies are carried out by the raising of prices; and the latter two by lowering them. (f) There is the government bank to buy the goods which the people cannot sell, and to lend them out when the people need them. In this way, the government adjusts the demand and supply, and prices are kept at a fixed level.

Fifth, all the transactions of buying and selling are done by bills of sale and purchase. These bills are made of one piece of wood, which is divided into two parts, one for the seller and the other for the buyer. They are issued by the government, in charge of the auditor of price, for the purpose of establishing confidence and preventing litigation. When the transaction involves a large sum, the long bill is issued; and, when it is small, the short bill is issued. If there is any litigation arising from the bills, and also from the written tally,[2] it is heard by the auditor of price. From

---

[1] In modern times, this policy has been changed to the opposite. During a famine, the price of grain is raised to induce merchants to bring in more grain.

[2] See *supra*, p. 432.

the time when the bill or the tally is issued to the time when the litigation is brought to the court, however, there are different limits according to the distance of the complainant. If he lives in the imperial capital, the period is ten days; in a suburb, twenty days; in the country, thirty days; in the surrounding cities, three months; in the feudal states, one year. Beyond these periods, the litigation shall not be heard.

Sixth, there is the police system. The gate of the market is guarded by policemen who hold whips and halberds. For every two shops, there is a policeman (*hsü*) to keep watch. For every ten shops, there is a captain (*ssŭ pao*) to take charge of fighters, noise-makers, peace-disturbers, offenders, and persons eating and drinking in parties. For every five shops, there is a detective (*ssŭ chi*). His functions are to find out the transgressor, to watch the stranger, to take note of the lounger who stops longer than a proper length of time, and to capture the thief. The punishments of the offender in the market are three—to declare his transgression by written notice, to set forth his body as a bad example, and to whip him as the most severe punishment. If it belongs to the criminal law, it goes to the court of justice.

All these regulations are given by the *Official System of Chou*.[1] Although this book was compiled by Liu Hsin, these regulations were the actual rules under the Chou dynasty. In fact, in the classical time, the government did interfere with the commercial life very minutely.

VII. INTERNATIONAL TRADE

Since the eighth of the nine standard rules is " the indulgent treatment of foreigners,"[2] foreign trade occupies a special category in the governmental system of Confucius. The practice of this rule is " to escort them on their de-

---
[1] Chs. xiv. and xv.
[2] See *supra*, pp. 318-19.

parture and meet them on their coming; to commend the good among them, and show compassion to the incompetent." Therefore, according to the principle of Confucius, a state should not only open the door to foreigners for foreign trade, but should also give them special favor because they live a long distance away.

The principle of international trade is based upon the geographical differences of economic condition. The "Royal Regulations" says:

The people of the Middle Kingdom and those of the tribes of the east, the south, the west, and the north, all have comfortable dwellings, delicious flavors, suitable dresses, useful implements, and finished articles. In these five regions, the languages of the people are not mutually intelligible, and their tastes and desires are different. To express their thoughts and to exchange their wants, there are the officers to handle foreign affairs: For the east, they are called transmitters; for the south, representatives; for the west, interpreters; and for the north, translators.[1]

According to this statement, the chief function of the officers in charge of foreign affairs is to promote foreign trade. Their duty is to interpret foreign languages for the expression of thoughts and the exchange of wants which are in the minds of the foreigners. Since the people of the five regions all have comfortable dwellings, delicious flavors, suitable dresses, useful implements, and finished articles, foreign trade is simply to supply the reciprocal demand of each other, and there are mutual gains. Moreover, since their tastes and desires are different, foreign trade can exchange their wants, so as to develop the different tastes, and to make use of anything which is not wanted in one region but demanded in another. Therefore, foreign trade is nec-

[1] *Li Ki*, bk. iii, pp. 229-230.

essary, and the policy of "the closed door" is not in harmony with the principle of Confucius.

According to the *Official System of Chou,* there is the commissioner of immigration (*huai fang shih*). His function is to give welcome to foreigners from all directions. He orders his subordinates to escort them on their departure and to meet them on their coming. He issues passports to them for their traveling. He takes care of their provisions, hotel, food and drink. By these means, he causes them to send their tribute and goods to the government.[1] This was the characteristic of foreign trade in the ancient times. Since the surrounding tribes were all inferior to the Chinese themselves, the opening of trade for them was really a favor to them. Therefore, when they came to China, they always brought their tribute to the government as an acknowledgment of its suzerainty; but at the same time, they imported their goods to exchange for Chinese goods. In return for their tribute, moreover, the government usually granted articles to them according to their wants. Therefore, it was really a foreign trade under the name of tribute; and these two things, tribute and trade, were connected with each other. A similar process continued throughout the whole history until the Opium War (2393, or 1842 A. D.). Since that time, foreign trade marks a great difference between the ancients and the moderns.

What we have discussed above is the trade between China and the subordinate nations. We now come to the trade between the equal nations within the Chinese world. As China was a great empire, and was divided up into different nations during the later part of the Chou dynasty,[2] the trade carried on among them was really an international trade, and not an internal trade. Therefore, international

[1] Ch. xxxiii.   [2] See *supra,* p. 131.

trade became a very important problem. According to *Tso's Commentary*, Duke Wên of Wei (118-84 B. K. or 669-635 B. C.) reorganized his ruined state by the promotion of trade. Hence, the term "international trade" has come to exist; in the original Chinese, it is called "communicating trade."[1]

When there is any international trade, there must be some sort of commercial treaty. If we want to trace back such treaties in the ancient times, we may give a few examples. In 100 B. K. (651 B. C.), there was a conference held in K'uei Ch'iu by the princes of seven states. One item of the fifth article of their agreement read: "Impose no restrictions on the sale of grain." Since grain was the chief article of food, they made it the object of free exportation. When Mencius spoke of this conference, he approved their agreement.[2]

Eighteen years before Confucius (569 B. C.), the advantages of peaceful intercourse between the Chinese and the barbarian tribes were pointed out by Wei Chiang, a minister of Tsin. He enumerated five advantages which came from the peaceful treaty made with the barbarians. The first of them was the profit of exchange; and the second, the continuity of production. He said:

The barbarians are continually changing their residence, and are fond of exchanging land for goods. Their lands can be purchased—this is the first advantage. Our borders will not be kept in apprehension. The people can labor on their fields, and the farmers complete their toils—this is the second.[3]

Eleven years before Confucius (562 B. C.), the princes of thirteen states made a covenant together in Po. The first

[1] *Classics*, vol. v, pt. i, p. 131.
[2] *Ibid.*, vol. ii, pp. 437-8.
[3] *Ibid.*, vol. v, pt. ii, p. 424.

two items of their treaty were: "All we who covenant together agree not to hoard up the produce of good years, and not to shut one another out from advantages we possess."[1] By this treaty, the first item referred to grain; and the second, to commodities in general which should come either from the natural resources of certain localities, or from the superior skill of certain people. It was a treaty to make exportation free.

The Confucian theory of international trade is an extreme doctrine of free trade. According to *Elder Tai's Record*, Confucius says: "Formerly, wise kings inspected travelers at the custom-houses, but did not levy duty upon commodities."[2] Such a statement is repeated by Mencius, Hsun Tzŭ, and the "Royal Regulations." Mencius mentions this doctrine several times; and, in one instance, he says: "If, at his custom-houses, there be an inspection of persons, but no taxes charged on commodities, then all the travelers of the whole world will be pleased, and wish to make their tours on his roads."[3] One day he says: "Anciently, the establishment of the custom-houses was to guard against violence. Nowadays, it is to exercise violence."[4] In another day he compares it with the thieving of fowls.[5] Indeed, Mencius condemns custom duties as unjust. When Hsun Tzŭ describes the effect of free trade, he says: "Transport the money, commodities and grain without any delay and stopping, in order to satisfy the reciprocal demand: it makes the whole world like a single family."[6] Therefore, according to the Confucians, international trade should be absolutely free. Since their principle is cosmo-

[1] *Classics*, vol. v, pt. ii, p. 453.
[2] Bk. xxxix.
[3] *Classics*, vol. ii, p. 200.
[4] *Ibid.*, p. 481.
[5] *Ibid.*, p. 278.
[6] Bk. ix.

politanism and their object is to equalize the whole world, it is no wonder that they advocate the doctrine of free trade in its extreme form.

Free trade was only a theory of the Confucians. There were custom duties under the Chou dynasty. According to the *Official System of Chou,* there was the director of custom-houses, who charged duties and storage. If any commodity was smuggled, it should be confiscated, and the smuggler should be punished. It was only during a famine or a great mortality, that the custom duties were suspended, but the persons were still under inspection.[1] From this example, we can see the difference between the *Official System of Chou* and the principles of the Confucians. The former is a record of facts, while the latter are theories. Sometimes they go along together, and sometimes they do not.

VIII. POSITION OF MERCHANTS

During the Chou dynasty, the position of merchants was very prominent. They were mostly individuals for the carrying on of their trade, but there was also associated and incorporated enterprise. The best example of the partnership was given by Kuan Tzŭ and Pao Shu (before the date of 143 B. K. or 694 B. C.).[2] In later times they both became famous ministers of Ch'i. Corporations are mentioned in the *Official System of Chou.* It says: " All the people who own commodities and money in common are regulated by the law of the state; and, if they violate the regulations, they shall be punished." [3] Cheng Chung says that these people are those who form joint stock companies

---

[1] Ch. xv.
[2] *Historical Record,* ch. lxii.
[3] Ch. xxxv.

Therefore, commercial corporations existed in the Chou dynasty.

There is another proof that the commercial corporation or trade guild existed in the Chou dynasty. In 26 A. K. (526 B. C.), Tzŭ-ch'an, the prime minister of Chêng and a good friend of Confucius, said:

Our former ruler, Duke Huan, came with the former merchants from Chou [222 B. K. or 773 B. C.]. Thus they were associated in cultivating the land, together clearing and opening up this territory, and cutting down its tangled southerwood and orach. Then they dwelt in it together. In every generation, our ruler has made a covenant with the merchants for the mutual faith. It reads: "You will not revolt from me, and I will not violently interfere with your traffic. I will not beg or take anything from you. You may have your profitable markets, precious things, and substance, without my taking any knowledge of them." Through this attested covenant, our rulers and the merchants have preserved their mutual relations down to the present day.

By this statement he protected a merchant from being compelled to sell a ring of jade to the prime minister of Tsin, a very powerful state.[1]

From these facts, we can see that the power of the merchants was very great. They helped the most powerful duke, uncle of the emperor, to establish a new state, and made a covenant with the princes in every generation. This shows the democratic movement, commercial freedom, and contractual society. From the time when Duke Huan moved his state to the time when Tzŭ-ch'an gave this statement, there was a period of 248 years, and the state did not violate the covenant. Such a thing never could be done by the individual merchants, and they must have in-

[1] *Classics,* vol. v, pt. ii, p. 664.

corporated themselves into a legal body. Hence, their corporation had a perpetual life for the making and preserving of the covenant with the state, from generation to generation. In order to guard this covenant, the statesman of the weak state even dared to refuse the demand for a ring raised by the envoy of the chief power. It proves that the internal contract between the state and the corporation was stronger even than the international relation. In fact, Chêng was a commercial state, and the corporation had a strong hold there.

Understanding that commercial corporations existed in the time of Confucius, we now come to consider the position of the individual merchants. For this purpose, we may mention a few of the most prominent merchants as examples.

In 76 B. K. (627 B. C.), when the army of Ch'in was going to invade Chêng, Hsien Kao, a merchant of Chêng, on his business journey, met it. Pretending that he was sent by his prince, he went with four dressed hides, preceding twelve oxen, to distribute them among the soldiers, and to delay the generals with compliments. At the same time, he sent intelligence of what was taking place with all possible speed to Chêng. Therefore, Chêng was saved.[1] This was a case where a merchant saved the country.

The chief figure in the " Biography of Merchants " in the *Historical Record*[2] is Tzŭ-kung. He was a pupil of Confucius, but he was also a merchant. He used his capital for speculative purposes, and sold his money. He made a great profit. Among all the pupils of Confucius, he was the richest one. Whenever he visited any prince, he was received and treated as if he were of the same rank with the prince.

---

[1] *Classics*, vol. v, pt. i, p. 224.
[2] *Historical Record*, ch. cxxix.

Therefore, the reputation even of Confucius was partly due to the effort of Tzŭ-kung.

A little later than Tzŭ-kung was Fan Li. He was the prime minister of Yüeh, and he became a merchant after his political success (79 A. K. or 473 B. C.). He took his economic theory from his teacher, and it is worth mentioning. Chi Jan, his teacher, says:

For skilful competition, one should make a preparation of supply; and for seasonal consumption, one should know the things demanded. When these two points appear, the situation of all commodities can be seen. . . . When there is a drought, one should store up the boats; and when there is a flood, one should store up the cars. . . .[1]

To keep the price of grain on a level, to put all commodities in the normal condition, and to make the custom-houses and the markets go on naturally without any interruption, all these are the principles of a good government.

The laws of accumulating capital are: One must keep all the capital goods intact. One must not allow money to be idle. An exchange is between commodity and commodity. The instruments which have worn out and cannot produce any thing should not remain.

Do not dare to keep goods when their price is high. By studying the amount of goods either over-supplied or under-supplied, that their price will either rise or fall can be known beforehand. When the high price rises to the extreme, it will turn down; and when the low price falls to the extreme, it will go up. At its highest price, the commodity should be got rid of as manure and clay; and at its lowest price, it should be taken as pearl and jade. All kinds of wealth and specially money should flow like the current water.

[1] This is the principle of accumulating a thing when it has no use, and waiting for the time when there is a demand for it. Since there can be neither a constant drought nor a constant flood, this policy usually leads to a great profit.

These are the economic principles of Chi Jan. After Fan Li had successfully applied these principles to the state, he wanted to apply them to his family; hence, he became a rich merchant. His methods were to select the right men, and to seize the right times. In fact, it was speculative. In a period of nineteen years, he accumulated wealth three times, and he distributed it to the poor twice. The amount of his wealth was over one hundred millions; hence, he distinguished himself by his wealth.

About the time of Mencius, there was Pai Kuei.[1] He was called the father of economics, but he looked upon economics as an art rather than as a science. He was mostly pleased to speculate upon the changes of times. His policy was: " Take what others throw away, and give away what others take." He was able to lessen food and drink, to restrain the passions and desires, to simplify dress, and to share both hardship and pleasure with his working servants. But when he was going to seize the right times, it was like the start of the cruel beast and the terrible bird. Therefore, he compared his economic principles with the politics of the greatest statesmen, the strategy of the founders of the military school, and the laws of the founder of the law school. He said:

If either his wisdom cannot see the changes of a thing, or his bravery cannot make out a decision, or his kindness is not enough for the giving of some thing, or his firmness is not strong enough to hold the principle, I shall never tell him about my methods, even though he may want to learn them from me.

Therefore, we are told by Ssŭ-ma Chien that the economists of the Chinese world recognized Pai Kuei as the father of

[1] He was accordingly a Confucian.

COMMERCE 459

economics. He says: "Indeed, Pai Kuei had proved his good practice. He possessed special genius, and his practical success was not by chance."[1]

---

[1] Tzŭ-kung had become minister in the states of Lu and Wei after his commercial enterprise. Fan Li had become the minister of Yüeh before his commercial enterprise, and became also the minister of Ch'i afterward. Pai Kuei was a commander of Marquis Wên of Wei, and conquered the state named Chungshan in 144 A. K. (408 B. C.); but he was also a merchant. They were the representatives of the prominent merchants of that time. In fact, these three men were really the founders of the commercial school.

During the Ch'in dynasty, the position of merchants was also very prominent. Lü Pu-wei, a great merchant, gained the state of Ch'in, and became the true father of the First Emperor (292 A. K. or 260 B. C.). *Historical Record*, ch. lxxxv. The First Emperor (306-342 A. K. or 246-210 B. C.) made a shepherd named Lo equal to the feudal prince; and he treated a widow named Ts'ing as a guest, and built a tower for her. They were both distinguished by their wealth. *Ibid.*, ch. cxxix. These illustrations prove that the position of the merchants was very honorable and powerful.

BOOK VII. DISTRIBUTION

CHAPTER XXIV

General Principles of Distribution: Rent, Interest and Profits

I. GENERAL PRINCIPLES OF DISTRIBUTION

In the economic theories of the Confucians, more importance is attached to the problems of distribution than to those of production, because the Confucians are more socialistic than individualistic. There are many principles in regard to the distribution of wealth, but we may classify them under three heads, namely, equality, productivity, and need.

1. Distribution According to the Principle of Equality

First, wealth should be distributed equally. By an equal distribution, it is not meant that everyone should have the same amount of income, but that everyone should have the same opportunity from which he will be enabled to get the same amount of income. Therefore, there is the minority of men who receive justly an unequal amount of wealth on account of their ability and service. But, as soon as the majority of men can have equal opportunity of production, and can live at the social standard without the suffering of poverty, it is an equal distribution. In fact, there never can be an absolute equality, but only a proximate equality.

Hsun Tzŭ says:

Now, to be as dignified as an emperor, and as rich as possessing the whole empire, are objects for which all men, according to human nature, have a common desire. But if we indulge the desires of men, there is no room for so many desires, and there is no sufficiency of things to satisfy them. The ancient kings accordingly established rites and justice for men in order to distribute wealth. They distinguished the classes between the honorable and the mean, the difference between the old and the young, and the separation between the wise and the ignorant, and between the able and the incapable. They made all men take up their work and get their justice respectively. Then, the different amounts of income either great or small, were all made suitable to everyone. This is the principle of harmony and unity of a society. Therefore, when the benevolent man is on the throne, the farmers will give all their strength to the farms; the merchants, their sagacity to wealth; the artisans, their skill to the articles; and all the officials, from the students up to the dukes, their virtue and abilities to their official duties. This is what is called perfect equality. Therefore, some receive income from the whole empire, [as an emperor], but they do not think that it is too much; and some receive it as a doorkeeper, or a waiter on a traveller, or a guard along the gate, or a watchman, but they do not think that it is too little. It is said: "Although it looks unequal, it is equal; although it looks partial, it is just; although it looks different, it is uniform." This is what are called social relations.[1]

According to the social principles of Confucius, there are two divisions of men. The one is in the honorable position, such as the emperor, the princes, the great officials, and the students, while the other is in the mean position, the common people. The class of honorable men should be rich, and the class of common people poor. Hence, the word rich comes together with the word honorable, and the word poor with the word mean. But there is nothing to confine

[1] Bk. iv.

anyone to either class, and he will either rise or fall according to his own ability. Among the five classes of men—the emperor, the princes, the great officials, the students and the common people—there is no equality of wealth. But among the common people themselves, the greatest number of men, wealth must be equally distributed. On the one hand, no one of them is enabled to get any special advantage over his fellow-members for the increasing of his income; and on the other, the upper classes are not allowed to take up any gainful occupation for competition with the common people. This is what Confucius means by an equal distribution.

We must understand that, according to the principles of Confucius, the two classes, rich and poor, should not be widely separated. They are simply comparatively rich and poor, but they should not have too much difference. During the Chou dynasty, there was a class struggle, and it is shown in the *Canon of Poetry*. It says:

> They have their good spirits,
> And their fine viands along with them.
> They assemble their neighbors,
> And their relatives are full of their praise.
> When I think of my loneliness,
> My sorrowing heart is full of distress.

The first four lines describe the wealth and jollity of the unworthy favorites of the court; the last two, the writer's distress in thinking of the existing disorder, and the coming ruin. It continues:

> Mean-like, those have their houses;
> Abject, they have their salary.
> But the people now have no maintenance.
> For Heaven is pounding them with its calamities.
> Those rich enjoy themselves;
> But alas for the helpless and solitary![1]

[1] *Classics*, vol. iv, pt. ii, pp. 319-320.

This poem was written during the reign of Yu Wang (230-220 B. K. or 781-771 B. C.), who ruined the Western Chou dynasty; and it shows that there was a great gap between the rich and the poor. Such an unequal distribution is the sign of ruin, and Confucius takes it as a warning for future generations. Therefore, the *Canon of History* says: "The former rulers, Wên and Wu, greatly equalized the wealth of the people."[1]

The reason why Confucius advocates equal distribution of wealth is from the psychological point of view. According to human nature, those who have too much of wealth are just as badly off as those who have too little of it. Confucius says:

The small man, when poor, feels the pinch of his straitened circumstances; and when rich, is liable to become proud. Under the pinch of that poverty, he may proceed to steal; and when proud, he may proceed to deeds of disorder. The social rules recognize these feelings of men, and lay down definite regulations for them, to serve as preventions for the people. Hence, when the sages distributed riches and honors, they made the rich not have power enough to be proud; and kept the poor from being pinched; and the honorable men not be intractable to those above them. In this way the causes of disorder would more and more disappear.[2]

Therefore, an equal distribution is to keep both the rich and the poor in good nature, and to preserve social peace. In short, Confucius means that the government is the distributor of wealth, and the controller of production and consumption.

In the book "Equalization" of the *Many Dewdrops of the Spring and Autumn*, Tung Chung-shu says:

[1] *Classics*, vol. iii, pt. ii, p. 566.
[2] *Li Ki*, bk. xxvii, pp. 284-5.

It is said by Confucius, "We are not troubled with fears of poverty, but are troubled with fears of a lack of equality of wealth." Therefore, when there is here a concentration of wealth, there must be an emptiness there. Great riches make the people proud; and great poverty makes them wretched. When they are wretched, they would become robbers; when they are proud, they would become oppressors; it is human nature. From the nature of the average man, the sages discovered the origin of disorder. Therefore, when they established social laws and divided up the social orders, they made the rich able to show their distinction without being proud, and the poor able to make their living without misery; this was the standard for the equalization of society. In this way, wealth was sufficient, and the high and low classes were peaceful. Hence, society was easily governed well. In the present day, the regulations are abandoned, so that everyone pursues what he wants. As human wants have no limit, the whole society becomes indulgent without end. The great men of the high class, notwithstanding they have great fortune, feel bad for the insufficiency of their wealth; while the small people of the low class are depressed. Therefore, the rich increase their avarice for money, and do not wish to do good; while the poor violate the laws every day, and no way can stop them. Hence, society is difficult to govern well.[1]

This is an explanation of the principle of Confucius.

Equality is a great principle of Confucius, and it has also its world aspect. Therefore, he advocates it from the international point of view. In the "Great Learning," the last and longest chapter is entitled, "The Equalization of the Whole World," in which the most important subject is administering wealth.[2] In the "Doctrine of the Mean," Confucius says: "The world, the states, and the families, may

---

[1] Bk. xxvii.   [2] See *supra*, p. 142.

be equalized."[1] Therefore, Confucius plans an equal distribution applied to the world as a whole.

During the time of Confucius, the princes of states and the chiefs of noble families made war against each other in order to extend their territory and to increase their people, because they thought that having more land and more population would make them richer. But the people not only had no interest in these wars, but also sacrificed their lives and property in them. Therefore, when the head of the Chi family was going to attack Chuan-yu, a dependent state of Lu, Confucius gave the great principle of equality. He said:

> I have heard that rulers of states and chiefs of families are not troubled lest their people should be few, but are troubled lest they should not have equality of wealth; that they are not troubled with fears of poverty, but are troubled with fears of a lack of peace among the people themselves. For, when the people have equality of wealth, there will be no poverty; when harmony prevails, there will be no scarcity of people; and when there is social peace among the people, there will be no fall of state or family.[2]

These three characteristics, equality, harmony and peace, are the aims of the economic theories of Confucius. But harmony and peace are the results of equality. Therefore, equality of wealth is the fundamental thing.

2. *Distribution According to Productivity*

Second, distribution should be according to productivity. Confucius says:

> The ceremony takes place before the silks offered in connection with it are presented:—this is intended to teach the people to make the doing of their duties the first thing, and

[1] *Classics*, vol. i, p. 389. [2] *Ibid.*, p. 308.

their salaries an after consideration. . . . It is said in the *Canon of Changes*, " He reaps without having ploughed that he may reap; he gathers the produce of the third year's field without having cultivated it the first year; it is an evil." [1]

Therefore, Confucius makes a rule for the Confucians: " They must first do the work, and then take the pay." [2] Hence, according to the principles of Confucius, distribution must be in accordance with the product. Even though it is difficult to find out the exact amount of productivity, this principle is a just one. The further discussion of it we shall defer till we take up the problem of wages.

3. *Distribution According to Need*

Third, distribution should be according to need. This is a very important principle in the *Spring and Autumn*. In the first year of Duke Yin of Lu, it records: " The emperor sent the sub-administrator Hsüan to return a present of two carriages and eight horses for the funerals of Duke Hui and his wife Chung-tzŭ." Now, as this present was not the old property of Lu, and just given by the emperor, why should Confucius use the word " return "? It is because he wants to indicate that the receiver, Duke Yin, should have a common ownership in those things with the Emperor. Ho Hsiu explains this principle as follows: " Wealth is produced by the power of Heaven and Earth, and it is not a possession of any single family. Therefore, those who have much wealth and those who have nothing should share it for their common interest." This is like the communistic idea. But we must understand it more clearly. Confucius recognizes the private ownership of wealth, but he denies that the owner has an absolute right to it. Therefore, he

---

[1] *Li Ki*, bk. xxvii, pp. 295-6.
[2] *Ibid.*, bk. xxxviii, p. 404.

makes society the supreme owner of everything, and the temporary possessor only a trustee. Since nature is a co-operator in production, no one can claim the absolute ownership of anything upon the occupation theory or the labor theory. Hence, distribution of wealth should be according to the needs of the members of society. In short, those who have much wealth should have the duty of giving, and those who have nothing should have the right of receiving. This is the principle of the *Spring and Autumn,* and it is illustrated by this case which does not mean that Duke Yin had no wealth.

In the *Analects,* Confucius says: "I have heard that a superior man helps the distressed, but does not add to the wealth of the rich."[1] This is his general principle of distribution.

The reason why distribution of wealth should be according to need is explained very clearly by Mencius. When he speaks to King Hsüan of Ch'i, he says:

It is only good scholars, who, without a permanent property, are able to maintain a permanent heart. As to the common people, if they have not a permanent property, it follows that they will not have a permanent heart. And if they have not a permanent heart, there is nothing which they will not do, in the way of self-abandonment, of moral deflection, of depravity, and of wild license. When they thus have been involved in crime, to follow them up and punish them is to entrap the people. How can such a thing as entrapping the people be done under the government of a benevolent man?

Therefore, a wise ruler will regulate the property of the people, so as to make sure that, for those above them, they shall have sufficient wherewithal to serve their parents, and, for those below them, sufficient wherewithal to support their wives and children; that in good years they shall always be abund-

[1] *Classics,* vol. i, p. 186.

antly satisfied, and that in bad years they shall escape the danger of perishing. After this he may urge them, and they will proceed to what is good, for in this case the people will follow after it with ease.

Now, the property of the people is so regulated, that, above, they have not sufficient wherewith to serve their parents, and, below, they have not sufficient wherewith to support their wives and children. Notwithstanding good years, their lives are continually embittered, and, in bad years, they do not escape perishing. In such circumstances, they only try to save themselves from death, and are even afraid they will not succeed. What leisure have they to cultivate propriety and righteousness?[1]

What Mencius means by "permanent property" is explained in the *tsing tien* system. After he has given this advice to the king, he immediately describes such a system in short outline. Indeed, what is necessary to make a man a good citizen is the basis of distributive justice. If his physical needs are not satisfied, with very few exceptions, no one can fully develop his intellectual and moral powers.[2]

II. RENT

1. *Absence of Land-ownership*

The *Spring and Autumn* does not allow the princes to confer feudal estates on anyone at their pleasure, nor the

---

[1] *Classics,* vol. ii, pp. 147-8.

[2] Prof. James Legge remarks: "His principle that good government should contemplate and will be seen in, the material well-being of the people, is worthy of all honor.... When Mencius teaches that with the mass of men education will have little success where life is embittered by miserable poverty, he shows himself well acquainted with human nature. Educationists now seem generally to recognize it, but I think it is only within a century that it has assumed in Europe the definiteness and importance with which it appeared to Mencius here in China two thousand years ago." *Chinese Classics,* vol. ii, pp. 49-50. Prof. Legge published his translation in 1894 A. D.

great officials to win the land exclusively. This principle means that none can be the true landlord except the emperor. The *Canon of Poetry* says: "Under the wide heaven, all is the king's land." [1] In ancient times, the king or emperor represented the sovereign power of the whole empire; hence, when anything belonged to the state, it belonged to the king or emperor. Therefore, according to the principles of Confucius, none should own the land except the state. Even the princes and the great officials have no right to take the land under their sway; how can the common people have any claim to its private ownership? We are sure that Confucius does not allow land to be subject to private ownership; hence, the form of rent does not exist in his system.

It should be noted that Confucius would justify the taking of rent, if the land had been the private property of its owner for a long time. Land is only one kind of capital goods; and, since Confucius does not condemn the taking of interest by the capitalist, he must not condemn the taking of rent by the landowner. Judging from his idea, if the land had not been private property, he would not let it go to private hands; but, if it had been so, he would not deny the owner the right of taking its rent.

2. *The Land Tax the Equivalent of Rent*

Confucius and his disciples give no theory about the rent of land, because in their day the land was under public ownership. The essentials of their principles, however, can be applied to the problem of rent. Since the government was the land owner, and the people paid the land tax to it, the land tax really took the place of rent. Although the term land tax is different from the term rent in modern times, they were not different in ancient times. Therefore,

---

[1] *Classics*, vol. iv, pt. ii, p. 360.

even in the Han and the Tang dynasties, the word rent was used in the sense of tax; and even in the present day, there is the so-called government rent which goes to the government for the use of public land. Hence, the principles of the land tax given by the Confucians are also the principles of rent.

3. *Amount of Rent*

According to the theory of the Confucians, the amount of rent should be one-tenth of the total produce of the land. This is the moderate rate of land tax; hence, it is also that of rent. There is also no-tax land, equivalent to no-rent land.

According to the historical facts, the earliest custom of paying rent was the *métayer* system. The cultivator retained one-half of the harvest, and paid the other half to the landowner as rent. This was strongly condemned by the Confucians. But such a practice has existed from the Ch'in dynasty [1] to the present day.

During the Wei and the Tsin dynasties, when people took land and oxen from the government for cultivation, the government got six-tenths of the harvest as rent, and the people got four-tenths. If the cultivators supplied private oxen and cultivated government land, they conformed to the *métayer* system.

In 1077 A. K. (526 A. D.), the Northern Wei dynasty regulated the land tax as five pints of rice for each acre. If the cultivator was a tenant of government land, each acre paid one peck of rice. Therefore, the amount of rent was equal to that of tax, five pints.[2]

The Kin dynasty obtained a great amount of rent from

---

[1] *History of Han*, ch. xxiv.
[2] *General Research*, ch. ii.

GENERAL PRINCIPLES OF DISTRIBUTION   471

the government land. In the year 1752 A. K. (1201 A. D.), the average of rent was five pecks of rice for each acre, including the land tax. At that time the tax on private land was only five and three-tenths pints of rice and fifteen catties of straw for each acre.[1]

In 2304 A. K. (1753 A. D.), the average rent of the government land for the support of public schools was about .0165 tael of silver for each acre, without paying land tax.[2]

In fact, the government rent is a form of land tax, and it is much lower than the private rent. The people can never pay as high rent to the government as to private landowners, because of the added cost of paying government rent, due to the cost of transportation and the corruption of the official administration. Therefore, the Sung and the Ming dynasties did great harm to the people, because they made the government rent equal to the private rent.

It is difficult to find the rate of rent paid to the private landowner outside the *métayer* system, but there are some statements. In 1345 A. K. (794 A. D.), Lu Chih, a great statesman, said:

Now, the government taxes each acre of land at the rate of five pints of rice. But the private families receive the rent at one bushel, which is twenty times the land tax. Even of the middle grade of land, its rent is still half this amount. The land is the possession of the emperor, and the agricultural works are the labor of the farmers; but the monopolistic capitalists get the benefits.

The break-up of the system of land distribution occurred not long before his time;[3] hence, Lu Chih did not recognize the

---
[1] *Continuation of the General Research*, ch. i.
[2] *General Research of the Present Dynasty*, ch. i.
[3] See *infra*, p. 520.

right of private receipt of rent. His conclusion was that land ownership should be limited, and rent should be legally reduced.[1] But he lost his position at the end of the year above mentioned, so his theory was not carried out. Passing through the Sung,[2] the Yüan and the Ming[3] dynasties, the general amount of rent was practically the same, one bushel of rice for each acre of good land. At the present day, the rent is paid partly in money.

III. INTEREST

In the Chinese language, there are two words, interest and profit. But the word profit can be used either for the word interest only, or for both interest and profit. Hence, there is great confusion.[4] The word interest, however, never can be used for the word profit, nor can it include the meaning of profit. Therefore, we shall discuss the problem of interest first.

1. *Justification of Interest*

The word interest in Chinese is called *hsi*, which means child. In the *Historical Record*, it is termed " the child money."[5] In the *Canon of History*, it is called *sheng*, which means produce. The oldest statement is in the *Canon of History*. It was said by P'an Kêng (850-823 B. K. or 1401-1374 B. C.): "I will not employ those who are fond of wealth and make their living upon the multiplication of interest."[6] Therefore, the capitalists making their living upon interest were very prominent during the Yin dynasty. The reason why P'an Kêng did not want to employ these

---

[1] *General Political History*, ch. ccxxxiv.
[2] *History of Sung*, ch. clxxiii.
[3] *History of Ming*, ch. lxxviii.
[4] *Cf. infra*, p. 475.   [5] Ch. cxxix.
[6] *Cf. Classics*, vol. iii, pt. i, p. 247.

men is that living upon interest is not a proper thing for the officials, because officials should not make any material gain like private persons.[1] But he did not prohibit the taking of interest. Therefore, anyone had the right of taking interest, and the only discouragement was that he would not be employed as an official. This is the principle of Confucius.

According to the principles of Confucius, taking interest is not wrong. Capital is the mother, and interest is her child. As an immediate cause, capital can produce interest because it is employed under the guidance of the entrepreneur. But as the remote cause, the entrepreneur can employ the capital for the producing of interest because he himself either is a capitalist, or can borrow it from the capitalist, for he cannot make interest out of nothing. Therefore, interest is imputed to capital just as a child is imputed to its mother. In Chinese literature, which calls it "child," there never has been a single question about its justification. It is justified very plainly by the language itself, and it causes no argument. The different usage in the European languages may account for part of the controversy about the taking of interest. Confucius gives no condemnation of it.

When Mencius quotes the words of Lung Tzŭ, who says that the farmers borrow money at the rate of one hundred per cent for the clearing-up of tax-payment, he does not blame the lender for the high rate of interest, but simply blames the system of taxation.[2] He knows that the rate of interest is determined by demand and supply, so that he does not say anything against it. Even of such a high rate of interest he gives no condemnation, and certainly he does

---

[1] See *infra*, pp. 543-8.
[2] See *infra*, pp. 623-4.

not condemn those who take interest at the natural rate. In fact, the Confucians justify the taking of interest.

2. *Rate of Interest*

Although interest is justifiable, what should be its natural rate? On this point, Confucius does not touch. Judging from the principles of the Confucians, and the common phrase, "the profit of one-tenth," we may venture to say that the ideal rate of interest from the Confucian point of view would be ten per cent.

In the *Annotation of the Official System of Chou*, Chêng Hsüan gives his theory as to the rate of interest as follows: When the government bank lends capital to the people, the annual rates of interest are different according to the residence of borrowers. If they live in the capital city, the rate is 5 per cent; if in the suburb, 10 per cent; if in the country, 15 per cent; if in the provinces, 20 per cent.[1] Therefore, the rate of interest is higher if the borrower lives further from the imperial city. We are not sure whether this rule was made by the Duke of Chou or not; but the theory of Chêng Hsüan is very interesting. Since he was one of the greatest Confucians, and his commentary had a great influence upon historical facts, we are safe in saying that it is the theory of the rate of interest of the Confucians. In explanation of this theory, we may make a suggestion: As the imperial city is the commercial center, the rate is the lowest one; while the further a locality is from the center, the higher will be the rate. This is the principle that demand and supply determine the rate of interest. But, as the highest rate is fixed at 20 per cent, it shows that the government bank is for the good of the people.

The rates just mentioned may have been theoretical or ideal rates. We now come to the historical facts concern-

[1] Ch. xv.

ing the rate of interest. According to the *Historical Record*, during the beginning of the Han dynasty, the annual rate of interest among all the farmers, the artisans and the merchants, was 20 per cent. This was the normal rate. In 398 (154 B. C.), when the princes borrowed money for a military expedition, the abnormal rate was as high as ten times the principal, because the risk was very great.[1] According to the *Law Code of the Ts'ing dynasty*,[2] the rate of interest is fixed at the limit of 30 per cent. But the commercial rate of the present day is much lower than that limit. Generally, it is 8 per cent, although varying to a great extent.

IV. PROFITS

The word profit has been loosely used for a long time. In ancient times, it included interest, insurance against risk, and wages of management. Indeed, besides the expense which was used for production, all gains were summed up by the word profit. In the case of the farmer, it included even rent, since he did not pay rent to anyone, except the land tax to the government; and even wages, since he himself was a laborer. Therefore, we must understand the scope of the word profit. Since the term profit applied to the net gain of an entrepreneur began only with F. A. Walker, we do not wonder that such a term was loosely used in ancient China.

1. *Profit Seldom Mentioned*

We are told by the *Analects* that Confucius rarely spoke of profit.[3] This statement is true. The reason for it is pointed out by Ssŭ-ma Chien. He says: "Oh, profit is really the origin of disorder. That Confucius seldom spoke of it was because he always prevented the germ of dis-

[1] Ch. cxxix. [2] Ch. xiv.
[3] *Classics*, vol. i, p. 216.

order." [1] Therefore, Confucius said: "He who acts with a constant view to his own profit will be much murmured against." [2] Indeed, Confucius was afraid that man would care too much for selfish gain. During the time of Mencius, the subject of profit became still more prominent. Therefore, Mencius not only seldom used, but also vehemently attacked, the word profit.[3] These facts indicate that the economic principles of the Confucians are from the social and moral points of view rather than from the purely economic point of view.

2. Justification of Profit

Although Confucius seldom spoke of profit, he did not give any statement against the common people who make profit. The *Canon of Poetry* says: "As a merchant gains a profit of three hundred per cent, a superior man has known it." [4] This means that the making of profit is a proper business of the merchant, but not of the superior man, the official. It is a condemnation of the official who makes profit like a merchant, but not a condemnation of the merchant. To gain a good profit is a proper thing for all the common people, either farmers, or artisans, or merchants; and it is justified by Confucius.

Even his own pupils Confucius did not condemn for the making of profit. As we have known, Tzŭ-kung was a very great merchant of that time, and the first one of the founders of the commercial school. One day, Confucius said: "There is Hui! He has nearly attained to perfect virtue. He is often in want. Tz'ŭ does not acquiesce in the appointment of Heaven, but accumulates commodities for the multi-

---
[1] *Historical Record*, ch. lxxiv.
[2] *Classics*, vol. i, p. 169.
[3] *Ibid.*, vol. ii, pp. 125-7, 428-30.
[4] *Ibid.*, vol. iv, pt. ii, p. 562.

GENERAL PRINCIPLES OF DISTRIBUTION 477

plication of wealth. Yet his speculations are often successful."[1] Hui was the personal name of Yen Yüan, and Tz'ŭ was that of Tzŭ-kung. Most of the commentators say that Confucius praised Yen Yüan and satirized Tzŭ-kung. But this was not the case. Confucius praised Yen Yüan indeed, but he praised Tzŭ-kung also. Yen Yüan distinguished himself by his virtue, and Tzŭ-kung by his ability; hence, they are both appreciated in this statement of Confucius. Of course, when Tzŭ-kung was compared with Yen Yüan, Yen Yüan was better than he; but when he was compared with all the pupils of Confucius, he stood as the second figure and next only to Yen Yüan.[2] Therefore, Confucius praised Yen Yüan first, and said that he had nearly attained to perfect virtue. But he praised Tzŭ-kung next, and said that he did not acquiesce in the appointment of Heaven and that his speculations were often successful. Let us think how difficult it is not to accept the appointment of Heaven and to succeed frequently in speculation. This showed the ability of Tzŭ-kung, and Confucius appreciated it highly. From the moral point of view, Yen Yüan was the best, because he had the best intellectual power but did not care for his economic life. From the intellectual point of view, Tzŭ-kung was a very able man, yet his moral character had no wrong. This is the true meaning of this statement of Confucius. Now, even though we grant that he did not praise Tzŭ-kung at all, he had nothing against him. For, the making of comparison between Yen Yüan and Tzŭ-kung does not mean that one is right and the other wrong. Therefore, we may say that Confucius did approve the making of profit by Tzŭ-kung. Even if he did not do so, he certainly did not condemn it.

In the *Debate on the Government Monopoly of Salt and*

[1] *Classics*, vol. i, p. 243.   [2] *Ibid.*, p. 176.

Iron,[1] Tzŭ-kung is defended. It says that he, in employing his capital, was not necessarily getting profit out of the people. He simply worked with his brains, exchanged commodities according to the conditions of the market, and took profit in the differences of prices. From this point of view, profit is the result of a skilful exchange, and it is not necessarily taken from the people.

3. *Amount of Profits*

Since the amount of profits is uncertain, we cannot make out the rate of profits. According to the statements of the ancient books, however, we may get a general idea about it. As we have just seen, the *Canon of Poetry* mentions a profit of three hundred per cent. The "Explanation of the Trigrams" also speaks about the profit of three hundred per cent in the market.[2] Therefore, we may say that three hundred per cent was considered as a good profit in the ancient times; but it was not an extraordinarily high profit.

In the *Plans of the Warring States*, there is a statement telling about the rates of profits as follows: Lü Pu-wei asks his father, "How many times more is the profit of cultivating land than the amount of capital?" "Ten times," answers his father. "How many times more is the profit of a jeweller than the amount of capital?" he asks again. "One hundred times" is the answer.[3] Judging from this statement, the rates of profits during the period of Warring States were very high. Such high rates of profits, however, began in the period of Spring and Autumn. Kuan Tzŭ says that the merchants may gain a profit of one hundred times the amount of capital, and that, for the pre-

---

[1] It was written by Huan K'uan during the reign of Han Hsüan Ti (479-503, or 73-49 B. C.). Bk. xvii.

[2] *Yi King*, p. 431.   [3] Bk. vii.

vention of it, a ruler must have a profit of ten times.[1] By this statement, he means that the ruler, the representative of the state, should get the profit for the social adjustment of wealth, and that private merchants gaining extraordinary profit should be prevented because they hurt the poor and destroy the equality of wealth. In conclusion, the rates of profits during the Chou dynasty were very high, but the word profit included many elements.

[1] Bk. lxxiii.

CHAPTER XXV

WAGES

1. ORIGIN OF WAGES

WHEN everyone works for himself, there are no wages to be paid out, although the element of wages will remain. Wages come when men work for others. The slave works for others, yet he receives no wages. Wages come when there are free laborers. In the historical period, China had no slavery as a general institution in the economic field. Every man was free, and every man received one hundred acres of public land from the government. Under such a system, no one would work for any private person, nor in public employment, unless he could get a return equal to what he could get on his farm. This is the origin of wages. It is expressed by Mencius and the " Royal Regulations " as " the substitute for tillage."

As the word salary is simply the higher form of wages, there is no essential difference between salary and wages. Now, in the Chinese language, salary is called *lu* and grain is called *ku*. The commentator of the " Royal Regulations " says that *lu* is *ku*. In other words, salary is grain. Just as, in modern times, wages paid by money are expressed in money, so, in ancient China, salary paid by grain was expressed in grain. But what we want to point out here is that the Chinese wages system came from the independent farmer. Instead of working his own farm, he worked for others, and received his wages in grain as a substitute for tillage.

In the western world, the wages system came from slavery.[1] But in China, this was not the case. In the Confucian writings, all public officers are regarded as laborers, and all their salaries as a substitute for tillage. Had China had a slave class, the public officers would not get any pay, because they would have slaves to do the tillage for them, and they should serve through their leisure the public for nothing. This had been done in ancient Greece. Moreover, even if the public officers should receive pay, why should Mencius call it a substitute for tillage? If they had had slaves, and had not tilled the land at all, why should their salary be called by a name which would not have been appropriate? We know perfectly now, that, because China had no slavery, and because the ancient Chinese all worked on farms, such an expression as the substitute for tillage came to be used. For this reason, even at the present day, in the English language, the public officers are called public servants; but in Chinese, they are called public laborers (*pai kung* or *ch'ên kung*). The word servant comes from the dependent slave, but the word laborer from the independent workman.

II. EMPLOYER AND EMPLOYEE

The wages system in China is very old, and we do not know its beginning. According to *Mo Tzŭ*, we know that Fu Yüeh arose from a wage-earner in the building business to be the prime minister of the Yin dynasty.[2] Therefore, the wages system must have existed long before that time (770 B. K. or 1321 B. C.).

In the beginning of the Chou dynasty, the hire system

---

[1] *Labor Problems*, by T. S. Adams and H. L. Sumner, p. 7.
[2] Bk. ix.

existed in agricultural life. The *Canon of Poetry* says: " There are the master and his elder son; his younger sons, and all their children; their strong helpers, and their hired laborers." [1] All of them work on the farms. The strong helpers are those who, after doing their own work, are able to go and give a hand where they are needed. The hired laborers are those who serve their master at his disposal. Here we find that there is a separation of these two classes —the master and the hired laborer.

According to the *Official System of Chou*, the separation of these two classes is very clear. It says: " The master gains the people with profit." This means that the employer, with the power of wealth which comes from his profits, can gain a great number of people who are the wage-earners. It is nothing against the employer, but rather indicates the fact that he is the leader of the people for the combination of economic forces. It divides the wage-earners into two classes—servants and laborers. The servants mostly work at home; their labor is somewhat easy; and their relation to the master is close and somewhat permanent. The laborers work anywhere; their labor is heavy; and their relation to the master is loose and not permanent.[2] It is a matter of fact that the class of wage-earners exists even under the most favorable conditions, because the abilities of men are unequal.

For dealings between employer and employee, there is a general rule given in the *Record of Rites*. When an employee wishes to undertake some work for an employer, he should measure his ability and duty, and all the labor conditions first, before entering on his employment. In this way, the one party has no ground for offense, and the other

---

[1] *Classics*, vol. iv, pt. ii, p. 601.
[2] Ch. ii.

WAGES

avoids all risk of guilt.[1] According to this rule, the employee should make a careful bargain in the beginning, and employer and employee should not fight against each other afterward. If laborers would observe this rule, labor disputes would be much fewer.[2]

III. THE PRODUCTIVITY THEORY

The wages theory of Confucius is a productivity theory. This means that the amount of wages of the laborer should be according to the product which he contributes. Confucius says: "By daily examinations and monthly trials, and by making their rations in accordance with their labors: this is the way to encourage all the classes of artisans."[3] This is the principle of justice governing the law of wages. Of course, labor should not be underpaid; yet neither should it be overpaid. If it were overpaid, or to state it clearly, if poor labor were as well paid as good labor, there would be no encouragement for all classes of artisans. The good laborer would be disappointed, the survival would be of the unfit, and the standard of workmanship would be lowered. But, if we want to pay wages according to product, daily examinations and monthly trials are necessary; otherwise we cannot know the amount of productivity of labor. This theory is the fundamental law of wages.

What Confucius refers to is the factory system under which the government is the employer. If the government wants to make the state rich, it must give the laborers just wages; this is the principle of inducing all the classes of artisans to come in. If it is not so, the artisans will neither

---
[1] *Li Ki*, bk. xv, p. 72.
[2] In Canton there are the so-called "seventy-two trade guilds;" trade unions have been organized on the side of the employees. Both have existed for centuries.
[3] See *supra*, p. 318.

immigrate nor stay, and the wealth of the state will not be sufficient. Kuan Tzŭ also recognizes the importance of encouraging artisans to come in, but his policy for carrying it out is to raise wages to a rate three times as great as that of other states.[1] This policy cannot be a general principle, but simply a temporary measure for an emergent demand for labor. From the statements of Confucius and Kuan Tzŭ, we know that, in the Chou dynasty, there was a free movement of labor, and there was international competition for the labor market; hence, the amount of wages was the determining factor in the movement of labor.

The productivity theory is applied not only to manual labor, but also to mental labor. Confucius says:

In the service of a ruler, when great words are spoken to and accepted by him, great advantages to the state may be expected from them; and when words of small importance are presented to him, only small advantages are to be looked for. Therefore, a superior man will not for words of small importance receive a great salary, nor for words of great importance a small salary.[2]

Even in regard to the value of words, they should be neither overpaid nor underpaid. This is the principle of justice, and it is the rule of accepting wages.

According to Confucius, however, a superior man may accept underpay, but not overpay. He says:

The superior man will decline a position of high honor, but not one that is mean; and riches, but not poverty. In this way, disorder will more and more disappear. Hence, the superior man, rather than have his emoluments superior to his worth, will have his worth superior to his emoluments.[3]

[1] Bk. li. [2] *Li Ki*, bk. xxix, p. 345.
[3] *Li Ki*, bk. xxvii, p. 286.

WAGES

This principle is based on moral and social reasons, but not on economic law. According to economic law, men should never be overpaid, nor underpaid.

According to the principles of the Confucians, division of labor is a very important thing for society, and all labor is productive. Not only is the farmer productive, but also the artisan and the merchant. Again, not only are these three classes of people productive, but also the political officer and the moral teacher. Referring to these two classes of men, there are many arguments saying that they are unproductive. For this reason, let us study their productivity.

First, let us see how the political officer is productive. When Chen Hsiang, formerly a Confucian, but converted by Hsü Hsing, visited Mencius, he quoted the words of Hsü Hsing to the effect that the ruler should cultivate the land equally and along with his people.[1] Mencius said: " I suppose that Hsü Tzŭ sows grain and eats the produce. Is it not so?" "It is so," was the answer. " I suppose also he weaves cloth, and wears his own manufacture. Is it not so?" "No. Hsü Tzŭ wears clothes of hair-cloth." "Does he wear a cap?" "He wears a cap." "What kind of cap?" "A plain cap." "Is it woven by himself?" "No. He gets it in exchange for grain." "Why does Hsü not weave it himself?" "That would injure his husbandry." "Does Hsü cook his food in boilers and earthenware pans and does he plough with an iron share?" "Yes." "Does he make those articles himself?" "No. He gets them in exchange for grain."

Mencius then said:

The getting those various articles in exchange for grain, is not oppressive to the potter and the founder, and the potter

[1] See *supra*, p. 385.

and the founder in their turn, in exchanging their various articles for grain, are not oppressive to the husbandman. How should such a thing be supposed? And moreover, why does not Hsü Tzŭ establish the pottery and foundery, supplying himself with the articles which he uses solely from his own establishment? Why does he go confusedly dealing and exchanging with all the artisans? Why does he not spare himself so much trouble?

Chen Hsiang replied: " The business of the artisans can by no means be carried on along with the business of husbandry."

Mencius resumed:

Then, is it the government of the empire which alone can be carried on along with the practice of husbandry? Great men have their proper business, and little men have their proper business. Moreover, even in the case of any single person, he may require various articles which are produced by all classes of artisans:—if he must first make them for his own use, this way of doing would lead the whole world into poverty.[1]

The doctrine of Hsü Hsing is extremely democratic. He teaches that everyone should support his mouth by his own hand, and that all rulers should be farmers. But it is impossible. Mencius' doctrine is based on the principle of division of labor. The governing class supported by others does not oppress the people, because the men of this class cannot cultivate the land at the same time they work in the government, and because their mental work cannot be done by the governed. It is merely an exchange of services, and the governing class and the governed class depend upon each other. The ruler exchanges his governmental work for food from the farmer just as the potter and the founder

[1] *Classics*, vol. ii, pp. 247-9.

exchange their articles for the grain of the farmer. From this point of view, we can justify not only the political relation between the ruler and the subject, but also the economic relation between manager and common laborer. Indeed, distribution according to productivity is universal justice.

Second, let us see how the moral teacher is productive. Followed by "several tens" of carriages and attended by several hundred men, this is the way Mencius traveled from one prince to another, and lived on their hospitality. P'êng Kêng, his pupil, thinking this excessive, says: "For a scholar, doing no business, to receive his support, is improper." Mencius answers:

> If you do not have interchange of service and exchange of productivity, so that one from his overplus may supply the difficiency of another, then the husbandmen will have a superfluity of grain, and the women will have a superfluity of cloth. If you have such an interchange, carpenter, mason, wheel-maker, and carriage-wright, may all get their food from you. Here now is a man, who is filial at home, and fraternal abroad; who keeps the principles of the ancient kings, awaiting the rise of future learners:—and yet you will refuse to support him. How is it that you give honor to the carpenter, mason, wheel-maker, and carriage-wright, and slight him who practises benevolence and righteousness?

Then P'êng Kêng says that those laborers should be fed by society because their purpose is for their living, but that the superior man should not be fed by society because his purpose is not for his living. Mencius replies: "What have you to do with their purpose? Anyone who is of service to you deserves to be supported, and should be supported." Then he asks P'êng Kêng whether he would pay a man for his purpose or for his service. To this P'êng cannot help but answer that he would pay him for his purpose.

Mencius asks him: "There is a man here, who breaks your tiles, and disfigures your painted walls with his knife; his purpose may be thereby to seek for his living, but will you indeed remunerate him?" "No," says P'êng. Then Mencius concludes: "That being the case, it is not the purpose which you remunerate, but the work done."[1] From Mencius' point of view, the formula of distributive justice is: to each according to his productivity, not his wants.

Kung-sun Ch'ou, pupil of Mencius, says to him: "It is said in the *Canon of Poetry*, 'He will not eat the bread of idleness.' How is it that we see superior men eating without farming?" Mencius replies: "When a superior man resides in a country, if its sovereign employ his counsels, he comes to tranquillity, wealth, honor, and glory. If the young in it follow his instructions, they become filial, fraternal, faithful, and sincere. What greater example can there be than this of not eating the bread of idleness?"[2]

The arguments of both P'êng Kêng and Kung-sun Ch'ou refer to Mencius himself. But he maintains that reward should be according to productivity, and that a moral teacher is much more productive than a carpenter, mason, wheel-maker, carriage-wright or farmer. In short, by productivity, he means production of utility, and not merely production of things. Since a moral teacher produces a great amount of social utility, he is justified in receiving a reward from society.

IV. STANDARD OF WAGES

As we have seen that wages are a substitute for tillage, the products of the former are therefore the bases of wages. Just as the amount of products is different among farmers, so the amount of wages is also different

[1] *Classics*, vol. ii, pp. 269-271.
[2] *Ibid.*, p. 467.

among laborers. Yet there must be an equality between the products of the farmers and the wages of other laborers, otherwise no one's wages would be enough to substitute for tillage, and no one would give up his farm for other employment.

According to Mencius and the "Royal Regulations," the standard of wages is something like this: Each farmer tills one hundred acres, together with some capital such as manure. Yet the products of the farmers are different from each other. They are classified into five grades. The products of the best farmer can support nine persons, and the products of those ranking next to him can support eight. The products of the average farmer can support seven persons, and the products of those ranking next to him can support six. The products of the poor farmer can support only five persons. These differences in their products are due to the fact that their efficiency is various. Yet they serve as the standard for the wage scale of common laborers. The salaries of the common people who are employed about the government offices are regulated according to these five grades.[1]

The wages theory of Mencius is quite like that of Henry George. Henry George takes the margin of production of the farmer as the standard of wages. The amount which the farmer can produce upon free land for himself is the basis of wages, otherwise he will not work for others. "The condition of labor in these first and widest of occupations," he says, " determines the general condition of labor, just as the level of the ocean determines the level of all its arms and bays and seas."[2] This is exactly what Mencius means. In the time of Mencius, there was no private ownership of

[1] *Classics*, vol. ii, p. 376, and *Li Ki*, bk. iii, p. 210.
[2] *Social Problem*, p. 190.

land; every man received free land from the government; and agriculture was the dominant industry. Under such conditions, the standard of wages was necessarily equal to the gain of the farmer, although the latter's gain was mixed with land values.

In the statements of Mencius and the "Royal Regulations," wages means real wages. Those statements do not measure wages in terms of money, nor in terms of any particular good, but in a certain amount of general products which can support a certain number of persons. This theory of real wages will hold true in all places and all times. Even the standard of living affects the rise and fall of wages, but it cannot affect the wage scale itself. If the standard of living is higher, it requires higher wages; if it is lower, it allows lower wages. But, in either case, the lowest wages in the scale must be sufficient to support five persons, and the relation among the different wages will remain the same in the scale. Because the scale is based on real wages, the principle of wage-measuring will not be changed by changes in the quantity of money, nor by the movement of price, nor by the standard of living.

The statements of Mencius and the "Royal Regulations" also fix the limit of the minimum wage. Cantillon says: "The lowest species of common laborers must everywhere earn at least double their own maintenance, in order that one with another they may be enabled to bring up two children."[1] Adam Smith said that in Great Britain the wages of labor seemed, in his day, to be evidently more than what was precisely necessary to enable the laborer to bring up a family.[2] But Mencius and the "Royal Regulations" give definitely the law of minimum wage—that is, the lowest rate of the wage of the poorest laborer must be

---

[1] *Wealth of Nations*, bk. i, ch. viii, p. 70.   [2] *Ibid.*, p. 75.

WAGES

large enough to support five persons. This is the smallest product of the poor farmer, and fixes the smallest wage of the lowest laborer.

V. IDEAL SCALE OF WAGES IN THE WHOLE SOCIETY

As we have said that the Confucians regard all public officers as laborers, and their salaries as wages, we can now form an ideal scale of wages in the whole society. From the Confucian point of view, we never could make such a mistake as to say that agricultural labor is the only productive labor. The farmer is a real farmer indeed, but the public officer is a substitute for the farmer. The difference between the farmer and the public officer simply is in the division of labor. Now, some officers are not only productive, but also in a much higher degree than the farmer. And in turn, society gives them a reward much higher than the ordinary wage. According to Mencius, the product of the best farmer forms the basis of the salaries of all public officers. The salary of the subordinate scholar is equal to the product of the best farmer; that of the middle scholar is twice as much as the product of the best farmer; that of the superior scholar is four times as much. The salary of the great official is eight times as much. All the salaries of the three classes of scholars and of the great officials are uniform throughout the whole empire. Then the salary of the minister of the small state is sixteen times the product of the best farmer, and that of his prince is one hundred sixty times; that of the minister of the second state is twenty-four times, and that of his prince two hundred forty times; that of the minister of the great state is thirty-two times, and that of his prince three hundred twenty times. The salaries of the ministers and princes vary according to the size of their state. Mencius does not mention the amount of the salary of the emperor, yet it is implied in the principle that the salary of the ruler is ten times that of his minister. We can say, therefore, that the salary of the emperor is three thousand two hundred times the product of the best farmer, because the income of his minister is equal to that of the prince of the great state. In short, the emperor and all other public officers are laborers who are substitutes for the farmers, working in the government; and all their salaries are wages, which are the substitute for tillage. Although their labor is not of the same kind, and their wages are not of the same amounts, the scale of their wages, nevertheless, is proportional to the product of the farmer.

Now, what is the scale of wages of common laborers? This scale has been stated before, but it should be made clearer now. The scale of common wages is based on the amount of product of the poor farmer, which is large enough to support five persons. Then the scale goes up to the different amounts of wages which can support six, seven, eight and nine persons. In this scale, there are five grades. The highest wage for common labor is sufficient to support nine persons, and the lowest, to support five.

Therefore, we can see the whole scale of all the various wages in the whole society. The so-called professional men or salaried class should belong to the official class. There are six main gradations in their wages. But, if we come to details, there are really eleven grades as shown by the different amounts of salary. The manual-labor or wage-earning class belong to the farmer class. Their wages are of five grades. The salary of the subordinate scholar and the product of the best farmer stand exactly on the dividing line between the official and the farmer classes. Taking two extremes in this scale, the poor farmer receives the lowest wage, the emperor the highest. Or, in other words, the minimum wage can support five persons, and the

WAGES

maximum wage can support two million eight hundred eighty thousand persons.

VI. EDUCATION AS A SOLUTION OF THE WAGES PROBLEM

Since there are officials, and their salary is great, how can we solve the problem of wages and distribute wealth justly? It is by education. Adam Smith says: "The difference between the most dissimilar characters, between a philosopher and a common street porter, for example, seems to arise not so much from nature, as from habit, custom, and education." This is exactly the view of Confucius.[1] He says:

Those who are born with the possession of knowledge are the highest class of men. Those who learn, and so readily get possession of knowledge, are the next. Those who are dull and stupid, and yet compass learning, are another class next to these. As to those who are dull and stupid and yet do not learn, they are the lowest of the people.[2]

Therefore, man is determined, not by nature, but by education. If he has education, even though he be dull and stupid, he will be ranked with those two classes of men in the final result.[3] And the really low class of people are only those who do not educate themselves. Since education determines the standing of men, it determines also their wages.

When Tzŭ-chang wants to learn something about the getting of an official salary, Confucius says:

Hear much and put aside the points of which you stand in doubt, while you speak cautiously at the same time of the others: then you will afford few occasions for blame. See much and put aside the things which seem perilous, while you

---

[1] See *supra*, p. 137.
[2] *Classics*, vol. i, pp. 313-4.
[3] *Ibid.*, p. 407.

are cautious at the same time in carrying the others into practice: then you will have few occasions for repentance. When one gives few occasions for blame in his words, and few occasions for repentance in his conduct, he is in the way to get a salary.[1]

One day Confucius said:" There is ploughing; even in that there is sometimes want. So with learning; an official salary may be found in it."[2] According to him, although education is not for the sake of getting a salary, it is the way of getting it. Therefore, he points out that the salary is the result of education, in order to encourage the people to learn.

According to Mencius, everyone may become like Yao and Shun;[3] and according to Hsun Tzŭ, anyone on the street may become like Yü. Their meaning is that everyone may become a sage. But Hsun Tzŭ explains this point more clearly. He says:

Let any man on the street addict himself to the art of learning with all his heart and the entire bent of his will, thinking, and closely examining; let him do this day after day, through a long space of time, accumulating what is good, and he will penetrate as far as a spiritual intelligence, and he will become a triumvir with Heaven and Earth. It follows that the characters of the sages were what any man may reach by accumulation.[4]

Hence, according to Hsun Tzŭ, education is the only thing which makes the mean noble, the fool wise, and the poor rich. Indeed, education has great power to make the man. Even if the educated man is poor, he is really rich on account of his worthiness.[5]

[1] *Classics*, vol. i, p. 151.
[2] *Ibid.*, p. 303.
[3] *Ibid.*, vol. ii, p. 424.
[4] *Ibid.*, pp. 85-6.
[5] Bk. viii.

WAGES

There is a poem written by Han Yü emphasizing the importance of education for the encouraging of his son, Han Fu, to study. In part it runs as follows:

> If you want to know the effect of education,
> It is that the wise and the fool are of the same origin;
> Because they cannot have the same learning,
> Different houses they are entering.
> Two families respectively have a son;
> The skill of the two babies is at the same condition.
> When they are a little older,
> As a couple of fishes they play together.
> Up to the age of twelve or thirteen,
> The differences in their appearance just begin.
> At twenty, they are more unlike:
> Clean canal and cesspool in the sight.
> At thirty, their physical development is certain:
> But one hog and one dragon.
> The latter flies away,
> And cannot help the toad on its way.
> The one is a driver before a horse;
> His back is flogged and becomes the home of insects.
> The other is a duke and a minister,
> Living in a mansion in a magnificent manner.
> Ask what is the reason,
> Education and non-education.
> Gold and jade although they come so dear,
> Soon waste away and disappear.
> Education is kept in your body;
> While the body exists, it is plenty
> That the people belong to either high or low class,
> Is not on account of their parents.
> Don't you see the duke and the minister,
> Raising themselves from the farmer?
> Don't you see the descendants of the nobles,
> Hungry and cold, go out without an ass?

All that we have said above concerns the relation between education and official salary. But how about the relation between education and ordinary wages? It will be the same thing. If the unskilled laborer wants to get the wage of the skilled laborer, he must first educate himself to be a skilled laborer. If he wants to get the salary of the manager, he must first educate himself as a manager. It is sometimes the case that he cannot get a good salary, even though he has a good education. But there is no hope of his getting a good salary without educating himself. Therefore, just as political democracy is based on education, so also is industrial democracy based on education. In short, from the Confucian point of view, education is the solution of the wages problem, which is the chief problem in the distribution of wealth.

BOOK VIII. SOCIALISTIC POLICIES

CHAPTER XXVI

The Tsing Tien System [1]

I. HISTORY OF TSING TIEN

The *tsing tien* system is the most important element in Chinese economic thought and history. According to a few modern scholars, this system was never in actual operation, but only a theory of Confucians. It is true that in ancient times, the *tsing tien* system could not have been as perfect as the Confucians taught; but it is also true that this system had been partly realized before the time of Confucius. Probably the original form of this system was not unlike the manorial system of England; it was then improved by many of the ancient great kings; and finally it was modified by the Confucians into an ideal system. But, so far as we can judge from Chinese literature, however imperfect the *tsing tien* system was originally, it was never as bad as the English manorial system, nor was the condition of the people so wretched as that of the villeins. Let us study the history of *tsing tien* system.

1. *The Reign of Huang Ti*

According to historians, the *tsing tien* system began in the legendary age. Huang Ti (2147-2048 B. K. or 2698-2599 B. C.), the founder of the Chinese Empire, was its

[1] For the meaning and the form of *tsing tien* see *supra*, pp. 352-5.

originator. He was the first one who established the rules of measure, and regulated the division of land into paces and acres, in order to prevent disputes and poverty. He made one *tsing* consist of eight families. Within the limits of one *tsing,* four roads were opened, the eight houses were separated, and a *tsing* (well) was dug in the center. The principles of this system were these: first, it did not waste land, because there was only one well for all eight families; second, it saved expense for each single family, because they had a well in common; third, it unified their customs; fourth, it improved their productive arts, because they could imitate one another; fifth, they exchanged easily their commodities; sixth, during the absence of some, others guarded for them; seventh, when they went out and came in, they took care for one another; eighth, they introduced intermarriage; ninth, in case of need, they lent wealth to one another; and tenth, in time of sickness, they cared for one another. Therefore, their feelings were harmonized without quarrels or litigation; and their wealth was equalized without deceit or oppression.

According to the political divisions, one *tsing* was also called a " neighbor;" three neighbors made up one " friendship;" three friendships, one " ward;" five wards, one " town;" ten towns, a " center;" ten centers, one " multitude;" and ten multitudes, one " province." By these divisions, the *tsing* was the starting point, because the settlement of the people was the basis; and when it came to the province, the statistics were complete. Through the Hsia and the Yin dynasties, this system of division was not changed.[1] Therefore, in the reign of Huang Ti, there was already the form of *tsing tien*, that is, the division of land, but the number of laws had not been completed.

[1] *General Research,* ch. xii.

2. *The Three Dynasties*

During the Three Dynasties, Hsia, Yin and Chou, the *tsing tien* system was developing step by step. According to Mencius, the Hsia dynasty allotted fifty acres to one man, and he paid the produce of five acres to the government as a tax; the Yin dynasty allotted seventy acres, and he paid that of seven acres; the Chou dynasty allotted one hundred acres, and he paid that of ten acres. Therefore the tax system of the Three Dynasties was really a tithe.[1]

We must understand, however, that the Three Dynasties did not change the size of the field as from the allotment of fifty acres to that of seventy, or from that of seventy to that of one hundred acres. The difference in the number of acres was due to the different units of measurement of the Three Dynasties. The form of field, as we know, was very complicated, and it would have been difficult as well as unnecessary to change it. There is, therefore, every reason to suppose that in each of the Three Dynasties the same amount of land was allotted to each family and each was required to pay the same tax.

During the Chou dynasty, the *tsing tien* system was completed. According to the *Official System of Chou*, the distribution of land was according to a definite principle; its quantity should be in accordance with its quality. In the neighborhood of cities, each family received one hundred acres of the unchanged land, which was cultivated every year; or two hundred acres of the second class of land, cultivated every other year; or three hundred acres of the third class of land, cultivated every third year. But in the country, there was a more favorable law. Of the superior land, one man, together with his wife, received a home of five acres in the town, one hundred acres of land, and fifty

---

[1] *Classics*, vol. ii, pp. 240-41.

acres of fallow land which was purposely left idle for the preparation of another crop. Of the ordinary land, one man received a home, one hundred acres of land, and one hundred acres of fallow land; and of the inferior land, one man received his home and one hundred acres of land together with two hundred acres of fallow land. If any family had a large number, the " supernumerary male " received an amount of land as follows: of the superior land, twelve and a half acres of fallow land; of ordinary land, twenty-five acres; of inferior land, fifty acres; while in all three grades, he received twenty-five acres of land to be cultivated.[1] The differences between the law which was applied to the neighborhood of cities and that which was for the country were these: around the cities, no fallow land was given as an addition to superior land, and nothing was distributed to the supernumerary males. The reason the countrymen were shown more favor was because the government gave special grace to those people who were far away from the cities. Moreover, near the cities, with a large population and a limited amount of land, it was impossible to use the same law as in the country. And the favorable law of the country might have been a policy of the government to draw the population from the cities. There is still another point: as the economic life of the cities was different from that of the country, the people of the cities did not need so much land as those in the country.

For the distribution of land, there was also another principle: the quality of land was in accordance with the size of the family. To a large family, from eight persons up to ten, superior land was distributed; to an ordinary family, from five to seven, ordinary land was distributed; and to a small family, from two to four, inferior land was dis-

[1] *Canonical Interpretation of the Ts'ing Dynasty*, vol. liii, ch. i.

tributed. For each grade of land, there was a sub-division; and altogether there were nine different classes of land.[1]

II. THE TSING TIEN SYSTEM OF CONFUCIUS [2]

Since we have already studied the form of *tsing tien* and its history, we now turn to the details which are described by the Confucians. First, we take up the *tsing tien* itself, and see what it is. According to Mencius, a square mile forms a *tsing*, and it contains nine hundred acres. The central square of the *tsing* is called the public field; and the surrounding eight squares are called private fields for assignment to the eight families.[3] In the center of the public field, twenty acres are taken out for the cottages of the eight families, each having a share of two acres and a half. The remaining eighty acres of the public field are cultivated in common by the eight families, each really cultivating ten acres. Each family receives one hundred acres of the private field from the public, and gives its labor to the public for the cultivation of ten acres in the public field; this is the system of tithe.

Since a *tsing* is the smallest community based upon common economic interest, it is not only a community of agriculture, but also a community of commerce. As the exchange of wealth is very small, a market-place is established in every *tsing*, and people can get the necessities of life

[1] These rules of distribution of land mentioned in these two paragraphs differ somewhat from those of the next section. As that section is based on the *Spring and Autumn*, the "Royal Regulations," and Mencius, it gives the theories of Confucians; the description in these two paragraphs is based on the *Official System of Chou* and may be assumed to correspond with the actual practice under the Chou dynasty.

[2] A complete description is given in the *Annotation of Kung-yang*, 15th year of Duke Hsüan.

[3] *Classics*, vol. ii, p. 245.

very easily. Because every *tsing* is at the same time a market, the common term "*shih tsing*" comes into existence; *shih* means market, and *tsing* is the *tsing tien*. This term is still used for the commercial district of the great cities.

To secure an equal distribution of the land there were the following rules: Generally, five persons make up a family—that is, husband and wife, together with parents and children. A farmer's family receives one hundred acres of the private field, five acres for the house in the town, two acres and a half for the cottage in the field, and ten acres of the public field; the total amount is one hundred seventeen and a half acres. If the family has more than five persons, its young man is called a supernumerary male, and he receives twenty-five acres without paying taxes.

The family of the student, artisan, and merchant also receives a share of land, but its amount is diminished. When these come to the age of maturity, they receive individually half the amount of the farmer—fifty acres; and their supernumerary male receives one-fifth the amount of the farmer—twenty acres.[1]

The age of maturity is twenty, and the people receive a full share of land, one hundred acres, at that time. But the land can neither be handed down to descendants, nor sold to others. It must be returned to the government at the age of sixty. From sixteen to twenty, youths are called supernumerary males, and receive a quarter of the full share. Among all the people, those above seventy years of age are supported by the state; those below ten are brought up by it; and those above eleven are compelled to practise by it.[2]

The land is divided into three grades, according to its

---

[1] *History of Han*, ch. xxiv. *Annotation of the Official System of Chou*, ch. xiii.

[2] *History of Han*, ch. xxiv.

quality. The superior land is cultivated every year; the ordinary land, every two years; and the inferior land, every three years. Each family receives one hundred acres of superior land, or two hundred acres of ordinary land, or three hundred acres of inferior land. Every three years the land and the residence of the various families are interchanged. In this way no one can always enjoy rich land, or suffer on the poor land. The rules described above are applied to the plain only. Among the mountain, hill, marsh, and salt lands, the distribution differs in quantity according to quality.[1]

According to Mencius, from the highest officers down to the lowest, each one must have his holy field, consisting of fifty acres. But according to Ho Hsiu, the local officers, such as the patriarchs and the justice, receive two shares of land, that is, two hundred acres. These statements are both correct. For Mencius refers to the government officers who receive salary; and the holy field is only for the purpose of religious worship. But Ho Hsiu refers to the local officers, who are elected by the people and receive no salary.

Third, we shall see how the works of the people are regulated. When they plant grain, they are not allowed to plant a single kind. Generally, they plant five kinds—rice, millet, panicled millet, wheat and pulse—in order to avoid bad crops. Within the field, no tree is allowed to be planted, lest it should give trouble to the grain. Around their cottages which are in the center of the public field, they plant mulberry trees; in their small gardens, different vegetables; and in the boundaries of their cottages, different fruits. Each family keeps five hens and two sows. The work of cultivating silkworms and weaving is the special profession of women.

[1] *History of Han*, ch. xxiv.

During spring, summer and autumn the people all work in the field. In the morning and evening, the patriarch and the justice, as overseers, sit in the houses which are in the two sides of the gate of the village. Those who go out too late are not allowed to go out, and those who do not bring some fuel back are not allowed to come in. When they bring fuel, they help each other according to the weight of their burdens, and assume the entire load of the grey-haired men. The patriarch and the justice can go back to their home only after the people have all gone out, or after they have all come in.

Besides the cottages in the field, the people have homes in the town, which is not far away from the field. A town covers several villages, and a village is made up of eighty families which come from ten *tsing;* while eight families occupy one street together. Around their homes, each occupying five acres, the space beneath the walls is planted with mulberry trees, with which the women nourish silkworms.[1] After the harvest, they all live in town. Then the justice hurries them to make the cloth. In the evening, men and women work together in the same street, spinning until midnight; hence, the work of women amounts to forty-five days' labor in the length of one month. This work commences in the tenth month, and ends in the first. They must work together to save light and heat, to disseminate the arts; and to make uniform their customs. All these rules tend to make their productive power alike, in order to equalize their wealth. In fact, the *tsing tien* system is a peculiar form of co-operative production.

Fourth, we shall notice that the *tsing tien* system is as individualistic as socialistic. Each man has his own land, his own cottage, his own home, his own mulberry trees, vege-

[1] *Classics*, vol. ii, p. 461.

tables, fruits and animals, and all other properties which belong to him. He reaps what he has produced in the field, varying from the amount which can support nine persons to that which can support only five. Moreover, from sixty to sixty-nine years of age, after he has returned the land to the public, he is supported, either by his children or by his accumulations. Therefore, from eleven up to seventy, he depends entirely upon his own. This is also individualism.

In conclusion, the *tsing tien* system is a group system based on territory. In the field, one *tsing* is the unit of division, and consists of eight families; in the town, one village is the unit, and consists of eighty families. Regardless of any blood-relationship, the only basis for the group system is territory. Therefore, the *tsing tien* system is not an ethnical society, but an economic, ethical, social, political and military society. From the foregoing description, everyone will see that it is an economic society. To prove that it is an ethical society, we may quote from Mencius, as follows:

When the land of the district is divided into different *tsing*, the people live together according to the same *tsing*. Therefore, they render all friendly offices to one another in their going out and coming in, aid one another in keeping watch and ward, and sustain one another in sickness. Thus the people are brought to live in affection and harmony.[1]

Since every village has a school house which serves also as an ethical church and a meeting house for social and political activities, it is a social and political society. The farmers are at the same time the soldiers, and ten *tsing* combine together to supply one chariot as the military duty. In time of peace, they are co-workers at home, and in time

[1] *Classics*, vol. ii, p. 245.

of war, they are co-fighters in the battle-field. Therefore, *tsing tien* is a military society. In short, the *tsing tien* is the basis of everything. As we describe many features of it in other places, we do not mention them here.

III. HISTORY OF THE DESTRUCTION OF TSING TIEN

Toward the end of the Chou dynasty, in 202 A. K. (350 B. C.), the state of Ch'in destroyed the *tsing tien* system. It was the policy of Shang Yang, minister of Ch'in. He thought that in the three neighboring states the people were poor and the land was not sufficient for them; and that in his own state the people were few and the land was more than they needed. Hence the land of Ch'in was not thoroughly cultivated, and the productive power of the soil was not fully utilized. Therefore, he lured in the people of the three neighboring states, with a special preparation of good farms and homes for them, and with an exemption of military duties for three generations; the only thing for them to do was the agricultural work at home. Then the native people undertook the charge of expeditions abroad. He destroyed the form of *tsing tien* which was created by the ancients, and opened the different roads and boundaries along the field for extensive cultivation. The people were allowed to take as much land as they wanted. The result of this policy was that within a few years, the state was rich and strong, and gained power for the consolidation of the whole empire.

This new law inaugurated a revolution in the economic history of China. It was the first time the people were given private ownership of land. From that time on, the land was not in the hands of the government, and the public could never control the wealth of the community.

In 336 A. K. (216 B. C.), the First Emperor of the Ch'in dynasty decreed that the people should themselves tell the amount of their land, in order to regulate the land tax. Since that year, throughout the whole empire, private ownership of land has prevailed, and everyone has been permitted to sell or buy land.

IV. HISTORY OF THE UNSUCCESSFUL ATTEMPTS TO REVIVE THE TSING TIEN SYSTEM

1. *Limitation Policy*

After the *tsing tien* system was destroyed, land was an object of sale and purchase. Therefore, the rich had an unlimited portion of land, and the poor had not even a single clod. In the reign of Han Wu Ti (about 432 A. K. or 120 B. C.), Tung Chung-shu was the first one to advocate the limitation of land-ownership. But his proposal was not carried out.

During the reign of Han Ch'êng Ti (520-545, or 32-7 B. C.), Chang Yü, the minister, owned forty thousand acres of the best land, and others who monopolized the land owned large tracts. In consequence the people were in a very bad condition. When Ai Ti came to the throne (545, or 7 B. C.), Shih Tan, the minister, proposed that there should be a limitation of property. Then a law was made which provided that all the princes, the marquises, the princesses, the landless marquises, the officials and the people should not own land beyond the limit of three thousand acres; and that the limit of slaves was two hundred persons for the princes, one hundred for the marquises and the princesses, and thirty for the landless marquises, the officials and the people. After a period of three years, this law was to take effect, and any offender against it should be punished by forfeiture. Then the price of land and slaves fell. But the favorites of the court did not like the law, and it was not enforced.

2. Confiscation Policy

During the time of Wang Mang, the poor had no land, and only borrowed it from the rich; hence they paid half of their produce to the rich. Therefore, the rich were vicious because of their haughtiness, and the poor were wicked because of their poverty; they both fell into guilt. In 560 (9 A. D.), Wang Mang decreed that the land of the whole empire should be called " imperial land," and slaves should be called " private dependents;" neither could be sold or purchased. Those families which had fewer than eight male members, but had land amounting to more than one *tsing*, should distribute the surplus of land to their relatives and townsmen. The offender should be punished by death. But the law was not justly fixed, and the officials took advantage of that fact to make fraudulent gains. Hence the whole empire was disturbed, and a great number of people fell into punishment. In 563, as Wang Mang understood the bad feelings of the people, he decreed that the " imperial land " and the " private dependents " could be sold without prohibition. Since all his policies were unwise, he did not succeed in anything.

V. HISTORY OF THE REVIVAL OF TSING TIEN

1. *The Tsin Dynasty*

In the decay of the Latter Han dynasty and throughout the period of the Three Kingdoms (735-831, or 184-280 A. D.), the whole empire was disturbed by warfare. In 831, the year that Tsin Wu Ti reunited the empire, the total population numbered only 16,163,863. Though these figures cannot be exact, the population was certainly greatly reduced since the warfare had continued about one century. Because the great empire had only a sparse population, because land-ownership was either destroyed or changed, and because the land practically belonged to the govern-

THE TSING TIEN SYSTEM 509

ment, Wu Ti was enabled to distribute the land to the people. Hence, from this time (831, or 280 A. D.) to the Tang dynasty (1264, or 713 A. D.), the *tsing tien* system of Confucius was practically carried into effect, although there was an interruption of about one century and a half.

(a) *Classification of People by Ages*

According to the law of 831 (280 A. D.), the men and women were classified by ages. The class from sixteen to sixty was called regular adult; from thirteen to fifteen, and from sixty-one to sixty-five, secondary adult; and from twelve down, and from sixty-six up, young and old, who were exempted from labor. This distinction among different ages embodied the same principle as modern labor laws; it gave more work to the regular adult, less to the secondary adult, and none to the old and young. As modern labor laws give special protection only to children and women, the law of the Tsin dynasty was more complete, because it gave protection to the old as well.

(b) *Equal Distribution of Land*

Among all the people, each man was given seventy acres of land, and each woman thirty acres. Besides these, for the regular adults, the man was given fifty acres of taxed land which was required to pay the land tax, the woman twenty acres; for the secondary adults, the man was given twenty-five acres of taxed land, and the woman was given nothing.

By this law, from sixteen to sixty years of age, every man got one hundred twenty acres of land, and every woman fifty acres. From thirteen to fifteen, and from sixty-one to sixty-five, every man got ninety-five acres of land, and every woman thirty acres. This law gave real rights to the women, who could become economically independent of the men. The reason women got less land than men was because they could not work so much as men. The law did not favor women less, but it pitied them more.

The historians tell us that in the reign of Wu Ti there was universal peace; taxation was equal, and everyone enjoyed his work. But no fuller details of the distribution of land are given.[1] Unfortunately, the successor of Wu Ti was most stupid, and the whole empire fell into disorder. How long this law remained in force is unknown, but it must have been about thirty years at the least.

2. *The Northern Wei Dynasty*

After the reign of Tsin Wu Ti, first came the Wars of the Eight Princes (851-857, or 300-306 A. D.), and next, the Rebellions of the Five Barbarians (855-990, or 304-439 A. D.). As a great part of the population was swept away, and also with them ownership of land, the Northern Wei dynasty was enabled to regulate again the distribution of land. Moreover, although the system of Tsin Wu Ti had been destroyed, something must have remained. In 1028 (477 A. D.), Hsiao-wên Ti decreed that one man should cultivate forty acres of land, and a young man twenty acres. This shows that there must have been a remainder of the system of Tsin, otherwise how could one man have forty acres for cultivation? At that time, the advocate of the equalization of land was Li An-shih (994-1044); his proposal was approved by the emperor, and carried out into actual law.

(a) *The Opened Land*

In 1036 (485 A. D.), Hsiao-wên Ti gave a decree for the equal distribution of land. From the age of fifteen

---

[1] *History of Tsin*, ch. xxvi.

years up, each man received forty acres of the opened land in which nothing had been planted, and each woman received twenty acres; the slave was treated like the free citizen. For each ox or cow, there was given a share of thirty acres, the limitation in number being four oxen. The poor land which was assigned for the oxen was generally given in double amount; if the land could be cultivated only the fourth year, it was given in quadruple amount; this was for cultivation by the oxen, and for a convenient way of distributing land. Those people who had reached the taxable age received land, and those who were old enough to be exempted from taxation, or who died, returned it.

The opened land was called the regular land, that on which the law of distribution of land was based. It was the most important point by which the equalization of land was carried out. After the destruction of *tsing tien,* the land had been under private ownership; if the government had taken it from the rich to give it to the poor, it would have caused great confusion and discontent. Now, in the Northern Wei dynasty, the land which was subject to the law of acceptation and return was the opened land on which nothing had been planted. The opened land might have been free land without private ownership, and belonged practically to the government.

(b) *The Flax Land*

There was a kind of land called flax land, on which flax was planted. When a man reached the taxable age, he was given ten acres of flax land; a woman was given five acres; the slave was treated like the free citizen. This land, too, was subject to the law of acceptation and return.

On all the lands which were to be returned, no mulberry, nor elm, nor date, nor any fruit was allowed to be planted. The offender should be punished as a violator of the constitution. After these lands were returned, they were distributed again.

(b) *The Mulberry Land*

There was another kind of land called mulberry land. When a man first received it, he had a share of twenty acres. It was not subject to the law of acceptation and return, and it was classified as the double land; that is, the regular land was the principal share of each person, and the double land was the auxiliary. If the amount of mulberry land was more than a man's share, it should not be counted as that of opened land; but if it was less than his share, he should take the opened land to fill up the amount of double land. This means that private land should not be substituted for public land, but that public land should be substituted for private land. The recipient was required to plant fifty mulberry trees, five date trees, and three elms. In the non-mulberry land, a man received one acre; he should plant here also elms and dates. The slave was treated like the free citizen. Within the limit of three years, the plantation should be finished; if it had not been finished, the unfinished part should be taken away. In the mulberry land, one was allowed to plant more mulberry trees and elms, or other kinds of fruit. All the mulberry land should be hereditary property; when the owner died, his land did not need to be returned. The distribution of mulberry land was in accordance with the then existing population only; he who held more of it than his share had no acceptation nor return, but he who held less of it than his share should accept a full amount and plant something according to the law. If he had more, he was allowed to sell the surplus; if he had less, he was allowed to buy it; but no one should sell his share, or buy more than the amount of his share.

The mulberry land was the private property on which the owner planted mulberries or elms. Under the law of the

Northern Wei dynasty, which took away house and mulberry land from those people only who were exiled to distant regions, or who had no descendants, the private property of the people in general was not touched. Hence, this law gave freedom of sale and purchase to the people in order to equalize their private property. There was a universal standard for such equalization, namely, twenty acres of the mulberry land as the share of one man. Although he who had more than that amount was allowed to retain it, no one was allowed to sell his share, nor to buy more than his share. It was a convenient way to equalize private land.

(d) *Privileges for the Weak People*

If the members of a family were all aged persons, children, and sick persons, who did not accept any land, a half share of the land of one man was given to each sick person and to each child over eleven years of age. The aged man over seventy years was not required to return his land. The widow who did not marry again, although she was exempted from taxes, was given the same share of land as the taxed woman, twenty acres of the opened land.

(e) *Adjustment between Land and Population*

In sparsely-populated places, the government leased the land to the people as far as possible. When any newcomer came in, land was distributed to him according to the general law. In densely-populated places, if a man who was to receive a new share of land on account of the increase in the members of his family, did not wish to move, the mulberry land of his family was taken into account as the share of the regular land; that is, taking his private land to fill the amount of public land which he should receive. If it was still not enough, he was not given the double land in addition; that is, he had only the amount of regular land. If it was still not enough, the shares of the members of his family should be reduced; that is, they should not get the full amount of the regular land. Those places where there were no mulberries were regulated by this law. Anyone who wished to move was allowed to settle in any place where land was plentiful; no discrimination was made against him who came from a different province or district. But, if he simply wished to escape from a place where there was difficulty, and to come to a place where there was ease, solely for the sake of his own advantage, it was not allowed. In those places where there was enough land, he was not allowed to move without reason.

For all the new settlers, one acre was given to every three persons for a home, and this amount was given to every five slaves also. From the age of fifteen up, each man or woman was required to plant on his share of the land vegetables covering one-fifth of an acre.

(f) *Miscellaneous Rules for Distributing Land*

All the acceptation and return of land took place in the first month. If anyone died after having accepted land, or sold or purchased slaves and oxen, the acceptation and return of land should take place in the first month of the following year.

For the share of one person, the regular land and the double land should be distinguished. The one should not be confounded with the other.

When a family increased its members, it should receive a new share of land, taken from its neighborhood. When two families were to receive land at the same time, and they were both near to that land, it should be given to the poor family first and then to the rich. This law was also applied to the double land.

If any were exiled to a distant place, or had no descendants so that the family was extinguished, all their houses and mulberry lands should become public land, in order to be distributed. In the order of distributing them, their relatives stood first; and before these lands were distributed, they should be loaned to the relatives.

When the officials took office, public land located near to their office was given to them. The governor was given one thousand five hundred acres; the prefect, one thousand acres; each of the different sub-prefects, eight hundred acres; and the district magistrate and the assistant sub-prefect, six hundred acres. When they left their offices, they were required to transfer the public land to their successors. If they sold it, they were punished according to the established law.

(g) *Criticism of the Law of the Northern Wei Dynasty*

In Chinese economic history, for the society as a whole, the equalization of land by the Northern Wei dynasty is next in importance only to the *tsing tien* system. The good points of the law have been stated above; we should now criticize its bad points. In the first place, slaves had their share of land. In the opened land, the flax land and the mulberry land, slaves were treated as citizens; and among the new settlers, five slaves were equal to three citizens. So far as they were dependent and could be sold and bought as property, the share of the slaves benefited only the slave-holder. In the second place, for each ox or cow, a share of thirty acres of opened land was assigned. Though there was a limitation to four oxen, this still gave the ox-owner a special benefit. From these two points, we may sum the matter up in a word—this law was especially favorable to the capitalist. Hence it diametrically opposed the fundamental principle of the equalization of land. But, as this law was good in general, this defect should not be unduly emphasized.

According to the taxation system of the Northern Wei dynasty, a husband and wife should pay one roll of silk and two bushels of grain as the direct tax, and this amount was the standard. Every four unmarried citizens above thirteen years of age, every eight slaves, when the male slaves could cultivate land or the female slaves could do spinning, and every twenty cultivating oxen were required to pay this amount. Probably the law-maker thought that since slaves and oxen paid a tax they should have the right to receive land.

The law of the Northern Wei dynasty was most important,[1] because it was the model of the Northern Ch'i, the Northern Chou, the Sui and the Tang dynasties.

3. *The Northern Ch'i Dynasty*

In the Northern Ch'i dynasty, the distribution of land took place in the tenth month of every year. The land was not allowed to be sold nor exchanged. In 1115 (564 A. D.), Wu Ch'êng Ti made a law providing that every man should receive land and pay taxes at eighteen years of age; should be enrolled as a soldier at twenty; should be freed from any forced labor at sixty; and at sixty-six, should return the land and should be exempted from taxes. Each man should receive eighty acres of opened land; each woman forty acres; and the slave was treated like the free citizen.

The limitation of slaves was: three hundred slaves for the princes of close relation; two hundred for the successive princes; one hundred and fifty for the successive princes from the second rank down, and the princes outside the imperial family; one hundred for the officials from the third

[1] *History of Wei*, ch. cx.

rank up, and the imperial clansmen; eighty for the officials from the seventh rank up; and sixty for the officials from the eighth rank down, and the common people. No land was given to the slaves who stood beyond this limit. For each ox, sixty acres were given; and the limit was four oxen.

Every man received twenty acres of mulberry land as perpetual property, which was not subject to the law of acceptation and return. When the land was not fitted to mulberry, flax land was given, to which the law of mulberry land was applied.[1]

(a) *Criticism of the Slavery of the Northern Dynasties*

There was slavery in the Northern Dynasties because the rulers of those dynasties came from the northern barbarian tribes. As they were accustomed to slavery, when they ruled a great part of China, they made it a positive institution. When they conquered a place, they took away both noblemen and commons, and made them slaves. Moreover, at that time, as the warfare continued, the condition of the people was very bad, so they would sell themselves as slaves. But, as the general civilization of the Northern Dynasties was lower than that of the Southern Dynasties, why should the Northern have shown greater concern for the equalization of land? It was because this system was established by Hsiao-wên Ti of the Northern Wei dynasty. During his reign (1022-1050, or 471-499 A. D.), when the power of the Wei dynasty was at its height, and there was a period of peace, he was especially fond of Confucianism, so that this system was formed. He moved his capital from northern China to central China at the old capital of the Chou and the Han dynasties; he forbade the wearing of barbarian costumes; and he changed nearly all the barbarian systems, and

[1] *History of Sui*, ch. xxiv.

adopted the Chinese civilization—he changed even the barbarian names for the Chinese names. Therefore, the equalization of land in the Northern Wei dynasty was the product of Confucianism, and the revival of the *tsing tien* system. Slavery was an institution of the Northern Dynasties, and was so firmly established that it was not changed even during the reign of Hsiao-wên Ti.

4. *The Northern Chou Dynasty*

In the Northern Chou dynasty, Wên Ti (1085-1107, or 534-556 A. D.) established the bureau of equality to deal with land. To a family of more than ten persons, five acres were given for their home; above seven, four acres, and above five, three acres. To a married man, one hundred and forty acres were distributed; to a single man, one hundred acres.[1] This law implied that a married woman had a real share of forty acres.

5. *The Sui Dynasty*

After the Northern Wei dynasty was divided up into the Northern Ch'i and the Northern Chou dynasties, the Northern Chou conquered the Northern Ch'i, and the Sui dynasty succeeded the Northern Chou. Therefore, their laws were similar. In distributing the opened land and the perpetual property, Sui conformed to the law of the Northern Ch'i. The people were also required to plant mulberries, elms and dates. On the average, every three citizens received one acre for their home and garden; and every five slaves received the same amount.

From the princes to the military commanders, all were given land for their perpetual property, its amount varying from forty acres to ten thousand acres. To the officials of the capital, the official land was given according to rank.

[1] *History of Sui*, ch. xxiv.

THE TSING TIEN SYSTEM

To those of the first rank was given the amount of five hundred acres; to those of the ninth rank, the last, one hundred acres; the difference between any higher rank and its next was fifty acres.[1]

6. *The Tang Dynasty*

There was a golden age in the Tang dynasty, and it came from the equalization of land. In 1175 (624 A. D.), a law provided that to every man above eighteen years of age, one hundred acres of land was to be given; to an aged or sick man, forty acres; to a widow, thirty acres; if she was the head of her family, twenty acres more were given to her. All of them took 20 per cent of the number of acres as perpetual property, and 80 per cent as mouth-share. Mouth-share means the share of each person belonging to the government. In the perpetual property, a certain number of mulberries, elms, dates and other trees which were fitted to the land, were to be planted.

Where the land was sufficient to be distributed to the people, the town was called "thinly populated town;" and where the land was not sufficient, it was called "thickly populated town." In the thickly populated town, there was distributed only half the amount of land distributed in the thinly populated town; if its land was cultivated every other year, double portions were given (100 acres). In the thinly populated town, if its land was cultivated every fourth year, it was given not at the rate of double portions—that is, if it should be given in double portions, it would be four hundred acres for a man; because it seemed too much, no double portions were given; but, if the law was so, those who received such poor land were unjustly treated. The artisans and merchants, in the thinly populated town, received half as much as the share of a farmer; in the thickly populated town, they received nothing.

[1] *History of Sui*, ch. xxiv.

Those people who moved to another town, or who were so poor that they could not even pay for their funerals, were allowed to sell their perpetual property. Those people who moved from the thickly populated town to the thinly populated one, were allowed to sell even their mouth-share. But after they had sold their land, nothing was given to them again. When the land-owner died, his land was taken by the government and given to those having no land.

In the tenth month of every year, the distribution of land took place, the government either taking it back or giving it out. The land was first distributed to the poor and those who paid taxes and served the public labor. If a town had more land than it needed for distribution, the surplus was given to neighboring towns; if such was the case in a district, it was given to the neighboring districts; if in a province, it was given to neighboring provinces.[1]

(a) *Criticism of the Law of the Tang Dynasty*

The chief defect of the law of the Tang dynasty was that it allowed the people to sell the land—both the perpetual property and also the mouth-share. Because the people were allowed to sell the land, there was no way to prevent the inequality of wealth. Hence, the rich bought up the land, and this system lasted only about one hundred years.

About 1201-1206 A. K. (650-655 A. D.), Tang Kao Tsung forbade the people to sell the perpetual property and the mouth-share; and later, he decreed that the buyer of land should return it to the owner, and that he should be fined. But, during the reign of Tang Hsüan Tsung (1264-1306, or 713-755 A. D.), land was monopolized by the rich. Since that time, all the lands of China have been almost entirely held by private owners. The *tsing tien* system never has been revived again.[2]

---

[1] *New History of Tang*, ch. li.
[2] Tables of land distribution are found on the next three pages.

THE TSING TIEN SYSTEM

Table Showing Systems of Land-distribution Under Six Dynasties

Kinds of Land		People Classified by Ages	Citizens[1]	People Classified by Condition	Slaves[1]	Ox[3]	Dynasties[2]					
							Tsin	Northern Wei	Northern Ch'i	Northern Chou	Sui	Tang
Subject to Reversion	Regular Land	Regular Adults		Man			12	40	80	100	80	80
				Woman				50	20	40	Man W. Wife 140	40
		Secondary Adults		Man			95					
				Woman			30					
				Sick Man				20				32
				Sick Woman				10				
				Widow				20				24
				Widow as head of Family								40
					Man			40	80			
					Woman			20	40			
						Ox		30	60			
	Flax Land		Man					10				
			Woman					5				
					Man			10				
					Woman			5				
Held in Perpetuity	Mulberry Land		Man					20	20		20	20
				Sick Man								8
				Widow								6
				Widow as head of Family								10
	Home[4]		3								1	
					5						1	
			5-6							3		
			7-9							4		
			10-							5		

[1] The figures under the column of citizens and that of slaves indicate the number of citizens and slaves.

[2] The remaining figures under the column of dynasties indicate the number of acres distributed among the people.

[3] Under the column of ox, the land was given for an ox.

[4] For their homes, the number of persons was counted not individually, but collectively.

TABLE OF AGE-LIMITS OF LAND-HOLDING

Age-classification	Dynasties[1]					
	Tsin	Northern Wei	Northern Ch'i	Northern Chou	Sui	Tang
Regular adult[2]..	16–60	15	18	18	18	18
Secondary adult.	13–15 61–65					
Old[2]	66–	[3]	66	65	60	60
Young	1–12					

VI. OPINIONS ON THE TSING TIEN SYSTEM

Since the *tsing tien* system was established by the celebrated emperors of the ancients, and its principles were worked out by Confucius, it has dominated the thoughts of scholars generation after generation. As the limitation policy of Tung Chung-shu and Shih Tan has been stated above, we shall study the most prominent thoughts of other Confucians.

1. *Hsun Yüeh*

During the Han dynasty, the landlords took half of the product of land as rent. Therefore Hsun Yüeh (699-760, or 148-209 A. D.) condemned the landlords as being more tyrannical than the Ch'in dynasty. He was not, however, in favor of the immediate abolition of land-ownership, because he thought that there would be great confusion rising

---

[1] The figures indicate the years of age. Except under the Tsin dynasty, the ages referred to men only.

[2] At the age of "regular adult", the people received the land; and at the age of "old", they returned it.

[3] Under the Northern Wei dynasty, nothing was said about old age; but it would be not less than sixty, nor more than sixty-six.

THE TSING TIEN SYSTEM

POULATION UNDER THE SIX DYNASTIES ROUGHLY CORRESPONDING WITH THE RESPECTIVE PERIODS OF LAND-DISTRIBUTION

Confucian Era[1]	Christian Era	Number of Population Under the Six Dynasties[2]					
		Tsin	Northern Wei	Northern Ch'i	Northern Chou	Sui	Tang
831	280	16,163,863					
1036	485		32,327,726				
1115	564			206,880			
1131	580				9,009,604		
1140	589					11,009,604	
1165	624						15,000,000 (about)

from the discontent of the landlords, and that the *tsing tien* sytem never could be carried out by such a measure.

His opinion is that the *tsing tien* system should not be established when population is dense, because the land is in the hands of the rich; and that it should be established only when population is small and there is much land.

His conclusion is still a limitation policy; but he makes his point more clear that the land should be neither sold nor purchased. He says:

As we cannot entirely revive the *tsing tien* system, there should

[1] At the dates given in this table, the land distributions took place. But 1131 is an exception, because the land of the Northern Chou dynasty was distributed by Wên Ti (1085-1107).

[2] The dynasties of Tsin, Sui and Tang ruled the whole empire of China. The Northern Wei ruled only the northern part of China; and the Northern Ch'i and Chou respectively took a division of the whole domain of Wei. Referring to these dates, Wei was at its best time; Tsin, Sui and Tang were at their beginning, just passing the period of war; and Ch'i and Chou were during the period of war.

be a limitation on the ownership of land according to the number of individuals. Everyone may cultivate land, but he is not allowed to sell or buy it. This method will enrich the poor and the weak, prevent the rich from monopolizing the land, and lay the foundation for realizing the whole system of *tsing tien*. Is it not a good thing?

2. *Su Hsun*

As Su Hsun (1560-1617, or 1009-1066 A. D.) was a great writer, he condemned the landlords very strongly. He said:

After the *tsing tien* system has been destroyed, the land is not owned by the cultivators, and the land-owners do not cultivate the land themselves. The land of the cultivators depends upon the rich. In a rich family, the land-owner has a great extent of land, and employs journeymen for the different parts of its cultivation. He whips them and enslaves them, treating them like actual slaves. He easily sits down and looks around for the issue of his direction; while among his employees, weeding the field for him in summer, and reaping the crop for him in autumn, none of them disobeys his regulations and takes a diversion. But, among the products of the land, the land-owner himself gets half, and the cultivators all together get the other half. There is only one land-owner, but there are ten cultivators. Therefore, the land-owner accumulates one-half of the land-products day after day, and grows richer and richer, stronger and stronger; the cultivators consume the other half day after day, and fall into poverty and starving without appeal.

Such a condemnation of the landlords suggests the condemnation passed by the socialists upon capitalists. In fact, the separation between land-owner and land-cultivator is the great evil growing out of the destruction of the *tsing tien* system.

Su Hsun, however, did not approve of the policy of reestablishing *tsing tien*. His argument is based not on the fact that the land of the rich cannot be taken away, but on the fact that the *tsing tien* system itself is impossible of full realization. He said that even though the rich should offer their land to the public and petition for the *tsing tien* system, it never could be re-established. Then he described all the details of this system under the Chou dynasty, and said that, even though this system were thoroughly re-established through a period of several centuries, the people would all have died long before. His theory is more advanced than that of Hsun Yüeh, since he thought that the form of *tsing tien* is impossible.

But he approved of the limitation policy, and pointed out that the reason this policy had not been realized was because the government was afraid that the rich would not give up their land which was beyond the limit prescribed. When he criticised the law of Han Ai Ti,[1] he said that the limit of this law, which permitted one man to own three thousand acres, was too high, and that the days of grace, which were only three years, were too short. Such a short period for the enforcement of this law meant forcing the people to destroy their own property. It was not in accordance with human nature, and it was difficult of realization.

Then he drew his conclusion, that the limit of land-ownership should be small, and that the limit should not be applied to the present day, but simply to the future. It should not take away the land which exceeded the limit before the limit was established; but it should merely prevent people in the future from owning more than the limit. After a few generations, the descendants of the rich would either fall into poverty and diffuse to others their land, which had been

[1] See *supra*, p. 507.

more than the limit; or they would divide it up among themselves. Then the rich could not own too much land, and there would be plenty of it. The poor could easily get the land, and they would not be enslaved by others. Although this policy is not the system of *tsing tien*, it would reach the same results as *tsing tien*.

3. *Chu Hsi*

Chu Hsi agreed with the theory of Hsun Yüeh, and said that the land could not be taken away from the people. The only opportunity for the re-establishment of *tsing tien* is after a great revolutionary war. Under such a condition, when the population is gone, and the land belongs to the government, the land-distribution can be realized. In time of peace, it can never be done.

He was the first one who discarded the limitation policy. He said that it was absurd. In general, at the beginning, it would be effective; but after three or five years, it would have no force. At the present even though the limitation of land-ownership might be fixed, year after year it would be only a dead letter. Then he gave his opinion, that if the *tsing tien* system could be realized, we should realize it; but if it could not be realized, we should leave the present institution untouched. The theory of limitation, according to him, was only a joke.

4. *Yeh Shih*

Yeh Shih was the first one who thought that the *tsing tien* system is not useful in modern times, and that it is not the basis of a good government. He said that even if the lands of the whole empire should belong to the government, and Wên Wang, Wu Wang and the Duke of Chou should rule again in the empire, there is no need of *tsing tien*, because its numerous and subtle rules cannot be carried out in modern times. The most important point he brought

THE TSING TIEN SYSTEM 527

out is the relation between feudalism and the *tsing tien* system. From the reign of Huang Ti to the Chou dynasty, the emperor governed only the imperial state, and the feudal princes also governed only their own states by hereditary right. Hence, the *tsing tien* system prevailed over the whole empire. But, in modern times, the whole empire is under a single government; although there are many officials, they all belong to the emperor, and the term of their office is not certain. Who shall be set to work for the formation of *tsing tien?* Even if the officials should work it out, it would require a long time—at least more than ten years. In the interval, how could the whole empire suspend the cultivation of the land? Indeed, as the feudal system has disappeared, it is impossible for the *tsing tien* system to remain alone.

Then he contributed a new idea, and looked for the solution of economic problems beyond the *tsing tien* system. He said that even under the *tsing tien* system, the amount of products was not different from that of modern times. Moreover, the use of great dikes and long banks, storing water from the mountains, and opening it for the need of irrigation, is a simpler and more convenient method; it costs a smaller amount of labor, but gives greater use. This shows that he had a dynamic mind, and was not satisfied with the form of *tsing tien*. Then he said that if the government of modern times were not inferior to that of the Three Dynasties, it would make the people support themselves through agriculture, and there would be no difference between the modern and the ancient. The reason why modern times are inferior to the Three Dynasties is not because the land is not divided into different *tsing*, but because poverty among the people cannot be abolished.

His conclusion looks not backward, but forward. Applying wisdom according to the times, and establishing law in harmony with the actual world—this is his main point. He discarded entirely the system of *tsing tien*, and emphasized the importance of legislation for the needs of the time. He said:

If the government will enact social legislation, ten years later the people will be neither too rich, nor too poor; encroachment by the wealthy will cease through its own nature; and the whole empire will get quickly the benefit of production;—this is the most important work that the emperor and the officials should hasten to do.

5. *Ma Tuan-lin*

The theory of Ma Tuan-lin is like that of Yeh Shih, emphasizing also the relation between feudalism and the *tsing tien* system. In ancient times, the feudal estate was small, and its people were few; hence this system was easily established. He says that it would be the same whether the ancient feudal princes distributed one hundred acres to each man or the modern landlords give their tenants the land of their ancestors. But in modern times, territory is extensive, and population is large; the governors take the place of feudal princes, and none can keep the office for his son; under such a condition, the *tsing tien* system never can exist. Therefore, under the Tsin, the Northern Wei, the Northern Ch'i, the Northern Chou, the Sui and the Tang dynasties, although the system of land-distribution had been realized, it did not last very long.[1]

VII. CONCLUSION

There is no doubt that the *tsing tien* system has passed away never to be revived. From the date of land-equalization by Wei Hsiao-wên to the first year of Tang Hsüan Tsung is two hundred twenty-eight years (1036-1264, or

[1] *General Research*, ch. i.

485-713 A. D.). But from the first year of Huang Ti to the date of destruction of *tsing tien* by Shang Yang is two thousand three hundred forty-eight years (2147 B. K.-202 A. K. or 2698-350 B. C.). The length of these periods shows the difference between the ancient and the medieval times. Because the ancient times were feudal, the *tsing tien* system lasted for thousands of years; and because the medieval times were under absolute monarchy, the system of equalization of land, which was not the exact system of *tsing tien*, did not continue ofr three hundred years. The fact is that the *tsing tien* system cannot exist without the feudal system.

Confucius was not in favor of feudalism. But, as the *tsing tien* system was bound up with feudalism, why was Confucius in favor of *tsing tien?* Because feudalism created political inequality, he hated feudalism; and because the *tsing tien* system created economic equality, he loved it. His idea was based entirely on the principle of equality. Moreover, as he lived in the feudal stage and so could not do away immediately with the feudal system, he was obliged to give his theory for the better condition of the people according to his stage. In his time, when the feudal estate grew up as a great nation, and the *tsing tien* system was decaying, the land was taxed at a higher rate than that of one-tenth of its product; the people were cruelly employed for military purposes at improper seasons; the forced labor took much more than three days; and the *tsing tien* system itself in its decay served to make confusion and inequality among the people. In a word, it was a transitional stage. Under such a condition, why should Confucius not advocate the *tsing tien* system? According to this system, not only could the people not own more land than their neighbors, but also the feudal lords could not tax the people more and make them work more. Indeed, it was a protection for the people against the feudal lords, and a remedy for the evils of the feudal stage.

Whenever there is a decay of any system, there must be confusion and trouble. During the decay of the *tsing* tien system, when Shang Yang saw it, he destroyed it entirely. It was a destructive policy. Shang Yang was condemned by many Confucians, but he was a great statesman. He invited foreigners to cultivate the land, and gave them private land-ownership, in order to send the natives abroad to engage in war. He cared more for the glory of the state than for the betterment of the people. His economic reforms were not for economic but for military reasons. The results were that the state got an immediate political advantage, but the people lost the economic equality based on land-ownership.

Mencius living at the same time with Shang Yang, when he saw the *tsing tien* system, wanted to make it as perfect as possible. It was a constructive policy. Mencius cared for the betterment of the people, and not for military glory. His economic reforms were for economic reasons, for the intellectual and moral education of the people, but not for the sake of war.

However, Mencius was also a great statesman. He thought that, if the *tsing tien* system were wisely established, it would conquer the whole empire. His theory is that the people are the most important element of the state; hence, if any prince could win the heart of the people in the neighboring countries, he would win those states. It seems impracticable. But, in his time, the princes took the people away in the agricultural seasons to make them engage in war, and caused hunger and loss to their families, and consequently the people had no love for their princes. Moreover, as the people of the whole Chinese world were practically one, and generally had no particular love for their own feudal state, it was easy for the virtuous ruler to unite the whole empire. If there were a truly virtuous

THE TSING TIEN SYSTEM 531

ruler, loving humanity for the whole empire, establishing the *tsing tien* system as Mencius said, and making the foreign people love him as his own people, he would be sure that when he attacked his enemies, their people would welcome him, and he would become the only ruler of the whole empire. This theory should be called universalism, which means to conquer the world by virtue. It differs from the theory of Shang Yang, whose theory should be called imperialism, which means to conquer the world by force.[1] Unfortunately, the policy of Shang Yang was put into actual practice, and it was successful; but the policy of Mencius remains only a theory, because no prince made him a minister. This was an unfortunate thing.

The system of *tsing tien* was good not because the land was divided into different *tsing*, but because its principles were based on equality. When we say that a book is good, we refer not to its binding, but to the work of the author. When Su Hsun and Yeh Shih argued about the form of *tsing tien*, Su thought that it was impossible, and Yeh thought that it was also unnecessary. Both were right. But, when we think about this system, we should consider, not its form, but its principles.

Superficially, the *tsing tien* system seems only an agrarianism; but this is not true. The word agrarianism might be applied to the system of equalization of land under the later six dynasties; but it cannot be applied to the *tsing tien* system itself. According to the theory of Confucius, the *tsing tien* system is the basis of everything, and is not merely a distribution of land. The essential ideas of this system are that everyone should get an equal share and an

[1] Universalism is the true sense of the Chinese word "king," and imperialism is that of "chieftain." See *Classics*, vol. ii, pp. 196-7. See also *ibid.*, pp. 134-7, 145-9, 181-5, 271-4, 300-301, 438-440, *etc.*

equal opportunity for the enjoyment of economic life, and also of social, political, intellectual and moral life.

In many of its essential ideas, the *tsing tien* system is similar to modern socialism. The two have the same object of equalizing the wealth of the whole society. Of course, by the changes of methods and organizations, the modern industrial stage must differ from the ancient agricultural stage. In ancient times, land was the most important form of wealth. Therefore, when land was equally distributed, the wealth of the people was practically equal. Under the *tsing tien* system, the people did not own even their houses, and their whole economic life was controlled by the state. It was an extreme socialism, or state socialism. In modern times, passing from the agricultural stage to the industrial stage, the land is not so important as before. Even if the land could be equally distributed or nationalized, the wealth of the people would still be unequal, because besides the land, there are many other capital goods. Therefore, modern socialism has more difficulties to overcome than that of the ancients. But the essential ideas of modern socialism are not different from those of the *tsing tien* system. By the *tsing tien* system, everyone got the whole of what he produced, because there was no landlord. When Su Hsun condemned the landlord, it was because he took half of the product from the cultivators. It is the same argument as that of the socialist, who would allow no capitalist to take half the product of the laborer. In a word, the *tsing tien* system and socialism both aim at equality of wealth, and at allowing the producers to get all that they produce.

However, the Chinese people have been a moderate people, and they never go to extremes. When the scholars thought about the *tsing tien* system, although they hated the landlord, they never thought that his land should be taken away by confiscation as in the theory of Henry George. Throughout the whole history of China, Wang Mang was the only one who nationalized the land by a policy of confiscation. However, even he did not touch those who owned no more than one *tsing*. If a family had only one hundred acres, it was saved from confiscation. Moreover, after three years, he abolished the law of land confiscation. As Wang Mang was condemned by the Confucians, no one thought thas his confiscation policy was right. Therefore, the land of China will probably remain in the hands of private owners forever, unless there shall be a new form of socialism.

CHAPTER XXVII

MONOPOLY

1. CONDEMNATION OF MONOPOLY

CONFUCIUS hated monopoly; but monopoly was condemned before the time of Confucius. In 298 B. K. (849 B. C.), when Chou Li Wang loved gain and was going to employ Duke Yung, Jui Liang-fu gave him a warning as follows:

Profit is the product of all things, and the fruit of heaven and earth. If one monopolizes it, he will cause much hatred. Since all people are getting profit from heaven and earth and all things, why should it be monopolized? . . . Even when one of the common people makes monopoly, he should be called a robber. If your Majesty practices it, there will be very few people who come to you.

Li Wang did not heed this admonition, and employed Duke Yung as minister. The result was that he was banished by the people.[1]

The theory of Jui Liang-fu is harmonious with that of Confucius. It will be convenient to treat Confucius' theory in accordance with modern categories, and we may classify monopoly first into two grand divisions, private and public. We may classify public monopoly as fiscal and social; private monopoly as personal, legal, natural, and business. Let us consider them in this order.

[1] *Narratives of Nations*, bk. i.

II. PUBLIC MONOPOLIES.

By public monopoly, we mean monopoly by the public at large, not by the ruler of any government. The ruler himself not only should establish no monopoly, but should make no profit at all. According to the principles of Confucius, if public monopoly is called for, in order to regulate production, distribution, or consumption, it would be approved. For example, the nationalization of land and the control of natural resources are principles of his. Judging from his ideas, all natural monopolies, such as wagon-roads, streets, canals, docks, bridges, ferries, waterways, harbors, lighthouses, railways, telegraphs, telephones, the postoffice, electric lighting, waterworks, gasworks, *etc.*, should be public monopolies, either municipal, or national, or even universal.

If the public monopolizes a thing simply for fiscal reasons, however, Confucius would not approve it. The government monopolies of salt and iron, originated by Kuan Tzŭ, would not conform to the ideal of Confucius, because prices are thereby raised. In short, public monopoly for social reasons is good, but public monopoly for fiscal reasons is not.

As to ordinary business, Confucius thinks that the state should control prices, but should not monopolize the whole market. So far as there is no natural monopoly, and competition is possible and desirable, Confucius will not let the state establish monopoly. Although the state should be the regulator of prices, such action is not monopoly, but simply helping to free competition and destroy private monopoly. These are the general principles of Confucius in regard to public monopoly.

III. PRIVATE MONOPOLIES

1. *Personal Monopolies*

Confucius opposes private monopoly, with few exceptions. Take personal monopoly first. Confucius is very glad, indeed, to give special honor and wealth to men who possess extraordinary virtue or ability. Therefore, honoring the virtuous and employing the able, and putting the distinguished men in high positions, is a principle of Confucius. But such a temporary personal monopoly is not for the sake of the individuals, but for that of society at large. Confucius says: " Employ the upright and put aside all the crooked; this way can make the crooked upright." [1] Therefore, to grant rewards to the individuals who hold personal monopoly is not only doing them justice, but also giving all others inspiration. Even personal monopoly, however, Confucius does not let alone, but he makes the people acquire it by education. Hence the system of universal free education arises, and the power of personal monopoly is diminished by popular education.

2. *Legal Monopolies*

As to legal monopoly, Confucius would not approve it. When Chung-shu Yu-he, an officer of Wei, showed military ability (38 B. K.), Wei rewarded him with a city. He refused it, and asked for the right to use the suspended instruments of music disposed incompletely, and the saddle-girth and bridle-trappings. These things were legally used only by the prince of a state, but such a right was granted to him. When Confucius later heard of this, he said:

Alas! It would have been better to give him many cities. It is only peculiar articles of use, and names, which cannot be granted to others than those to whom they belong; to them a

---

[1] *Classics*, vol. i, p. 261.

ruler has particularly to attend. By the right use of names he secures the confidence of the people. By that confidence he preserves the articles distinctive of ranks. In those articles the ceremonial distinctions of rank are hid. By those ceremonial distinctions justice is practised. By justice, social profit is produced. By social profit the people are equalized. Attention to these things is the condition of good government. If they be conceded where they ought not to be conceded, it is giving away the government to the recipients. When the government thus perishes, the state will follow it; it is not possible to arrest that issue.[1]

If, according to the principles of Confucius, even the right to use certain articles should not be granted, there is no reason why the government should grant legal monopoly. The legal right of establishing monopoly is included in the word "names" used by Confucius. It is a part of sovereign power, and should not be given to any private person. This is for the profit of the whole society and for the equality of the people.

In Chinese history, no legal monopoly has been given to private persons by the government, except in one instance. In 1837 (1286 A. D.), Yüan Shih Tsu granted the seals of paper money to Chang Hsüan and Chu Ts'ing, and let them make paper money, on account of their service in sea-transportation. When their wealth was equal to that of the state, the government killed them on some excuse, because it was afraid that they would be a danger to the state.[2] Legal monopoly is generally not good for society at large.

A limited legal monopoly, such as copyrights and patents, however, Confucius would approve. Since his philosophy is based on a justice that is practised by a system of rewards,

[1] *Classics*, vol. v, pt. i, p. 344.
[2] *Continuation of the General Research*, ch. ix.

he would grant a limited monopoly to the author or inventor, in order to reward him and to encourage others. But the Chinese did not develop such a monopoly. Hence the people had no encouragement for invention, and many inventions were lost. In old times, the people generally did not care to invent anything. Even the scholars who did invent things, did so, not for the sake of economic interest, but for the sake of curiosity, or to show their ability. Therefore their inventions died with them. In those times the people lived in an isolated way, communication and transportation were poor, and there were no newspapers and magazines, so that the people could not have known anything about new inventions had there been any. Moreover, even if they had known about them, how could they have understood the secret of the inventors and have duplicated them? Therefore, many old inventions are simply recorded in history, without producing any great effect, and many others, such as gunpowder, and the art of printing, are by unknown inventors. There were many causes which retarded Chinese invention, but the absence of a patent system was a very important one.

There arises a question—how did the ancients develop and preserve their inventions? Because they had a quasi-legal monopoly—the hereditary right of holding office in different sciences and arts. For each profession and each line of workmanship, there was a government office which was hereditarily held, even throughout different dynasties. Since their division of labor extended to details, and their specialization lasted for many generations, they would naturally invent new things or improve old methods. Even if it were not so, the old would scarcely have been lost, because the government was its preserver, even though the family should die out. Therefore, although the hereditary offices were a bad thing, they still produced some good effects.

Confucius, however, did not approve the inheritance of offices, and since the Han dynasty such a system has been destroyed. Because the people could not get legal monopoly, they resorted to secret monopoly,—that is, when they invented or discovered anything, they kept it secret, as a natural monopoly. Professor Friedrich Hirth says:

It is a feature of Chinese social life that specialities in art and workmanship are treated as the monopoly of certain families on which no outsider is allowed to trespass. Such was the case under the Han dynasty with certain patterns of silk brocade. Many trades, such as the superior lacquer industry in Foochow and the manufacture of bronze drums in Canton, have been family secrets; and these secrets are so well guarded that a branch of art may die out with the last scion of the family that created it, as in the case of the celebrated Foochow lacquer, the secret of which was lost during the T'ai-p'ing rebellion.[1]

Such a secret monopoly was not legally protected, but existed simply because there was no competition on the same level. It had two evils: First, the time of monopolization was unlimited, lasting from generation to generation. Second, the secret was easily lost, because the family did not teach it to outsiders. It is much better to create legally a limited monopoly, and let the monopolist teach others. This is the way to develop secret monopoly to open monopoly, and society will benefit from it much more than the monopolist. Since 2449 (1898 A. D.) the tendency in China is in this direction.

In short, regarding legal monopoly, Confucius would give it for a limited time to those who contribute something to society, but not to those who are simply favorites of the court.

[1] *The Ancient History of China*, p. 117.

3. *Natural Monopolies*

As to natural monopoly, Confucius positively does not allow any private person to hold it. According to the principles of the *Spring and Autumn*, the famous mountains and great meres are not conferred to the feudal princes. "Because they are the natural resources of heaven and earth, which are not produced by human power, they ought to be shared in common with all the people."[1] This principle is also set forth in the "Royal Regulations."[2] If such natural resources were conferred on the feudal princes, they would be their owners, and the people could not make use of them. Therefore, they are left as common property for all the people, and the princes are not allowed to hold such a natural monopoly. Since Confucius does not permit even the feudal princes to own the natural resources, how can any private person have the right to own them? Subject to this principle is the modern development of franchise monopolies, such as railways, waterworks, *etc*.

This principle is applied not only to local or national monopoly acquired by natural advantages, but also to international monopoly. Explaining this principle, the *General Discussion in the White Tiger Palace* says:

It makes all the people share the advantages, and does not allow any single nation to monopolize them. The riches of mountains and forests, the advantages of water and rivers, should be commonly distributed over thousands of miles. It is for the equalization between those who have something and those who have nothing, and for the fill of insufficiency.[3]

Since Confucius takes the whole world as an economic unit,

---

[1] *Annotation of Kung-yang,* 16th year of Duke Huan.
[2] See *supra*, p. 349.
[3] Bk. iv.

MONOPOLY

he forbids not only private persons, but also individual nations, to monopolize the natural advantages. Indeed, if there is any natural monopoly affecting the whole world, it should belong to the government of the world-state. This is the basis of the free-trade doctrine of Confucius and that of his world-socialism.

During the Han dynasty, when Sang Hung-yang defended the government monopoly of salt and iron (471, or 81 B. C.), he referred to this principle, and said that the people should not be allowed to monopolize the natural resources.[1] When the Tsin dynasty (816, or 265 A. D.) and the Liang dynasty (1053, or 502 A. D.) distributed the feudal estates, the famous mountains and great meres were not conferred; and all the regions producing salt, iron, gold, silver, copper and tin, and bamboo-gardens, capital cities, public buildings and different parks were not included in any feudal estate.[2] These facts show the influence of Confucianism upon actual law.

4. *Business Monopolies*

Confucius does not permit private persons to have business monopolies, a principle which is thus indicated by Mencius:

In old times, the market-places were for the exchange of the articles which they had for those which they had not. There were simply some officers to keep order among them. It happened that there was a mean fellow, who looked out for a conspicuous mound, and got up upon it. Thence he looked right and left, to catch in his net the whole profit of the market. The people all thought his conduct mean, and therefore they

---

[1] The *Debate on the Government Monopoly of Salt and Iron*, bk. vi.
[2] *General Research*, chs. cclxxi-ii.

proceeded to lay a tax upon his business. The taxing of traders took its rise from this mean fellow.[1]

Confucius does not allow any monopoly profit. If there is any, a tax on such profit is necessary, in order to discourage the monopolist and to equalize the distribution of wealth.

For the prevention of business monopoly, there are two great principles, the exclusion of the ruling class from the economic field and the government control of demand and supply. We shall discuss them in the following chapters.

The Chinese hate business monopoly. According to the *Law Code of the Ts'ing Dynasty,* any business monopoly is forbidden. For example, people are not allowed to open a general company to control completely a branch of trade in order to prevent the merchants from going to other companies; nor to divide up territory within which no competitor can stand; nor to control transportation either by shipper or by carrier. He who monopolizes the market either as a seller or as a buyer shall be punished with eighty blows of the long stick. If any has made profit through such monopolistic schemes, that profit shall be regarded as booty, and he shall be punished as a robber according to the amount of booty.[2]

As a result of the taxation system, however, there are some businesses mixed with the element of monopoly. They will be discussed under the subject of taxation.

---

[1] *Classics,* vol. ii, pp. 227-8. Hence the Chinese sometimes use the two words, conspicuous mound, for the word monopoly.

[2] Ch. xv.

CHAPTER XXVIII

Exclusion of the Ruling Class from the Economic Field

1. GENERAL PRINCIPLES

In modern times the socialist advocates modern socialism against capitalism for the laborers. In ancient times the Confucians advocated Confucian socialism against feudalism for the farmers. These two doctrines are the same in principle, because in the ancient days feudal lords were at the same time capitalists, and the farmers were themselves laborers. But, when we compare these two doctrines, Confucianism seems to go further than modern socialism. There would be no capitalist under either. Under Confucianism, the important means of production should belong to the public, and the ruling class should get only their salary. When the official class got their salary, however, they could accumulate it and make themselves capitalists. The modern socialist does not exclude salaried officials from the gainful occupations, but the Confucians excluded them entirely. We may say that the difference between the two is due to the fact that in ancient times aristocracy allowed the officials to hold their office by hereditary right, and that in modern times it is not so; hence the Confucians necessarily excluded them. This is true, and it would be the original idea of Confucius. But Confucian socialism means still more. In the first place, Confucianism does not allow aristocracy; no one should hold office by hereditary right. In the second place, even after the abolition of feudalism and aristocracy, and even for those temporary officials, this principle of exclusion was applied. From this it is clear that Confucian socialism goes further than modern socialism.

At the time of Confucius, feudalism prevailed over the whole empire. The feudal princes and the noble families occupied all the lands, so that they were the landlords. They owned also a great number of cattle and many other capital goods, so that they were the capitalists. There was small room, indeed, left for the common people. Moreover, they could oppress the people as they would, and the condition of the people must have been very bad. As they had all the political powers and social dignities, if they should become competitors with the people in the economic field, they would take all the profits, and the people could have no foothold to compete with them. Then the people would be reduced to the condition of actual slavery. Therefore, on the one hand, Confucius concentrated the political power in an absolute monarchy, and denied the hereditary right of office-holding, in order to destroy feudalism and to transform aristocracy into democracy. On the other, he excluded all officials from the economic field, in order to give full opportunity to the people.

The general law is as follows: " The emperor ought not to talk about whether he has wealth or not; the feudal princes ought not to talk about whether they have more wealth or less; and all the families which enjoy a public salary ought not to compete with the people for profit."[1] Promoting the character of the ruling class to a higher ethical standard, taking away their favorable condition and powerful competition from the economic field, and giving a great chance to all common people,—these are the objects of this principle. It has been a great scheme of social reform, and its tendency has been toward economic equality.

[1] *History of Latter Han*, ch. lxxiii.

1. *Exclusion of the Emperor*

The principle of exclusion should be first applied to the rulers,—the emperor and the feudal princes. In the *Spring and Autumn*, there is a law stating that the emperor should not demand anything pecuniary from the feudal princes. When an emperor asked the prince for anything, he was condemned by Confucius. The demand for money was condemned most of all. Since the emperor had the taxes from the imperial state and the tribute from the feudal states, he should be a most moderate man and an example to the whole empire. If the emperor should care for money, it would make the princes avaricious, the great officials miserly, and the students and common people sly. Therefore, the *Record of Rites* says: " The emperor plants only gourds and flowering plants, not such things as might be stored." [1]

2. *Exclusion of the Feudal Princes*

In the *Spring and Autumn*, there is a condemnation of the fishery of Duke Yin of Lu. The value of his fishes amounted to one hundred catties of gold, which was equal to one million of copper money in the Han dynasty. Ho Hsiu states that he should not leave the government and compete for profit with the people. To do so is a great shame, and not fitting to a ruler.

3. *Exclusion of All Salaried Officials*

According to Confucius, all the salaried officials should be excluded from the economic field. He says:

The superior man does not take all the profit, but leaves it for the people. It is said in the *Canon of Poetry:*

> " There shall be handfuls left on the ground,
> And here ears untouched,
> For the benefit of the widow."

---

[1] *Li Ki*, bk. ix, p. 433.

Hence, when a superior man is in office and enjoys its emoluments, he does not do farming.[1]

Leaving profit for the people is the fundamental idea of this principle. Its aim is to protect the weak against the strong. Therefore, when Confucius spoke of Tsang Wên-chung, a great official of Lu, he condemned him as wanting in virtue, because he made his concubines weave rush mats for sale.[2]

The "Great Learning" says: "He who keeps horses and a carriage does not look after fowls and pigs. The family which keeps stores of ice does not rear cattle or sheep."[3] The first sentence refers to the one who is beginning to be a great official; and the second, to the great official and minister. Indeed, none of the officials should do any business.

II. THE ESTABLISHMENT OF THESE PRINCIPLES.

1. *Example of Kung-yi Hsiu.*

The best example illustrating the exclusion of officials from gainful occupation is given by Kung-yi Hsiu. After taking the professorship of Lu, he became the prime minister of Duke Mu (145-176 A. K. or 407-376 B. C.). He was the first one who enacted the Confucian theory of exclusion as a legal law. Under his administration, the salaried officials were not allowed to compete for profit with the people. When some one gave him a fish, he declined. The giver said, "I have heard that you like fish. Why do you refuse my present of fish?" "Because I like fish, I do not accept it," answered the minister. "Now, as I am a minister, I am able to buy fish myself. If I should accept the fish and should lose my position, who will give me fish in the future? For this reason I do not accept it." From his

---

[1] *Li Ki*, bk. xxvii, p. 296.
[2] *Classics*, vol. v, pt. i, p. 234.
[3] *Classics*, vol. i, pp. 379-380.

statement, we may surmise that there was a law forbidding officials to accept anything from any person. It is stated: " He who has received one great thing is not allowed to take the small one." When Kung-yi Hsiu ate the edible mallow, he pulled it in his garden and threw it away. When he had seen his wife weave cloth, he burned the loom and divorced her. He said: "As I have received salary, why should I snatch, too, the profits of gardener and weaver?"[1] In the *Historical Record*, his words are put in this way: " How can the farmer and the working girl find a place to sell their commodities?"[2] The essential point is that the officials should get only their salary and leave the whole economic field free for the common people.

2. *Statement of Tung Chung-shu*

In 412 (140 B. C.), Tung Chung-shu gave to Han Wu Ti an answer that has become famous. In criticizing the social conditions of his time, he says:

Heaven has also the law of distribution. For example, those animals which are given upper front teeth have no horns; the bird, having wings, has only two legs. This means that those who have received great things are not allowed to take small ones. In ancient times, the salaried officials did not live by physical labor, and did not touch industrial occupations. This also shows that those who have received great things are not allowed to take small ones. It is the same idea as that of Heaven. If a man had received the great things and took the small ones too, even Heaven could not satisfy his covetousness—how could man satisfy him? This is the reason people suffer in poverty. A man whose personality is already honorable, and who has risen to high position, whose family, in addition, is already rich, who receives a large salary,

---

[1] Quoted by Tung Chung-shu, *History of Han*, ch. lvi.
[2] *Historical Record*, ch. cxix.

and then uses his powers of wealth and dignity to compete for profit with the people who are below him; how can the people compete with him? Therefore, he increases the number of his servants, keeps more cattle, extends his land and houses, accumulates all kinds of property, and saves the surplus. He pursues those things without an end, in order to oppress the people. Day after day, and month after month, the people are robbed by him, then they fall into great poverty. While the rich have luxury and superabundance, the poor are in grievous distress. If the public should not save the poor from distress and grievance, the people could have no pleasure in life. When the people have no pleasure in life, they do not escape even death; how can they escape from crime? This is the reason why punishments are numerous and criminals increase.

Therefore, the families of salaried officials should get only their salaries, and should not compete with the people in gainful occupations. Thus profits may be equally distributed to the people, and each family of them may have sufficient. This is the natural law of Heaven, and the principle of antiquity as well. The emperor should imitate it in his laws, and the officials should practise it in their conduct.

In conclusion, he quotes this interesting passage from the *Canon of Changes*: " Bearing on the back and riding in the carriage causes robbers to come." He explains that " riding in the carriage " refers to the position of the higher class, " bearing on the back " to the business of the lower class. If one occupies the position of an official, and takes up the business of the common people, calamity must ensue.[1] These statements of Tung Chung-shu have had great influence on Confucian socialism.

3. *Laws of Different Dynasties*

The exclusion of officials from all gain has been carried into actual law by many dynasties. During the Tsin

---

[1] *History of Han*, ch. lvi.

dynasty, after Wu Ti reunited the whole empire (831, or 280 A. D.), he decreed that the princes and dukes should regard their feudal estates as their families, and that they should not have lands and houses in the imperial capital as private property. The only two things each should have were the residence within the city and the pasture near the suburb. Then he made the following limitation: In the capital, the princes, the dukes, and the marquises were allowed to have one residence. If their residence was not in the city, but out of it, it was allowed to remain there. Near the capital, those who had a great feudal estate were allowed to have one thousand five hundred acres of suburban land; those of second estate, one thousand acres; and those of small estate, seven hundred acres.

There was also a limitation upon the ownership of land by officials. The amount of land was in accordance with their rank. To the first rank five thousand acres were given; to the second, four thousand five hundred acres; to the third, four thousand acres; to the fourth, three thousand five hundred acres; to the fifth, three thousand acres; to the sixth, two thousand five hundred acres; to the seventh, two thousand acres; to the eighth, fifteen hundred acres; and to the ninth, the last, one thousand acres. Moreover, their descendants had the hereditary right to hold the land, and the limit of time was also according to their rank. The longest hereditary right came down through nine generations, and the shortest through three generations.[1]

During the Tang dynasty, in 1175 (624 A. D.), a law was enacted that all the families which had received salaries were not allowed to compete for gain with the people.[2]

According to the *Law Code of the Ts'ing Dynasty*, all the officials are not allowed to buy land and houses in those

[1] *History of Tsin*, ch. xxvi.
[2] *Old History of Tang*, ch. xlviii.

places where they hold their office. The transgressor shall be beaten with a small stick fifty times. He shall be deprived of his office, and his land or house shall be confiscated.[1]

If officials lend money at interest, or hold property on mortgage, although conforming to the legal rate of interest, they shall be punished with eighty blows with the long stick. If they take interest beyond the legal rate, such interest shall be considered as a bribe, and they shall be punished accordingly.[2]

If the officials buy salt from the government and sell it to the people for the sake of making profit, they shall be punished with one hundred blows of the long stick and banished to another part of the same province for three years. Their salt shall be confiscated.[3] All these laws keep the officials from competing with the people.

III. CONCLUSION

Hu Yin (died 1702, or 1151 A. D.) gives a criticism of this exclusion of officials. He says:

This exclusion is a good institution, inspiring moderation in the officials. In ancient times the government employed men who were fitted to their position. Then they held their office without change, sometimes for life, and sometimes even to their descendants. Their salary was permanently given. . . . At that time, if they competed with the people for profit, they should have been blamed. In modern times, as the men are not carefully employed, their rise and downfall are uncertain. In the morning they may enjoy the grain of the imperial garner, but in the evening they may be obliged to eat at home. Since they may have parents, wives and children, if they are not superior men who can be self-contented in a poor position, how can they live without taking up gainful occupations? For

[1] Ch. ix.   [2] Ch. xiv.   [3] Ch. xiii.

example, Lu Huai-shên [died 1267, or 716 A. D.] was a minister of the Tang dynasty. But when he died, he had only a servant who sold himself for the expense of his funeral. What can the other officials whose position is lower than that of minister do?

According to reason, when the officials take their office, land should be given to them in accordance with their rank. During their employment, they have salaries in return for their work; even if they are dismissed, they have land by which to make their living. Only in the case of some great disgrace which cannot be excused will their land be taken back by the government. In this way the exclusion of the officials from gain may be practised, and the spirit of moderation will prevail.[1]

The argument of Hu Yin is very reasonable, and it holds true in modern times, because feudalism has died out. But this principle of excluding officials from gainful occupation has a great influence on Chinese economic life. In China's history there are very few officials who accumulated a great fortune in any way they could. Modesty and purity were the general spirit of the officials. As they did not compete with the common people for profits, the people had much more chance to compete among themselves, and enjoyed full freedom of economic activity without being in unfavorable competition with those who had added power. Very recently, public sentiment is beginning to depart from this principle. Owing to the international struggle with foreign countries, China unfortunately needs more men for the economic war. Formerly, it was not suitable for the officials to compete with the people at home, but to-day, everyone should compete with the foreigners abroad. In fact, in old times this principle was established for the object of equal distribution, and in the present day it is going to be renewed for the object of large production.

[1] *General Research*, ch. ii.

CHAPTER XXIX

Government Control of Demand and Supply

I. GENERAL PRINCIPLES

In economic society there are two sets of interests, those of producers and those of consumers. But nothing more markedly affects the interest of both sides at once than prices. Therefore, price is a great problem for society as a whole. According to the Confucian theory, the government should level prices by the adjustment of demand and supply, in order to guarantee the cost of the producer and satisfy the wants of the consumer. Its chief aim is to destroy all monopoly, so that the independent or small producer can be protected on the one side, and the consumer on the other. It prevents the middleman from making large profits, and gives the seller and buyer full gain. Originally this theory was purely for the benefit of the people and brought no gain to the budget of the government. In later times this theory became a financial scheme by which the government made a large profit. However, if this scheme is carried through successfully, it is a benefit to society, because it takes away profit from the great merchant only and lightens the taxation of everyone. On the principle that the ruling class should be excluded from the economic field, the conservative Confucians always opposed this scheme, because they said that the government should not compete with the people for profit. But we should distinguish two divisions in the budget of a government,—one part for the ruler himself, and the other for the state as a whole. As to the ruler himself, he, of course, should be excluded from any gainful occupation and should not compete with the people. But as to the state as a whole, the collective representation of the people, it should be allowed to get its revenue in the most convenient way. If the state competes with a few great merchants and lessens the burden of the majority, it is a good plan for meeting the public expense. Moreover, if the administration is as good as that of Liu An (1267-1331, or 716-780 A. D.), these three things result: the state gets profit, the people constantly enjoy a reasonable price, and distribution is nearly equal. But such an administration is very difficult. Therefore, Wang Mang and Wang An-shih both failed. This theory is applied to all commodities; but as grain and money have very important problems which are treated independently, this chapter will be concerned with only the price of commodities in general.

When we discuss the theory of Confucianism, we must refer to the Confucian Bible. The *Canon of Changes* says: " The superior man diminishes where there is an excess, and increases where there is any deficit, in order to bring about a level according to the nature of things."[1] Excess and deficit here relate to relations between supply and demand. In the former case, supply should be diminished, and in the latter case, supply should be increased. Both cases may arise at different times; or at the same time but in different places; or at the same time, in the same place, but concerning different goods. It is the task of the superior man to adjust demand and supply so as to keep prices on a level.

In the *Canon of History* there is a passage saying, " To transport the commodities from where there was plenty to where there was nothing was to exchange the accumulated stores. In this way all the people got rice to eat and all

[1] *Yi King*, p. 286.

the states began to come under good rule." [1] This commercial policy was the deed of Yü. When there is plenty, the supply side is sufficient; but when there is nothing, the demand side is unsatisfied. Then transportation for both sides is necessary. For instance, in the mountain region there is a store of timber, and at the seaboard there is a store of fish and salt; they need to exchange with each other. No one can be only a getter from others; he must be also a giver to others. Hence the results of commerce are not only that the people get sufficient food, but also that all the states have a good feeling toward one another. This is the theory of commerce.

According to the *Official System of Chou*, one of the functions of the government bank is to control the demand and supply of commodities. When commodities cannot be sold because supply exceeds demand, the bank buys them, at their market price. When the demand for them rises and exceeds the supply, it sells them at their original price, which has been carefully written on a label of each commodity. In the first case, the producer is benefited ; in the second, the consumer; but the government itself does not make money out of the transaction. The buyers must get a certificate from their magistrate before the commodities are sold to them. This excludes those merchants who may wish to buy cheap goods from the government and sell them again for profit. Generally, after the price has fallen, it rises again; hence, the government should supply the needs of the common people only.[2]

There is a fragment of the *Doctrine of Music* which was preserved by Liu Tê (died in 422, or 130 B. C.), that says:

The emperor selects the scholars from the feudal princes in

[1] *Classics,* vol. iii, pt. i, p. 78.   [2] Ch. xv.

order to establish the "five equalizations." Therefore, the markets have uniform prices, and the four classes of people [the students, farmers, artisans and merchants] are equal. The strong cannot oppress the weak and the rich cannot take advantage of the poor. Then public finances will be more than sufficient, and benefit will come to the small people.[1]

"Five equalizations" is the title of an office whose function is to equalize market prices. According to Ma Tuanlin, there was such an office in ancient times. Although we cannot find out its history, we know that it is at least a theory of Confucianism.

II. SANG HUNG-YANG

1. *Systems of the Equal Transportation and the Level Standard*

For the practice of controlling demand and supply, in the Han dynasty, there was a marvelous financier named Sang Hung-yang (421-472, or 131-80 B. C.), son of a merchant. At the age of thirteen (433) he became a favorite of the emperor on account of his economic genius. In 436 he became the second secretary of the treasury, and he began to practise the "equal transportation" scheme. In 442 he was made secretary of the treasury to control the government monopoly of salt and iron. He saw that, owing to the independent and competitive purchases of the officials, the price was raised; and that by the old way of sending products as the taxes to the capital from each place, the value of the goods sometimes did not cover even the cost of wages. Then he proposed that several dozens of subordinate officers of the treasury department should be appointed, and that they should be definitely charged with the affairs of a given state or province. Each of them should

[1] *History of Han*, ch. xxiv, (commentary).

appoint subordinate officers in each district to establish the office of "equal transportation." Then, even in remote regions, the people should be required to pay their taxes in the form of merchandise which was formerly exchanged by the merchants; and the merchandise should be exchanged among the officers themselves. All the merchandise offered as taxes should be the staple products of the locality, so that their price would be reasonable. Then the government should sell them in other places, and get a profit. It would save the cost of transportation of the localities, and give the remote regions convenience, equal to their neighborhood.

In the capital, the office of "level standard" should be established to control all the transportation of the whole empire. All the articles needed by the officials should be supplied by the treasury department. By all the officers of the treasury department, the commodities of the whole empire should be controlled. When their price was high, they should be sold, and when it was low, they should be bought. In this way, rich merchants could not make great profits, and prices would return to the normal level. Because the price would be artificially kept down, this office should be called "level standard." His proposal was approved by Han Wu Ti, and carried into practice. During the reign of Wu Ti the expense of the government was extraordinarily great. But by the schemes of equal transportation and level standard, the public finances sufficed without increasing taxes.[1]

[1] The policy of controlling demand and supply by the state was worked out very successfully by Kuan Tzŭ (died 93 B. K. or 644 B. C.). His work contains several books dealing with this question, but he uses the terms "lightness and heaviness" instead of demand and supply. Lightness means supply over demand, and heaviness means demand over supply. His policy may be summed up in a few words: the government should control the ratio between money and commodities by issuing and redeeming money, in order to level rich and poor, and to make the state the dominant power in economic life. His theory is like state socialism, and he was the real precursor of Sang-Hung-yang.

It would be hardly accurate to say that Sang Hung-yang was a strict Confucian, but as he was born (421) after Confucianism had been made a state religion (412), he was a Confucian in the broad sense.[1] In 471 (81 B. C.), there was a debate between him and the representatives of the people on the abolition of equal transportation. His opponents were good scholars and strict Confucians. Their argument was based on the ethical teaching that the government should not take up commercial business, and they were in favor of agriculture rather than industry. But Confucianism is a great philosophy which gives its principles to both sides, so that Sang Hung-yang based his argument also on Confucianism. His statement was in favor of industry, but not, however, against agriculture. He said that where there is plenty of rich land but not plenty of food, the improvement of tools is needed; and where there is a great amount of natural resources but not a great amount of wealth, commerce and industry are needed. All the staple commodities of different places are waiting for the manufacture of artisans, and for the exchange of merchants. According to the ancient sages, agriculture is not the only subject of political economy. Therefore, the representatives did not win the debate and this system was not abolished.

Sang Hung-yang's system encountered much popular opposition, but it was justifiable. From the social aspect, it took away profits from rich merchants and helped the poor in time of need. From the economic aspect, it saved the expense of sending goods from each place to the capital and made great revenue. Moreover at that time there was a military struggle for national expansion so that the revenue from the system of equal transportation was neces-

[1] Huan K'uan calls him a widely and thoroughly educated man. His son, Sang Ching, was a Confucian scholar.

sary. If we judge Sang Hung-yang from the viewpoint of nationalism, it was he who enabled Han Wu Ti financially to expand the Chinese empire. His services to the nation as a whole were great and lasting. He was the first one to practise state socialism successfully on a gigantic scale;[1] but his system died out after his death, because no one was able to administer such a plan.

III. WANG MANG

1. *System of the Five Equalizations*

From the phrase, " five equalizations," in the *Doctrine of Music*, Wang Mang established an office called " five equalizations." Its purpose was to equalize the mass of the people and do away with monopoly. In 561 (10 A. D.), in the capital, three bureaux were opened; and in each of the five chief cities there was one bureau. In each bureau there were five officers in the trade department and one officer in the banking department. During the second month of each season the controller of markets in each bureau fixed the prices for the three grades of each commodity. Despite differences in other places, each bureau used its own fixed prices as the " market level." When the people could not sell their commodities, after the officers examined the facts, the commodities were bought by the bureau at the cost price, in order to prevent loss to the producers. When the price was higher than the level by one penny, the bureau sold its commodities at the level price. When the price was lower than the level, it left the people to exchange commodities among themselves, in order to prevent speculators from storing the commodities. But Wang Mang did not succeed.[2]

[1] *Historical Record*, ch. xxx; *History of Han*, ch. xxiv.
[2] *History of Han*, ch. xxiv.

CONTROL OF DEMAND AND SUPPLY

IV. LIU AN

During the Tang dynasty, Liu An, commissioner of transportation, was the greatest financier. In his time there was a great rebellion (1306-1313, or 755-762 A. D.) The population was diminished over two-thirds. Many districts were occupied by military commanders who, being somewhat independent, and opposed to the central government, sometimes broke out in rebellious war. The government got only a small revenue; but with rebellions within the country, and barbarian wars on the boundary, it had to defray great expenditures. The happy outcome of this bad condition was due entirely to Liu An Basing his operations on the system of level standard, he controlled the natural resources, drove out the great merchants, fixed the prices of commodities, and made great profit for the government. Without increasing taxation, he made revenue sufficient to meet expenditures. This was his part in the restoration of the Tang dynasty.

1. *His Administration of the Equal Transportation*

Liu An was a great statesman. He thought that taxation is based on social ability; hence, his financial policy began on the social side; love for the people was the first thing. Before his administration, magistrates had forced the rich to take charge of transportation and communication, and forced them to pay beyond the requirements of taxation. Then the people became brigands and pirates for over ten years. But Liu An began to use the government ships for transportation and to employ clerks for communication, and he abolished all unlawful imposts.

In different provinces he established local stations. All these stations established numerous postoffices and employed the best runners there at high wages. The prices and other circumstances of the four corners, even from a great distance, were known to Liu An in not over four or five days. Hence he was able to determine the weight of all commodities and keep their prices in normal relation. Thus he made great profit for the government, and, in addition, the people were benefited, as the producer did not suffer from too low a price, or the consumer from one that was too high.

Liu An thought that a good government should show its love for its people not by bounty, but by the adjustment of their production. In normal years he bought commodities at the market price, and in bad years he sold them for the relief of the people. On an average, the commodities were annually increased one-tenth, and he wisely controlled them in accordance with the situations. He appointed officials in charge of the local stations. Every ten days and every month they reported the weather conditions of the different districts. When they saw signs of a bad year, they told him beforehand how much taxation should be exempted and in which month, and how many commodities should be sold. In due time, without waiting for the demand of the magistrate, he satisfied the wants of the people with the exact supply. Therefore, the people never actually fell into bad conditions and the population was increased. When Liu An was made commissioner of transportation (1311 A. K.), the number of families was less than two millions (1,933,-125), but in his last year (1331 A. K.) it was nearly four millions (3,805,076). However, the increase of population was under his administration only; under other administrations there was no increase. He increased the revenue also. In his first year the annual revenue was not more than four millions of strings, but in his last year it was more than ten millions.

It was argued that he should simply give commodities to the people instead of selling them at a cheap price. His

CONTROL OF DEMAND AND SUPPLY

theory in reply was that prevention was better than cure. In free distribution, there would be two disadvantages First, if the distribution was too small, it could not save their lives, or if it saved many, it would exhaust the revenue and bring about increase of taxation. Second, distribution was near to injustice. The officers would be corrupted, and the strong would get more than the weak; and this could not be prevented even by punishment by death. But in sale, there were two advantages. First, in the places where bad crops occurred, although the inhabitants were in want of food, they possessed other products. Selling the food supply at a low price to exchange their commodities, then transporting these commodities to places where the season was good, and selling them, or using them by the government, these schemes would make public finances sufficient. Second, it brought a great supply of food into the market, and let the people sell and transport it to a great extent. When the retailers came into the villages, those poor people who could not go to the market could indirectly get the benefit, and escape hunger. Moreover, following the system of "constantly normal granary," Liu An kept in storage a great amount of rice—in each prefecture the average storage of rice was three million bushels. Indeed, he was a great statesman, for the people as well as for the state.

The chief article from which Liu An got large revenue was salt. In his time, western China consumed the salt of the Shansi province, which was controlled by the treasury department; and eastern China consumed that of the sea, which was controlled by him. He thought that by salt, which is necessary to people, a large revenue could be obtained. At the places where salt was produced he created the officials of salt; and in all other places there were no such officials, because he thought that too many officials would trouble the people. According to the times, he gave different orders to teach the people how to produce salt. As salt was a government monopoly, the officials bought salt from the people who produced it and sold it to the merchants, who were allowed to go anywhere. Formerly, the magistrates taxed the salt when the merchants transported it through their passes. Liu An abolished such a bad custom, and salt enjoyed free trade. Doing away with smuggling, he especially appointed able officials to the local stations without touching the magistrates.

He transported the government salt to those regions which were far away from the salt-producing places, and stored it up. When merchants did not come to those places, and the price of salt was high, he sold it at a low price. This scheme was called " constantly normal salt." The government made great profit, and the people did not suffer from a high price. When the price of salt at the capital was high, Liu An was ordered by the emperor to transport there thirty thousand bushels. It came from Yangchow (Kiangsu) to Sian (Shensi) in only forty days, and the public thought it miraculous.

In the first year of Liu An's administration (1311), the annual profit from salt amounted to six hundred thousand strings, but in his last year (1330) it was more than ten times this amount. In 1330, out of the total revenue of twelve million strings, the profit from salt was over six millions. The public finances were sufficient, but the people bore no burden. Comparing it with the salt of Shansi, the profit there was only about eight hundred thousand strings, and the price was also higher than that of the salt of the sea.

In the time of Liu An, the native products of the southern provinces which were offered as a sort of taxation were heavy, rough, cheap and defective. Liu An thought that even if they were transported to the capital, it could not cover the cost. Then he stored them up in the valley of

Yangtze, and exchanged them for copper, lead, fuel and charcoal. The annual coinage was more than one hundred thousand strings. This shows his economic policy. On the one hand, native products became more useful, and on the other, circulation of money was made sufficient.

His administration was remarkable, partly because of his own genius, and partly because of his choice of men. He selected several hundred of the best scholars to have charge of the business, because he said that scholars care for fame more than for money. Among his subordinates, even at a great distance, no one deceived him. After he died, these also became famous financiers for a period of twenty years. This shows the wisdom of Liu An.[1]

V. WANG AN-SHIH [2]

1. *Plan of Equal Transportation*

Under the Sung dynasty, in 1620 (1069 A. D.), Wang An-shih revived the system of equal transportation. It was proposed because, owing to the old custom, the officials of public finance did not know the relation between the central government and local conditions, and they were unable to fill the deficiency with the surplus. The amount of stipulated annual contribution of products by the provinces to the capital was fixed by rule. It was not allowed to be more than the fixed amount, even in a year of plenty, and when transportation was easy; nor could it be less, even in bad years and at a high price. In the latter case, the provinces contributed their commodities at a cost two-fold or five-fold the normal price; but when they reached the capital, they

---

[1] *New History of Tang*, ch. cxlix; *etc.*

[2] From this section and the following statements (pp. 589-94, 667, 673-6), the reader will see that the article "How Socialism Failed in China," written by General Homer Lea, published in *Van Norden's Magazine* (September and October, 1908), is incorrect.

perhaps realized only half of their value. This simply enabled the great capitalists and merchants to take advantage of the embarrassment of the government and people and to exercise arbitrary power in the markets. Now, the commissioner of transportation was charged with all the revenue of the six rich provinces; his function was to deal with the taxes of tea, salt, alum and liquor; and from him came the greater part of the public revenue. Hence he should be trusted with money and goods, and he should dispose of them according to the financial condition of the six provinces. Among all commodities which were purchased by the government, or were offered to the government as taxes and contribution, he should be allowed to make substitution and exchange. When their price in one place was high, let him get them from other places where their price was low. When their transportation was not convenient, let him exchange them in the neighborhood, instead of at a distance. He should be informed beforehand of the amount needed for the annual expenses of the central government; thus he might conveniently buy or hold or exchange the commodities, as circumstances demanded. In this way the public would control the demand and supply, in order to facilitate transportation, to reduce expense, to remove heavy taxes, and to relax the burden on the farmers. Then the public finances would suffice, and the wealth of the people would not be exhausted. This proposal was approved by the emperor, and the commissioner of transportation, named Hsieh Hsiang, was charged with the task of carrying into effect this system. The emperor granted him five million strings of cash and three million bushels of rice for the development of it, but the plan was a failure.

2. *System of Exchanges*[1]

In imitation of the system of level standard, Wang An-shih established the "exchange." It was first proposed by a man of the common people named Wei Chi-tsung. He said that the capital was the center of all commodities; but the market had no regular price, and whether things were dear or cheap depended only upon speculation. A good government should be able to take something from the rich and give it to the poor. Now, as rich men and great families, taking advantage of the emergencies of the people, made large profits, doubling their capital many times, wealth was accumulated by a few, and public finances were also made insufficient. Money should be given to the commodity-taxing bureau to establish a constantly normal exchange. For this undertaking, financial officers should be selected; and to carry out the business, good merchants should be employed. They should know the market price of all commodities. When things were cheap, the exchange should buy them at a higher price; and when they were dear, it should sell them at a lower price. Then the profit would go to the state. In 1623 (1072 A. D.) this proposal was carried out. In the capital an "exchange" was established with 1,870,000 strings of cash as its fund. Over the whole empire there were numerous branches established for a short period of time.

In the capital, the general rules of the exchange were as follows: The guild-merchants and brokers could be merchants and brokers of the exchange; but the merchants should pledge themselves by property, either their own or borrowed, and five men should join together as a guarantee. When the people could not sell their goods, they were allowed to sell them at the exchange. After the bargain between the seller

[1] See also *infra*, pp. 592-3.

and the merchant was settled at a reasonable price, according to the amount of commodity purchased by the merchant, the price was paid in money by the exchange; if the seller wished to exchange his commodity for government commodities, it was allowed. By a pledge of salable goods, people were allowed to borrow money or to buy government commodities on credit, in accordance with the value of their pledge; the rate of interest was 10 per cent for a half year, or double that rate for a whole year. All kinds of goods, which might not be immediately wanted by the merchants but could be stored up and exchanged in the future, should be bartered for or bought by the officers, and should be sold at the market price without any effort to make a special profit. When the officials wanted anything, they should buy it from the exchange. When these rules were framed, there was an article saying that if the capitalists should make unjust profit by monopolistic schemes and injure this new law, such a proceeding should be investigated by the exchange and punished by the treasury department, but the emperor struck out this article.

As to the capital of the exchanges, the exchange of the capital city had 1,870,000 strings. In the same year (1623), in the military station of Chênt'ao (Kansu) an exchange was established with capital of about 500,000 strings. In 1624, the exchange of Hangchow (Chekiang) was established, with 200,000 strings. In 1625, the emperor granted a loan of 2,000,000 strings to the exchange of the capital city. In 1626, to the exchange of Canton (Kuangtung) were given 100,000 strings; and to that of Yünchow (Shantung), 300,000 strings. In 1627, to the exchange of Hsiho (Kansu) were given 150,000 strings. In 1628, the amount of capital in the exchange of the capital city was fixed at 7,000,000 strings; if this amount diminished, it should be filled up by the interest annually received. When the exchange borrowed money from the private treasury of the emperor, the annual interest was 20 per cent. In fact, the capital of the exchanges was very large.[1]

The system of the exchange had three characteristic features: the loan bank, the pawn shop, and the market place. We shall discuss the first two characteristics under the subject of government loan, and here discuss the last one only. The exchange was administered by Lü Chia-wên, but he was not successful. Wang An-shih tried in every way to imitate Sang Hung-yang and Liu An, but he did not succeed because he had no such men as Sang and Liu. From the side of the people, the exchange caused a great deal of trouble. Buying at a cheap price and selling at a dear one, it monopolized the market. Its original idea was to do away with the monopoly of the rich, but its real result was to ruin even the occupations of the poor. It sold even ice, the sesame, and fruits; hence the price was high, and it was hard for retailers to make a living. But from the side of the government, it did not make very much money. In 1627, when the exchange had been established about five years, its total interest and profit from these three features amounted to only 1,332,000 strings. At that time the merchants did not come to the capital city, and passed through other ways with their commodities, because they thus escaped the compulsory power of the exchange, forcing them to sell their goods at the exchange. Therefore, the small gain of the exchange did not cover even the loss of the commodity tax. In 1637 this system was abolished; in 1648 it was reestablished; and in 1679 (1128 A. D.) it was finally abolished because its gain did not cover its expense.

[1] These figures are collected from the *History of Sung* (ch. clxxxvi), and the others, not given by history, are not to be found out.

CHAPTER XXX

GOVERNMENT CONTROL OF GRAIN

I. EQUALIZING THE PRICE OF GRAIN [1]

As a food supply has been necessary for human life through all ages, and China has been an agricultural country for thousands of years, the grain problem has been one of the greatest problems in its economic history. The theories and laws concerning grain are numerous. We shall select only the most important of them. On the whole, the policy of equalizing the price of grain is of chief importance, because it affects the interest of the whole society.

The policy of equalizing the price of grain is very old. According to the *Official System of Chou*, the superintendent of grain (*ssŭ chia*) looked around the fields and determined the amount of grain to be collected or issued, in accordance with the condition of the crop. He equalized the food of the people, fulfilling the deficit of their demand and adjusting their supply.[2] This policy was also carried out by Kuan Tzŭ and Fan Li. But Li K'o was the first one to give special emphasis to it and to establish complete rules. Therefore we shall take up his rules first.

1. *Rules of Li K'o*

When Li K'o became the minister of Wei, he said that if the price of grain were too high, it would hurt the con-

---

[1] This is a particular phase of government control of demand and supply.
[2] Ch. xvi.

GOVERNMENT CONTROL OF GRAIN

sumers, and that if it were too low, it would hurt the farmers. If the consumers were hurt, the people would emigrate, and if the farmers were hurt, the state would be poor. The bad results of a high price and a low price are the same. Therefore, a good statesman would keep the people from injury and give more encouragement to the farmers. After describing the bad condition of the farmers,[1] he gives the following law for equalizing the price of grain:

Those who want to equalize the price of grain must be careful to look at the crop. There are three grades of good crops: the first, the second and the lowest. In an ordinary year, one hundred acres of land yield one hundred fifty bushels of grain. In the first grade of good crop, the amount is fourfold,—that is, one hundred acres yield six hundred bushels. Throughout one year, a family of five persons needs two hundred bushels for their living, so that they have a surplus of four hundred bushels. The government should buy three hundred bushels from them, leaving them a surplus of one hundred bushels. In the second grade of good crop, the amount of grain is threefold,—that is, one hundred acres yield four hundred fifty bushels. The family would then have a surplus of three hundred bushels.[2] The government should buy two hundred bushels, leaving them one hundred bushels. In the lowest grade of good crop, the amount is twofold,—that is, three hundred bushels. The family would then have a surplus of one hundred bushels. The government should buy fifty bushels, and leave them the other half. The purchase of the government is for the purpose of limiting the supply according to the

[1] See *supra*, p. 270.
[2] That is, of course, speaking roughly. According to an exact calculation, there are only 250 bushels remaining, since the family itself consumes 200 bushels.

amount demanded by the people, and it should be stopped when the price is normal. This policy will prevent the price of grain from falling below the normal and keep the farmers from injury.

There are also three grades of famine: the great famine, the middle famine and the small famine. During the small famine, one hundred acres yield two-thirds as much grain as in the ordinary year,—that is, one hundred bushels. The government should then sell at the normal price what it has bought in the lowest grade of good crop. During the middle famine, the hundred acres yield one-half as much grain as in an ordinary year,—that is, seventy bushels. The government should now sell what it has bought in the second grade of good crop. During the great famine, the amount of grain is only one-fifth of what it is in an ordinary year,—that is, thirty bushels. The government should sell what it has bought in the first grade of good crop. Therefore, even if famine, flood and drought should occur, the price of grain would not be high, and the people would not be obliged to emigrate. This would come about because the government takes the surplus of good crops to fill the insufficiency of bad years. In other words, the government controls the excess of supply in a good year in order to meet the demand in a bad year.

The policy of Li K'o is for the benefit of both society as a whole and the agricultural class. His main idea is for the welfare of the people only, and not for the finances of the state. Therefore, he is the real Confucian who stands on the side of the people and represents the purely economic doctrine in a practical scheme. When his scheme was carried out in Wei, he not only made the people rich, but also made the state strong.[1]

[1] *History of Han*, ch. xxiv.

GOVERNMENT CONTROL OF GRAIN 571

2. *Statement of Mencius*

In the writings of Mencius we find also the same principle of adjusting the supply and demand of grain. Mencius said to King Hui of Laing:

When the grain is so abundant that the dogs and swine eat the food of man, you do not make any collection for storage. When there are people dying from famine on the roads, you do not issue the stores of your granaries for them. When people thus die, and you say, " It is not owing to me; it is owing to the year," in what does this differ from stabbing a man and killing him, and then saying, " It was not I; it was the weapon? "[1]

3. *System of the Constantly Normal Granary*

The principle of equalizing the price of grain advocated by Li K'o and Mencius was adopted into the system of " constantly normal granary." During the reign of Han Hsüan Ti, when there were good crops for many years, the price of one bushel of grain was as low as five pennies. Then the farmers suffered greatly. In 498 (54 B. C.), Kêng Shou-ch'ang proposed that the government should buy grain from places near the capital instead of transporting it from the eastern provinces. According to the old custom of the Han dynasty, the government transported annually from the eastern provinces four million bushels of grain to supply the capital, which was in the province of Shensi, in northwestern China. As this transportation was by means of the waterway, the number of laborers amounted to sixty thousand. By the plan of Kêng Shou-ch'ang, which was approved and carried out by the emperor, the government saved more than half the expense of transportation, and the farmers got more profit. Then

[1] *Classics*, vol. ii, p. 132.

Kêng Shou-ch'ang proposed that all the provinces along the boundary of the empire should establish granaries. When the price of grain was low, they should buy it at the normal price, higher than the market price, in order to profit the farmers. When the price was high, they should sell it at the normal price, lower than the market price, in order to profit the consumers. Such a granary was called "constantly normal granary." As the result was good for the people, the emperor gave Kêng Shou-ch'ang the title of marquis.[1] This system has continued from the time the constantly normal granary was established, in 498, to the present day. Although it was sometimes in practice, and sometimes out of practice, according to the political conditions of different ages, its name has nominally existed in nearly all ages. Despite the modifications of this system in later times, the fundamental law of Kêng Shou-ch'ang remains the same. Therefore, we shall not mention the different laws of different dynasties.[2]

[1] *History of Han*, ch. xxiv.

[2] Through all ages, the amounts of addition to and of deduction from the market prices of grain under the system of "constantly normal granary" varied. During the reign of Tang Hsüan Tsung, about 1293-1305 (742-754 A. D.), for the purchase of grain, three pennies were added to the market price of each peck. In 1363 (812 A. D.), Tang Hsien Tsung ordered that ten pennies per peck be added. During the reign of Sung Chên Tsung (1557, or 1006 A. D.), these rates were fixed: in purchasing, three or five pennies were added to the market price; and in selling, three or five pennies were deducted from the market price; the deduction was not below the original price at which the grain was bought. About 1712-1740 (1161-1189 A. D.), the law of the Kin dynasty stated that the purchase-price was to be two-tenths higher than the market price, and that the selling-price was to be one-tenth lower than the market price. In 1741, the selling-price was reduced to one-third of the market price. In 2308 (1757 A. D.), Kao Tsung of the present dynasty ordered that the selling-price of one bushel of grain should be three maces of silver lower than the market price. From the facts mentioned above, we can get some idea of the range of prices.

GOVERNMENT CONTROL OF GRAIN

4. *Criticism*

(a) *Its Strength*

The equalization of the price of grain is a very beneficial and practical scheme. It benefits the people without cost to the state. When the price is too low, though the government buys the grain at a price higher than the market rate, this does not mean a waste to the government. When the price is too high, though the government sells the grain at a price lower than the market rate, it does not mean a loss to the government. Even if it should be an expense to the government, the social benefit is much greater than the public expense. On the contrary, as a matter of fact, the government can make profit out of this system. In ancient times, Kuan Tzŭ used a similar scheme to enrich the state of Ch'i. During the Tang dynasty, this scheme made money to meet the need of public finances. During the Sung dynasty, it became of great importance for the food supply of the standing army along the boundary. We do not touch here the side of public finance, however, but the side of the people only, which was the original consideration of this system.

According to the *laissez-faire* doctrine, this system seems unnatural, and will do more harm than good, but this is not true at all. In the first place, the farmers are short-sighted and cannot look out for their own interests. As Ch'iu Chün (1971-2046, or 1420-1495 A. D.) said, the farmers have no farther thought; when the crop is good, they exchange the grain for money, and exchange the money for consumption goods. In a little while the whole crop is gone. When a bad year comes, they fail to make a living.

In the second place, the farmers are helpless to protect their own interests, even if they are not short-sighted.

From the statements of Li K'o and Chao Tsao,[1] everyone can see that in ancient times the condition of the farmers was very bad. But conditions are about the same in modern times. Because the condition of the farmers is very bad, they are bound to sell their crops at any price. When the harvest is finished, every farmer is obliged to sell grain at the same time. As there is a great supply of grain, its price must naturally be lower than usual. When the artificial suppression of the merchants is added, the farmers have no way to escape suffering. Moreover, as the farmers almost always borrow money from the merchants at a high rate of interest, their crop is practically sold before the harvest. In a word, the life of the farmers is controlled by the merchants.

In the third place, as grain is necessary to human life, its price has the greatest influence upon society at large. If the merchants controlled its price by keeping it in storage and limiting its supply in the market, the consumers would suffer severely. From a study of Chinese history in famine times, it appears that the high prices of grain usually disturbed national peace, at least locally, and sometimes even produced great revolutions. Even at the present day, the people are alarmed at a high price. Therefore, besides the system of constantly normal granary, the Chinese have now numerous laws to forbid exports of grain to foreign countries, local prohibitions of exportation, the special storage of the merchants, *etc.* In fact, the price of grain serves as a barometer of Chinese economic conditions.

In the fourth place, last and most important, as agriculture is subject to nature, the crop does not follow the law of demand and supply. A bad year may come simultaneously with a great demand, and several good crops may

---

[1] See *supra*, pp. 270, 395-7.

come successively. If we adopt a *laissez-faire* policy, in the former case the people would die of hunger, and in the latter case the farmers would get nothing but grain, because the lowest price would not be sufficient to exchange for other commodities. If they sold their crops at the lowest price, the merchants would profit at the expense of the farmers. If the consumers bought grain at the highest price, the merchants would profit at the expense of the whole society. Such a condition is especially true in China, where there is a great population and the people use rice as the principal food. Before the Opium War, China had little foreign trade, and did not get much food through importation. Even at present, foreign trade does not help China in this respect, because the western nations do not supply her with rice.[1] As the people cannot depend upon nature, they must necessarily adjust artificially the price of grain.

Because of these four considerations, the system of equalization of the price of grain has done immeasurable good to China. Owing to the difficulty of transportation and the absence of importation, this system was more important in old times than it is at present, but it is still very important. Take the province of Kuangtung, for example, where transportation by water is very convenient, and where the importation of rice from Annam and Siam and from the neighboring provinces of China is very large. When the crop is bad, it is a policy of the government to give a fund together with the subscription of the people, to buy rice everywhere and sell it at a low price, in order to compete with the rice-merchants and make the price low. Artificial limitation of supply by the merchants and unreasonable raising of price are not allowed. The chief reason is because the people

[1] The only importation of rice is from Annam and Siam.

depend so much on rice, and demand it in large amount. It seems that a change of taste or habit, and a resulting smaller consumption of rice, would be desirable.

(b) *Its Weakness*

Although the system of constantly normal granary is good, it still has weaknesses. The first one to object to this system was Liu Pan (570-629, or 19-78 A. D.). When Han Ming Ti wished to establish it. Liu Pan said that it had the name of benefiting people, but that it did not do so in fact, because the rich took advantage of the system, and the people failed to get the benefit.

In 1637 (1086 A. D.), Ssŭ-ma Kuang (1570-1637, or 1019-1086 A. D.) describes very clearly the weakness of this system in his day. Some of the magistrates have no public fund to buy grain, and some do not want to buy it because they like to save themselves trouble. In some cases, the officials do not know the real price, and let the employees, together with the merchants, defraud them. When the farmers hurry to sell their grain, the employees purposely give a lower price, in order to make the farmers sell it not to the government but to the merchants. After the merchants buy enough of it, they begin to raise the price. Therefore, the farmers get only a low price, and the government pays always a high price; the profits go only to the merchants. In some other cases, even if the officials want to buy it at proper times, they are obliged to send word from the district to the prefecture, from the prefecture to the superior of the province, and from the province to the imperial capital. When the answer comes back, months have passed, and the price is doubled. Therefore, a few years later, the original price of the purchase of the government is still higher than the market price. Such grain cannot be sold, and becomes a waste. But he said that these defects come from the administration of man, not from the law itself, which is true.[1]

As the criticism of Ssŭ-ma Kuang refers to the purchase only, we shall give a criticism referring to the sale. Chu Hsi says that as the constantly normal granary is established only in cities, it benefits only the lazy suburbans. As for the good farmers in the mountain districts, even if they are dying of hunger, the grain cannot reach them. Moreover, the law is too complicated; its result is that even when the officials see victims of famine, they do not dare to issue the grain. Usually they lock the granary up and hand it down to their successors without its being touched for several decades. During an emergency when the grain is necessarily issued, it has become dust and dirt which cannot be eaten.[2] But all these weaknesses are the results not of the original law itself, but of the administration of man.

To-day, although the constantly normal granary exists not only in name, but in fact, it is not of great importance. Usually, keeping the old grain in the granary, the officials neither buy new grain nor sell old. Therefore, the fundamental principle of this law has lapsed, and the granary has nothing to do with the market price. The chief reason for this is that it is difficult for officials to undertake commercial functions along with political duties.

II. DISTRIBUTION OF GRAIN [3]

1. *System of the Free Granary*

From the system of constantly normal granary, the system of "free granary" was introduced by the Sui dynasty. There are these differences between the two systems: the

[1] *General Research*, ch. xxi.   [2] *Ibid*.
[3] All occasional distributions of grain, during any calamity, are entirely left out.

578 GOVERNMENT CONTROL OF GRAIN

constantly normal granary belongs to the government, and the grain is bought and sold by means of payment; while the free granary belongs to the people, and the grain is collected as an addition to taxation, and is distributed freely. In 1136 (585 A. D.), Ch'ang-sun P'ing, a high official, basing his plan on the Confucian doctrine of storing grain,[1] proposed that each village should establish the free granary. During harvest, each farmer should be advised and encouraged to contribute voluntarily rice and wheat, proportionately to his crop. This should be stored up in the granary, and the committee of that village should be in charge of the annual collection, the care of storage and the account. During a bad year, if the inhabitants of that village should be in want of food, the grain of the granary should be given to them. This proposal was carried out by Sui Wên Ti, and this system prevailed over many provinces.

In 1147 (596 A. D.), Wên Ti decreed that the free granary should also be established in the city of each district. In the same year, he changed the voluntary contribution into a tax, and regulated it in three grades: the well-to-do family should be taxed not more than one bushel of grain; the ordinary family, not more than seven pecks; and the poor family, not more than four pecks.[2]

The free granary was also called "village granary." This system was highly esteemed by Hu Yin, who said that, for the relief of famine, nothing is more important than that the granary should be near to the people. Therefore, the system of free granary of the Sui dynasty was much better than that of modern times, when the granary was located in the cities only.[3]

---

[1] See *supra*, p. 360.
[2] *History of Sui*, ch. xxiv.
[3] *General Research*, ch. xxi.

During the Tang dynasty, in 1179 (628 A. D.), Tai Chou, a high official, also making use of the Confucian doctrine of storing grain, proposed to reestablish the system of free granary. Then Tang T'ai Tsung carried his proposal into law. According to the products of different soils, each acre was taxed two pints of grain. During a bad year, if the crop lost four-tenths, half of the tax was remitted; if it lost seven-tenths, the tax was remitted entirely. As the merchants had no land, their families were classified into nine grades, and the variation of their offering of rice was from five bushels down to five pecks. The poorest families and the barbarian tribes were exempted. When the crop was bad, grain was distributed to the people, or in the spring it was loaned for seed, and in the autumn it was returned.[1]

Under the Sung dynasty, the system of free granary practically died out. But there was a proposal which should be mentioned. About 1585-1588 (1034-1037 A. D.), Wang Ch'i proposed that this system should be reestablished. The tax should begin from the fifth grade of family up; and its rate should be one-twentieth of the regular tax. It should be collected together with the regular tax, and remitted in bad years. Since the average amount of the regular tax in the ordinary prefecture was one hundred thousand bushels, the free granary would get an addition of five thousand bushels. The rich families, owning more land, would pay more taxes to the free granary; while the ordinary and poor families, owning less land, would pay only a small tax. But, during bad years, while the rich families might not need the distribution of grain, the ordinary and poor families might really receive the benefit. This would follow the principle of " taking away the surplus to fill the insuffi-

[1] *New History of Tang*, ch. li.

ciency," and it would be a benefit to the whole empire.[1] Although his proposal was not enacted into law, his statement points out clearly the principle of the system of free granary.

This system was a socialistic measure: it got more taxes from the rich and gave more benefit to the poor. But no one has thought that this system is not welcomed by the rich. First, the tax was very small, and it was in accordance with ability, so it was easy for the people to pay it. Second, the rich could participate in the social benefit just as much as the poor, otherwise they would lose more than the poor by the disturbance of peace. Third, as they lived together in a small community, the rich for ethical reasons were willing to help the poor. Fourth, as the account was in the hands of the rich, they knew perfectly its financial condition, and had no fear of the corruption of the officials. The first cause made them able to pay the tax, and the last three causes made them willing to pay it. These points are the strength of this system.

III. GOVERNMENT LOANS OF GRAIN

1. *Classical Theories*

In ancient China the whole empire was an agricultural community, so that the grain was not only the subject of production and consumption, but also the means of exchange and distribution. In fact, in modern times money is a most important factor of industrial capital, but in ancient times grain was the most important. As the agricultural class formed the majority of people, if they were suffering the whole empire would be in distress. In that agricultural stage, there was nothing worse than usury for the hurt

---

[1] *General Research*, ch. xxi. His theory is the faculty theory of taxation, as against the benefit theory.

of the farmers. But fortunately, the ancient Chinese did not enact any law to forbid usury, because they knew that it could not be done away with by law.[1] The only protection given by the government to the farmers against usury was the lending of capital, grain, to them at the lowest rate of interest, or no interest at all. Although the loan was in the form of grain, since the country was in the agricultural stage, the same principle would apply even in the industrial stage. This is the socialistic theory of Confucianism.

The *Canon of Poetry* says: " Bright are those extensive fields, a tenth of whose produce is annually levied. I [2] take the old stores and with them feed our farmers."[3] Chêng Hsüan comments:

When the granaries were more than sufficient, the people were allowed to borrow grain on credit or on payment of interest. Taking the old stores to feed the farmers, on the one hand, was to change the old grain of the government; and on the other hand, it encouraged the people to keep their new grain. This was the law of ancient times practised in good years.

Even in good years there might be poor people in want of food; hence the government helped them out by lending them the old grain, while it kept the new grain in its granary.

According to the *Official System of Chou*, there is a collector of the taxes of the country (*lü shih*), who takes

---

[1] Historically, the usury law first appeared in the Han dynasty; in 436 A. K. (116 B. C.), Marquis P'ang-kuang was deprived of his feudal estate partly because he made interest beyond the legal rate (*History of Han*, ch. xv). There is a usury law in the *Law Code of the Ts'ing Dynasty* (ch. xiv) ; but it is not enforced.

[2] The prince.

[3] *Classics*, vol. iv, pt. ii, p. 376.

charge of the three kinds of grain which come from the three kinds of taxation. First, when the grain is distributed to the people, he calls them up by the names of the tax roll, and distributes proportionately the stores. Some are for the maintenance of life or consumption, and some are for use in business or production; for both purposes the people are required to pay the same rate of interest. Second, there is also another law for the lending of grain without interest. In spring, when the people are in want of grain, he gives it to them. In autumn, when the people have plenty of it, they return it to him. In this way the government exchanges the old grain for the new, and the people are enabled to meet their needs. It benefits the people, but costs the government nothing.[1]

During the Chou dynasty, the lending of grain to the people was a policy for winning their hearts. Therefore it was practised by many noble families—such as the Han of Chêng, the Yo of Sung, and the Chen of Ch'i.[2] The result was that they all became controllers of their states. These facts are sufficient to show the importance of lending grain by the government. First, it relieved the people; and second, it strengthened the power of the ruling house.

2. *System of the Village Granary*

From the system of free granary, a system of " village granary " was developed. The difference between these two systems was that the former distributed grain freely, while the latter loaned it. But, since the free granary was also called village granary, and since the grain of the free granary in the Tang dynasty was also allowed to be loaned, the system of village granary was practically the same as that

[1] Ch. xvi. The second rule was adopted by Wên Ti of the Northern Chou dynasty.
[2] *Classics,* vol. v, pt. ii, pp. 548, 589.

of free granary. However, the main purpose of the free granary was distribution, and that of the village granary was loan, so it is best to make a distinction between them. Moreover, the sources of the free granary came from an addition to the taxes, and the granary was interfered with by the government; but those of the village granary came entirely from voluntary contributions, and the granary was controlled solely by the people. Therefore, the system of village granary was an independent institution, an outgrowth from the free granary.

The system of village granary was established by Chu Hsi. In 1719 (1168 A. D.), when the people of his district (Fuhkien province) were hard pressed for food, he asked the prefect to give him six hundred bushels of rice from the constantly normal granary for the purpose of relief. In the summer the people received the rice, and in the winter they returned it, together with 20 per cent interest. After that year, this was repeated every year. When the crop was not good, one-half interest was remitted, and when it was very bad, the total interest was remitted. Throughout fourteen years, three granaries were established for the storing of the rice which came as interest. After he returned the original amount of rice to the prefect, the existing amount in the granaries was three thousand one hundred bushels. Then no interest was required; but when the people returned their loan, for each bushel three pecks of rice were added to the principal in order to save waste. Hence, around his village, even when bad years occurred, there was no want of food. This system was called village granary. In 1732 (1181 A. D.), when he suggested this system to the government, it was given by the government to all districts as a model.

The details of this system were that among all borrowers. ten families formed a *chia*. In each *chia*, a head man was elected. Among fifty *chia*, a village elder was chosen by the committee of the granary. In the first month, the village elder began to form the *chia*. Those people who kept deserted soldiers, who did not behave themselves, and who were well-to-do, were excluded; but none was compelled to come in. When they wanted to come in, they gave the number of the adults and children of their families. For an adult, one bushel of grain was loaned, and for a child, half that amount. Below five years, no child could apply for a loan. The head man of the *chia* could apply for a double amount. The village elder, after his examination, took signatures of all the members to the granary, and they were examined again. Their names were registered according to the arrangement of the *chia*, and the amount of loan for each family was written down. For the total amount of the loan of each *chia*, a certificate was given to the head man for his withdrawing of grain. Yet the issue of the loan was divided in two—one part for the seeding and the other for the weeding. After harvest, the loan should be entirely paid back not later than the last day of the eighth month. If the returned grain was not good, the returner was liable to a fine. These details were the general rules of the system of village granary.

The system of village granary was similar to that of " green sprout money," [1] but the former was much more successful than the latter. The reasons for this have been pointed out by Chu Hsi himself. He said that the idea of the law of " green sprout " was not bad; but its issue was not of grain, but of money; its location was not in villages, but in cities; its control was not by the people, but by the officials; and its practice was not with the motive of charity, but with the aim of revenue. Therefore, this law was suc-

[1] See *infra*, pp. 589-592.

cessful when Wang An-shih applied it to a district, but it was unsuccessful when he applied it to the whole empire. Now, this system of Chu Hsi was of the same principle as that of Wang An-shih, but his application was different. Its issue was of grain; its location was in villages; its control was by the people; and its practice was with the motive of charity. These were the reasons of the success of the village granary system.[1]

Since the system of village granary was established by Chu Hsi, it has been practised by many followers. Under the Sung dynasty there were some modifications—the grain was also loaned to farmers who owned no land, while originally it was loaned to land-owning farmers only, and no interest was required.[2] In the present dynasty this system still exists. In 2275 (1724 A. D.), the following was the rate of interest: for one bushel of grain loaned in summer, two pecks should be paid in winter as interest, that is, a semi-annual interest at the rate of 20 per cent. According to the situation of bad crops, a remission of either a half or the whole of the interest was made. After ten years, when the interest would be more than double the amount of the original grain, the rate of semi-annual interest should be reduced to 10 per cent.[3] Although there were small modifications in later times, its essentials remain the same.

[1] *General Research*, ch. xxi.
[2] *Continuation of the General Research*, ch. xxvii.
[3] *General Research of the Present Dynasty*, ch. vi.

CHAPTER XXXI

Government loans and public relief

II. GOVERNMENT LOANS.

1. *Classical Theories*[1]

THE principle of government aid for the farmer was noted by Mencius. He says:

When the emperor visited the princes, it was called a tour of inspection. When the princes attended the court of the emperor, it was called a report of office. It was a custom in the spring to examine the ploughing, and supply any deficiency [which might be either of seed, or of instruments, or of money]; and in autumn to examine the reaping, and assist where there was a deficiency of the crop.[2]

In fact, whenever the emperor and the princes went out, it was necessary for them to help the farmers in any way. Before the seeding, and after the harvest, any deficiency was filled by the aid of government,—that means the government should aid the farmers at all times when they need it. But, as Mencius does not tell whether the farmers should return what they had received to the government or not, we cannot decide that with certainty. It would seem, however, that the farmers must have returned it, otherwise the government could not have given aid as often as Mencius says. But there would be no interest.

[1] See also the classical theories about the government loan of grain, *supra*, pp. 580-2.
[2] *Classics*, vol. ii, pp. 159, 436.

GOVERNMENT LOANS AND PUBLIC RELIEF

Among all the Confucian texts, there is no theory of lending money at interest by the government. Such theory is given only in the *Official System of Chou*. Unfortunately, Wang Mang and Wang An-shih were the only two who applied this law of the *Official System of Chou*, and both failed. Therefore, the question was raised as to whether this law was originated by the Duke of Chou or not. Many Confucians denied it, and thought that this law was put into the *Official System of Chou* by Liu Hsin, in order to support Wang Mang's law. But the affirmative side is very strong. Although Liu Hsin did put his own words into the *Official System of Chou* in many other places, it seems sure that this law was originated by the Duke of Chou. During the beginning of the Chou dynasty, the government completely controlled the economic life of the people, and there was no capitalistic class. If the government would not lend money to them in time of need, how could the people get money to meet their expenses? And how could the productive forces be sufficient? As the government was paternal in form, and the Duke of Chou was a great sage, there is no doubt that he did establish a government bank for the benefit of the people.[1]

According to the *Official System of Chou*, the government bank is called *ch'üan fu*—*ch'üan* means money, and *fu* means treasury. It gives credit and loans to the people. Since this bank has commodities for sale, the people are allowed to buy them on credit without paying interest. But such credit is given on only two occasions—sacrifice and funeral. As these two things are religious matters and are necessary to the people, the government gives them credit in order to satisfy their needs in emergencies. The limit of time is fixed thus: for sacrifice, payment shall be made in

[1] *General Research*, chs. viii, xx.

not over ten days; and for funeral, in not over three months. Whenever the people want to borrow money or commodities from the bank, it first investigates their cases with the aid of their magistrate, and then grants them the loan. In this way it makes sure that they use the loan for production and not for consumption, so that there is no danger to creditor or borrower. For necessary consumption, as sacrifice and funeral, the government does not require interest; but for productive capital, it requires interest. On the one hand, this prevents the people from making private profit at public expense; and on the other hand, it benefits them without loss to the government, because the total interest would be sufficient against the risk. There is a rule that the interest is paid according to the business of the locality. For example, if the principal business of the locality of the borrower A is agriculture, the interest is paid in agricultural products, and if that of the borrower B is manufacture, it is paid in manufactured goods. This is for the convenience of the borrower, so that he can easily pay off his debt. Since the rate of interest is not given by the text, it is unknown; but it must be very low, because its purpose is not for revenue, but for the benefit of the people.[1]

During the Chou dynasty, the government loan was part of a policy of developing the economic interest of the people. For example, when Marquis Tao of Tsin wanted to give his people rest and prosperity (13 B. K. or 564 B. C.), all the accumulated stores of the state were given out for the borrowing of the people. From the marquis downwards, all who had such stores brought them forth. Hence, the state had no store which was not in circulation, and there was no one exposed to want.[2]

---

[1] Ch. xv. Chêng Hsüan gives the rate of interest in his Annotation (see *supra*, p. 474), but it is only a guess.
[2] *Classics*, vol. v, pt. ii, p. 441.

GOVERNMENT LOANS AND PUBLIC RELIEF

2. *Their Application*

(a) *The System of Credit and Loans*

Wang Mang imitated closely the Duke of Chou. In 561 (10 A. D.), he decreed that the banking department in the office of "five equalizations" should give credit and loans to the people. When people were called on for sacrifice or funeral, but had no money to meet their needs, it should lend them the money which came from the income tax on simple credit without requiring interest. The limit of time was: for sacrifice, not later than ten days; and for funeral, not later than three months. When people were in want and wished to borrow money for the purpose of production, it should give them loans according to the order of application. Besides the covering of their cost of production, the government got a tithe of their annual net profit for the profit of the government, as an income tax. The rate of interest was 3 per cent monthly.[1] As there was a distinction between interest and profit, it shows that there was an advance in economic theory and practice. But Wang Mang was killed in 574, and thus this scheme did not last very long.

(b) *System of the Green Sprout Money*

Under the Sung dynasty, the system of constantly normal granary was changed into the system of "green sprout money." This was the most important law of Wang An-shih. His law was based on the statement of Mencius and the law of the *Official System of Chou*. But the peculiar features of his law were that it lent to the people not grain, but money; and that it lent money not only to the farmers but also to the burghers. However, the primary purpose of this law was to lend money to the farmers. Hence the

---

[1] *History of Han*, chs. xxiv, xcix.

name of green sprout money was given it,—meaning that before harvest, when the grain was only a green sprout, the government lent money to the farmers.

This law was introduced in 1620 (1069 A. D.). If people wished to get money in advance, they were allowed to borrow it from the government; and when they paid taxes, they should return grain for the money they had borrowed. If they wanted to borrow grain instead of money, or if they wanted to return money instead of grain because at the time of return the price of grain was high, they were allowed to do so. For the crop of summer, the money was lent in the first month; and for that of autumn, in the fifth month. If the crop was bad, the farmers were allowed to return grain at the coming of another good crop. This law was intended to enable the farmers to start to work without delay, and to prevent private money-lenders from taking advantage of the interval of the harvest to get usury.

According to history, the practice of this law was that the loan of the government and the payment of the people were both in money, not in grain. The annual rate of interest was 20 per cent. In 1625 (1074 A. D.), Wang An-shih said that the government received annually total interest from its loans amounting to three million strings. In 1634 (1083 A. D.), the total issues of loan were fixed at 11,037,772 strings, and the total collections on the same at 13,965,459 strings, including interest. These two sums were the average amounts of three years, for the issue and the collection. But, when there was a fixed amount for issuing loans, the officials had to lend as much money as the fixed amount; and when they wanted to get special rewards or to show their ability, the money was lent even beyond the fixed amount. Therefore, the officials forced the people to make loans. Again, when there was a fixed amount for

GOVERNMENT LOANS AND PUBLIC RELIEF 591

collecting payment, the officials forced the people to pay their debts together with interest. For the immediate interest of the government, it brought a large sum of revenue.

What were the results to the people? The officials wanted to get interest rather than to help the people, so they lent as much money as possible. As the rich did not wish to borrow, they gave them large sums; and as the poor needed to borrow, they gave them small sums. According to the grades of wealth, the loans were distributed. For example, the rule of Wang Kuang-lien was that, for the first grade of family, fifteen strings of cash were given; for the second, ten strings; for the third, five strings; for the fourth, one string and five hundred; and for the fifth, one string. Taking the rich and the poor together, ten men guaranteed each other, and the rich man was made the head of them. Hence the rich and the poor were both overburdened with debts, and were pressed by the officials for the return of payment.

Although the purpose of this law was good because it intended to help people getting away from usury, the practice of it was bad, because in the beginning it forced people to take loans, and in the end it forced them to pay debts. Generally, when it was too easy for the people to get loans, even good citizens would be careless and use them for other purposes; and when they paid debts, even rich men would delay their payment. Then the officials must have had a great deal of trouble. Moreover, in issuing loans and collecting debts, there was no way to prevent administrative corruption. This was the chief reason for the failure of this law.

Furthermore, the law itself was rather to get revenue than to help people. First, it made the annual interest 20 per cent; and second, it issued loans twice a year. In spring, it might be said that the green sprout money was needed by the farmers; but in summer, when the crop was just reaped, why should this money be lent again for the crop of autumn? The loan of the fifth month was at the same time when the debt of spring was collected. How could the people make profit out of such a loan? It was clear that the government purposely wanted to get interest.

From 1620 to 1636 (1069-1085 A. D.), the green sprout law continued for seventeen years. In 1637, when the new emperor, Sung Chê Tsung, came to the throne, and the party opposing Wang An-shih, Ssŭ-ma Kuang, came into power, this law was abolished. In 1645, after the empress dowager, the regent, had died, when the followers of Wang An-shih returned to power, this law was revived. But they made some reforms in the law. First, the annual interest was reduced to 10 per cent. Second, the amount of loans was not fixed, so the officials were not obliged to force the people to borrow money. Third, there was no special reward for the officials who made more interest, so it prevented them from forcing the people to make loans. In 1674 there was still another decree to regulate the loans. This law was ended by the fall of the Northern Sung dynasty (1677, or 1126 A. D.).[1]

(c) *System of Exchanges*[2]

Besides the system of green sprout money, in 1623 (1072 A. D.), Wang An-shih established the government exchange. In that exchange the people were allowed to borrow money. There were two ways: one was that they could pledge their land, houses, gold, silver, *etc.*; and the other was that when they had no pledge, they should get three men together to form a guarantee. In the first case, this resembled a pawn shop; in the second case, it resembled

---

[1] *History of Sung*, ch. clxxvi. *General Research*, ch. xxi.
[2] See also *supra*, pp. 565-7.

GOVERNMENT LOANS AND PUBLIC RELIEF 593

a loan bank. The annual rate of interest in both cases was 20 per cent. If the payment was later than the due time, besides the regular interest, there was a fine at the rate of 2 per cent a month.

When the people fell into debt and could not pay even the interest, however, how could they pay the fine? Even the punishment of imprisonment was in vain. In 1630 a new law was enacted that the loan should be issued only on a pledge of property, and that the annual rate of interest should be reduced to 12 per cent. Those people who had no pledge but a simple guarantee, should not be given loans. Except the principal and interest, all fines before the date when the law was enacted should be remitted, and these amounted to several hundred thousand strings. For the indebted people, days of grace were given, the length of a half year for the payment of principal and interest.

In 1631 the amount of loan due to the exchange of the capital city was fixed at not more than three million strings; and in all provinces it should not be more than one-fourth of that amount. In 1633 the emperor decreed that debts due to all the exchanges should be paid off at the length of three years, and by the way of monthly instalments. This was for the benefit of the people.[1]

(d) *System of Pawn Shops*

Besides the exchanges which had the characteristics of pawn shops, there were also real government pawn shops, under that name. In 1632 (1081 A. D.), by the proposal of Chia Ts'ing, four pawn shops were established in the capital. In 1633 they were established in the districts near the capital, and in the next year they were over the whole empire. Among the five provinces, each had one hundred

[1] *History of Sung*, ch. clxxxvi. *General Research*, ch. xx.

thousand strings for the capital of the pawn shops; and among the rest, each had fifty thousand strings. The annual rate of interest was not over 20 per cent.

The pawn shop also did commercial business, because it was allowed to exchange commodities with the people. The functions of pawn shops and of exchanges overlapped each other, and the two institutions were connected with each other. How long the system of pawn shops lasted is unknown, but since the date of 1679 (1128 A. D.) it does not appear in history.[1] Probably it died out not very long after that date.

3. *Conclusion*

The lending of money by the government presents the difficulty of accomplishing two things at the same time:— namely, aid to the poor people and revenue to the state. If it is a purely social scheme, as advocated by Mencius and in the *Official System of Chou*, it may be successful for the help of the people. If it is a purely financial scheme, with a good administration like that of a private business, it may be successful for the interest of the state. But if it tries to accomplish the two objects at the same time, it must fail on both sides. As the primary purpose of this scheme is for the help of the poor, the loan ought to be given only to the poor. But, when the poor borrow money, it is certainly difficult for them to pay back not only the interest, but also the principal. How should the government treat them? If their indebtedness should be swept away, it would be a loss to the state; if it should be demanded, it would be a great trouble to the people. It must fail either way. Wang Mang and Wang An-shih are examples of this.

However, why did the green sprout money still bring a

---

[1] *History of Sung*, ch. clxxxvi.

great revenue to the state? Because this money was lent more to the rich than to the poor, and because the rich were obliged to guarantee the credit of the poor. The scheme of green sprout money was partially for the purpose of revenue, so that it was somewhat successful in this aspect; but it was hardly of any great benefit to the poor. However, from the experience given by history, the loan on pledge is much better than on personal guarantee, because the pledge is convenient to both lender and borrower, and saves the trouble of the third party.

In the opinion of Liu An, government loans were not a good thing, so he never extended any loan to the people. When some one criticized him for this policy, he replied:

To allow the people to obtain money without labor is not the blessing of the state, and to let the officials collect debts in an arbitrary manner is not the convenience of the people. Although I do not lend anything to them, I know the crops and the prices of every place in a short time. When the price is low, I buy the commodities, and when it is high, I sell them. Thus no place has ever suffered the trouble which comes either from a very high price or from a very low price. Why should I need to give them any loan?[1]

This statement is good, but it is good only for Liu An, because no man can make the condition of the people such that they do not need loans, as he did. Generally, the people do need the loan of money; if the government provides loans to them at the lowest rate of interest, it may help them a good deal, and do away with usury. But it must not be mixed up with the purpose of raising revenue; if it is, how can this be better than private lenders?

[1] *History of Sung*, ch. clxxvi.

According to the theory of Ma Tuan-lin, government loan is good in the feudal stage, but not good in the stage of absolute monarchy with a provincial system. Under the Three Dynasties, not only could such a great sage as the Duke of Chou successfully lend money to the people, but even ordinary men could do so. After that period, not only could Wang Mang and Wang An-shih not succeed, but even a sage would have failed. The reasons are simply that in the feudal stage the interests of the ruler are identified with those of the people, because the ruler holds by hereditary right, and the administration is easy because the imperial state and the feudal state are all small; and that, in the provincial system, with a temporal administration of the officials, they are strangers in the beginning, and cannot accomplish their work before they go away after a term of three years. Therefore, when the government attempts to apply the laws of the *Official System of Chou*, it is a useless trouble to the government as well as to the people. Hence, from the Ch'in dynasty down, the government has preferred the *laissez-faire* policy.[1]

This theory of Ma Tuan-lin is correct, but it seems to us that some laws of the *Official System of Chou* can be applied in the modern democratic society. Take the government loan for example. If the government were really in the hands of the people, the interest of the people and that of the government would be the same. Under such a condition, the government, especially the officials, can do no wrong to the people, and with a good system of administration in every way, the government loan at lowest interest may not only help out the needs of the people, but also raise revenue for the state. Wang An-shih was a great statesman indeed, but he lived either too late or too early.

[1] *General Research*, ch. clxxx.

Had his whole plan been carried out, China would have been a modern state one thousand years ago.

II. PUBLIC RELIEF

1. *Principles of Confucius*

Although Confucius wishes everyone to be economically independent, there are many unfortunate people who cannot have economic independence. Hence they need public relief. The " Royal Regulations " says:

One who while quite young loses his father is called an orphan; an old man who has no son is called a solitary one; an old man who has no wife is called a widower; and an old woman who has no husband is called a widow. These four classes are the poorest of Heaven's people, and have none to whom to tell their wants. They all should receive regular allowances.[1]

This is the law of Confucius. Mencius gives an historical fact to support this theory. He says: " Wên Wang, in the institution of his government with its benevolent action, made them the first objects of his regard." [2]

These four classes are either too young or too old for work; hence the state supports them by a regular allowance without requiring them to labor. But there is another kind of unfortunate people who can work but have difficulty in finding their particular kind of employment by themselves. Therefore, the " Royal Regulations " says: " The dumb, the deaf, the lame, those have lost a member, the pygmies, and the artisans, are all fed according to what work they are able to do." [3] Except the last class, all the

---

[1] *Li Ki*, bk. iii, pp. 243-4.
[2] *Classics*, vol. ii, p. 162.
[3] *Li Ki*, bk. iii, p. 244. See also *Hsun Tsŭ*, bk. ix.

five kinds of people have physical defects, and find it very difficult to make their own living. Even among the last class, those who have a particular profession or art, may be out of employment under many circumstances and cannot be self-supporting. Therefore, public relief is necessary. Since they are neither too old nor too young, and their physical condition still allows them to work although having some defect, and since the artisans have their handicrafts, they are not given regular allowances, but simply supported by their own labor at tasks which are provided by the state. The state gives great help to them, but does not waste the public money. The people get some dependence, but still live upon their own work without disgrace. This way is in the middle course between charity and justice.

2. *Historical Facts*

The principle of giving special favor to the widower, widow, *etc.*, was first put in practice by Han Wên Ti (373 A. K. or 179 B. C.), but it was well established by the Sung dynasty. After 1608 (1057 A. D.), the government established a granary in each district for the storing of rice which came from the public land as a rent. From the first of the eleventh month to the end of the third month of the next year, one pint of rice was given to each person every three days, and the children received half the amount. In 1654 (1103 A. D.) this idea was carried too far, and it became too expensive. In the almshouse, food, clothes, and beds were all given; servants, cooks, and nurses were all supplied. In 1671 (1120 A. D.) the following law was fixed: when the poor lived in the almshouse, one pint of rice was given to each every day, and the children got half this amount. The old regulations, that ten coins were daily distributed, and five coins for charcoal were added from the eleventh month to the first month, were abolished.[1]

[1] *History of Sung*, ch. clxxviii.

GOVERNMENT LOANS AND PUBLIC RELIEF 599

Yüan Shih Tsu issued decrees ten times for the relief of the widower, widow, *etc.* We may give a few examples. In the eleventh month of 1820 (1269 A. D.), he decreed that all the provinces give monthly two pecks of rice to each of the poor; and in the first month of 1822, he decreed that they establish almshouses for the shelter of the poor, and give them fuel, besides food. In 1842 (1291 A. D.) he granted clothes for summer and winter to the widows, and in the following year he gave the poor five catties of fuel every day.

Ming T'ai Tsu decreed several times to support the widower, widow, *etc.* In 1937 (1386 A. D.) he made the following law: among poor people, if the age was above eighty, five pecks of rice, three pecks of wine, and five catties of meat were given to each of them monthly. If the age was above ninety, one roll of silk and one catty of cotton were added to this amount annually. Those who owned some farm land were not given rice. To all the four classes, —widower, widow, orphan, the solitary,—six bushels of rice were given annually.[1]

In the present dynasty, every district has an almshouse. According to the *Law Code of the Ts'ing Dynasty*, if the officials do not support the four classes, the very sick person and the infirm and superannuated who need public support, they shall be punished with sixty blows of the long stick.[2] Therefore, the principle of Confucius has been put into actual law, and its effect differs only because of the efficiency of administration.

What we have mentioned is only one phase of public relief which is maintained permanently. The occasional public relief which is issued during any calamity, such as fire, flood,

---

[1] *Continuation of the General Research*, ch. xxxii.
[2] Ch. viii.

or famine, is entirely left out. Here we have simply indicated that, according to the system of Confucius, there is a positive institution for the support of the poor.

3. *Private Charity*

Working along with public relief is private charity. Confucius does not like to have anyone possess a disproportionate amount of wealth over others; but if one has a great fortune and deserves it, he likes to encourage him to diffuse it in a proper way. Hence charitable works are good things.

Tzŭ-kung says to Confucius: " Suppose the case of a man extensively conferring benefits on the people, and able to sasist all, what would you say of him? Might he be called a philanthropist?" " Why speak only of philanthropy in connection with him?" replies Confucius. " Must he not have the qualities of a sage? Even Yao and Shun were still solicitous about this." [1] From this conversation we can see how highly Confucius praises the one who can confer extensively benefits on the people and assist all. Indeed, there is even yet no one who can attain such an ideal.

When Tzŭ-lu asks about the wishes of Confucius, the Master says: " They are, in regard to the old, to settle them comfortably; in regard to friends [who are about the same age as mine], to make them confident [of getting what they want without seeking for it] ; [2] in regard to the young, to treat them tenderly [like a father or a teacher]." [3] In fact, this is the principle of universal love; none will be left behind unsatisfied. It is like heaven, covering everything. Charitable works cannot reach such an ideal, but they are moving in this direction.

[1] *Classics*, vol. i, p. 194.
[2] *Cf. Li Ki*, bk. xxiii, p. 257.
[3] *Classics*, vol. i, p. 183.

For the conduct of a Confucian, Confucius says: "Almsgiving and wealth-distributing is the diffusion of humanity."[1] Mencius says: "The imparting by a man to others of his wealth is called kindness."[2] When Hsun Tzŭ describes the characters of a scholar, he says that a scholar delights in diffusing his wealth to others, and he feels ashamed if he be rich alone.[3] Here we simply point out that private charity is the principle of Confucius, but we have no need to give the historical facts.

To-day, charitable institutions, great or small, are all over different localities. They are controlled by a body of private men, and maintained by voluntary contributions. But they are really quasi-public institutions, and far more important than the government institutions. Take those of Canton, for example. They carry their policy beyond the sphere of Kuangtung province, and assume the burden of inter-provincial tasks. Beside social works, they come into even political and industrial activities. They may have a great development in the future, provided that they have good men.

[1] *Li Ki*, bk. xxxviii, p. 409.
[2] *Classics*, vol. ii, p. 253.
[3] Bk. vi.

PART IV
PUBLIC FINANCE

BOOK IX. PUBLIC FINANCE

CHAPTER XXXII

Public Expenditures

1. THE TERM: PUBLIC FINANCE

PUBLIC finance deals with the revenues and expenditures of governments and is a part of economics. In China, public finance has occupied nearly the whole field of economics, because statesmen and scholars have given their attention mostly to it rather than to private finance. Therefore, when the Chinese use the term economics ("administering wealth"), the hearer may generally narrow its meaning to public finance. But in the Chinese language there is a special term for public finance—"national expenditures" (*kuo yung*). This term first occurs in the "Royal Regulations," and it is used by Ma Tuan-lin as the name of a book in his great encyclopedia.[1] It seems unscientific, because it indicates expressly only expenditures. But it includes revenue as well as expenditures, since there can be no expenditures without revenue. The reason why this term includes only expenditures is because it is characteristic of the Chinese language generally to avoid using more than two characters to express a single concept.

However, if we want to adopt a term more scientific than "national expenditures," we may use the more popular term "national accounting" (*kuo chi*). This term is very old,

[1] *General Research*, chs. xxiii-xxvii.

and it is used for the title of a book during the Tang dynasty. Or, we may use the word "accounting" only (*kuei chi*). This term is used by Confucius.[1] Furthermore, we may adopt the term "wealth and expenditures" (*ts'ai yung*), a better translation being revenue and expenditures. It occurs in the "Great Learning" and the "Doctrine of the Mean," and is spoken of by Mencius.[2] All these three terms may be used in the sense of the English term, public finance. The only difference among them is that, while the first denotes public finance only, the last two may be applied to both public and private finance.

II. NECESSITY OF PUBLIC FINANCE

The question may be raised, why should we have public finance at all? In other words, why should we have government? According to the theory of Hsü Hsing, the ruler should live individually by his own labor, and should not have granary, treasury, or arsenal. If a ruler has such things, he is an oppressor of the people for his own support.[3] Although Hsü Hsing was not an anarchist, his theory is that, while there is a government, there should not be public finance. This is an impossible ideal.

As we have seen, the government exists chiefly for the economic interest of the people. Now, if it is productive, why should they not support it? According to Confucius, government is the result of the division of labor, and public finances are necessary for the support of the public laborers Mencius says:

There is the saying, "Some labor with their minds, and some labor with their strength." Those who labor with their minds

[1] *Classics*, vol. ii, p. 383.
[2] *Classics*, vol. i, pp. 380, 409; and vol. ii, p. 483.
[3] *Cf. supra*, p. 385.

PUBLIC EXPENDITURES

govern others; those who labor with their strength are governed by others. Those who are governed by others support them; those who govern others are supported by them. This is a principle universally recognized.[1]

III. PROPER PROPORTION BETWEEN SOCIAL INCOME AND PUBLIC EXPENDITURES

Since public finance is necessary, we must ask, what is the proper proportion between the total social income and the part devoted to public expenditures. As the produce of the land is the chief source of income of the whole agricultural society, and the land tax is the only source of income of the government, we may say that, according to Confucius' system, the proper proportion is ten to one; that is to say, ten per cent of the total income should go to the state. This is a deduction from the taxing system of Confucius.

The tax of one-tenth is the standard of Confucius' system, which cannot be made heavier nor lighter. The *Spring and Autumn*, the *Great Commentary of the Canon of History*, and Mencius, all stick to this point. Not only a heavier tax than a tithe is bad, but also a lighter tax. Chieh, the last emperor of the Hsia dynasty, was a tyrant; if the tax took four-tenths or five-tenths, it should be called great Chieh; if two-tenths or three-tenths, it should be called small Chieh. Mo was a common name for the barbarous tribes on the north; if the tax took only one-fourteenth or one-fifteenth, it should be called great Mo; if one-twelfth or one-thirteenth, it should be called small Mo. In short, a heavier tax injures the people, so it is imposed only by a tyrant; and a lighter tax cannot defray the necessary expense, so it is found only among barbarians.

Pai Kuei said to Mencius: " I want to take only a twen-

[1] *Classics*, vol. ii, pp. 249-50.

tieth of the produce as the tax. What do you think of it?" Mencius said: "Your way would be that of the Mo. In a country of ten thousand families, would it do to have only one potter?" Pai Kuei replied: "No; the vessels would not be enough to use."

Mencius went on:

In Mo all the five kinds of grain are not grown; it produces only millet. There are no fortified cities, no edifices, no ancestral temples, no ceremonies of sacrifice; there are no princes requiring presents and entertainments; there is no system of officers with their various subordinates. On these accounts a tax of one-twentieth of the produce is sufficient there. But it is the Middle Kingdom that we live in. To banish the relationships of men, and have no administration of superior men—how can such a state of things be thought of? With but few potters a kingdom cannot subsist—how much less can it subsist without superior men?[1]

According to Confucius, the rule of taxation is not the lighter the better, and the rule of public expenditure is not the smaller the better. A tenth of the social income for public expenditures is the proper limit; above this the people are over-burdened, and below this the state is unable to develop its activities.

IV. GENERAL PRINCIPLES OF PUBLIC EXPENDITURES

The financial condition of the state is determined by its political conditions. Therefore, a statistical study of all the departments is necessary as the basis of making a budget. The "Royal Regulations" says:

The minister of accounts prepares the complete accounts of the year to be submitted to the emperor, which are reverently received by the prime minister. The grand director of music,

[1] *Classics*, vol. ii, pp. 441-3.

the grand minister of justice, and the minister of commerce, these three officers, follow the minister of accounts with the completed accounts of their departments to be submitted to the emperor. The grand minister of education, the grand minister of war, and the grand minister of works, reverently receive the completed accounts of their several departments from their various subordinates, and examine them, then presenting them to the emperor. Those subordinates then reverently receive them after being so examined and passed upon. This being done, the aged are feasted and the royal sympathy shown to the husbandmen. The business of the year is concluded, and the national expenditures are regulated.[1]

According to this statement, the national expenditure of next year is determined in the tenth month, when all the departments have reported their completed accounts to the emperor. It seems to identify the fiscal year with the calendar year, but the budget is really prepared two months in advance.

Again, the " Royal Regulations " says:

The prime minister must regulate the national expenditures toward the end of the year. When the five kinds of grain have all been gathered in, he then regulates the national expenditures. They should be according to the size of the territory, as large or small, and the returns of the year, as abundant or poor. On the average of thirty years, he regulates the national expenditures, controlling the outlay to make it conform to the income.

A tenth of the year's expenditures is for sacrifices. . . . A tithe of three years' expenditures is allowed for the rites of funeral. When there is not sufficient for the rites of sacrifices and funeral, it is owing to lavish waste; when there is more than enough, the state is described as affluent. In sacrifices there should be no extravagance in good years, and no niggardliness in bad.

[1] *Li Ki*, bk. iii, p. 239.

The conclusion is that he must regulate the national expenditures in such a way that the government has a surplus sufficient for ten years.[1]

The regulating of national expenditure is really the making of the budget. In the system of Confucius, the budget is prepared by the prime minister. Since the government is monarchical in form, the monarchy cannot be changed easily and frequently, except by peaceful deposition or by great revolution. But the monarchy is not always good, and the people may suffer from a bad ruler. Under such a government, Confucius gives the prime minister a great power, and makes him responsible for the whole administration. Although he is next to the emperor in name, he has the real power of the whole government—as was the case of Shun and Yao, Yü and Shun, Yi Yin and Ch'êng T'ang and T'ai Chia, Fu Yüeh and Kao Tsung, the Duke of Chou and Ch'êng Wang. This is somewhat like the responsible ministry of modern constitutional government. Therefore, the prime minister is empowered to prepare the budget, because he takes the political responsibility. Although there is no parliament to control the budget, it is better in the hands of the prime minister than in those of the emperor.

The principle that expenditure should be according to income is important. It has been recognized that this principle should be applied not only to public finance, but also to private finance. Since the modern development of the budgetary system, however, some people may think that it is good only for private finance, while in public finance this principle should be reversed—the income should be according to the outgo. This is quite a superficial view. From the constitutional standpoint, income is determined after

[1] *Li Ki*, bk. iii, pp. 221-2.

expenditure is decided upon; but from the economic standpoint, expenditure is always regulated by income. The budgetary system is simply a legal process; but, fundamentally, a budget never can go beyond the social income. In fact, social income is the basis and the regulator of public expenditure; hence this principle is quite correct.

Moreover, in ancient China there was no vote for the budget, nor for an increase in taxation. How could the government augment its income to meet its expenditures? To do so it would have to make use of its arbitrary power to tax the people. Of course, Confucius does not allow such a thing. Since he sets forth certain rules for taxation which cannot be freely increased, expenditure must be regulated by income.

Although expenditure is subject to income, it is still elastic. In the first place, a budget is determined according to the returns of the year. If the returns are abundant, the taxes which come from the produce of the field increase; hence expenditure may be raised. If the returns are poor, the taxes decrease; hence the expenditure may be cut down. This is elasticity depending upon the conditions of the particular year. In the second place, it takes the average of thirty years. Therefore, even when there are many successive good years, the government may keep the surplus without waste; and even when there are many successive bad years, it can defray the expense without difficulty.

There rises a question, why should the government keep a surplus sufficient for the use of ten years? In order to understand this rule, we must remind ourselves that ancient China was in the agricultural stage. In ancient times agriculture depended mostly upon nature. Both flood and drought might do great harm to the crops. Therefore, the crops were very uncertain, and the yield from taxation was correspondingly irregular. Under such circumstances, if the government did not keep a surplus, how could it provide for the perpetual life of the state during a period of successive bad years? Therefore, in every three years there must be a surplus sufficient for one year. Taking this as the standard, by the end of thirty years the government should have a surplus sufficient for ten years. After the surplus has reached this amount, the government may remit the future taxes to the people, or may increase its expenditure by extending its functions or activities. The need for the surplus being understood, there is no danger that the surplus will do harm to the government by encouraging extravagance.

As we shall see, public finance in ancient times was mixed up with the private finances of the ruler. Therefore, economy was the chief principle. Confucius attaches great importance to this principle, as we have indicated above.[1] Passing through all ages to the present day, this principle has been recognized as the chief maxim of public finance. The *General Research on the Literature and Authorities of the Present Dynasty* makes " economy " the first section of the book of " national expenditures." In fact, economy is a very sound rule, which is specially important for a monarchical government.

In Chinese history, there are many emperors who practised this principle. But the most conspicuous representatives of this type are Han Wên Ti and Sui Wên Ti. They both began their reigns under very unfavorable conditions, but they made not only the government but also the whole empire rich. They taxed the people little, yet they spent liberally a great amount of money for the public welfare. The fundamental thing that allowed them to do

[1] *Cf. supra*, pp. 81, 363-4.

so was economy. They were frugal in their own expenditures. For example, Han Wên Ti did not dare to build an opened tower because it would cost one hundred pieces of gold coin. He was dressed in black silk, and his curtains and screens were not embroidered. Sui Wên Ti did not eat more than one meat, unless it was at a public banquet; and he did not allow the use of the cloth-bag for keeping dry-ginger, nor the woollen-bag for presenting incense.[1] They seemed too parsimonious, but they were like the type of Yü who was praised by Confucius as being frugal in personal expenditures and liberal in social expenditures.[2]

V. CLASSIFICATIONS OF PUBLIC EXPENDITURES

Although Confucius gives no classification of expenditures, we may deduce two classifications from his writings. But before we give these classifications, we should like to present the classification of the *Official System of Chou*, in order to show the ideas (and perhaps the actual conditions) of the ancient Chinese. According to this, there are nine classes of public expenditures: (1) expenditure for sacrifices, (2) expenditure for entertaining guests, (3) expenditure for funerals, and for famine relief, (4) expenditure for food and clothes of the imperial family, (5) expenditure for various works, (6) expenditure for ceremonial presents, (7) expenditure for keeping oxen and horses, (8) expenditure for general distribution to the officials and (9) expenditure for special gifts on certain occasions. These nine expenditures are separately supplied by the nine taxes which come either from different localities or from different objects. Each expenditure has its fixed standard regulated annually by the prime minister. Therefore, the expenditures of the

---

[1] *History of Han*, ch. iv; *History of Sui*, ch. xxiv; Ma Tuan-lin's remark in his *General Research*, ch. xxiii.

[2] *Cf. supra*, p. 245.

emperor are controlled by the prime minister and governed by laws.[1]

Such a classification, however, is incomplete. If we make an analysis, the first and part of the third are religious expenditures; the second and the sixth are social and diplomatic expenditures; part of the third is charitable expenditure; the eighth may be called general governmental expenditure, as a distribution of salary to officials; the fifth and the seventh may come under both the public expenditures and the private expenditures of the emperor, since the fifth may include the expenditures of public works and the seventh may include military expenditures; the fourth and the ninth are the private expenditures of the emperor.

If we want to make a classification of expenditures according to Confucius' theory, we may base our classification either on the "Great Model" or on the "System of Yao." According to the "Great Model," the classification will be:

    I. Expenditure for economic functions.
        1. Agriculture.
        2. Industry and commerce.
    II. Expenditure for religious services.
        1. Sacrifices.
        2. Funerals.
    III. Expenditure for public works.
    IV. Expenditure for educational functions.
    V. Expenditure for judicial functions.
    VI. Expenditure for social and diplomatic intercourse.
    VII. Expenditure for military protection.

This classification is based on the eight objects of government given in the "Great Model." The first two objects are combined in the first class, while we add the word funerals to the second class.[2]

---

[1] Chs. ii, vi.   [2] *Cf. supra*, pp. 52-53.

According to the "System of Yao," the classification will be:
I. Expenditure for physical welfare.
   1. Public works dealing with the natural environment, such as water and earth.
   2. Agriculture.
   3. Labor.
   4. Natural resources, such as forests, animals and mines.
II. Intellectual and moral welfare.
   1. Education.
   2. Religion, including spiritual services and social entertainment.
   3. Music.
III. Expenditure for governmental business.
   1. Justice.
   2. Secretarial office.

This classification is based on the nine departments of the "System of Yao."[1]

These two classifications are quite similar to each other. The expenditures are mostly for the people, and not for the government itself. They both leave out the private expenditure of the monarch. It shows that Confucius does not ascribe much importance to the expenditure of the ruler.

So long as there is a monarch, however, he must make expenditures, and these form a part of public expenditures. In these two classifications, to what class should the expenditures of the monarch belong? His expenditures should be regulated by the prime minister, and the money is supplied by the department of the treasury. By these two classifications, there is no such department, because Confucius lays more emphasis on the side of the people than on that

[1] *Cf. supra*, p. 75.

of the state. But since this department is necessary, its function may be included in the department of agriculture (or, according to the "Great Model," it may be absorbed by the department of industry and commerce). Even in the Han dynasty, the secretary of the treasury department was still called "the great minister of agriculture." Therefore, these two departments are to be combined into one.

Between these two classifications there is only one great difference, that is, military expenditure.[1] As long as war has not been abolished, Confucius still recognizes that military protection is a necessary expenditure. Therefore, the army is one of the eight objects of the "Great Model." But the "System of Yao" represents the ideal society of Confucius, and there is no war at all. Therefore, it needs no military expenditure, and this classification is more advanced than the first one.

VI. CHARACTERISTICS OF THE PUBLIC EXPENDITURES OF THE ANCIENTS

We wish here to point out the marked features of the public expenditures of the ancients. First, in ancient times, the head of the government represented the sovereignty of the state, and his income involved the total revenue of the state. Therefore, there was no distinction between his private expenditures and public expenditures, and the former were parts of the latter. Or, we may even say that public expenditures were merely the greater parts of his private expenditures, because he was responsible for the public welfare and all public expenditures. All the heads of the government, whether the emperor, or the princes of the feudal states, or the great officials of the noble families—in short, anyone who owned the land of his

---

[1] Since the sixth class of the first classification is included in the religion of the second one, there is no great difference at that point.

domain, whether large or small—received the land tax as income, and this tax was the chief revenue of the whole government. Therefore, there was great confusion in the theories of public finance.

In the " Royal Regulations," however, a distinction is drawn between imperial and official expenditures, althought it is not clear. It is said: " The land tax from the first hundred miles square of the emperor serves to supply the needs of the various public offices; that from the rest of the thousand miles square is for the imperial expenditures." [1] This shows an advance in the principles of finance, because it separates the expenditures used in the various offices from those used by the emperor. But this separation is not complete, because imperial expenditures still involve a large part of public expenditures. The official expenditures used in the various offices are only the general expenditures common to all the different departments, in order to keep the offices going. The reason why the limited revenue which comes from the first hundred miles square only can supply the needs of the offices, will be explained by the next point.

According to the *Official System of Chou*, besides the great treasury which controlled all the revenues, there were the treasury of jade, the inner treasury, and the outer treasury. These three treasuries seemed to be separated from the great treasury, and supplied the expenditures of the imperial family, although they were mixed up with some public expenditures.[2] Therefore, since the Han dynasty, the government has always had two kinds of treasuries: one for public expenditures, and the other for the private expenditures of the emperor. The good emperor may use the private treasury for public expenditures, and the bad em-

[1] *Li Ki*, bk. iii, p. 212.   [2] Ch. vi.

peror may use the public treasury for private expenditures. This is the sign of a government, either good or bad.

Second, the salaries of the officials included the administrative expenditure of their offices. Just as the income of the head of the government included the general expenditure of the state, so the income of the officials included the particular expenditures of their departments. There were two kinds of officials: most of the high officials were granted the public land and collected the land tax at a certain rate for their salaries, the other or low officials received salaries directly from the government. In both cases they were responsible for their administrative expenditure. Therefore the land tax from the first hundred miles square might be sufficient to supply the general needs of the various offices. If the officials were good, they spent liberally of their salaries for the public expenditures; if they were bad, they did the opposite, for their personal use, but they might lose their offices. The salary of the officials was the chief item of public expenditures, because it included administrative expense; but its larger part was not paid out by the public treasury at all, because the land tax which belonged to the officials went directly to them.

Among the nine standard rules of a government, Confucius gives the fifth as " kind and considerate treatment of the whole body of officers." As to the details and purpose of this rule, he says: "According to them a generous confidence, and making their salaries large: this is the way to encourage the body of officers."[1] In fact, when the officers do not own any public land and receive salaries directly from the government, Confucius advocates the principle of giving them large salaries. For the salary-system of Con-

[1] *Classics*, vol. i, pp. 408-410.

fucius, we have already referred to Mencius and the " Royal Regulations." [1]

Third, the military expenditures were small in comparison with modern times. (1) There was no special class called soldiers. All the men at a certain period of life were soldiers, so there was no need of expenditures for the support of a standing army. (2) The people furnished much of their own equipment for military service, while the government paid neither salaries nor wages. (3) There was no transportation of food. When the army went out, the men carried some food, but except for this, it was supported by the feudal states through which it passed or in which it stayed. Therefore, military expenditures were not an important part of public expenditures, and it was chiefly for this reason that only a small amount of public revenue was needed.

Fourth, religious expenditures were too great. The ancients spent a large part of public money for the service of spiritual beings, and such expenditures were really private expenditures of the monarch. In the " Royal Regulations," Confucius sets the limits to such expenditures, as we indicated above. Since sacrifices are regular, the expenditure for them is limited to a tenth of the total expenditure of one year; and, since funerals are irregular and infrequent, the expenditure for them is confined to a tenth of that of three years. Although the expenditure appropriated for funerals is greater than that for sacrifices, the former is really smaller than the latter when we compare them through a period of years. But, during the time of mourning, most of the sacrifices are omitted. This is one reform of Confucius. Yet, according to his ideals, the limits for the religious expenditures set forth in the " Royal Regulations " are

[1] *Cf. supra*, pp. 491-3.

still too large. In fact, they serve as a check for the ancients only, and they should be narrowed to the smallest limit as society progresses.

In conclusion, we may say that the chief part of public expenditure is shifted according to the Three Stages: In the Disorderly Stage, the greater part of public expenditures is spent for the monarch himself, including religious expenditures; in the Advancing Peace Stage, for the state, military expenditures being the chief item; and in the Extreme Peace Stage, for the people, the fostering of their physical, mental and moral welfare being the chief aim. This is the principle of the Three Stages of Confucius. And we may judge the nations or ages by this standard and see in which direction they are tending.

CHAPTER XXXIII

TAXATION IN GENERAL

SOME of the socialistic policies which we have discussed provide special sources of public revenue. But, according to the principles of Confucius, those policies should be adopted not for the sake of getting revenue, but for that of distributing equal wealth to the people. Therefore we shall not consider them in our discussion of sources of revenue. Under this head we shall take up only taxes.

I. DEVELOPMENT OF TAXATION IN THE EARLIEST TIMES

Some information in regard to the development of taxation is given by the terms applied to the tax systems of the Three Dynasties. According to Mencius, the tax system of the Hsia dynasty was called *kung*, "tribute;" that of the Yin dynasty, *tsu*, "assistance;" and that of the Chou dynasty, *ch'ê*, "assessment." Mencius does not explain the word *kung*, because it is clear by itself. He comments on the other two words as follows: "*Ch'ê* means an exaction [from the people], and *tsu* means dependence [of the government]."[1]

During the Hsia dynasty, when the central government was first well organized, the people were glad to pay their tax as a present. Hence the tax system was called *kung*, a voluntary gift of the people to the government. During the Yin dynasty, the people felt that they were doing the government a favor. Hence it was called *tsu*, an assistance of

---
[1] *Classics*, vol. ii, pp. 240-241.

the people for the government, or a "dependence" of the government upon the people. During the Chou dynasty, the government had the independent power to tax the people. Hence it was called *ch'ê*, a universal assessment upon the land, and a compulsory exaction from the people. It is interesting to see that these three terms are sufficient by themselves to indicate the historical development of the tax system.[1]

Although the system of the Chou dynasty reached the highest development, the Confucians preferred the system of the Yin dynasty. The " Royal Regulations " says: "Anciently, the public fields were cultivated by the united labors of the farmers, who paid no tax from the produce of their private fields."[2] Mencius says: " If a ruler require the farmers' assistance for cultivating the public fields, and exact no other taxes from them, then all the farmers of the world will be pleased, and wish to plough in his fields."[3]

The reason why the Confucians preferred the system of Yin grows out of their concern for the good of the people. When the people render their labor to the public fields without paying other taxes, it does not necessarily mean that they would neglect their duty. On the contrary, if there were a good government, they would care first for the public and then for their private interests. The *Canon of Poetry* says: " May it rain first on our public fields, and then come to our private!"[4] This is the sentiment of unselfish people under a good government. Therefore, *Ku-liang's Commentary* says: " When the crop of the private fields is not good, the officials should be blamed; when that of the

[1] *Cf.* Seligman's *Essays in Taxation*, pp. 5-7.
[2] *Li Ki*, bk. iii, p. 227.
[3] *Classics*, vol. ii, p. 200.
[4] *Ibid.*, vol. iv, pt. ii, p. 381.

public fields is not good, the people should be blamed."[1] The former case shows that the officials urge the people to work especially for public interest and leave out private onest while by the latter is meant that the people pay special attention to private and neglect public interests. Therefore, the system of assistance or services binds the government and the people as one body. The government should look after private, and the people after public interests. This is the socialistic idea of Confucius.

His principle is like the political philosophy of the West, " no taxation without representation." For, by the " assessment " system, the government has arbitrary power, and the people are merely tax-payers; but by the " assistance " system, the government is a dependent, and the people are the assistants. Therefore, Confucius makes the latter, from his philosophical point of view, a model tax system, irrespective of the fact that the former is, historically, a more developed form. To-day, in the constitutional governments whose people control taxation, there is fundamentally the same principle as that of the " assistance " system advocated by Confucius.

Furthermore, a tax system should accord with the ability of the people. Mencius quotes a statement of Lung Tzŭ an ancient worthy, as follows:

For regulating the lands, there is no better system than that of assistance, and none is worse than that of tribute.[2] By the tribute system, the regular amount of taxation is fixed by taking the average of several years. In good years, when the grain lies about in abundance, much may be taken without its being oppressive; but the actual exaction is small. In bad

[1] Fifteenth year of Duke Hsüan.

[2] What Lung Tzŭ means by the system of tribute is not the system of the Hsia dynasty, but the practice of the period of Warring States.

years, the produce being not sufficient to repay even the manuring of the fields, this system still requires the full amount. A ruler is the parent of the people. But the people are made to wear looks of distress, that they, after the whole year's toil, are not able to nourish their parents. Furthermore, they are obliged to borrow money at one hundred per cent interest to remit their deficit due to the paying of the tax. Owing to this, old people and children are found lying in the ditches and water-channels. Where, in such a case, is his parental relation to the people?[1]

Now, according to the system of "assistance," the government requires no regular amount of tax from the people, and the people pay taxes in accordance with their annual condition. It is the same principle as that of the modern budget which is renewed every year. In short, the system of "assistance" conforms to the faculty theory.

In Chinese economic history, however, outside of the tax systems of the Three Dynasties advocated by the Confucians, all the tax systems of different dynasties prescribe a fixed amount—an amount not only of the average of several years, but also of a custom of several centuries. This is opposite to the principles of Confucius.

II. SOURCES OF TAXATION

The sources of taxation are not in the government itself, but in the people. Therefore to enrich the people is the way to increase taxation. When Duke Ai of Lu asked Confucius about government, he replied: " There is a policy which makes the people rich. . . ." " Why?" asked the Duke. " By lightening the taxes," replied Confucius, " the people will be rich. . . ." " If so," said the Duke, " I myself shall be poor." Confucius said: " It is said in the *Canon of Poetry*, ' The happy and courteous sovereign is the parent

---

[1] *Classics*, vol. ii, p. 241-2.

TAXATION IN GENERAL

of the people.' I have not seen that the parents are poor when their sons are rich."[1] This conversation indicates the relation between the government and the people, and shows that the social income is the real criterion of the burden of taxation.

One day Duke Ai inquired of Yu Jo, saying: "The year is one of scarcity, and the returns for expenditures are not sufficient; what is to be done?" "Why do you not simply tithe the people?" replied Yu Jo. "With two-tenths," said the Duke, "I find them not enough; how could I do with that system of one-tenth?" Yu Jo answered: "If the people are rich, who will make the ruler alone in want? If the people are in want, who will make the ruler alone rich?"[2] Indeed, to enrich the people is the only way of enriching the government, and to lighten taxation is the most important policy of giving the people the means of developing their economic interest.

The principle of Confucius is like that of Hales, who says: "A king cannot have treasure when his subjects have none." Hsun Tzŭ says: "When the people are poor, the government is also poor; when they are rich, it is also rich."[3] Therefore, the social income is the source, and taxation is only its flow.

The condition of a state can be judged by the policy of taxation. Hsun Tzŭ says:

One who can become an emperor, is to enrich the people in general. One who can become a leader of the feudal princes, is to enrich the soldiers. The state which scarcely stands intact, is to enrich the great officials. The state which is ready to ruin, is to enrich the baskets and to fill the treasuries. When

[1] *Park of Narratives*, bk. vii.
[2] *Classics*, vol. i, p. 255.
[3] Bk. x.

the baskets have been enriched and the treasuries have been filled, the people are impoverished; it is so-called "overflowing above but running away at the bottom." Such a state cannot defend itself at home, nor engage in war abroad. It is simply waiting for its immediate fall.[1]

In 1345 A. K. (794 A. D.), Lu Chih gave a good theory of taxation. He said:

To create offices and to establish government is for the end of nourishing the people. To tax the people and to get revenue is for the means of supporting the government. A wise ruler does not increase the means at the expense of the end. Therefore, he must first pay his attention to the business of the people, and give them a full chance for their economic activities. He must first enrich every family, and then collect the surplus of their income.[2]

This statement points out why government should be established, why the people should be taxed, and how the tax can be collected. In fact, the existence of the government is for the benefit of the people at large, the justification of taxation is for the defraying of governmental expenses, and the paying of taxes is dependent on the ability of the people.

III. DOCTRINE OF THE LIGHT TAX

Since the people are the tax-bearers, and the amount of taxation is dependent on the social income, Confucius advocates the doctrine of the light tax. We must remember that feudalism existed during his time. The princes taxed the people at their will, and did not concern themselves much about the welfare of the people. Therefore, the

---

[1] Bk. ix.
[2] *General Political History*, ch. ccxxxiv.

TAXATION IN GENERAL 627

lighter the tax system was, the better. Confucius said to his prince, Duke Ai: "Employing them only at the proper times, and making the imposts light, this is the way to encourage the people."[1] Mencius says: "By teaching the people to cultivate their land well, and making the taxes light, the people may be made rich."[2] Indeed, the light tax is an important economic principle of Confucius, because it retains the wealth in the hands of people, and helps the development of their economic interest.

During the feudal age, the monarch was the chief consumer of the public revenue. To increase public revenue was to do harm, rather than good, to the people. Hence, Confucius strongly condemned the public financier.

Jan Yu distinguished himself by his economic statesmanship. He said to Confucius: "Suppose a state of sixty or seventy miles square, or one of fifty or sixty miles square, were governed by me for three years, I could make the people rich."[3] Confucius also recognized his statesmanship.[4] But when Jan Yu became the chief officer of the head of the Chi family, who was richer than the Duke of Chou had been, and collected his imposts for him, Confucius reproved Jan Yu: "He is no disciple of mine. My little children, beat the drum and assail him."[5] Mencius comments: "Looking at the subject from this case, we perceive that when a ruler is not practising benevolent government, all his officials who enrich him should be punished by the law of Confucius."[6] Jan Yu was a great disciple of Confucius, so his collecting of imposts would not be in an unjust way. He increased the revenues through his administrative ability. But this was bad enough, because

[1] *Classics*, vol. i, p. 410.
[2] *Ibid.*, vol. ii, p. 462.
[3] *Ibid.*, vol. i, p. 247.
[4] *Ibid.*, p. 175.
[5] *Ibid.*, pp. 242-3.
[6] *Ibid.*, vol. ii, p. 305.

Confucius did not like to enrich a ruler who was not an ideal one.

Mencius gives a strong condemnation of public financiers as follows:

Those who nowadays serve their rulers say, "We can for our rulers enlarge and develop the cultivated land, and fill their treasuries and arsenals." Such persons are nowadays called "good ministers," but anciently they were called "robbers of the people." If a ruler does not follow the right way, nor has his mind bent on benevolence, to seek to enrich him is to enrich a Chieh.[1]

Under the influence of Confucius, the public financiers of different dynasties have been unfavorably criticized. The term "collecting imposts" has become an odious term. On the whole, such a spirit is good, because the Chinese government is monarchical in form, and the court is still the chief consumer of public revenue. When the emperor is good, a small amount of taxes is sufficient, and the nation is also prosperous. When the emperor is bad, especially extravagant, even a large revenue cannot suffice, and the nation is impoverished. Therefore, the teachings of Confucius help the people a great deal in their economic life.

However, the Chinese have carried this point a little too far, and it has retarded the science of finance. Generally, when the government needs more money, the times are not good, especially if a war is in progress. Hence, the people have an impression that the increase of taxation is a bad thing. But as soon as there is need of money, we cannot avoid enlarging the revenue, and the tax system, together with all details, is very important for the national life. If we pay attention to it, we may get a better result; if we

[1] *Classics*, vol. ii, pp. 440-441. For Chieh *cf. supra*, p. 607.

ignore it, we must perish as a nation. Since the Chinese scholars are afraid of talking about money-making, even for public use, China is hampered in the natural development of her financial system. Even when good systems have been originated, they have been abolished or suspended, or at least unjustly criticized.

The fundamental obstacle to the development of the financial system is the form of government. So long as the government is monarchical in form, and the monarch has the greatest power over the public treasuries, the Chinese never appreciate the increase of revenue. The financial system will not be developed to full extent until the establishment of a true constitutional government in the future.

IV. GENERAL PRINCIPLES OF TAXATION

Mencius gives a comprehensive statement covering all the principles of taxation. He says: "A worthy ruler will be gravely complaisant and frugal, showing a respectful politeness to his ministers, and taking from the people only in accordance with certain regulations."[1] This statement is quite general—in short, there must be certain regulations of taxation in order to check the arbitrary power of the government; and all the regulations must be harmonious with the principles, because the regulations are based upon the principles.

The first principle of taxation is equality—a tax must be equally imposed on everyone and in whatever place. It is illustrated in a poem of the *Canon of Poetry*. This poem was written by a great official of the imperial state, who came from T'an, one of the smaller states of the East, showing the inequality of taxation between the East and the West, the imperial state. The most important sentence of

[1] *Classics*, vol. ii, p. 240.

this poem is: "The way of Chou is like a whetstone." It means that the tax system of the Chou dynasty was as equal as a whetstone, contradicting the present condition of the author. Then he describes the misery of the East with the following stanza:

> In the states of the East, large and small,
> The looms are empty.
> Thin shoes of dolichos fibre
> Are made for walking on the hoar-frost.
> Slight and elegant gentlemen
> Walk along the road of Chou.
> Their going and coming
> Makes my heart ache.

Having devoted another stanza to describing the restless hardship of the East, he contrasts the economic condition of the East and that of the West as follows:

> The sons of the East
> Are charged only with heavy burdens without encouragement.
> The sons of the West
> Shine in splendid dresses.

It is evident that the East is poor and the West rich, and that unequal taxation is unjust.[1] In short, a system of taxation must be as equal as a whetstone.

In the *Canon of Poetry* there is a passage: "The pitcher has been exhausted; it is the shame of the jar."[2] Chêng Hsüan explains this passage by the tax system. K'ung Ying-ta explains Chêng's theory as follows:

It means that this is the shame of the drinker who takes charge of the jar. The large jar is like the rich and large family; the small pitcher, the poor and small family. If both the jar and the pitcher are arranged for drinking, one should drink more

[1] *Classics*, vol. iv, pt. ii, pp. 353-4.   [2] *Ibid.*, p. 351.

from the jar and less from the pitcher until both are exhausted; this is the pinciple of equality. It is just the same principle as that of taxation: when both the rich and the poor are taxed, in money as well as in labor, one should tax the rich more and the poor less, up to the point that both can bear the burden; this is also the principle of equality.

Although such explanation may not be the original meaning of the text, it is the theory of taxation of the Confucians. According to Chêng and K'ung, a tax should be progressive rather than proportional, because it should put the rich and the poor on the same footing in accordance with their ability.

The second principle of taxation is universality—a tax must reach everybody. This principle is illustrated by a poem of the *Canon of Poetry*. As we shall see that personal service is one kind of taxes, this poem speaks of this duty. It was written by an officer who complains of the arduous and continual duties unequally imposed upon him, and keeping him away from his duty to his parents, while others are left to enjoy their ease. We may select from it three stanzas, as follows:

> Under the wide heaven,
> All is the king's land.
> Within the sea-boundaries of the land,
> All are the king's citizens.
> His great officials are unfair,
> Making me serve as if I were the only one having ability.
>
> My four horses never halt;
> The king's business allows no rest.
> They praise me as I am still not old;
> They think very few are as vigorous as I.
> While the backbone retains its strength,
> I must plan and labor in all parts of the kingdom.

> Some enjoy their ease and rest,
> And others are worn out in the service of the state.
> Some rest and loll upon their couches,
> And others never cease to march forward.[1]

Although this poem speaks only of personal duties, it points out clearly the principle of universality. Indeed, any kind of taxes must be based on universality, preventing anyone's escaping from supporting the state.

Although universality is the general principle of taxation, there are some exceptions. Take for example the land tax. Mencius says: "From the highest officers to the lowest, each one must have his 'holy field,' consisting of fifty acres."[2] The "Royal Regulations" says: "No tax was levied from the 'holy field.'"[3] The holy field was assigned to the families of the officials for the sacrifices to their ancestors. It served as a social distinction for worthy men, so it was exempted from taxation.

In the social system of Confucius there are two classes, the governing class and the governed. The governing class being the salaried class, pays no land tax. Their salaries come from the produce of the land, which is paid by the farmers as tax. The governed class is the only class of taxpayers who receive public land from the government and pay one-tenth of its produce to the government as tax. Therefore, the members of the former class are called superior men; those of the latter, country-men. Mencius says: "If there were no superior men, there would be nobody qualified to rule the country-men. If there were no country-men, there would be nobody having ability to support the superior men."[4]

---

[1] *Classics*, vol. iv, pt. ii, pp. 360-2.
[2] *Ibid.*, vol. ii, p. 244.
[3] *Li Ki*, bk. iii, p. 227.
[4] *Classics*, vol. ii, p. 244; cf. also *supra*, pp. 606-7.

In fact, according to the Confucians, the land tax is practically the only tax. Because the officials do not cultivate the land, they are not required to pay land tax. Although they receive the land tax as their salary, such an income is the compensation paid by the state for their service, so that it is not subject to taxation. Besides the officials, even the common people employed in the government offices do not pay the land tax, because they cultivate no land. This shows that the officials really do not get any special privilege, and that the exemption of fifty acres of the " holy field " of each official does not affect the principle of universality.

Take personal service for another example. While common people are required to serve the state physically, officials serving the state mentally are exempted from physical service. However, all officials, whether high or low, are responsible for military service in time of war. Therefore, the partial exemption of officials from physical labor, such as the different kinds of public works, does not affect the principle of universality.

Moreover, under Confucius' system, these two classes are interchangeable. It is not a system of caste, but a division of labor. It simply gives just reward to the higher class, and inspires the ambition of the lower class, because anyone can get the same exemption as soon as he raises himself to the higher class. To-day, there is no distribution of public land nor any personal service; everyone is on the same footing. Therefore, the tax system is apparently quite universal.

V. CLASSIFICATION OF TAXES

As to the classification of taxes, there is a complete statement of the tax system given in *Elder Tai's Record*.[1] Confucius says:

[1] Bk. xxxix; *cf. Li Ki*, bk. iii, p. 227.

Formerly, the wise kings inspected the travelers at the custom houses, but did not levy duty upon commodities. They established public warehouses in the market-places, but did not tax commodities. They taxed one-tenth of the produce of the land. They employed the labor of the people not more than three days in one year. The entering into the mountains and the meres by the people was limited to the proper times by regulations, but not by tax. All these six things [custom-houses, market-places, land, personal labor, mountains and meres], may be regarded as the ways of getting revenue. But the wise kings taxed only two things [land and personal labor], in a moderate way, leaving the other four untaxed.

From this statement of Confucius we know that there were six kinds of taxes in his time. But according to his idea, there should be only two kinds of moderate taxes.[1] His fundamental point is to abolish all kinds of indirect taxes.

There is another passage given by Confucius describing the tax system of the ancient kings, which is arranged according to the ability to pay. He says:

The ancient kings, having regulated the land, required labor from the people to cultivate the public fields as a tax on their private fields in accordance with their strength; and the location of their residence from the public fields was also made equal in distance. They taxed the ground of their residence according to their income, but the general condition of each family was also taken into consideration. They made the people serve in the public works according to the number of men, but the old and the young were exempted. Moreover, widowers, widows, orphans and sick persons, were exempted from these three taxes, except in time of war. Even in time of war, the total amount of annual tax paid by nine hundred acres of land was not over six hundred and forty bushels of

---

[1] The ground tax of the house is included in the term land tax.

the whole plant of the grain, two hundred and forty pecks of straw, and sixteen pecks of rice.[1]

According to this statement of Confucius, there are three kinds of taxes. One is the land tax; another, the ground tax; and the third, a tax in the form of personal service. The ground tax needs a little explanation. As silk is made by women from the mulberry trees grown around the house which is on public land and under public control, the ground of the house is required to pay hempen-cloth or silk. This is a contribution of the women just as the land tax paid in grain is a contribution of the men. This is also a tax on income derived from the ground. Therefore, the general condition of the family, rich or not, should be considered. Under such a consideration, it is not a tax on gross income, but on net income, because, when the poor family has no net income left, it is exempted. This tax has become the family tax in later times, known as the "door tax," a tax on property and income.

These three kinds of taxes should be required at different times. The ground tax paid in cloth and silk is required in summer; the land tax paid in grain, in autumn; and the personal-service tax, in winter. Mencius says:

There are exactions of hempen-cloth and silk, of grain, and of personal service. The superior man in the government requiries but one of these at once, deferring to collect the other two. If he require two of them at once, then the people die of hunger. If he require the three at once, fathers and sons are separated.[2]

During the Chou dynasty, when the common laborer

[1] *Narratives of Nations*, bk. v.
[2] *Classics*, vol. ii, p. 491.

under his employment could not render the public personal service, he was required to pay money as the poll tax (*fu pu*); and, when nothing was planted around the house, money was required as the ground tax (*li pu*). These were justifiable. But in Mencius' time the princes required the poll tax from the people even though they had served the public labor, and the ground tax from the houses even though they had already contributed silk and cloth. It meant that the person and the ground were taxed twice. Therefore, Mencius said: " If, in the residential districts, a ruler did not impose the poll tax and the ground tax paid in money, then the people of the world would be pleased, and wish to become his citizens." [1]

In China there is no legal separation of local from national revenue. Every tax is national. It is simply collected by local officers who are appointed by the central government. The local officers have no legal power to impose or expend any tax at all, except one approved by the emperor through the recommendation of the minister of finance.

However, as a matter of fact, there has always been a division of local and national revenue. We shall see that such a division began at the time of Yü.[2] During the reign of Tang Hsien Tsung (1357-1371, or 806-820 A. D.), the revenue of the whole empire began to be divided into three parts—one for the central government, one for the provincial government, and one for the prefecture. The Sung dynasty did the same way. Even at the present day there are two parts of revenue—one is reserved for the defraying of local expenditures, and the other sent to the central government. Therefore, we may say that China has

[1] *Cf. Classics,* vol. ii, p. 200. Since the ground tax is only a subordinate of the land tax, we shall not discuss it any farther.
[2] *Cf. infra,* pp. 639-640.

the principle of separating local from national taxes. But it is a separation only of uses, not of sources. This has caused great trouble in the financial system. Although the Chinese government has been a centralized government since the Hsia dynasty, its practices become a decentralized government because the sources of taxation are not separated. However, it is promised that they shall be separated during the present year.

Since China has no separation of the sources of taxation,[1] we shall classify the taxes not into national and local taxes, but into direct and indirect taxes.

[1] In reality, China has a separate category of local taxes. Besides the local officers illegally collecting imposts, the people themselves assess and collect the true taxes for the local welfare. In the country towns, they are controlled by the gentry and the elders; in the cities, by the merchants. They are justly imposed, and their administration is efficient and democratic. Hence the people do not even know that they are taxes, and they are not called taxes.

CHAPTER XXXIV

DIRECT TAXES

I. LAND TAX

1. The Oldest System of Land Tax Described by Confucius

ALTHOUGH the land tax began with Huang Ti, there is no older system than that of the " Tribute of Yü," and this system is authorized by Confucius. According to the " Tribute of Yü," the land of the nine provinces is classified into nine grades; and the amount of tax to be collected from these nine provinces, into nine degrees. These grades and degrees are intended to afford merely a rough method of classification and do not correspond in individual cases. Thus, within any province, all the land cannot very well be of the same grade, and the tax, therefore, cannot be of the same degree. The grades of land and the degrees of tax are merely averages. Moreover, taking a province as a whole, the degree of tax does not necessarily correspond with the grade of land. For, if the cultivation of the people is good, the one-tenth tax on the lower grade of land will afford more revenue; when it is poor, the one-tenth tax on the higher grade will afford less. Although the amount of tax of the nine provinces varies in nine degrees, the rate of tax, it must be clearly understood, is uniform throughout the whole empire, that is, one-tenth. It is because the territory of each province and its population differ from those of the other provinces that its contribution to the total tax fund must be different.

DIRECT TAXES

There is a significant principle in the "Tribute of Yü," that is, the distinction between the central and the local taxes. Both the central and the local governments tax the land at the same rate, yet there is a distinction.

In the imperial province, Ki Chow, the tax is paid in kind. Five hundred miles constitute the "imperial domain," that is, five hundred miles from the capital as a center to the north, south, east and west; or, in other words, a square of 1,000 miles, making the imperial domain equal to an area of 1,000,000 square miles. In fact, the imperial domain is divided up on each side of the capital into five zones, each having the same width, namely, one hundred miles. From the first hundred miles, the people bring, as tax, the whole plant of the grain; from the second, they bring the ears; from the third, they bring only the straw, but attend to the transportation of the grain which comes from the fourth and the fifth hundred miles; from the fourth, they give the grain in the husk; and from the fifth, the grain cleaned.

This is, of course, a primitive system of taxation, but its principle is admirable. Since the first zone surrounding the capital is the nearest, they bring the whole plant. The second is a little farther away, so they bring only the ears. The third is still farther, so they bring only the straw without grain; this is least valuable of all, but they give also personal service. The fourth is much farther, so they give the grain in husk; and the fifth is the farthest, so they give only the grain cleaned. From the first zone to the third, they all bring the produce to the capital themselves; but the fourth and fifth do not bring the grain to the capital, but convey it only to the third zone. This is the principle of justice. The contributions of different zones are arranged with reference to their distance from the capital and the resulting labor of transportation. The plan takes both the amount of taxation and the cost of transportation into consideration, and aims to make all the people bear the same burden.

This system of taxation in the imperial domain is the standard for the whole empire. The princes of different feudal states tax the land in the same way, so that the " Tribute of Yü " does not give the details in the states. But what marks the difference between the central and the local taxes is that, the local tax paid to the central government by the princes is not in kind, but in value.

The princes tax the people at the rate of one-tenth. Besides retaining a part of it for the expenditure of their states, they pay a certain part of the total amount of land tax to the imperial government. The great states pay one-half; the middle class of states, one-third; and the small states, one-fourth. The princes take the sum of the fixed amount to buy the principal articles of their states, and send them to the imperial capital. Such payment, known as "tribute." is a part of the local tax due to the central government. While the imperial province pays its tax in kind directly to the government without sending tribute, all the other eight provinces pay no other tax, except the tribute, which is itself a tax.

All the tribute goes to the government factories. However, some of the tribute is put in baskets of bamboo, which go to the female factory. Hence there is a distinction between the tribute in general and the " baskets " in particular For the convenience of our readers, we shall make a table showing the different articles paid as tribute or baskets by the provinces and the barbarous tribes. Fron the following table we can imagine the economic development during the Yü dynasty (1704-1655 B. K. or 2255-226 B. C.).

DIRECT TAXES

LIST OF COMMODITIES SENT AS TRIBUTE

Provinces	Taxes		Contributions not Taxes
	Tribute	Baskets	Tribute from the Barbarians
Ki Chow.	—	—	Dresses of skins from the barbarians of the islands.
Yên Chow.	Varnish, silk.	Woven ornamental fabrics.	—
Ts'ing Chow.	Salt, fine grass-cloth, various productions of the sea, silk, hemp, lead, pine-trees, and strange stones, from the valleys of the Tai.	Silk from the mountain mulberries.	—
Sü Chow.	Earth of five different colors, variegated feathers of pheasants from the valleys of the Yü, solitary dryandra from the south of Mount Yi, sounding stones that seem to float near the banks of the Sze.	Deep azure silks, checkered silk with a black warp and white woof, and fabric white and unornamented.	Oyster pearls and fish from the barbarians about the Hwai.
Yang Chow.	Gold, silver, copper, *yao* and *kun* stones, bamboos small and large, ivory, hides, feathers, hair, and timber. Small oranges and pummeloes rendered when required.	Woven variegated silks.	Garments of grass from the barbarians of the islands.
King Chow.	Feathers, hair, ivory, hides, gold, silver, copper, *ch'un* tree, wood for bows, cedars, cypresses, grindstones, whetstones, stones for arrow-heads, cinnabar, three-ribbed rush. *Ch'un* and *lu* bamboos, *hu* tree, rendered when required. Great tortoise presented when caught.	Deep azure and purple silken fabrics, and white strings of pearls that are not quite round.	—
Yü Chow.	Varnish, hemp, finer hempen cloth, coarser hempen cloth. Stones for polishing sounding-stones rendered when required.	Fine silken fabrics, and fine floss-silk.	—
Liang Chow.	Musical gem-stones, iron, silver, steel, stones for arrow-heads, sounding-stones.	—	Skins of bears, great bears, foxes, and jackals, and articles woven with their hair, from the barbarians of Hsi-ch'ing.
Yung Chow.	*Ch'iu* and *lin* gem-stones, and the *lang-kan* precious stones.	—	Hair-cloth and skins from the western barbarians.

From this table we learn that there are two knids of people: the civilized and the barbarian. The nine provinces are divided into five domains, namely, (1) the imperial domain, (2) the domain of the nobles, (3) the peace-securing domain, (4) the domain of restraint, and (5) the wild domain. Each domain consists of one thousand miles square, and the five domains amount to five thousand miles square. The first three domains are called Middle Kingdom, and the last two, the barbarians. Beyond the five domains, all the territories still belong to the nine provinces. Those regions without the nine provinces are occupied by the barbarians and called " Four Seas." These are the political divisions of ancient China, and they form the basis of taxation.

Within the Middle Kingdom the land is divided into *tsing tien*, and the people pay a regular tax at the rate of one-tenth of their produce. All the fields are classified with reference to their soils into three classes, which are subdivided into nine classes. The classification of the soils forms the basis of the degree of tax. In fact, the amount of tax must be in accordance with the soils; this is the principle of faculty, or ability to pay.

The lands occupied by barbarians, whether within or without the nine provinces, are not divided into *tsing tien*, and the barbarians are not required to pay regular taxes. Those who live in the nine provinces, are the subjects of the empire, and are obliged to send tribute. Those who live in the " Four Seas," are not imperial subjects, and send tribute only as an acknowledgment of the supreme civilization. All the barbarians send their tribute by the different waterways which are used by different provinces.

The tribute from the different provinces consists mostly of native products. The articles distinguished by the names of particular localities such as silk, hemp, lead, pine-trees and strange stones from the valleys of the Tai, variegated feathers of pheasants from the valleys of the Yü, *etc.*, must be products of these localities. When a state is located out of such localities, it should, therefore, buy these articles from the neighboring states, and send them as its tribute. In this way a state which has no distinguishable product, is still held to the obligation of sending tribute. This system proves that there was a certain degree of commercial development.

The sending of tribute instead of agricultural products is really an advancement of civilization. Because the imperial domain is near the capital, the people pay produce instead of tribute; and because the other four domains are far from the capital, the people pay produce to the local governments of their states, and the princes convert them into tribute and send it to the capital. This is for the convenience of both the people and the princes, and has the advantage of saving the cost of transportation. It was this that Sung Shên Tsung referred to when he said that the "Tribute of Yü" conforms to the idea of the system of "equal transportation."[1]

The question naturally arises, why the princes should not send money instead of tribute, since money would be still more convenient. In all probability the economic development of that time had not yet reached the stage of money economy. Even if it had, however, there were also other reasons for sending tribute. First, the government was the greatest consumer of the whole empire, and it needed all the varied things which came as tribute. Secondly, since the government was the only large single consumer, and the general economic condition of the people was still very low, the government would find it very difficult to buy such

[1] *General Research*, ch. xx.

things from the merchants, since they would not bring many of them to the imperial capital, there being no commercial demand for them to make this profitable. Therefore, if all the provinces had sent money instead of tribute, it would have been of less use to the government than the tribute, because the government would have been unable to convert the money into the articles which it needed. Thirdly, money was not generally used in a large amount by the people, so the princes could more easily secure the articles than collect money from their subjects. Fourthly, even if they could collect a large sum of money, it would not have been good for the provinces to send away their circulating money to the imperial capital, since the money circulating in their markets was small in amount. Nor would it have been good for the capital to receive the additional money from all the pirovinces, as this would have raised the prices in its markets. In short, we must remember that there were no bills of exchange, so money if sent at all, would have to be sent in cash, and that, since the feudal states were semi-independent, and the central government did not generally spend money outside of the imperial domain, no exchanges were made. Therefore, the sending of money would really not have been a good policy. Although the paying of taxes in tribute is not so highly developed a form of taxation as paying them in money, it is still a great advance, since there is a conversion of the tax paid in kind into the tax paid in value, which is represented by the tribute.

In Chinese economic history there are two institutions contrary to the principles of the " Tribute of Yü." The one is the canal-transportation of rice from the provinces to the capital. According to the " Tribute of Yü," only the imperial domain pays agricultural products as taxes, while other provinces send only their tribute. In fact, the capital depends upon its own domain for its food supply, and does not require the farther provinces to transport their rice to it. The system of transporting rice to the capital began with Han Kao Ti (350-357 A. K. or 202-195 B. C.). At the beginning, the annual transportation amounted to only several hundred thousand bushels. But, during the reign of Han Wu Ti, it increased to six million bushels. From that time to the present day the food supply of the capital has come from great distances, and the cost of transportation is a great waste of the public revenue.

Since this system is against the principles of the " Tribute of Yü," and involves economic waste, why has it continued for so long a time? Why did none of the statesmen of different dynasties abolish it? To explain this we may consider it from different standpoints. First, it has economic reasons. (a) As the capital is the center of industry and commerce, but not of agriculture, it needs the provinces to supply its food. But this is a sign of the neglect of agriculture. As China was supposed to be an agricultural country, every locality should have a sufficient supply of food. Although the capital itself cannot produce sufficient rice, why should its neighborhood not be able to supply its demand? This is the chief defect of the government, that it does not develop the land in its surrounding districts. (b) In general, at the beginning of a dynasty, the transportation of rice is small in amount, but in its middle or end has become great. This shows the increasing extravagance of the government. Whenever the government becomes extravagant, it consumes more rice; hence this transportation cannot be stopped. (c) Even though the neighbors of the capital did not produce rice enough, and the government was extravagant, why should the government not buy rice from merchants in the capital instead of transporting it from a long distance? Because there was no private transportation of rice on a sufficiently large scale to support the government. In old times, transportation, especially of rice, was extremely difficult. The cost of transportation was so great that the merchants might make no profit, but actually lose. Therefore, the government itself transported rice, and appointed high officials to take charge of it. This was the fundamental reason for the existence of this system.

Secondly, there are military and political reasons. The chief consumers of rice are not the members of the court, but the soldiers. The amount of rice transported corresponds with the number of soldiers. In order to strengthen the power of the capital, the government must have its own transportation of food, employing its own ships and its own employees, irrespective of any circumstance.

To-day, although the capital needs the food supply from the southern provinces, the system of canal-transportation should be abolished. First, the government should develop the land to the north for the fundamental solution of this problem. Secondly, it may depend on the private transportation of the merchants, since the transportation is now much easier than it was formerly. Thirdly, even if the government transportation were necessary, the rice can be transported either along the sea-coast or by the railways This is much simpler and more economical. Therefore, the abolition of canal-transportation, and the change from a tax paid in rice for the transportation to a tax paid in money must occur in the near future.

The other institution contrary to the principles of the " Tribute of Yü " is the requirement of tribute from different localities. What the " Tribute of Yü " calls ribute is really the land tax, which is the only tax of the government. But, from the Han dynasty, the government required the famous products of different places as tribute. At the beginning, it always said that the value of the tribute should be substituted for the amount of the regular taxes. But in later times it demanded the tribute in addition to the regular taxes. Sometimes bad rulers wanted such things, and sometimes bad officials presented them in the expectation of receiving some special favor. This was really an unlawful tax, and the people suffered a great deal. Such a bad custom is nominally abolished by the present dynasty, and those products needed by the government are bought with public money by the officials.[1] But the purchases by the officials still give trouble to the people, and such bad results will be extinguished only under a real constitutional government.

We have already seen that the Three Dynasties taxed the land at the same rate of one-tenth, and that such rate was uniform throughout the whole empire.[2] But this might be simply the ideal plan of Confucius, not conforming in fact to the system of the ancients. Take, for example, the *Official System of Chou*. The tax on the gardens and the houses of the cities was at the rate of one-twentieth of their income; that on the land of the suburbs, one-tenth; that on the land of the country, three-twentieths; that on the land of the crown domain governed by the imperial officers, two-tenths; and that on the timber land, five-twentieths.[3] This system had different rates in regard to different lands or to the same land in different localities. It has been disputed because it is not harmonious with the principles of Confucius. Of course, it does not conform to Confucius' system, but it might nevertheless have been the actual system of the Chou dynasty.

Confucius approves of the system of tithes, and such a

[1] The tribute sent by the dependencies is not under this rule, because the dependencies do not pay regular taxes.
[2] *Cf. supra*, p. 499.
[3] Ch. xiii.

theory is justifiable. Prof. Edwin R. A. Seligman says: " Since land itself is not private property, since land is not bought and sold, the faculty of the taxpayer can be measured not by the value of the land, but by the value of its produce, which is in some proportion to the quantity of the land." [1] Therefore, although a tithe is a tax on the gross produce, it is a good test of ability to pay.

According to Ricardo, the chief objection to tithes is that they are not a permanent and fixed tax, but increase in value, in proportion as the difficulty of producing corn increases.[2] This is true, but under Confucius' system this objection practically does not exist. Every man receives the same amount of land, one hundred acres, from the government, produces a similar amount of product, and pays a similar amount of tax. There is no great difference in regard to either the increasing difficulty of producing corn, or the value of the tax. Although the productivity of the farmers varies in five grades,[3] the majority of them must be the ordinary farmers, neither the best nor the worst. Therefore, a rate of tax equal to one-tenth of the produce is really a permanent and fixed tax.

It should be noted that the tithe is a tax for the state, not for the church. The church in China has no revenue from taxation whatever, since it is without the taxing power.

2. *Later Development of the Land Tax*

The land tax is the chief tax of China, so there are numerous interesting facts about it. We shall not go into all the details, but shall merely pick out the most important events to show its development. Since the tax system of the Three

---

[1] *Essays in Taxation*, p. 14.
[2] *Political Economy*, Bohn's edition, pp. 158-9.
[3] *Cf. supra*, pp. 390-391.

DIRECT TAXES 649

Dynasties is mixed up with the theories of Confucius, and has been explained above, we shall begin with the end of the Chou dynasty.

In 43 B. K. (594 B. C.), Duke Hsüan of Lu began to tax the land of the people by acres. Formerly, as the public fields existed, the people simply contributed their labor to the public fields, and paid only its produce as a tax. This was for the enlargement of the people's wealth. But, since Duke Hsüan did not care much for the people, they did not pay much attention to the public fields. Therefore, he taxed their private fields directly by acres, and abandoned the system of public fields. Although the rate of tax was still one-tenth, the government exercised more power over the people, and the tax was more efficient and regular. This was really an advance in the tax system. But Confucius did not like it, because he thought that Duke Hsüan would exhaust the wealth of the people, and he recorded his disapproval in the *Spring and Autumn*.[1]

In 204 A. K. (348 B. C.), just after the destruction of *tsing tien* (202 A. K.), the state of Ch'in began to enact a tax system. This was an important event, because the land began to be subject to private ownership, and the basis of taxation was changed from gross produce to property. The rate of tax was unknown, but this system was really an advance.

The rate of land tax was low during the Han dynasty. At the beginning, the rate was one-fifteenth of its produce. But the most economical emperor was Han Wên Ti. In the twelfth year of his reign, he remitted half the land tax. In the next year (385 A. K. or 167 B. C.) he remitted it entirely. In the second year of his son's reign (397 A. K. or 155 B. C.) the government began to renew

---

[1] *Cf. Classics*, vol. v, pt. i, p. 329.

the land tax which had been remitted for twelve years. Then its rate was reduced to one-thirtieth, and it was paid according to the number of acres.

During the first part of the reign of Han Chang Ti (about 627-629 A. K. or 76-78 A. D.), the land tax was paid in money. In 716 A. K. (165 A. D.), Han Huan Ti began to require ten copper coins for each acre. It was the first time that money was required for the land tax. Han Ling Ti did the same in 736 A. K. (185 A. D.) Both were bad emperors, and such a tax was an addition to the regular tax. However, this was not a permanent system.

From the Tsin dynasty to the first part of the Tang dynasty the land tax was mixed up with the poll tax and the family tax. The person or the family was the basis of taxation. Each person or family paid a uniform rate of taxes. At that time there was an equal distribution of public land, so that the faculty of everyone was practically equal, and each person was able to pay an equal tax.

After the Three Dynasties, the most famous system of taxation was the three-taxes system of the Tang dynasty. In 1175 A. K. (624 A. D.), the law was made as follows: Among all the recipients of public land, each adult man annually contributed two bushels of rice, which was called land tax. According to the native products of its town, each family annually contributed any of the three kinds of silk—*chüan, ling* and *shih*—twenty cubits in all, and three taels of floss-silk; if there was no silk industry, it paid twenty-five cubits of cloth and three catties of flax; such a tax was called the family tax. The regular length of time for the public service was twenty days in one year. During a leap year, two days were added. He who did not serve it gave three cubits of silk for each day. Such a tax was called a labor tax, or poll tax. In some special cases, if fifteen days were added, the family tax was remitted; if thirty days were added, both the land tax and the family tax were remitted. But, on the whole, the service was not longer than fifty days.[1]

All these three taxes were in harmony with the faculty of the people. Since each man received one hundred acres of public land, he was able to pay the land tax; since he had a family, he was able to pay the family tax; and since he had his own body, he was able to pay the labor tax. All the requirements were based upon what he had, not upon what he had not. But the distribution of the public land was the fundamental thing which enabled him to pay all the taxes. This is the reason that this law was famous.

Under the system of the three taxes, the person was the basis of taxation, and the taxes were paid in kind, not in money. But after the decay of this system, Yang Yen, the prime minister, established the famous system of summer and autumn taxes in 1331 A. K. (780 A. D.). The decree reads as follows:

All families, no matter whether native or stranger, should be registered according to their present residence. All persons, no matter whether adult or young, should be classified according to their wealth. . . . The taxes of the permanent residents are collected twice a year, in summer and autumn. Those who find it more convenient may pay them in three periods. All other direct taxes are abolished. But the fixed amount of poll tax will remain. The total land tax is fixed according to the amount of land which has been cultivated in the year of [1330 A. K.]. The summer tax should be paid not later than the sixth month, and the autumn tax not later than the eleventh month.[2]

[1] *Old History of Tang*, ch. xlviii. *General Political History*, ch. ccxxxiv. *General Research*, ch. ii.
[2] *Old History of Tang*, ch. xlviii.

Yang Yen was a great reformer. He abolished all other direct taxes, and reduced them to the land tax only. The poll tax was included in the land tax. This was the first time that the system of "single whip"[1] was originated. He made no difference between the stranger and the native, nor between the young and the adult. The only basis of direct taxation was the land, not the person. It was simple and uniform. The officials could not practice corruption, nor could the people evade their dues. Since this time the land tax has been collected in money, and in two periods of the year. This was an epoch-making revolution in the financial systen. It changed entirely the tax system of the ancients, and served as a model for all succeeding dynasties.

In 1345 A. K. (794 A. D.), Lu Chih criticized the system of summer and autumn taxes as follows:

The production of wealth is dependent upon the labor of men. Therefore, when the ancient kings regulated taxation, they took the person as the basis. They did not increase one's land tax because he was diligent in agriculture, nor diminish it because he was lazy; hence the land products were plentiful. They did not augment the family tax because the family accumulated its property, nor exempt it because the family was not a native; hence the people were firmly attached to their locality. They did not give the person more work because he was good, nor relieve anyone of personal service because he was neglectful; hence the people were diligent. Therefore the people were comfortable in their living, and tireless in their efforts for the production of wealth.

Now, the establishment of the summer and autumn taxes takes only income and property, not the person, as the basis But, among the classes of income and property, some are kept in a pocket or a box, and some are stored up in gardens or granaries. In the former case, although they are very

---

[1] *Cf. infra*, pp. 656, 667-8.

valuable things, nobody can see them. In the latter case, although their value may be little, everyone thinks that their owner is rich. Some are circulating and productive capital goods, and some are used for consumption, such as houses and furniture. The former may be in a small quantity, but they receive income every day. The latter may be capitalized at a high price, but they do not bring any profit even in a whole year. There are many cases similar to these. If we take them as a whole for the assessment, it must lose equity and increase fraudulence. Hence, those who keep personal property and move anywhere usually escape taxes, and those who pursue agriculture and establish their permanent home always have to pay. Such a system induces the people to commit fraud, and tends to drive them away because of their desire to escape public labor. Their productive effort must be weakened, and the public revenue must be insufficient.[1]

The theory of Lu Chih represents the old theory of taxation. Its first part clings to the old system, the person being the basis. It held true in the ancient time, since each person was nearly equal to every other, and received an equal share of land. But it was not true in the medieval time, when the ancient system of land-distribution was broken up, and the wealth of the people had become unequal. Moreover, his theory is contrary to the fundamental principle of taxation. According to him, taxes on income and property are a penalty upon the efficient producer. He failed to realize the principle of faculty. However, the latter part of his theory is good, because it points out the defects in the summer-and-autumn-taxes system. The objections which he urges are practically the same as those brought against the general property tax to-day.[2]

According to the opinion of Ma Tuan-lin, the basis of

---

[1] *General Political History*, ch. ccxxxiv.
[2] Seligman's *Essays in Taxation*, pp. 24-33.

taxation from the Tsin dynasty to the Tang dynasty was the family rather than the land. But, since every family received a share of land, the family tax really included the land tax. Although the Tang dynasty separated the three taxes, the payer of them was also the land-holder. In the middle part of this dynasty land became private property, being sold and bought, and the system of land distribution was entirely broken down. The people who formerly paid the three taxes were mostly not landholders. How could they be taxed in the same way as the rich? Moreover, after the rebellions (1306-1313 A. K. or 755-762 A. D.) the population was changed, and the census could not be the basis of taxation. The only thing unchanged was the land. Therefore, to take the amount of land cultivated in the year 1330 A. K. as the fixed amount for the establishment of the summer and autumn taxes was a good system for the time being, although it was not the permanent plan of the state. If the three-taxes system should be reestablished, the land-distribution system must be first reestablished. As long as the land could not be equally distributed, the system of summer and autumn taxes was the best.

Another tax, the "mouth tax" of different dynasties, always took the person as the basis, modification being made only in accordance with age. But inequality in wealth has existed for a long time. According to the old system, although a young boy may inherit a great fortune, he pays a small tax; while the adult, although he may be very poor, is burdened with a heavy tax. Is this not unjust and absurd? Now, the system of summer and autumn taxes classified the people according to their wealth without regard to their age. This is quite correct. The defects of this system pointed out by Lu Chih rest on the administration, but not on the system itself. For both agriculture and commerce can get riches. Although the merchants find it easier to evade taxes, and the farmers suffer from the burden, the sufferers are nevertheless the rich people. Is it not comparatively better than to tax the people according to the original census without regard to their wealth?

Ma Tuan-lin goes still a step further, to show the defects of a tax system based on the person. According to Chinese history (before the present dynasty), the acres of land cultivated increased, but the population decreased. He cites this to show that the "mouth tax" and the "door tax" made the people dishonest. Then he points out the incorrectness of the theory of Lu Chih, who urged that the basis of taxation should be the person, by saying that the abilities of men are not equal. Although they are all human beings, some are clever and some are stupid. Although they all do business, some are successful and some fail. There are people who rise from deep poverty to become millionaires, and who have additional ability to support others. There are other people who cannot preserve even a little of their inheritance, and who regard even their lives as burdens. Even sages cannot make men alike. Therefore, he concludes that to take land as the basis of taxation, and income as the test of ability to pay, was a necessary policy of that time.[1]

The theory of Ma Tuan-lin is the doctrine of faculty. Its fundamental point is still true, but its application to modern times must be modified. Since land is not the only test of ability to pay, land cannot be the basis of taxation.

The payment of the land tax in silver began in the Sung dynasty. In 1628 A. K. (1077 A. D.) the summer tax consisted of 31,940 taels of silver, and the autumn tax of 28,197 taels. The Kin and the Yüan dynasties never col-

[1] *General Research*, ch. iii.

lected the land tax in silver. Under the Ming dynasty, in 1927 (1376 A. D.), there was an ordinance that silver be allowed to be substituted for rice; and during the reign of Ch'êng Tsu (1954-1975 A. K. or 1403-1424 A. D.) the annual tribute consisted of 300,000 taels of silver. But these were simply for the convenience of payment, and the silver was regarded like other commodities. It is only since 1987 A. K. (1436 A. D.) that the land tax has begun to be regularly paid in silver. In this year the land tax of all the southern provinces was paid in silver, and one tael was equal to four bushels of rice. In 2038 A. K. (1487 A. D.) this system was extended to all the northern provinces, and one tael was equal to only one bushel. These figures show the fluctuation in the value of metal in comparison with that of rice. But this system was a revolution in economic history, and it has continued to the present time.[1]

In 2132 A. K. (1581 A. D.) the system of "single whip" was universally established. The total amount of land tax and poll tax of each district was fixed, and the poll tax was equally distributed to the land. Whenever there was public labor, the officials employed laborers with payments. All the different kinds of contributions, tribute, *etc.*, were simplified into a single item, and they were supplied by the officials with the money of the land tax. Land was the only object of direct taxation, and was taxed according to acreage.

[1] The payment of the land tax in gold began with the Sung dynasty. In 1528 (977 A. D.), one tael of gold was equal to eight thousand copper coins. In 1948 (1397 A. D.), Ming T'ai Tsu decreed that the land tax may be paid in gold, one tael being substituted for twenty bushels of rice. In these cases, gold was used only like commodities. In fact, whether the tax is paid in kind or in money depends on the economic condition of the people. The old Chinese usually held the opinion that it is better for the farmers to pay tax in kind, because they need not exchange their products for money, and their products are not subject to market price. Such a view was quite true, since China was an agricultural country.

DIRECT TAXES

The worst thing in the financial system of the Ming dynasty was the constant increase of the land tax. Formerly, the annual revenue of the national treasury was about 2,430,000 taels of silver, and the expenditures were not over 2,000,000 taels, sometimes only seven or eight hundred thousand taels. There was a rule that the government spent seven-tenths, but reserved three-tenths for any emergency, such as famine or military expenses. This was in harmony with the principles of Confucius. But in 2065 A. K. (1514 A. D.) Ming Wu Tsung increased the land tax temporarily to the amount of 1,000,000 taels for the reconstruction of a palace, because he had exhausted the reserve fund. This was the first time of increasing tax. In 2102 A. K. (1551 A. D.), when the military expenditures were increased, Ming Shih Tsung got a temporary addition of tax, 1,200,000 taels, distributing it to the land tax of Kiangsu and Chekiang. From 2169 to 2171 A. K. (1618-1620 A. D.), when the rebellion broke out in Manchuria, Ming Shên Tsung increased the land tax of the whole empire three times, the total addition being 5,200,000 taels; and this became a permanent addition. In 2181 A. K. (1630 A. D.) Ming Chuang-lieh Ti made an addition of more than 1,650,000 taels. In 2186 A. K. he raised the land tax one-tenth, which was called a subsidy. Again, he made an addition of 2,800,000 taels in 2188, and another addition of 7,300,000 taels in 2190. From 2169 to this year, the total increase in the annual land tax amounted to 16,900,000 taels. The government wanted to get money in order to put down the rebels and the banditti, but the people could not bear the burden, so that they were driven to become banditti. This was one cause of the downfall of the Ming dynasty. Therefore, in 2207 A. K. (1656 A. D.) the present dynasty abolished all the additions to the land tax and brought it back to the original amount.

In 2263 A. K. (1712 A. D.) the present dynasty made a great revolution in the tax system. This was by making the amount of the poll tax of 2262 A. K. a fixed burden and freeing the increasing population from any further poll tax.[1] From 2274 to 2280 A. K. (1723-1729 A. D.) the poll tax of different provinces was added to the land tax. Hence, China has to-day no poll tax, and the people who own no land pay no direct tax whatever.

For a long period the land has been taxed by acreage. In 755 A. K. (204 A. D.) Tsao Tsao taxed each acre at four pints of rice. In 881 A. K. (330 A. D.) the Tsin dynasty taxed each acre at three pints, which was called one-tenth of its produce; and in 912 A. K. (361 A. D.) this rate was reduced to two pints. In 1321 A. K. (770 A. D.) the Tang dynasty fixed the land tax as follows: For the summer tax, each acre of the higher grade of land paid six pints, and that of lower grade, four pints; for the autumn tax, one pint was deducted from both grades. In 1831 A. K. (1280 A. D.) the Yüan dynasty regulated the land tax at the rate of three pints for one acre, paid in paper money. In the beginning of the Ming dynasty (1919 A. K. or 1368 A. D.), each acre was taxed at $3\frac{35}{100}$ pints. All these rates were but general rates. Since the middle part of the Tang dynasty there has been no uniform rate, and the amount of rice has mostly been paid in a fixed equivalent sum of money

The land tax of the present dynasty varies greatly in the different provinces. For example, each acre in the Kansu province is taxed from .0002 to .1504 tael of silver, from .03 to 8.11 pints of rice, and from .3 to .46 of a bale of straw.[2] Each acre in the Sian prefecture (Shensi province) is taxed 2.3817 taels of silver, and from 5.25 to 5.85 pints

---

[1] *Cf. supra*, pp. 340-41.
[2] A bale weighs fifteen catties.

DIRECT TAXES 659

of rice. These rates are determined by custom rather than by any scientific measure of ability to pay.¹

The requirement of extra taxes besides the regular tax began in the Five Dynasties. In 1477 A. K. (926 A. D.) the extra tax of ten per cent was abolished. In 1501 A. K. (950 A. D.) the extra tax was increased to twenty per cent. It was pretended that the extra tax was to provide against any loss or waste of the regular tax, because the tax was collected in kind. In the middle part of the Ming dynasty, although the land tax was paid in silver, the extra tax was required upon another pretext—to make good the loss from melting. Since 2275 A. K. (1724 A. D.), the present dynasty has taken the extra tax from the local officers into the central government, and fixed its amount, varying to a great extent, from two per cent to twenty per cent. But it is distributed again to the magistrates of the districts, as an addition to their salaries and for other local expenditures.

This is not a good system. If we wish to get more revenue for legitimate expenditures, we should directly increase the tax itself, but should not impose an additional tax. It is unequal and complicated, and is a source of corruption. The magistrate in the first place requires an addition, and then his clerks require another addition. The people pay fifty per cent more than the amount of the regular tax. Moreover, the poor suffer more than the rich, because their payment is smaller and their resistance is weaker. Therefore, the extra tax should be abolished.

In conclusion, the land tax is the oldest and the most important tax of China. According to the budget of this year (2462 A. K. or 1911 A. D.) the total land tax is 48,101,346 taels of silver. But, since 1331 A. K. (780 A. D.), there has been no great change in the land-tax system. Every

¹ *Cases of the Institutes of the Ts'ing Dynasty* (*Ta Ts'ing Hui Tien Shih Li*), ch. clxii.

dynasty has simply followed in the footsteps of the preceding dynasty, and the people are bound to pay the tax, not according to any sound principle, but according to what they had paid before. It is far from justice. In short, China must reform the land tax fundamentally, and this should also increase largely the public revenues.

II. PERSONAL SERVICE

In ancient times the revenue system was simple, the land tax practically being the only tax. But there were many kinds of work which were necessary to the government and could not be paid for out of the small revenues. Therefore, the people contributed their labor for all kinds of public work without receiving any payment. This was the oldest form of poll tax, although the tax was not paid with money, but with labor. Hence, Confucius regards forced labor as a tax.

1. *Principles of Confucius*

In the feudal stage the people suffered from forced labor a great deal. Therefore, Confucius condemned any war,[1] and any unnecessary construction or repair of buildings,[2] because the people were oppressively employed for those things. The general principle of this tax was the employment of the people at the proper season.[3] Mencius said: "If the seasons of husbandry be not interfered with, the grain will be more than can be eaten."[4] Indeed, the personal-service tax might easily interrupt the occupations of the people. But Confucius did not advocate the abolition

---

[1] *Cf. supra*, pp. 144-6.
[2] *Cf. supra*, p. 247.
[3] *Cf. supra*, pp. 81, 627.
[4] *Classics*, vol. ii, p. 130.

DIRECT TAXES

of this tax, because the people at large at that time were unable to pay money in its place. He merely advocated its reform, and its abolition was later the achievement of Chang Yüeh, Yan Yen, and Wang An-shih.[1]

Confucius prescribes an age limit for personal service According to the "Royal Regulations" and the authorities of the Modern Literature, a man begins to serve in public work at twenty, and retires at fifty; he begins to serve in the army at thirty, and retires at sixty.[2]

For the service of public work, no more than three days within a year are allowed. In all employments of the people on public work, even the strong men are given only a small amount of work, the same as that of old men; and even old men are given ample rations, the same as strong men. In this way favorable treatment is accorded to the people. Moreover, according to this principle, public work is not forced labor, but hired labor, since it receives subsistence.[3]

The most important form of personal service is military duty. The people contribute not only their labor, but also their equipment. According to the *tsing tien* system, ten *tsing* together (eighty families) contribute one chariot. But many other kinds of equipment are supplied by the government.

Kuan Tzŭ was the first one to require the people of sixteen *tsing* (one hundred and twenty-eight families) to supply seven buff-coats.[4] Duke Ch'êng of Lu followed this example in 39 B. K. (590 B. C.). But Confucius condemned this law in the *Spring and Autumn*, because the making of buff-coat was not the profession of the ordinary people, and such a requirement was oppressive.[5]

[1] *Cf. infra*, pp. 665-7. [2] *Cf. Li Ki*, bk. iii, p. 241.
[3] *Ibid.*, pp. 227-8. [4] Bk. v.
[5] *Cf. Classics*, vol. v, pt. i, p. 337.

The exemption from personal service is as follows: First. there is an exemption for educated men. The "selected scholars" brought to the notice of the minister of education are exempted from services in their districts. The "eminent scholars" promoted to the imperial university are exempted from all services under the department of education. Secondly, there is an exemption for the benefit of those families which have aged persons or sick persons, or deaths. When a person becomes eighty, one of his sons is free from all services; when he becomes ninety, all the members of his family are free. In a family whose member is disabled or ill, requiring the attendance of others to wait upon him, one man is discharged from services. Parties mourning for their parents have a discharge for three years, and those mourning for one year or nine months have a discharge for three months. Thirdly, there is an exemption for emigrants and immigrants. When one is about to move to another state, he is discharged from service for three months beforehand. When one comes from another state, he is discharged for a round year. These are the rules of Confucius.[1]

2. *Rules given in the Official System of Chou*

The *Official System of Chou* gives many rules in regard to personal service. Although they are somewhat different from those of Confucius, they are important because they were the actual laws of the Chou dynasty. Therefore, we shall mention some of them. In the capital city those from twenty to sixty, and in the country those from fifteen to sixty-five, paid the service tax.[2] Five men formed the smallest group, a *wu;* twenty-five men made up a *liang;* one

---

[1] *Cf. Li Ki*, bk. iii, pp. 232, 243.

[2] Since the people of the capital city served the public labor much oftener than those of country, the period of service was shorter.

DIRECT TAXES 663

hundred men, a *tsu;* five hundred men, a *lü;* two thousand five hundred men, a *shih;* and twelve thousand five hundred men, an army. This standard was for the raising of soldiers, for the undertaking of hunting expeditions and public works, for the driving away of an enemy, for the capturing of robbers, and for the collecting of taxes. The average numbers of those people who were strong enough to serve in the public labor were as follows: In the families consisting of seven persons, each family had three men; in those consisting of six persons, two families together had five men; in those consisting of five persons, each family had two men. But, in all kinds of public labor, each family was required to contribute not more than one man. It was only for hunting, or for driving an enemy away, or for capturing robbers, that all the able-bodied persons in each family were required to take part.[1]

There were many local officers who controlled all local affairs. Five families formed the smallest group, and over them was the lowest officer. Then came some higher officers—one for twenty-five families, one for one hundred families, one for five hundred families, and one for two thousand five hundred families. The larger the group, the higher the officer. They were chosen from among the people themselves. All the personal services were directed by them. They were both civil and military officers. In time of peace they were administrators, in time of war, commanders.[2]

There was an equalizer (*chün jên*) who equalized the personal services performed either through physical labor, or through the use of animals and vehicles. In all cases, the equalization of personal services was according to the year. In a good year the period of public labor was three

---

[1] Chs. xi, xii.   [2] Ch. xii.

days; in an ordinary year, two days; and in a bad year, one day. If there was famine or epidemic, there was no requirement of personal service.[1]

3. The "Rotation Tax" of the Han Dynasty

During the Ch'in dynasty the people served the local government for one month, and then the central government. In the whole year, the amount of service, both as a soldier at the frontier and as a workman on public work, was thirty times more than that of the ancients.[2] This was the worst example in Chinese history.

At the beginning of the Han dynasty, the example of the Ch'in dynasty was followed. However, in later times, the law was fixed in this way: The personal service was called "rotation." The "soldier rotation" was service for one month. The "fulfilling rotation" was a payment of two thousand copper coins for the length of one month, which might be substituted for the soldier rotation. The "passing rotation" was the payment of three hundred coins in substitute for the three days' service at the frontier.

Therefore, under the Han dynasty, the system of hired labor was well established. The wage of such labor was called "level price," one hundred coins for one day's labor. Hence, the total amount of "rotation tax" for one man in one year was two thousand three hundred coins. This was really too much.[3] But, if the Chinese in general had been rich enough to pay this tax, there would have been no forced labor. The fundamental cause for the existence of forced labor was the economic condition of the people.

---

[1] Ch. xiv.

[2] *History of Han*, ch. xxiv.

[3] *Ibid.*, ch. vii (commentary). Besides this tax, there were also the poll tax and the family tax (*cf. infra*, pp. 669-671).

4. *Reformation of Chang Yüeh*

From the beginning of Chinese history, the people have been responsible for military service. In 1273 A. K. (722 A. D.) a great revolution in the military system took place. At that time the soldiers of the standing army in the military stations served the army from twenty-one to sixty. Moreover, their families were not exempted from other services. Hence, they became poor and weak, and deserted from their stations in large numbers. The people suffered from this system. Then Chang Yüeh, the prime minister, proposed to hire strong men for imperial guards. By exempting them from other services and giving them favorable treatment, deserting soldiers were induced to offer themselves for such an employment. Tang Hsüan Tsung put this proposal into effect. Within ten days he got one hundred and thirty thousand good soldiers. They were distributed to different stations, and ordered to come to the capital in rotation. This was the first time that the soldiers were separated from the farmers.[1]

Since this revolutionary change in the military system, the Chinese have not been required to serve in the army. From the military point of view, there are many objections to this change. From the social and economic points of view, however, the people derive great benefits. Although the people pay more taxes for the support of soldiers, they are free from all troubles. Moreover, there is no necessity for every man to be a soldier, and the specialized soldier is better than the ordinary man. Indeed, the separation of the people and the soldiers is justified by the principle of division of labor. Chang Yüeh, although criticized by many, was a great reformer, and his innovation was comparable to the " forced-labor emancipation law " of Wang An-shih.

[1] *General Political History*, ch. ccxii.

5. *Reformation of Yang Yen*

We have already learned that under the three-taxes system of the Tang dynasty the poll tax was paid either by a contribution of labor or by a payment of silk.[1] This was in harmony with the principles of Confucius, because there was no double taxation upon the person, and the people were not required to contribute both labor and payment We have also learned that, by the reformation of Yang Yen, the poll tax was combined with the land tax.[2] This meant a great advance in civilization, because there was neither poll tax paid in money nor forced labor. Therefore, from that time on (1331 A. K. or 780 A. D.) China should not have poll tax or forced labor at all. This was the great achievement of Yang Yen, and we should give him not less credit than we give to Wang An-shih (a justice which the Chinese have never done him).

6. *Reformation of Wang An-shih*

However, there was another kind of forced labor coming into existence. During the Tang dynasty the families were classified into nine classes, according to their wealth, and the rich families were required to take up the public service We must remember that this service was an honorable service, different from ordinary public labor. The position of the rich people who undertook the public service was like that of the local officers of the Chou dynasty.[3] But, after 1262 A. K. (711 A. D.) this position began to be dishonorable, and it gradually became similar to forced labor. Hence we speak of it as forced labor. But we must not forget that this forced labor was different from the ordinary forced labor which was abolished by Yang Yen. The former was based on property, and the latter on person.

[1] *Cf. supra.*   [2] *Cf. supra*, pp. 651-2.
[3] *Cf. supra*, p. 663.

In the Sung dynasty this forced labor became intolerable. The kinds of public labor were such as the keeping and transporting of government property, collecting taxes, policing, carrying messages, *etc.* It was a great burden especially put on the higher grades of families, and it destroyed the property and lives of many people.

In 1621 A. K. (1070 A. D.), Wang An-shih established "the forced-labor emancipation law," and it was a great revolution in the economic history of China. The fundamental point was to change forced labor to hired labor. Wang An-shih based his principle on the institutions of the ancient kings—that is, to tax the people for the wages of the government employees. In fact, this law substituted a money tax for personal service. We shall discuss the law itself under the head of property taxes.

7. *Final Settlement*

The system of hired labor is the best institution established by Wang An-shih. Even for this alone he deserves all honor. But the system of forced labor was revived in 1637 A. K. (1086 A. D.), and it was abolished again in 1645 A. K. (1094 A. D.). After 1686 A. K. (1135 A. D.) the wages provided for hired labor were used for military expenses, and forced labor was revived again. Hence, both the ordinary public service and the higher public service came into existence. Since the Kin dynasty, there has been a distinction between the service assigned to the families paying the land tax and the service assigned to those paying no land tax. But their character was that of forced labor just the same.

When the "single whip" system was universally adopted in 2132 A. K. (1581 A. D.), the land tax was increased to take the place of forced labor. The government got money from the land for the wages of hired labor, and the people were freed from forced labor. But this system was not thoroughly established until the present dynasty (2263-2280 A. K. or 1712-1729 A. D.).[1] To-day no one is obliged to take up any public labor.

As to the reasons for the existence of forced labor, besides the fundamental one which we have mentioned above—the economic condition of the people—three others may be given. First, the amount of taxes was so small that it could not defray the wages of hired labor. Secondly, except for Yang Yen's abolition of forced labor by an augmentation of the land tax, there was no one who had the wisdom and courage of Wang An-shih to devise a new tax to take the place of forced labor. Therefore, although the optional payment of money in lieu of personal service had been an institution of the Chou and the Han dynasties, forced labor itself had never been abolished; and, although Wang An-shih had abolished it, it was revived again when the money for hiring laborers was used for other purposes. Thirdly, since there was no separate source of revenue for local expenses, the public labor that had to be performed for the local government was necessarily imposed upon the people of the locality. Therefore, although military duty, the chief service to the nation, was abolished by Chang Yüeh, local service continued to be burdensome enough to the people; and, although the ordinary forced labor was abolished by Yang Yen, the higher forced labor still existed in the localities. These are the three reasons for the existence of forced labor.

As to the evils of forced labor, it seems that they resulted from the ignorance and weakness of the mass of the people. If they had been intelligent and strong, their lives and property would not have been destroyed by forced labor, such as

[1] *Cf. supra*, pp. 340-41, 658.

the collecting of taxes and police duty. They might even derive benefit from it, since there was some compensation and exemption for them. But, as a matter of fact, they were somewhat timid and weak, so they were apt to be imposed upon by the officials and their servants. Therefore, even after forced labor had been changed to hired labor, they were still robbed by the officials and their servants. In fact, the best protection for the people is to teach them how to protect themselves. If we want to reform anything at all, we must go to the very bottom. Political education is the fundamental thing.

III. POLL TAX

The "mouth tax" was a poll tax. It does not appear in the Confucian texts, so that there is a presumption that this tax did not exist in ancient times. But, according to Kuan Tzŭ, the amount of the mouth tax was ten coins annually.[1] In the *Official System of Chou* it was called *fu*.[2] Pan Ku says that *fu* was for military expenditures, for the reserve of the treasuries, and for the gifts of the rulers.[3] Therefore, we are sure that the mouth tax must have existed in ancient times; but it was probably very light. This tax was not approved by Confucius, because a person having contributed his personal service should not be taxed twice.

In 349 A. K. (203 B. C.) the mouth tax first occurred in Chinese history at a regular rate. Every man, from fifteen to fifty-six, paid annually one hundred and twenty copper coins for the tax of his body. This amount was later reduced either to a half, one-fourth, or one-third. But merchants and slaves paid double this amount. In 363 A. K. (189 A. D.) an ordinance was issued that unmarried women, from fifteen to thirty, should be taxed at a rate five

[1] Bk. lxxvi.   [2] Ch. ii.
[3] *History of Han*, ch. xxiv.

times that amount. It was probably intended to increase the population. Every boy, from seven to fourteen, paid the "mouth money," twenty coins a year. During the reign of Han Wu Ti, a boy began to pay "mouth money" at three years old, and three coins were added. In 508 A. K. (44 B. C.) the tax age was changed to the original, seven years old, but the amount remained the same, twenty-three coins.

Since the Tsin dynasty, the poll tax has been mixed up with the land tax. In 928 A. K. (377 A. D.) the mouth tax was three bushels of rice; and in 934 A. K. it was increased to five bushels. But each person received seventy acres of public land without paying the land tax.

After 1331 A. K. (780 A. D.) the poll tax was included in the land tax by Yang Yen. Therefore there should be no poll tax. But during the Five Dynasties it was revived, and it lasted throughout the Sung dynasty.[1]

The Yüan dynasty regulated the poll tax in 1831 A. K. (1280 A. D.). Each adult man paid three bushels of rice, and each young man, one bushel. This was the standard. In some families, each adult or young man paid only half this amount, or each adult man paid only one bushel. Therefore, there was a gradation in the poll tax.

The amount of the poll tax in the present dynasty has varied to a great extent. The smallest amount was .001 tael of silver for one person, and the greatest amount 8.7786 taels. However, since the total amount of the poll tax of the empire was combined with the land tax (2263-2280 A. K. or 1712-1729 A. D.) China has had no poll tax.

IV. FAMILY TAX

Since the Han dynasty there has been the "door tax," a tax upon the family. It was connected with, and similar to,

---

[1] *General Research*, chs. x, xi.

the mouth tax. But this tax under the Han dynasty was not heavy, the annual rate being two hundred copper coins for each family.¹

The increase of the door tax began in the Wei dynasty In 755 A. K. (204 A. D.) Tsao Tsao made a law that each family should pay annually two rolls of silk and two catties of floss-silk.

After 831 A. K. (280 A. D.), Tsin Wu Ti regulated the door tax as follows: A family consisting of an adult man (from sixteen to sixty) paid three rolls of silk and three catties of floss-silk annually. A family consisting of an adult woman or a man of the secondary adult class (from thirteen to fifteen or from sixty-one to sixty-five) paid half this amount. In the prefectures along the boundaries, a family sometimes paid only two-thirds of this amount; in the regions remote from the capital, only one-third.²

The door tax or the family tax of the Tsin dynasty seemed to include the land tax. Hence, it was heavier than that of the Han dynasty. But, since there was a distribution of public land,³ there was no family that held no land. Therefore, the family tax could be required. Moreover, there was no poll tax upon the individual person.

The gradation of the family tax began in 1101 A. K. (550 A. D.). Wên-hsüan Ti of the Northern Ch'i dynasty first divided the families into nine classes. The rich paid their money, and the poor contributed their labor.⁴ Hence, the character of the family tax began to change to that of a property tax.

The family tax of the Yüan dynasty was heavy. One family paid one catty and $6\frac{40}{100}$ taels of silk, and five

---

¹ *Historical Record*, ch. cxxix.
² *History of Tsin*, ch. xxvi.   ³ *Cf. supra*, p. 509.
⁴ *History of Sui*, ch. xxiv.

taels of silver. This was the standard, and the different grades of family paid different amounts less than this standard. It was really a property tax. Besides the family txx, there was also a poll tax, three bushels of rice.[1]

In the present dynasty there is no family tax.

Our conclusion is, that when the wealth of the people is equal, the family tax upon the family as a whole is justifiable, because it includes the income made by the housewife. Such is the case of ground tax or the exaction of cloth and silk mentioned by Confucius and Mencius.[2] But, when wealth is not equally distributed, there should be no family tax. Therefore, the family tax has been changed to the property tax since the middle part of Tang dynasty.

V. GENERAL PROPERTY TAX

In 69 A. K. (483 B. C.) Lu began to establish a property tax, basing it upon the ratio of the land tax. For instance, the land tax was formerly one-tenth of its produce, but it was now doubled, the second one-tenth being the tax upon general property. It was the first time that the general property tax was invented, but it excluded land. Confucius condemned this new tax, because it was simply an addition to the land tax.[3]

In 570 A. K. (19 A. D.) Wang Mang taxed the wealth of both the officials and the people at the rate of one-thirtieth. This was the first time that the general property tax was levied throughout the whole empire.[4]

In 1320 A. K. (769 A. D.) Tang Tai Tsung regulated the family tax as follows: All the families, either of the

---

[1] *Continuation of the General Research*, ch. xvi.
[2] *Cf. supra*, pp. 634-5.
[3] *Cf. Classics*, vol. v, pt. ii, p. 826.
[4] *History of Han*, ch. xcix.

DIRECT TAXES

people or of the princes, were classified into nine classes, and were required to pay their taxes in money. Each family of the first class paid four thousand copper coins; each of the second, three thousand five hundred; each of the third, three thousand; each of the fourth, two thousand five hundred; each of the fifth, two thousand; each of the sixth, one thousand five hundred; each of the seventh, one thousand; each of the eighth, seven hundred; and each of the ninth, five hundred. The officials were classified according to their nine ranks in correspondence with these nine classes. If one family had several officials holding their position in different places, each of them paid his tax in his place according to his rank. Those people who had hotels, firms, or factories were raised two grades above their proper class for purposes of taxation. The families of farmers living out of their native districts were regarded as the seventh class; and those of temporary residents as the eighth class. All journeymen and boarders were classified under either the eighth or the ninth classes according to their income. The farms situated in different places but owned by one person or one family were separately taxed in the respective localities. The soldiers, during their service, had the special privilege of being classified under the ninth class.[1]

This was a combination of general property tax and income tax. But the chief importance was still laid upon the land, except the salaries of the officials and the business of the merchants. This tax was changed in 1331 A. K. (780 A. D.), when the system of summer and autumn taxes was established.

The "forced-labor emancipation law" of Wang An-shih, established in 1621 A. K. (1070 A. D.), was really a general property tax. Its details were as follows: The families

[1] *Old History of Tang*, ch. xlviii.

who paid money for the emancipation of forced labor or for the aid of emancipation were classified into five grades according to their real and personal property. They contributed this money twice a year, in summer and autumn, according to their grade. The families of the country from the fourth class down, and those of the cities from the sixth class down, were exempted.[1] When they held property in two districts, the higher grades paid money to each district, and the ordinary grade paid it to one district only, including its property in any other district. Those families which divided up their possession were classified into new grades according to the division of their property. The families of officials, those consisting of only women or minors, and the monasteries, paid half the amount. All the money was used to hire those whose family paid taxes, from the third class up, for the execution of public labor. The amount of wages was regulated according to the amount of work. For example, the number of families in the district of K'aifung was over 22,600, and the annual contribution of this money amounted to 12,900 strings. Ten thousand and two hundred strings were used for wages, and the remainder, 2,700 strings, was reserved to make good any deficit which might occur during a bad year.

All the families which formerly served in public labor paid money according to their grade; this was called "the forced-labor emancipation money." All the families of officials, women, single men, bonzes, *etc.*, who were formerly exempted from the public labor, were required to pay money; this was called "the forced-labor emancipation aid money." This tax was rated according to the estimated amount of wages needed in each district, the inhabitants of which were required to make the assessed amount good, in

---

[1] We should remember that, before this law was passed the families were classified into nine classes according to their wealth.

accordance with the grade of their families. Besides the fixed amount, an extra charge of twenty per cent was collected to provide against such contingencies as years of famine and inundations, when the people might be deprived of all means of paying taxes. This charge was kept as a reserve fund, which would enable the government to remit this annual impost in necessitous times.

The forced-labor emancipation law was good, but it encountered much opposition. In the first place, it created a new tax paid in money. In the second place, it taxed all the higher classes which were formerly freed from forced labor. Since the common people got the real benefit from the emancipation, the higher classes who especially suffered by this tax made a loud outcry. But both Sung Shên Tsung and Wang An-shih were strong enough to maintain this law. Shên Tsung said: " This change of institution is, indeed, not welcomed by most of the officials; but what is the inconvenience to the people?" This law meant a social revolution for China—the higher classes paid more taxes, and the lower classes were not only emancipated from forced labor, but also freed from the general property tax.

This tax was levied upon the five grades of family. Such classification was based either on the amount of the land tax which the family paid, or on the acreage of land, or on the accumulation of cash, or on the amount of rent received. Since it was necessary that hired labor be substituted for forced labor, and that the hired labor be paid by some means, this tax was justifiable. It brought in large revenues to the government. Therefore, besides paying wages to hired labor, it was also used for the salaries of government clerks and for the famine-relief fund.

However, this tax had two defects. One was that the land was subject to double taxation. The other was that the law ought not to have required at all the extra charge, which was reduced in 1645 A. K. (1094 A. D.) to ten per cent.

In 1625 A. K. (1074 A. D.), after Wang An-shih was dismissed, Lü Hui-ch'ing, formerly a personal friend of Wang, devised " the self-proving law " to make the forced-labor emancipation law effective. The government determined the average prices of all real estate, personal property and live-stock. Then it let the people assess themselves according to the aggregate value of their property. The houses were classified according to whether they had income or not. Five units of stored-up money were equal to one of income-making money. Anyone who concealed his property was liable to be informed against. If the information proved true, a third of the value of the concealed property was paid to the informer as a reward. A schedule of taxable property to be returned in the roll was issued to every house, and the magistrate of each district received and registered it. According to the prices of their property, five classes of families were distinguished. Therefore the total amount of the wealth of an entire district could be known. Judging by the original amount of the " forced-labor emancipation money " of the whole district, the government decided how much each should pay.

This law imposed a tax upon property which brought in income, consumption goods being exempted. But the difficulty was encountered of distinguishing between goods for consumption and goods for production, because the products of agriculture and industry might be used for either purpose. Moreover, a worse thing was the inducement given to informations. Therefore, when Wang An-shih came back to the government, this law was abolished (1626 A. K. or 1075 A. D.), while the " forced-labor emancipation law " remained practically the same throughout the Sung dynasty.[1]

[1] *General Research*, chs. xii, xiii.

The general property tax of the Kin dynasty was like this: All lands, gardens, houses, carriages, live-stock, plants and money, were counted as property, and the tax was levied upon them according to their quantity. This was a universal tax, none being exempted. But, since the property-owner had paid the land tax beside this, it involved double taxation so far as land was concerned. In 1746 A. K. (1195 A. D.) the total amount of this tax was 2,604,742 strings.[1]

After the Kin dynasty there was no general property tax, except in the form of the family tax. During the present dynasty there is neither general property tax nor family tax.

VI. HOUSE TAX

According to Confucius, there is no separate tax levied upon the house itself, except the ground tax.[2] But, during the Chou dynasty, there was the house tax. Besides the tax on the shops, factories, warehouses and residences of the commercial districts, mentioned in the *Official System of Chou*,[3] Kuan Tzŭ says: " The rich families who build their beautiful houses pay a large tax, while the ordinary families who make the common houses pay a small tax."[4]

However, in later history, there is only one instance in which the house tax was levied upon all kinds of buildings. In 1334 A. K. (783 A. D) Tang Tê Tsung divided the houses into three classes. The tax for the first class was two thousand copper coins; that for the second class, one thousand; and that for the lowest class, five hundred. He who dared to conceal one house was beaten with the heavy bamboo sixty times, and the informer was rewarded with

[1] *Continuation of the General Research,* chs. xiii, xv.
[2] *Cf. supra,* pp. 634-5.
[3] Ch. xv.
[4] Bk. lxxiv.

fifty thousand coins, paid by the transgressor. But this tax was abolished in the following year.¹

In the present dynasty, since 2452 A. K. (1901 A. D.), the provincial governments have tried to impose a universal tax upon all houses. But they succeed only in the cities, and fail to reach the houses in the country districts because the people do not want to pay this new tax.

Therefore, our conclusion is that China never has had a special house tax universally imposed upon the houses of the whole empire. Kuan Tzŭ may have taxed the houses in the country districts, but his state was only a feudal state. This is the difference between the administration of a feudal state and that of a large empire. Although the general property tax of different dynasties did include the tax on houses, it was not a special house tax, but a general property tax.

VII. INCOME TAX

Every tax finally falls upon income. According to Confucius, there is no objection to an income tax, especially a tax on the monopolistic profits of merchants.² The income tax began in the Chou dynasty, and it took the form of taxing profits. According to the *Official System* of *Chou*, the remainder of the government goods which were not used up by the government itself were sold to the merchants, and their profits were taxed for the gifts of the emperor.³

According to the law of the Han dynasty, all those who had to pay income tax were to make a self-assessment in accordance with their property. It was made by the head of the family himself. If the assessment was not true, or if

---

¹ *New History of Tang*, ch. lii. This tax, we might suppose, would have reached only the houses in the cities.

² *Cf. supra*, pp. 541-2.

³ Chs. ii, vi.

it was not written down by the head of the family himself, the fine was two catties of gold, and, moreover, the unassessed property and its income were confiscated.[1] Since this law is not well known, we may take two cases to show its effects. In 436 A. K. (116 B. C.) Marquis P'ang-kuang was deprived of his feudal estate because he did not assess the income which he derived from a loan. In 471 A. K. (81 B. C.), when the government abolished the monopoly of liquors, the people were allowed to distill spirits on condition that they should pay the income tax according to law.[2] Therefore, the income tax was well established in the Han dynasty.

Wang Mang levied an income tax upon every one. In 561 A. K. (10 A. D.) he made a law that all hunters, fishers, foresters, miners, shepherds, weavers, tailors, mechanics, physicians, witches, fortune-tellers, priests, and all other kinds of professional men and business men living in shops, residences and hotels, were required to report themselves and their business to the magistrate of the district where they lived. After deducting their expenses, they should turn over one-tenth of their net income to the government. Those who did not report, or reported falsely, were punished by the confiscation of their total production.[3] There was no exemption,[4] nor differentiation, nor graduation. Therefore, the people suffered a great deal. Yet there was a good point about this tax, that is, that it was not on gross, but on net income.

---

[1] *History of Han*, ch. vii (commentary).

[2] *Ibid.*, chs. xv, vii.

[3] *Ibid.*, ch. xxiv.

[4] Since Wang Mang nationalized the land in 560, there was no income derived from land. And since he did not give salaries to officials until 567 (even at that time officials received no true salaries), there were no salaries to be taxed.

In China there is a practice that, when the government needs money, salaries and pensions are reduced. This is really a tax on income, stopping it at its source. Such a practice began with the Sung dynasty of the House of Liu. In 1001 A. K. (450 A. D.) the deduction from salaries was one-third.[1]

In 1333 A. K. (782 A. D.) the Tang dynasty reduced salaries in this way: The amount of monthly salaries above one hundred strings was reduced by one-third; above eighty strings, by one-fifth. The reduction of the lower salaries was made in a similar way. But the salaries which were under thirty strings were not reduced. In 1335 A. K. salaries were paid according to their full amount.[2] Such a reduction of salaries had two good points: a progressive tax upon large salaries, and an exemption of small salaries.

In 1673 A. K. (1122 A. D.) the Southern Sung dynasty taxed the salaries of officials at one per cent. Gradually this rate was raised to 5.6 per cent in 1716 A. K. (1165 A. D.). Ma Tuan-lin criticized this practice on the ground that the government might abolish some unimportant offices or reduce salaries openly, but that it should not keep back part of what it had promised to pay.[3] His theory is true. But, if there were a universal income tax, there would be no objection to proportional reduction of salaries.

At the present day, it is the practice in Kuangtung for the people themselves to tax their houses one month's rent for local purposes. One-half of this amount is paid out of the rent, retained by the tenant, and the other half is contributed by the tenant himself. Such a practice prevails in the cities. It is really an income tax upon two elements. rent and profit. At present, the provincial government taxes the houses in the same way.

[1] *History of Sung*, ch. v.
[2] *General Research*, ch. lxv.   [3] *Ibid.*, ch. xix.

DIRECT TAXES

VIII. INHERITANCE TAX

In the kingdom of Latter Shu (1458-1516 A. K. or 907-965 A. D.), when people married, their dowries were assessed and taxed. This was the first time that the dowry tax occurred in history. But it was abolished in 1524 A. K. by Sung T'ai Tsu.

The true inheritance tax began in 1670 (1119 A. D.). All the testaments, or bequests to daughters, were required to be stamped with the official seal and to pay a tax. But this tax was abolished after a short time.[1]

According to the stamp-tax act of 2458 A. K. (1907 A. D.), every testament was required to be pasted with a stamp of one thousand copper coins. But this act has not been universally enforced.

IX. PUBLIC DEBT

Although public debt is not a tax in name, it is a tax in fact. Ma Tuan-lin has put it under the head of miscellaneous taxes. It began with the Sung dynasty of the House of Liu. In 1001 A. K. (450 A. D.), when national defense was important, the princes, princesses and officials mostly gave voluntary contributions to help the state. Among the rich people, some offered several tens of millions. Then a system of public debt was introduced: one-fourth of the wealth of those people who had five hundred thousands, and of those monks and nuns who possessed two hundred thousands, was borrowed by the state. If their wealth was over these amounts, it was borrowed at the same rate. The government promised that, when the war was over, the debt should be immediately paid off.[2]

When Tang Su Tsung came to the throne (1307 A. K. or 756 A. D.), the government could not get revenue on ac-

---

[1] *General Research*, ch. xiv.   [2] *Ibid.*, ch. xix.

count of a great rebellion. Hence he borrowed money from the southern people, taking away twenty per cent of their wealth. It was called " the borrowing at percentage," and it was really a forced loan. For the same reason, necessary military expenditures, Tang Tê Tsung issued the ordinance of " borrowing from the merchants " (1333 A. K. or 782 A. D.). It did great harm to the people, and, moreover, the total collection in the capital was only two million strings.[1]

Under the present dynasty, a public debt has been created several different times. In 2445 A. K. (1894 A. D.), on account of the war with Japan, the government borrowed ten million taels of silver from the merchants. In 2449 A. K. (1898 A. D.), in conforming to the proposal of Huang Ssŭ-yung, the government tried to borrow one hundred million taels, but the actual collection was only about four million taels. These two sums were really forced money. Yüan Shih-kai tried to establish a public debt of the modern type in 2456 A. K. (1905 A. D.), but did not succeed. Besides borrowing one million eight hundred thousand taels by force, he secretly borrowed from The Yokohama Specie Bank three million taels in order to carry out his plans. Many other officials tried to imitate his scheme, but nobody was successful. In short, China cannot establish a domestic debt until she shall have a constitutional government.[2]

[1] *New History of Tang*, chs. li, lii.

[2] The foreign debt began in 2425 A. K. (1874 A. D.), when a loan of £627,675, bearing 8 per cent interest, was contracted through the Hongkong and Shanghai Bank. After the war with Japan and the Boxers' movement, the foreign debt was largely increased. During the last few years, foreign capital has been borrowed in large amounts for the development of industries and other reforms. Economically, there is no objection to the foreign debt, but politically, the present government is not fitted to borrow foreign money at all.

CHAPTER XXXV

INDIRECT TAXES

CONFUCIUS does not like indirect taxes. According to his view, there should not be any such taxes at all. This opinion appears to be justified not only by reason but by reference to the history of taxation in China. During the first part of the Han dynasty (346-422 A. K. or 206-130 B. C.), the Sui dynasty (1134-1168 A. K. or 583-617 A. D.), and the first part of the Tang dynasty (1169-1306 A. K. or 618-755 A. D.), there were practically no indirect taxes. Yet the government was very rich, and the people were very prosperous at this period, except during the revolution at the end of the Sui dynasty (1162-1173 A. K. or 611-622 A. D.). In later times, however, the government has never been able to get along without indirect taxes. This will appear from the account of the historical development of the indirect taxes from the Chou dynasty to the present day, to which we will now proceed.

I. CUSTOMS DUTIES

Confucius is an extreme free-trader, in regard to both internal and foreign trade.[1] But, according to the *Official System of Chou*, there were three places where commodities were taxed—the external custom-house (*kuan*), the internal custom-house (*mên*), and the market-places (*shih*). Commodities might be taxed at only one of these three places, but it was necessary to show receipts for the taxes paid be-

[1] *Cf. supra*, pp. 453-4.

fore they could pass any one of them. When a commodity was imported, a receipt was issued by the external custom-house when the import duty was paid, and this was examined on passing into the internal custom-house and market. When a commodity was exported, a receipt for the export duty was first issued by the controller of the market, and then examined as it passed through the internal and external custom-houses. The three authorities coöperated in order to prevent smuggling. Therefore, the Chou dynasty did not allow free trade in any commodity.[1]

1. *Customs Duties on Internal Trade*

After the Ch'in dynasty had consolidated the feudal states into a single nation, the internal trade of China was far more important than the foreign trade. Therefore, we shall first consider the inland customs of different dynasties.

According to history, from the Ch'in dynasty to the first part of the Tsin dynasty, customs duties did not exist. Therefore there was free trade, internal as well as external.

Customs duties were first revived by the Eastern Tsin dynasty. From the Eastern Tsin to the Southern Chen (868-1140 A. K. or 317-589 A. D.) custom-houses were established along the waterways. Such commodities as fuel, charcoal, fish, *etc.*, were taxed at ten per cent.

Under the Sung dynasty, the general rate of commodity tax when the commodity passed through inland customs was two per cent *ad valorem*.[2]

In later history, there was only one period during which the Confucian doctrine of absolutely free trade was realized. In 1713 A. K. (1162 A. D.) Kin Shih Tsung abolished all customs duties, and the custom-houses were ordered to in-

[1] Chs. xiv, xv.
[2] *General Research*, ch. xiv.

spect passengers only. This reform was proposed by Chang Chung-yen.[1]

The present dynasty has twenty-six principal custom-houses of the old type. They are both inland and maritime custom-houses. All the sub-stations established by each of them for the collection of duties and for inspection and search are confined to certain places. The general rate of duties is three per cent *ad valorem*. Many custom-houses require a customs fee, one-tenth of the duty itself, for administrative expenses. If there is no fee required, the expenses are defrayed by "the additional amount." The amount of collection of each custom-house is fixed, and it is divided into two parts, "the regular amount" and "the additional amount." When the duties collected fall below these fixed amounts, the director is responsible for the deficit; when they are above these limits, he should send to the government the actual amount collected.[2]

(a) *Tax on Ships*

Han Wu Ti began to tax the ships of merchants (423 A. K. or 129 B. C.). A ship over fifty feet long paid one hundred and twenty coins annually. It was simply a tax upon the instrument of trade. During the Five Dynasties (1458-1510 A. K. or 907-959 A. D.) there was a tax on ferry-boats. It was abolished by Sung T'ai Tsu (1511), but revived in later times (at least in 1622). In 1630 A. K. (1079 A. D.) the government established public warehouses and transported merchants' goods with government ships, in order to charge a tax for the ships. Yet private ships were freed from tax. It was only during the Southern Sung dynasty that ships were illegally taxed

---

[1] *Continuation of the General Research*, ch. xviii.

[2] The *Institutes of the Ts'ing Dynasty (Ta Ts'ing Hui Tien)*, chs. xxiii, lviii, lx. *General Research of the Present Dynasty*, ch. v.

by local officials. The regular tax upon ships, as a tonnage duty collected by special officers, really began at the end of the Yüan dynasty, but was repealed after three years (1888-1891 A. K. or 1337-1340 A. D.).

The Ming dynasty established seven inland custom-houses for the collection of tonnage duties in paper money in 1980 A. K. (1429 A. D.). In 2076 A. K. (1525 A. D.) their number was twelve. All of them collected only tonnage duties from the ships, with the exception that two collected the commodity tax also. From 2031 to 2080 A. K. (1480-1529 A. D.) all the " paper-money custom-houses " gradually substituted for the collection of paper money the collection of silver. In the present dynasty, tonnage duties still exist.

(b) *Tax on Passengers*

The most objectionable form of taxation in Chinese history was the tax upon passengers. In 451 A. K. (101 B. C.) Han Wu Ti taxed the passengers in Wukuan, an important pass, for the expenses of its keepers. In the Northern Wei dynasty (1077 A. K. or 526 A. D.) and the Northern Chou dynasty (1131 A. K. or 580 A. D.), people coming to the market-places were taxed, one coin for one person; but such tax was abolished in 1132. Fortunately, these were the only cases.

(c) *Likin*

Besides the customs duty, there is the *likin*, or contribution of one-thousandth. It is a tax on commodities when they pass through any *likin* barrier. In 2404 A. K. (1853 A. D.), when the T'ai-p'ing rebels captured Nanking, the sources of revenue for military expenditures were cut off. Therefore, Lei Yi-hsien, a military officer, created the *likin* tax. At the beginning, it was a voluntary contribution from the merchants, and the government promised that it should be abolished as soon as the rebellion should be put down. This tax was an important factor in preserving the present dynasty. But the government has not kept its promise, and the tax has now become an intolerable burden. Its legal rates vary in different provinces—some are one or two per cent, and some are five or nine per cent. According to the budget of this year (2462 A. K.), the total sum of *likin* is 43,187,907 taels.[1] It will be abolished in the near future.

2. *Customs Duties on Imports and Exports*

Before the Sung dynasty, the import duty levied on foreign goods was unknown. In 1522 A. K. (971 A. D.) the first maritime custom-house was established in Canton. Its purpose at first appears to have been regulation rather than revenue. The rate of customs duty was first made twenty per cent in 1542 A. K. (991 A. D.). During the reign of Sung Jên Tsung (1574-1614 A. K. or 1023-1063 A. D.), three maritime custom-houses were established in different places—Hangchow, Ningpo and Canton. Ten per cent of commodities was taken as import duties, and the government bought thirty per cent at reduced prices. In 1698 A. K. (1147 A. D.) the annual revenue, raised from both the duties and the purchases, amounted to two million strings. In 1715 A. K. (1164 A. D.) the system of government purchase was abolished, and the rate of duty was fixed at ten per cent.[2]

The tariff of the Yüan dynasty was changed several times. In 1828 A. K. (1277 A. D.) general commodities were taxed at the rate of one-tenth, and coarse commodities one-fifteenth. A distinction was drawn between native goods

[1] This sum is mixed up with other minor taxes.
[2] *General Research*, ch. xx.

and foreign goods. The former paid duties only half as high as the latter. This was the germ of protection. In 1834 A. K. (1283 A. D.) the tariff was changed so that fine goods paid one-tenth, and coarse goods five-tenths. In 1843 A. K. (1292 A. D.) the rates of tax on the sale of imported goods which had paid duties and were sold in the province where the custom-house was located, were fixed: fine goods paid one-twenty-fifth, and coarse goods one-thirtieth, and were exempt from other taxes. When the merchants bought commodities at the custom-houses, the commodities were not taxed twice; and they simply paid the tax at the place where they were sold. In the following year, the duties at all maritime custom-houses were regulated at the rate of one-thirtieth.

The Ming dynasty treated foreigners liberally, and sometimes made foreign trade free. In 1920 A. K. (1369 A. D.) a law was enacted that foreign goods imported by those who brought tribute should be exempted from paying duties, but sixty per cent of them should be bought by the government at a low price. The object of this policy was to show generosity to foreigners; it was more political than economic. Generally, imported commodities were required to pay duties.[1]

Under the present dynasty, a revolutionary change in Chinese policy was brought about by the Opium War. Before the war foreign trade was of the old type, and since the war it has been of a new one. We may first take up the old type. In 2236 A. K. (1685 A. D.), all foreign ships which brought tribute were exempted from duties. During the same year the rate of tonnage duty was reduced.[2] In 2249 A. K. (1698 A. D.) all foreign ships were

---

[1] *Continuation of the General Research*, ch. xxvi.

[2] Formerly, under the Ming dynasty, the import duty on foreign

classified into four classes, and the rates of tonnage duty were reduced to 1,120, 880, 480 and 320 taels. Owing to the difficulty of detecting them and assessing their value correctly, jewels, pearls, precious stones, *etc.*, were exempted from import duty in 2335 A. K. (1784 A. D.) by Kao Tsung.

Rice brought into China has not been subject to duty. In 2273 A. K. (1722 A. D.) the rice imported from Siam was freed from import duty. In 2276 A. K. her other commodities brought along with rice were also freed. In 2279 A. K. (1728 A. D.) a general law was enacted that rice and grain might be imported free. In 2294 A. K. a law lowering the duties on commodities brought in on foreign rice-ships was enacted: When a ship imported ten thousand bushels of rice, one-half of the duties on its other commodities was taken off; when it imported five thousand bushels, the exemption was thirty per cent.[1]

After the Opium War, the character of foreign trade was changed. In 2394 A. K. (1843 A. D.) the five ports—Canton, Foochow, Amoy, Ningpo and Shanghai—were opened to foreign trade; and since 2405 A. K. (1854 A. D.) maritime customs of the new type have been administered by foreigners. Hence there is a distinction between the old customs and the new ones. The tariff is five per cent *ad valorem*. Even this rate was not effective until 2452 A. K. (1901 A. D.). In 2456 A. K. (1905 A. D.) the total sum collected in the new customs was 35,111,004 taels. If China

goods had been changed to the system of taxing foreign ships according to their size (2122 A. K. or 1571 A. D.), because the frauds practiced by foreigners were not easily detected. European ships were classified into nine grades, each paying a fixed amount of duty according to its size. At a later time in the Ming dynasty, thirty per cent of the fixed amount was taken off in deference to the foreigners' petitions. In the same year (2236 A. K.), twenty per cent more was taken off.

[1] *General Research of the Present Dynasty*, ch. vi.

will abolish *likin*, the foreign countries have agreed to pay a surtax equivalent to one and one-half times the original rate, which would make the total amount twelve and one-half per cent.

According to the agreement made between China and Great Britain in 2409 A. K. (1858 A. D.), the following goods were duty-free: gold and silver bullion, foreign coins, flour, Indian meal, sago, biscuit, preserved meats and vegetables, cheese, butter, confectionery, foreign clothing, jewelry, plated ware, perfumery, soap of all kinds, charcoal, fire-wood, candles (foreign), tobacco (foreign), cigars (foreign), wine, beer, spirits, household stores, ships' stores, personal baggage, stationery, carpeting, druggeting, cutlery, foreign medicines, and glass and crystal ware. They paid no import or export duty; but if transported into the interior, with the exception of personal baggage, gold and silver bullion, and foreign coins, they paid a transit duty at the rate of two and one-half per cent *ad valorem*.[1]

These duty-free goods began to be liable for import duty in 2452 A. K. (1901 A. D.), the rate being five per cent *ad valorem*. Yet foreign rice, cereals, and flour, gold and silver, both bullion and coin, printed books, charts, maps, periodicals and newspapers are not liable to pay import duty.[2]

Until this unjust tariff has been revised, it will be difficult, if not impossible, for China to put a special excise upon native liquors and native tobacco. If she were to do so, the excise would be not only unjust, but also unproductive. Unfortunately, this is true in regard to many kinds of taxes. In fact, under the present system foreigners are portected at the expense of the Chinese.

[1] Hertslet's *China Treaties*, vol. i, p. 36.
[2] *Ibid.*, p. 170.

INDIRECT TAXES

In regard to exports, they were formerly almost free. Although there were some regulations to forbid the exportation of certain goods, goods exported paid practically no duty, except in a few instances. The regular export duty was first fixed in 2393 A. K. (1842 A. D.), at about the rate of five per cent *ad valorem*. If China will abolish *likin*, she may raise the export duty to seven and a half per cent.

Under the treaty of peace made between China and Great Britain in 2409 A. K. (1858 A. D.), the tonnage dues have been fixed in this way: " British merchant-vessels, of more than 150 tons burden, shall be charged tonnage dues at the rate of 4 mace per ton; if of 150 tons and under, they shall be charged at the rate of one mace per ton." [1]

In conclusion, as her history shows, China has practically adopted the doctrine of free trade in her maritime customs. But, since public expenditures have been increasing all the time, China has been obliged to get revenue from customs duties. Therefore, although she has not adopted a protective tariff, she has been compelled to maintain a tariff for revenue. But, whenever she has wanted to derive revenue from her customs, her sovereign power has been interfered with by foreign nations. This is a great injustice. It checks China's industrial development and opposes needed financial reforms. It must be done away with.

II. BUSINESS TAXES

1. *Tax on Buildings*

According to Mencius, the buildings of merchants should not be taxed.[2] But, according to the *Official System of Chou*, the taxes on merchants took many forms, namely, a tax on shops, a tax on open grounds upon which those who had no shops stood to conduct their business, a

---

[1] Hertslet's *China Treaties*, vol. i, p. 28.
[2] *Cf. infra*, p. 697.

tax on residences and warehouses, *etc.* These taxes were mostly paid in money. But some were paid in produce. For example, the tax of the butcher was collected in the form of skins, horns, muscles and bones—the by-products of his industry which were manufactured in the government factories.[1]

In 1077 A. K. (526 A. D.) the Northern Wei dynasty classified the buildings of the markets into five grades for the purpose of taxation. Under the Ming dynasty, the buildings of merchants were taxed in paper money, monthly or quarterly, in accordance with the kinds and the size of their business. In 2303 A. K. (1752 A. D.) the " firm tax " in Peking was regulated by the present dynasty. as follows: Firms whose capital was large were classified into the first class, and were required to pay five taels of silver annually; the middle class paid half this amount; and the lowest class was exempted. The magistrates personally inspected the firms every year and classified them according to their actual condition.

The tax on water-power mills began in the Sung dynasty (about 1630 A. K. or 1079 A. D.). In 2261 A. K. (1710 A. D.) the present dynasty taxed the water-power mills of Szechuan at the rate of $5\frac{88}{100}$ taels of silver. This was a factory tax.

2. *Tax on Carriages*

The tax on the carriages of merchants began with Han Wu Ti (423 A. K. or 129 B. C.). In 433 A. K. (119 B. C.) the tax was extended to the common people. If not an officer or a soldier, a person was required to pay one hundred and twenty coins annually for the possession of a carriage. But the carriage of the merchant paid double this rate.[2] This tax did not last very long.

---

[1] Ch. xv.   [2] *History of Han*, chs. vi, xxiv.

The Ming dynasty began to tax carriages for hire (1980 A. K. or 1429 A. D.). The tax was paid in paper money.[1] Under the present dynasty, carriages have not been subject to taxation until recently, when a new system of police was established. But this tax is insignificant.

3. *Tax on Money*

In 433 A. K. (119 B. C.), Han Wu Ti began to tax reserved cash according to the number of strings. All business men who carried on manufacturing, banking, trade, storage and transportation were required to make a self-assessment of their reserved cash. The rate of tax was six per cent. The cash of all craftsmen who made money by selling their products was taxed at three per cent. One who did not assess or did not tell the whole truth, was banished to the boundaries for one year, and his money was confiscated. If there was an informer, half of the concealed money was given to him as a reward. Hence, in 435 A. K. (117 B. C.) such informations were frequent over the whole empire, and the well-to-do families were often prosecuted. This tax applied to practically all classes, many rich families were destroyed, and the people were led to care only for present consumption and to desist from saving. In 439 A. K. (113 B. C.) the government lent the people mares for the making of interest at ten per cent every three years—that is, the people returned ten mares and one young horse at the end of three years. Since the government expected to get " horse interest," Wu Ti abolished this tax in that year.[2]

The tax on reserved cash was a tax on capital, but an exception was made on behalf of craftsmen. Their

---
[1] *Continuation of the General Research*, ch. xviii.
[2] *History of Han*, ch. xxiv.

money was taxed at only half the rate on that of merchants. This was because they depend upon their labor more than do merchants, and cannot make as much profits as merchants. This was the first time that a tax was levied directly on cash. The worst result of it was the encouragement it gave to informers.

During the first year of the reign of Tang Su Tsung (1307 A. K. or 756 A. D.), when the great rebellion broke out, the provincial governments taxed the merchants for military expenses. Cash in excess of one thousand coins was taxed. In 1333 A. K. (782 A. D.) Tang Tê Tsung taxed merchants' cash transported through the internal customs, at the rate of two per cent.[1] These were the only cases where the money of merchants was legally singled out to be taxed. In other cases, money was included in the general property tax.

4. *Tax on the Guilds as a Whole*

During the Sung dynasty, all the different trades in the capital had guilds. When the government needed anything, the guilds were responsible for supplying it. They frequently suffered loss. Lü Chia-wên proposed to assess the amount of the income of each guild, and make it pay a tax instead of supplying goods. When the government wanted commodities, it bought them through the officials, and the guilds were freed from the obligation of supplying them. This was called "the emancipated-guild tax," enacted in 1624 A. K. (1073 A. D.). It was a tax upon the guild as a whole. Each trader had to register in the public office as a member of the guild and to pay this tax monthly.[2]

---

[1] *New History of Tang*, chs. li, lii.
[2] *Continuation of the General Political History*, edited by Pi Yüan (2280-2348, or 1729-1797 A. D.), ch. lxix.

INDIRECT TAXES

III. LICENSE TAXES

1. Tax on Fishery

According to the principles of Confucius, the people should be allowed to fish in any water without paying a tax. Mencius describes the government of Wên Wang, saying that he gave no prohibitions respecting the ponds and weirs.[1] Indeed, when fishing is on a small scale and conducted by the poor for their daily living, it should not be taxed at all.

The tax on fishery, however, was an old tax. According to the *Official System of Chou*, its proceeds came to the "treasury of jade" for the use of the emperor.[2] The state of Ch'i made the sea the state treasury, and controlled fishery as a government monopoly.[3] The Han dynasty had the "sea rent," a tax upon fishermen. During the reign of Han Wu Ti the government itself fished in the sea. From the Han dynasty to the Ming dynasty there has been a tax levied upon rivers, lakes, ponds, *etc.*, paid by fishermen, although it has been remitted or exempted many times. The Ming dynasty made this tax prominent, and established officers to take charge of it, known as the *ho po so*.

In the present dynasty, the license to fish belongs in the class of miscellaneous taxes. Each of the twelve provinces has a fixed amount of this tax. As to the license fee, each license in Kinchou (Fungtien) costs annually a half tael of silver. But each net in Pehtuna (Kirin) must pay twenty taels.

2. Tax on Brokers

This tax must be a very old one, but we cannot discover its origin. It was once abolished during the Yüan dynasty

---

[1] *Classics*, vol. ii, p. 162.
[2] Ch. iv.
[3] *Classics*, vol. v, pt. ii, p. 683.
[4] *Cases of the Institutes of the Ts'ing Dynasty*, ch. ccxlv.

(1836 A. K. or 1285 A. D.). Under the present dynasty, the brokers' license are issued by the commissioner of finance in each province, and their number is limited. When any firm is incorporated for conducting the transfer of certain goods from seller to buyer at fixed rates of commission, it must get a license. Such license has three classes. Take, for example, Kiangsi province. The first class annually paid three taels of silver; the second, two taels; the lowest, one tael (2311 A. K. or 1760 A. D.). In 2343 A. K. (1792 A. D.) ten firms were established in Nanning (Kuangsi) and each was annually taxed at five taels of silver.

3. *Tax on Pawnshops*

In 2203 A. K. (1652 A. D.) the license fee for pawnshops established in the provinces was fixed by the present dynasty at five taels a year.[1]

IV. EXCISE TAXES

1. *General Excise Taxes*[2]

We have already learned that Confucius does not approve of indirect taxes, and exempts all commodities either passing through custom-houses or sold in market-places from taxation.[3] We may quote one more passage from

---

[1] Closely related to the license taxes are the incorporation fees established by the present dynasty in 2455 (1904 A. D.). All kinds of business may be incorporated in the Department of Agriculture, Industry and Commerce. The fees for incorporation vary from fifty *yen* to three hundred, according either to the number of partners in a partnership, or to the amount of capital in a stock company. The incorporation fee for the different kinds of banks incorporated in the Department of the Treasury is four taels of silver. It was fixed in 2459 (1908 A. D.).

[2] Such a term is only approximate, and does not mean that everything is subject to excise tax.

[3] *Cf. supra*, p. 634.

INDIRECT TAXES

Mencius: "If, in the market-places, a ruler simply establish public warehouses without taxing commodities, and simply enforce commercial regulations without taxing merchants' residential houses, then all the merchants of the world will be pleased, and wish to store their goods in his market-places."[1] In another place Mencius declares that a tax imposed either in the custom-house or in the market-place is as unjust as the stealing of a neighbor's chickens.[2] Therefore, according to the principles of Confucius, no commodity should be taxed.

As a matter of fact, however, the tax on commodities is very old. According to the *Official System of Chou*, the tax in the market-places was suspended only during a famine or an epidemic. Such a suspension was for the purpose of lowering prices.[3]

In 1331 A. K. (780 A. D.) the Tang dynasty taxed the commodities of merchants at the places where they carried on their business, the rate being one-thirtieth *ad valorem*. In the following year, on account of military expenses, this rate was raised to one-tenth.[4]

In 1509 A. K. (958 A. D.) the Latter Chou dynasty taxed live-stock at three per cent of the selling price. In the Sung dynasty the general rate of commodity tax was the same.[5]

Under the Kin dynasty the rates of the commodity tax were regulated in 1731 A. K. (1180 A. D.). The tax on gold and silver was one per cent, and that on other commodities three per cent. Subsequently the first rate was increased to three per cent, and the second to four. In 1758 A. K. (1207 A. D.) the minister of finance wished to tax gold and silver at the same rate as other commodities, be-

---

[1] Cf. *Classics*, vol. ii, p. 199.
[2] *Ibid.*, p. 278.   [3] Ch. xiv.
[4] *General Political History*, ch. ccxxvi.
[5] *General Research*, ch. xiv.

cause they are precious things and possessed by the rich. Such a theory was just. But other officials said that it would encourage concealment. Therefore, the rates remained unchanged.

The Yüan dynasty fixed the commodity tax at the rate of one-thirtieth in 1821 A. K. (1270 A. D.), and raised the rate to one-twentieth in 1849 A. K. (1298 A. D.). Therefore, in 1821 A. K. the total amount of this tax was fixed at 45,000 ingots of silver, each ingot being fifty taels; but in 1880 A. K. (1329 A. D.) the actual amount was over 939,568 ingots. The tax was oppressive.

In 1915 A. K. (1364 A. D.) Ming T'ai Tsu regulated the commodity tax at the rate of one-thirtieth. In 1919 A. K. he exempted books and agricultural implements from tax. The total amount of the annual tax in 2095 A. K. (1544 A. D.) was 156,204 taels of silver. One of the worst abuses of the Ming dynasty was the sending of eunuchs to the provinces as tax commissioners (2147-2171 A. K. or 1596-1620 A. D.). This was one of the causes of the fall of the Ming dynasty.[1]

In the first year of the present dynasty (2195 A. K. or 1644 A. D.) the tax on the sale of domestic animals was regulated at three per cent *ad valorem*.[2]

Lo-ti-shui is a tax upon commodities when brought to market. Such a term appeared in the Ming dynasty. The present dynasty classified it under the head of miscellaneous taxes. It is insignificant now, but it should be abolished.

(a) *Farming Out the Commodity Tax*

The farming-out of the commodity tax began in the Sung

[1] *Continuation of the General Research*, ch. xviii.
[2] *Cases of the Institutes of the Ts'ing Dynasty*, ch. ccxlv.

dynasty. The farmers paid a fixed price, which was really a tax, and it was used for local and national expenditures. Formerly, farmers were the keepers or transporters of government property (a forced labor), and it was intended that they should derive profits from their farming. They were required to pay a pledge, and the right of collecting the tax expired at the end of a certain term. In 1621 A. K. (1070 A. D.), when forced labor was changed to hired labor, the price of such right became a competitive price. The government sold it to anyone who offered the highest price. In the following year the farmer was taxed at five per cent of the price he paid. Generally the farmer could not make a good profit, and even met with loss, because the price was too high.

Such a farming-out of taxes was confined to a certain market-place for the taxes on all commodities or to a certain trade in a definite locality. It has never applied to direct taxes. The purposes of this system were to insure the regularity of the revenue and to avoid the trouble of collection. Since the market-place in a country town was small, and the particular trade simple, it was not economical for the government to establish a special office to collect the insignificant taxes. Moreover, the government sometimes utilized the farmers only as pioneers for a new or undeveloped tax, and itself collected the tax as soon as this was worth while. It would have been even better to abolish such taxes; in lieu of this, the system was at that time justifiable.

Under the Yüan dynasty a strange thing occurred. In 1790 A. K. (1239 A. D.) a merchant bought the right of taxing commodities in all the provinces for 2,200,000 taels of silver. Of course, this was a barbaric way of the Mongol. Except for this instance, China has never farmed out a tax on a national scale. Even this case was confined to northern China only, because southern China was at that time held by the Sung dynasty.

In the present day this system still exists. One form of it is for the government to bestow a monopoly of the taxed product upon certain merchants, the salt merchants being the best example. The other is for the government to confer on the merchants the right of collecting a tax, *e. g.*, the particular guilds in Canton which collect the particular taxes levied upon their particular goods. But China has no excuse for not abolishing this system to-day.

2. *Special Excise Taxes*

The special excise taxes are far more important than the general excise taxes. Historically, they were sometimes the chief sources of revenue. Most of them have the characteristic of government monopoly, either in their original development or in the present administration, but they are really taxes. A fair characterization is to say that they were originally public prices and have developed into excise taxes.

According to the principles of Confucius, all natural resources should be opened to the people as a whole, and should not be monopolized by the government. But if they were opened to the people freely, the rich would get a monopolistic power over them, and the poor would be excluded. Therefore, the Confucians in later ages held the opinion that natural resources should be controlled by the government. The government should allow everyone to have access to them, and should tax their products, but should not monopolize them. The taxes on the products derived from natural resources are justified by the fact that large use is made of them only in connection with the capitalistic production of the rich, not by the poor. For the same reason, a tax upon the profits of manufacturers or

INDIRECT TAXES

merchants would be better than one upon the land of farmers. Although excise taxes are shifted, they are nevertheless taxes on profits, because the products taxed come from highly capitalistic enterprises. This is true of the businesses of salt, iron, and the like. China has not produced great industrial kings since the middle part of the Han dynasty, because the government has either monopolized natural resources or taxed them at a high rate. In short, little room has been left for capitalistic enterprises.

(a) *Tax on Timber*

According to the *Official System of Chou*, the forests were controlled by the government, and all the natural products, such as the teeth, horns, bones and feathers of animals, *pueraria* and other grasses, fuel, charcoal and coal, fruits and vegetables, were subject to taxes. Timber was taxed at the rate of twenty-five per cent.[1]

When Kuan Tzŭ became the minister of Ch'i, he put forests and grasses under government monopoly. The woods of the mountains were classified into three classes—for fuel, for buildings and for coffins—and were required to pay three rates of tax.[2] Such a monopoly of natural resources lasted to the end of Ch'i.[3] But these practices were not in harmony with the principles of Confucius.

The tax on the transportation of bamboo and timber began with the kingdom of Latter Ch'in (about 944-967 A. K. or 393-416 A. D.). The Tang dynasty revived this tax in 1333 A. K. (782 A. D.), and it was abolished in 1335. During the Southern Sung dynasty this tax was revived again.

---

[1] Chs. xvi, xiii.
[2] *Kuan Tsŭ*, chs. lxxx, lxxiv.
[3] *Classics*, vol. v, pt. ii, p. 683.

The Kin dynasty established a special bureau for taxing bamboo, and fixed the amount of the annual tax. During the Yüan dynasty, bamboo was a government monopoly.

The Ming dynasty also taxed bamboo and timber at different percentages—ten, twenty, or thirty per cent. Under the different dynasties, the bamboo and timber collected through the tax were used for buildings and other purposes. In 2022 A. K. (1471 A. D.) the tax was paid in money, and it was turned into the department of labor for the expenses of building and manufacture. Under the present dynasty, the tax on timber is three or ten per cent.

(b) *Tax on Mineral Products*

The tax on mineral products began in the Chou dynasty. According to the *Official System of Chou*, gold, jade, tin and precious stones were subject to a government monopoly.[1] Kuan Tzŭ pursued the same policy, and all mines of iron, lead, silver, cinnabar, gold, copper, *etc.*, were brought under a government monopoly.[2]

The chief product under the government monopoly of Kuan Tzŭ was iron. It was taxed at thirty per cent.[3] Kuan Tzŭ regarded this tax as important as that on salt.[4] In 433 A. K. (119 B. C.), Han Wu Ti first made iron a government product exclusively. The government estblished " iron officers " over different prefectures, and made iron wares for sale. Since that time iron has sometimes been under a government monopoly and sometimes under a special tax. Over the entire period of Chinese history the system of government monopoly has been the more frequent, although the government rarely undertook to make

---

[1] Ch. xvi.
[2] Ch. lxxvii.
[3] Ch. lxxxi.
[4] *The Ancient History of China*, p. 204.

INDIRECT TAXES 703

iron wares, contenting itself with controlling the raw material merely.

In 1065 A. K. (514 A. D.) the Northern Wei dynasty established "silver officers" to take charge of the mining and manufacturing of silver. Under this dynasty there were also more than one thousand families in Hanchung (Shensi) who were called "gold families," getting gold in the Han River and sending it at the end of the year to the government.[1]

The tax on mineral products began to assume great importance in the Tang dynasty. Under this dynasty there were 168 mines of gold, silver, iron, tin, *etc.*[2] In the Sung dynasty there were also 271 mines.[3]

Over all mines there were special officers. Some mines were opened by the government with its own capital, and some were bought by people who paid a certain percentage of the products to the government, usually twenty per cent. But, in any case, the government had monopolistic power over the mines, because it not only taxed their products, but also bought them at a fixed price.

Through the Yüan, the Ming, and the present dynasty no great changes in policy have been made. In the present dynasty, when the tax on mineral products was twenty per cent, the government bought forty per cent of the product at a fixed price, and permitted the remaining forty per cent

---

[1] *History of Wei*, ch. cx.

[2] During the reign of Tang Hsien Tsung (1357-1371, or 806-820 A. D.), the annual taxation of different mines was at the following amounts: 12,000 taels of silver; 266,000 catties of copper; 2,070,000 catties of iron; 50,000 catties of tin; lead having no regular amount.

[3] In 1629 (1078 A. D.), the amounts of taxes levied upon different mines were as follows: 10,710 taels of gold; 215,385 taels of silver; 14,605,969 catties of copper; 5,501,097 catties of iron; 9,197,335 catties of lead; 2,321,898 catties of tin; 3,356 catties of quicksilver; 3,646 catties and more than 14 taels of vermilion.

to be sold freely by the miners; or, the tax might be ten per cent, when the government might buy the remaining ninety per cent; or, the tax might become thirty per cent, when the rest was sold by the miners themselves. Sometimes the government used its own capital, and made contracts with the merchants for the execution of such business. Sometimes the government itself opened the mines.

The government monopoly of alum began in the Tang dynasty. It was abolished in 1389 A. K. (838 A. D.), and the alum mines were left to be controlled by the local governments. The Five Dynasties established special officers to monopolize them. During the Sung dynasty the alum tax became important. In 1634 A. K. (1083 A. D.) the annual tax was 337,900 strings.[1]

Passing through the Kin, the Yüan and the Ming dynasties, there was also government monopoly of alum. In the *Law Code of the Ts'ing Dynasty* an article provides that the punishment for unlicensed alum is according to that for unlicensed salt.[2] Therefore, although the alum tax at the present day is insignificant, alum still has the character of a government monopoly.

The present dynasty put the mining regulations into their present form in 2455 A. K. (1904 A. D.). The license tax is one hundred taels for ten square miles, and one tael is added for each additional square mile, thirty square miles being the limit. Operators are also required to pay one year's land tax. When mineral products are extracted out of ores, no more land tax is required, but the products are taxed according to the following rates: The tax on coal, antimony, iron, alum and borax is five per cent *ad valorem;* that on kerosene oil, copper, tin, lead, sulphur and vermilion,

[1] *History of Sung*, ch. clxxxv.
[2] Ch. xiii.

seven and a half per cent; that on gold, platinum, silver, quicksilver and spelter, ten per cent; that on diamonds, quartz crystals, and other precious stones, twenty per cent. When these products are exported, they are also required to pay custom duties.

There are many reasons why the mineral resources of China have not been extensively developed. First, the government did not want to open the mines. Take, for example, Tang T'ai Tsung, a typical emperor. In 1187 A. K. (636 A. D.) Ch'üan Wan-chi, a favorite of his, told him that an annual revenue of several million strings could be obtained by opening two silver mines. T'ai Tsung said in part: "What I want is not money. I am only sorry that I receive no good advice which can benefit the people. You have never recommended a worthy person nor dismissed an unworthy person. But you speak only of the profit of taxing silver. Do you want me to be Huan and Ling?" Then he dismissed Wan-chi immediately.[1]

Second, the opening of mines sometimes did harm to the people, because the officials required a fixed amount of tax from the miners without regard to their output. About the end of the Ming dynasty (2147-2156 A. K. or 1596-1605 A. D.) mining was looked after by the eunuchs, and this was one cause of the fall of that dynasty. Hence the opening of mines came to be regarded as disadvantageous.

Third, there was an economic consideration. Since China was an agricultural country, she did not like to let the people leave their farms for the mines. Moreover, the laborers working under ground were usually not good citizens, because good men would not engage in this labor. Hence there was a dread that a great number of bad men

---

[1] Huan Ti and Ling Ti were the two bad emperors of the Latter Han Dynasty. *General Political History*, ch. cxciv.

or adventurers coming from different regions to the mines would disturb the peace of the empire. For, since mines are subject to the law of diminishing returns, although it is easy to get laborers when mining is profitable, it would be difficult to send them home when the profit was exhausted. This theory was well expressed in an edict of Ts'ing Shih Tsung (2275 A. K. or 1724 A. D.).

Added to these three reasons which operated in the past, the lack of capital, science and machinery are other causes at the present time. For all these reasons together, the Chinese mines have not been greatly developed. This may prove a very fortunate thing for the future, since China has thus preserved her natural resources while western countries have been exhausting theirs at a rapid rate.

(c) *Tax on Salt*

The government monopoly of salt began with Kuan Tzŭ.[1] This tax continued practically throughout all dynasties, and has become the chief item among the excise taxes. There are many theories and regulations about this tax, but we have no need to enter into them. According to the budget of this year (2462 A. K.), the total tax on salt is about forty million taels. When the present method of collecting the tax has been reformed, the government will get a greater revenue than it does now, while at the same time the people may enjoy a lower price.

(d) *Tax on Liquors*

According to the principles of Confucius, there is no absolute prohibition against liquors, but they should be regulated. If there is a gang gathering for unlawful drinking and plotting against the government, they may be put to death. If the drinkers have simply fallen into a bad habit,

---

[1] *The Ancient History of China*, pp. 203-4.

they should be taught instead of being put to death.¹ According to the *Official System of Chou*, there was an officer (*p'ing shih*) to inspect liquors and regulate them.² The law of the Han dynasty provided that if three men or more should drink together without special reason, they should pay a fine of four taels of gold.³ Therefore, the people had no right to drink at a gathering, unless the government gave them a special permit. There were two reasons for the prohibition of spirits: one moral and the other economic, the latter being that distilled spirits waste grain, which is the food of the people.

The government monopoly of liquors began with Han Wu Ti (454 A. K. or 98 B. C.). Since that time liquors have been sometimes prohibited, sometimes made by licensed private distillers, and sometimes controlled as a government monopoly. During the reign of Sung Jên Tsung (about 1600-1604 A. K. or 1049-1053 A. D.) the annual tax on liquors and distillers' grains amounted to 14,986,196 strings. In the present dynasty there is no government monopoly of liquors, but the tax on them has been greatly increased since 2452 A. K. (1901 A. D.). In China there are no saloons, so there are no saloon licenses.

(e) *Tax on Vinegar*

Connected with the tax on liquors was the tax on vinegar. The government monopoly of vinegar began in the Wei dynasty. It was practised during the Five Dynasties, the Sung, the Kin and the Yüan dynasties. The Ming dynasty did not monopolize it, but levied on it a license tax. In the present dynasty vinegar is not subject to a special tax.

---

[1] *Classics*, vol. iii, pt. ii, pp. 411-2.
[2] Ch. xxxvi.
[3] *History of Han*, ch. iv (commentary).

(f) *Tax on Tea*

Tea was first taxed in 1333 A. K. (782 A. D.), but this tax was abolished in 1335. In 1344 A. K. (793 A. D.) tea first became the object of a permanent tax. It was taxed in both the tea-growing districts and the important passes— ten per cent *ad valorem*. Before 1372 A. K. (821 A. D.) the annual tax amounted to four hundred thousand strings. The rate of tax was doubled in 1372. Li Yü expressed a protest in the following words: Since tea is necessary to the people, a heavy tax must increase its price and hurt the poor. Since tea is naturally produced in large amount, and since an increase of tax depends upon its sale, a high price will cut down the demand. His reasoning is correct, and it is true in regard to other excise taxes in general. But the government did not accept it. In 1386 A. K. tea began to be monopolized by the government, but the monopoly was abolished in the same year. In later times the tax on tea became higher and higher.

At the beginning of the Sung dynasty the government monopolized tea. In 1585 A. K. (1034 A. D.) the total tax was annually 1,500,000 strings. In 1610 A. K. (1059 A. D.) there was the system of "free trade," that is, the government simply taxed the tea-farmers and the tea-merchants without monopolizing tea. In later times, tea was sometimes under government monopoly and sometimes under the "free-trade" system. The Yüan, the Ming, and the present dynasty have adopted the latter system. When the merchants want to buy tea from the tea-farmers, they must first buy tea-certificates from the officials. Then they pay taxes to the inland customs according to the certificates. If the amount of their tea does not correspond with the certificates, or if their tea is separated from the certificates, they are punished as smugglers. Nor are the tea-farmers allowed to sell tea to those who have no certificates. Accord-

INDIRECT TAXES

ing to the budget of this year (2462 A. K.), the total tax on tea is about six million taels.

(g) *Tax on Incense*

During the Sung dynasty, besides tea, salt and alum, there was a great revenue coming from frankincense or gum olibanum. It was bought up exclusively by the government from foreigners, and then sold directly to consumers. Sometimes the government sold it to the merchants, who in turn sold it to consumers. In short, frankincense was a government monopoly.[1]

(h) *Tax on Ginseng*

Ginseng is a plant the root of which is supposed to resemble the human body in shape. In Hsü Shên's *Dictionary*, published in the Han dynasty, it was recognized as a medicine. In the Tang dynasty it became an item of tribute to the emperor from the prefecture of T'aiyüan, Shansi. Today the Chinese value it very highly.

Since the best kind of ginseng is found in Manchuria, the present dynasty, from its very beginning, put the ginseng mountains under special governmental control. The ginseng-gatherers must get a license, and the number of licenses is limited. The gatherers are strictly controlled as to where they shall go and when they shall return. In Shêngking, the tax for each license is five maces of ginseng, and in Kirin, two taels. After the ginseng-gatherers have offered to the government the best ginseng, the remaining ginseng is allowed to be sold to the merchants in the government firms. The price was fixed in 2360 A. K. (1809 A. D.) at twenty taels of silver for one tael of the best ginseng. The merchants are not allowed to bring with them the ginseng which they have bought into Shanhaikuan, the pass at the

[1] *History of Sung*, ch. clxxxv.

east end of the Great Wall. The government transports it for them with the government ginseng, and charges them the freight and customs duty. One catty of the ginseng of Shêngking pays four taels of silver for the freight and customs duty, and that of Kirin pays six taels. Therefore, ginseng is subject to a very strict excise tax.[1]

(i) *Tax on Tobacco*

Tobacco began to be used during the Ming dynasty. It was called "evil thing" at the beginning of the present dynasty, and it was proposed to prohibit it during the reign of Jên Tsung (2347-2371 A. K. or 1796-1820 A. D.). According to the old regulations of 2331 A. K. (1780 A. D.), one hundred catties of tobacco pay four maces and six candareens of silver to the inland customs. In 2435 A. K. (1884 A. D.) the Department of the Treasury began to propose a license tax for the tobacco firms. This tax will become important in the future.

(j) *Tax on Opium*

Originally China prohibited opium. In 2390 A. K. (1839 A. D.) the prohibition were made extremely stringent. The importers, producers, sellers, planters and smokers were all punished with death, although by different methods. But English merchants smuggled in opium constantly. Through the Opium War (2393 A. K. or 1842 A. D.), England forced China to accept opium. Hence the Chinese prohibition of opium was done away with, and the Chinese have since planted the native opium. This was the consequence of England's importation of opium. In 2455 A. K. (1904 A. D.) the tax on native opium collected by the customs was 3,750,598 taels, while the import duty on foreign opium amounted to 6,025,121 taels.

[1] *Institutes of the Ts'ing Dynasty*, ch. xx. *Cases of the Institutes of the Ts'ing Dynasty*, chs. ccxxxii, ccxxxiii.

INDIRECT TAXES

In 2457 A. K. (1906 A. D.) a decree was issued that opium should be absolutely prohibited for a period of ten years. The acreage of opium-growing land and the number of opium-smokers have been greatly reduced.

V. TAXES ON TRANSACTIONS

Taxes on transactions began in the Chou dynasty. According to the *Official System of Chou*, all commercial transactions were done by bills (*chih chi*), long ones for large transactions and short ones for small transactions. There were also the written tallies (*shu ch'i*) used as checks and receipts.[1] The bills and tallies were made by the government, with stamps upon them. Their nature resembled that of stamp tax, and there were fines for the punishment of fraud and evasion.

From the Eastern Tsin dynasty to the Chen dynasty (868-1140 A. K. or 317-589 A. D.), transactions in slaves, horses, cattle, land and houses were made binding by means of documents or title-deeds. The tax was four per cent *ad valorem*—three per cent being paid by the seller and one per cent by the buyer. Even if the transaction was not effected by means of a document, the value of the object was determined and taxed also at four per cent.[2]

In 1334 A. K. (783 A. D.) a tax on money-payments was created. In all public and private payments, fifty coins out of one thousand were retained for the government, making the tax-rate five per cent. When there was a payment in things or an exchange of commodities, such a transaction was figured out in terms of money. The brokers were given records for the writing down of their daily transactions, the total amount of which was calculated on the

[1] *Cf. supra*, pp. 432, 448-9.
[2] *History of Sui*, ch. xxiv.

following day. Those whose transactions did not pass through brokers were given records for themselves, and those who received no records offered the deduction themselves, together with the statements of facts. If one concealed one hundred coins, two thousand coins were confiscated, and sixty blows with the long stick were inflicted upon him. The informer of the concealment was rewarded with ten thousand coins, paid by the evader. When this law was put into effect, the brokers monopolized the power of collection, and there was great fraud. The government got less than half the tax, and discontent prevailed over the whole empire. In the following year (1335) the law was abolished.[1] This tax was a bad one but it made use of the method of stoppage at the source.

The tax on title-deeds became a great source of revenue during the Sung dynasty. All purchasers and mortgagees of real estate and cattle were required to present their title-deeds to be stamped with the official seal and to pay an ad *valorem* tax. The time limit for doing so was not over two months. If this limit was exceeded, the tax was doubled. Without the seal, deeds received no legal protection. Deeds were also sold by the government, at a profit. From 1595 to 1672 A. K. (1044-1121 A. D.) the tax was four per cent *ad valorem;* but in 1722 A. K. (1171 A. D.) it was raised to 12.12 per cent. This tax was an important item for the meeting of military expenditures.

Shortly before 1771 A. K. (1220 A. D.) the people were allowed to buy the stamped document to be pasted on to a private deed, and this was sufficient. This was quite like a stamp tax. But some trouble arose in connection with the land-tax system, as the government did not know where the purchaser of the land was. Therefore, it was again re-

[1] *Old History of Tang,* ch. xlix.

quired that transactions should pass through the hands of officials (1771).[1]

In the present dynasty, the tax on title-deeds was fixed at three per cent *ad valorem* (2198 A. K. or 1647 A. D.) Since 2286 A. K. (1735 A. D.) mortgages have not been taxed. In 2340 A. K. (1789 A. D.) the time-limit for paying the tax was fixed at one year. But this tax does not produce any great revenue; for the purchasers of lands and houses are not compelled to have their deeds stamped, because when they do so, they may conceal the acreage or the price, and because the clerks and officials are often corrupt. Moreover, the law itself is not good, since it fixes a certain amount for certain districts or provinces.

In 2458 A. K. (1907 A. D.) the stamp tax was enacted. While there were different rates for different transactions, the general rate was .2 per cent upon a transaction whose value was above ten thousand copper coins. But this act has not been universally put in force.

VI. CONCLUSION

To the extent that a state needs revenue, it cannot follow strictly the principles of Confucius for the abolition of all indirect taxes. But, to conform to his ideas, and at the same time to supply the fiscal needs of the state, we might adopt this program: China should abolish all customs duties on internal trade, leaving only those on imports and exports; it should abolish all excise taxes in general, except a very few on special products. Transactions should not be taxed at all. There should be no stamp tax. The business tax and the license tax should be changed to direct taxes, so as to make them taxes on net income In these ways indirect taxes could be reduced to a minimum.

As regards direct taxes, we might adopt this program:

---

[1] *General Research*, ch. xix.

The poll tax, family tax, and general property tax, which China abolished long ago, should not be revived. The land tax should remain, and the house tax should be universally adopted. The income tax should be highly developed, and the inheritance tax should be re-introduced. In short, China should tax income rather than property.

As to her financial system as a whole, China must make a radical change and make her system conform to the principles of modern finance, modified to suit the customs, ideals, and economic needs of the Chinese people.

PART V
CONCLUSION

CHAPTER XXXVI

CONCLUSION

SINCE we have discussed and criticized topic by topic, all the subjects which we have considered, it remains only for this final chapter to bring together our conclusions.

According to the order we have adopted, we should first say something about consumption. Confucius prescribed different standards for different classes—somewhat as in a sumptuary law. There is no doubt that this has checked economic development to a certain extent. But the fundamental idea of Confucius' sumptuary regulations was not so much social as economic. He feared that the production of wealth would not be sufficient for everyone if everyone extended his wants without restraint. He perceived the law of diminishing returns, and his idea was justified by the fact that in ancient times production was on a very limited scale. Again, under the monarchical government of the old type, a sumptuary law was necessary for the preservation of social classes. Moreover, since Confucius permitted anyone to raise himself to the higher classes, everyone might consume more as his social standing became higher. Therefore, sumptuary regulations do not really prevent economic development, provided the individual is capable of elevating himself. The word noble and the word rich are interchangeable. In Chinese history the sumptuary regulations have had little or no effect, and rich people may consume anything except a few things connected with official distinctions. We must therefore seek the explanation for the stationary production of China in other causes. Confucius is not responsible for it, because different standards for different classes in accordance with their incomes are natural and inevitable.

We must now explain why Chinese economic life has been stationary for so many centuries and production has made so little progress. The first cause is in the ethical field. A man always has two kinds of motives, economic and ethical. But the economic motive is generally stronger than the ethical motive. Confucius, however, teaches men to subject the former to the latter. Such a teaching is not always accepted and acted upon, but it has been followed in China to a remarkable extent. For this reason the Chinese are ashamed to talk about money-making, and production is checked. Confucius is responsible for it, but we should not wish to criticize him on this account.

Second, there has been a philosophical reason for China's lack of progressiveness. Both Taoism and Buddhism are too spiritual, disregarding material welfare. Under the Tsin dynasty and the Southern Dynasties, the scholars were fond of "pure conversation," abstract and mystical. This was because of the influence of Taoism. Wang Yen (807-862 A. K. or 256-311 A. D.), who did not even speak the word "money," is an example. The philosophy of Buddhism is to extinguish human wants, and to make life as hard as possible. Under its influence the scholars of the Sung, the Yüan, the Ming, and even the present dynasty, were little concerned about economic problems. Of course, this was due not only to Buddhism, but also to Confucianism. But Confucianism never goes to extremes. Even the Confucian scholars have been somewhat influenced by Buddhism. The philosophical views of these three religions have, therefore, combined to check economic progress, but especially Taoism and Buddhism.

Third, there has been an educational reason for China's

CONCLUSION 719

backwardness. After the Han dynasty China had practically no public education adapted to the daily needs of the people. From the Wei dynasty to the Tang dynasty, literature in the narrow sense was most popular. From the Sung dynasty to the present day, although the study of the *Four Books*[1] and the *Five Canons* has been very popular, students generally have not made much use of them. The worst feature of all was the requirement known as the "modern essay" (*pa ku* or "eight parts.") It was established in 1921 A. K., and finally abolished in 2453 (1370-1902 A. D.). Every official had to pass civil-service examinations, so that all students had to learn how to write the modern essay. Therefore, the object of their study of the *Four Books* and the *Five Canons* was, generally speaking, not to make use of them, but to pass examinations. This was really a profanation of the Confucian Bible. The modern essay was of no practical use, but its styles were various and complex, and its mastery required long practice. Even the best of this form of writing, however, is not good enough to be ranked with other kinds of literature. The study of it simply wasted time and energy. Of course, there were good scholars who studied deeply and widely many subjects besides writing modern essays. But how many minds of ordinary students were befogged by such a bad system of education! Even among the good scholars, how much better off they would have been if they had been freed from such a requirement! It is true that many great men did come to the front through the civil examinations. But this was not because the examinations produced great men, but simply because the great men happened to pass the examinations. This is the chief cause for the weakness of China, and the stagnation of its economic life is one of its results.

[1] It contains the "Great Learning," the "Doctrine of the Mean," the "Analects" and "Mêng Tzŭ."

But we must understand that Confucianism did not make China weak. She is weak not because she followed the teachings of Confucius, but precisely because she did not truly follow his teachings.

For the education of farmers, artisans and merchants there was practically no provision. There was no school of agriculture, nor of mining, engineering, chemistry, or commerce. The only education that the farmers got was from their farms; that of the artisans, from their apprenticeship; and that of the merchants, from their firms. Under this system China may keep her economic condition stationary, since her people receive good practical training, but she cannot make great advance, because the farmers, the artisans and the merchants lack scientific instruction.

Fourth, there are social reasons for China's situation. We have already shown that China has classified the people into four classes — students, farmers, artisans and merchants. According to Confucius, they are all equal. But in Chinese society the highest esteem has always been paid to students. Therefore, the best men of the nation always try to become students, and leave the industrial world to the inferior people. Of course, we cannot say that the student class is all wise, and that the other three classes are all ignorant. But the tendency has been for the intelligent men to be driven out of these three classes because of social prejudice. Since the industrial world has lost the help of the student class for so long a time, it is no wonder that the farmers, the artisans and the merchants have not made any great improvements or inventions. Although the students have invented some things, they have done it not to turn them to practical account but from scientific curiosity. How can we expect that ordinary men should develop scientific curiosity and the power of invention?

CONCLUSION

Besides these four classes of people, we may mention two more classes, namely, the Buddhists and the Taoists. We criticize them not from the religious, but from the social standpoint. They do not belong to any of the four classes, but form two separate classes by themselves. They do not cultivate the land, but eat. They do not weave cloth, but dress. According to history, they have been exempted from many taxes. Generally speaking, they are the parasites of society. Although we may say that the student class is also somewhat idle, there are many great differences between the students and the Buddhists and Taoists. For instance, the students are working for society, while the Buddhists and the Taoists live by themselves, out of society, yet depending upon society. There is a proverb, "The monks are fat, but the students are lean." The monks are fat because of their idleness, and the students are lean because of their hard study. Since a great number of the Chinese have become Buddhists and Taoists, there are two idle classes, and the productive force of society as a whole has been weakened. Moreover, they have spent a large amount of social income in unproductive ways. Therefore, the Buddhists and the Taoists are also responsible for the retarded economic development.

Now, we may divide the people by sexes, and look upon the women as a class. The Chinese women are productive indeed, but there is no social emancipation of women. Most of them stay at home. Although they are productive, their productive power is limited. In the industrial world practically no women are found. Moreover, from the middle class up, the women are generally idlers. Here we disregard every other aspect of the place of women in society except the economic, and declare that the lack of the social emancipation of women greatly retards economic development.

Fifth, there is a political reason. Since the Ch'in dynasty consolidated the feudal states, China has been under a single imperial government. In governing such a great empire, without a good system of communication and transportation, the administration is necessarily inefficient. Therefore, since the Han dynasty the Chinese government has adopted the doctrine of Lao Tsŭ, the *laissez-faire* policy. After the Yüan dynasty the administration became worse, because the size of the provinces was too large. Consequently the government stands aloof from the people, and the officials are not true administrators but mere tax-collectors. How can such a government help the people to develop their economic interests?

However, if the government really adopted the *laissez-faire* policy and let the people alone, the results would be better than those that are found to-day. Unfortunately, the government made a bad combination. Its interference was not efficient in developing the economic interests of the people at large, and its *laissez-faire* policy was not sufficient to allow the large producers to develop their own interests. The manufacturers and merchants have been frequently interfered with. If China had allowed capitalists to exist as a class, she would have passed the stage of capitalism long since. But, because she adopted socialistic measures a little too early, and destroyed the existence of capitalism, there has been no large production.

Sixth, there is an economic reason. Many things have retarded the economic development of China: (a) The lack of revolutionary changes in the methods of production. (b) The lack of combinations of capital on a large scale except in the form of trade guilds. (c) The lack of a great increase in capital. (d) The failure to develop the natural resources. (e) The constant growth of population.[1] (f) The com-

---

[1] As this book goes to press, Professor Edward Alsworth Ross, of

paratively equal distribution of wealth. There is no need of discussing any of these points except the last one. In China the distribution is perhaps more equal than in any other modern nation. This is peculiar to the Chinese. It has advantages indeed, but it has also serious disadvantages, namely, the discouragement of large production.

As to the subject of finance, we find many principles of Confucius which hold true even to-day. The only difference is that, under the monarchical government of ancient times, the taxation was as light as possible, while under the constitutional government of modern times we have to increase taxation to provide for growing social needs. But the Chinese have not shown any great advance in their financial system, because the government needs have been limited and the administration has been inefficient.

As to the whole economic life of the Chinese, we may

the University of Wisconsin, has published in *The Century Magazine* for July, 1911, an article entitled, "The Struggle for Existence in China." He says that one general cause for a grinding mass-poverty is the crowding of population upon the means of subsistence. His conclusion is: "For at least a generation or two China will produce people rapidly, in the Oriental way, who will die off slowly in the Occidental way. ... In forty or fifty years there will come a powerful outward thrust of surplus Chinese. ... To Mexico, Central and South America, South-eastern Asia, Asia-Minor, Africa, and even Europe, the black-haired bread-seekers will stream; and then 'What shall we do with the Chinese?' ... will become a world question." The crowding of population is indeed one of the chief causes for the poverty of China, but, as pointed out above, it is not the only one. In regard to Chinese emigration in the future, we may say that China should and will first move her surplus population to Manchuria, Mongolia, Chinese Turkestan and Tibet, before any great eastern emigration takes place (*cf. supra*, pp. 306-7). Before the whole Chinese empire is filled with the Chinese, a long period of time must elapse, and by that time the population will probably be more nearly stationary than at present, or will have a low birth rate. Only if there is still a surplus of population for which there is not enough room at home, will it be necessary for them to emigrate.

say that it is more socialistic than that of any western people. Take consumption for example. Consumption is more individualistic than production. Yet the Chinese consume much wealth socially. A single man in China must spend a greater sum of money for others beside himself than in America. Outside of the family group, there are the ties of clan, of town, of marriage and of friendship. These relations are extended beyond the limit of territory and last for many generations. Since the social relations are very close, complex and expanded, the social expenditures in the individual budget are very large. Therefore, there is a proverb: " Social expenditures are more urgent even than debts." [1]

Production also shows this difference. Agricultural life in China is somewhat socialistic, but we need not discuss this here. But even in commercial life, the trade guilds are different from the American trusts. Although the guilds are organizations for the private interest of their members, they are not so selfish or individualistic as the trusts, and they also have social functions like clubs. The Chinese trade unions are about the same as those in America, but they do not interfere with the liberty of others. Therefore, although the guilds and the unions have existed for many centuries, public sentiment is not opposed to them. In a word, their competition is not extremely sharp, and their selfishness is not great enough to invite the hatred of the public at large.

Distribution also is more socialistic in China than in western nations.

Furthermore, in regard to taxation, the Chinese usually

[1] For instance, the mother of T'ao K'an (810-885, or 259-334 A. D.), a poor widow, cut off her hair and sold it in order to entertain her son's friend, who came to visit him unexpectedly. *History of Tsin*, ch. lxvi.

CONCLUSION

have the social concept. The business tax, the tax upon title-deeds, the government monopoly of salt and iron, *etc.*, are believed or alleged to be for the benefit of society. Therefore, we may say that Chinese economic life as a whole tends in a socialistic direction. Such an idea was fostered before the time of Confucius, and it was much strengthened by him.

Now, there remains one general cause which has made the Chinese different from other people, namely, their natural environment. Why was Chinese economic life stationary? Why was it more socialistic than that of other people? Because China was an isolated country. The Chinese regarded China as a world: the territory outside of China was not counted, and the people not Chinese were mere barbarians. Such a wrong conception was supported by the fact that they did not during thousands of years find any land or people as good as those in China. Since there was no national struggle, the only thing for them to do was to make the people live at home peacefully. They did not want rich men, because they felt that the rich would be enriched at the expense of the poor. Hence agriculture was preferred over industry and commerce. Some cunning and selfish emperors did not want even wise men, because they feared that the wise would be a menace to their government. Hence public education was seriously narrowed. This was a single all-important cause from which many other causes have developed to prevent China from progressing.

Therefore, the periods of Spring and Autumn and of Warring States reached a high mark of civilization which the latter ages have not surpassed. More heroes were produced in time of war than in time of peace. The beginning of every dynasty was good, because the ruling house had fresh vigor and energy, and the great men had just been tested in the revolutionary struggle;

but the middle part or the end of almost every dynasty was bad, because the rulers were weak and ignorant, and the people in general were the same. After the Sung dynasty the national strength became less and less, on account of the philosophical schools of the Sung—too abstract and unpractical, too refined and unwarlike. Therefore, China was for the first time conquered by the Mongol.

We have criticized the Chinese thus far as severely as possible. Now, what can be claimed for the Chinese? (1) The Chinese have the best religion—Confucianism. This point, of course, would not be agreed to by all people. But we may make a concession, and say that Confucianism is, at least, one of the best religions. (2) The Chinese have the highest standard of morality. Even though it may not be superior to those of other peoples, it is certainly equal to them. (3) The Chinese have the most widely-spoken language. Although it is difficult for foreigners to learn, it is the national language of four hundred million people. In addition, the written language is used in Annam, Corea and Japan. (4) The Chinese have produced the best literature of all kinds. This is beyond dispute. Since the golden ages of different dynasties lasted for a long time —much longer than the Periclean age, the Augustan, the Elizabethan, or the age of Louis XIV,—and since the Chinese language has been used throughout the whole historical period, it is no wonder that Chinese literature has reached the highest development.

(5) In referring to fine arts, we may take them up separately. The ancient music of China is unknown, but its modern music is inferior to that of the West. The architecture of the present day is not good, but the buildings of the Ch'in dynasty and the Han dynasty were superior even to those of Greece. In later dynasties there were also many good buildings. Unfortunately there is no proof ex-

cept the description in books. Sculpture in China has not yet been taken up by a high class of people. The chief obstacle to the development of sculpture is that Chinese custom has not permitted the nude figure to be exposed. Painting has suffered from the same disadvantage, but China did produce many famous painters. Similar to the art of painting, the Chinese possess one kind of fine art which is peculiar to them only—penmanship. It is regarded as equal to painting.

(6) The Chinese system of government is moderate, democratic, centralized and permanent. Before the modern type of government appeared, it was the best type of government that had existed for such a long period.

If we take the whole history of China and compare it with the whole history of the West, the Chinese should not be ashamed. The civilization of the Chou dynasty was better than that of Greece. The civilization of the Han dynasty was better than that of Rome. We need not make any comparison with the Dark Age. The great trouble has been that, when the Chinese government was at its worst, the modern nations, rising just a little earlier than China, entered into her door and interfered with her affairs. Therefore, China is inferior, in some respects, to the West in the present day.

Now, what shall China do? China must accept all the good things from the outside world and retain the good things of her own. Should China adopt Christianity as her state religion? No.[1] The Chinese would appreciate Christianity only from the ethical standpoint. But the ethical teachings in Christianity are not so many as those in Confucianism. In a word, all the good points of Christianity

---

[1] The author has nothing against Christianity, nor against the missionaries, nor against the native Christians. In the following discussion he has sought simply to tell the truth.

are found in Confucianism, and besides, Confucianism gives still more. From the philosophical standpoint, Christianity is not so deep and rich as Confucianism, nor as Buddhism and Taoism. From the practical standpoint, Christianity is not so human or so related to man as Confucianism. Hence it is extremely difficult to convince Chinese scholars to become Christians. When it comes to the common people, it is still worse. They are afraid even to talk about the word Christianity. It is most opposed to the feelings of the people. In the first place, it is antagonistic to their ancestor-worship. In the second place, it has been introduced by arms, protected by treaties and extraterritoriality. It has cost China many lives, many miles of land and many millions of dollars. Many missionaries are not well behaved, and interfere with the people's affairs, such as lawsuits and religious worship. They look upon themselves as ambassadors, and take advantage of the officials and of the people. Therefore, the so-called " missionary cases," of which the Boxers' trouble was the greatest, have occurred many times. In the third place, there are exceedingly few Chinese who honestly become Christians. Most of them are converted for the sake of two things—protection and advantage. If weak people simply seek for protection, they may still be good citizens. But in many cases, as soon as they are protected by the church, they do something out of revenge, or even commit great wrongs. And sometimes they were outcasts before they became members of the church. About those who seek for advantage we need not say anything. Therefore, whenever a native becomes a Christian, China loses a citizen, and the people have more trouble brought in by the Christian.

If foreign countries really care for the spread of Christianity, they would be much wiser to let the Chinese alone. Send freely the Christian Bible to every Chinese, and see whether he will accept it, but do not convert him by force, nor by appealing to his self-interest. By so doing, missionaries do great harm rather than good to Christianity; but foreign countries will not believe this, because the missionaries serve as a means of exercising influence over China.[1] This is exactly the reason that the Chinese will not accept Christianity; besides, they are not satisfied with the Christian Bible. Hence, all of the foreign religions but Christianity have acquired a foothold in China without trouble, and even Christianity did not bring any trouble to China until after the Opium War. Therefore the Chinese look upon the missionary cases not as religious disputes, but as political uprisings.

Some Christians say that China cannot become a strong nation unless she be a Christian nation. This is quite absurd. We may simply point out some historical facts. If Christianity can make every nation strong without regarding other elements, why did the Roman Empire fall? Why have Spain and Portugal become weaker? Why do not the nations in South and Central America become strong? The chief maker of modern nations is not Christianity, but militarism and industrialism. Even the religious revolution was the product of the Renaissance. We are sure that Christianity did, and does, much good for the Christian nations and for the world as a whole, but there is no reason to think that only Christianity can make a nation strong. If a nation cannot be strong without Christianity, why was China strong for a long time until the Opium War, and why did Japan become a modern nation? The originators of the political revolution in Japan were not Christians, but Confucians. Even one branch of Confucianism—

[1] Even Japan has tried to send missionaries to China in order to teach the Chinese Buddhism—a most ridiculous thing, since Japan got Buddhism from China.

the doctrine of Wang Shou-jen—was sufficient to transform old Japan into modern Japan. Why should the whole school of Confucius not be able to modernize China?

The future of China is bright. With an uninterrupted history extending over five thousand years, with an intelligent, diligent, prudent, and vigorous people of four hundred million, with an extensive but connected territory of four and a quarter million square miles,[1] with abundant natural resources, under one centralized government, one uniform language, one highly-developed religion, one national idea, China will, without doubt, become a strong nation, but the world need not be afraid of the so-called yellow peril. China will indeed adopt both militarism and industrialism. But China will not injure anyone not Chinese as the western nations take advantage of other people. After China shall be strong, the Great Similarity of Confucius will come, and the world-state will appear. Then the brotherhood of nations will be established, and there will be no war, but perpetual peace.

[1] English miles.

APPENDIX I
TABLE OF CHINESE CHRONOLOGY

Era of Confucius	Era of Christ	Name of Dynasty[1]	Name of Period	Grand Division
2402-2288 B. K.	2953-2839 B. C.	Pao Hsi	Five Emperors	Ancient
2287-2148 "	2838-2699 "	Shên Nung		
2147-2048 "	2698-2599 "	Huang Ti		
1806-1707 "	2357-2258 "	Yao		
1704-1655 "	2255-2206 "	Shun		
1654-1215 "	2205-1766 "	the Hsia dynasty	Three Dynasties	
1215-571 "	1766-1122 "	the Yin dynasty		
571-220 "	1122-771 "	the Western Chou dynasty		
219 B. K.-393 A. K.	770-249 "	the Eastern Chou dynasty	Spring and Autumn and Warring States	
331-346 A. K.	221-206 "	the Ch'in dynasty		
346-557 "	206 B. C.-6 A. D.	the Former or Western Han dynasty		
576-771 "	25-220 A. D.	the Latter or Eastern Han dynasty		
771-816 "	220-265 "	Wei — Shu	Three Kingdoms	
772-814 "	221-263 "	Wu		
780-871 "	220-280 "			
816-867 "	265-316 "	the Western Tsin dynasty		
868-971 "	317-420 "	Eastern Tsin		
971-1030 "	420-479 "	Sung (House of Liu)		
1030-1053 "	470-502 "	Ch'i		
1053-1108 "	502-557 "	Liang		

Dates	Dynasty	Period	Era
502–557	Liang	Southern and Northern Dynasties	Medieval
557–589	Chen		
386–534	Northern Wei		
534–550	Eastern Wei		
535–557	Western Wei		
550–577	Northern Ch'i		
557–581	Northern Chou		
581–618	the Sui dynasty		
618–907	the T'ang dynasty		
907–923	Posterior Liang	Five Dynasties	
923–936	Posterior T'ang		
936–947	Posterior Tsin		
947–951	Posterior Han		
951–960	Posterior Chou		
960–1127	the Northern Sung dynasty		Modern
1127–1279	Southern Sung		
937–1125	Liao		
1115–1234	Kin		
1260–1368	the Yüan dynasty		
1368–1644	the Ming dynasty		
1644–	the Ts'ing dynasty		

[1] The period of the Five Emperors is legendary; their dates given here are simply the conventional statements; a much longer period of time must have elapsed. The word "the" before the name indicates that the dynasty ruled the whole empire except in the case of the Northern Sung dynasty; others ruled only parts of China. Small kingdoms are omitted. Adding the Wu kingdom to Eastern Tsin, Sung, Ch'i, Liang and Chen, they are called the Six Dynasties.

APPENDIX II

LIST OF AUTHORITIES IN ENGLISH AND CHINESE [1]

1. *Analects* (*Lun Yü*, James Legge's translation given in the *Chinese Classics*, vol. i), 31.
2. *Annotation and Explanation of the Thirteen Canons* (*Shih San Ching Chu Shu*).
3. *Biography of Noteworthy Women* (*Lieh Nü Chuan*), 34.
4. *Book of the Lord of Shang* (*Shang Chün Shu*), 412.
5. *Book on the Great Similarity* (*Ta T'ung Shu*), 71.
6. *Canon of Changes* (*Yi King*, translated by James Legge, contained in the *Sacred Books of the East*, edited by F. Max Müller, vol. xvi, Clarendon Press, 1882 A. D.), 25-6.
7. *Canon of Filial Piety* (*Hsiao King*, contained in the *Sacred Books of the East*, vol. iii), 31.
8. *Canon of History* (*Shoo King, Chinese Classics*, vol. iii), 24-5.
9. *Canon of Mountains and Seas* (*Shan Hai Ching*), 388.
10. *Canon of Poetry* (*She King, Chinese Classics*, vol. iv), 24.
11. *Canon of Rites* (*Li Ching*), 25. The Chinese have made the great mistake of omitting this Canon in what they call the *Five Canons*, and put *Younger Tai's Record of Rites* in its place. The number of chapters given in the notes refers to the edition of the *Annotation and Explanation of the Thirteen Canons*.
12. *Canonical Interpretation of the Ts'ing Dynasty* (*Huang Ts'ing Ching Chieh*), a series of one hundred eighty separate books or volumes, 7.
13. *Cases of the Institutes of the Ts'ing Dynasty* (*Ta Ts'ing Hui Tien Shih Li*), 659.

[1] This is by no means a complete list of the Chinese books utilized by the author, but, with the exception mentioned in the next sentence, merely a list of those books whose names have been mentioned in this treatise. Nos. 2, 15, ·31 and 54 have not been mentioned, but are printed here because they are the collective names of a series of books. The figures following the titles of the books refer to the pages of this treatise. In the first list is contained the translation of the titles in English, followed by the Chinese names in English letters. In the second list the titles are given in the Chinese characters.

APPENDIX II

14. *Chuang Tsŭ*, 29.
15. *Continuation of the Canonical Interpretation of the Ts'ing Dynasty* (*Huang Ts'ing Ching Chieh Hsü P'ien*), a series of two hundred and nine separate books or volumes.
16. *Continuation of the General Political History* (*Hsü Tsŭ Chih T'ung Chien*), 694.
17. *Continuation of the General Research on Literature and Authorities* (*Hsü Wên Hsien T'ung K'ao*), 333.
18. *Correction of the Youth* (*Chêng Mêng*), 61.
19. *Debate on the Government Monopoly of Salt and Iron* (*Yen T'ieh Lun*), 477-8.
20. *Elder Tai's Record of Rites* (*Ta Tai Li Ki*), 31-2.
21. *General Discussion in the White Tiger Palace* (*Pai Hu T'ung*), 62.
22. *General History of Institutes* (*T'ung Tien*), 296.
23. *General Political History* (*Tsŭ Chih T'ung Chien*), 320.
24. *General Research on Literature and Authorities* (*Wên Hsien T'ung K'ao*), 300.
25. *General Research on Literature and Authorities of the Present Dynasty* (*Huang Ch'ao Wên Hsien T'ung K'ao*), 333.
26. *Great Commentary of the Canon of History* (*Shang Shu Ta Chuan*), 89.
27. *Han's External Commentary of the Canon of Poetry* (*Han Shih Wai Chuan*), 197.
28. *Han Fei Tsŭ*, 29.
29. *Hsün Tsŭ*, 33.
30. *Hsü Shên's Dictionary* (*Shuo Wên*), 357.
31. *Imperial Edition of the Seven Canons* (*Yü Tsuan Ch'i Ching*).
32. *Institutes of the Ts'ing Dynasty* (*Ta Ts'ing Hui Tien*), 685.
33. *Ku-liang's Commentary* (*Ku-liang Chuan*), 32.
34. *Kuan Tsŭ*, 141-2.
35. *Kung-yang's Commentary* (*Kung-yang Chuan*), 32.
36. *Lao Tsŭ* (or *Tao Tê King*), 115.
37. *Law Code of the Ts'ing Dynasty* (*Ta Ts'ing Lü Li*), 148.
38. *Lieh Tsŭ*, 72.
39. *Many Dewdrops of the Spring and Autumn* (*Ch'un Ch'iu Fan Lu*), 58.
40. *Mêng Tsŭ*, 33.
41. *Mo Tsŭ*, 29.
42. *Narratives of Nations* (*Kuo Yü*), 35.
43. *New Narrations* (*Hsin Hsü*), 34.
44. *Official System of Chou* (*Chou Kuan*, miscalled *Chou Li*), 35. The number of chapters given in the notes refers to the edition of the *Annotation and Explanation of the Thirteen Canons*.
45. *Oldest Chinese Dictionary* (*Erh Ya*), 352.

APPENDIX II

46. *Park of Narratives (Shuo Yüan)*, 34.
47. *Plans of the Warring States (Chan Kuo T'sê)*, 478.
48. *Record of Industry (K'ao Kung Chi)*, 354.
49. *Research on the False Bible of the School of Hsin (Hsin Hsiao Wei Ching K'ao)*, 36.
50. *Research on the Reformation of Confucius (K'ung Tsŭ Kai Chih K'ao)*, 30.
51. *Seven Adjuncts (Ch'i Wei)*, 33.
52. *Spring and Autumn (Ch'un Ch'iu, Chinese Classics,* vol. v), 26-7.
53. *Tso's Commentary (Tso Chuan, Chinese Classics,* vol. v), 35.
54. *Twenty-four Histories (Er Shih Sŭ Shih),* a series of twenty-four different histories, *e. g., Historical Record, History of Han.* The individual names are omitted in this list.
55. *Younger Tai's Record of Rites (Li Ki,* contained in the *Sacred Books of the East,* vols. xxvii-xxviii), 31-2.

引用書目略表

論語注疏	一
三傳	二
列女傳	三
商君書	四
大戴禮	五
易經	六
孝經	七
書經	八
山海經	九
詩經	十
禮記	十一
皇清經解	十二
大莊續正鹽鐵論	十三
皇清經解續編	十四
荀子	十五
貧文獻通考	十六
蒙通考	十七
經解	十八
事類賦	十九
續通鑑考	二十
解通	二十一
論語	二十二
戴禮	二十三
禮記	二十四
通鑑考	二十五
獻通	二十六
文獻傳	二十七
大外子	二十八

白通資文皇尚韓韓	一
御纂七經會傳	二
說文解字	三
大戴禮記	四
管子	五
公羊傳	六
老子道德經	七
列子	八
大清律例	九
春秋繁露	十
孟子	十一
墨子	十二
國語	十三
新序	十四
周官	十五
爾雅	十六
說苑	十七
戰國策	十八
考工記	十九
新學僞經考	二十
孔子改制考	二十一
七緯	二十二
春秋左氏傳	二十三
十二小戴禮	二十四
四禮記	二十五
史記	二十六

INDEX

A. K., after K'ung Fu Tzǔ or after Confucius, 5.
Acre or *mou*, 421-2.
Aesthetics, principles of, 250-9.
Age, of maturity, 502; classification of people, 509; law of Northern Ch'i, 516; table of limit, 522; limit for personal service, 661.
Agriculture, School of, 42; department of, 73; Confucius refers to, 74-5; not mentioned in the nine standard rules, 316-7; ch. XXI; importance of, 380-3; not the only productive occupation, 383-6; science of, 384; methods of, 386-9; agricultural life, 392-7; compared with commerce, 413; not the only subject of political economy, 557.
Ai, duke of Lu, 64, 624-5.
Ai Ti, of Han, 507.
Alexander, 320.
"Alternative fields," 386-7.
Alum, tax on, 704.
Amoy, 689.
An Tzǔ or An Ping-chung, 8, 240; as the representative of parsimony, 242.
Ancestor-worship, 197, 728; participated in by woman, 153; expenditure for, 283-8; as companion of God, 284-6; reason for, 287.
Ancient Literature, School of, 34-6, 46.
Annam, 415, 575, 726.
Annotation of Kung-yang, 32.
Annotation of the Canon of Poetry, 36.
Annotation of the Canon of Rites, 36.
Annotation of the Official System of Chou, 36.
Annotation of the Record of Rites, 36.
"Appendix" of the *Canon of Changes* (Hsi T'zǔ), 32, 48, 52, 59, 120-128; *etc.*
Appointed people, 197-8.
Arbitration, wishes of Tzǔ-kung, 144.
Archery, one of the six arts, 12; game of, 231-6; description of the game of, 232-3; as a national game, 233-4; great, 234; social, 234; directed by Confucius, 234; usefulness of, 234-6.
Architecture, 726-7.
Aristocracy, absent in Confucianism, 88; absent in China, 92.
Aristotle, 41.
Artisans, position of, 406-7; condition of, 407-410; under public relief, 597-8; taxed more lightly than merchants, 693-4.
Augustan age, 726.
B. K., before K'ung Fu Tzǔ or before Confucius, 5.
Bale, 658.
Banks, government, 434-5, 554, 587-8; "money association," 434; private banks of the people of Shansi, 434; banking department, 589.
Bible or Canons of Confucius, 23-4; influence of, 36-7; accepted as a state religion, 43; as a legal code, 44; as a profanation of, 719.
"Borrowing field," 360, 381-2.
Bounty, theory of Liu An, 560.
Boxers' trouble, 682, 728.

Brokers, tax on, 695-6; as a collector of tax, 711-2.
Buddha, 255.
Buddhism, 44, 718, 729; compared with Confucianism, 191-2; compared with Christianity, 728.
Buddhist, Confucius' influence upon, 287; church, 430; as idler, 721.
Budget, two divisions, 552-3; making of, 608-12; of 2462 A. K., 659, 687, 706, 709.
Buildings, absence of, 119; of later ages, 120, 125; comparison between China and Europe, 131-2, 726-7; no repair in bad year, 143; no construction in bad year, 204; extravagance of, 245-6; Confucius' house, 256; of Hsüan Wang, 257; description of, 257-9; Brilliant Hall, 259; height of, 261-2.
Bushel or *hu*, 421.
Business taxes, 691-4, 713.
Caesar, 320.
Canals, Han Canal, 419; Imperial Canal, 419-20; Tung-chi Canal, 419; Yung-chi Canal, 419-20; Southern Canal, 420; transportation of rice, 644-6.
Canon of Changes, 12, 25-7, 46, 59; principle of, 122-3; *etc.*
Canon of History, 8, 11-2, 20, 24-5, 46, 63, 73, 77, 244-5, *etc.*
Canon of Music, 8, 11-2, 25, 226.
Canon of Poetry, 8, 11-2, 24, 64, 66, 77, 81, 90, 95, 149, 152, 153, 154, 156, 238, 249, 257, 393-5, 630-2, *etc.*
Cantillon, 490.
Canton, 483, 566, 601, 687, 689, 700.
Capital, 294, 355-62; importance of, 177; industrial, 318; the word, 355-7; as important as labor, 405; accumulation, 180, 457; grain as, 580-2.
Capitalist, Chinese view toward, 700-1, 722.
Carriages, tax on, 692-3.
Catholics, 86.
Catty or *chin*, 421, 422.
Cha, 205, 227-8.
Chang Chung-yen, 685.
Chang-chü, 388.
Chang Hêng, 415.

Chang Hsüan, 537.
Chang Hung, 7.
Chang Shih, 191.
Chang Ti, of Han, 650.
Chang Tsai, 60.
Chang Yung, 433.
Chang Yü, 507.
Chang Yüeh, 665.
Ch'ang-sun P'ing, 578.
"Changelings," name of paper money, 433, 434, 442.
Chao Sh'i, 328.
Chao the Great, 210.
Chao Tso, 304-5, 312, 360, 382-3, 395-7.
Charity, foolish generosity and unwise alms not approved by Mencius, 103-4; private, 600-1.
Chê Tsung, of Sung, 592.
Chekiang, 657.
Chemistry, agricultural, 388.
Chen, state of, 11; a noble family of Ch'i, 582; dynasty of, 684, 711.
Chen Hsiang, 426, 485-6.
Chen Huan, 356.
Chen Tsin, 104.
Chên Tsung, of Sung, 572.
Chêng, state of, tunes of, 74, 218, 226; development of the tunes of, 225; knife of, 404; commercial state, 218; commercial and democratic state, 455-6.
Chêng Chung, 432, 454.
Chêng Hsüan, 35-6, 474, 581, 630-1.
Ch'êng, duke of Lu, 661.
Ch'êng-fêng, 65.
Ch'êng T'ang, one of the Three Kings, 6, 19, 29, 78, 360, 610.
Ch'êng Ti, of Han, 507.
Ch'êng Tsu, of Ming, 656.
Ch'êng Wang, of Chou, 6, 19, 610; mother of, 137.
Ch'êng Yi, 148.
Chênkiang, 420.
Chênt'ao, 566.
Chi, state of, 28.
Chi-chi, 65.
Chi Jan, economic theory of, 457.
Chi-sun, 110, 465, 627.
Ch'i, state of, 8, 9, 43; chief state for industry and commerce, 128-9; 573, 695, 701.
Chia, group of ten families, 583-4.
Chia K'uei, 389-90, 429.
Chia Ts'ing, 593.

INDEX 739

Chia Yi, 113, 262, 359-60, 439, 440.
Chiao Ko, 373.
Chieh, 607, 628.
Chieh-ni, 388.
Chih, music-master, 216.
Ch'ih Jên, 405.
Ch'ih Yu, 415.
Children, treatment of, 265-6; fed by the king of Yüeh, 323.
Chin Shih, 92.
Ch'in, state of, 43, 308, 404, 506, 649; dynasty of, 34, 43, 46, 130, 174, 299-300, 376, 430, 459, 470, 596, 664, 684, 722, 726.
China, history before Confucius' time, 4; in Confucius' time, 17; national spirit of, 212-3; national expansion of, 557-8.
Ching, duke of Ch'i, 113.
Ching, prince of Wei, 207-8.
Ching chi, 48-9.
Ching Chiang, 348.
Ching Ti, of Han, 360, 397, 440.
Ch'iu, a surname, 409.
Ch'iu, personal name of Confucius, 7.
Ch'iu Chün, 573.
Chou, last emperor of the Yin dynasty, 62; the strongest example of extravagance, 246.
Chou, Duke of, 4, 6, 19, 35, 128, 285, 353, 393, 415, 587, 610, 627.
Chou dynasty, 4; Eastern Chou line, 5; 15, 29, 74; beginning of, 128-9, 336; foundation of, 393-5; industry of, 401-3; 428-9, 430, 432, 481-2, 499-501, 582, 587, 588, 621-2, 630, 662-4, 677, 691-2, 702, 711, 727.
Chou Tun-yi, 186.
Christianity, compared with Confucianism, 61, 86, 159-60, 192-4, 727-8; could not be state religion of China, 727-30.
Christians, Chinese, 728.
Chu, 421, 432.
Chu Hsi, 45, 526, 577, 552-5.
Chu-ko Liang, 416.
Chu Ts'ing, 537.
Ch'u, state of, 10, 11, 43, 308, 390, 429.
Ch'üan Wan-chi, 705.
Chuang-lieh Ti, of Ming, 657.
Chuang Tzŭ, 29, 282.
Chung-kung, 46.
Chung-mou, name of city, 8.

Chung-ni, designation of Confucius, 7.
Chung-shu Yu-he, 536.
Chung-tu, name of city, 8.
Chung-tzŭ, 65, 466.
Church, no taxing power, 648.
Civil-service competitive examinations, 90, 719.
Clan system, 167.
Clark, J. B., 181.
"Code of Po," 24-5.
Commerce, functions of, 73; referred to by Confucius, 74-5; resort of the poor, 178; ch. XXIII; importance of, 411-3; compared with agriculture, 413; commercial regulations, 445-9; theory of, 553-4.
Communication, 414.
Communistic idea, 466-7.
Competition, should not be absolutely free, 168-170; not very sharp in China, 175; results of free, 178, 179.
Confucianism, 4, 31, 32; influence of, 36-7; economic teachings, 37; historical movements of, ch. IV; the word, 39; as a new religion, 40-42; struggled with other religions, 42-3; as a state religion, 43; during the Han, 43-4; decline of, 44-5; from the Sung to the Ming, 45; renaissance of, in the present dynasty, 45-6; summary on historical movements of, 46; development of, hampered by the government, 47; future development of, 47; theory of creation, 58; highest theological stage, 59; doctrine of trinity, 60; freedom of thought, 61; freedom of belief, 84-5; no conflict with science, 85-6; no conflict with politics, 86-7; key to the ethical teachings of, 117-8; as a religion of the economic world, 127; final aim of, 136; cosmopolitanism, 141; golden mean, 175; more human than any other religion, 186; compared with Buddhism, 161-2; compared with Christianity, 61, 159-60, 192-4, 727-8; first step to, 208-9; a great philosophy, 557; as a check to

economic progress, 718; not truly followed by China, 720; as the best religion, 726.
Confucians, compared with the priests and ministers of Christianity, 39; divided into eight branches, 43; common point of economic theory of, 179; in a poor condition, 209-10.
Confucius, life of, ch. I; time of, 4-6; birthplace of, 6; ancestors of, 6; birthday of, 7; as a teacher, 7-8; visit to the imperial capital, 7-8; went to Ch'i, 8; prepared the Canons, 8; considered accepting the invitations of the rebels, 8; political career of, 8-9; travels of, 9-11; relation of, with God, 10-11; teachings of, 12; pupils and followers of, 12; death of, 12; worship of, 13; descendants of, 13; as a founder of a great religion, 13-4; fundamental concepts of, ch. II; writings of, 11-2, 23-30; methods of, 27-8; character of his writings, 28-30; claims of, 30; influence of, 36-7; not primarily an economist, 37; a religious reformer, 40-42; struggling for the captured game, 106; wishes of, 144-5, 600; as an evolutionist, 168; system of, 189-90; in a poor condition, 213-4; taste and work of, on music, 216-8; food of, 251; dress of, 253-4; house of, 256; standard of living of, 263-4; a good worker, 373, *etc.*
Conscience, 102-3.
Constantly normal granary, system of, 561, 571-7, 589.
Consumption, social control of, 196-200; relation to distribution, 196, 199; relation to production, 182, 199-200; financial control of, 200-2; according to times, 202-5; according to places, 205-6; of rich and poor, ch. XIII; conclusion on, 717-8; socialistic, 724.
Contentment with means possessed, 207-8.
Co-operative production, 504.
Copyright, 537.

Corea, 726.
Corporation, 454-5, 696.
Creation, 58-9.
Creatures, conservation of, 345-6.
Credit, 587-8, 589.
Crop, effect in consumption, 204-5; two-crop system, 388-9; effect in public labor, 663-4.
Cultivation, by pairs, 387-8; with ox or cow, 388; extensive and intensive, 389-391.
Customs duties, 454, 683-4, 713; on internal trade, 684-7; on imports, 687-91; duty-free goods, 690; on transit, 690; on exports, 691.
Dance, two kinds of, 223; origin of Chinese drama, 224; relation to singing, 224; not taken by women, 225; taken by man and woman, 225.
Dead, having no knowledge, 279.
Demand and supply, 423-5, 457; government control of, ch. XXIX.
Democracy, 62, 73, 77-9, 88, 92-3, 152; taking people for the participation of pleasure of a ruler, 238-9; industrial, 406; covenant between ruler and merchants, 455; banishment of the emperor by the people, 534; Confucius' policy, 544; responsible ministry, 610; people as tax-controllers, 622-3.
Diminishing returns, 347, 391-2, 706, 717.
Diplomacy, School of, 42; of Tzŭ-ch'an, 455-6.
Distribution, a function of the state, 171; unequal, 174; comparatively equal in China, 175, 723; under free competition, 178-9; relation to production, 181; relation to consumption, 196; Confucius' view, 310; general principles of, 460-8; according to equality, 460-5; class struggle, 462-3; psychological view, 463-4; international view, 464-5; according to productivity, 465-6; according to need, 466-8; law of Heaven, 547; socialistic, chs. XXVI-XXXI, 724.

INDEX

District-drinking, as one way of getting pleasure, 227-231; for four occasions, 227; description and explanation of, 228-231; economic principle of, 230.

Divorce, seven grounds for, 148; three considerations of, 148; corrupt custom of, 149; issued to woman, 150; rare in China, 151.

"Doctrine of the Mean," "*Chung Yung*"), 13, 127, *etc.*

Doctrine of Music, (*Yüeh Yü*), 554-5.

Door tax or family tax, cause of inaccurate census, 335, 655; abolition of, 338, 672; origin of, 635; of Tang, 650; of Han, 671; of Wei, 671; of Tsin, included land tax, 671; gradation of, 671; of Yüan, 671-2; conclusion on, 672.

Drama, origin of, 224.

Dress, of root-grubbing period and of later ages, 119-20; change from savage life to civilized life, 123-4, 126; comparison between China and Europe, 130-1; work of woman, 152-3; system of, 197, 254-6; of Confucius, 253-4; of young men and women, 264-5.

Drink, 252; of water, 201, 213.

Economic development, woman as a promoter of, 68; government as a promoter of, 76-7; test of a good government, 91; ch. IX; root-grubbing period, 119-120; hunting and fishing stage and pastoral stage, 121; agricultural stage and primitive commercial stage, 122, 126; primitive industrial stage, 126; national economy, 129; world economy, 129; stages of, 129-30; comparison between China and Europe, 130-132; capitalistic stage, 173-4, 179; handicraft stage, 410; coming to modern factory system, 410; during the Yü dynasty, 640-1, 643; reasons of slow, 96-7, 718-23; socialistic, 723-5.

Economics, to other sciences in general, ch. V; definition of, 48-9; the term in Chinese, 48-9; and sociology, ch. VI; basis of sociology, 52-7; basis of religion, 57; basis of politics, 73-6; Confucius' political economy, 79; basis of ethics, 94-7; as the first item of reformation, 96; harmony with ethics, 97-101; choice between economic life and ethical life, 101-3; identification with the doctrine of filial piety, 157; divisions of, 180-2; household economy, 207-8; music as the greatest principle of, 222-3.

Economy, 79, 361-2, 612-3.

Education, 71; religion included, 82; universally free, 82-4; local school, 83; different grades of schools, 83; training, 83-4; examinations, 84; election system, 87-93; gestatory, 136-7; family, 137-8, 371; archery, 234-6; industrial, 409; economic condition as the basis of, 467-8; as a solution of wages problem, 493-6; political, 669; chief cause for the weakness of China, 716; of farmers, artisans and merchants, 720.

Eight objects of government, 50-51.

Eight rites, 25.

Eight trigrams, 26, 121.

Election, 87-93, 236.

Elizabethan age, 726.

Ely, R. T., 51.

Emperor, not the head of the church, 61; merely a title, 62; as a farmer, 152; parent of the people, 172; salary of, 492; excluded from economic field, 545.

Empress, as a weaver, 152-3.

England, 318, 690, 691; compared with China, 93; imported opium by force, 710.

Epicureanism, 116.

Epicurus, 42.

Equal transportation, system of, 555-6; administration of Liu An, 559-63; plan of Wang An-shih, 563-4; in harmony with the "Tribute of Yü," 643.

Equality, universal, 61-2; social, 368; economic, 544.

Ethical Culture Society, 41.

Ethics, to economics, 49-50, ch. VIII; compared with law, 81-2; economics as the basis of, 94-7; harmony with economics, 97-101; choice between economic life and ethical life, 101-3; economic progress and moral perfection, 136; combined with economics, 189-90; self-control of wants, 195-6; happiness of the poor, 208-15; checked production, 718; highest moral standard, 726.
Europe, 92, 130-2, 320-1.
Evolution, doctrine of, 26, 122-3, 168-170.
"Evolution of Civilization" ("Li Yün"), 59, 119-20, etc.
Exchange, a part of production, 181; included in the term commerce, 411; system of Exchanges, 565-7, 592-3.
Excise taxes, 696-711, 713; general, 696-700; not in harmony with Confucius' principles, 696-7; special, 700-711; theory of Li Yü, 708.
Exemption, of taxes, 632-3, 634, 662, 674, 680, 688-9, 721.
Expenditures, general standard of, ch. XV; particular, ch. XVI; according to income, 610-1.
Explanation of Mao's Commentary of the Canon of Poetry (Shih Mao Shih Chuan Shu), 356.
Extreme North, a Utopian state, 72.
Extreme Peace Stage, 135-6.
Factories, development in Yin, 400-1; in Chou, 401-2; in all the four dynasties, 402-3; government, 407-8.
Faculty theory, 579-80, 623-4, 634, 642, 651, 653, 653-5.
Family, 18-20, 70-72; the smallest economic organization, 145-167; the term, 146, 502; happy life of, 146; Chinese type, 163-7; of the virtuous men, 212; perpetuation of, 328-9; monopoly of, 539.
Famine, 436-8, 448, 454, 570, 578, 697.
Fan Ch'ih or Fan Hsü, 375, 384.
Fan Li, 457-8, 459, 568.
Fang, name of city, 6.

Farmers, being students at the same time, 90; in the end of the Chou dynasty, 268; as the second group of people, 367; in the beginning of the Han dynasty, 396-7; conditions of, 573-4; government loans to, 586.
Farming-out of the commodity tax, 698-700.
Fate, doctrine of, 106-111; definition of, 106; three kinds of, 107; three viewpoints, 107; subject human nature to, 107-8; passive policy, 108-9; active policy, 109-111.
Father, no absolute power over his son, 62.
Fei, name of city, 8.
Fênhu, name of state, its wood for arrow, 404.
Feudalism, 5; "Essay" on, 55-6; 78, 529, 543-4, 596, 627; differences between absolute monarchy and, 299-300, 527, 528, 596, 678.
Filial piety, 19, 112; relation of father and son, 155-167; great filial piety, 156; doctrine of, 156-163, 328-30; summary of the duties of a son, 156-7; of the common people, 157; support of parents, 158-163; five unfilial things, 158-9; parents and wife, 159-60; filial daughter, 161; love for trees and animals, 193; of the poor, 201; service of parents, 265; return to the parents, 329-330; of the feudal princes, 361.
First Emperor of the Ch'in dynasty, 43, 459, 506-7.
Fishery, tax on, 695.
Five Barbarians, disturbances of the, 378.
Five blessings, 170-2.
Five Canons, 25, 27, 31, 719.
"Five chu," name of coin, 431.
Five colors, 190.
Five Dynasties, 45, 659, 670, 685, 704, 707.
Five elements, 340-1.
Five equalizations, 554-5, 558, 589.
Five grains, 382, 503.
Five moral constants, 19-20.
Five notes, 190.

INDEX 743

Five social relations, 19-20, 25.
Five tastes, 190.
Flemish workmen, 318.
Foochow, 689.
Food, of root-grubbing period, 119; of later ages, 120; inventor of kitchen and cookery, 121; refinement of, 124; comparison between China and Europe, 130; work of woman, 152; eating of meat, 193-4; of Confucius, 251; and art of cooking, 251-3; of different classes, 261; of the old, 266-7.
Food and commodities, 50; "Record" of, 51.
Foot or *chih*, 421, 422.
Forced-labor emancipation law, 666-7, 673-6.
Foreign debt, 682.
Foreigners, in China, 315; protected at the expense of the Chinese, 690.
Forests, conservation of, 346; government monopoly of, 701.
Forest of K'ung, 12.
Four Books (*Ssŭ Shu*), 719.
Four groups of people, 367-9; equally useful to society, 412; social prejudice toward, 720.
"Four Seas," 642.
Frankincense, tax on, 709.
Free distribution, compared with selling at a low price, 560-1.
Free granary, system of, 577-80.
Free trade, on exportation, 452, 453; doctrine of, 453-4; of salt, 562; practiced by Ch'in, Han, Wei, Tsin, 684; practiced by Kin, 684-5; of rice, 689; of certain goods, 690; practically adopted in maritime customs, 691.
Freedom, of movement and speech, 6; of thought, 47, 61; of speech, 80-81; of belief, 61, 84-5; economic, 179-180; of movement, 311-2; of occupation, 369-371.
Fu, professor, 89.
Fu Yüeh, 373, 481, 610.
Funeral, expenditures for, 201, 272-283; reasons for an expensive, 274-8.
Gabelentz, G. von der, on Confucius, 3-4.

General property tax, objections to, 652-3; came from the family tax, 671-672; as an addition to the land tax, 672; first applied to the whole empire, 672; of Tang, 672-3; of Sung, 673-6; of Kin, 677; did not exist after Kin, 677.
Generalization, School of, 42.
George, Henry, 296, 489, 533.
Giddings, F. H., 156.
Ginseng, tax on, 709-10.
God, relation with Confucius, 10-11, 13-14; meaning of the word, 20-21, with the word *Yüan*, 58-9; man as his assistant and co-ordinate, 59; fatherhood of, 60; everyone the son of, 61; all men children of, 62; helps only the strongest, 169; relation with father or ancestor, 284-6.
Gold, present to Mencius, 104; as a standard of money, 428; ratio to silver and copper, 429; decrease of quantity, 430; ratio to copper, 545; ratio to copper and rice, 656.
Golden mean, 14; for distribution, 173; for consumption, 203; for social institutions, 241; for consumption, 242-3; for funeral and mourning, 283.
Goods, economic and free, 424-5; sent as tribute, 641.
Government, mixed with religion, 4; monarchical, 19, 78; influence on religion, 47; eight objects of, 50-51; existed for economic reasons, 73-6; as a promoter of economic life, 76-7; general principles of, 77-82; state, 79; local, 79-80; dependent on man, 87; effect of good, 96; three requisites of, 101; regulation of economic life, 168-175; final end of, 170-1; ideal form of, 171-2; difference between modern and ancient, 174; nine standard rules of, 316-7; under Confucius' influence, 335-6; control of industries, 407-8; theory of Wei Chi-tsung, 565; modern democratic, 596; obstacle to centralization, 637;

inefficient, 722; the Chinese type as the best in the past, 727.
Grain, as capital, 358-60; five kinds, 382; policy of giving high value to, 383; as money, 437; free exportation of, 452; for salaries, 480; government control of, ch. XXX; equalization of the price of, 457, 568-77; government transportation of, 571; distribution of, 577-80; government loans of, 580-2; system of village granary, 582-5; free importation of, 689.
Grand Summit, 59.
Great entertainment, 67.
Great floods, 342.
"Great Learning," ("*Ta Hsiao*") 63, 74, 77-8, 97-9, 127; outline of, 139-140; 140-2, 151, 180, 293, 546.
"Great Model," 24-5, 46, 50-51, 57, 170-2, 614.
Great Scholars, Board of, 43.
Great Similarity, 17-20, 46, 47, 57, 70-72, 135, 730.
Great uniformity, 57, 307.
Grand Unity, 59.
Greece, 131, 379, 481, 726, 727.
Greeks, 320-1.
Green sprout money, compared with the village-granary system, 584-5; system of, 589-92, 594-5.
Gresham's law, 430-1, 444-5.
Hales, 625.
Han, a noble family of Chêng, 582.
Han dynasty, 33, 34, 42, 43, 44, 46, 92, 129, 130, 333, 334, 430, 541, 617, 646, 669-70, 678-9, 683, 695, 707, 719, 722, 726, 727.
Han Fei Tzŭ, 29, 43, 150.
Han Fu, 495.
Han River, 703.
Han Ying, 197.
Han Yü, 44, 495.
Hanchung, 703.
Hangchow, 302, 420, 566, 687.
Helen, 67.
Hire system, 481-2.
History, economic, 51; economic interpretation of, 120-6; interpreted by the figures of population, 336-7; summary of Chinese, 725-7.

Ho, or Huang Ho, or Yellow River, 418.
Ho Hsiu, 32, 58, 466, 503.
Ho-po-so, 695.
Ho Yi-sun, 432.
Hongkong and Shanghai Bank, 682.
Horse, for transportation, 124, 415; "horse interest," 693.
Hou Chi, 285, 386, 387.
House tax, 677-8, 680, 714; ground tax, 635-6; tax upon the buildings of merchants, 691-2.
Hsia dynasty, 15, 28, 29, 74, 176, 428, 429, 498, 621, 637.
Hsiang An-shih, 357.
Hsiao-wên Ti, of Northern Wei, 510-6, 517-8.
Hsieh, name of city, 104.
Hsieh Hsiang, 564.
Hsien Kao, saved the country, 456.
Hsien Tsung, of Tang, 432, 572, 636.
Hsiho, 566.
Hsun Tzŭ, 33-4, 39, 43, 46, 52-3, 88, 135, 187, 188, 343-4, 362, 453, 460-1, 494, 625-6, *etc.*
Hsun Yüeh, 522-4.
Hsü Hsing, 385, 485-6, 606.
Hsü Kan, 300.
Hsüan, king of Ch'i, 75, *etc.*; duke of Lu, 649.
Hsüan Ti, of Han, 478, 571.
Hsüan Tsung, of Tang, 520, 572, 665.
Hsüan Wang, 257, 381.
Hu, where the Huns lived, 404.
Hu Yin, 550-1, 578.
Huan, duke of Ch'i, 173; duke of Chêng, 455.
Huan K'uan, 478, 557.
Huan Ti, of Han, 650, 705.
Huan Tui, 10-11.
Huang-fu Mi, 333.
Huang Ssŭ-yung, 682.
Huang Ti, 122-6, 353, 415, 420, 497-8, 638.
Huang Tsung-hsi, 45.
Human nature, change of, 135-8; view of Confucius, 135; view of Hsun Tzŭ, 135; view of Mencius, 135; selfish, 170; view of Adam Smith, 493.
Human wants, 176, 185-7; characteristics of, 187; satisfaction of, 188-194; regulation of, 195-206; moral control, 195-6; so-

INDEX   745

cial control, 196-200; repressing, 248.
Hui, king of Liang, 96, 99, 238, 308, 571; duke of Lu, 466.
Huns, 130, 360, 376.
Hunting, 239-241.
Hwai, name of river, 418, 419.
Imperialism, 313, 531.
Income tax, 589, 635, 673, 678-80, 714.
Independence, individual, 62-3.
Incorporation fees, 696.
Indirect taxes, abolition of, 634; ch. XXXV; did not exist in some periods, 683; conclusion on, 713.
Individualism, of Confucius, 18-20.
Individualistic, 504-5.
Industry, referred to by Confucius, 74-5; in the earliest period, 126; ch. XXII; the word, 398; importance of, 318, 398-9, 406-7; divisions of, 399-403; in Yin, 399-401; in Chou, 401-2; subject to government promotion, 402-3; four elements of, 403-5; government control of, 407-8; definition of the word, 408.
Inheritance tax, 681, 714.
Interest, mixed up with the word profit, 472; justification of, 472-4; rate of, 473-5; against usury, 580-2; required by the government, 587-8, 589; rates of, 583, 585, 589, 590, 593, 594, 624; tax on, 679; "horse interest," 693.
International relation, 16-20, 140-2, 315, 551.
International trade, one of the nine standard rules, 449-50; based on geographical difference of economic conditions, 450-1; old characteristic of, 451; within the Chinese world, 451-2; the term, 452; commercial treaty, 452-3; free exportation of grain, 452; peace made with barbarians, 452; free exportation in general, 453; free-trade doctrine, 453-4; customs duties, 454, 687-91; importation of rice, 575, 689, 690; germ of protection, 688.

Interpretation, of the writings of Confucius and his disciples, 37-8.
Inventions, technical, 119; of earliest times, 120-5; basis of civilization, 127-8; not encouraged in China, 538; not favorable for, 720.
Iron, tax on, 702-3.
Jade, use of, 262.
Jan Kêng or Jan Po-niu, 388.
Jan Yu, pupil of Confucius, 94-5, 375; distinguished by economic statesmanship, 627.
Japan, 92, 682, 726, 729-30.
Japanese, 41, 48, 92, 356.
Jên Tsung, of Sung, 687, 707; of Ts'ing, 710.
Jesus, 42, 159, 192, 255.
Ju, 39, 209.
Jui Liang-fu, 534.
Jung, duke of, 534.
Justice, relation with love, 94.
Kai-yüan coin, 431.
K'aifung, 674.
Kang Yu-wei, 30, 36, 46, 71, 145, 194.
Kansu, 658.
Kao Kung, 338.
Kao Ti, of Han, 13, 376, 411-2, 645.
Kao Tsu, of Tang, 431-2.
Kao Tsung, of Sung, 442; of Tang, 520; of Ts'ing, 572; of Yin, 610.
Kao Tzŭ, 135, 186.
Kao Yao, 170.
Kêng Shou-ch'ang, 571-2.
Ki Chow, 417, 639.
Kiang or Yangtze Kiang, 418, 419.
Kiang-tu, prince of, 96.
Kiangsi, 696.
Kiangsu, 657.
Kin dynasty, 334, 431, 470-1, 572, 667, 677, 684-5, 697-8, 702, 704, 707.
Kinchou, 695.
King, meaning of the word, 54, 60, 313; no divine right, 61-2.
King or King Chow, 404, 428.
Kirin, 709, 710.
Knowledge, 85.
Ku Yen-wu, 45.
Kuan Chung or Kuan Tzŭ, mercantilism and state socialism, 141-2; as the representative of extravagance, 242, 246; 129, 368, 373, 435-6, 454, 478-9, 484, 556,

568, 573, 661, 669, 677, 678, 701, 702, 706.
Kuan Chü, name of poem, 216, 217, 218.
Kuang-wu Ti, of Han, 377-8.
Kuangtung, 575, 680.
K'uang, name of city, 10.
K'uei Ch'iu, name of city, 452.
K'ühfeu, 7.
Kung-liang Yü, 11.
Kung Liu, 392.
kung-po Liao, 110.
Kung-shan Fu-jao, 8.
Kung-sun Ch'ou, 488.
Kung Tsi-chin, 46.
Kung-yi Hsiu, 546-7.
K'ung, family of Confucius, 3, 6-7.
K'ung Chi, 440.
K'ung-fu Chia, 6.
K'ung Fu Tzŭ, 7.
K'ung Ying-ta, 123, 173, 630-1.
Labor, ch. XVIII; department of, 73; division of, 368, 485-7; necessity, justice and honor of, 371-4; all kinds productive, 407; relation between employer and employee, 481-3; free movement of, 484; relation between manager and common laborer, 487; legislation, 230-1, 509.
Laboring class, 482.
Laissez faire policy, 175-80; defects of, 168-170, 573-5; practiced after the Ch'in dynasty, 596, 722.
Land, 294, 295; limited in quantity, 350; various in quality, 350-2; different in location, 352; form of field, 352-5; absence of private ownership, 468-9; see the *tsing tien* system, ch. XXVI; " opened," 510-11; " flax," 511-2; " mulberry," 512-3; table of distribution of, 521; officials' ownership limited, 549.
Land tax, classification of Ch'u, 389-90; equivalent of rent, 469-70; of Northern Wei, 470; of Kin, 471; in the form of government rent, 471; of Tang, 471; of Ch'in, 506-7; amount in the ordinary prefecture, 579; in ancient times, 616-7, 618, 622, 632-3, 638-48; described in the " Tribute of Yü, 638-44; different rates during the Chou dynasty, 647; first directly levied upon acres, 649; changed from gross produce to property, 649; of Han, 649-50; money first required, 650; of Tsin, 650; mixed up with poll tax and family tax, 650; of Tang, 650-2; collected in money, 652; paid in silver, 655-6; single-whip system, 652, 656, 658; paid in gold, 656; constant increase of, 657; amounts of, 658-9; extra tax, 659; conclusion on, 659-60, 714.
Landlords, 522-3, 524.
Language, Chinese, 605, 726.
Lao Tzŭ, 7, 42, 115; economic doctrine of, 190; *laissez-faire* policy of, 722.
Latter Ch'in, kingdom of, 701.
Latter or Posterior Chou dynasty. 697.
Latter Shu, kingdom of, 681.
Law, School of, 29, 42; principles of, 52-3; same punishment for both father and son, 63; responsibility confined to certain member of the family, 63; basis of economic development. 76-7; compared with ethics, 81-2; universal and equal, 171; social legislation, 527-8.
Law Code of the Ts'ing Dynasty. 148, 150, 155, 160-1, 165-7, 287, 414, 475, 542, 549-50, 581, 599, 704.
Legge, James, 16-7, 23, 39, 468.
Lei Yi-hsien, 686.
Level standard, system of, 556.
Li An-shih, 510.
Li K'o, 267-8, 391, 568-70.
Li Ssŭ, 43, 46.
Li Wang, of Chou, 534.
Li Yü, 708.
Liang dynasty, 541.
Liang Chow (Kansu province), 378.
Liberty, 46, 62-3.
License taxes, 695-6, 713; for mining business, 704.
Life, principle of, 201-2.
Likin, 686-7, 689-90.
Lincoln, Abraham, 378.
Ling Ti, of Han, 650, 705.
Ling Wang, of Chou, 7.

Liquors, tax on foreign, 690; prohibition against, 706-7; tax on, 707.
Literature, burning by the Ch'in dynasty, 34; highest development of the Chinese, 726.
Liu An, 553, 559-63, 595.
Liu Chung-yüan, 55-7.
Liu Hsiang, 34, 46.
Liu Hsin, 34-6, 449, 587.
Liu Pan, 576.
Liu Tê, 554.
Lo, name of a shepherd, 459.
Lo-ti-shui, 698.
Loans, of grain by the government, 580-2; of grain by the people, 583-5; government, 586-97.
Local taxes, collected along with the national regular tax, 578-80; not separated from national taxes, 636-7; existed not as taxes, 637; distinguished from that of central government, 639-40.
Loh, name of river, 419.
Logic, School of, 42.
Louis XIV, age of, 726.
Love, 20-21, 54; universal, 60-61, 600; relation with justice, 94; for the same kind, 155-6; toward all creatures, 193-4.
Lu, state of Confucius, 3, 6, 43, 404, 672.
Lu Chih, 471-2, 626, 652-3.
Lu Chiu-yüan, 63.
Lu Huai-shên, 551.
Lü Chia-wên, 567, 694.
Lü Hui-ch'ing, 676.
Lü Pu-wei, 459, 478.
Lü Tsu-chien, 441.
Lung (Kansu province), 378.
Lung Tzŭ, 623.
Luther, Martin, 45.
Luxury and extravagance, evils of, 243-7; reasonable luxury, 244-5; choice between parsimony and extravagance, 259; of the government, 645.
Ma Chün-shao, 415.
Ma Jên-wang, 335-6.
Ma Tuan-lin, 300, 442, 528, 555, 596, 605, 653-5, 680, 681.
Malthus, 161-2, 186-7, 307-8.
Malthusian doctrine, suggestion of, 338-9.

Man, origin of, 58-63; brotherhood of, 60; as a spiritual being and a material being, 185; feelings of, 185; business, 293-4; first factor of production, 295-6.
Manchuria, 657, 709.
Market, 122, 447, 501-2, 541.
Marriage, ceremonies of, 64-5, 269-70; tie of, 70-72; as the starting-point of Confucius' social system, 146-7; customs in China, 147; to a second husband, 147-8; consummation of, 148-9; views of Confucianism, Christianity and Buddhism, 192-3; expenditure for, 269-272; without music, 271; importance of, 321-2; day of, 322-3; exogamy, 324-5; polygyny, 325-7; Confucius in favor of monogamy, 327.
Measures, standard of, 420-1; comparison between the ancient and the modern, 421-2; comparison between Chinese and English, 422; importance of, 422-3.
Mencius, 13, 29, 42, 43, 46, 75-6, 78, 96-7, 98-9, 102-3, 103-6, 116, 135, 136, 142-4, 160, 169, 186, 210-2, 238-9, 266, 313, 328, 346, 370, 373, 423, 426, 453, 467-8, 473, 476, 480, 485-8, 489-93, 499, 501, 503, 505, 530-1, 541-2, 571, 586, 597, 601, 606-7, 607-8, 621, 627, 628, 629, 635, 636, 695, 697, etc.
Menelaus, 67.
Mèng Hsien-tzŭ, a worthy great official of Lu, 98.
Mèng Yi-tzŭ, 7.
Mercantile school, 141.
Merchants, productive, 368; in the beginning of Han, 395-7; two classes, 411; suppression of, 411-2; position of, 454-9; founders of commercial school, 459; taxed at double rate, 669, 692, 693.
Merit, examination of, 91.
Métayer system, 470.
Methods used by Confucius, 27-8.
Mi Tzŭ, 110.
Middle Kingdom, 17, 60, 608, 642.

INDEX

Migration, freedom of movement, 311-2; encouragement of immigration in general, 312-5; contrast between the Chinese and the Occident, 314-5; encouragement of immigration of artisans and merchants, 316-9.
Mile or *li*, 421, 422.
Military force, the army, 50-51; the soldiers, 101; of ancient times, 505-6, 619, 661; called for transportation of food, 646; great revolution in the system, 665.
Mind, 116-8.
Mineral products, tax on, 702-5.
Mines, conservation of, 346-7; mining regulations, 704-5; reasons for the undevelopment of, 705-6.
Ming dynasty, 45, 46, 334-5, 471, 472, 656-7, 658, 659, 686, 688-9, 692, 693, 695, 698, 702, 703, 704, 705, 707, 708, 710, 718.
Ming Ti, of Han, 13, 576; of Wei, 415.
Missionaries, 728-9.
Missionary cases, 728-9.
Mo, 607-8.
Mo Tzŭ or Mo Ti, 29, 42, 64-5, 111; economic doctrine of, 190; against music, 225-6; attacked Confucius' rites of funeral and mourning, 280-1; economic theory of, 281.
"Modern essay," 719.
Modern Literature, School of, 33, 34, 35-6, 46.
Moism, 29, 42, 43, 111, 190; criticism of, 282.
Money, history of, 428-435; three metals, 428-9; gold standard, 428, 435; ratio of the three kinds of, 429; two kinds of, 430; why gold not as money, 430-1; silver, 431; copper, 431-2; paper, 432-4, 442-3, 537; "flying money," 433; silver standard, 435; principles of, 435-445; next only to food, 435; as a commodity, 435; a medium of exchange, 435; standard of value, 436; quantity theory, 436-9, 556; coined at a period of natural calamities, 436-8; coinage, 440-1; government the only coiner, 440; prevention of illicit coining, 440-1; free coinage, 441; evil of bimetallism, 445; coinage of Liu An, 563; first required for land tax, 650; tax on, 693-4.
Mongolians, 378, 699.
Monopoly, ch. XXVII; condemnation of, 534; public, 535, 700-1; private, 536-42; personal, 536; legal, 536-9; family, 539; natural, 540-1; international, 540-1; business, 541-2; prevention of business, 542, 552; of forest and grasses, 701; of bamboo, 702; of mines, 702-4; of liquors, 679, 707; of vinegar, 707; of tea, 708; of frankincense, 709; of ginseng, 709-10.
Morse, H. B., 431-2.
Mourning, for parents, 280, 283.
Mouth tax or poll tax, as the cause of inaccurate census, 335, 655; in the Chou dynasty, 635-6; of Tang, 650-2; injustice of, 654; single-whip system, 652, 656, 658; existed in ancient times, not approved by Confucius, 669; of Han, 669-70; mixed up with land tax, 670; included in land tax, 670; revival of, 670; gradation of, 670; abolition of, 338-9, 670.
Mu, duke of Ch'in, 24; duke of Tsau, 308; duke of Shan, 346-7; duke of Lu, 546.
Mu, marquis, 67.
Music, as an institution of the government, 74-5; as one way of getting pleasure, 216-231; Confucius fond of, 216-7; necessary to daily life, 217; arrangement of Confucius, 217-8; reformation of Confucius, 218; theory of, 218-223; origin of, 218-9; definition of, 218-9; two functions of, 219-20; relation to society, 220-1; usefulness of, 221-3; economic value of, 222-3; four component parts of, 223; best for changing the influence of the people, 225; condemned by Mo Tzŭ, 225-6; of the Chinese, 226-7; not employed at marriage, 271;

compared with that of the West, 726.
Name, of married woman, 65; doctrine of, 111-6; as a substitute for profit, 114; as a reward and a punishment, 115.
Nanking, 686.
Nanning, 696.
Nan-kung Ching-shu, 7.
Natural environment, population and, 301; influence of, 347-9; determining industry, 404; as a single all-important cause for the Chinese life, 725.
Natural resources, department of, 73; conservation of, 345-7; determining industry, 404; tax on the products derived from, 700-1.
Natural selection, 53, 168-170.
Nature, forces of, 340-2; control over, 343.
Nine departments, 73.
Nine provinces, under the Hsia dynasty, 351, 641-2.
Nine sects, 42.
Nine services, 341-2.
Ningpo, 687, 689.
Northern Ch'i dynasty, 516-8, 523.
Northern Chou dynasty, 44, 431, 518, 523, 686.
Northern Wei dynasty, 44, 378, 430, 470, 510-6, 523, 686, 692, 703.
Occupation, "own occupation," 304; freedom of, 369-371; effects upon the character of man, 370; hereditary, 408-9; for a life time, 409.
Officers, election system, 87-91; holding of public land, 503, 515, 518-9; hereditary, 538; excluded from economic field, 545-51; difficult to undertake commercial functions, 576-7; salaries of, 618-9; local, 663.
Old, living of the, 266-7.
Opium, tax on, 710; prohibition against, 710-11.
Opium War, 315, 451, 688, 710, 729.
Ox or cow, for transportation, 124, 415; for ploughing, 388; tax on, 516; share of public land, 515, 517.
Pai Kuei, father of economics, 458-9; theory of taxation, 607-8.
Pai-li Hsi, 373.
Painting, 727.
Pan Ku, 53-4, 62, 132-3, 173-4, 370.
P'ang K'êng, 372, 472.
P'ang-kuang, marquis, 581, 678.
Pao Hsi or Fu Hsi, one of the Five Emperors, 4, 25-6, 120-121, 428.
Pao Shu, 454.
Paris, 67.
Parsimony, evils of, 249-250; choice between parsimony and extravagance, 259.
Partnership, 454, 696.
Passengers, tax on, 686.
Patents, 537.
Paul, 159, 192.
Pawn-shops, established by the government, 592, 593-4; tax on, 696.
Peace, 16, 73, 133; doctrine of, 142-5; harmony with economics, 143-4; made with barbarians, 452; of the future, 730.
Peck or tou, 421.
Pehtuna, 695.
Pei-kung Yi, 29.
Peking, 420, 692.
P'êng K'êng, 487-8.
Penmanship, 727.
Periclean age, 726.
Personal honor, 44; general of defeated army and great official of fallen state excluded from archery meeting, 234.
Personal pride, 208-13.
"Personal receiving," 64-5, 270.
Personal service, 631-2, 633; age limit for, 516; of Tang, 650-1; principles of Confucius, 660-2; as hired labor, 661; according to the *Official System of Chou*, 662-4; rotation tax of Han, 664; reformation of Chang Yüeh, 665; reformation of Yang Yen, 666; reformation of Wang An-shih, 666-7, 673-6; two kinds of forced labor, 666-7; single-whip system, 667-8; reasons for the existence of, 660, 668; causes of the evils of, 668-9.
Personality, 63.
Physiocrats, 93.
Pi Hsi, 8.
Pi Yüan, 694.

Pin, the original state of the Chou dynasty, 24, 392-5.
Ping Wang, 5.
Pint or *shêng*, 421, 422.
Pitch-pot, one kind of game, 236-7.
Plato, 145, 321.
Pleasure, for the common people, 96; in truth, 213-5; different ways of getting, ch. XIV; general principle of enjoying, 216; connection with labor, 230-1.
Po-chi, 65.
Po-yi, 113.
Poetry, collecting of, 69-70; form of, 80-81; part of music, 223.
Pointing-south car, 415.
Police system, 449.
Political, divisions, 498, 642; conditions in the past, 596; divisions of the imperial domain, 639.
Politics, three stages of, 17; to economics, 49, ch. VII.
Poor, consumption of, 201; happiness of, 208-15; hopes of, 373-4; public relief, 597-600; four classes, 597.
Popular council, 91.
Population, 295-6, ch. XVIII; importance of, 297-300; and land, 300-7; government control of, 301-2; description of governmental distribution of, 304-6; reasons for government control of, 306; and food, 307-309; and wealth, 309-311; migration of, 311-21; conditions in China, 321-30; policy of increasing, 323-4; historical study of, 331-9; table of, 332; in the beginning of the Chou dynasty, 336; destroyed by war, 336-7; increasing in the Sui dynasty, 338; increasing in the present dynasty, 338-9; evil effects of over-population, 392; adjusted to land, 513-4; table showing relation to land-distribution, 523; increase under Liu An's administration, 560; future emigration, 306-7, 723.
Portugal, 729.
Poverty, cause of, 547-8.
Prayer, not in Confucianism, 40.

Present, for traveling, 104; for marriage, 272; for funeral, 273-4; of introduction, 288-290.
Prices, 425; Confucius doing away with fraudulent, 425-6; Hsü Hsing's theory of, 246; Mencius' theory of, 426-7; relation to consumers' wants, 427-8; relation to the quantity of money, 438-9, 443; controlled by the government, 447-8, ch. XXIX, 595; Chi Jan's theory, 457; affected by law, 507; of grain, 568-77; affected by taxation, 697.
Prime minister, 610.
Princes, excluded from economic field, 545.
Private property, 18-20; woman's ownership, 155; of a family, 163-7; theory of, 466-7; regulation of, 467-8; land-ownership, 468-9, 471-2; see the *tsing tien* sysem, ch. XXVI; first time of land-ownership, 506-7; limitation policy, 507; confiscation policy, 508.
Production, natural process of, 177; over consumption, 180-1; should be rapid, 181; including exchange and distribution, 181; in ancient China, 200; three factors of, ch. XVII; branches of, 177-8, ch. XX; reasons of slow progress of, 718-23.
Productivity, 152; distribution according to, 465-6; theory, 483-8.
Profits, the word, 475; seldom mentioned, 475-6; justification of, 476-8; amount of, 478-9; of a master, 482; sources of, 534; tax on, 541-2, 678, 679, 680, 700-1; left for the people, 545-6; taken from merchants by the government, ch. XXIX; distinguished from interest, 589.
Progress, 20; theory of, 132-8; economic, 132-4; summary of the theory of, 134-5; domination of different industries along with the general direction of, 402-3; why slow in China, 337, 717-26.

Public debt, 681-2.
Public expenditures, 383, ch. XXXII; proper proportion between social income and, 607-8; general principles of, 608-13; classifications of, 613-6; characteristics of the ancients, 616-20; according to the three stages, 620; rule of Ming, 657.
Public finance, 552-3, 555-67, 573, 589-97; the term, 605-6; necessity of, 606-7; surplus reserved, 611-2; department of the treasury, 615-6; mixed up with private finance of the ruler, 616-8; obstacle to the development of, 627-9; great trouble, 637; surplus reserved, 657; conclusion on, 714, 723.
Public park, 237-9.
Public relief, 597-600.
Public work, 204-5, 228, 245, see personal service.
Quesnay, 93.
Race question, absent in China, 319-20; in Europe, 320-1; in America, 321; commingling, 324.
Rebellions of the Five Barbarians, 510.
Reciprocity, 21-2; basis of world economy, commercial policy and international law, 141.
Recording-miles-drum car, 416.
Records of the Seventy Disciples and their Followers, (*Ch'i Shih Tzŭ Hou Hsiao Chi*), 32.
Religion, three stages of, 17; Chinese old, 40; basis of, 57; no blood ever shed on account of, 61; included in education, 82; social, 84-7; particular character of the Chinese, 287-8; foreign, in China, 729.
Religious, worship, 85; piety, 152; expenses, 205, 260-1, 619-20.
Rent, absence of land-ownership, 468-9; land tax the equivalent of, 469-70; amount of, 470-2; theory of Lu Chih, 471-2; theory of Hsun Yüeh, 522; theory of Su Hsun, 524; tax on, 680; "sea rent," 695.
Representation, 89-91.
Representatives, of the people, 557.
Responsibility, 63.

Revolution, great, 62; Confucius' opinion on, 78.
Ricardo, 648.
Rice, 124, 382, 553; transported by sea, 418-9; storage of, 561; consumption too large, 575-6; canal-transportation of, 644-6; not subject to import duty, 689, 690.
Rites, doctrine of, 187-206; scope of the word, 187; origin of, 188-90; as the golden mean, 243.
Roads, along the fields, 354; general system, 416; system given in the *Official System of Chou*, 417; imperial, 419.
Roman Empire, 729.
Romans, 320-1.
Rome, 131, 379, 727.
Roscher, 51.
Ross, E. A., 722-3.
Ruler, meaning of the word, 54, 77-8; expenditures of, 615-6, 616-8.
Ruling class, excluded from economic field, ch. XXVIII.
Sage of Times, Confucius, 14.
Sage rulers, 4, 10.
Salaries, the word, 480-1; ideal system of, 491-3; means of getting, 493-4; amount of, 618; reduction of, 680.
Salt, policy of Liu An, 561-2; farmed out to the merchants, 700; tax on, 706.
Sang Ching, 557.
Sang Hung-yang, 541, 555-8.
Saving, general rule of, 358; principle of, 361; importance of, 362; affected by taxation, 693.
Sculpture, 727.
Self-help, 40-41, 109.
Self-proving law, 676.
Seligman, 622, 648, 653.
Senior, N. W., 199.
Settlement, 300-2, 347-8.
Shang Yang, 385, 412, 506, 530-1.
Shanghai, 225, 689.
Shanhaikuan, 709.
Shao, duke of, 224.
Shao, name of music, 74-5, 216.
Shao-chêng Mao, 9.
Shao Hao, 415.
Shên Kai, 442.
Shên Nung, 121-2, 176, 385.

Shên Tsung, of Sung, 643, 675; of Ming, 657.
Shêngking, 709, 710.
Shêntaoism, 41.
Shih Chiao or Shih Tzŭ, 385.
Shih Tan, 507.
Shih Tsu, of Yüan, 537, 599.
Shih Tsung, of Ming, 657; of Kin, 684-5; of Ts'ing, 706.
Ships, tax on, 685-6.
Shu, kingdom of, 333.
Shu (Szechuan province), 378.
Shu-chi, 65.
Shu-ch'i, 113.
Shu-chün, 388.
Shu-liang Ho, 6.
Shun, one of the Five Emperors, 20, 29, 75; type of a republic, 77; 104, 122-6, 373, 386, 422, 610.
Shun Ti, of Sung, 415.
Siam, 575, 689.
Sian, 562, 658.
Silk, industry, 126; work of woman, 152-3; silk-worm's house, 153; for the old, 266.
Simplicity and moderation, 247-8.
Singing, men and women, 69, 80; of Confucius, 217; the word, 217; description of, 223; relation to dance, 224.
Single-whip system, 338-9, 652, 656, 658, 667-8.
Six arts, 12.
Six calamities, 170-1.
Six Canons, original order, 24-6; changed order by Liu Hsin, 34.
Six imperial factories, 400-1.
Six treasuries, as natural production, 341-2; storing products, 399-401.
Slavery, absent in China, 374-9, 480-1; resulted from crime, 374-5; absent in Confucius' system, 375; in the Ch'in dynasty, 376; in the Han dynasty, 376; first announcement against, 376-7; first abolition, 377; abolished by Kuang-wu, 377-8; final abolition, 379; of the Northern Dynasties, 517-8.
Slaves, rights of public land, 515; direct tax of, 516; limitation of, 516-7; taxed at double rate, 669.
Small Tranquility, 17-20, 46, 70.

Smith, Adam, 100, 211-2, 490, 493.
Socialism, of Confucius, 18-20; state, 142, 172, 173-4, 478-9; Confucian, 175, 466-7, 543-4; compared with *tsingtien* system, 532; idea of Confucius, 623.
Socialists, 524.
Sociology, to economics, 49, ch. VI; How and why society comes to exist, 52-7; origin of man, 58-63; five social orders, 196; social usurpation, 246-7; contractual society, 455-6; two classes of men, 95-6, 461-2, 632, 633; group system, 662-3.
Soul, doctrine of, 116-8; the synonyms, 116; belief of Confucius, 286; existence of, 286-7.
South and Central America, 729.
Southern Dynasties, 684, 711, 718.
Southern and Northern Dynasties, 44, 430.
Spain, 729.
Spiritualism, 42.
Spring and Autumn, 12, 15-7, 26-7, 32, 46, 58, 64, 65, 69, 77, 85-6, 88, 115, 143, 204, 245-6, 319, *etc.*
Spring and Autumn, period of, 42, 129-30, 173-4, 336, 725.
Ssŭ Hsia, 217.
Ssŭ-ma Chien, 7, 46, 51, 112, 176-9, 349.
Ssŭ-ma Kêng or Ssŭ-ma Tzŭ-niu, 388.
Ssŭ-ma Kuang, 320, 576-7, 592.
Stamp tax, in the Chou dynasty, 711; in the Sung dynasty, 712-3; of the present dynasty, 681, 713.
Standard of living, identified with standard of morality, 198; social, 260-8; general survey, 260-2; of the great officials, 263-4; of the students, 264-6; of the common people, 266-8.
Stone or *shih*, 421.
State, taking up functions of the family, 71; size of different, 238.
Statistics, of the expenditures of the common people, 268; of the population, 297-9; reported by different departments, 608-9.
Stoics, 41.

Stoppage at the source, 680, 712.
Struggle, for safety and subsistence, 54.
Student, type of, 63; not necessary to be a farmer, 384-5; for fame than for money, 563; highest esteem paid to, 720.
Su Hsun, 524-6.
Su Shih, 424.
Su Tsung, of Tang, 681-2, 694.
Sü Chow (Kiangsu), 377.
Sui Dynasty, 44, 92, 338, 518-9, 523, 577-8, 683.
Sun-shu Ao, 373.
Sung, state of, 6, 28, 43, 104, 404.
Sung dynasty, of the House of Liu, 680, 681.
Sung dynasty, the Confucians of, 45, 46, 96-7, 127, 250, 726; population of, 334; 471, 472, 573, 579, 585, 598, 636, 655, 656, 667, 670, 680, 684, 685-6, 687, 692, 694, 697, 698-9, 701, 703, 704, 707, 708, 709, 712-3, 718, 719, 726.
Switzerland, compared with China, 93.
"System of Yao," 24-5, 73, 615-6.
Sze, name of river, 418.
Szechuan, 433, 692.
Tael or *liang*, 421, 422.
Tai Chou, 579.
Tai Mountain, 12, 311.
Tai Shêng, 31-2.
Tai Tê, 31-2.
Tai Tsung, of Tang, 672-3.
T'ai Chia, 610.
T'ai Kung, 128-9, 150, 428.
T'ai-p'ing rebellion, 339, 686.
T'ai Tsu, of Ming, 599, 656, of Sung, 681, 685.
T'ai Tsung, of Tang, 319-20, 579, 705.
T'ai Wang, 322.
T'aiyüan, 709.
T'an, name of state, 629.
Tang, nation of, 249.
Tang dynasty, 44, 319-20, 334, 418, 430, 470, 519-20, 523, 549, 573, 579, 658, 666, 680, 683, 697, 701, 703, 704, 709, 719.
Tao, marquis of Tsin, 588.
T'ao, surname, 409.
T'ao K'an, mother of, 724.

Taoism, 7, 29, 42, 44, 111, 115-6, 190-1, 718; compared with Christianity, 728.
Taoist, Confucius' influence upon, 287; as idler, 721.
Tartars, 378.
Taxation, policy of Chao Tso, 383; system of Sui, 338; system of Yin, 400; system of Northern Wei, 516; system of Han, 555-6; policy of Liu An, 559, 562-3; faculty theory, 579-80, 623-4; in general, ch. XXXIII; development in the earliest times, 621-4; system of different dynasties, 624; sources of, 624-6; doctrine of the light tax, 626-9; with certain regulations, 629; principle of equality, 629-31; progressive, 631, 680; principle of universality, 631-3; classification of, 633-7; in time of war, 634-5; double, 636, 675, 677; legal separation between local and national, 636-7; three-taxes system of Tang, 650-1; summer-and-autumn-taxes system, 651-5; extra taxes, 659, 675; social concept of, 724-5.
Tê Tsung, of Ts'ing, 46; of Tang, 677-8, 682, 694.
Tea, tax on, 708-9.
Theater, 224-5.
Thousand-miles ship, 420.
Three businesses, 341-2.
Three Dynasties, 4, 15, 499, 596, 621-2.
Three Kingdoms, 333, 508.
Three Kings, 4.
Three Stages, 16-20, 72, 132, 194, 327.
Three Systems, 15-6.
Three things worthy of honor, 211-2.
Tientsin, 225.
Timber, tax on, 701-2.
Tithe, 499, 607, 625, 647-8.
Title-deeds, tax on, 711, 712-3.
Tobacco, tax on foreign, 690; tax on, 710.
Tonnage duties, 686; on foreign ships, 688-9, 691.
Tools, importance of, 405.

INDEX

Trade guilds, 455; seventy-two in Canton, 483; tax on, 694; different from American trusts, 724.
Trade unions, 483, 724.
Transactions, tax on, 711-3.
Transportation, earliest development, 124; by land, 414-7; uniformity for, 416; by water, 417-420; by sea, 418-9, 537; of grain, 571; of rice, 644-6.
Tribute, really the land tax, 640; of native distinguishable products, 642-3; reasons of sending, 643-4; as an unlawful tax, 646-7; connected with foreign trade, 451, 688.
"Tribute of Yü," 24-5, 417-8, 638-44.
Trojan War, 67.
Tsai, state of, 11.
Tsang Wên-chung, 546.
Tsao Tsao, 44, 658, 671.
Ts'êng Tzǔ, 21, 30, 31, 63, 157-8, 203.
Tsin, state of, 8, 369, 455; dynasty of, 44, 340, 470, 523, 541, 548-9, 658, 670, 671, 684, 711, 718.
Tsin, name of river, 66.
Ts'in, name of river, 420.
Tsing tien system, 69, 70, 75, 79, 80-81, 82, 85, 132-4, 266, 374, 376, 468; meaning of the words, 352-3; form of, 352-5; ch. XXVI; history of, 353, 497-501; principles of, 498; of Confucius, 501-6; destruction of, 506-7; unsuccessful attempts to revive, 507-8; revival of, 508-522; opinions on, 522-8; conclusion on, 528-33; applied to the Middle Kingdom only, 642.
Ts'ing, name of a widow, 459.
Ts'ing Chow (Shantung), 377.
Ts'ing dynasty or present dynasty, 45-6, 657-9, 670, 682, 685, 686-7, 688-91, 692, 693, 695, 696, 698, 702, 703-4, 704-5, 707, 708-9, 709-11, 713, 718.
Tso-ch'iu Ming, 35.
Tsou, name of city, 6.
Tsu Chung-chih, 415, 420.
Tsui Shih, 302.
Tu Yu, 296.

Tung Chung-shu, 43, 46, 58, 88, 95, 96, 376, 463-4, 507, 547-8, *etc.*
Turks, 319-20.
Twelve tubes, 420-1.
Tyrannicide, 78.
Tzǔ, 33.
Tzǔ-ch'an, 455.
Tzǔ-chang, 175-6, 463.
Tzǔ-chung, son of, 225.
Tzǔ-han, 340.
Tzǔ-hsia, 31, 32, 43, 60, 267, 375.
Tzǔ-kung, 12, 13, 31, 101, 230; wishes of, 144; as a merchant, 456-7, 459, 476-8.
Tzǔ-lu, 85, 110, 200, 234, 385; wishes of, 144; as a type of strong man, 209.
Tzǔ-nang, 369.
Tzǔ-ssǔ, grandson of Confucius, 46, 202-3.
Tzǔ-yu, 31, 46, 119, 201.
United States, the, 92, 93, 314, 318, 321, 379.
Unity, 20-22.
Universalism, 313, 314-5, 530-1.
Usury, 580-1.
Utility and scarcity, 423-5.
Value, 423-5.
Village of K'ung, 13.
Village granary, system of, 582-5.
Vinegar, tax on, 707.
Wages, origin of, 480-1; productivity theory, 483-8; standard of, 488-91; ideal scale in whole society, 491-3; education as a solution, 493-6; Liu An's policy, 559; for public work, 661, 664, 667; tax on, 679.
Wan Chang, 105.
Wang An-shih, 45, 563-7, 584-5, 589-93, 666-7, 673-6.
Wang Chi, 322-3.
Wang Ch'i, 579-80.
Wang Chung, 245.
Wang Fu-chih, 45.
Wang Mang, 34, 377, 429, 430, 431, 508, 533, 558, 587, 589, 672, 679.
Wang Shou-jen, 45, 63, 730.
Wang Yen, 718.
War, destroyer of population, 336-7; 465.
Warring States, period of, 42, 129-30, 173-4, 336, 725.
Wars of the Eight Princes, 510.
Water-channels, 353-4.

Wealth, relation to virtue, 98; acceptance of, 103-6; the first of the five blessings, 170, 172; the word, 356-8; nature as a producer of, 466-7.
Wei, state of, 94, 218, 570.
Wei, name of river, 66.
Wei, nation of, 249; dynasty or kingdom of, 44, 333, 470, 671, 707, 719.
Wei Chi-tsung, 565.
Wei Chiang, 452.
Wei Ts'ing, 376.
Wei Tzŭ, 6.
Wei Yüan, 46.
Wên, marquis of Wei, 43, 267; marquis of Têng, 43, 75; duke of Tsin, 173; duke of Kuo, 381; duke of Wei, 452.
Wên-hsüan Ti, of Northern Ch'i, 671.
Wên Ti, of Han, 197, 360, 383, 397, 598, 612-3, 649; of Northern Chou, 518, 582; of Sui, 419, 578, 612-3.
Wên Wang, one of the Three Kings, 10, 19, 26, 29; type of constitutional monarchy, 77; mother of, 137; park of, 238-9; excursions or hunting of, 240; 244, 285, 597, 695.
Wheat, 382.
Wife, meaning of the word, 64; like brothers, 64; respect to, 64-5; choice of, 137; relation to husband, 146-155; equal to husband, 154-5; parents and, 159-60.
Woman, position of, 63-72; equal to man, 64-5; respect to, 64-5, 154; name of married, 65; separated from man, 65-9; as a promoter of economic progress, 68; social intercourse with man, 66-7, 69; man can be teacher of, 69; political right of, 69-70, 407; absolute independence of, 70-72; economic position of, 151-5, 407; nourishing a child, 151-2; participating in ancestor-worship. 153; ownership of property, 155; not dancing with men, 225; in the theater, 225; dancing with men, 225; special profession of, 503; work of, 504; rights to public land, 509-10, 518, 521; five-times the regular rate of poll tax upon the unmarried woman, 669-70; not help economic development, 721.
Wooden oxen and flowing horses, 416.
World, 16-20; as the largest economic organization, 139-145; two things for the equalization of, 140; to be united, 145; economic relation, 317; no division of people, 311.
Wu, name of state, 323-4, 404, 419; kingdom of, 333.
Wu, name of music, 74-5, 224.
Wu or Wu Wang, 19, 29, 62, 75, 78, 115.
Wu-ch'êng Ti, of Northern Ch'i, 516.
Wu Ti, of Han, 43, 430, 431, 556, 645, 670, 685, 686, 692, 693, 695, 702, 707; of Tsin, 333-4, 508-10, 549, 671; of Liang, 431.
Wu Tsung, of Ming, 657.
Wun Yen-po, 319-20.
Ya and *sung*, 218, 219, 226.
Yang, marquis, 67.
Yang Chow, 418, 428.
Yang Chu, 42, 115-6, 191.
Yang Hu, 100.
Yang Ti, of Sui, 33, 419-20.
Yang Yen, 651-2, 666, 670.
Yangchow, 419.
Yao, one of the Five Emperors, 20, 24, 29; type of a republic, 77; 122-6, 173, 360, 386, 415, 610.
Yeh Shih, 302-3, 392, 412, 444, 526-8.
Yeh Tzŭ-ch'i, 442-3.
Yellow cup, the standard of measures, 420-1.
Yellow peril, 730.
Yen, name of state, 404.
Yen Chêng-tsai, 6.
Yen Chou-yu, 110.
Yen Yüan or Yen Hui, 74; wishes of, 144-5; poor condition of, 214, 263, 476-7.
Yi Chow (Szechuan province), 378.
Yi Yin, prime minister of Ch'êng T'ang, 104, 610.
Yin, duke of Lu, 466, 545.

Yin or Shang dynasty, 6, 15, 28, 29, 74; development of industry, 399-401; 429, 472, 481, 498, 621-2.
Yo, a noble family of Sung, 582.
Yokohama Specie Bank, 682.
Yu or Yu Wang, last emperor of the Western Chou, 153, 463.
Yu Chow, 418.
Yu Jo, 13, 625.
Yü, name of the dynasty of Shun, 176, 402, 428, 429, 640-1.
Yü, one of the Three Kings, 19, 29; spending of, 243; founder of the really monarchical empire, 336; repressed the great floods, 350; universal establishment of the *tsing tien* system, 353; originator of water-channel system, 353; 360, 386, 553-4, 610.
Yüan, 20-21, 58-9.
Yüan, daughter of, 225.
Yüan dynasty, 45, 418, 433-4, 472, 658, 670, 686, 687-8, 695, 698, 699, 702, 703, 704, 707, 708, 718, 722.
Yüan Hsieh, 444-5.
Yüan Shih-kai, 682.
Yüeh, name of state, 323-4, 404.
ɪungchia, School of, 45.
Yünchow, 566.

ERRATA

Vol. I

Page 33, line 13, *prohibited by several emperors, and* should be omitted.
Page 65, note 2 should be inserted: ² *cf. infra*, pp. 111-5.
Page 69, line 9, instead of *weaving* read *spinning*.
Page 73, line 17, instead of *,rst* read *first*.
Page 73, note 1, *infra*, pp. 553-4.
Page 75, note 1, *infra*, p. 467.
Page 125, note 1, *infra*. pp. 277-8.
Page 134, note 1, *infra*, pp. 142-5.
Page 134, note 3, *infra*, pp. 343-4.
Page 134, note 4, *infra*, pp. 497-506.
Page 188, line 7, instead of *Tsun* read *Hsun*.
Page 205, note 1, *infra*, p. 667.
Page 268, note 2, *infra*, pp. 568-70.
Page 300, note 1, *infra*, pp. 333-6.
Page 308, line 13, instead of *Mo* read *Mu*.
Page 310, note 1, *infra*, p. 465.
Page 313, note 3, *infra*, pp. 530-1.

Vol. II

Page 404, line 16, instead of *Hu* read *Fênhu*.
Page 422, note 1, instead of *Present* read *Ts'ing*.
Page 534, lines 4 and 14, instead of *Duke Yung* read *Duke of Jung*.

VITA

CHEN HUAN-CHANG, author of this monograph, was born on the twenty-sixth day of the tenth month, 2431 A. K. (November 28th, 1880 A. D.). His father was Chen Chin-ch'üan, and his mother is Li P'êng-hsien. He is a native of the Inkslab Island (Yen Chou) in the West River (Si Kiang), belonging to the district of Kaoyao, the chief district of the prefecture of Chaok'ing, Kuangtung province. His family was very poor, but his father educated him with extraordinary effort, sacrificing everything for his education. In 2443 (1892 A. D.), he passed the examinations conducted by the Imperial Commissioner of Education in the city of Chaok'ing, and obtained the first degree, *Hsiu Ts'ai*. He studied several years in the large schools of Canton, the capital city of that province, but he acquired his knowledge very largely through his own study. After becoming interested in the writings of Kang Yu-wei, he came to Kang's school in 2449 (1898 A. D.), but he first met Kang Yu-wei in Hong Kong when Kang had been excluded from China on account of political reforms, in the later part of that year. Then he became editor of *The Chinese Reformer (Chih-hsin Pao)*, a political magazine edited in Macao, three issues in one month. In 2453 (1902 A. D.), he taught in the Shih-min High School in Canton; in the next year, he became the superintendent of that school. In this year (1903 A. D.), by passing higher examinations, he was enrolled by the Imperial Commissioner of Education as a Salaried Student

VITA

(*Lin Shêng*), and was later selected also by him as an Excellent Student (*Yu Shêng*). Then he passed the still higher examinations in Canton, and obtained the second degree, *Chü Jên*. In 2455 (1904 A. D.), he passed the highest examinations in Peking, and obtained the highest degree, *Chin Shih*. He was thereupon appointed by the emperor a Secretary of the Grand Secretariat, and became a member of the Chin Shih College. In the next year, he was sent by the government to America for study. He landed in San Francisco about the end of that year (January, 1906). He studied in Columbia University under the Faculty of Political Science since 2458 (March, 1907). His major subject was economics, and his minors were sociology and constitutional law. During a vacation (the summer quarter of 1908), he studied in the University of Chicago. At Chicago, he studied under Professors H. J. Davenport and J. E. Russell. At Columbia, he studied with Professors Seligman, Clark, Seager, H. L. Moore, Simkhovitch, Mussey, McCrea, Giddings, J. B. Moore, Burgess, Beard, Montague and others. He did seminar work with Professors Seligman, Clark, Seager, and Hirth.

图书在版编目(CIP)数据

孔门理财学＝The economic principles of Confucius and his school：英文/陈焕章著.—北京：商务印书馆，2015
(中华现代学术名著丛书.英文本)
ISBN 978-7-100-11220-8

Ⅰ.①孔… Ⅱ.①陈… Ⅲ.①经济思想史—研究—中国—古代—英文 Ⅳ.①F092.2

中国版本图书馆 CIP 数据核字(2015)第 074899 号

所有权利保留。
未经许可，不得以任何方式使用。

中华现代学术名著丛书
孔门理财学
(英文本)
陈焕章 著

商 务 印 书 馆 出 版
(北京王府井大街36号　邮政编码100710)
商 务 印 书 馆 发 行
北 京 冠 中 印 刷 厂 印 刷
ISBN 978-7-100-11220-8

2015年12月第1版　　　开本 787×1092　1/16
2015年12月北京第1次印刷　印张 48 1/2　插页 1
定价：145.00元